Israel, the Church, and Millenarianism

Since the calls of the Second Vatican Council, Roman Catholic theologians have sought to overcome an overarching problem facing Jewish–Christian relations, the concept of "supersessionism"; the idea that God has revoked the spiritual and historical promises made to the Jewish people in favour of granting those same privileges to a predominantly Gentile Church.

Israel, the Church, and Millenarianism breaks new ground by applying an ancient principle to the problem of Israel's "replacement": the early Church's promotion of millennialism. Utilizing the best in Patristic research, Aguzzi argues that these earliest Christian traditions made room for the future of Israel because Christ's reign in the Church was viewed as provisional to his historical reign on earth—Israel's role in salvation history was and is not yet complete. Aguzzi's research also opens the door for a greater Catholic understanding of the millennial principle, not shying away from its validity and relevance for understanding the importance of safeguarding Jewish particularity, while concluding that the Synagogue and the Church are indeed on a parallel trajectory; ". . . what will their . . . [Israel's] . . . acceptance be but life from the dead?" (Romans 11:15). Ultimately, the divine will is fulfilled through both Christian and Jewish means, in history, while each community is dependent, in different ways, upon the unfolding of God's future and the coming Parousia of Christ.

Steven D. Aguzzi is an ordained minister in the Presbyterian Church, and on the adjunct faculty of Duquesne University's theology department. He earned his PhD in Systematic Theology from Duquesne University in December of 2013, with a research specialization in Jewish–Christian comparative theology. He is widely published on the topic of supersessionism and Jewish–Catholic relations, particularly in ecumenical journals, and his work is constructive in its attempts to utilize traditional eschatologies in an effort to express a Christian theology that takes Judaism seriously, on its own terms. Aguzzi also holds an M.Div. from Princeton Theological Seminary, with specializations in comparative theology and ecumenical ecclesiology. Aguzzi has established ecumenical relations in the Pittsburgh area, and speaks nationally on the topic of post-*Shoah*, post-replacement theology.

Routledge New Critical Thinking in Religion, Theology and Biblical Studies

The *Routledge New Critical Thinking in Religion, Theology and Biblical Studies* series brings high-quality research monograph publishing back into focus for authors, international libraries, and student, academic and research readers. This open-ended monograph series presents cutting-edge research from both established and new authors in the field. With specialist focus yet clear contextual presentation of contemporary research, books in the series take research into important new directions and open the field to new critical debate within the discipline, in areas of related study, and in key areas for contemporary society.

For a full list of titles in this series, please visit https://www.routledge.com/religion/series/RCRITREL

New Voices in Greek Orthodox Thought
Untying the Bond between Nation and Religion
Trine Stauning Willert

Divine Power and Evil
A Reply to Process Theodicy
Kenneth K. Pak

Leaving Christian Fundamentalism and the Reconstruction of Identity
Josie McSkimming

Feminist Eschatology
Embodied Futures
Emily Pennington

The Soul of Theological Anthropology
A Cartesian Exploration
Joshua R. Farris

The Church, Authority and Foucault
Imagining the Church as an Open Space of Freedom
Steven G. Ogden

Israel, the Church, and Millenarianism
A Way beyond Replacement Theology
Steven D. Aguzzi

Israel, the Church, and Millenarianism
A Way beyond Replacement Theology

Steven D. Aguzzi

LONDON AND NEW YORK

First published 2018
by Routledge
2 Park Square, Milton Park, Abingdon, Oxon OX14 4RN

and by Routledge
711 Third Avenue, New York, NY 10017

Routledge is an imprint of the Taylor & Francis Group, an informa business

© 2018 Steven D. Aguzzi

The right of Steven D. Aguzzi to be identified as author of this work has been asserted by him in accordance with sections 77 and 78 of the Copyright, Designs and Patents Act 1988.

All rights reserved. No part of this book may be reprinted or reproduced or utilised in any form or by any electronic, mechanical, or other means, now known or hereafter invented, including photocopying and recording, or in any information storage or retrieval system, without permission in writing from the publishers.

Trademark notice: Product or corporate names may be trademarks or registered trademarks, and are used only for identification and explanation without intent to infringe.

British Library Cataloguing in Publication Data
A catalogue record for this book is available from the British Library

Library of Congress Cataloging in Publication Data
Names: Aguzzi, Steven D., author.
Title: Israel, the church, and millenarianism : a way beyond replacement theology / Steven D. Aguzzi.
Description: New York : Routledge, 2017. |
Series: Routledge new critical thinking in religion, theology, and biblical studies | Includes bibliographical references and index.
Identifiers: LCCN 2016057293| ISBN 9781472485229 (hardback : alk. paper) | ISBN 9781315590141 (ebook)
Subjects: LCSH: Millennialism. | Church—History of doctrines. | Judaism—Relations—Christianity. | Christianity and other religions—Judaism.
Classification: LCC BT892 .A38 2017 | DDC 231.7/6—dc23
LC record available at https://lccn.loc.gov/2016057293

ISBN: 978-1-4724-8522-9 (hbk)
ISBN: 978-1-315-59014-1 (ebk)

Typeset in Times New Roman
by Florence Production Ltd, Stoodleigh, Devon, UK

Contents

Foreword by Jürgen Moltmann ix
Preface and acknowledgements xi
List of abbreviations xv

Introduction 1

PART I
Supersessionism and *Nostra Aetate* 23

1. **The problem of supersessionism** 25

   Types of supersessionism 25
   Supersessionist hermeneutics and the Bible 29
   Supersessionism: a theological problem 39

2. ***Nostra Aetate* and its reception: supersessionism challenged** 57

   The shift to the relation to non-Christian religions 58
   Nostra Aetate *and its reception: the irrevocable call 60*
   Theological tensions after Nostra Aetate *69*

PART II
Millenarianism: a valid part of Church history 87

3. **Millenarianism explored** 89

   Millenarianism defined and contextualized 91
   Revelation 20: an intentionally chiliastic text 93
   The amillennial interpretation of Revelation 20 is flawed 97
   Millenarianism in the Gospels and Pauline corpus 100

4. Millenarianism and early Church tradition 115

Millenarianism as orthodox eschatology 115
Responding to the refutation of chiliastic normativity 118
The earliest detractors of chiliasm: Marcion, Gaius, Origen 121

5. A shift in eschatology: the Church becomes the kingdom 133

Eusebius (ca. 263–339 C.E.): the Church and the Roman kingdom 134
Augustine (354–430 C.E.): the Church and the kingdom of God 135

PART III
Millenarianism, heresy, and contemporary Catholic theology 143

6. The hermeneutics of heresy 145

St. Vincent of Lérins: determining valid doctrine 148

7. Millenarianism: creeds, Ecumenical Councils, and heresy? 159

The Apostles' Creed 160
An early Council responding to Montanism, not Chiliasm 164
Nicaea (325 C.E.) and Rome (382 C.E.) 165
Constantinople (381 C.E.): "whose kingdom shall have no end" 171
Ephesus (431 C.E.): no direct or indirect reference to millenarianism 174

8. Recent magisterial statements on millenarianism 189

Pius XII and the declaration against millenarianism 189
The 1994 Catechism and millenarianism 192
Benedict XVI and the spiritual, Eucharistic millennium 194

PART IV
Millenarianism and post-supersessionism 203

9. Prolegomena to a Christian millenarian theology of Judaism 205

Jewish eschatological hope in relation to supersessionism and millenarianism 209
Moltmann's mitigated millenarianism and the provisional Church 217
Three problematic questions 222

10. Millenarianism, supersessionism, and the messianic kingdom   235

Millenarianism, amillennialism, and economic supersessionism 236
Millenarianism, amillennialism, and punitive supersessionism 247
Millenarianism, amillennialism, and structural supersessionism 255
Constructing ideas on the nature of the millennial age 262

Conclusion   287

Bibliography   291
Index   319

Foreword

This book came out of the author's dissertation "Israel, the Church and the Eschatological Question: Moltmann's Millenarianism and the Jewish–Catholic Question", Duquesne University 2013. I take the chance to praise the author's erudition and to give reason for my "mitigated" millenarianism.

The problem is the internal connection between the relationships of the Church to Israel and to the kingdom of Christ.

The author describes in Part I how recent Catholic theologians deal with their traditional identification: "The Church is the kingdom of Christ". In Part II he presents his own thesis: the expectation of the kingdom of Christ is an essential element in the history of the ancient Church: the Church of Christ is not yet the kingdom of Christ. In Part III he returns to the declaration of the Catholic Church today on the Christian–Jewish question. And finally in Part IV he explains his own messianic millenarianism and "post-supersessionism". The expectation of the messianic kingdom of Christ unites already today the Church and Israel to a partnership on the way.

The attentive reader may wish another book of the author on the millenarianistic discussions in the protestant Churches since Johann Heinrich Alsted, Herborn 1627, his famous student Amos Comenius and the great rabbi of Amsterdam Mennaseh ben Israel and his influential book *Spes Israelis* 1650. Today the evangelical dispensationalism is widespread; remember the *Day After* series.

My own expectation is an eschatology in the light of Christ's resurrection. This is the true eschatological event in the history of humankind and nature. I refuse the speculations of the seven ages of the world (Talmud), the three world kingdoms (Joachim of Fiore) and the five monarchies (Quintomonarchianism) and with these any form of dispensationalism.

The apostle Paul is teaching us to understand the resurrection of Christ not as an exception but as the beginning of a process: "Christ the firstfruit, afterward they that are Christ's at his coming, then comes the end when he shall have delivered the kingdom to God . . . the last enemy that shall be destroyed is death" (1 Corinthians 15:22–28). Those "who belong to Christ" will experience a resurrection "from the dead" as Christ was raised "from the dead". Christ's Parousia will happen in the time of death, and with the destruction of death the universal resurrection of the dead is reached: "For since by man came the death, by man came also the resurrection of the dead" (1 Corinthians 15:21). The kingdom of Christ is a kingdom in between the Church of Christ and the kingdom of the triune God, where God will be "all in all" (1 Corinthians 15:28). When Israel will meet her redeemer her acceptance will be like "life from the dead" (Romans 11: 15). Paul used the same formula "from the dead" for Israel's redemption which he used for the kingdom Of Christ. In Revelation 20:1–15 the same eschatological event is meant, but described with the symbol of the "thousand years".

Traditional eschatologies speak of the "end", the end of life, the end of history, the end of this world. In the eschatological light of Christ's resurrection we speak of the beginning, the beginning of new life, the beginning of the new world of God and are ourselves new creatures, born to a living hope.

I am very grateful to Steven Aguzzi for this fine book: he has opened the Church–Israel question and the millenarianistic question in new ways.

Tübingen at the first of Advent 2016
Jürgen Moltmann

Preface and acknowledgements

The question of the relationship between Jews and Catholics has come to the fore in recent Christian theological debate, especially over the issue of whether the Church, comprised predominately of Gentiles, "takes up," "replaces," or "supersedes," either in part or totality, the spiritual promises that were made to the People Israel. Since the Vatican II declaration *Nostra Aetate*, the presumptions of supersessionism in the Roman Catholic tradition have been seriously questioned and Catholic theologians, both from within and outside the ecclesial hierarchy of the Church, have sought to overcome this dangerous and often violent presupposition. Because supersessionism is deeply embedded in the fabric of the Catholic tradition, the search for various root causes has led Christian scholars to examine both the ecclesiological and eschatological dimensions of the problem. Truly post-supersessionist theology must point toward an ecclesiology whereby the Church views itself as a partner in history with Judaism and whereby the Church views the final consummation of both the Church and the synagogue as a tertiary reality—the coming kingdom of God. The early Christian interpretation of Revelation 20: 4–6 and the millenarian hope of earthly messianic expectation borrowed from Jewish apocalyptic traditions were replaced during Constantine's era with a historicized and allegorized version, setting up the Church as the all-surpassing pinnacle of God's kingdom-reign on earth. The Church has never formally condemned the alternative to amillennial eschatology, millenarian eschatology. The work of the Protestant theologian Jürgen Moltmann, to which I am deeply indebted, addresses the issue of supersessionism and calls for a reassessment of Patristic, *eschatological millenarianism* as a means of overcoming supersessionism and as a call to examine eschatological theories that are acceptable to both the Church and synagogue. I argue that since *eschatological millenarianism* was a strong aspect of the early Catholic tradition, it should be reassessed within that same tradition as a way forward beyond supersessionism. Eschatological millenarianism is able to overcome aspects of supersessionism because it leaves theological space for an in-breaking of God's kingdom apart from the Church of history—a space that values Jewish religious participation toward the future eschaton, in line with Christian views of salvation, but without demanding the envelopment of Jews into the predominanetly Gentile Church specifically. In this work, I seek to utilize a wide range of ecumenical sources, Catholic, Orthodox, and Protestant, in order to reassess and transcend traditionally anti-Jewish theologies of consummation. The goal is to bring together, in major brushstrokes, the constructive aspects of ancient and contemporary Christian theology for the purposes of moving beyond the 'theology of abrogation,' and creating a more functional dialogue between Jews and Christians, in the most fraternal sense possible.

As a sign of appreciation to those who have helped to mold my thoughts on the topic of God's character, and to those who have helped me discern my vocation, I would like to acknowledge their contribution toward this book on the Jewish–Catholic question. First, I want to express gratitude for my wife, Robyn, for the endless support and countless hours of sacrifice she has made in order for this research to be possible. You have always been my anchor in life—you, and no other. I want to thank my daughter, Arden, for reminding me of all that is good and pure in this world. It has always amazed me how a 6-year old is able to have theological insights that rival those of history's greatest thinkers. I am also most grateful to my parents, Mr. Fabio Aguzzi and Mrs. Maria Aguzzi, and my in-laws, Mr. James Young and Mrs. Sandra Young, for their influence, prayers, and encouragement. To my brothers, David, Robert, and James, I am grateful for your support and always thoughtful discussions. I'd like to thank my brother-in-law, Scott Young, his wife Karin, and my friends, Andrew VonArx, Alexander Herd, Craig Britcher, Hilary Brown, Devon Jennings, Danielle Graham-Robinson, Raymond Robinson, John and Lynn Schrott, Neil Brem, and Dr. Bob Maravalli. I also acknowledge the inspiration of those in my home church, the pastors, staff, elders, deacons, trustees, members and friends of the Mt. Lebanon Evangelical Presbyterian Church. I would especially like to thank the worship team members of MLEPC, whose support I cherish. Special thanks are due to my friends and colleagues in academic work, for countless hours of stimulating theological discussion, including Dr. Daniel Lattier, Dr. Ryan Patrick McLaughlin, Dr. Damon McGraw, Fr. Michael Darcy, Dr. Jimmy Menkhaus, Dr. Kevin Storer, and Dr. James Platt. I'd like to thank Fr. Drew Morgan and those at the *National Institute for Newman Studies* in Pittsburgh, especially for the Institute's investment in me as a theologian. My own work has been influenced extensively through the opportunity to sit on the editorial board of the *Newman Studies Journal*. I'd like to thank my good friend Jason Kravitz, whose upbringing in a Jewish home has given me a new appreciation for the nuances of the Jewish tradition. And for the foundation to think critically and theologically, I want to acknowledge the professors at Princeton Theological Seminary, specifically Dr. Darrell Guder, Dr. Daniel Migliore, Dr. William Stacy Johnson, and Dr. Diogenes Allen— especially for their contribution to my own thought on post-Holocaust theology and the issue of supersessionism. Last, I would like to thank the entire theology faculty at Duquesne University, in particular, Dr. George Worgul, Dr. William Wright, Dr. Bogdan Bucur, Dr. Gerald Boodoo, Dr. Marie Baird, and Fr. Dr. Radu Bordeianu. Special thanks go to Dr. Aimée Light for her thoughtful insight, patience, careful critique, and overall encouragement. For assistance in proofreading this volume, I would like to acknowledge the tireless work of Dr. Margaret

Puskar-Pasewicz, and Christopher Herd. To the entire editorial and publication staff at the former Ashgate Publishing Company, and Taylor & Francis, I offer my heartfelt gratitude for the opportunity and guidance in the publication of this manuscript. I'd like to thank Prof. Dr. Jürgen Moltmann for his kind review of this work, and for his personal correspondence. This book is offered in loving memory of Fr. Matthew Baker, priest, scholar, and friend.

Steven D. Aguzzi
Pittsburgh, Pennsylvania
October, 2016

Abbreviations

Translations of the Bible

NASB   New American Standard Bible
NIV   New International Version

Books of the Bible

The same abbreviations are used as found in the New International Version

Ancient Works

Ambrose

De Spir. San.   On the Holy Spirit

Augustine

De Civ Dei.   City of God

Barnabas

Let. Barn.   Letter of Barnabas

Cyprian

Ep. Ad. Mag.   Epistle to Magnus
Ep. Ad. Jan.   Epistle to Januarius

Epiphanius

Adv. Haer.   Against Heresies
Pan.   Panarion

Eusebius

Hist. Eccl. — Church History
Vit. Const. — Life of Constantine

Gennadius

De Dogm. Eccles. — History of Dogma

Hermas

Pastor Vis. — The Shepherd of Hermas

Hippolytus of Rome

Dan. — Commentary on Daniel

Irenaeus

Contra Haer. — Against Heresies

Jerome

Com. Dan. — Commentary on Daniel
Comm. on Ez. — Commentary on Ezekiel
De Vir. Illustribus. — On Illustrious Men

Justin Martyr

1 *Apol.* — First Apology

Lactantius

Inst. Div. — Divine Institutes

Origen

Con. Cel. — Against Celsum
De princ. — On First Principles

Papias

Frag. — Fragments

Philiaster

de Haeres. — Of Heresies

Tertullian

Adv. Marc.	Against Marcion
De Praescript.	The Prescription against Heretics
De Anima.	A Treatise on the Soul

Collections and modern publications

ANF	Roberts, Alexander, and James Donaldson, eds. *Ante-Nicene, Christian Library Translations of the Writings of the Fathers Down to AD 325*. Whitefish, MT: Kessinger, 2004.
CP	Moltmann, Jürgen. *The Church in the Power of the Spirit: A Contribution to Messianic Ecclesiology*. 1st Fortress Press ed. Minneapolis, MN: Fortress Press, 1993.
DI	*On the Unicity and Salvific Universality of Jesus Christ and the Church: Dominus Iesus*. Boston, MA: Pauline Books & Media, 2000.
HD	Moltmann, Jürgen. *On Human Dignity: Political Theology and Ethics*. Minneapolis, MN: Fortress Press, 2007.
NA	*Nostra Aetate* in Flannery, Austin. *The Conciliar and Post Conciliar Documents, Vatican Council II*. Dublin: Dominican Publications, 1975.
NPNF	Roberts, Alexander, James Donaldson, Philip Schaff, and Henry Wace, eds. *Nicene and Post-Nicene Fathers: Second Series*. 14 vols. Buffalo, NY: Hendrickson Publishers, 1994.

Introduction
Introducing the problem of supersessionism in relation to eschatology

In our age, the question of Catholicism's relationship to Judaism has come to the fore, partly due to the awareness among Christian scholars that there is a need for a post-Holocaust theology, and partly due to the reality of the modern State of Israel. Prior to Vatican II, the Roman Catholic Church had not drafted a definitive statement on the Church's positive relationship with the Jewish people.[1] This means that approximately 1,965 years passed without the Church explicitly mentioning the positive nature and influence of Christianity and Judaism on one another in either a doctrinally or pastorally binding manner.[2] Certainly, there were papal bulls and various encyclicals issued, but the majority of these documents were either antagonistic to the plight of the Jewish people or announced decisions that would ensure the survival of Catholic authority at the expense of Jewish political and social existence.[3] The Church of the medieval period went to great lengths to reiterate certain aspects of rhetoric and legend that portrayed the Jews as rejected by God, cursed to live a "wandering existence" with no land, libel for the blood of Christ, and singled out and charged for the crime of deicide with all its implied consequences.

The Catholic Church's history with the Jewish people is at best a series of transgressions against humanity, and at worst a trajectory marked by anti-Judaism in theological form, leading in many ways to anti-Semitism.[4] The long history between these connected religions has been a continual exercise in the Christian desire to define itself against the other in such a manner that its own theological roots were damaged.[5] Christianity's philosophical assumptions led to a form of fratricide, resulting in the Church being unable to accept the "other" that was actually a part of itself. The beginnings of this phenomenon may be traced to the New Testament period, in which an inner conflict between Jews belonging to the "Way" of Jesus, and those rejecting the messianic identity of Jesus, ultimately resulted in a "parting of the ways." This phenomenon was made particularly evident when the Pauline mission to the Gentiles took shape.[6]

The Patristic period saw the formation of a harsh polemic between the Greek-inspired Gentile Christians, and the Torah-observant rabbinic Judaism that transpired after the destruction of the Jewish Temple by the Romans. This polemic contained within it the seed for a very specific reading of the salvation narrative which interpreted the Hebrew Scriptures in an almost exclusively typological manner whereby the Hebrew Bible itself, God's relations with the chosen people

Israel, and the covenantal promises made to this people for both present and future blessing and prosperity were seen solely in light of the Church.[7] In the Church, *all* the covenantal promises of God were allegorized, spiritualized and then historically fulfilled in such a way that left no room for God's continued covenantal life with the Jewish people.[8] The new people of God, the Church, with its spiritual ethos and law of faith and love superseded that which was perceived to be the old, carnal people of God—along with what was taken to be their legalistic yet equally disobedient history. With its roots in these earlier theological works, and with the help of Justin Martyr and Irenaeus, a new reading of the salvation narrative had taken form which espoused an explicitly *supersessionist* tone.[9] For the most part, many forms of supersessionism continue to influence aspects of theology today.[10] Aside from some preparatory statements and declarations that occurred during or after Second World War, the Second Vatican declaration, *Nostra Aetate* (hereafter, *NA*), stands as the most definitive and authoritative statement on the relationship of the Catholic Church with the Jewish people, along with its positive impact and influence which has become evident in the document's reception.[11] *NA*'s reception is significant because it sparked a renewed understanding of the Church's role in partnership with Judaism and was the first official document from an Ecumenical Council that appeared to question the Church's supersessionist history.

According to the Catholic theologian Rosemary Radford Ruether, the source and origin of both anti-Judaism and supersessionism is twofold. First, it is Christological in that the Church's affirmation that Jesus is the messiah is ". . . a refutation of the synagogal reading of the Scriptures."[12] Second, it involves ". . . the historicizing of the eschatological event,"[13] whereby "the message of messianic expectation is imported into history and reified as a historical event in a way that makes it a reality-denying, rather than a reality-discerning principle."[14] I agree with Ruether in part, but I will claim in this book that a strong Christology must be preserved, maintaining that Jesus in his earthly history indeed fulfilled part of God's consummative act, not merely paradigmatically and proleptically, but within history. Both a high Christology and the universally salvific nature of Jesus Christ are maintained in the work of the German Protestant theologian Jürgen Moltmann, though Moltmann is likewise able to stress the imperative and necessary value of Jewish religious reality in the contemporary moment.[15] According to Moltmann, the synagogue and the Church each have a valid religious value, but both are provisional and will be *superseded* by the kingdom of God itself.[16] Moltmann's primary contribution to overcoming Christian supersessionism is centered on his ability to maintain the traditional Christological categories of orthodoxy while at the same time challenging the concept that the Church has forever replaced Israel, through a careful re-apprehension of ancient Christian eschatologies that left space (whether intentionally or not) for a continued theological significance for Judaism.

In this book, I will argue that one powerful means of overcoming supersessionism—a theological problem admitted, identified, and addressed recently in the Catholic scholarly tradition—is by the re-evaluation and reintegration of certain positive attributes of the *millenarian* approach to eschatology.[17] This is an approach, however, which has been rejected in Catholic ecclesial documents since 1944, yet has its roots in the Catholic tradition and is evident throughout Catholic history.[18] Millenarianism, or chiliasm, which will be examined in detail in part two of this book, refers to the following for the purposes of this project:

> the best-documented and most persistent eschatology in the first two Christian centuries was chiliasm, the belief that God would establish a future kingdom on earth centered in Jerusalem. The term chiliasm comes from the Greek word for "thousand" (*chilias*) and refers to the belief, first stated in the book of Revelation, that Christ would one day return to rule on earth for a period of a thousand years before the heavenly Jerusalem comes down from the heavens.
> (Revelation 21)[19]

One major distinction between Moltmann's conception of millenarianism and the above definition has to do with the earlier millenarian insistence on a definitive end to Christ's kingdom and then a resurgence of it, although Fathers such as Irenaeus seem to preview Moltmann's model.[20] Because Moltmann believes that the "Thousand Years' reign" need not be taken literally in terms of *length of time*, and because the period of Christ's earthly reign is a transcendent, "in-between" period located in the middle of history and eternity, Moltmann's version may be considered a highly modified or mitigated form of millenarianism.

I will argue that Moltmann's insistence on a modified millenarian approach to Christian eschatology is necessary if one is to overcome supersessionism. Such replacement theology, which is theologically and ethically problematic, may be overcome only by acknowledgment of a salvific future for the Jews that necessitates a renewed conversion to the kingdom of God through the messiah, but does not require a conversion to Catholicism or the Church. Millenarianism is deeply imbedded in the early Christian tradition and Judaism, and allows for a salvific future for Jews without mandating conversion to the predominantly Gentile Church, specifically.

A large section of this book will be dedicated to illustrating that millenarianism is biblical, traditional, and was never formally declared a heresy in the Church's history. There was an element within Catholic ecclesial history that sought to reject millenarianism since the fourth century, but it was never done so in any canonically binding manner. If one considers heresies as associated with declarations or formal rejections of doctrine, taking the form of either an *ex cathedra* papal declaration or a statement from the canons of an Ecumenical Council, then millenarianism was never precluded from orthodox thought. Granted, the ordinary Magisterium of the Catholic Church has rejected a specific form of historicized millenarianism: "The church has rejected even modified forms of this falsification of the kingdom to come under the name of Millenarianism."[21] Yet when the Catechism reads that the Church has rejected millenarianism, it means it has done so officially beginning with a statement by Pope Pius XII in July of 1944—hardly

4 *Introduction*

sufficient grounds for claiming its utter rejection throughout all of Catholic history.[22] Likewise, the form of millenarianism to which the Church has an aversion, and the context of the Church's rejection, is important before any sweeping judgments are made. It is imperative to show that millenarianism has a place in Catholic history and was adopted as a part of the deposit of faith, not only by the significant, normative proportion of the Church Fathers, but likewise by pious men and women later in Catholic history—persons who were never censured by the church.[23] Although more recent statements by ecclesial authorities point toward certain "dangers" inherent in a millennial eschatology, absent of a formal condemnation, the concept of millenarianism, treated as an antidote to supersessionism is important and promising as a point of exploration for contemporary Catholic theologians.[24]

That which promoted the unfolding neglect and near abandonment of millenarian theology, with millenarianism itself acting as a theology which deeply and positively penetrated the earliest Patristic consciousness, was the writing of Augustine of Hippo.[25] Augustine's *City of God* decisively interpreted the Thousand Years' reign of Christ in non-literal terms, equating the period of blessedness for the saints and their reign with Christ, as the era of the historical Church. This amillennial concept has since more or less solidified as Roman Catholic theology. I will argue that Moltmann's eschatological millenarianism, aspects of which were popular and normative in the witness of the early Church, has the ability to overcome supersessionism, primarily because it allows for an alternate messianic hope which is not fulfilled *in toto* by the Church of history, yet simultaneously maintains Jesus Christ as the Jewish messiah who redeems Gentile Christians and the entire world, in terms of identity.

The Church's later resistance to millenarian thought, solidified in Augustine's *City of God*,[26] is related to its desire to ". . . legitimate political or ecclesiastical power, and is exposed to acts of messianic violence and the disappointments of history."[27] The writings of Moltmann shed light on the need to reject what he calls "historical millenarianism," in which the historical Church is considered the fulfillment of the Thousand Years' reign of Christ on earth mentioned in Revelation 20, in favor of "eschatological millenarianism" in which Christ's Thousand Years' reign is a future event in history, prior to the full and final consummation.[28] Moltmann considers that both views are forms of "millenarianism," while one is an allegorical reading of the Revelation narrative in the line of Origen, and the other is a more literal interpretation. Yet this does not mean that the "Thousand Years" or "Thousands Years" reign of Christ needs to be taken as a literal period in terms of temporality. There are multiple variations of millenarianism, with Moltmann's functioning as a highly qualified and modified version of the more radical political forms that led to violence in the sixteenth century. Moltmann's primary problem with historical millenarianism is the ecclesiological picture that it produces. He claims that:

> the condemnations of eschatological millenarianism always have their basis in a historical millenarianism. Those who proclaim that their own political

or ecclesiastical present is Christ's Thousand Years' empire cannot put up with any hope for an alternative kingdom of Christ besides, but are bound to feel profoundly disquieted and called in question by any such hope.[29]

I will argue that some of the condemnations to which Moltmann refers are ambiguous and were not explicit condemnations of millenarianism but other theological errors, such as Apollinarianism and Marcellianism.[30] Nevertheless, there is an overarching fear within Catholic theology that disallows for an eschatological millenarianism on the grounds that ecclesial authority may be usurped by competing claims to Christ's kingdom—including Jewish messianism.[31]

It must be said that the Catholic Church has some legitimate reasons to reject millenarianism, reasons that raise serious questions regarding how Christians should view time and history. Those concerns will be examined in this book, predominantly in the sections that reference Joachim of Fiore and also modern, secularized forms of political millenarianism—ones that have led to violence because of a borrowed set of millennial terminologies and principles. Yet these concerns do not preclude the re-evaluation of the millenarian topic as a whole as it regards an eschatological outlook more conducive to Jewish–Christian relations and in line with non-supersessionism.[32]

Moltmann stresses the eschatological and ecclesiological elements of supersessionism in an attempt to overcome the kind of replacement theology that has been a major part of the Catholic ethos up until recent times—thus I will utilize his primary text on eschatology, *The Coming of God*, in addition to his text on ecclesiology, *The Church in the Power of the Spirit*. It is the Church which sees *itself* as the total fulfillment of eschatological reality because it cannot distinguish itself as the Body of Christ in time and history, from what it will become, or be converted to in its universalized and future state alongside Israel. The Church has attempted to maintain an *already/not-yet* theological trajectory, specifically through the Second Vatican Council, but the Church's insistence on an unmodified historical millenarianism has limited its ability to accept Judaism's alternative messianic hope and view it in terms of what Moltmann would call "a partnership in history."[33] Thus, the Church has a tendency to see itself as the kingdom of God already manifest on earth, excluding any other historical vehicle whereby God may consummate history and usher in the kingdom.[34]

Ruether, building on some of Moltmann's ideas and applying them to Catholicism, points to the reality of historical millenarianism when she claims that ". . . the Church settled down into the new historical era that had opened up between Jesus' historical coming and his future return . . . the Church came to see its own times as the 'Christian era.'" Ruether's point that the Church era became the eschatological millennium[35] (referring to the allegorized and historicized interpretation of Revelation 20:4 popular since the time of Augustine), is the precise problem and the primary focus of this book.

I will argue that by re-appropriating the aspects of eschatological millenarianism that were once prevalent in the Church's history and tradition—namely, space and expectation for Jewish messianic hope which is at least marginally within history and associated with a specific geographic location, Jerusalem—the Church may be able to see in Israel a "partner in history," working toward a future that is coming toward history from outside it. The Church identifies this future as the kingdom of God—specifically, as the eschatological reign of Jesus Christ, whereas adherents of Judaism do not, but have their own eschatological and messianic expectations for the "world to come." The theological error that has surfaced over much of Christian history is the equating of the future kingdom of God, i.e. Christ's universal reign over history, and the Church of today. Thus, millenarianism is a reversal of the totalization that occurs in *pre-millennial history* as a result of the majority Christian eschatological and ecclesiological understanding that the future kingdom of God has been made historical and "incarnated" in the Church. The in-between state of the Thousand Years' earthly reign of Jesus Christ and the end of time/history acts as a deterrent to the Church's view that *it* is the totalization of all otherness into the sameness that constitutes historical Christianity.[36] It is in this in-between state that the beginning of the end of God's consummation occurs, moving closer to the point when ". . . Christ is all and is in all" (Colossians 3:11).

As mentioned by R. Kendal Soulen, the primary difference between Catholic and Jewish conceptions of the messiah is actually centered upon *function* and not *identity*. If Jesus of Nazareth fulfilled *all* of the Jewish expectations for restoration during the first earthly advent, it is unlikely that Judaism and Christianity would currently be two separate religions. Some may argue that the kingdom has crept in, in some sort of silent or hidden manner (which it has, to some extent), but regardless, that which is still missing is the value it carries for the Jewish people in the here and now. Quite the contrary; the Christian era has produced violence, suffering, and death for the Jewish people, thus diminishing the Church's powerful witness.

I will argue that in millenarianism, the Church takes a theological stance that opens a door for the possibility of a future messiah who will usher in the kingdom of God outside the formal boundaries of the Church. To some, this view may appear as a "postponed triumphalism," in the guise of a Christian concession to Jewish religious reality—a critique that has been made in reference to Moltmann's work.[37] Though I will explore the theological effects of millenarian thought on the eradication of supersessionism, this project will generally remain ambiguous regarding the topic of what the millennial reign of Christ or the Parousia would look like in all its details, with the exception of a very brief experiment in constructive chiliastic exegesis at the end of the book. Overall, we will leave the bulk of such speculative details to other Christian theologians.[38] The primary point is that by viewing the full eschatological reign of Jesus Christ as an event that is future in form, the Church cannot claim its own "reign" in history, or that it as an institution possesses the only messianic vision or hope for the future. Likewise, the Church must view itself as provisional—converting to the coming kingdom of God on earth, and converting again and again to the way of Jesus the messiah.

Because this book is addressed to those within the Christian tradition, specifically Roman Catholics, we must ask to what degree Jesus has been stripped of his "Jewishness"—not solely for the sake of interreligious dialogue, but for the sake of Christian theology itself. I will argue that any reassessment of supersessionism must begin with the assumption that God is not "done" with the Jewish people and that the earliest Christian traditions espoused primarily Jewish forms of eschatology. The Jewish aspect of divine personhood is precisely that which is missing from the collective consciousness of Western Christianity—Judaism is a constitutive part of God's workings within history, in light of the fact that God's gifts and calling are irrevocable.

As a Christian theologian, I write as one who has a personal stake in maintaining the divinity of Jesus Christ and the Trinitarian nature of God. The Lordship of Christ and the divinity of Jesus are no doubt obstacles to messianic notions among the Jewish people, yet these issues will be left relatively unexplored for the sake of the larger purpose of this project—to point out that *the Church's sedimentary view of itself* may be opened up to an alternative hope, through a millenarian approach. A re-apprehension of early Christian millenarian theology has the ability to overcome ecclesial supersessionism while simultaneously reminding contemporary theologians of the Jewish roots of Jesus's own eschatological emphasis.

According to Moltmann, through its rejection of millenarianism,

> the church has set itself up as the kingdom of God on earth in absolute form. But in setting itself up as absolute through this claim, it is bound to detach itself from the history of Israel, because it is unable to recognize any other representation of divine rule on earth, or to promise the world any other future than itself. This absolutism has divided the church from its origin and future. Christian hate of the "impenitent" Jews is ultimately based on Christians' self-hate of their own impossible claim, namely "hatred of one's own imperfection, of one's own "not yet", which constantly has to be repressed through this absolute assertion.[39]

Here Moltmann points out an important concept in post-Holocaust theology: the sentiment that the Church is not "perfect" because it is working toward a *future*, somehow in relation to other historical entities. The historical entity that is Judaism is a special case for the Church because, despite the obvious need to respect the otherness of Judaism, it is nevertheless a religious phenomenon *constitutive* of Catholicism itself. Without the Hebrew Bible, without the God if Israel, without the people Israel, and without the Jew named Jesus of Nazareth, Catholicism would have nothing to say about the God of Israel and the covenantal and divine relationship initiated for Gentiles through the root of Judaism.[40]

Ultimately, my work will demonstrate that there are two important ecclesiological aspects of consequence for Jewish–Catholic relations, reintroduced by millenarian thought: first, the resurgence of a messianic hope for the future outside the canonical boundaries of the Church, namely, for the Jews, and second, the acceptance of the contingent reality of the Church, i.e., that the Church is able to maintain the proposition that it somehow possesses a revelatory reality, while at the same time understanding that it will be "surprised" by the future brought to it by God. This view perceives the Church as an entity within time and history, as opposed to an absolutized form of the kingdom of God on earth. In this revised theology, Jesus Christ is the fulfillment of messianic promises, but is so in a way that relates the future of Christ to the future of human beings. There exists a contingency and an openness because the future has not yet been realized. Though the future must include the Jewish people because of God's covenant faithfulness, exactly how this will take place remains a mystery. We know that it will occur in "eschatological ways." Moltmann's work helps in this regard because ". . . he sees the resurrection of Jesus as the anchor of hope in history, the bridge between the universal hope of Jewish prophecy and apocalyptic and the eschatological mission of the Church in world history."[41] The Church is called to proclaim Jesus as messiah, but the synagogue has its own mission in the world—one not yet fully known, remaining undefinable within Christian theology. If Christian theologians ponder the ways Jewish religion contributes to salvation history and its future, those theologians do so only from a highly conditioned perspective—through the eyes of a follower of Jesus the messiah.

This book is for the use and benefit of the confessional Christian theological community, first and foremost. We couch this project in confessional terms because some Christian participants in the Christian–Jewish dialogue have "put the cart before the horse," pretending that the propositional, dogmatic cart is not in reality an obstacle, and then wondering why only incremental progress is made. The theological cart that stands before the horse of Jewish–Catholic dialogical progress is supersessionism—a silent assumption that lives within the shadows of Constantinian Christianity, and deeply rooted in a certain kind of ecclesiological eschatology.

A key question that will be raised is that of *why* millenarianism is the way forward beyond supersessionism in terms of eschatological systems, instead of some other system. Certainly, critics of eschatological millenarianism would argue that the appearance of Jesus Christ on earth for a period of time prior to the general resurrection is not necessary in maintaining a healthy relationship with the Jews. Is not the restoration of all things in Christ and the eschatology espoused in Catholic history since the fourth century adequate in expressing the concerns that Moltmann has raised concerning "historical millenarianism?" Richard Bauckham's book *God will be All in All* is unique in that it features a dialogue between Bauckham (a student of Moltmann), and Moltmann himself on the issue of millenarianism, and it will be cited in this book to examine this issue. Moltmann claims that the primary way in which the Church usurped Israel's identity was by denying Israel the right to any future messianic eschatological hope of its own. There is no way in which the modern church acknowledges the validity of the manner in which the Jewish people are still waiting for their personal messiah—one who is to fulfill all the prophetic expectations of the Hebrew Bible as interpreted by the rabbis throughout the history of restoration theology.[42] Moltmann argues that the confessional documents of the Reformation period mention the Jews only once and this one mention contained the rejection of millenarianism as a "Jewish dream" in the seventeenth article of the Augsburg Confession.[43] Prior to this period, such as that which is reflected in the canons of the Fourth Lateran Council, all confessional documents either made no mention of the Jews, or were utterly pejorative. Thus, in millennial eschatology, Moltmann sees a reiteration of Jewish hope that had previously been appropriated by allegorical or historicized readings of the Thousand Years' reign of Christ:

> This designation of the millennium as a Jewish dream is generally explained historically: it is supposed to have been due to movements within the Judaism of the time. But I understand it theologically. Christ's kingdom of peace is evidently associated with hope for Israel's future in the fulfillment of God's promises to Israel in the kingdom of the Son of man (Daniel 7). But *for Christians* this kingdom of the son of man is identical with Christ's kingdom of peace at the end of time.[44]

The Christian "reign" with Jesus Christ is to be marked by its character as a reign of martyrs and oppressed saints.

In the final chapter of this book, I will argue for ways in which Christian theologians might begin to envision such an eschatological convergence, which must logically lead the Church into understanding itself as a consistently *converting* entity, moving away from an institution which seeks to harbor power, toward an entity which seeks to serve in partnership with other historical entities, respecting their alternative "otherness," while still maintaining its evangelistic witness.[45] This conversionary element within the Church and the unique hope for Israel *as* Israel is found primarily within the millenarian paradigm.[46] Though Moltmann's language of Israel and the Church operating as "two parallel detours" in history toward an eschatological future is foreign to Catholic thought, one need not adopt a two-covenant theory in order to accept the premise of the Thousand Years' reign of Christ. This is because the discrepancies that follow between the Jewish and Christian conceptions of the messiah appear to have more to do with function than identity, and there could be a unified covenantal understanding of Judaism and Christianity containing within it a very diverse and variable expression that allows both traditions to be what they currently are.[47] In other words, the millenarian paradigm views Jews as Jews, and Christians as Christians, worshipping the God of Israel and the Lamb of God together during the eschaton, but without necessarily *becoming the other* in totality.

Moltmann's insistence on millenarian hope in the Christian tradition is rooted in his understanding of the Book of Revelation's Thousand Years' reign of Christ, and its connection with Paul's "apocalyptic mystery" in Romans 11:25–32. For Moltmann, the absence of the recognition of Jesus as the Christ of Israel is to be viewed as a means for Jewish messianic hope in the Christian tradition:

> Paul justifies his mission to the Gentiles, which he wanted to pursue to the ends of the earth, on the grounds of all-Israel's rejection of the gospel: that is the starting point; while all-Israel's acceptance and salvation through the One 'who will come from Zion', the Christ of the Parousia, is the final goal.

>His mission to the Gentiles is the detour he is making for the purpose of Israel's redemption. Israel's future does not lie in the church. It is to be found in the kingdom of the Messiah/Son of man, as God has promised Israel. Paul describes the End-time 'timetable of salvation' *geographically*, and according to our terminology this also means *within history. That is to say it has in view already the end of time, not just the eternity of the new creation.*[48]

Moltmann's argument for the necessity of a "futurist" millenarian approach is rooted in his interpretation of St. Paul's understanding of the return of Jesus Christ, and not in the current Catholic interpretation which essentially limits the eschatology of the Church to the Augustinian approach, an approach rendered authoritative, though not formally so, in the fourth century A.D. In the current Catholic view, death ushers in heaven for members of the Church, while Christ's return will immediately usher in the eternity of the new creation and not the end of time, whereas for the millennialist, the end occurs within history and in a specific geographical location, namely Zion. For many Jews, these historical and geographical points are *imperative* because redemption occurs at the coming of the messiah and the "flooding in" of the nations to a specific geographical and earthly location, Zion, or Jerusalem.

The disregard for the ancient heritage of millenarianism by the formulation of fifth century Roman Catholicism set the stage for an a priori dismissal of any futurist expression of chiliasm in the majority of Western Christianity. For example, in traditional Lutheran theology, ". . . eschatology consisted essentially of an apocalyptic expectation of an imminent Last Judgment."[49] The space in between time and eternity that was maintained in the millenarian emphasis on material history was neglected in favor of an almost entirely spiritualized understanding of the afterlife, counter to the Judaism of the earliest Jesus followers. Nevertheless, there were notable exceptions to the resistance to millenarianism in the West. Moltmann claims that it is in the apocalyptic tradition of England that we see a theology of hope for the Jews. This English theology ". . . was aligned towards the resurrection and God's coming kingdom. Hand in hand with the expectation of the overthrow of the Antichrist went the expectation of Israel's redemption and the establishment of Christ's thousand years' empire."[50] For the millenarian Christian, the redemption of Israel and the *first* resurrection of the dead happen in close proximity, because Paul's words are not taken as allegory but as literal eschatological reality: "For if their rejection is the reconciliation of the world, what will their acceptance be but life from the dead?" (Romans 11:15, NAB).[51] In this Romans passage, "acceptance" simply refers to the acceptance of the Jewish people by God. Moltmann claims that millenarian ideas are implicit in the writings of Paul, pointing primarily to the chapters on the Jewish reality in Romans and various passages that draw a sharp distinction between the resurrection *of* the dead and resurrection *from* the dead.

For Moltmann, the issues raised by millenarianism are important, not only for how the Church views the continuing significance of Judaism, but likewise for how Christians themselves view eschatology and the reality of the bodily resurrection, outside of interreligious implications. If there is truly a distinction between the resurrection *from* the dead and the resurrection *of* the dead, and if in fact there are issues raised regarding temporality and geography in the writings of Paul and John, a millenarian reading of the New Testament must at minimum be re-evaluated by its opponents, and should not be rejected a priori.

Moltmann believes that the root of the near-equating of the Church with the kingdom of God is the rejection of an alternative hope for the future messiah outside of the Church—a hope emphasized and protected by millenarianism, but rejected as a "Jewish dream," even by many Reformation Churches.[52] Following Joachim of Fiore, Moltmann posits a new preaching of the gospel in the End-time, ". . . a preaching which calls people, no longer to the church but to the kingdom—converts no longer to the Christian faith but to hope for the kingdom."[53] The Christian Church of the Last Days walks alongside Israel in a mutual and continual conversion to the kingdom.[54] Wisely, Moltmann does not define what the kingdom is exactly, as to leave space for a Jewish understanding of it—but for Moltmann, the kingdom is a Christian one—the expected reign of God as expressed in the life, death and resurrection of Jesus.

In the first part of this book, I will frame the question of supersessionism utilizing contemporary Catholic theology. Beginning with *NA*, and working through the documents and theologians within the Catholic tradition associated with its reception, I will illustrate how supersessionism is increasingly viewed as an infeasible theology in Catholic circles, and oftentimes identified as a theology that is dangerous and should itself be replaced. Nevertheless, supersessionism remains a strong deterrent to Jewish–Catholic relations. Utilizing the work of Rosemary Radford Ruether, Philip Cunningham, Walter Kasper, Pope John Paul II, and various Protestant theologians, I will demonstrate how the roots of supersessionism have been associated with certain trends in both eschatology and ecclesiology. I will also identify and examine modern Catholic theology that seeks to maintain aspects of supersessionism. I will claim that the Roman Catholic conception of fulfilled messianism, ecclesiologically fulfilled promises that negate the Jewish covenantal relation with God, and the tradition's propensity for favoring the "already" over the "not yet," particularly in ecclesiological terms (vis-à-vis historical millenarianism), have acted as major roadblocks to overcoming the theological problem of supersessionism. I will demonstrate that *NA*'s challenge to Roman Catholic theologians, and its utilization of key biblical and theological terms, makes it a watershed ecclesial document as it is applied to Jewish–Catholic questions. I will pose the question as to whether a millenarian eschatology, one deeply imbedded in the early Church tradition, may be able to overcome the aspects of traditional Catholic ecclesiology and eschatology that allow supersessionism and forms of replacement theology regarding the Jews to flourish.

I will begin the second part of this book by defining millenarianism, and will intersperse the section with the words of authors who have challenged it as a legitimate eschatology in Roman Catholicism. I will trace millenarianism's roots to Jewish apocalypticism in addition to its early Christian roots in the Gospels, Pauline literature, and the Book of Revelation. I will introduce Moltmann's version of millenarianism and describe its connection with the Jewish–Christian question. I will subsequently examine the doctrine's popularity and normativity among the Church Fathers, both orthodox and heretical and trace its decline (but not its disappearance) in the third and fourth centuries. I will add a brief section in which I critique a relatively recent book that argues from silence while suggesting that amillennialism was common in the early Church. I will support the claim that millenarianism was the ante-Nicene Church's universal eschatology, taken as an apostolic deposit. Next, I will examine the pivotal turning points of eschatology in Catholicism, namely, the works of Gauis and Origen. I will likewise explore Eusebius' political amillennialism and Tyconius' ecclesiological amillennialism, with a focus on Augustine's *City of God* and the bishop's later rejection of millenarianism—pointing toward the establishment of "historical millenarianism" in the tradition. With the Augustinian tradition, the Church came to see itself as the kingdom of God on earth.

In the third section, I will briefly turn to the subject of orthodoxy versus heresy, and utilize a segment of the work of Vincent of Lérins, applying it to the millenarian question. The issue at hand will revolve around whether the early Church viewed millenarianism as heretical, even up through the fifth century, or as unilaterally normative and preferable. I will examine the early creeds and general Ecumenical Councils, and I will argue against scholars who claim that millenarianism was formally rejected as heretical in these Councils, basing my argument on sound contemporary scholarship. By contrast, I will show how millenarianism actually helped to form the basis of the early Church creeds. For the sake of brevity, I will then look at the modern and contemporary rejection of millenarianism in official Catholic pronouncements and documents, provide the context that may help explain such statements, and question whether they stand as authoritative definitions regarding the whole of Catholic eschatology. I will examine the official pronouncements of the Catholic Church regarding millenarianism, beginning in the 1940s with Pope Pius XII and going through the statements of Pope Benedict XVI. I will pay special attention to the circumstances and the context concerning these pronouncements against millenarianism, stressing that these were the first official ecclesial statements regarding millenarianism—statements occurring many centuries after the doctrine took root in various parts of the Christian tradition. I will touch upon a version of Eucharistic millenarianism supported by the Church, specifically because it maintains clerical and papal authority. Finally, I will explore both the legitimate and illegitimate reasons for the Catholic resistance toward millennial eschatologies in order to flow into the next chapter regarding Moltmann's modified version of millenarianism.

In the final sections I will provide brief prolegomena to the concept of Moltmann's Jewish and Christian messianic kingdom by exploring some general concepts within Jewish eschatology. I will explain how Moltmann's mitigated millenarianism is an extension of the thought of the early Fathers, but also how his modified version is poised to overcome the supersessionism that is part of Christianity and Catholicism in particular. By viewing the Church as a provisional entity within history, leading to the kingdom, Moltmann critiques traditional amillennialism and illustrates how millenarian theology opens a way for an alternative messianic hope—future Judaism. The understanding that the Church is a transitional and initiatory reality, moving as a "partner in history" with Judaism finds its culmination and confirmation in Moltmann's millenarianism, as an authentic and traditional alternative to current Roman Catholic eschatology. I will likewise explore the question of whether amillennialism is necessarily supersessionist, and whether Moltmann's millenarian approach is necessary in overcoming supersessionism. I will utilize distinctions in the philosophy of history and time that exist between millennialists and amillennialsts in order to show the necessity of millenarian approach in order to refute replacement theology. Last, I will take a brief look at the millenarian exegesis of Moltmann and others regarding both Revelation 20, and Romans 11, and use the passages in constructing a post-supersessionist view of the world to come. Overall, this final chapter will seek to illustrate how a millenarian reading of history within the Roman Catholic Church may allow for an alternative Jewish messianic hope that is not totalized through problematic understandings of the institutional Church and its function in history—all while attempting to maintain traditional Christological categories and also what theologians call "the unicity and universality" of Jesus Christ for the Church and the world.

The focus of this study is that of overcoming supersessionism, synonymous with "replacement theology," both of which will be defined as a problematic theological constructs. We will also explore how a millenarian reading of history and the Last Days has a positive impact on the question of Jewish and Catholic coexistence and future hope. The theme therefore imposes some limitations on the project as a whole. This project examines four concepts specifically. First, I examine the questioning and rejection of traditional supersessionist theological readings of the Jewish–Catholic interaction in contemporary Catholic theological scholarship. Second, I illustrate the biblical and Patristic root of millenarian eschatology, which was normatively held as a part of the apostolic deposit of faith. Third, I explore the possibility that millenarianism—an eschatological system that has been recently rejected by the Catholic hierarchy, but was never formally condemned as a heresy prior to the modern period—is an acceptable eschatology for Roman Catholic theologians to examine. Finally, I argue that the Protestant theologian Jürgen Moltmann has contributed greatly by illustrating how a millenarian view of history has the power to protect and expand a positive Christian position on the Jews and their continued participation in salvation history, essentially overcoming supersessionist presumptions, while at the same time maintaining orthodox views on the person of Christ. My work suggests that through the theological exploration of the implications of this millenarian approach, Roman Catholic theology may experiment with and adopt a position that clearly limits ecclesial triumphalism through the concepts of alternative hope that are inferred by millenarian presuppositions. The hope of the nations and of Israel is Jesus Christ, but this book argues that the distinctions between Jew and non-Jew are God-ordained, and play heavily into salvation history.

Though this book may provide a dialogical ground for the future, it is an exercise in Christian theology specifically, and not a work on Jewish–Christian "inter-religious dialogue," or even inter-theological dialogue. It is an intra-theological work. This book is focused on the issue of supersessionism as a problem in Roman Catholic, and to a great extent, Christian theology and in it I argue that the tension may be overcome by adopting eschatological and ecclesial aspects that have been a part of the Catholic tradition but were in the past relegated to a non-dominant position throughout Catholic history. This book is written from the perspective of a theologian who is a member of the Protestant Christian tradition, with a special eye toward uprooting supersessionist foundations as perceived within Roman Catholic theology. My deep exposure to Catholicism and continued growth in the knowledge of Catholic theology and philosophy will aid in accomplishing the goals of this project. Though Christianity is a polyvalent phenomenon, based on the author's presumption that both Protestantism and Catholicism are in multiple ways part of one faith tradition that views itself as "Christian," dialogue and critique within these traditions will be an assumed mode of systematic study. This work is intended neither as a treatise on the ethical ramifications of the *Shoah*, nor as a philosophical, ethical, or historical analysis of the connections between Christian anti-Judaism, supersessionism, and anti-Semitism. When the terms "Jew," "Jewish,""Judaism," "People of the Covenant," "Israel," and "People of Israel" are used in this book, the meaning is to be bracketed and limited to a specific Christian understanding of these terms, as this is the only legitimate epistemic location from which the author may gauge and analyze the theological problem of supersessionism. To attempt otherwise would be to speak on behalf of the other in a manner that is unrepresentative, unfair, and damaging, both to the Jewish philosophical and theological tradition, and to the Christian. Judaism itself is as complex, varied and diverse as Christian denominationalism and cannot be totalized, as if any one piece of scholarship is able to describe a given religious phenomenon in its entirety.[55] Because a baseline understanding of Jewish religious expression is necessary for the purposes of Christian discourse on the subject, certain broad attributes will be applied to some aspects of Jewish religious experience with the understanding that these aspects by no means encompass the whole of Judaism in a religious or ethnic sense.

This study is not intended as a thorough historical analysis of supersessionism and Christian millenarian readings, though the Catholic ecclesial decisions regarding these issues will be examined in detail and will trace back centuries—particularly as it regards millenarianism and the Councils. The historical analysis will serve the theological implications that are imperative to define and explore in this study, for the ultimate purpose of going beyond the supersessionism of past centuries. In the initial chapter on supersessionism, not every voice of the subject will be given a hearing, but only those which have either pioneered discussion in the modern and contemporary period, or those who represent the contemporary Roman Catholic resistance to replacement theology through ecclesiological and eschatological means, inspired by the Second Vatican Council.

The objective of this study is limited in both quantity and degree, insofar as it is designed as a study on the eschatological and ecclesial implications of a specifically Christian millenarian thought, the reasons for the contemporary Catholic rejection of such thought, and the various ways in which such thought is powerful in the positive or negative role it ascribes to Judaism, both in relation to the future and coming kingdom of God, and the current historical significance of certain Jewish eschatological and soteriological ideas. I do not intend to resolve each complexity embodied in the idea of Jewish–Christian eschatological hope, although the issues of the Trinity and the incarnation will be brought up throughout because of their obvious bearing on messianic expectations in the two faith traditions. In this project I will not attempt to resolve the differences between Judaism and Catholicism, especially questions surrounding the divinity of Jesus, but instead will look to offer possible venues for further clarification, namely shifts in ecclesiology and eschatology within the Catholic tradition. This project exists in order to close certain doors on the theological assumptions that stem from Christian supersessionism while at the same time open doors to overcoming supersessionism by examining damaging ecclesial and historical principles and adopting alternative ecclesiological and eschatological awareness, specifically as garnished from the rich millenarian circles of theology that have been and continue to be very much alive in the Church today. The objective of this study, because it involves supersessionism, millenarianism as it has been historically received in the Catholic tradition, millenarianism as it is read through Jürgen Moltmann's messianic ecclesiology and theology of history, and finally the overall implications of examining these areas for a potentially new Catholic theology of Judaism, each section will be treated modestly, analyzed primarily in its relation to the Jewish–Catholic question, and will rely heavily on the expert scholarship that is existent.

This book will contribute to both post-Holocaust theology and to the changes in theological discourse signaled by *NA*, particularly the move toward *theological* dialogue between Judaism and Catholicism, and not merely dialogue on an ethical or comparative level as it regards religion. Nevertheless, this project is merely a precursor to further dialogue between the Jewish and Catholic traditions—a precursor aimed at overcoming anti-Jewish Christian theologies. Specifically, this book will continue and enhance the contemporary discussion on developing a non-supersessionist theology in light of the New Testament and progress made regarding the historical Jesus, the context of Second Temple Judaism, and the Catholic theological tradition. It is my intention that the book go a step further than the current scholarship regarding supersessionism by utilizing Jürgen Moltmann's millenarian theology. I plan to use this messianic ideology as a means of constructing a theology of ecclesial self-conversion, overcoming some of the eschatological and ecclesiological barriers in Catholicism that stand in the way of acknowledging the continued role in salvation history that the Jewish people possess—a role implied by *NA*. Considering that Moltmann is one of the most prominent Protestant theologians today, an application of a major theme in his messianic thought should contribute well to modern Christian theologies of

Judaism. In addition, Moltmann's thought on millenarianism and the Jewish–Christian question was never systematized in any formal manner, though it played a considerable role in almost all of his writings. To consider the various ways in which Moltmann's theology of common hope adds to the specific ways in which Catholic theology has struggled with the issue of supersessionism will contribute to a long-term and ongoing effort toward solutions.

One other major contribution of this study will be the ecclesiological implications that it will have for Roman Catholic theology. The official documents of the Second Vatican Council express a desire for the Catholic Church to view itself as a developing entity, complete and fulfilled in some ways, yet provisional and secondary to the kingdom of God in other ways.[56] The Second Vatican Council describes the Church as partnering with other entities and other religious systems through history, working toward a common future.[57] The Council documents are somewhat ambiguous as to what that future will hold or resemble, but as a Catholic statement, it places the reign of God and the continued significance of Jesus at the center of it. The work of Moltmann and the questions raised by theologians seeking to propose a post-supersessionist understanding of Judaism have much to say regarding how the Church is to view itself, and how its ecclesiological stance in relation to the future kingdom of God is pivotal to the way it views other religions, particularly Judaism with its covenantal terms, and the constitutive aspects Judaism carries for Christianity. The aspects of millenarianism that will be discussed as a legitimate way forward in a positive Christian theology of Judaism, aspects recently rejected by the Magisterium, have profound implications for Catholicism, considering that these aspects have never fully disappeared from Catholic theology.

My thesis that a millenarian reading of Revelation 20:4–6, which is both traditional in Catholic history and central in the work of Moltmann, is capable of overcoming supersessionist tendencies in Catholic theology—because of its eschatological and ecclesial implications regarding Judaism—will hopefully mark the beginning of the reconsideration of other eschatological systems in relation to the Jewish–Catholic question.

Notes

1 In this book, the terms "Judaism," "Jewish People," "Jew," "People of Israel," "Jewish," "People of the Covenant," and "Israel," will be understood, in an intentionally ambiguous manner, as ". . . the biblical and theological view of the Jews before God as this is expressed today through religious Judaism in the synagogues and in the land of Israel." Jürgen Moltmann, *The Coming of God: Christian Eschatology* (London: SCM, 1996), 197.

2 The First Scottish Confession of 1560 was the only creed of the Christian Church as a whole to refer to God's history with the Jews. See Philip Schaff, *The Creeds of Christendom*, 6th ed. (Grand Rapids, MI: Baker, 1998), vol. 3, 442–443. In The Augsburg Confession XVII: "The Return of Christ for Judgment," there is a cursory treatment of Christ's "Thousand Year Reign," which is rejected as a "Jewish Dream." This will be extremely important for my overall argument.

Introduction 17

3   From the papal letter of Gregory I in 598 entitled "Sicut judaeis non," to the 1755 "Beatus Andreas" by Benedict XIV, a steady litany of anti-Jewish documents are historically traced.
4   See Robert Michael, *A History of Catholic Antisemitism: The Dark Side of the Church* (New York: Palgrave Macmillan, 2008), 10. For the distinction between anti-Judaism and anti-Semitism, see Helen M. Valois, "Anti-Judaism vs. Anti-Semitism: Was Christianity Itself Responsible for the Nazi Holocaust?" *Lay Witness*, October 1998, 1–4.
5   David Mamet, *The Wicked Son: Anti-Semitism, Self-Hatred, and the Jews, Jewish Encounters* (New York: Schocken, 2006), 10. Robert W. Jenson has claimed that the Church and the synagogue have walked in such close parallel that it is nothing short of remarkable. Carl E. Braaten, and Jenson, *Jews and Christians: People of God* (Grand Rapids, MI: William B. Eerdmans, 2003), 3. See also Edith Schaeffer, *Christianity is Jewish* (Wheaton, IL: Tyndale House, 1975), 8.
6   See James D.G. Dunn, *Jews and Christians: The Parting of the Ways, A.D. 70 to 135*; the Second Durham-Tübingen Research Symposium on Earliest Christianity and Judaism, Durham, September 1989 (Grand Rapids, MI: Eerdmans, 1999), 24.
7   Michael J. Vlach, *The Church as a Replacement of Israel: An Analysis of Supersessionism*, Edition Israelogie (Edis) (Frankfurt and New York: Peter Lang, 2009), 25–26. For Augustine, there was a more nuanced and reciprocal relationship between the Old and New Testaments, expressed in his dictum "Novum Testamentum in Vetere latet, et in Novo Vetus patet" (*Quaest. in Hept.*, 2, 73: CSEL 28, 3, at 141).
8   Walther Eichrodt, *Theology of the Old Testament*, The Old Testament Library (Philadelphia, PA: Westminster Press, 1961), 14. See further, Patrick D. Miller, *Israelite Religion and Biblical Theology: Collected Essays* (Sheffield: Sheffield Academic Press, 2000), 473.
9   R. Kendall Soulen, *The God of Israel and Christian Theology* (Minneapolis, MN: Fortress Press, 1996), 34–51.
10 Ronald E. Diprose defines supersessionism, or replacement theology as the view that "the church completely and permanently replaced ethnic Israel in the working out of God's plan and as recipient of Old Testament promises to Israel." Diprose, *Israel in the Development of Christian Thought* (Rome: Istituto Biblico Evangelico Italiano, 2000), 2. On the continued influence of supersessionism on contemporary theology, see the Institute for Christian and Jewish Studies document entitled "Supersessionism," found at http://www.icjs.org/library/flashpoints/supersessionism.php/.
11 Philip A. Cunningham, "Official Ecclesial Documents to Implement the Second Vatican Council on Relations with Jews: Study Them, Become Immersed in Them, and Put Them into Practice," *Studies in Christian–Jewish Relations* 4, no. 1 (2009): 1–36. For references to *Nostra Aetate*, see Austin Flannery, *The Conciliar and Post Conciliar Documents, Vatican Council II* (Dublin: Dominican Publications, 1975).
12 Rosemary Radford Ruether, *Faith and Fratricide: The Theological Roots of Anti-Semitism* (New York: Seabury Press, 1974), 12. Ruether's work remains a definitive tool in assessing the roots and theological underpinnings of modern anti-Judaism.
13 Ibid., 246.
14 Ibid.
15 In this sense, the church is a "missionary anticipation of the kingdom," pointing to Christ through the proclamation of the gospel. Richard Bauckham, *The Theology of Jürgen Moltmann* (Edinburgh: T&T Clark, 1995), 146. Moltmann states, regarding the Christological question: "Every eschatology that claims to be Christian, and not merely utopian or apocalyptic or a stage in salvation history, must have a Christological foundation." See Moltmann, *The Coming of God*, 194.
16 Bauckham, *The Theology of Jürgen Moltmann*, 146. See also Alva J. McClain, *The Greatness of the Kingdom: An Inductive Study of the Kingdom of God as Set Forth in the Scriptures* (Grand Rapids, MI: Zondervan, 1950,) 15.

18 *Introduction*

17 Paula Fredricksen, "Tyconius and Augustine on the Apocalypse," in Richard K. Emmerson and Bernard McGinn eds., *The Apocalypse in the Middle Ages* (Ithaca, NY: Cornell University Press, 1993), 20–37, 20.

18 A considerable number of the early Church Fathers accepted a literal reading of Christ's Thousand Years' reign and rejected the idea that the Church itself was the reign of Christ on earth. Much of this was related to the early Church's expectation of the imminent return of Christ. For a full rendering of the Catholic Church's intersections with millenarianism, see Karl A. Kottman, *Millenarianism and Messianism in Early Modern European Culture*, Vol. 2: *Catholic Millenarianism: From Savonarola to the Abbé Grégoire* (Dordrecht: Kluwer Academic, 2001). For the Catholic Church's recent rejection of millenarianism, see *Catechism of the Catholic Church* (New York: Doubleday, 1995), 194. The 1995 Catechism carries the Imprimatur Potest, authorized by Joseph Cardinal Ratzinger for the argument that the Roman Catholic and Orthodox Churches viewed millenarianism as a theological concept not held "everywhere by all, always," see Laurent Cleenewerck, *His Broken Body: Understanding and Healing the Schism between the Roman Catholic and Eastern Orthodox Churches* (Washington, DC: Euclid University, 2007), 122.

19 R.L. Wilken, *The Land Called Holy: Palestine in Christian History and Thought* (New Haven, CT: Yale University Press, 1992), 56.

20 The form of millenarianism espoused by Moltmann is to a large degree a variant of its earlier forms, and this will become evident throughout this book.

21 *Catechism of the Catholic Church: Revised in Accordance with the Official Latin Text Promulgated by Pope John Paul II*, 2nd ed. (Vatican City and Washington, DC: Libreria Editrice Vaticana, 1997), #67.

22 Pope Pius XII's statement is rendered as such: "Systema Millenarismi mitigati tute doceri non posse" (A mild millennial system is not able to be taught safely). Henricus Denzinger, ed., *Enchiridion Symbolorum: Definitionum et Declarationum de Rebus Fidei et Morum,* 36th emended ed., ed. Adolfus Schönmetzer (Freiburg: Herder, 1976), 759.

23 See Henri Grégoire, *Histoire Des Sectes Religieuses* (Paris: Potey, 1814). Among those whose millenarian approaches were not formally censured are first and foremost the Patristic saints and Doctors of the Church who had advocated millenarian ideals, namely St. Justin Martyr, St. John Chrysostom, St. Papias (a friend of Polycarp), St. Irenaeus, the African bishop Nepos, St. Hippolytus of Rome. See Alexander Roberts, et al., *The Ante-Nicene Fathers, Translations of the Writings of the Fathers Down to A.D. 325* (New York: C. Scribner's Sons, 1899). It is important to note that the Orthodox Church officially condemns millenarianism based on an erroneous claim that the Second Ecumenical Council of 381 C.E. likewise rejected it. See "Chiliasm" in "Orthodox Christian Beliefs and Practices," accessed at http://www.uocc.ca/en-ca/faith/beliefs/, January 28, 2011. Some other Orthodox texts make the claim that millenarianism was rejected at the Councils. See Damascene, *Father Seraphim Rose: His Life and Works* (Platina, CA: St. Herman of Alaska Brotherhood, 2003). Other Orthodox periodicals admit of the nuances of heresy and question if Chiliasm was ever formally rejected in the canons: ". . . a scholarly and impartial review of the primary sources shows that the Councils have never explicitly condemned premillenialism [sic]." "Q. 486" in "Orthodox Answers," at http://www.orthodoxanswers.org/answer/485/, accessed January 28, 2011. One notable supporter of millenarian ideals after both the Patristic supporters and Joachim, was Henri Grégoire, otherwise known as Abbé Grégoire, a Jesuit priest, constitutionally elected bishop, and French revolutionary. Grégoire was so well known for his denunciations of anti-Jewish violence that the Nazis of eastern occupied France destroyed his statue in 1942. See Richard S. Levy, *Antisemitism: A Historical Encyclopedia of Prejudice and Persecution*, 2 vols (Santa Barbara, CA: ABC-CLIO, 2005), 284. According to

Introduction 19

R. Hermon-Belot, Grégoire was emphatic in his ". . . statement that the intermediary Advent of Jesus-Christ, and his visible reign upon the entire earth, consists in a 'doctrine almost universally taught by the Fathers of the first three centuries.' As a matter of fact, it has been distorted and made odious by heretics, but it was never positively rejected by the church." R. Hermon-Belot, "God's Will in History: The Abbé Grégoire, the Revolution and the Jews," in Kottman, *Millenarianism and Messianism in Early Modern European Culture*, 96. Again, Herman-Belot states that Grégoire ". . . saw the Millennium in history. In his eyes, the prophecies were about what was going to come to earth," and that "Grégoire always emphasized the extremely important part . . . [Figurist millenarian writings] . . . assigned to the Jewish people." Ibid., 97. See also Massimo Introvigne, "Catholic Apocalypticism and the Army of Mary" in Stephen Hunt, *Christian Millenarianism: From the Early Church to Waco* (Bloomington, IN: Indiana University Press, 2001), 151. Thus, throughout Catholic history there have been pockets of millenarian belief—systems of thought not censured by the church until the reign of Pope Pius XII.

24 See Catherine Cornille, ed., *Many Mansions?: Multiple Religious Belonging and Christian Identity* (Maryknoll, NY: Orbis Books, 2002).

25 Though other Church Fathers argued against millenarian principles, Augustine's writing was the major death-blow to chiliasm.

26 The early Augustine, like many of his contemporaries, was a firm supporter of millenarian ideas. G. Folliet, "La Typologie Du Sabbat Chez Saint Augustin: Son Interprétation Millénariste Entre 388 Et 400," *Revue des études augustiniennes 2* (1956): 371–391.

27 Moltmann, *The Coming of God*, 192.

28 See Moltmann, *The Coming of God*, 192–194; 146. Moltmann states that he is ". . . distinguishing between historical millenarianism, which interprets the present as Christ's Thousand Years' empire and the last age of humanity, and eschatological millenarianism, which hopes for the kingdom of Christ as the future which will be an alternative to the present, and links this future with the end of "this world" and the new creation of all things.

29 Ibid., 194.

30 For example, the line in the Nicene Creed, and likewise in the later Athanasian Creed which reads "and his kingdom will have no end . . ." in reference to Jesus' return (missing in the version from the First Council of Nicaea in 325 but added during the First Council of Constantinople in 381), was not included to emphasize that a literal reign of Christ upon the earth for a time within history was impossible, but instead to illustrate that the Trinitarian reality is an eternal reality—not one which "came into being," as in the Marcellianism, a heresy whereby adherents claimed that the Divine Logos was immanent from eternity in God, but issuing from God in the act of creation. Marcellus himself never explicitly agreed that Christ's kingdom was "permanent," but the context of the dispute that led to the Epiphanian–Constantinopolitan additions to the Athanasian Creed never entailed millenarian ideas whatsoever. Expert of apocalyptic writings, Richard Bauckham, has confirmed my point.

31 The Catholic insistence on historical millenarianism solidified with Augustine's *De civitate Dei* 20.9: "Therefore, the Church even now is the kingdom of Christ and the kingdom of heaven." One would think that with the developments in ecclesiology in the *Lumen Gentium* concept of the "Pilgrim Church" that the concept of the Church as the kingdom would have died down, but such is not the case. For example, Pope Benedict XVI expresses that the Catholic Church holds to an ". . . interpretation of the kingdom of God we could call the ecclesiastical: the kingdom of God and the Church are related in different ways and brought into more or less close proximity." Pope Benedict XVI, *Jesus of Nazareth* (London: Doubleday, 2007), 49–50.

20 *Introduction*

32 For a list of the Catholic concerns surrounding millenarianism, see Benedict XVI, *Eschatology, Death, and Eternal Life*, 2nd ed. (Washington, DC: Catholic University of America Press, 2007), 212–213.
33 This logically means that the Church and modern Israel, though part of the same covenant, lead to the same telos. Moltmann states that "The common focus of Jewish and Christian hopes is the coming of the Messiah to his messianic kingdom. Only the Christ of the Parousia will save 'all Israel' (Rom. 11:26). The acceptance of all Israel will be 'life from the dead' (Rom. 11:15f.). Consequently Israel's Messiah must be the risen One." Moltmann, *The Coming of God*, 198. Moltmann maintains the salvific universalism of Jesus Christ while opening space for Jewish religious significance for Christianity.
34 The words of Pope Benedict XVI regarding the 'proximity' between the Church and kingdom suggest this kind of realized ecclesiology. Ratzinger, *Jesus of Nazareth: From His Transfiguration through His Death and Resurrection*, 49–50.
35 Ruether, *Faith and Fratricide*, 247, emphasis mine.
36 See Moltmann, *The Coming of God*, 201.
37 Stephen R. Haynes, *Prospects for Post-Holocaust Theology*, American Academy of Religion Academy Series (Atlanta, GA: Scholars Press, 1991), 136.
38 See for example, Wilfred Cantwell Smith, *The Meaning and End of Religion* (Minneapolis, MN: Fortress Press, 1991), Paul F. Knitter, *No Other Name?: A Critical Survey of Christian Attitudes Toward the World Religions* (Maryknoll, NY: Orbis Books, 1985), 179; 199.
39 Jürgen Moltmann, *The Church in the Power of the Spirit: A Contribution to Messianic Ecclesiology* (Minneapolis, MN: Fortress Press, 1993), 136–137.
40 Moshe Aumann, *Conflict & Connection: The Jewish–Christian–Israel Triangle* (Hewlett, NY: Gefen Books, 2003), 118.
41 Rob Yule, "A Review of Literature on Eschatology with Special Reference to Jürgen Moltmann's Theology of Hope," *Journal of the New Zealand Theological Students Fellowship* (April 1968): 5–9.
42 For the Jewish understanding of belief in the resurrection as a requisite for resurrection, see Jon Douglas Levenson, *Resurrection and the Restoration of Israel: The Ultimate Victory of the God of Life* (New Haven, CT: Yale University Press, 2006), 19.
43 Richard Bauckham, ed., *God Will Be All in All: The Eschatology of Jürgen Moltmann*, 1st Fortress Press ed. (Minneapolis, MN: Fortress Press, 2001), 150.
44 Ibid., emphasis mine.
45 See Darrell L. Guder, *The Continuing Conversion of the Church*, Gospel and Our Culture Series (Grand Rapids, MI: W.B. Eerdmans, 2000), 195.
46 Moltmann states, "The historical paths [of church and synagogue] are separate and individual, the eschatological goal universal. Up to now I have seen no positive Israel theology on the Christian side which fails to integrate Christ's chiliastic kingdom of peace into eschatology." Moltmann as quoted in Bauckham, *God Will Be All in All*, 150, n. 41.
47 See Soulen, *The God of Israel and Christian Theology*.
48 Bauckham, *God Will Be All in All*, 151, n.41, emphasis mine.
49 Ibid., 152. Standing as an exception to this aversion to millenarianism are certain English Lutheran theologians of the nineteenth century, some of whose ideas are adapted by Moltmann. See note 41.
50 Ibid., See also Avihu Zakai, "The Poetics of History and the Destiny of Israel: The Role of the Jews in English Apocalyptic Thought during the Sixteenth and Seventeenth Centuries," *Journal of Jewish Thought and Philosophy* 5 (1966): 313–350.

51 The Greek word for "acceptance" or "reception" here is *apodoché* (in the Vulgate, *assumptio*), which connotes a future reception into the kingdom of God. Joseph Henry Thayer, Carl Ludwig Wilibald Grimm, and Christian Gottlob Wilke, *Thayer's Greek-English Lexicon of the New Testament: Coded with the Numbering System from Strong's Exhaustive Concordance of the Bible* (Peabody, MA: Hendrickson, 1996), 548. We must ask if by "reception," Paul meant the ushering in of the Jews in Christ's Thousand Years' reign on earth.
52 *Creeds of the Hungarian Reformed Christians: The Second Helvetic Confession and the Heidelberg Catechism* (Ligonier, PA: Bethlen Freedom Press, 1968), ch. 11.
53 Moltmann, *The Coming of God*, 199.
54 See Guder, *The Continuing Conversion of the Church*, 181.
55 See Jacob Neusner, *Judaism When Christianity Began: A Survey of Belief and Practice* (Louisville, KY: Westminster John Knox Press, 2002), 6.
56 On the one hand, in "The Mystery of the Church" of *Lumen Gentium*, it is stated that "The church . . . is the kingdom of Christ already present in mystery," while on the other hand, in the same section it is states that "while it slowly grows to maturity, the church longs for the completed kingdom and, with all its strength, hopes and desires to be united in glory with its king." Austin Flannery, *The Conciliar and Post Conciliar Documents, Vatican Council II*, 2–4, emphasis mine.
57 See the section in *Lumen Gentium* entitled "The Pilgrim Church," in addition to *NA*, 4, paragraph 4. In "The Pilgrim Church," the conciliar fathers claim "The church . . . will receive its perfection only in the glory of heaven, when the time for the renewal of all things will have come (Acts 3:21). At that time, together with the human race, the universe itself . . . will be perfectly established in Christ . . ." Ibid., 72, emphasis mine.

Part I

Supersessionism and *Nostra Aetate*

1 The problem of supersessionism

Though we have briefly defined supersessionism in the section above, a more detailed examination of the phenomenon will take place later in our text, along with contemporary prospects for a post-supersessionist theology. First, we must examine why supersessionism is considered a theological *problem* and why alternatives to supersessionism are appropriate. In many ways, the question is centered on the biblical interpretations that allow for supersessionism and the theological premises that follow—interpretations and premises that do not necessarily follow from the texts themselves. We must ask, along with all responsible theologians, if the philosophical and biblical presuppositions of a supersessionist theology correspond to the traditional Christian understanding of the character of God and the reality of salvation history as viewed through the lens of the Christian life. We must keep in mind the ethical ramifications of our theological understanding of Judaism in light of the atrocities of the past, namely, the *Shoah*. In line with the theology of Rosemary Radford Ruether, we must recognize whether a supersessionist view of history is a "reality-denying" rather than a "reality-discerning" principle.[1] Last, we must examine whether the theological propositions of Jews and Christians are ultimately convergent and reconcilable, resulting in a coherent "Jewish–Christian reality," if the Church, comprised predominantly of Gentiles, must be viewed as the fulfillment of Judaism in totality, rendering the Jewish theological heritage obsolete in soteriological form and function,[2] or neither of these options.

Types of supersessionism

Supersessionism, though active in numerous writings and practices in the Christian tradition, is a phenomenon and theological construct that only recently has been studied in-depth and parsed out in its various forms. Supersessionist theology was a normative Patristic historical hermeneutic, as is evidenced by the writings of Justin,[3] Barnabas,[4] and Origen,[5] yet it was so due to heavy competitions and polemical issues that were specific to the time and historical context. Supersessionist theology has taken on a great deal of critique by many skilled theologians in recent decades as an outside response from Jewish scholars, as a reaction to problems with replacement concepts by Christian theologians in search of a specifically positive Christian theology of the Jews, and by Jews who seek to critique Jewish counter-supersessionism—a critical response to millennia of Christian abuse aimed at usurping the God of Israel. According to David Novak, "... the ultimate coup de grâce of the Jewish counter-supersessionists is to assert that Christians do not worship the Lord God of Israel as do the Jews, but rather, another God altogether."[6] Thus, it is evident that Christian supersessionism has unleashed a considerable degree of theological virulence in both Christian and Jewish theological camps, and has created an avalanche of hermeneutical ramifications that have become deeply imbedded in the minds of both Jewish and Christian scholars. Though this book is about the problem of supersessionism in the Christian tradition, we will occasionally and deliberately interface with Jewish thinkers, beginning with the assumption that Judaism and Christianity, though distinct religious phenomena, are traceable to the same historical roots and should be viewed in a fraternal or sororal sense.

Overall, contemporary experts on the subject, writing from the Christian perspective, have come to identify three major and distinct types of supersessionism, though multiple variants of replacement theology and the philosophical assumptions that underlie them have been identified and exposed—primarily as theologically unimaginative, and ultimately harmful.[7]

The first type of replacement theology, *punitive supersessionism*, appears to have roots in early Christian sources and claims "... that God has rejected and punished carnal Israel on account of its failure to join the Church."[8] Such theological discourse is seen in John Chrysostom's *Eight Homilies against the Jews*, although this was a later text that was inspired by a few centuries of *adversus Judaeos* tradition.[9] In punitive supersessionism, the opposition between Church and synagogue was stressed "... until the Jewish people became the embodiment of all that is unredeemed, perverse, stubborn, evil, and demonic in this world."[10] This imagery of the perversity of the Jewish people stemmed from rejection of Christ and the perceived willingness of Jews to kill him, putting the weight of punishment and the liability for Christ's blood on their shoulders. This punishment upon the Jews, according to Christian tradition, included the removal of all the promises of the God of Israel, placing them instead upon the non-carnal, spiritual and universal entity that came to be known as the Church.[11] The voices that advocated a punitive supersessionism also included in the list of chastisement things such as the sacking of Jerusalem, the destruction of the Temple, and the myth associated with the Jews wandering aimlessly in Diaspora as a "witness people"[12]—those who pointed to the punishment due when an entire people group rejects the predominantly Gentile understanding of Jesus as the messiah. Eventually, this line of theological thought led to concrete political ramifications, including the reduction of civil rights, legal protections, and eventually, targeting by the State.[13]

The primary theological question raised by punitive supersessionism has to do with God's faithfulness to the Jewish people up until the time of Christ, and the purely Deuteronomic theology espoused by a punitive or retributive concept of the God of Israel at the expense of the Restoration theology also reflected in the Old and New Testaments.[14] For Soulen, the main problem with punitive supersessionism is that in it, "... God abrogates God's covenant with Israel (which is already in principle outmoded) on account of Israel's rejection of Christ and the Gospel ... because the Jews obstinately reject God's action in Christ, God in turn angrily rejects and punishes the Jews."[15] The primary theological weakness that arises as a result of punitive supersessionism has to do with the nature of God and the authority with which God's promises are made. Are the promises of God, reiterated over and over again in the Bible as *permanent*, in reality, *transient*? Though Karl Barth was ultimately unable to overcome all forms of supersessionism, his concept of election put the question of punitive supersessionism in the proper theological light: if God has rejected the Jewish people and punished them by applying the promises originally due them to the Church, what kind of certainty does the Church have regarding the nature of God's free and sovereign election?[16]

Through the second type of supersessionism, *economic supersessionism*, the claim is made that "... everything that characterized the economy of salvation in its Israelite form becomes obsolete and is replaced by its ecclesial equivalent."[17] Soulen associates the roots of economic supersessionism with the "foreground" of the new Christian narrative interpretation of salvation history, whereby God's interaction with Israel is simply a "background" to the main importance of the story–the NT and Apostolic Witness. This framework, the interpretive structure created by Justin and Irenaeus, is dubbed the "standard model," a system we briefly described earlier in our project. Economic supersessionism, rooted in this standard model or narrative, leaves out, almost entirely, God's interactions with the people of Israel, the Abrahamic promises, and the concept that God's promises are eternal for Israel. God *as the God of Israel* is rendered highly indecisive in the economy of salvation since that economy is taken up completely and in totality through Jesus the Redeemer, vis-à-vis *the Church*, making any given theme of ransom, redemption, or salvation in the Hebrew Bible a simplified *type* of what was to come.[18] At the heart of the issue, the theological problem with economic supersessionism is that it is a modified and concealed form of Gnosticism, an early Church heresy. Soulen claims that economic supersessionism, resulting from a standard model reading of the OT, "... rejects Gnosticism at the level of ontology but not at the level of covenant history."[19] What Soulen means is that as Gnosticism 'collapsed' creation into the fall of humankind, nullifying the goodness of creation itself, economic supersessionism collapses God's covenant with Israel into the economy of redemption in a prefigurative form.[20] This causes a serious theological problem because it makes God's consummative economy with Israel *dependent* upon sin, death, and ultimately, a later redemptive work.[21] Economic supersessionism treats salvation history in such a way that God's elective grace in the events of the people Israel, and God's intention, purpose, and will in consummating the plan of salvation for Israel is interrupted by sin in such a manner that God becomes *dependent upon sin* to the degree that *consummation* is thwarted and becomes wholly dependent upon God's *redemptive economy*. What Soulen argues is that God's consummative activity and economy with the people Israel is a particularity that cannot be subsumed into God's redemptive economy, made in and through Jesus Christ. Karl Barth and Karl Rahner are two theologians among a small group who would agree with Soulen's assessment of the distinction between God's consummative and redemptive economies in salvation history.[22] Barth, for example, claims that God's covenant with Israel is a covenant of *grace*, and that it "... is supremely gracious *in its own right* antecedent to sin and the need for redemption."[23] Later, will examine in fuller detail Soulen's reasons for rejecting economic supersessionism.

The third kind of supersessionism that is evident in the Church's history is *structural supersessionism*, a form that is less so a dogmatic construct and more so a formal extension of the "standard model of canonical narrative," set up by Justin and Irenaeus. Structural supersessionism "... refers to the narrative logic of the standard model whereby it renders the Hebrew Scriptures largely indecisive for shaping Christian convictions about how God's works as Consummator and as Redeemer engage humankind in universal and enduring ways."[24] In economic supersessionism, Judaism plays a role *de jure*, but not de facto, while in structural supersessionism, Judaism plays no decisive role at all. The theological problem with structural supersessionism is that, at its core, it advocates a veiled form of Marcionism—it attempts to rid the canonical narrative of anything having to do with Israel or the God of the Hebrew Bible.[25] Soulen claims that structural supersessionism came to the fore with the Enlightenment thinkers, Immanuel Kant and Friedrich Schleiermacher.[26] Essentially, Kant and Schleiermacher cut away as "alien and obsolete" the Israelite background of the Christian narrative, while accepting only the most universalized aspects of the standard model's foreground. The Jewish–Christian link that existed prior to the Enlightenment, based primarily on the incontrovertible connection between Christianity and the God of Israel, was now gone. For Kant, religion was rational and rested on an analysis of universal moral experience.[27] In Kant, Jesus is portrayed as the single morally perfect person ... the embodiment of the archetype and ideal of a morally good humanity. Thus, for Kant, the Christian religion is thoroughly about the moral law and its universal claim concerning rational creatures—it has nothing at all to do with Judaism, a religion that, according to this view, is concerned with a messiah who will simply bring "earthly fortunes."[28] Because of the stress on universal categories, the rejection of the notion of a "thing in itself" outside of subjective perception, and a spiritualized, universalized religious principle in the philosophical roots of German Idealism, Kant depicts "... the Jews as socially ... conditioned to the material"—a condition to which Kant himself has a serious aversion.[29]

If Kant universalizes Christianity to a form of moral, rational law, Schleiermacher universalizes it in reference to a natural human experience of that which is "greater."[30] They both "... exploit the structure of the standard model in order to consolidate the victory of the creaturely-universal spirit over the historical-particular flesh."[31] Thus, in structural supersessionism, there is no abiding need to connect the universal aspects of Christocentrism—through moral law or transcendental experience—with the *particularity* inherent in viewing the Gospel as an event that views the God of Israel as working in Jesus Christ, a Jew from Nazareth, for the sake of the world.

In sum, there are three major forms of supersessionism: punitive, economic, and structural. Each is a problematic theology for its own specific reasons. Punitive supersessionism does not take seriously the character of the God of Israel as expressed in the Hebrew Bible, namely, a God whose "anger lasts only a moment, but his favor lasts for a lifetime" (Psalm 30:5), and a God whose elective will and promises are eternal, specifically for the people to whom they were addressed. The idea that God would eternally punish even the Jewish people of the future because of their historically tempered rejection of Jesus as messiah is an unnecessary and flawed concept, rooted in the "standard model's" interpretation of the narrative canon—an interpretation that ignores alternative readings of the Hebrew Bible and the later Apostolic Witness. Economic supersessionism is theologically problematic because, according to Soulen, it espouses a form of Gnosticism by collapsing God's election of carnal Israel, ultimately a salvific economy of consummation, into the economy of redemption that took place under the Christian historical era of Jesus of Nazareth—rendering God's work as consummator to be dependent upon the fall of humankind, sin, and the standard model of redemption. Structural supersessionism is theologically problematic because it champions a universalized form of Christianity based on a moral philosophy, as in Kant, or a universal and natural experience of that which is "greater," as in Schleiermacher. Because structural supersessionism renders the Hebrew Bible *entirely* indecisive for the Christian religion, it is in essence a form of the early heresy of Marcion.

Supersessionist hermeneutics and the Bible

Among the several cogent reasons why Christian scholars have considered supersessionism problematic, three stand out as representative of the rest: the hermeneutical, the biblical, and the systematic-theological. In this section, we will examine the hermeneutical and biblical roots of supersessionism, while the systematic-theological issues will be taken up through an exploration of various non-supersessionist theologians at a later point. First, according to Vlach and Soulen, supersessionists utilize a hermeneutical principle that is inherently flawed. This is not to say that the New Testament was never considered a fuller or more progressive form of revelation by non-supersessionists.[32] For example, when Jesus makes the statement "do not think that I came to abolish the Law or the Prophets; I did not come to abolish but to fulfill" (Matthew 5:17), non-supersessionists believe he is indeed saying something new and proclaiming a further fulfillment. Nevertheless, nonsuperessionists seek to resist any interpretation of Jesus's words that would claim that the Law is unimportant or that the previous dispensation is illegitimate or has been made utterly obsolete by the new.

The first hermeneutical flaw that becomes apparent in supersessionist thought is that of the "either-or" construct and its priority in replacement ideology. Vlach, an evangelical theologian, claims that:

> there may be two referents to an OT promise—the first referent is Israel while the second referent is the Gentiles, the Church, or both. The fact that an OT

promise or covenant is applied/fulfilled with the Church does not mean that the original referent—Israel—is no longer related to the promise or the covenant. Thus, at times there are both-and constructs.[33]

This hermeneutical principle of "either-or" reflects the profound degree to which supersessionists emphasize a New Testament priority over the Old—the Old Testament is viewed almost exclusively in a typological manner. This is not to say that, for non-supersessionists, the Old Testament does not provide types for the New. But it does mean that Old Testament typological constructs contain within them a "surplus of meaning" whereby the intent inherent in the language has significance in reference to its origin (the Jews), may have an application to the Church, and may *also* refer to elements within the Jewish and Christian community that will apply in the eschatological future.[34] It is the eschatological dimension of the hermeneutical approach of supersessionists that will be addressed at length later in this book, with special focus on the problem of viewing the previous covenant(s) that God made with the Jews as fulfilled by the Church in such a manner as to leave no room for a future fulfillment. Superesessionist hermeneutical commitments have a profound effect on ecclesiology as well. Vlach points out the primary error that necessarily flows from a purely supersessionist reading of the Old Testament when he asks if the texts of the Old Testament might include:

> other referents in a *partial fulfillment* of OT passages (i.e. Gentiles) but not doing so in such a way that excludes a fulfillment with the nation Israel. Is this an unreasonable expectation *in light of the fact that there are two comings of Jesus*? Should we not expect already/not yet and partial fulfillment constructs in light of this? Thus, new applications of OT passages or new referents do not mean the original meaning has been jettisoned.[35]

Traditional Catholic exegesis has also left room for the possibility of a future fulfillment of Old Testament passages that are likewise considered fulfilled to some degree by the advent of Jesus Christ and the establishment of the Church. For example, the Anglican turned Catholic Cardinal John Henry Newman managed to find room for a double meaning in the texts of the Old Testament:

> I would say that the prophecies in question have in their substance been fulfilled literally, and in their present Dispensation . . . *not that there may not be both a figurative and a future accomplishment besides*, but those will be over and above, if they take place, and do not interfere with the direct meaning of the sacred text and its literal fulfillment.[36]

That which comes into question is the meaning of the term "literal fulfillment." For Newman, this was the fulfillment of the old dispensation in the new—the prophetic typology fulfilled in the life, work, passion, death, and resurrection of Jesus Christ. But is it also possible that a further literal fulfillment may occur, connecting the modern day Jews with the prophetic texts that referenced the Jews originally? Certainly such a reading would not render the fulfillments attributable to Jesus Christ obsolete. It would simply admit of a future for God; that the consummation of God's plan for Israel, in salvation history, has not yet met its end.

Contemporary Roman Catholic texts seem to be moving in this direction of a "dual-significance" to Old Testament prophecy. For example, the *Pontifical Biblical Commission* document entitled "The Jews and their Sacred Scriptures in the Christian Bible" emphasizes the continuing significance of the Old Testament in ways that move beyond the purely typological reading espoused by supersessionists:

> Christians can and ought to admit that the Jewish reading of the Bible is a possible one, in continuity with the Jewish Sacred Scriptures from the Second Temple period, a reading analogous to the Christian reading which developed in parallel fashion. Each of these two readings is part of the vision of each respective faith of which it is a product and an expression. Consequently, they cannot be reduced one into the other.[37]

Further into this book we will examine the nuances of the Commission's seminal text and its implications, but for now it is sufficient to point out that if the Jewish reading of the Old Testament "cannot be reduced" to the Christian interpretation, this leaves supersessionists hard-pressed to support their overarching hermeneutic regarding the sole fulfillment of prophetic texts through adoption of the strict priority of the New Testament and the interpretations of the Christian tradition. It appears that in the Roman Catholic tradition, at least in reference to the "literal" reading of the canon as a whole, a typological understanding of certain Hebrew Bible texts is appropriate, but *does not preclude* a literal reading of the original text in relation to the people of Israel. Thus, the Catholic Church is able to conceive of an interpretation of the Hebrew Bible which is outside the bounds of total fulfillment by the advent of Christianity or the Church, and is yet supplemented by alternative interpretive mechanisms, such as Masoretic readings.

According to Hans W. Frei, though the assemblage of the NT canon was done so with the intention of creating one, unified whole, through the adoption of typology and fulfillment language extracted from the OT and applied to the NT, the rejection of the value intrinsic to the original OT texts was not necessarily required or advocated within the tradition.[38] Regarding the task of the precritical realistic reading of the Bible—one reading associated with biblical interpretation prior to the Protestant Reformation—Frei suggests that in order to view all the biblical stories as falling in line with one temporal sequence:

> the several biblical stories narrating sequential segments in time must fit together into one narrative. The interpretive means for joining them was to make earlier biblical stories figures or types of later stories and of their events and patterns of meaning. *Without loss to its own literal meaning or specific temporal reference, an earlier story (or occurrence) was a figure of a later*

one. The customary use of figuration was to show that Old Testament persons, events, and *prophecies were fulfilled in the New Testament.*[39]

The issue that is raised concerning supersessionist hermeneutics is the application of OT prophetic writing to the NT in such a manner that makes the NT or ecclesial interpretive fulfillment the *sole* fulfillment of the text. For example, we might ask in what way the eschatological language of Isaiah 11 retains its own "literal meaning" or "specific temporal reference"—that of the wolf living with the lamb on God's holy mountain; a text read among Jews as pivotal to the final restoration of carnal Israel—if the text is rendered by Christians as *exclusively* referencing the new, "spiritual" Jerusalem? Referencing this hermeneutic, Soulen writes, "the standard model is structurally supersessionist *because it unifies the Christian canon in a manner that renders the Hebrew Scriptures largely indecisive for shaping conclusions about how God's purposes engage creation in universal and enduring ways.*"[40]

Along with Vlach, Soulen traces and identifies a hermeneutical problem that has existed in supersessionist readings of the Hebrew Bible since the Church's earliest traditions. Soulen attributes the supersessionism of today to the hermeneutical commitments of the past. This is what Soulen calls the "standard model," which he likewise refers to as "a flaw in the heart of the crystal" of Christian Scriptural exegesis. This interpretation, a canonical narrative invented and applied by Justin Martyr and Irenaeus, conceives of "God's history with human creation in four crucial episodes: God's intention to consummate the human pair whom God created, the first parents' disobedience and fall, the redemption of lost humanity in Christ, and final consummation."[41] This reading, Soulen claims, either leaves out everything from the first few chapters of Genesis through the advent of Christ, or collapses the history of Israel into the fulfillment of God's consummative act in the person of Christ, rendering Israel's role in salvation history almost entirely inconsequential. If one thinks in terms of the theological implications of exegesis, this standard canonical narrative makes Israel's history merely a "stepping stone" to its fulfillment in the person of Jesus Christ and the Church. On its own, Israel has neither covenantal nor soteriological significance apart from God's future acts through the incarnation and the Apostolic Witness. Though continuity between the history of Israel and the advent of the Church is emphasized in both Justin and Irenaeus, Israel's history is simply a preparatory stage—a "prehistory." Few early Christian writers express this reality better than Melito of Sardis, whose works, of which we now only have fragments, serve as evidence for the early roots of such thought:

> In the same way that the type is depleted, conceding the image to what is intrinsically real, and the analogy is brought to completion through the elucidation of the interpretation, so the law is fulfilled by the elucidation of the Gospel, and the people is depleted by the arising of the Church, and the model is dissolved by the appearance of the Lord. And today those things of value are worthless, since the things of true worth have been revealed.[42]

This early expression of Christian supersessionism creates within the Hebrew Bible an interpretive narrative structure that is foreign to its original meaning—the Hebrew narrative, with the exception of the beginning of Genesis, is considered a mere background to the foreground which is the Apostolic Witness. Soulen states that:

> above all, the Scriptures are concerned with the history that transpires between the God of Israel, Israel, and the nations, a history that the Scriptures appear to regard as virtually coextensive with human history as a whole. Characteristically, the standard model brings all of this unruly material under the hermeneutic control of the foreground story of creation, fall, redemption, and final consummation.[43]

Ultimately, this hermeneutic which was popular among the early Christian apologists has become the standard Christian reading of the Hebrew Bible and has been considered the only appropriate means of reading the Old Testament in light of the New. What is typically missing in reference to the examination of this early interpretive lens in its application to contemporary reading of the Bible is the context and motive behind such language, namely the apologetic significance of the Church Fathers. The Fathers, in their hermeneutical constructs, were defending the fledgling Church against three serious threats: Jews, pagans, and Gnostics.[44] Against the Jews and the Gnostics, the Fathers had to uphold the belief that the God of the Hebrew Bible acted in the person of Jesus Christ; that the message of the Apostolic Witness was intimately connected with the Hebrew Bible. Against the pagans, the Fathers had to uphold the belief that the Gospel of Jesus Christ, the Son of the God of Israel, acted in such a way that was significant for *universal* salvation. As an apologetic structure in response to all three of these threats, the "standard model" fit the bill. The fourth-century anti-Judaic rhetoric of Chrysostom in his "Eight Homilies against the Jews" was set in place as a means to thwart Antiochian Christians from falling under the 'mystical temptation' of Jewish worship in the synagogues, and also as a means to stem the tide against the "Judaizers." Likewise, the hermeneutical allegiance to supersessionist readings of the Hebrew Bible acted to solidify the Christian identity against its detractors in the first few centuries after Jesus.[45] Yet the supersessionistic reading of salvation history was "buffered" within the tradition of the Patristics through a system of eschatology that balanced their emphasis on the ecclesial fulfillment of God's promises to the Jews with a continuing, immanent expectation for a messianic future that would likewise include the Jews as a particular entity apart from the future Gentile Church.[46] Hermeneutically, today's Church has adopted the Patristic supersessionist reading, but has relegated the immanent eschatological expectations of the Fathers to the place of myth and imagination.

The second major reason why supersessionism is considered a problem goes beyond the *reading* of the Bible and salvation history. This point involves the compilation of the LXX and its use in the New Testament, and some specific NT texts that have been used in the past to support supersessionism. This biblical aspect of the debate over supersessionism has been the subject of attack by non-supersessionists in recent years, because there are a handful of NT texts used by supersessionists in an attempt to "prove" beyond doubt that the Christian revelation unequivocally expresses a replacement of Israel by the Church—either by usurping OT language that applies to Israel, or through a biblical passage that has been read as a rejection of Israel and its subsequent replacement by the kingdom of God as manifest through the Church. Though it is outside the scope of this work to analyze each of these texts, a sampling of them along with their non-supersessionist response is helpful to our overall statement that supersessionism is a problem and that alternatives are possible and to be explored. Vlach states that he has ". . . found that most of the arguments supersessionists offer for holding that the Church is the complete replacement or fulfillment of Israel are based on implications they believe are true but in reality are not biblically accurate or logically consistent."[47] Because it is important to explore the ways in which supersessionism is a problem, we will briefly examine three New Testament passages in order to explain the supersessionist reading and to offer an alternative to those readings—two concerning the application of "Israel" language to the Church, and one concerning the punishment of God upon the Jewish people who rejected Jesus as messiah. The purpose of this exercise is to illustrate how alternative readings—interpretations that run contrary to the supersessionist readings of the three texts, logically exist and may be applied.

Some scholarship on the side of supersessionist readings of the NT suggests that because the same terms are used for "Israel" and the new Jesus-follower movement in the LXX rendering of the Hebrew Bible, the continuity between the groups is smooth to the point of subsumption.[48] The Hebrew words *ēḡâ* and *qāhāl* both refer to the "assembly" or "congregation" of the Hebrew people, while *qāhāl* specifically refers to the group as it is gathered before God. There is a special significance to the word *qāhāl* in its use in Deuteronomy 5:22 at the ratification of the Sinai covenant, whereby the Jewish people are formalized as the "people of God" in a special way that connects their peoplehood with God's election of them as a Torah-based community. It must be admitted that the NT rendering of these Hebrew words as *ekklēsía*, echoed in the LXX, suggests a radical continuity between the assembly which gathered as the people Israel and the Church as the new covenant community assembled under Jesus Christ. The term *ekklēsía* as used in the NT and LXX means "those called out," derived from the roots *ex* and *kaleo*, and was perhaps used to distinguish the early Jesus movement comprised of the Jewish messianic community, from the synagogue, or the primary expression of Second Temple Judaism practices by the rabbis. According to Geoffrey Bromiley, ". . . in both the LXX and the NT, *qāhāl* determines the meaning of *ekklēsía*, not vice versa."[49] This is significant insofar as the context of the term *ekklēsía* was considered in the Apostolic Witness in such a manner as to portray the Jewish assembly of the People of God as a root for the establishment of the new covenant.

Yet another significant point must be made because it undermines the supersessionist assumption that the entire spiritual identity of Israel is taken up by the Church in the NT and LXX. The Hebrew terms that are rendered as *ekklēsía* in the LXX are not done so absolutely, in each and every case. Bromiley tells us that "in the LXX, *qāhāl* is *frequently, though not exclusively,* translated by *ekklēsía*. This is the case in Deuteronomy (except 5:22), Joshua, Judges, Samuel, Kings, Chronicles, Ezra, and Nehemiah; in the remainder of the Pentateuch *qāhāl* is rendered *synagōgé*. *Ēḏâ* is usually rendered *synagōgé*, never *ekklēsía*."[50] One must ask why the translators of the LXX frequently, *but not uniformly*, translated the Hebrew Bible's term for the gathering or assembly of the people of God using the same word that was applied to the early gathering of Jesus followers. After all, the "remainder of the Pentateuch" referenced above by Bromiley is a considerable portion of the Hebrew Bible, suggesting that the compilers of the LXX, and by default those who quoted it in the NT, sought to leave some distinction between the *ekklēsía* and the *synagōgé*. Otherwise, the idea that the early Church was a "sprout" or a "shoot" attached to the root that was the congregation of Israel would have never made it into the NT canon (Romans 9–11).

I contend that the continuity between the two covenant peoples was rendered in the LXX and the NT in such a manner that the theological context of the times—the NT as an expression of the somewhat tolerated subset of Jesus followers among the larger category known as "Israel"—conveyed a real continuation between the religious peoples, yet not with the intention of drawing a *one-to-one* correspondence between the messianic community of Jesus and the Jews as a whole.[51] Indeed, the term "Church," at least in the manner it is used today by supersessionists—applied to the contemporary and predominately Gentile Christian community *in contrast to* the Jewish community that existed as an extension of the ministry of Jesus of Nazareth—never appears in the NT. Rausch claims that the original NT term *ekklēsía* carries with it cultic and eschatological nuances often missing from today's conception of "Church."[52] This eschatological dimension associated with those involved in the Jesus community expresses a movement forward toward a common hope that is nestled within the expectations of Second Temple Judaism, not the dualistic, sedimentary, and exclusionary conception of Church espoused by modern supersessionist readings.

According to Vlach, some NT texts used as Scriptural support for replacement theology concern this application of Old Testament language to the Church—the notion that the Church has *become* the "new Israel."[53] Paul's Epistles to the Galatians and Ephesians are favorites of the supersessionist camp because they seem to suggest a conflation between Jew and Gentile, or that in the Church the two groups somehow *completely* merge, in the present moment, under a messianic fulfillment brought by Jesus Christ. One example of this occurs in Galatians 3:26–29, in which Paul, speaking within the context of baptism, states that "you [who are baptized] are all one in Christ Jesus . . . if you are Christ's, then you are Abraham's offspring." Some scholars take this to mean that Paul was denying *any* distinction between Jew and Gentile, because the spiritual significance of the Jew, Abraham's "seed," is transferred to the new community of Jews and Gentiles who embrace Jesus as messiah—the Church. Elisabeth Schüssler Fiorenza claims that the passage ". . . proclaims that in the Christian community all distinctions of religion, race, class, nationality, and gender are insignificant. All baptized are equal, they are one in Christ."[54] This application of the principles of liberal egalitarianism to the text, though noble in its intention, misreads the passage. It is less, for Paul, that the distinctions between ethnic and religious groups dissolve within the fledgling Christian community, and more that the Gentile community is brought into the covenantal relationship that God has already established with the ethnic "seed of Abraham." Baptism does not erase *all* distinctions between Jew and non-Jew, but allows for the spiritual status of the Jew to be applied to the non-Jew—those who are in Christ are given a new identity, adopted into the community of the baptized. Galatians says nothing of a change to the status of God's original people, the Jews, let alone their usurpation—it simply is referring to the profound change in status and identity that occurs to one who undergoes the ritual of baptism.[55] Thus, in Galatians, there is not a one-to-one correspondence between "Church" and "Israel," and such a correspondence is missing from the New Testament at large: "In spite of the many attributes, characteristics, privileges and prerogatives of the latter [Israel] which are applied to the former [Church], the Church is not called Israel in the NT."[56] Later, in discussing the work of George Lindbeck, we will examine how the NT does indeed use the language of Israel and applies it to the Church, but does not do so in the way supersessionists would have us believe.

Another Scriptural example used by supersessionists is Ephesians 2:11–22. Less so a usurpation of the title "Israel" by the title "Church" as it relates to Galatians 3, this text in Ephesians is used by supersessionists to claim that since now, in Christ, there is unity between the "circumcised" and "uncircumcised," a unity applied to Jews and Gentiles who believe in Jesus as messiah, Israel is now the Church, and the original Israel has no future outside the Church. The text reads:

> Therefore, remember that formerly you who are Gentiles by birth and called "uncircumcised" by those who call themselves "the circumcision" (which is done in the body by human hands)—remember that at that time you were separate from Christ, excluded from citizenship in Israel and foreigners to the covenants of the promise, without hope and without God in the world. But now in Christ Jesus you who once were far away have been brought near by the blood of Christ. For he himself is our peace, who has made the two groups one and has destroyed the barrier, the dividing wall of hostility, by setting aside in his flesh the law with its commands and regulations. His purpose was to create in himself one new humanity out of the two, thus making peace, and in one body to reconcile both of them to God through the cross, by which he put to death their hostility. He came and preached peace to you who were far away and peace to those who were near. For through him we both have access to the Father by one Spirit. Consequently, you are no longer foreigners and strangers, but fellow citizens with God's people and also members of his household, built on the foundation of the apostles and prophets, with Christ Jesus himself as the chief cornerstone. In him the whole building is joined together and rises to become a holy temple in the Lord.

And in him you too are being built together to become a dwelling in which God lives by his Spirit.

(Ephesians 2:11–22, NIV)

The context of this passage is important, as it gives readers insight as to how the author's surroundings and historical situation gave rise to the language that was used.[57] If the letter was written by Paul, the language of exclusion, citizenship, unity, and peace may correlate to the projected date and location of its writing—written by a Jew to a Gentile audience from a Roman prison cell during the time of the *Pax Romana*.[58] Likewise, the text mentions "the dividing wall of hostility" that is broken down by Christ—a wall which kept Gentiles from worshipping in the house of God, alongside their Jewish counterparts. The supersessionist reading of this passage takes the text a step beyond its context and applies an interpretive framework that suggests that the two groups, "the uncircumcision" comprised of Gentiles, and "the circumcised" comprised of Jews who believed in Christ, by virtue of the cross of Christ, had come to form "one new humanity" in Christ—one established in sharp contrast from either a distinct group of Jews who believed in Jesus as messiah, or the Jewish people as a whole. Furthermore, according to the "replacement" reading, this new community, made up of both believing Jews and Gentiles, is one which is unified and established as the *real* or *true* Israel into which both ethnic groups have "citizenship." If the supersessionist reading were to end at this point, little controversy would have surrounded the exegesis of Ephesians 2. But the supersessionist reading does not end here. The supersessionist reading applies a value system to the text in Ephesians that is found nowhere in the text itself, nor in its implied context—the idea that *no future salvific unification* between the Jews and the covenant is attainable or applicable outside the formal boundaries of this new, unified community, the now Gentile Church. As Vlach points out, biblical scholar Wayne Grudem states that this passage in Ephesians "... gives no indication of any distinctive plan for Jewish people *ever* to be saved apart from inclusion in the one body of Christ, the Church."[59] Anthony A. Hoekema states that when reading Ephesians 2:

> the entire discussion ... would be pointless if Paul was not making a distinction between Jews and Gentiles. The fact, however, that the New Testament often speaks of Jews in distinction from Gentiles does not at all imply that God has a separate purpose for Israel in distinction from his purpose for the Church ... The New Testament makes quite clear that God has no separate purpose for Israel.[60]

Both Grudem and Hoekema argue that because Ephesians 2 does not explicitly mention the possibility of a salvific future for Jews who find themselves outside the Church, such a future must not exist. Additionally, Hoekema argues that no such future is mentioned within the NT canon itself—an obvious neglect regarding both the historical and eschatological dimensions of the Epistle to the Romans, which draws a sharp distinction between those members of Israel who believe in

Jesus as messiah, and those who do not—and promises a future restoration of the latter which is engulfed in theological mystery (Romans 11:25).[61] According to Vlach, the idea that the Church is incorporated into the entity known as "Israel" as the category is understood in terms of its Hebrew Bible usage, the covenantal people of God ratified at Sinai; this idea is utterly missing from the Ephesians text and not implied, even remotely. Vlach claims that there are four reasons for this: first, "... while Eph. 2:13,17 indicates that Gentiles are 'made near' and are no longer excluded from the 'commonwealth of Israel,' this does not necessarily mean that believing Gentiles *become* Israel."[62] Thus, *nearness* does not equal utter incorporation or subsumption, let alone the converse often espoused by supersessionists—the concept that Israel *became*, in totality, the predominately Gentile Church. Just as Gentiles are not incorporated into Israel in a manner resulting in a complete surpassing of the former, neither does Israel become subsumed into the Church. There is a radical connection made in the NT between these two communities—Israel and the messianic community of Jesus—but not to the neglect of particularity. Second, Vlach argues that if the author intended to say that Gentiles were now Israel, he would have explicitly said so, which he did not.[63] Instead, Paul emphasizes that in Christ, Jew and Gentile form "one new man"— not one new entity known as "Israel."[64] Third, the 'one new man' mentioned in Ephesians is a 'soteriological community'—an organism that is attached to Jesus Christ and the Apostolic Witness, whereas "Israel" is not an entity which is of NT origins, and has its own history dating back to the Abrahamic covenant.[65] Last, the use of the Greek *syn* compounds, terminology which means "to share" or "to fit together" in the greater context of Ephesians 2–3 precludes any idea of the Church becoming Israel. Instead the passage expresses the idea that the Gentiles and Jews now have an equal footing together as the people of God.[66]

In addition to texts that appear on the surface to communicate that the early ecclesial community *became* Israel in a way that eradicated the people of God of the Hebrew Bible, perhaps the most popular text among replacement theologians is Matthew 21:43. In the Gospel, Jesus makes the statement: "Therefore I say to you, the kingdom of God will be taken away from you and given to a people, producing the fruit of it." The supersessionist reading of the above passage insists that the "you" to which Jesus was referring applies to the Jewish people in general, while the "people," *ethnei*, refers to the Church. Ewherido, for example, claims that this sequence of text expresses that "Israel was unproductive and hardhearted and therefore loses God's favor, and the blessing that was hers is given to a productive and obedient people."[67] Though popular among some biblical scholars,[68] Ewherido's assessment is by no means the consensus. Snodgrass, for example, interprets the "you" as referring to the Jewish leaders alone. The text in verses 45–46 states emphatically that the chief priests and Pharisees took Jesus' parable as referring to them, *not the nation of Israel as a whole*.[69] In seeking to seize Jesus as a response to his words, the Gospel claims that the religious leaders "... feared the people, because they considered Him to be a prophet" (21:46). This language is hardly applicable if Jesus was referring to the Gentile Church becoming the new recipient of the promises made to the Jews in general—in light of the fact that his audience and all his disciples were Jews. M. Eugene Boring surmises that:

> this text does not speak explicitly ... of Israel's being rejected, but of the "kingdom of God" being taken from "you"; in Matthew's view, the saving activity of God continues in that community where taking up the "yoke of the kingdom" means adherence to the Torah as fulfilled in the teaching of Jesus.[70]

Because the saving activity of God within a previous community continues in a later community, it does not necessarily follow that God's saving activity, or the future prospect of it, has ceased from the previous community. Therefore, the supersessionist reading is not the sole reading of this text in Matthew, and supersessionist scholars have not adequately illustrated that the Matthean text is in fact referring to the kingdom of God which is to be taken from all the stock of Israel and given to the Gentile Church. According to Anthony J. Saldarini, some:

> commentators understand this *ethnos* ... [the term "nation" as used in the Matthew text] ... as the Gentile Church replacing Israel. Numerous problems beset this interpretation and the supersessionist replacement theology which motivates it. First, the addressees of the parable are unclear. Second ... in Matthew the vineyard [the Jewish people as a whole] is faultlessly fruitful and only its tenants [the leaders of the people] are unsatisfactory ... *The author of Matthew does not say that ... believers-in-Jesus are a new or true Israel, nor a replacement for Israel.*[71]

A third way that supersessionists defend their reading of history, beyond the hermeneutical and biblical justifications mentioned above, is through a systematic-theological paradigm. This theological paradigm will be the subject matter of what follows, and will be brought to light under the critiques of Protestant and Catholic theologians. Finally, critiques of the theological paradigm of supersessionism will be extracted from the implied language of Roman Catholic ecclesial documents, with a primary focus on *NA*. Thus, it will be illustrated that theological shifts in the Roman Catholic conception of supersessionism and official pronouncements of the Catholic Magisterium call for adequate alternatives to the general theology of a replacement of the Jewish people by the Roman Catholic Church.

Supersessionism: A theological problem

In an effort to continue to illustrate why supersessionism as a theological construct is problematic, a condensed analysis of both contemporary Protestant and Catholic theological reflections on the subject is in order. After exploring a basic understanding of post-supersessionist[72] thought, we will examine the three most common *theological* problems that arise from a supersessionist framework, aligning these issues with the various theologians who have brought the problem to light or have proposed alternatives.

Supersessionism gives rise to various theological problems by utilizing a combination of questionable biblical exegesis and uncreative ways of upholding traditional categories regarding covenant and election, all at the expense of Jewish religious existence and value. Specifically, a vast majority of supersessionist scholars make assumptions based on certain interpretations of Scripture and past theological consensus that avoid alternative understandings of the relationship between Judaism and the Church—alternatives which leave space for a Judaism that contributes theologically to Christian ecclesiology, eschatology, and history.[73]

Post-supersessionist theology came to the fore in Christian studies through the advent of two-covenant theology, a thought process inspired by the Jewish theologian and philosopher Franz Rosenzweig. This scholarship was developed later through advances in the study of the history of religions after the Holocaust, circa 1950.[74] According to Craig A. Blaising, post-supersessionism is closely linked to one's idea of covenantal reality, stating that:

> The key feature of two-covenant theology is the belief that Jews and Christians are related to God separately by distinct covenants. Christianity offers a covenant relationship to God for Gentiles through Jesus the Christ. Judaism offers a covenant relationship to God for Jewish people through Torah . . . Quite consistent with this, those who take this dual-covenant view of Judaism and Christianity have repudiated Christian evangelism and mission to Jewish people not just as an affront, but as a theological violation of God's covenant with Israel.[75]

Though not all Christian post-supersessionist theologians are two-covenant or "dual covenant" theologians—i.e., the belief that God's covenant with the Jewish people through Abraham is entirely separate from the new covenant God initiated with the ecclesial community through Jesus Christ—the idea that the covenantal relationship that God has with the Jewish people is special, particular, and still in effect, is consistent among post-supersessionists. Some post-supersessionists regard God's covenant with the Jews and covenant with the Christians as two entirely different paths, while others regard it as a double-detour rooted in the one covenant, one Jewish and one Christian. Regardless of these distinctions, *the continued validity of God's covenant with Israel* is central to Christian post-supersessionism.

For Rosenzweig, "covenantal movement" throughout history means that the Jews as a whole, particular as the carnal chosen people, but not particular if understood in the sense of "each and every one," by virtue of their existential situation, have an innate and permanent relationship with the God of Israel outside of the current "messianic mediation" of Jesus of Nazareth.[76] In a famous statement in a letter from Rosenzweig to Rudolf Ehrenberg,[77] Rosenzweig claimed that:

> we . . . [Christians and Jews] . . . are wholly agreed as to what Christ and his Church mean to the world: no one can reach the Father save through him. No one can reach the Father! But the situation is quite different for one who

does not have to reach the Father because he is already with him. And this is true of the people of Israel (though not of individual Jews).[78]

In the quotation above, Rosenzweig points to the first theological problem that arises in supersessionist theology—the irrevocable character of God's covenant with the people Israel. Several prominent Christian theologians including Robert W. Jenson have addressed this concept of the permanent nature of the covenant and pinpointed it as central to the supersessionist debate. In light of this, the irrevocable nature of God's covenant with a specific group of people designated as "Israel," is a concept that is impossible to deny based upon Scriptural exegesis alone.

Since the first historical era in which post-supersessionist theology came to the fore—as an effort to examine how anti-Jewish Christian ideologies may have played a role in the rise of National Socialism and the Holocaust—the Church's *standard view* of the irrevocable character of God's covenant with the Jews was thought to be a problematic issue. Questions were raised as to whether the covenant that God made with Abraham, in biblical terms the father of the Jewish people, was unconditional, permanent, and meant specifically for the ethnic and spiritual offspring of the then-established community—those who would later become the national people "Israel" (Genesis 15:18–21). The Genesis passage above specifically promises land and a "blessing to be a blessing" to Abraham and his offspring—a land that will abide with Israel *forever* and a blessing that will come through Abraham's seed for the benefit of the rest of the world, eschatologically. We see in the Genesis 15 narrative that God requires *nothing* of Abraham for this initial covenant to be put into effect, and that in Genesis. 17:7, the covenant is expanded to apply not only to Abraham, but also to his "seed" after him. Jeremiah 31:35–36 expresses the nature of God's covenant with Abraham, Isaac and Jacob, but expands the promises associated with Abraham beyond simply land and blessing, to that of an *eternal peoplehood* in relation to YHWH:

> Thus says the LORD, who gives the sun for light by day and the fixed order of the moon and the stars for light by night, who stirs up the sea so that its waves roar—the LORD of hosts is his name: "If this fixed order departs from before me, declares the LORD, *then shall the offspring of Israel cease from being a nation before me forever.*"
>
> (Jeremiah 31:35–36, ESV).

According to the NT, this eternal nature of the covenant with Abraham is not limited to the Jews, but the Jews remain central to it in a permanent sense. For example, Paul makes the statement that, ". . . if you are Christ's, then you are Abraham's offspring, heirs according to promise" (Galatians 3:29). Paul's text in Galatians refers to a double-legitimacy to Abraham's legacy, insofar as both Jewish and Gentile persons have a religious connection associated with the Abrahamic covenant. Therefore, post-supersessionists do not read this to mean that the special promises of God to the Jewish people were circumvented or made obsolete in any way.[79] Newness and expansion does not, a priori, negate the original and the specific—it simply supplements them.[80] The words of the author of Deutero-Isaiah, written during the post-exilic period, address Israel by name and makes the following promise that explicitly speaks of the *enduring, permanent, and all-encompassing* relationship between God and the people Israel:[81]

> But Zion said, "The LORD has forsaken me, the Lord has forgotten me." "Can a mother forget the baby at her breast and have no compassion on the child she has borne? Though she may forget, I will not forget you! See, I have engraved you on the palms of my hands; your walls are ever before me. [and vs. 26]: "I will contend with those who contend with you, and your children I will save. I will make your oppressors eat their own flesh; they will be drunk on their own blood, as with wine. Then all mankind will know that I, the LORD, am your Savior, your Redeemer, the Mighty One of Jacob."
> (Isaiah 49:14–16, 26, NIV)

In reference to scriptural passages such as the one above, post-supersessionists ask if it is truly rational to believe that these pieces of the Bible, explicitly intended for a specific people, have since been applied to Christians in such a manner that makes the original promises and recipients null and void? If such is the case, what then is to be said of the character of God and the nature of God's promises for Christians?

One major point allows for post-supersessionists to frame the question of the continued relevance of the covenant with the Jews in terms that refuse to give in to the supersessionist Christian paradigm. It is simply the fact that the Jews, as a diverse religious reality, *still exist*. As Jenson puts it, "From a certain angle of vision, the mere existence of Judaism looks much like a refutation of Christianity—and may indeed be just that."[82] Yet for scholars such as A. Roy Eckardt, Christianity goes unharmed by a repudiation of supersessionism because Christology is less a problem in contributing to Christian anti-Jewish fervor than is a binary way of thinking that insists that Judaism and Christianity, in covenantal terms, are mutually exclusive: "He [Eckardt] argued that the Christian affirmation of Jesus as Christ did not exclude Jews from the salvation of God and that their own covenant was not diminished or superseded."[83] The same may be said regarding ecclesiology. According to Jenson, the problem with supersessionism is not that the Church claims to be "Israel," but more that supersessionists hold "... the theological opinion that the Church owns the identity of Israel in such fashion as to exclude any other divinely willed Israel-after-Israel."[84] George Lindbeck echoes this thought, insofar as he sees the value of a semi-technical usage of the term "Israel" for the Church, but is against the "... supersessionist belief that Christians alone are now the true Israel, the chosen people, because God has rejected the Jews..."[85] If the Church owns the moniker "Israel" in such a manner that Israel itself, in its original form prior to the coming of Jesus of Nazareth becomes abrogated by the Church, then why do the Church's current "messianic fulfillments" of the eschatological promises made to the Jews in Jesus (see Isaiah 65:17–25) *appear to be so unfulfilled*? Again, for post-supersessionists such as Jenson, it is because "until he [Jesus] comes, as we sometimes say, "in glory," the Messiah is not yet come in such a way as to end history, or therefore, to *conclude the promises*."[86] Ultimately, Jenson argues that since the promises of God were to the descendants of Abraham and Sarah specifically, ". . . that God wills the Judaism of Torah-obedience as that which alone can and does hold the lineage of Abraham and Sarah together during the time of detour. And that lineage must continue, until the day when lineages shall end."[87] The time of detour here is the dual movement of Judaism and Christianity in covenant history. Thus, for Jenson, the problem with supersessionism is that its adherents fail to see the reason, *de jure*, behind Judaism's continued existence as a recipient of covenantal promises.[88]

Commenting in reference to ecclesial documents from various Christian denominations, Mary C. Boys frames the problem of supersessionism in a similar way, stating that language of confirmation regarding the old covenant is a good starting point, but must result in a positive reason by the Jewish peoples' continued existence.[89] Various supersessionist responses to the existence of the Jews acting as a theological splinter in the replacement argument have been formulated, particularly among more traditionalist Catholics who claim that because supersessionism was the "central posture" toward Judaism among the Church Fathers, it should remain so today.[90] Certainly other aspects of Catholic theology which were once taken for granted have since been reevaluated and reinterpreted, such as the traditional Cyprianic formula *Extra Ecclesiam nulla salus*, which was redeveloped through *Lumen Gentium*'s concept of pneumatological activity outside the canonical bounds of the Church, expressed in the term "*subsistit in*."[91]

The second theological problem that post-supersessionists see with replacement theology is the anti-Judaic nature of a predominately Gentile Church that has been overly influenced by elements of Platonic philosophy—an organism and entity which claims to take on the identity of Judaism, yet is content in abandoning the traditional particularities of that identity, the very context in which the followers of Jesus of Nazareth sprouted. In evaluating the reality of the Church now, we find an entity that has stripped Jesus and the early Christian movement of the Jewish elements that were once constitutive of it—primarily due to supersessionist assumptions regarding the nature and persistent significance of Judaism.[92] With modern Christianity resembling so little of its first-century Jewish roots, questions are raised as to whether there must be a *reason* for Torah-observant Judaism, as enacted by a "national peoplehood," to be in existence today.[93] Supersessionists must contend with the fact that Judaism exists as a very carnal and specific religious reality—it is a people, a nation, a religious expression tied to the Torah observance of a people group, and in some Jewish expressions, it is still initiated through the most fleshly of means—circumcision. Is this Jewish "carnal reality" in existence simply as a 'shameful holdover' from times past, because of the rejection of the supreme and spiritualized/allegorized advent of the Church, as some writers have suggested?[94] For Paul M. van Buren, the reason for the Church's resistance and rejection of the Jewish roots of Christian existence is due to the fact that the two faiths *share one covenant* and exemplify two "detours" within it, yet many Christians refuse to see both the continued connection between Judaism and Christianity, and the particularity of the contemporary Jewish *witness* to the world. Such a rejection is antithetical to Christianity, which has, since its inception, sought to maintain the importance of the *flesh* in terms of its doctrine of the incarnation and the resurrection, in response to Gnosticism, Docetism, and Marcionism.[95] Thus, there is a deep parallelism between the Jewish and Christian notions of the flesh and its importance. For van Buren, the "fleshly witness" of Israel is Torah observance in relation to Judaism's elect status, and a continued desire among the Jews to be a "blessing to the nations." Van Buren states that:

> A Christian theology of the people Israel, as it has been defined, is obliged to point out to the Church that it has failed to listen to the witness of Israel on this matter of the substance of election. The content or substance of election is life lived according to God's Torah. That is freedom. This may not be discounted under a misconceived charge of "works-righteousness."[96]

The context of van Buren's challenge is the Abrahamic covenant that God established as a relational link to Israel—a covenant that *was and is* both unconditional and permanent, and was ratified at Sinai as an extension of its original permanence.[97] The Torah observance of Judaism today is the continued means by which Judaism validly operates as a particular religious people, and to ignore or attempt to rescind such means is an act of Christian self-hatred[98] due to a shared covenantal reality and the obligation of Christianity to view the Apostolic Witness as a confirmation and affirmation of, among other things, *God's promises to the Jews* in light of their God given laws.[99] This truth is exemplified in the fact that Jesus of Nazareth, the one whom Christians view as both divine and the fulfillment of all messianic expectation, was a Torah-practicing Jew, despite his propensity to reveal and exemplify the "heart of the law."[100] The Christian view of the incarnation is and cannot be otherwise, that of the God of Israel taking on the *particularity of Jewish flesh* in a unique way. Jesus's particularity, physical existence, and life as a Jew in first-century Roman Palestine are rendered largely superfluous in the theological construct of supersessionism, primarily in its "structural" variety. According to Jewish scholar and rabbi, Michael Wyschogrod:

> Gentile Christianity absorbs much of the [Platonic] attitude, which is easily converted into a flaunting of the spirituality of the New Israel over the carnality of the old. And yet, the Jewish dimension of the Church never disappears. Modified by the gentile Greek consciousness, severed from its roots in the Hebrew and Aramaic of Jesus and the apostles, estranged from the land of Jesus, head-quartered at the old central office of the Roman Empire, the Church clings to the Hebrew Bible, even as it proclaims it superseded and fulfilled in the New Testament. And above all, the Church clings to the crucifixion and the resurrection, and later comes to define the incarnation, all carnal conceptions rooted in the Judaism of its origin.[101]

If, as supersessionists suggest, the Jewish liturgical elements, promises, prophetic utterances, messianic expectations, and eschatological restorative components are fulfilled in Jesus of Nazareth in such a fashion as to be transferred, absolutely, to the Church, why then must the Church, bragging about its spiritualized triumph over the merely literalistic, carnal, and legalistic, "cling" to the roots of its Hebrew origins, as Wyschogrod suggests, in order for its most fundamental doctrines to survive and make theological sense? Why not simply stand content with the uprooted and Gnostic religion of Marcion, or Valentinus,[102] or as discussed previously, the universalized religion of Kant, or Schleiermacher? Such are the questions that arise when supersessionist readings are measured against the Jewish particularity of Jesus, the Scriptures, and the early Torah observance of the Apostles.

The third problem that arises with a supersessionist view of salvation history is that of the ecclesiological[103] and eschatological construction that exists, either as the root-cause or the logical consequence of viewing Judaism as an obsolete religious system in light of the Church.[104] Among supersessionists, the kingdom of God is typically viewed as a reality that has not only come to earth in its *preliminary* form through the ministry of Jesus, but has been granted to the Church of history and considered to *be* the new Israel, which is at one and the same time its *custodian* and its *essence*. The question at hand has to do with the supersessionist understanding of the kingdom of God as *equated* with the Church of history.[105] In this book, I secondarily argue that though the bulk of the early Church Fathers were supersessionist in their view that the Church had replaced Israel, they held such a view in tension with an *expectation for the immanent return of the messiah* and borrowed Jewish apocalyptic imagery in such a manner as to allow for a kind of parallel restoration of Israel during Christ's Parousia.[106] Thus, the Patristic era held to a *modified* supersessionism that had yet to solidify into a theology void of any *future expectation or hope for the Jewish people*, even if this hope meant, in an eschatological sense, acceptance by God of Jews "outside" of the Gentile Church.[107] Likewise, there were exceptions to supersessionism in Patristic history, such as the notable Church Father and critic of Gnosticism, Clement of Alexandria.[108]

Robert A. Sungenis argues that supersessionism must "remain" an aspect of official Roman Catholic Church teaching because it was the *unmitigated consensus* of the Fathers. Quoting the Council of Constantinople, Sungenis advocates for supersessionism and applies any concept contrary to this understanding of Judaism to the following account:

> But whoever presumes to compare or to introduce or to teach or to pass on another creed to those wishing to turn from the belief of . . . the Jews or from any heresy whatsoever to the acknowledgement of truth, or who (presumes) to introduce a novel doctrine or an invention of discourse to the subversion of those things which now have been determined by us, [we declare] these, whether they are bishops or clerics, to be excommunicated.[109]

Sungenis's application of the canons of Constantinople to the issue of supersessionism is a blatant oversight in context.[110] First, the Council statement referenced is applicable only to those *wishing to convert from their current faith*, including Judaism, to the Catholic faith. This quote from Constantinople says nothing of those who wish to *remain* Jewish! Post-supersessionism speaks to the reality of Judaism as it is a separate religious expression than that of the Christian Church—it rarely intends to speak of those who wish to convert between the two faiths, except to say that Christian attempts to overtly proselytize are unnecessary, either because the Jewish people are in valid covenantal relation with God already, or because they will be in the future, outside of the Church as we know it. Second, there is no hard proof that the basic tenants of post-supersessionism are absolutely *novel* theological ideas, as evidenced by the words of Clement.[111]

The indirect openness to an alternative to supersessionism among some of the Patristics was the result of an eschatological outlook that did not utterly conflate God's consummative activity intended for the created order, through Israel, with the economy of redemption found in Jesus Christ and operative in the Church. The kingdom of God was still considered a *future reign* that could not be equated with the Church in a manner that emphasized the "already" of God's consummative promises over the "not yet," *unrealized elements* of the kingdom.[112] This chapter previously showed how Soulen argued for an alternative to supersessionism by viewing God's consummative plan for humankind, active through Israel, as distinct from the economy of redemption, and the dependency on human sin, and the entrance of death into the human condition.[113] Soulen argues that *blessing*, not redemption, is the central theme of the Old Testament and that God's intention to consummate creation, *antecedent* to God's redemptive work through the Church, will ultimately result in the peace (*shalom*) of Israel.[114] This *peace*, with the earthly and centralized role of Jerusalem as an essential tenant, is the alternate messianic hope of Israel. Soulen says that:

> the goal of God's work as Consummator is that future reign of *shalom* in which the economy of difference and mutual dependence [between Israel and the nations] initiated by God's promise to Abraham and Sarah is fulfilled in a way that brings fullness of life to Israel, the nations, and to all of creation. Three strands of biblical testimony combine to illuminate this vision of final consummation.[115]

Jesus speaks of the *future consummation* as something that will include the restoration of Israel:

> He [Jesus] appeared to them [the apostles] over a period of forty days and spoke about the kingdom of God. On one occasion, while he was eating with them, he gave them this command: "Do not leave Jerusalem, but wait for the gift my Father promised, which you have heard me speak about. For John baptized with water, but in a few days you will be baptized with the Holy Spirit." Then they gathered around him and asked him, "Lord, are you at this

time going to restore the kingdom to Israel?" He said to them: "It is not for you to know the times or dates the Father has set by his own authority. But you will receive power when the Holy Spirit comes on you; and you will be my witnesses in Jerusalem, and in all Judea and Samaria, and to the ends of the earth."

(Acts 1: 3b–8, NIV)

There are two telling aspects regarding this text in Acts. First, the events described occur *after* Jesus was crucified, died, and rose again. Since supersessionists believe that God's consummative intentions have already been fulfilled in history and *in totality* through the life, death, and resurrection of Jesus and the establishment of the Church, any expectation for future restoration of the kingdom of Israel *qua* Israel, must be nullified. It is the kingdom of God that is *granted* to the Church upon the finished work of Jesus Christ and the call of the Apostles. Yet it would be a logical fallacy to think that the 'the restoration of the kingdom of Israel' took place immediately upon the establishment of the Church at Pentecost, at the beginning of Acts 2.[116] There is nothing in the text of Acts 1 to suggest such an interpretation. Second, Jesus, in Acts 1 says nothing to correct an erroneous understanding of the earthly restoration of Israel. To the contrary, Jesus claims that the Father, through divine authority, *has set a time for the restoration of the kingdom to Israel*, but that the witnessing nature of the Church is a mediative reality that must take place prior to Israel's restoration and the consummation of salvation history.[117] The primary problem with many supersessionist interpretations of the Bible and supersessionist formulations of ecclesiology is that they lead to a conclusion that suggests the Church has replaced Israel. Further, the majority of supersessionist biblical and ecclesiological interpretation is rooted in "realized eschatology."[118] Without either an implicit or explicit adoption of realized eschatology, the theology of replacement could not be adequately defended because its advocates would have to admit of a *distinction* between the kingdom and the Church. If such a distinction exists, it would be impossible to claim that the kingdom of God was taken from Israel and given to the Church, as some supersessionist exegetes of Matthew 21:43 have claimed.[119] Contemporary biblical scholarship has declared this eschatological view infeasible despite its continued use and *necessity* in the logic of supersessionism:

> Is it not possible to understand the high pitch of expectance and hope that were admittedly present during the ministry of Jesus to mean that the guarantee of the eschaton was with them? That is to say, the preliminary events had begun to appear. *But there seems to be no warrant for saying that the disciples believed that the 'event' itself had yet arrived.*[120]

This third problem of supersessionism, the root doctrine of eschatological hope realized or historicized in the Church/Church era, will be the focus of the remaining chapters of this book. In that which follows, the concept of supersessionism as raised by *NA* and its reception will be examined, as will the rejection

48 *Supersessionism and* Nostra Aetate

of supersessionism by contemporary Roman Catholic theologians. We will trace a certain shift, albeit incremental, away from supersessionism in the consciousness of the Catholic tradition.

Notes

1. Ruether, *Faith and Fratricide*, 246.
2. Paul M. van Buren, *A Theology of the Jewish Christian Reality*, Vol. 2: *A Christian Theology of the People Israel* (San Francisco, CA: Harper & Row, 1987), 343.
3. Justin and R.P.C. Hanson, *Selections from Justin Martyr's Dialogue with Trypho, a Jew* (New York: Association Press, 1964), ch. 29.
4. *Let. Barn.*, 5:11–13; 6:7; 7:5; 8:2; 12:5 in Jack N. Sparks, *The Apostolic Fathers* (Nashville, TN: T. Nelson, 1982). In examining the works of Barnabas and Justin, Erich Zenger offers a brief survey of a misreading of the *Epistle to the Hebrews*, insisting that the context of the text reveals issues of contention over Temple sacrifice vs. the sacrifice of Jesus on the cross, rather than expressing a *removal or displacement* of the first covenant with a second covenant. Erich Zenger, "The Covenant that was Never Revoked: The Foundations of a Christian Theology of Judaism," in Philip A. Cunningham, Johannes Hofmann, and Joseph Sievers, eds., *The Catholic Church and the Jewish People: Recent Reflections from Rome* (New York: Fordham University Press, 2007), 94–96.
5. Origen, *Against Celsus* 4.2.3. in *History: Selected Readings*, 3 vols, 1st ed. (Chicago, IL: University of Chicago, 1948).
6. David Novak, *Talking with Christians: Musings of a Jewish Theologian*, Radical Traditions (Grand Rapids, MI: Eerdmans, 2005), 9.
7. Kessler and Wenborn claim that the post-supersessionist movement ". . . represents the most significant development in Christian teaching on the Jewish people since the second and third centuries, when supersessionism originally solidified as the Church's dominant outlook." Edward Kessler, and Neil Wenborn, *A Dictionary of Jewish–Christian Relations* (Cambridge and New York: Cambridge University Press/Cambridge Centre for the Study of Jewish–Christian Relations, 2005), 350.
8. Soulen, *The God of Israel and Christian Theology*, 181, n. 6.
9. Chrysostom's *Eight Homilies* was penned in the fourth century in the context of the Jewish and Christian relations in Antioch and the "temptation" of Antiochene Christians to worship in Jewish synagogues. See also John Chrysostom, *Discourses against Judaizing Christians* (Washington, DC: Catholic University of America Press, 1979).
10. Ruether, *Faith and Fratricide*, 13.
11. See Samuel James Andrews, *God's Revelations of Himself to Men as Successively Made in the Patriarchal*, 2d ed. (New York and London: G.P. Putnam's Sons, 1901), 346.
12. The concept of the "witness people" is attributable to Augustine, who insisted that Jews should be protected and not killed as to not interrupt God's plan that they might witness, through their earthly sufferings, to that which happens to those who reject Christ. Stephen R. Haynes, *Reluctant Witnesses: Jews and the Christian Imagination* (Louisville, KY: Westminster John Knox Press, 1995), 28. During the time of Constantine and through the era of Justinian, the concept of the witness people slowly began to fade. Finally, by the time the political and economic riots hit in Germanic parts of Europe, the protection afforded by this concept was gone. The first, second, and third Crusades of later centuries attest to its loss. See Steven Bayme, *Understanding Jewish History: Texts and Commentaries* (Hoboken, NJ: KTAV, in association with the American Jewish Committee, 1997), 164.

13 James Carroll, *Constantine's Sword: The Church and the Jews: A History* (Boston, MA: Houghton Mifflin, 2001), 446.
14 Though according to the Hebrew Bible, YHWH consistently "punished" the people of Israel in countless occasions due to "disobedience," "idolatry," "stiffneckedness," etc., the God of Israel as expressed in the Old Testament narrative is known more for steadfast love and patience than for *permanent* rejection. See Katharine Doob Sakenfeld, *The Meaning of Hesed in the Hebrew Bible: A New Inquiry* (Missoula, MT: Published by Scholars Press for the Harvard Semitic Museum, 1978).
15 Soulen, *The God of Israel and Christian Theology*, 30.
16 Ibid., 87. According to Soulen, the logic of supersessionism is significantly altered, though not completely eradicated in Barth, because Barth saw God's election of Israel as an act of *grace*. For an examination of Barth's ambiguity on the subject of supersessionism, see Mordecai Paldiel, *Churches and the Holocaust: Unholy Teaching, Good Samaritans, and Reconciliation* (Jersey City, NJ: KTAV, 2006), 22.
17 Soulen, *The God of Israel and Christian Theology*, 28.
18 Irenaeus and others referred to Israel as a "training ground" for salvation. According to Paul Van Buren, there indeed was a training ground, but it was the covenant God made with Noah. For Van Buren, God did not know in advance how salvation was going to play out, so it was not until Abraham that God "got it right." The Abrahamic covenant, ratified for the Jews at Sinai, and made applicable to the rest of the world at Calvary, is the one and only abiding covenant for Van Buren. Paul Matthews van Buren, *A Theology of the Jewish–Christian Reality* (Lanham, MD: University Press of America, 1995), 134.
19 Soulen, *The God of Israel and Christian Theology*, 110.
20 Ibid., Soulen calls the collapsing of the creation of humankind into the theology of the fall of humanity "historical Gnosticism."
21 Kevin Madigan and Jon Douglas Levenson argue that the consummative concept of resurrection appears in the eschatological passages of the OT, in light of sin, but outside a specific framework of substitutionary redemption as espoused in the NT. Kevin Madigan and Jon Douglas Levenson, *Resurrection: The Power of God for Christians and Jews* (New Haven, CT: Yale University Press, 2008), 172.
22 Soulen, *The God of Israel and Christian Theology*, 84.
23 Karl Barth, Geoffrey William Bromiley, and Thomas F. Torrance, *Church Dogmatics IV.1: The Doctrine of Reconciliation* (London: Continuum, 2004), 27, emphasis mine. For Barth, God's elective purposes are simply summed up when God declares to Israel, "I will be your God, and ye shall be my people." This declaration is a *permanent expression* of God's relation to the People of Israel.
24 Soulen, *The God of Israel and Christian Theology*, 181, n. 6.
25 Marcion of Sinope, ca. 85–160 C.E. was one of the most prominent of the early Christian heretics, advocating a belief in two distinct Gods—one of the OT and one of the NT. Marcion, and James Hamlyn Hill, *The Gospel of the Lord: An Early Version which Was Circulated by Marcion of Sinope as the Original Gospel* (New York: AMS Press, 1980) and Sebastian Moll, *The Arch-Heretic Marcion* (Tübingen: Mohr Siebeck, 2010), 47.
26 Soulen, *The God of Israel and Christian Theology*, 58.
27 Stanley J. Grenz and Roger E. Olson, *20th Century Theology: God & the World in a Transitional Age* (Downers Grove, IL: IVP, 1992), 28.
28 Soulen, *The God of Israel and Christian Theology*, 64. The irony behind Kant's statement is that the Messianic idea, rooted deeply in Judaism, is less concerned with "earthly fortunes" than with a "place in the life [world] to come." See Maimonides' *Guide of the Perplexed* and his "Messianic Tutorial."
29 Michael Mack, *German Idealism and the Jew: The Inner Anti-Semitism of Philosophy and German Jewish Responses* (Chicago, IL: University Of Chicago Press, 2003), 40.

50 *Supersessionism and* Nostra Aetate

30 Schleiermacher ultimately reduces Christian divinity to "the human creature's natural capacity for consciousness of God." Soulen, *The God of Israel and Christian Theology*, 78.
31 Ibid., 79.
32 Michael J. Vlach, *Has the Church Replaced Israel?: A Theological Evaluation* (Nashville, TN: B&H, 2010), 92.
33 Ibid., 94.
34 According to Paul Ricoeur, the "semantics career" of a text lasts longer than its "semiotics status," resulting in any given text becoming a "trace" of the past in the present or *future*. See Paul Ricœur, *Interpretation Theory: Discourse and the Surplus of Meaning* (Fort Worth: Texas Christian University Press, 1976), 6.
35 Vlach, *Has the Church Replaced Israel?*, 96, emphasis mine.
36 John Henry Newman, "The Christian Church a Continuation of the Jewish," in *Sermons on Subjects of the Day*, 181, http://www.newmanreader.org/works/subjects/sermon14.html, accessed on January 17, 2010, emphasis mine. See further, Steven D. Aguzzi, "John Henry Newman's Anglican Views on Judaism," *Newman Studies Journal* 7, no. 1 (2010): 56–72, 56.
37 Pontificia Commissio Biblica. *The Jewish People and Their Sacred Scriptures in the Christian Bible* (Boston, MA: Pauline Books & Media, 2002), § 22, available at http://www.vatican.va/roman_curia/congregations/cfaith/pcb_documents/rc_con_cfaith_doc_20020212_popolo-ebraico_en.html/.
38 Daniel 9:24–27; Isaiah 11:1–2; Isaiah 35:4–7; Ezekiel 36:22–27; Isaiah 53; Psalm 22; Zechariah 9:12, 13; and Wisdom 2:12–24, among other texts, appear in early Christian literature in a typological sense, referring either to Jesus' work in history or the establishment of the Church. Judaism, in general terms, interprets these Scriptural texts as referring to either a future messianic reality, or to Israel itself.
39 Hans W. Frei, *The Eclipse of Biblical Narrative: A Study in Eighteenth and Nineteenth Century Hermeneutics* (New Haven, CT: Yale University Press, 1974), 2, emphasis mine.
40 Soulen, *The God of Israel and Christian Theology*, 31.
41 Ibid., 25, emphasis in original.
42 Melito and Alistair Stewart-Sykes, *On Pascha: With the Fragments of Melito and Other Material Related to the Quartodecimans*, Popular Patristics Series (Crestwood, NY: St. Vladimir's Seminary Press, 2001), 47–48, §43.
43 Soulen, *The God of Israel and Christian Theology*, 52.
44 Ibid., 33.
45 Robert Louis Wilken, *John Chrysostom and the Jews: Rhetoric and Reality in the Late 4th Century*, The Transformation of the Classical Heritage (Berkeley, CA: University of California Press, 1983), 116.
46 Michael J. Vlach, "Rejection then Hope: The Church's Doctrine of Israel in the Patristic Era," *TMSJ* 19, no. 1 (2008): 51–70, 51.
47 Vlach, *Has the Church Replaced Israel?*, 3.
48 The LXX is the second-to-third century B.C.E. Koine Greek translation of the Hebrew Bible. The term is used in distinction from the Masoretic Text (edited by a group of Jews in the seventh century A.C.E but linguistically traceable to the much earlier Qumran texts, or the Latin Vulgate (translated primarily from the LXX in 382 by Jerome). Among the supersessionists who read the New Testament through the lens that the Church has become the new Israel in light of the rejection of the messiah by the Jews in the time of Jesus is J.D.G. Dunn, *The Theology of Paul's Letter to the Galatians* (Grand Rapids, MI: Eerdmans, 1994), 100, and J.S. Feinberg, *The Epistle of Paul to the Churches of Galatia* (Grand Rapids, MI: Eerdmans, 1994), 227.
49 Geoffrey William Bromiley, *The International Standard Bible Encyclopedia*, 4 vols, rev. ed. (Grand Rapids, MI: Eerdmans, 1979), 761.

50 Ibid., emphasis mine.
51 Even with the earliest placement of a parting of the ways to the time of the Bar Kokhba revolt (132–135 C.E.), common knowledge points to a later Hellenization of the predominately Jewish movement that formed the Jesus *ekklēsía*—mainly during the time of Marcion, Justin, Tertullian, Origen, Eusebius, and Chrysostom, chronologically.
52 Thomas P. Rausch, *Towards a Truly Catholic Church: An Ecclesiology for the Third Millennium* (Collegeville, MN: Liturgical Press, 2005), 47.
53 Vlach, *Has the Church Replaced Israel?*, 123.
54 Elisabeth Schüssler Fiorenza, *In Memory of Her: A Feminist Theological Reconstruction of Christian Origins* (New York: Crossroad, 1983), 213.
55 Ellen Juhl Christiansen, *The Covenant in Judaism and Paul: A Study of Ritual Boundaries as Identity Markers* (Leiden and New York: E.J. Brill, 1995), 311.
56 Peter Richardson, *Israel in the Apostolic Church* (London: Cambridge University Press, 1969), 7.
57 Most scholars agree that although Pauline authorship for the Letter to the Ephesians is difficult to prove, the text clearly indicates authorship by a person familiar with Paul's themes and theology—perhaps even a scribe of Paul. Delbert Royce Burkett, *An Introduction to the New Testament and the Origins of Christianity* (New York: Cambridge University Press, 2002), 371. The letter itself identifies Paul as the author in several places: Ephesians 3:1; 4:1; 6:20.
58 William Barclay, "The Letters to the Galatians and Ephesians," in *The New Daily Study Bible*, 3rd ed. (Louisville, KY: Westminster John Knox Press, 2002), 67.
59 Wayne A. Grudem, *Systematic Theology: An Introduction to Biblical Doctrine* (Leicester, UK, and Grand Rapids, MI: Zondervan, 1994), 862, emphasis mine, as quoted in Vlach, *Has the Church Replaced Israel?*, 133.
60 Anthony A. Hoekema, *The Bible and the Future* (Grand Rapids, MI: Eerdmans, 1979), 199.
61 According to Joel A. Weaver, there are interpretations of the text in Romans 11 which ascribe a dual-mediation of salvation for Jews which highlights both their distinctive and future roles in history: "Plag asserts that there are two distinct ways of salvation for Israel presented in Romans 11: the way of conversion (vs. 11–24 & 28–31) and the way of the Deliverer (vs. 25–27). He sees vs. 25–27 as a secondary insertion, albeit Pauline, of a Jewish apocalyptic tradition that is likely borrowed from another Pauline letter. This tradition is, according to Plag, added in response to the failure of the way of conversion, Plag, *Israels Wege zum Heil*, 66. Joel A. Weaver, *Theodoret of Cyrus on Romans 11:26: Recovering an Early Christian Elijah Redivivus Tradition* (New York: Peter Lang, 2007), 23, n. 51. We shall see in subsequent chapters how Moltmann's reading of Romans 11 is strikingly similar to the interpretation of Plag.
62 Vlach, *Has the Church Replaced Israel?*, 152, emphasis mine.
63 Ibid.
64 See further, C.B. Hoch, Jr., "The New Man of Ephesians 2" in *Dispensationalism, Israel and the Church: The Search for Definition*, ed. Darrell L. Bock, Walter C. Kaiser, and Craig A. Blaising (Grand Rapids, MI: Zondervan, 1992), 113.
65 Vlach, *Has the Church Replaced Israel?*, 153. See also, Margaret Y. MacDonald and Daniel J. Harrington, *Colossians and Ephesians* (Collegeville, MN: Liturgical Press, 2000), 243.
66 Ibid., See further, Thomas Marberry, Robert E. Picirilli, and Daryl Ellis, "Galatians through Colossians," in *The Randall House Bible Commentary* (Nashville, TN: Randall House, 1988), 176, and Francis Foulkes, "The Letter of Paul to the Ephesians: An Introduction and Commentary," in *The Tyndale New Testament Commentaries*, 2nd ed. (Leicester, UK, and Grand Rapids, MI: IVP and Eerdmans, 1989), 81.

52 *Supersessionism and* Nostra Aetate

67 Anthony O. Ewherido, *Matthew's Gospel and Judaism in the Late First Century C.E.: The Evidence from Matthew's Chapter on Parables (Matthew 13:1–52)* Studies in Biblical Literature. New York: Peter Lang, 2006, 220.
68 Cf. Douglas R.A. Hare, "The Rejection of the Jews in the Synoptic Gospels and Acts," in Alan T. Davies, ed., *Antisemitism and the Foundations of Christianity* (New York: Paulist Press, 1979), 27–47.
69 Klyne Snodgrass, *Stories with Intent: A Comprehensive Guide to the Parables of Jesus* (Grand Rapids, MI: Eerdmans, 2008), 290–291. See further, Snodgrass, *The Parable of the Wicked Tenants: An Inquiry into Parable Interpretation*, Wissenschaftliche Untersuchungen Zum Neuen Testament (Tübingen: J.C.B. Mohr, 1983), 68–69, and John S. Kloppenborg, *The Tenants in the Vineyard: Ideology, Economics, and Agrarian Conflict in Jewish Palestine*, Wissenschaftliche Untersuchungen Zum Neuen Testament (Tübingen: Mohr Siebeck, 2006), 195.
70 M. Eugene Boring, "The Gospel of Matthew: Introduction, Commentary and Reflections" in *The New Interpreter's Bible: General Articles & Introduction, Commentary, & Reflections for Each Book of the Bible, Including the Apocryphal/ Deuterocanonical Books*: Vol. *VIII, New Testament Articles, Matthew, Mark* (Nashville, TN: Abingdon Press, 1994), 415.
71 Anthony J. Saldarini, "Reading Matthew without Anti-Semitism," in D.E. Aune, ed., *The Gospel of Matthew in Current Study: Studies in Memory of William G. Thompson, S.J.* (Grand Rapids, MI: Eerdmans, 2001), 170–172, emphasis mine.
72 According to *A Dictionary of Jewish–Christian Relations,* Post-supersessionism ". . . designates not a single viewpoint but a loose and partly conflicting family of theological perspectives that seeks to interpret the central affirmations of Christian faith in ways that do not state or imply the abrogation or obsolescence of God's covenant with the Jewish people, that is, in ways that are not supersessionist." Kessler and Wenborn, *A Dictionary of Jewish–Christian Relations*, 350.
73 For an excellent analysis of the theological short-sightedness of supersessionist preconceptions, see Larry M Wishon, *Redigging The Wells of Our Fathers*, vol. 2 (Chattanooga, TN: CreateSpace, 2010).
74 For a topical history on the life and thought of Franz Rosenzweig, who wrote his watershed philosophical-theological volume *The Star of Redemption* in 1921, see Franz Rosenzweig, and Nahum N. Glatzer, *Franz Rosenzweig: His Life and Thought*, 2nd rev. ed. (New York: Schocken Books, 1961). Rosenzweig's philosophical system self-entitled "The New Thinking," was a response to problems he saw in the totalizing philosophical framework of German Idealism, namely the philosophy of Hegel. Rosenzweig sought to free the theological concept of revelation from the grips of metaethics, metalogic, and metaphysics, by positing the profound particularity and initial separateness of God, man, and world. Franz Rosenzweig and Barbara E. Galli, *The Star of Redemption*, Modern Jewish Philosophy and Religion: Translations and Critical Studies (Madison, WI: University of Wisconsin Press, 2005), 9–19. By adopting an understanding of philosophy known as speech-thinking (in contrast to the sedimentary and totalizing thought-thinking, Rosenzweig believed he could unleash the dialogical potential of particularity, expressed by the reality of name-surname (Rosenzweig, *The Star of Redemption*, 60). Ultimately, Rosenzweig understood there to be three "elements" (God, world, and man) which intersected through the three "paths" of creation, revelation, and redemption, maintaining an *otherness* between them. Nadine Schmahl, *Das Tetragramm als Sprachfigur. Ein Kommentar zu Franz Rosenzweig's letztem Aufsatz.* (Tübingen: Mohr Siebeck, 2009), 38. Cf. Rosenzweig, *The Star of Redemption*, 336–337.
75 Craig A. Blaising, "The Future of Israel as a Theological Question," in The National Meeting of the Evangelical Theological Society (Nashville, TN: Evangelical Theological Society, November 19, 2000).

76 Rosenzweig believed that the '"... connection of the innermost heart with God' which the heathen can only reach through Jesus is something the Jew already possesses ... he possesses it by nature, through having been born one of the Chosen people ..." Rosenzweig and Glatzer, *Franz Rosenzweig: His Life and Thought*, 27.
77 Ehrenberg was Rosenzweig's cousin and close friend, and a convert to Christianity. Rosenzweig, following in the footsteps of Ehrenberg and under the influence of Eugen Rosenstock-Heussy had decided to convert to Christianity, but only after living as an orthodox Jew in preparation before baptism. In a revelatory experience in a Yom Kippur service at an Orthodox synagogue in Berlin on October 11, 1913, Rosenzweig reversed his decision. Emil L. Fackenheim, *To Mend the World: Foundations of Future Jewish Thought* (New York: Schocken Books, 1982), 60.
78 Eugen Rosenstock-Huessy and Franz Rosenzweig, *Judaism despite Christianity: The Letters on Christianity and Judaism between Eugen Rosenstock-Huessy and Franz Rosenzweig*, Tuscaloosa, AL: University of Alabama Press, 1969), 73–75.
79 For an alternative, post-supersessionist reading of Galatians 3:28–29, see David J. Rudolph, "Messianic Jews and Christian Theology: Restoring a Historical Voice to the Contemporary Discussion," *Pro Ecclesia* XIV, no. 1 (2005): 78.
80 For an argument that the Epistle to the Hebrews is more an example of "fulfillment theology" than strict supersessionism, see L. Kim, *Polemic in the Book of Hebrews: Anti-Semitism, Anti-Judaism, Supersessionism?* (Eugene, OR: Pickwick Publications, 2006). For an argument that Hebrews has been misread altogether in support of supersessionism, see Zenger, "The Covenant that was Never Revoked," 94.
81 James Luther Mays, Joseph Blenkinsopp, and Society of Biblical Literature, *The HarperCollins Bible Commentary*, rev. ed. (San Francisco, CA: HarperSanFrancisco, 2000), 523.
82 Robert W. Jenson, "Toward a Christian Theology of Judaism," in Braaten and Jenson, *Jews and Christians*, 4.
83 Paul R. Bartrop and Steven L. Jacobs, *Fifty Key Thinkers on the Holocaust and Genocide* (Abingdon, UK, and New York: Routledge, 2010), 97.
84 Jenson, "Toward a Christian Theology of Judaism," in Braaten and Jenson, *Jews and Christians*, 5.
85 G. Lindbeck, "The Church as Israel: Ecclesiology and Ecumenism," in Braaten and Jenson, *Jews and Christians*, 78–79.
86 Jenson, "Toward a Christian Theology of Judaism," in Braaten and Jenson, *Jews and Christians*, 6.
87 Ibid., 9.
88 Jacques Dupuis has posited making a distinction between religious pluralism as a reality de facto, which expresses the diversity simply as a fact, and pluralism as a reality *de jure*—more as an intentional and purposeful construct of reality with its own positive repercussions. See Jacques Dupuis, *Toward a Christian Theology of Religious Pluralism* (Maryknoll, NY: Orbis Books, 1997), 312. As we will see later, an inclusivism but not a pluralism is the most helpful construct in dealing with supersessionism.
89 "The Enduring Covenant," in M.C. Boys, ed., *Seeing Judaism Anew: Christianity's Sacred Obligation* (Lanham, MD: Rowman and Littlefield, 2005), 17–28, 25.
90 Those Catholic scholars in the supersessionist camp include Avery Cardinal Dulles, Brian W. Harrison, and Robert Sungenis. See Avery Dulles, "'Covenant and Mission,'" *America* 187/12 (October 21, 2002): 9; Brian W. Harrison, "The Catholic Liturgy and'Supersessionism,'" and Christopher Blosser, "Robert Sungenis and the Jews," *Fringe Watch*, September 9, 2006, http://fringewatcher.blogspot.com/2006/09/on-robert-sungenis-and-jews.html/.
91 Early theologians argued that salvation occurs outside the canonical boundaries of the Church, such as when Augustine explained the following: "How many sheep there

are without, how many wolves within!" St. Augustine, *St. Augustine On Homilies On the Gospel of John, Homilies On the First Epistle of John and Soliloquies: Nicene and Post-Nicene Fathers of the Christian Church, Part 7*, Tractate XLV (Whitefish, MT: Kessinger Publishing, LLC, 2004), 254.

92 For various examples of the stripping of Jesus' Jewish particularity within the Christian tradition, see "Jesus the Jew" in Carroll, *Constantine's Sword*, 71.

93 Augustine's theory was that the continued existence of the Jews could be explained as Israel acting as a "witness people" in order to point toward the dangers of not accepting Christ and the punitive issues that arise from rejecting him. See Paula Fredriksen, *Augustine and the Jews: A Christian Defense of Jews and Judaism*, rev. ed. (New Haven, CT: Yale University Press, 2010), 326.

94 Since the time of the nineteenth century German philosopher Bruno Bauer, there has been a steady stream within the Christian philosophical tradition that has suggested the obsolescence of Jewish ritual practice in light of either a greater Christian revelation, or in light of a universal moral imperative. Jacob Katz, *From Prejudice to Destruction: Anti-Semitism, 1700–1933* (Cambridge, MA: Harvard University Press, 1980), 214.

95 Laurie Guy, *Introducing Early Christianity: A Topical Survey of Its Life, Beliefs, and Practices* (Downers Grove, IL: IVP, 2004), 251.

96 Van Buren, *A Theology of the Jewish–Christian Reality*, Vol. 2: *A Christian Theology of the People Israel*, 157.

97 Wyschogrod and Soulen state that "were the election of Israel contingent upon Israel's behavior, then Israel could walk out on its calling. It could then abrogate the covenant and blend back into the nations of the world instead of living at the white-hot contact point where God meets humankind. But Israel does not have that choice . . . The election of Israel is seared into its flesh and not only its consciousness." "Judaism and the Land" in *Abraham's Promise: Judaism and Jewish–Christian Relations*, ed. Michael Wyschogrod and R. Kendall Soulen, *Radical Traditions* (Grand Rapids, MI: Eerdmans, 2004), 96.

98 According to Richard John Neuhaus, in its rejection of supersessionism and embrace of its Jewish roots, ". . . the Church does not go outside herself but more deeply within herself to engage Jews and Judaism. This is consonant with Rosenzweig's observation that Christianity becomes something else when it is not centered on the Jewish 'man of the cross.'" Richard John Neuhaus, "Salvation Is from the Jews," in Braaten, *Jews and Christians*, 73. *NA* likewise speaks of the "mystery of the Church" when it speaks of the spiritual bond linking the New Covenant with Abraham. *NA*, 4.

99 James H. Wallis, *Post-Holocaust Christianity: Paul Van Buren's Theology of the Jewish–Christian Reality* (Lanham, MD: University Press of America, 1997), 82. Van Buren, *A Theology of the Jewish–Christian Reality*, Vol. 2: *A Christian Theology of the People Israel*, 158. See also, Van Buren, "Torah: God's Generosity—Torah as grace" in *A Theology of the Jewish–Christian Reality*, 210. Cf. Martin Hengel, "The Attitude of Paul to the Law in the Unknown Years between Damascus and Antioch" in *Paul and the Mosaic Law*, ed. James D.G. Dunn, (Grand Rapids, MI: Eerdmans, 2001), 25.

100 Van Buren, *A Theology of the Jewish–Christian Reality*, Vol. 2: *A Christian Theology of the People Israel*, 256–257.

101 Wyschogrod and Soulen, *Abraham's Promise: Judaism and Jewish–Christian Relations*, 97.

102 The *Gospel of Truth*, a Coptic text attributable to Valentinus both in textual inscription and by Irenaeus, speaks of a world and carnal reality created out of utter ignorance. Jesus is said to have come to redeem humankind to a greater cosmic significance and given a renewed and proper ontological reality in contrast with their former bodily existence. Marvin W. Meyer, *et al.*, *The Nag Hammadi Scriptures* (New York: HarperOne, 2007), 31–32.

103 For a critique of the ecclesiological consequences of supersessionism and an alternative "bilateral Jewish–Gentile ecclesiology," see Mark Kinzer, *Postmissionary Messianic Judaism: Redefining Christian Engagement with the Jewish People* (Grand Rapids, MI: Brazos Press, 2005), 12.

104 J. Ross Wagner, *Heralds of the Good News: Isaiah and Paul in Concert in the Letter to the Romans* (Boston, MA: Brill, 2003, 299), n. 236.

105 The concept that the Church is the kingdom of God came into Christian theology in the fourth century with the work of Augustine: "Ergo ecclesia et nunc est regnum Christi regnumque caelorum." Augustine, *et al.*, *The Confessions; the City of God; on Christian Doctrine*, 2nd ed. (Chicago, IL: Encyclopædia Britannica, 1990), XX.9. See further, F. Kattenbusch, "Kritische Studien zur Symbolik," *ThStKr* 51 (1878): 179–253. Kattenbusch is said to be the first scholar to draw attention to Augustine's close identification of the Church with the *apocalyptic* kingdom. *Lumen Gentium*, Article 3 equates the Church with the kingdom, but modifies the statement by claiming that the Church envelops the ultimate, consummated kingdom in a mystical and sacramental way. Avery Dulles, *Models of the Church* (Garden City, NY: Doubleday, 1974), 106. For examples of supersessionism motivated by "realized eschatology," see John Pawlikowski, "The Historicizing of the Eschatological; the Spiritualization of the Eschatological: Some Reflections," in *Antisemitism and the Foundations of Christianity*, 151–166.

106 Vlach, "Rejection then Hope: The Church's Doctrine of Israel in the Patristic Era," 52. See also Samuel M. Frost, *Misplaced Hope: The Origins of First and Second Century Eschatology* (Colorado Springs, CO: Bimillennial Press, 2002), 90–91.

107 See Michael Joseph Brown, "Jewish Salvation in Romans According to Clement of Alexandria in *Stromateis* 2," in Kathy L. Gaca and L.L. Welborn, eds., *Early Patristic Readings of Romans* (New York: T&T Clark, 2005), 42–62. Brown makes a strong argument for a highly charitable reading of Clement in regard to the Jews. According to Brown, Clement interprets Romans 10–11 in a way that puts supersessionism in question, alluding to the idea that ". . . Judaism and Christianity are two respectable paths to salvation in the eyes of the biblical God." Gaca, *Early Patristic Readings of Romans*, iv.

108 Kessler and Wenborn, *A Dictionary of Jewish–Christian Relations*, 19. Clement never made the claim that the Church replaced Israel in a 'wholesale' sense, but always maintained that God's relationship with Israel was permanent and abiding.

109 See Council of Constantinople III: DS, 556–559 as quoted in Catholic Church. *The Companion to the Catechism of the Catholic Church: A Compendium of Texts Referred to in the Catechism of the Catholic Church* (San Francisco, CA: Ignatius Press, 1994), 149. See also, R. Sungenis, "The Old Covenant: Revoked or Not Revoked," (paper presented at the annual meeting of the Bellarmine Theological Forum, Louisville, KY, February 9, 2008). It should be noted that Sungenis was sanctioned from teaching on the subject of Catholics and Jews by Bishop Kevin C. Rhoades.

110 Sungenis's contextual oversight of the statements of the Fathers likewise explains why he has fought hard to have any hint of post-supersessionism removed from the *United States Catholic Catechism for Adults*, which states boldly that ". . . the covenant that God made with the Jewish people through Moses remains eternally valid *for them*." *United States Catholic Catechism for Adults* (Washington, DC: United States Conference of Catholic Bishops, 2006), 131, emphasis mine.

111 For an interesting argument that *post-supersessionist theology* is a valid development of doctrine that has been in the Catholic tradition implicitly, see John L. Drury, "Testing the Tests: Post-Supersessionist Theology and Newman's Notes of a Genuine Development of Doctrine," http://www.drurywriting.com/john/Testing%20the%20 Tests%20-%20Senior%20Thesis.htm (accessed February 21 2011).

112 Frost states that Origen "... certainly believes that Christ had not yet subjected all of his enemies under his feet. He held that the consummation of all things was not yet, and he does not seem to indicate when this will happen. To him, then, the reality of physical death was a sign that Christ had not yet conquered death. Origen, *De Princ.*, 1.6.1. He believes that when the "age to come" arrives, it will bring with it a new heaven and new earth. It is at this time that the promises of salvation will be fully restored. Here, Origen is most consistent with the orthodoxy of the apostolic fathers. *Everything was future.*" Frost, *Misplaced Hope*, 134, emphasis mine.
113 "Redemption is for the sake of consummation, not consummation for the sake of redemption." Soulen, *The God of Israel and Christianity Theology*, 175, emphasis in original.
114 Walter Kasper likewise states that the coming of the kingdom of God, a living hope among the Jews of Jesus's time, "... coincided with the establishment of the eschatological *shalom* . . ." Walter Kasper, *Jesus the Christ* (London and New York: Burns & Oates and Paulist Press, 1976), 73.
115 Soulen, *The God of Israel and Christian Theology*, 131.
116 On the theological complexities of this passage, see Anders E. Nielsen, *Until It Is Fulfilled: Lukan Eschatology according to Luke 22 and Acts 20*, Wissenschaftliche Untersuchungen Zum Neuen Testament (Tübingen: Mohr Siebeck, 2000), 258.
117 Robert W. Wall states that "with minds opened by Jesus to understand the witness of Scripture to the salvation of Israel, the disciples ask Jesus whether God's promise of the Spirit is coordinate with God's promise to restore the kingdom to Israel (1:6). Jesus is instructive both in what he says and what he does not say in response (1:7–8). He does not reprove the Apostles for they are right in making the connection: Pentecost has *everything* to do with God's fidelity to the biblical promises made to the Jews. Nowhere does Jesus suggest that God's promise to restore "real" Israel has been reclaimed and given to the Church as a spiritual or "true" Israel. Christianity has not superseded Israel in the plan of God's salvation so that God's future now belongs to the Church. Jesus rather indicates to his apostles that the fulfillment of God's promise to revitalize Israel is not a matter of "when" (1:7) but "how" (1:8): God's concern for what happens at the "end of the earth" or at its very center in Jerusalem is evinced by the Church's *mission*. The Gentile mission is *not* the result of Jewish rejection. It is God's idea from the very beginning according to biblical prophecy, and it is made possible only because of God's prior saving work among repentant Jews mediated by the Church's *Jewish* mission. Robert W. Wall, "Acts 1:3–14 Reflections," in *The New Interpreter's Bible* (Nashville, TN: Abingdon Press, 46), emphasis in original.
118 See "Realized Eschatology," in D.K. McKin, ed., *Westminster Dictionary of Theological Terms* (Louisville, KY: Westminster John Knox Press, 1996), 92.
119 "The Gentiles come to salvation when the *basileia* is taken away from Israel." Ulrich Luz and Helmut Koester, *Matthew 1–7: A Commentary*, rev. ed. (Minneapolis, MN: Fortress Press, 2007), 195.
120 Donald Joseph Selby, "Changing Ideas in New Testament Eschatology," *Harvard Theological Review* 50 (January 1957): 23, emphasis mine.

2 *Nostra Aetate* and its reception
Supersessionism challenged

Perhaps there is no greater historic manifestation of the Roman Catholic Church's shift in attitude toward the Jews than the *Nostra Aetate* (*NA*) of the Ecumenical Council Vatican II.[1] Much debate has occurred as a result of the sweeping changes initiated by Vatican II, particularly surrounding issues that marked a shift in power and authority in Catholicism—a shift from the "rubber stamp of the *Curia*" to a more collegial and truly episcopal process relevant to the modern world.[2]

According to *Dei Filius* of Vatican I, the bishops assembled in the context of a called Ecumenical Council act as the subjects of the "supreme magisterium"[3] and are "equipped to enunciate binding and irrevocable doctrines concerning faith . . ."[4] A source of contemporary debate over Vatican II concerns whether the Council aspired to be, or was intended to make, binding doctrinal pronouncements, considering that overall, ". . . there are no clearly developed criteria for determining *when* a valid Ecumenical Council is in fact teaching with the charism of infallibility."[5]

NA and other Vatican II documents have been relegated to the status of mere pastoral authority, both by Pope Paul VI who completed the Council, and through the interpretive framework of Pope Benedict XVI[6]—all this in spite of the fact that two of the documents produced by the Council are dogmatic constitutions (*Dei Verbum* and *Lumen Gentium*) containing wide implications for the interpretation of Scripture for the modern world, and even wider implications for ecclesiology.[7] Benedict XVI used the following terms to make the distinction between the pastoral and dogmatic elements of the Council: "The truth is that this particular council defined no dogma at all, and deliberately chose to remain on a modest level, as a merely pastoral council; and yet many treat it as though it had made itself into a sort of superdogma which takes away the importance of all the rest."[8]

Though *NA* is a declaration and not a dogmatic constitution, this book will treat the document as an extension of the teaching authority accepted by the Catholic tradition within the context of its Latin original,[9] *acta*, and the Council's historical and theological context.[10] Although other aspects of dialogue will be addressed, the theme of this section specifically concerns the impact and influence of *NA* regarding the Catholic Church's reassessment of its traditional supersessionist theology, particularly in its reception. This theological basis makes *NA* very significant as the declaration informs contemporary Catholics regarding Jewish–

Catholic relations. According to Erich Zenger, after the wake of *NA*, supersessionism has come to be seen as a theology of the past, despite the fact that various quarters of the Church cling to the dangerous ideology:

> at least in the realm of Catholic and Protestant theology, an *ecumenical consensus* has been reached on various fundamental principles of a possible Christian understanding of Judaism . . . [the first of which may be summarized as claiming that] . . . at no point in time did God revoke his covenant with Israel. Israel is and remains the chosen people of God, even if it does not accept Jesus as its own Messiah.[11]

In addition to Zenger's claim, Walter Kasper has made significant statements regarding the concept of supersessionism in relation to the reforms of *NA*: "The old theory of substitution [of the synagogue by the Church] is gone since the Second Vatican Council. For us Christians today the covenant with the Jewish people is a living heritage, a living reality."[12]

Though *NA* itself does not explicitly reject supersessionism, its reception in various ecclesial documents[13] and its interpretation by Pope John Paul II and various Catholic theologians suggests that the declaration's intent and scope was to advocate a post-supersessionist theology. Because of the declaration's style and approach, there is a level of hermeneutic ambiguity implicit in its study that has led to divergent readings of the text.[14] In this section, *NA* will be examined in light of the *intentions* of its authors, its assessment of God's covenant promises to the Jews utilizing the language of Romans 11, its reception by Pope John Paul II and official ecclesial documents, the tensions among its interpreters, its reading in light of the ecclesiology and eschatology of *Lumen Gentium*, and its impact on the theology of supersessionism.

The shift to the relation to non-Christian religions

Nostra Aetate, Latin for "in our age," was promulgated during the second session of the Second Vatican Council, by Pope Paul VI on October 28, 1965, and was approved by an episcopal vote of 2,221 to 88.[15] Though officially entitled "Declaration on the Relation of the Church to non-Christian Religions," the original intention of its authors was to address the Jewish–Catholic question only.[16] Lobbying by the *Arab League* was so strong that it initially caused a near swing of voting in favor of withdrawing entirely the fourth paragraph of the declaration, the section on the Jews, as "the Syrian prime minister, Selah el-Bitar was harshly outspoken: the proposed declaration was 'Zionist-inspired and part of a plot to mobilize Catholic opinion against the Arabs for reigniting the Palestinian question . . .' "[17] Opposition by some traditionalist bishops also led to a near dismissal of the declaration in its entirety.[18]

The dramatic history behind the inception of *NA*'s fourth paragraph is not common knowledge among many theologians who work outside the field of conciliar history. Eugene J. Fisher states the following:

Between 1962 and 1965, the debate on the draft raged furiously both on the floor of the Council and behind the scenes. Anti-Semitic tracts were passed out to the Council Fathers and debunked by defenders of the statement. Intense diplomatic pressure was put forth by Arab governments. *Compromises in wording and nuance were made and remade. The document was originally intended to be a lengthier one put out on its own.* Then it was thought to attach it to the statement on ecumenism. *The final compromise was to include it in a statement on "Non-Christian Religions" in general.* Thus it was that the Council Fathers took up the issue of dialogue with Islam, Hinduism, Buddhism and the native traditions, in a real sense, in order to take a positive approach to Judaism.[19]

We may only guess as to what the compromises "in wording and nuance" were, especially if such compromises toned down an original intent in the language of *NA* that would have repudiated supersessionism in a more formalized and explicit manner.[20] The series of events leading up to the declaration's inclusion of many non-Christian religions are important for our evaluation, primarily because of the issue of supersessionism and the election of the Jews, and likewise the focus of critique aimed at the document as a whole. Though there were many benefits because of the inclusion of various religious traditions in *NA*, the "clumping in" of Judaism with the remainder of the world's religions communicates a significant theology: all non-Christian religions are on the same plain, regardless of claims to direct revelation (the Hebrew Bible), particular election as a nation or carnal reality, and covenantal priority. As Moltmann claims in his critique:

> The Second Vatican Council ... still talks about Israel in the framework of the 'non-Christian religions' and the Church's general relationship to them. It is only more recent Catholic declarations about Israel that go beyond this view of Israel as one of the 'non-Christian religions'. But up to now neither the Vatican nor Geneva [the Reformed Church] has drawn appropriate conclusions as far as organization is concerned. Israel is still allocated to the secretariats for relations with non-Christian religions.[21]

Yet if *NA* was originally intended to be a treatment of the Jewish people separate from the reality of the Church in relation to other non-Christian religions—this reality lends itself to the idea that the God of Christianity is at work in modern Judaism in a way that is unique and somehow covenantal, albeit, "imperfect."[22] Likewise, things have changed since Moltmann wrote his critique, insofar as there are no official "missionary" organizations within the Catholic Church at the Vatican level that seek to convert the Jews specifically, and perhaps most significantly, contemporary dialogue with the Jews is done under the auspices of the Commission of the Holy See for Religious Relations with the Jews, which works in tandem with the Pontifical Council for Promoting Christian Unity—*not* the *Sacra Congregatio de Propaganda Fide*."[23] Why dialogue with the Jews is organized in this manner is related to the overall attitude toward the Jews that surfaced *after* the reforms of *NA* and continue to impact Jewish–Catholic relations today: "Many Christians and some Jews feel that Vatican II is an important turning point in the relations between Christianity and Judaism: Catholics may no longer regard Judaism as an anachronism that was abrogated by the advent of Jesus. Rather, Catholics may regard contemporary Judaism as a meaningful religion in itself..."[24]

The ways in which *NA* and the documents of its reception history have moved Catholic theology away from supersessionism and toward new understandings of viewing God's covenant with the Jews in light of the coming kingdom of God is the subject matter of what follows. Though there is disagreement among members of the Catholic curia as to whether Jews must accept the Gospel in the eschatological future, *NA*'s reception appears to definitively ring the death toll for *ecclesial supersessionism*[25]—the idea that contemporary Jews must convert to and become members of the Roman Catholic Church that exists now, in history, in order to obtain salvation and live into their covenantal calling. Indeed, this is the position of the Catholic Church regarding other religions—that one need not be Catholic in order to obtain salvation, which is nevertheless possible because the Church of Christ subsists in the Catholic Church and because the Holy Spirit may work outside its canonical boundaries.[26] But *NA*'s reception points to something beyond the mere "subsists in" formulation—Jews are not superseded by the Church *precisely because they are Jews and because they have their own divinely ordained witness to the nations*. Augustine Cardinal Bea, the individual in charge of presenting *NA* at Vatican II made the claim that the Jews "... are still very dear to God for the sake of their fathers and it is still their privilege that the Gospel and the kingdom of God *belong to them in the first place* ... just as they were the first to receive the messianic promises."[27] According to Bea, criticism has been aimed at the concept that the Jewish people are "special" or "chosen" in the eyes of God, to which he reminds retractors that there is no "racist" implication regarding a strong sense of Jewish election in light of the fact that God's choices are gratuitous and that the mission of Israel is meant as a blessing to all nations.[28] The way the Jews have been treated in history is a testament to the fact that emphasis on the special status of the Jews as eternally loved by God could go a long way in reforming the Church's traditional "teaching of contempt." In light of this reality, we will examine the official documents issued by the Vatican in relation to *NA*, along with significant sections of *NA* itself, and finally we will explore the statements of Pope John Paul II and the bishops regarding the declaration.

Nostra Aetate and its reception: The irrevocable call

It is imperative that *NA* no. 4, what Gregory Baum has deemed "... the most profound change in the ordinary magisterium of the Church to occur at Vatican II,"[29] not be viewed as an isolated and rigid document. The reception of the declaration throughout the brief Catholic history since its promulgation has been so transformative for the ways Catholics are to view Jews and Judaism that the official ecclesial and popular aspects of this reception must be used as a means of interpretation for the document itself.[30] There have been multiple official documents released by the Church in relation to *NA*, in addition to strong statements issued by John Paul II, and the USCCB interpretation of the document. Though *NA* made enormous changes through its repudiation of the charge of deicide against the Jews[31] and its utter rejection of anti-Semitism, which led to a formal apology by John Paul II,[32] the primary focus of this section will involve only those aspects of the text that relate to the problem of supersessionism.

The fourth article of *NA* begins its section on Judaism, and does so by relating the roots of Jewish election to the *mystery* of the Church:

> Sounding the depths of the mystery which is the Church, this sacred council remembers the spiritual ties which link the people of the new covenant to the stock of Abraham. The Church acknowledges that in God's plan of salvation the beginnings of its faith and election are to be found in the patriarchs, Moses and the prophets.[33]

As Eugene J. Fisher interprets it, "*Nostra Aetate* 'acknowledges the Church's indebtedness to Judaism, in which 'the beginnings of her (the Church's) faith and her election are already found.' Far from replacing or superseding Jewish faith, Christians are 'included in the patriarch's (Abraham's) call.' "[34] Though no explicit mention is made of the post-exilic Jewish tradition, the "stock of Abraham" refers to the Jewish people as they stand today, and not merely as they were at the time of Abraham.[35] The 1974 "Guidelines and Suggestions for Implementing the Conciliar Declaration *Nostra Aetate*" (hereafter "Guidelines") released by the *Vatican's Commission for Religious Relations with the Jews* expanded the declaration by reminding its readers that "[t]he history of Judaism did not end with the destruction of Jerusalem" (III, 7) and expresses the Jewish and Christian traditions as 'interrelated' (IV, 1).[36] Pressing the clarification further, the 1985 "Notes on the correct way to present the Jews and Judaism in preaching and catechesis in the Roman Catholic Church" (hereafter, "Notes") proclaims that "the *permanence of Israel* . . . is a historic fact and a sign to be interpreted *within God's design* . . ." (VI, 25) suggesting that modern Judaism is a religious phenomenon *de jure* and not merely de facto.[37] *NA* claims that ". . . the salvation of the Church is mystically prefigured in the exodus of God's chosen people from the land of bondage,"[38] but nowhere in the document is it claimed that the religious phenomenon that acted as a prefiguration became obsolete. Quite the contrary, the Vatican "Notes" claim that a "typological reading only manifests the unfathomable riches of the Old Testament, its inexhaustible content and the mystery of which it is full, and should not lead us to forget that it *retains its own value as Revelation* . . ."[39] Further, in "Notes" the claim is made that typology itself has an *eschatological* dimension that points to the period when the "divine plan" will be consummated, thus there is a sense of "surprise" and a resistance to absolute statements in regard to the consummation of God's plan with the Jews.[40] The document *NA* begins to point toward Paul's *Epistle to the Romans*, as it claims that "... [the Church] cannot forget that it draws nourishment from that good olive tree onto which the wild olive branches of the Gentiles has been grafted."[41] Thus, in *NA* an attempt is made to balance an approach that preserves the good, lively, and permanent aspects of God's covenant with the Jews and the insistence that the covenant is *one*.[42] The Letter to the Romans is quoted again, insofar as the declaration reads:

> the Church keeps ever before its mind the words of the apostle Paul about his kin: 'they are Israelites, and it is for them to be sons and daughters, to them belong the glory, the covenants, the giving of the law, the worship, and the promises; to them belong the patriarchs, and of their race according to the flesh, is the Christ.
>
> (Romans 9:4–5)[43]

The significance of how this New Testament passage is treated hermeneutically cannot be overlooked because, unlike previous supersessionist and pre-conciliar renderings, the declaration translates the original Greek properly, in the *present tense*:

> οἵτινές εἰσιν Ἰσραηλῖται, ὧν ἡ υἱοθεσία καὶ ἡ δόξα καὶ αἱ διαθῆκαι καὶ ἡ νομοθεσία καὶ ἡ λατρεία καὶ αἱ ἐπ αγγελίαι, ὧν οἱ π ατέρες, καὶ ἐξ ὧν ὁ Χριστὸς τὸ κατὰ σάρκα: ὁ ὢν ἐπ ὶ π άντων θεὸς εὐλογητὸς εἰς τοὺς αἰῶνας, ἀμήν.
>
> (Romans 9:4–5, GNT)

The phrases "They *are* Israelites . . ." and "to them *belong* the glory," imply that the Jewish people are still the recipients of the promises of the covenant, and not merely that the Jews used to be the recipients until the dawn of the age of Christ, and then the Church became the sole bearer of such promises.[44] The declaration goes on to state that although the Jews, in general, did not accept the Gospel, the Church, along with Paul:

> maintains that the Jews remain very dear to God, for the sake of the patriarchs, since God does not take back the gifts he bestowed or the choice he made. Together with the prophets and the same apostle, the Church awaits the day, known to God alone, when all people will call on God with one voice and "serve him shoulder to shoulder."[45]
>
> (Soph 3:9; see Isaiah 66:23; Psalm 65:4; Romans 11:11–32)

This section of the document reiterates the Pauline doctrine of unrepentant choice on the part of God and confirms the election of carnal Israel. The declaration likewise implies an internal mission that binds together the synagogue and the Church: a witness to the idea that Israel's election was for the blessing of the nations,[46] and a witness to the eschaton. Some Jewish commentators take the "all people" above to refer specifically to the Jews, interpreting the declaration's emphasis of God's election of the Jews merely in light of a specifically inferred Pauline anticipation that "... they [the Jews] remain not without hope because in the fullness of time it is anticipated that they will finally see the light and join the Church."[47] Yet this ecclesial supersessionist projection appears nowhere in the text or in the official ecclesial documents that aid in interpreting *NA*. Quite the contrary, the 1985 "Notes" claim that Jews and Christians:

> have to witness to one same memory ... [referring to the witness of the Hebrew prophets and the messianic hopes of the Second Temple period] ... and common hope in Him who is the master of history. We must also accept our responsibility to prepare the world for the coming of the Messiah by working together for social justice, respect for the rights of persons and nations and for social and international reconciliation. To this we are driven, Jews and Christians, by the command to love our neighbor, by a common hope for the Kingdom of God and by the great heritage of the Prophets.[48]

There is no hint in this statement that the Jews are to convert *en masse* and become members of the Catholic Church in order to initiate or participate in the common messianic and eschatological witness. It is not until the 1999 writings of then Cardinal Joseph Ratzinger (now Pope Emeritus Benedict XVI) in his *Many Religions—One Covenant: Israel, the Church and the World*, and its influence upon Catholic catechesis that the eschatological claims of *NA* take on a more traditionalist tone, despite Benedict's determination to continue the positive relations with the Jewish people begun by John Paul II.[49] The supplementary scriptural texts cited in *NA* immediately after the phrase "... the Church awaits the day, known to God alone ..." appear to exist simply in order to strike a balance between the particularity of Jewish election and the universality of the Gospel as proclaimed to the nations through the Church. Soph 3:9 speaks of God's care for the elect, Isaiah 66:23 of how, from one Sabbath to another, all mankind will bow before the Lord, Psalm 65:4 reiterates the language of God's sovereign choice, and Romans 11:11–32 is the Pauline narrative suggesting that there will come a time when Israel's "deliverer will come from Zion," quoting Isaiah 59:20, 21; 27:9 (LXX). Nowhere in *NA* or in the Pauline text, is Jewish membership *in the Church* mentioned or necessarily implied. Though the Christian conviction is that "the deliverer" coming from Zion is none other than Jesus, even this point is couched in what Paul calls a μυστήριον that demands from Gentile Christians a kind of humility, "so that you may not be conceited" (Romans 11:25).[50] "Notes" takes the theological problem of the Jewish "no" to Jesus as messiah and grapples with it as a *positive* sign of Israel's abiding election,[51] reiterating that "[w]e must in any case rid ourselves of the traditional idea of a people punished, preserved as a living argument for Christian apologetic. It *remains a chosen people*, "the pure olive on which were grafted the branches of the wild olive which are the gentiles."[52]

In general, the public statements and writings of Pope John Paul II agree with *NA*'s reception through the various Vatican documents, with special attention given to the theology which surfaces from a certain interpretation of the Romans 11 passages.[53] John Paul II, following in the tradition of the declaration, was the first pope in history to renounce supersessionism by claiming that the Jews *are*—not *were*—". . . the people of God of the old covenant, *never revoked* by God . . ."[54] ". . . *partners* in a covenant of eternal love which was *never revoked*,"[55] and ". . . the present-day people of the Covenant concluded with Moses."[56] A responsible reading of the phrase "the people of God of the old covenant, never revoked by God . . ." would take that which was "never revoked by God" to apply to both the covenant *and the people*—the Jews. Modern scholarship interprets Paul's language of the covenant in Romans, the Epistle to which John Paul II was referring in his statements, as inseparable from "Israel."[57] Likewise, in these statements, the term "old covenant" refers to God's agreement with Abraham, as it was ratified through the Mosaic dispensation on Sinai.[58]

Parsing out these papal statements has been a matter of great debate among theologians, though in light of the bulk of the Vatican documents that interpreted *NA* prior to the pope's commentary, the various contours of John Paul II's thought are definitively discernible. John Paul II's ideas that the Jews remain God's people, that the covenant God made with them was not revoked and then reapplied to the Church, and that there is some kind of ongoing covenantal witness or mission that the Jewish people retain by virtue of the fact that they are members of the community of Israel—these are all post-supersessionist in tone and content. The root of John Paul II's theology of Judaism is the concept that there is both a sameness and otherness that is unique to Jewish and Christian existence, thereby reading Romans 11 and *NA* as advocating a symbiotic relationship between the two traditions. Supersessionism becomes an absurd prospect precisely because the Church cannot participate in God's covenant apart from the "good olive tree" to which it has been grafted. The Church has become a part of Israel, sharing in Israel's covenantal blessing, without Israel relinquishing its own original identity. If advocates of supersessionist theology seek to remove or blot out God's enduring relationship with the Jews, resulting in a kind of "self-hate of their own . . . imperfection . . . [and] . . . 'not yet,' " as Moltmann argues,[59] or a fratricidal posture as Ruether argues,[60] John Paul II's revisions, by contrast, point to the dignity of the Church, precisely by upholding the unrevoked covenant given to its 'elder brother,' the Israel of then and now.[61] As Bruce D. Marshall states in reference to the pope's comments to the rabbis at the Great Synagogue of Rome:

> In his interpretation of Romans 11:29, he [John Paul II] apparently goes further than does *Nostra Aetate*, no. 4 (and *Lumen Gentium*, no. 16). The Jews remain 'most dear to God,' indeed, but they are more than that. The electing love of God which made Abraham, Isaac, Jacob, and their descendants according to the flesh 'the firstborn of the Covenant' continues to make their descendants today, the Jews of Rome, the covenant's firstborn. God's original covenant with the Jewish people remains in force . . . Not only is faithful Israel before Christ the root from which the gentiles live in Christ, *but faithful Israel now*, the Jews gathered with their chief rabbi in the Great Synagogue of Rome, are

the root from which the gentile Church *now lives in Christ*. This is a very strong reading of Romans 11, and a very strong sense in which the Jewish people are 'elder brothers' to us Christians.[62]

In this manner, John Paul II broke with his predecessors and moved beyond the moderate language expressed in *NA* by positing a post-supersessionist theology that centered on the *Jews of today* and their ongoing significance in God's plan of salvation for the world. John Paul II's consistent reiteration that the Jews are "partners"[63] with the Church does not imply that the Jewish community is on its way to *becoming* the Church, although for John Paul II, Judaism is in a sense already constitutive of the Church.[64] Instead, the term partnership may represent the incomplete character of both Judaism and Christianity in its "Pilgrim Church,"[65] and the Jewish and Christian participation in a God-ordained reality that has yet to approach human beings entirely, and has yet to fully break into history. For John Paul II and the contemporary Catholicism that followed *NA*:

> Judaism constitutes a *sui generis* category, falling under the rubric of neither Christian nor non-Christian . . . As the religion that gave birth to Christianity, as the community to which God made unbreakable covenantal promises, Judaism has, in John Paul II's language, a special status *within* the Church as a beloved (elder) brother . . . [This] *sui generis* category for Judaism suggested by contemporary Church leaders is a comfortable compromise; by preserving Jewish distinctiveness, it conforms better with Judaism's self-image.[66]

On the one hand, precisely because God's covenant with the Jews is eternally valid and a source of salvation, the Church's participation in Israel vis-à-vis Jesus Christ allows it to share and participate in the coming reality of God's reign and the hope of the fullness of salvation: "Remember, therefore, that at one time you gentiles in the flesh . . . were separated from Christ, separated from the commonwealth of Israel, and strangers to the covenants of promise, *having no hope* . . ." (Ephesians 2:11–12).[67] On the other hand, according to the contemporary Catholic perspective initiated by John Paul II's understanding of Vatican II, the Jewish people participate in the Church by virtue of their role as "elder brothers"—ones sharing the same parent, the God of Israel, and sharing the same historical root of the Second Temple period. Teetering between possessing the fullness of salvation[68] and moving as a pilgrim Church in partnership with other entities in history,[69] the Catholic Church enjoys the seeds of the kingdom of God that are likewise present through Judaism's eternal covenant, while looking forward to a consummation of history and a messianic hope that is *yet to come*.[70] Thus, two aspects of Pope John Paul II's reception of *NA* have come to bear fruit in contemporary Catholic theology—one ecclesiological and one eschatological. First, by viewing Judaism as constitutive of the Church, with the Church likewise drawing spiritual nourishment from Judaism, Judaism is placed in a *sui generis* religious category that protects it from being subsumed into the Catholic Church without its otherness and distinction, while at the same time resisting traditional supersessionism by claiming that there is an element of *contemporary* Judaism that is constitutive of the Church—if the Church claims that the synagogue has been abrogated, the Church abrogates a part of itself. Second, because the Jews are still the people of God, as we shall examine in the upcoming section, and because the Jews are even now, "partners" in covenant history, the Church moves along *in time* with the synagogue,[71] participating in a common witness of messianic hope. For both the synagogue and the Church, the messiah has a future coming.

The most substantial statement concerning the issue of supersessionism in *NA* is the qualification of the phrase "people of God," the biblical term used often at Vatican II and later adopted by John Paul II in reference to the Jewish people. The document reads: "It is true that the Church is the new people of God, yet Jews should not be spoken of as rejected or accursed as if this followed from holy Scripture."[72] Cunningham states that "chapter 4 of this document [*NA*] repudiated the foundational principle of supersessionism by stating that 'the Jews remain very dear to God' and by quite explicitly instructing that 'the Jews should not be presented as rejected or accursed by God'."[73] The declaration does not refrain from using the term "people of God," expressing a newness to the biblical phrase that is found in the New Testament and since the advent of Jesus of Nazareth, yet the Church no longer claims that the Jews are *not* the "people of God."[74] "Notes" reiterates this point by claiming that the Jews are to be viewed as ". . . the people of God of the Old Covenant . . ." and that the Jews are still "a chosen people."[75] Another interpretive document entitled "*Within Context: Guidelines for the Catechetical Presentation of Jews and Judaism in the New Testament*," (hereafter, "*Within Context*") commissioned by the Secretariat for Catholic–Jewish Relations in 1986 clarifies the concept of the "People of God" by stating that "The Second Vatican Council *clearly taught* that God's covenant with and therefore *presence among the Jewish people as God's own people* has not been abrogated by the coming of Christ . . ."[76]

In light of the declaration's reception in relation to the problem of supersessionism and statement that ". . . Jews should not be spoken of as rejected or accursed as if this followed from Holy Scripture," we must ask a pivotal question: does this imply that they instead are accepted and blessed, *as Jews*? As Boys affirms, "to assert that the 'old covenant' has not been revoked carries little import if there is no *theological reason for the existence of Judaism* after the coming of Jesus Christ."[77] The traditionally supersessionist Pope Emeritus Benedict XVI likewise admits of this reality of an ongoing mission of contemporary Jews.[78] Benedict insists that though the Church may reflect theologically on the continued witness of modern Jews in the world, it is only for the Jews themselves to articulate their own mission in light of their own experience.[79] Thus, Benedict's instinct is correct, in leaving the defining work of a mission only to the community from whose epistemic location the mission may be formulated—but this counters Benedict's previous work on Judaism, which suggests that Judaism is valid only in light of its relation to the Church.

Though the Jewish community is the sole community responsible for a full articulation of Jewish mission, *NA*'s call for theological dialogue has forced

Catholic theologians to rethink the concept of a "parallel mission" between Jew and Catholic. One of the nuances that have surfaced since Vatican II is the idea that the way in which Judaism is viewed within its own tradition has a theological bearing on how the Church views itself, suggesting that the Church develops doctrinal understanding by moving toward its eschatological reality, in a sense, "converting" to itself and beyond with the help of other historical partners.[80] This "conversionary" element that takes place in interreligious theological dialogue, the kind of dialogue inspired by *NA*, has been emphasized in the work of Jacques Dupuis insofar as he believes that it is actually through the process of interreligious dialogue that we learn something new, viewing interreligious dialogue as an ongoing revelation of sorts. Dupuis relates dialogue as an aspect of mission, as does the Vatican document "Dialogue and Proclamation,"[81] and claims that ". . . as a specific element of evangelization, dialogue does not seek the 'conversion' of others to Christianity but the convergence of both dialogue partners to a *deeper shared conversion to God and to others . . .*"[82] Francis Cardinal George takes great offense at such a conception of the Church's mission in relation to recent interpretations of *NA*, because he believes that giving priority to dialogue over proclamation ". . . posits the incompleteness of both . . ."[83] Christianity and the other faith in question.[84] The eschatological and ecclesiological issues raised by *NA*'s reception and the idea that Judaism has a mission outside the scope of the Church, forces theologians to reevaluate what it means to witness to the kingdom of God, and the proximity to which the kingdom is made in reference to the Church. George continues:

> Forms of Kingdom-centered missiology that separate the Kingdom from the Church and also from Christ, so that mission becomes "promoting the so-called 'values of the Kingdom' (peace, justice, freedom, fraternity) as well as dialogue between peoples, cultures, and religions with the goal of mutual enrichment" are misleading and inadequate. The mission of the Church is to announce a Kingdom *already present within her*.[85]

Certainly, the call of the Church is to passionately proclaim the Gospel of Jesus Christ, yet the weakness that becomes evident in George's objection is that Jesus's own mission also contained a promotion of the "values of the Kingdom," within the context of imminent Jewish messianism and restoration theology. The restoration of Israel was an emphasis of missiology *prior* to the inception of the Church. The equating of the Church with the kingdom occurred after the Church took on a purely supersessionist attitude, gave up its roots in the imminence of Jewish apocalypticism, and began to ignore the language that Jesus used in describing the kingdom—as an entity related to the Church but existing far beyond it.[86]

Overall, perhaps the most significant theological reason for the continued existence of the Jewish people, one that has been reiterated in ecclesial and episcopal documents since *NA*, is that the Church shares with the Jewish people in this partnership of witness to the future (coming) kingdom of God: ". . . the

Catholic Church has come to recognize that its mission of preparing for the coming of the kingdom of God is one that is shared with the Jewish people, *even if Jews do not conceive of this task* Christologically as the Church does."[87] If the reception of *NA* has collectively had the effect of discerning that the synagogue and the Church are called to work together to witness to God's coming reign and the consummation of the kingdom,[88] this realization has a significant impact on whether any form of supersessionism is any longer appropriate for Catholic theology, and beyond this, whether the conversion of the Jews to the Church specifically should be a part of Catholic evangelization. The USCCB *Reflections on Covenant and Mission* made the following bold statement regarding the issue of partnership in witness and the place of evangelization among and toward the Jews:

> If the Church, therefore, shares a central and defining task with the Jewish people, what are the implications for the Christian proclamation of the Good News of Jesus Christ? Ought Christians to invite Jews to baptism? This is a complex question not only in terms of Christian theological self-definition, but also because of the history of Christians forcibly baptizing Jews. In a remarkable and still most pertinent study paper presented at the sixth meeting of the International Catholic–Jewish Liaison Committee in Venice twenty-five years ago, Prof. Tommaso Federici examined the missiological implications of *Nostra Aetate*. He argued on historical and theological grounds that there should be in the Church no organizations of any kind dedicated to the conversion of Jews. This has over the ensuing years been the *de facto* practice of the Catholic Church.[89]

The idea that there are no Catholic organizations dedicated to the conversion of the Jews—that this is a de facto, unofficial practice, and not one formally and dogmatically expressed by the Vatican—does not detract from the overall manner in which *NA* has been received in Catholic theology as a whole. The reception of *NA* in officially released documents from the Vatican, statements made by Pope John Paul II, and documents released by the USCCB, have largely done away with the theology of supersessionism, replacement, and abrogation, and have advocated for a view of contemporary Judaism that assigns it a positive role in the realm of eschatology and a partnership in witnessing to the coming kingdom of God. Yet this kind of positive theological development will have "staying power"[90] only if the Church adopts an ecclesiology which is different in kind from its past conceptions—an ecclesiology which stresses the "not-yet" of eschatology in balance with the "already" of tradition, and establishes and dogmatically approves in a logically consistent manner the idea that the coming kingdom of God is not expressed in totality by the Church on earth. As Boys mentions in reference to *Reflections on Covenant and Mission*, ". . . the Church has come to a newfound recognition that it shares with Jews the mission of preparing for the *coming of God's reign*. One might infer that the writers are suggesting that the Catholic Church does not have a mission to the Jews, but rather a mission with the Jews to the world."[91] In order for the Church's "newfound recognition" of the eschatological dimension of its relationship with Jews to become permanent, it must mine its own tradition for theologically viable solutions to its unfortunate history of ecclesio-centric supersessionism.

Theological tensions after *Nostra Aetate*

Though the bulk of literature including papal statements, papal writings, and official ecclesial documents interpreted *NA* as a conciliar call to move beyond supersessionism, there are a few exceptions that caused tension in the overall move toward overcoming the "theology of abrogation" which still lingers in Roman Catholic theology. In the section that follows, primacy will be given to the brief examination of one of the documents which has put a check on the Church's move toward a fully post-supersessionist understanding of the Jews: Joseph Cardinal Ratzinger's *Many Religions—One Covenant: Israel, the Church, and the World*, published in 1999.[92] I have chosen an exploration of *Many Religions* because it is a widely read text, expresses Ratzinger's primary views on Judaism, and is regarded as an authoritative piece of scholarship in light of the fact that Ratzinger is now Pope Emeritus Benedict XVI. In order to illuminate the ecclesiological and eschatological aspects of Ratzinger's thought—the two themes emphasized in our study of supersessionism—we will also include his dogmatic work entitled *Eschatology: Death and Eternal Life*, published in German in 1977. For the purpose of context, we will first examine briefly two other documents associated with Joseph Cardinal Ratzinger before the treatment of *Many Religions—One Covenant*, those being, *Dominus Iesus* and the *Catholic Catechism*, exploring briefly their interaction with the Jewish–Catholic question of covenant.

Although the Vatican declaration *Dominus Iesus*, issued by the Congregation for the Doctrine of the Faith in September 2000, has been viewed as a document that advocates for supersessionism in an absolute manner, it has been vigorously clarified by the Vatican hierarchy as *inapplicable* to the Jewish people and Judaism in general—indeed, it hardly mentions Judaism at all.[93] Despite the damage *DI* has done, according to some scholars, for decades of ecumenism and interreligious dialogue, it is argued that the document cannot be applied to Judaism because the universal elements of salvific unicity in Jesus Christ and the Church cannot and do not abrogate the covenant God has made with the Jews. Nevertheless, it is clear that *DI* implies an intentional relapse back to the era of supersessionism in the document's #13, where the authors claim that Christianity enlightens Judaism with a "fulfillment of salvation that went beyond the law," harkening back to dualistic representations of Judaism's Mosaic heritage, as if the Law itself was and is some cold, callous conception, having nothing to do with God's grace (related to the concept of *hesed* in the Old Testament) or promises. *DI* also reiterates very traditionalist views of the Church and the eschaton, and emphasizes the dogmatic link between the canonical Church and a very strong Christological expression.[94] One aspect of *DI* that is particularly applicable to our study of supersessionism is the way in which its authors speak—counter to the

Vatican II reforms—of the *Church*, as the universal vehicle whereby salvation is applied to an individual:[95] "Therefore, in connection with the unicity and universality of the salvific mediation of Jesus Christ, the unicity of the *Church* founded by him must be *firmly believed* as a truth of Catholic faith."[96] The document makes the strong statement supporting the "*... the universal salvific mediation of the Church.*" Indeed, if it is said that not only Jesus Christ, but the Roman Catholic Church itself, is the necessary mediation for Jewish people unto salvation,[97] then logically speaking, *DI* is a supersessionistic document. The ecclesiology indicative of *DI* is also firmly embedded in a specific understanding of the kingdom of God in extremely close proximity to the Church. For the authors of *DI*, the kingdom, in a sense, *is* the Church: "If the kingdom is separated from Jesus, it is no longer the kingdom of God which is revealed ... *Likewise, one may not separate the kingdom from the Church*" (*DI*, 18). Though the document claims that there is a "distinction" between the kingdom of God and the Church, it does not elaborate, thus confirming more traditionalist strands of Catholicism, i.e., that the Church is the kingdom of God in the world.[98] The traditional eschatological concept that the Church is God's reign and closely identifiable with God's consummative act regarding the kingdom is reiterated in *DI*, but rooted in the new Catholic Catechism (CCC) that was promulgated in Latin in 1997—originally drafted in 1994 and influenced primarily by Cardinal Ratzinger.[99] As we shall see further into this project, the close approximation of the Church with the kingdom reflects only one aspect of the Christian tradition, leaving out other ancient expressions that are traced to the earliest eschatological models of the faith.[100]

The new Catechism teaches that the "*Ecclesia simul via est et scopus consilii Dei: in creatione praefigurata, in Vetere Foedere praeparata ...*"[101] We must ask, if the Church is the *goal* of God's plan for human history, how may there exist another consummative and future expression of this plan? If Judaism has its own unique witness and mission to the world, as is expressed in a variety of official ecclesial documents since *NA*, what does is meant when it is stated in the Catechism that the Church has its own unicity and is necessary for salvation, and is in itself the *telos* of God's consummative plan? According to the Catechism, the Church has "become the kingdom of our Lord and of his Christ," and in the Church, Christ is viewed as reigning, "forever and ever." If the Church is what was prefigured "in creation," and particularly prepared for in the revelation historically expressed in the Old Covenant—note that the Catechism does *not* read "Old Testament"—how may there be an alternative expression of God's consummative economy, particularly in Judaism? The reality is that there cannot be an alternative, if one takes literally the statements of the Catechism, in line with *Dominus Iesus*. According to Boys, the Catechism, the ecclesial document that was influential later for *DI*, promotes the view of Judaism only as "... a preparation for and figure of that new and perfect covenant which was ratified in Christ ..." (CCC, #781), and in sum, "... gives its readers virtually no sense of Judaism as a living, vital tradition."[102]

It must be said that Ratzinger, in his written scholarship on Catholics and Jews, has indeed referred to an "alternate" mission for the Jews outside the Church, and has given a rationale for the Jewish rejection of Jesus as messiah based on Old Testament prophecy.[103] Ratzinger has gone so far as to say that the Jewish "alternate mission" is one with its own sense of value, not only for the Jewish community, but for the entire world:

> The Fathers define this mission . . . [of the Jews] . . . in the following way: the Jews must remain as the first proprietors of Holy Scripture with respect to us, in order to establish a testimony to the world. But what is the tenor of this testimony? . . . I think we could say that two things are essential to Israel's faith. The first is the Torah, commitment to God's will, and thus the establishment of his dominion, his kingdom, in this world. The second is the prospect of hope, the expectation of the Messiah—the expectation, indeed, the certainty, that God himself will enter into this history and create justice, which we can only approximate very imperfectly.[104]

Even the "no" of the Jews appears to play a part in their God-ordained witness to the world, according to Ratzinger: ". . . while history still runs its course, even this standing at the door . . . [i.e., rejection of Jesus] . . . fulfills a mission, one that is important for the world. In that way this people still has a special place in God's plan."[105] In the quotes above, Cardinal Ratzinger appears to take seriously the reforms initiated by Vatican II, but for the sake of theological honesty, one must put these statements in the context of Ratzinger's unequivocal support of the document *Dominus Iesus*, which in essence reiterates the idea that outside of various aspects of the Church's mediatorial role, the kingdom of God is unattainable.[106] Cardinal Ratzinger's statement on the special mission of the Jewish people appears to simply be a reiteration of the words of Pope John Paul II, and appears to be an anomaly. Overall, the content and tone of the majority of Ratzinger's scholarship has advocated the view that the Jewish people's covenantal status has indeed been replaced, and the logical interpretation of his work leads one to believe that the temporary Jewish "no" to Jesus, and by default their rejection of the Church, leaves the Jews with no hope without the Church as indispensable mediator, either through the divinely revealed vehicle of Torah as a ratification of covenant, for which the faithful response of obedience is a mainstay of Jewish religious expression, or for a future prospect of messiah or messianic kingdom outside the Church's sphere of influence. Thus, it is not surprising that the *Catholic Catechism*, *Dominus Iesus*, and *Many Religions*, which were either authored or heavily influenced by Cardinal Ratzinger, continued the legacy he began in his 1966 *Theological Highlights of Vatican II*—a document almost entirely void of any significant treatment of the contributions of *NA*.[107] Cardinal Ratzinger's evaluation of supersessionism and his attitude toward the Jewish people appear either highly ambiguous, or seem to move toward pre-conciliar attitudes as it regards the Catholic Church's overall theological stance regarding the Jewish people.[108]

The primary focus of our thought, *Many Religions—One Covenant*, was written as a means of clarifying the question of the divine covenant among Christians,

72 *Supersessionism and* Nostra Aetate

Jews, and essentially all world religions, but it is also evident that in it Ratzinger intended to challenge some of the assumptions made in the more developed, contemporary examples of Jewish–Christian scholarship. The Cardinal alludes to and challenges various points brought up in Rosemary Ruether's *Faith and Fratricide*. As articulated previously in this book, Ruether's pinpointing of Christological propositions as the source of supersessionism appears faulty. In this sense, I agree with Cardinal Ratzinger's assessment that some post-supersessionist works attempt to overcome replacement theology by throwing the proverbial baby out with the bathwater and making any Christian claim about Jesus' messiahship, or the need for non-Christians to embrace Jesus Christ impossible to hold. In reference to the hostility between Jews and Christians in history, Ratzinger asks:

> Does this hostility result from something in the very faith of Christians? Is it something in the "essence of Christianity", so that one would have to prescind from Christianity's core, deny Christianity its heart, in order to come to real reconciliation? . . . Do confession of Jesus of Nazareth as the Son of the living God and faith in the Cross as the redemption of mankind contain an implicit condemnation of the Jews as stubborn and blind, as guilty of the death of the Son of God?[109]

In reference to the critique above, I would wholeheartedly agree. The problem arises in Ratzinger's work when, in an attempt to protect traditional Christology and the Christian universal kerygma from what he views as the relativism marked by certain forms of post-supersessionist theology, Ratzinger's theology of covenant utilizes some of the language of *NA*, but ultimately reverts back to dualistic and rigidly typological readings of the Hebrew Bible in relation to the Apostolic Witness. For example, in one section, Ratzinger makes the positive claim that in the Catholic tradition inspired by the Augustinian and Thomistic ideas of covenant, ". . . the relationship between the Torah and the proclamation of Jesus is never seen dialectically,"[110] yet in another section treating the Mosaic covenant, Ratzinger appears to adopt a strictly supersessionist theology, claiming that "God's pedagogy with mankind operates in such a way that *its individual props are jettisoned* when the goal of the educational process is reached. *Particular paths are abandoned*, but the meaning remains."[111] The path to which Ratzinger refers, the one which is "jettisoned" and "abandoned," is the mediation and the ratification of the covenant through God's revelation on Sinai, as accepted and expressed as the pinnacle of religious experience in much of modern Judaism.[112] The covenant in its earlier expression in Judaism is portrayed *only* as a temporary pedological element pointing its pupils to the consummation of the kingdom revealed in the New Testament, and ultimately (this indeed is the source of the problem), in the Church. The language of "pedagogy" is a hallmark of previous supersessionistic models that harken back to the idea that the "witness" of the Jewish people is to teach the world of what horrible things happen to those who reject the offer to join the Church. Indeed, Ratzinger's impetus for portraying the "many covenants"[113] of the Old Testament as having a unicity with the one, new, and eternal covenant[114] appears to be to reiterate the concept that in the Church, the covenant is fulfilled and the central Jewish expression of the unconditional promises of God to Abraham, reified at Sinai, is abrogated and has become obsolete:

> Thus, *the Sinai covenant is indeed superseded*. But once what was provisional in it has been swept away, we see what is truly definitive in it. So the expectation of the New Covenant, which becomes clearer and clearer as the history of Israel unfolds, does not conflict with the Sinai covenant; rather, it fulfills the dynamic expectation found in that very covenant.[115]

This language, though likely unintentional, ultimately results in a rather extreme prospect: every otherness and particularity in modern Judaism that is associated with the centrality of the remembrance of the giving of Torah on Sinai is pulverized and subsequently enveloped by the Church. We see from the above statement that it is not merely the Jewish expression of covenant that is superseded, but it is the Mosaic covenant itself. Sinai is replaced by Calvary, so *therefore*, the synagogue is replaced by the Church. As a logical extension of this claim, Ratzinger circumscribes again to Israel the roles typical of supersessionist history—conditionality, temporality, carnality, blind casuistry, limitation, and provisional status.

In another section, instead of dissolving Jewish particularity and universalizing it into the existence of the "new people of God," Ratzinger stresses Jewish *uniqueness* in order to claim its abolition:

> With regard to the Sinai covenant, we must again draw a distinction. It is strictly limited to the people of Israel; it gives this nation a legal and cultic order (the two are inseparable) that as such cannot simply be extended to all nations. Since this juridical order is constitutive of the Sinai covenant, the law's "if" is part of its essence. To that extent it is conditional, that is, temporal; within God's providential rule it is a stage that has its own allotted period of time.[116]

In line with replacement theology, Ratzinger seeks to stress the conditionality of the Sinai covenant, reiterating that its temporal period has indeed passed. Whatever was the intent of God in giving the Law at Sinai as a ratification of the Abrahamic covenant, and whatever its essence and value, it is now superseded by the new covenant and the new community—the Church. The problem with this view, both exegetical and theological, is that the "conditional elements" of the covenant on Sinai have little to do with its standing as either eternal or limited: the covenant at Sinai was as much a grant of privileged status as the initial "unconditional" covenant made with Abraham. Sinai took place not because the Jewish people were obliged to follow the Law at risk of forfeiting their election, but by contrast, they were called to follow the Law precisely *because* of their election:

The grant treaties, where property or privileged position is granted by the king, or god, constitute a general parallel which, while it has been explored in relation to the Abrahamic and Davidic covenants, has been all but ignored so far as the Sinai covenant is concerned. The strong contrast which is sometimes drawn between conditional and unconditional covenantal commitments is seen to be untenable and the Sinai covenant shares many features with those covenants which are regarded as belonging to the 'grant' type.[117]

Mary C. Boys best sums up the perspective expressed in *Many Religions—One Covenant:* "However sophisticated and nuanced Cardinal Ratzinger's reading of the covenants is, in the end it seems thoroughly *supersessionist.*"[118] If what Boys writes is correct, we must inquire as to the central eschatological and ecclesiological notions that govern the theology of covenant present in Ratzinger's writing. If Ratzinger views the old and new covenants as referring *solely* to promises made to one people group, the Church, then supersessionism is not merely an aspect of his thought, but the *foundation* of his writing on Jewish–Christian dialogue. Ratzinger does not go so far as to state that the promises made to the Jewish people are no longer applied to them, but, as we will see, he insists that any true consummation of God's promises to the Jewish people ultimately come through the Church.

In must be noted, that in a positive step, Cardinal Ratzinger, in his *Many Religions*, utilizes distinctions and nuanced language as it regards the problem of the traditional portrayal of "hardened legalism" in relation to the Pharisees— something Ratzinger accuses liberation theologians of promulgating through their critique of those in religious authority (30). Ratzinger likewise rejects certain interpretations of the Pauline epistles which render the antithesis between Law and Gospel, old and new, flesh and spirit "too stiffly" (54).[119] Further, he expresses, to some extent, the influence of Vatican II reforms on his own theological purview in light of a certain degree of covenantal value ascribed to *biblical* Israel. Though Ratzinger mentions a continued legacy and even a qualified form of witness for contemporary Jews along with today's Christians,[120] his overall reading of Christian history suggests that biblical Israel's existence was almost solely predicated upon its ability to prepare for the revelation of Jesus Christ. If his assessment ended with the Hebrew preparatory stage pointing toward Christ, it would be defensible on the grounds of the Apostolic Witness as articulated in the NT. But significantly, Ratzinger applies the preparatory nature of the Sinai covenant to *today's Church*, comprising a composite of "the nations" and the Jews, which becomes the New people of God ". . . through acceptance of the Davidic kingdom."[121] For Ratzinger, the Davidic kingdom is almost entirely summed up in the Church,[122] even the Church of history, although he claims that the kingdom is not manifest as a political organization expressed through force. For example, Ratzinger adamantly critiques ". . . Alfred Loisy's 'modernist' separation of the kingdom and Church"[123] (although Jesus never mentions the Church proper, as understood today, in the Synoptic Gospels—only the kingdom), and on another occasion, Ratzinger emphasizes what he interprets to be the "ecclesial" understanding of the kingdom of God, common in the early Fathers, in which ". . . the kingdom of God and the Church are related in different ways and brought into more or less close proximity."[124] Curiously missing from Ratzinger's assessment of the eschatology and ecclesiology of the early Fathers—a point that will be addressed later in this project—is the concept, overwhelmingly popular in the early Church, that the kingdom of God was an imminent reality, coming in the future, which would be established in visible form during an interregnum period, with Christ's Second Coming. The idea that there could be a specifically earthly and future, political "kingdom of God," as is held by a large constituency in modern Judaism,[125] is utterly rejected in Ratzinger's critique of Jürgen Moltmann's "Theology of Hope," and its connection with liberation theology, as it is expressed in *Eschatology: Death and Eternal Life*:

> The Kingdom of God, not being itself a political concept, cannot serve as a political criterion by which to construct in direct fashion a program of political action and to criticize the political efforts of other people. The realization of God's Kingdom is not itself a political process. To misconceive it as such is to falsify both politics and theology. The inevitable result is the rise of false messianic movements which of their very nature and from the inner logic of messianic claims finish up in totalitarianism.[126]

Here we see Ratzinger pointing to the dangers of messianic hope in Christianity without critiquing the concept that the Catholic Church has emphasized its own existence as the imperial realization of such hopes and as the implied political reign of Christ on earth. Indeed, it is undeniable that the Church has embedded itself into the political fabric of the greater worldwide society. Thus, it is not surprising that Aidan Nichols, in his introductory note on Eschatology, points to Augustine's *City of God* and its fourth-century re-interpretation of the millennial reign of Christ expressed in the Book of Revelation as a primary influence on Ratzinger and his understanding of the kingdom of God.[127] Ratzinger, though he expresses that he is not critiquing Moltmann's theology as a whole, and that it contains within it "gleams of real gold," insists that viewing the messianic kingdom as a "political concept," is both an affront to politics, and an ". . . emasculation of Christian hope."[128] Certainly, in Ratzinger's defense, a kind of hesitance to blend political and *secular* messianic conceptions is understandable since the time of the Nazis, who used such ideas to gain power for the Third Reich. Nevertheless, it must be admitted that the primary messianic conception for both Judaism and early Christianity was an immanent messianism combined with an expectation for political liberation from oppression and a longing for justice in the realms of earthly power. This is frequently argued as the very reason why Jesus modified the political aspects of messianism *without rejecting them entirely*, modeling a political response to power in the form of martyrdom and silent witness in the face of false accusation and violence. It is impossible to say that Jesus's conception of the kingdom of God was apolitical.[129]

It is interesting to note that Ratzinger is particularly sympathetic to C.H. Dodd's realized eschatology[130] without mentioning the obvious connection between fulfilled apocalypticism and traditional Post-Nicene Catholic ecclesiology. The Church *did* become the political criterion by which a political effort was fashioned, particularly, in the time immediately succeeding Constantine, later during the Crusades, and historical periods manifest in the multiple pogroms against the Jewish people, as Jews were natural enemies of the Church vis-à-vis their alternative messianic claim—a point brought up by Moltmann on numerous occasions.[131] The Church, for a great duration of history, was an ecclesiastical manifestation of that which Ratzinger critiques—the totalitarianism of political messianism. Ratzinger's glowing review of Dodd is centered upon an *already present* interpretation of the kingdom, focused on the Church's mediation, particularly as it celebrates the Eucharist, "a sacrament of realized eschatology."[132] Ratzinger writes that "Dodd connects this interpretation of Jesus' message of the kingdom with a Christological and sacramental view of things fully in continuity with the inner development of historic Christianity."[133] Though he is partially correct, the problem with Ratzinger's reflections on the "inner development of historic Christianity" is that it leaves out a significant aspect of Christian development which followed Jesus' emphasis on the immanence of the kingdom, and not solely its already-present content—the phenomenon of millenarianism, adopted in Christian thought from its Jewish precursory forms.

Modern scholarship, including the biblical work of N.T. Wright and Dale Allison, confirms that the emphasis of Jesus' preaching was an imminent expectation of the kingdom, with Allison tracing Jesus' words and the traditions associated with them to parallels common in the first century, ". . . found above all in millenarian movements."[134] Steven M. Bryan states the following:

> Few today would want to follow C. H. Dodd in seeing Jesus' eschatology as fully realized. In fact, if the way Jesus' eschatology is understood changed substantially over the course of the last century, the perception that Jesus expected an imminent end of some sort seems very much the same. To be sure, most would acknowledge a certain realized dimension to Jesus' eschatology. But for many scholars the realized aspect of Jesus eschatology in no way occupies the centre of his thought. Rather, it is often made subservient to his imminent expectation . . .[135]

Overall, we notice the near *equating* of the kingdom of God with the Church in Ratzinger's comments, contrary to modern scholarship, insofar as the Davidic kingdom is a thing that is accepted by the new people of God because it is *already present*.[136] Though some of Ratzinger's work leaves room for a distinction between the Church and the kingdom,[137] Ratzinger definitively emphasizes the "already" of the kingdom of God as present via the mystery of the Church. The equating of the messianic kingdom of David with the Church of history is a hallmark of the supersessionist trajectory because there may be no alternative historical, future, and political vehicle for the kingdom of God, if the Roman Catholic Church has a "monopoly" on the divine reign, as we shall see in detail further into this book. Thus, the inner logic of Ratzinger's understanding of the typological function of the old covenant for the new, the unity of Torah, and the Christian message insofar as Christ subsumes Torah entirely, and the emphasis of a realized eschatological framework that ties the Church inextricably to the kingdom of God to the point of equating the two phenomena and making the Church the sole mediating entity between God and humanity, fails to adequately take into account developments in post-supersessionist theology since *NA*, and the common elements of the declaration's reception. In sum, Ratzinger's insights regarding Judaism and covenantal history, though well-articulated and erudite, emphasize elements of ecclesiology and eschatology that are basically supersessionist in both tone and content. Though Ratzinger indicates that Judaism has its own "mission in the world" and its own distinct witness, it is difficult to ascertain what that mission might be, considering that Judaism's unique features are portrayed as being taken-up or entirely fulfilled in the Roman Catholic Church, which is essentially viewed as God's kingdom on earth. In this sense, the main problematic issue within contemporary Roman Catholic theology, as exemplified by Cardinal Ratzinger in relation to replacement theology is not one of Christology or even proclamation, but one of a realized and sedimentary eschatological structure with the Church as consummation, pinnacle, and *telos* of the kingdom related language.

Notes

1 Zenger, "The Covenant that was Never Revoked," 93.
2 See "Eventful Sociology and Vatican II" and "Trying to Ensure a Rubber-Stamp Council: The Curia on the Eve of Vatican II" in *Vatican II: A Sociological Analysis of Religious Change*, ed. M.J. Wilde (Princeton, NJ: Princeton University Press, 2007), 15–16.
3 J. Dupuis and J. Neuner, *The Christian Faith in the Doctrinal Documents of the Catholic Church* (New York: Alba House, 2001), 42.
4 M.L. Lamb and M. Levering, *Vatican II: Renewal within Tradition* (New York: Oxford University Press, 2008), 34.
5 R.R. Gaillardetz, *Teaching with Authority: A Theology of the Magisterium in the Church* (Collegeville, MN: Liturgical Press, 1997), 202.
6 Pope Paul VI claimed that "in view of the pastoral nature of the Council, it avoided any extraordinary statements of dogmas endowed with the note of infallibility, but it still provided its teaching with the authority of the Ordinary Magisterium which must be accepted with docility according to the mind of the Council concerning the nature and aims of each document." Pope Paul VI to a General Audience on January 12, 1966.
7 Walter Brandmüller, who sympathizes with a reading of Vatican II in the light of previous Church tradition, states that "... practically every Council, including Vatican II, has unique elements in its structure, development and content; *what they all have in common is the collegial wielding of supreme doctrinal and pastoral authority.*" Walter Brandmüller, "Vatican II in the History of Church Councils," *L'Avvenire*, November 29, 2005, at §9, emphasis mine. See also, Brandmüller, *Light and Shadows: Church History amid Faith, Fact, and Legend* (San Francisco, CA: Ignatius Press, 2009), 226.

78 *Supersessionism and* Nostra Aetate

8   Joseph Cardinal Ratzinger, "Remarks to the Bishops of Chile Regarding the Lefebvre Schism" (lecture, Santiago, Chile, July 13, 1988).
9   The Latin original is the only official and authoritative text of the Vatican II pronouncements. It is accessible in its published form as *Sacrosanctum Oecumenicum Concilium Vaticanum II: Constitutiones, Decreta, Declarationes* (Vatican City: Typis Polyglottis Vaticanis, 1967).
10 In research preparation for this section of the book, the development of *NA* was reviewed. Its subject matter, in detail, may be found in *Acta Synodalia Sacrosancti Concilii Oecumenici Vaticani Secundi* IV, part IV, Congregatio Generalis CLXIV (Vatican City: Typis Polyglottis Vaticanis, 1978).
11 Zenger, "The Covenant that was Never Revoked," 92.
12 Walter Kasper, "Dominus Iesus" (paper delivered at the 17th Meeting of the International Catholic–Jewish Liaison Committee, May 1, 2001), 3. Available at: http://www.ccjr.us/dialogika-resources/documents-andstatements/analysis/497-kasper01may1.html.
13 See Cunningham, "Official Ecclesial Documents to Implement the Second Vatican Council on Relations with Jews: Study Them, Become Immersed in Them, and Put Them into Practice," 1–36.
14 Uri Bialer, Neville Lamdan, and Alberto Melloni, *Nostra Aetate: Origins, Promulgation, Impact on Jewish–Catholic Relations: Proceedings of the International Conference, Jerusalem, 30 October-1 November 2005: Essays* (Berlin: LIT, 2007), 103. See also John L. Allen, *Cardinal Ratzinger: The Vatican's Enforcer of the Faith* (New York: Continuum, 2001), 248.
15 Bialer, Lamdan, and Melloni, *Nostra Aetate*, 102.
16 See Thomas Stransky, "The Genesis *of Nostra Aetate*: An Insider's Story," in Bialer, Lamdan, and Melloni, *Nostra Aetate: Origins,* 29.
17 Bialer, Lamdan, and Melloni, *Nostra Aetate: Origins*, 50. The accusation of various Jewish "plots" and "schemes" is part of the anti-Semitic history of the gentile nations. For the culmination of these viewpoints in the phenomenon of German fascism, see L.A. Wagner, *Hitler: Man of Strife* (New York: W.W. Norton, 1942), 101.
18 G. Alberigo, and J.A. Komonchak, *History of Vatican II: The Council and the Transition, the Fourth Period and the End of the Council, September 1965-December 1965* (Maryknoll, NY: Orbis, 2005), 231.
19 Eugene J. Fisher, "*Nostra Aetate*: Transforming the Catholic–Jewish Relationship," *ADL* 16, no. 1–3 (April 2006): 161, emphasis mine, accessed at http://www.adl.org/main_Interfaith/nostra_aetate.htm? Multi page_ sections=sHeading_2 on January 28, 2011.
20 Gregory Baum, a theological adviser who was present during the drafting of *NA* at Vatican II alluded to a "postsupersessionist intention" behind the document. Gregory Baum, "Dialogue between Believers and Secular Thinkers." In Doctoral Colloquium, Theology Dept., Duquesne University, October 7, 2009. Cf. Gregory Baum, "Rethinking the Church's Mission after Auschwitz," in E. Fleischner, ed., *Auschwitz: Beginning of a New Era?: Reflections on the Holocaust* (Jersey City, NJ: KTAV, 1977).
21 Moltmann, *The Church in the Power of the Spirit*, 146.
22 "Though *already* present in his Church, Christ's reign is nevertheless *yet* to be fulfilled 'with power and great glory' by the King's return to earth." (*Catechism of the Catholic Church*, Art. 7, #671).
23 See http://www.vatican.va/roman_curia/pontifical_councils/chrstuni/index.htm, accessed May 18, 2011.
24 David G. Singer, "Has God Truly Abrogated the Mosaic Covenant? American Catholic Attitudes toward Judaism as Reflected in Catholic Thought, 1945–1977," *Jewish Social Studies* 47, no. 3/4 (1985): 243.

25 For the intimate connection of supersessionism with both eschatology and ecclesiology, see Diprose, *Israel in the Development of Christian Thought*, 4.
26 See *Lumen Gentium* 8 and Steven D. Aguzzi, "Florovsky's 'The Boundaries of the Church' in Dialogue with the Reformed Tradition: Toward a Catholic and Charismatic Ecumenical Ecclesiology," *Ecumenical Trends* 39, no. 3 (2010), 8–14.
27 Augustin Bea, *The Church and the Jewish People: A Commentary on the Second Vatican Council's Declaration on the Relation of the Church to Non-Christian Religions* (New York: Harper & Row, 1966), 100, emphasis mine.
28 Ibid., 62.
29 See Ruether, *Faith and Fratricide*, 181, and John T. Pawlikowski, "The Christ Event and the Jewish People," in Tatha Wiley, ed., *Thinking of Christ: Proclamation, Explanation, Meaning* (New York: Continuum, 2003), 109.
30 See G. Alberigo, J.P. Jossua, J.A. Komonchak, and M.J. O'Connell, *The Reception of Vatican II* (Washington, DC: Catholic University of America Press, 1987), 362.
31 See *NA*, no.4: ". . . neither all Jews indiscriminately at that time, nor Jews today, can be charged with the crimes committed during his passion . . ." (Flannery, *The Conciliar and Post Conciliar Documents* 573). Solomon Zeitlin, "The Ecumenical Council Vatican II and the Jews," *The Jewish Quarterly Review* 56, no. 2 (1965): 93–95.
32 *NA* states that the Church ". . . deplores all hatreds, persecutions, displays of anti-semitism leveled at any time or from any source against the Jews . . ." *NA*, no. 4 in Flannery, 573. For John Paul II's apology to the Jewish people, see Y. Landau, M.B. McGarry, L. Boadt, and K.T.P.D. Camillo, *John Paul II in the Holy Land—In His Own Words: With Christian and Jewish Perspectives* (Mahwah, NJ: Paulist Press, 2005), 121.
33 Ibid., 572.
34 Eugene J. Fisher, "Official Roman Catholic Teaching on Jews and Judaism: Commentary and Context," in L. Klenicki and E.J. Fisher, eds., *In Our Time: The Flowering of Jewish–Catholic Dialogue* (Mahwah, NJ: Paulist Press, 1991), 5.
35 F. Mussner, *Tractate on the Jews: The Significance of Judaism for Christian Faith* (Minneapolis, MN: Fortress Press, 1984), 251.
36 See http://www.vatican.va/roman_curia/pontifical_councils/chrstuni/relations-jews-docs/rc_pc_chrstuni_doc_19741201_nostra-aetate_en.html, accessed on May 19, 2011.
37 See http://www.vatican.va/roman_curia/pontifical_councils/chrstuni/relations-jews-docs/rc_pc_chrstuni_doc_19820306_jews-judaism_en.html, accessed on May 19, 2011, emphasis mine.
38 *NA*, no. 4 in Flannery, *The Conciliar and Post Conciliar Documents*, 572.
39 "Notes," II, 7.
40 Ibid., 8.
41 *NA*, no. 4 in Flannery, *The Conciliar and Post Conciliar Documents*, 572.
42 See Gregory Kaplan, "In the End Shall Christians Become Jews and Jews, Christians?: On Franz Rosenzweig's Apocalyptic Eschatology," *Cross Currents* 53, no. 4 (Winter 2004): 511–529.
43 *NA*, no. 4 in Flannery, *The Conciliar and Post Conciliar Documents*, 572.
44 See Fisher, "Official Roman Catholic Teaching," 6. See also Bialer, *Nostra Aetate: Origins*, 149 and A.J. Cernera, *Examining Nostra Aetate after 40 Years: Catholic–Jewish Relations in Our Time* (Fairfield, CT: Sacred Heart University Press, 2007), 122.
45 *NA*, no. 4, in Flannery, *The Conciliar and Post Conciliar Documents*, 573.
46 *Catechism of the Catholic Church: Revised in Accordance with the Official Latin Text Promulgated by Pope John Paul II*, #762. See also Pontifical Commission on Justice and Peace, "Church and Racism: Toward a More Fraternal Society," III.20.

47 Ben Zion Bokser, "Vatican II and the Jews," *The Jewish Quarterly Review* 59, no. 2 (1968): 149.
48 "Notes," II, 11, cf. "Guidelines," IV, 11.
49 Mary C. Boys, "The Covenant in Contemporary Ecclesial Documents," *Two Faiths, One Covenant?: Jewish and Christian Identity in the Presence of the Other*, ed. E.B. Korn and J. Pawlikowski (Lanham, MD: Rowman & Littlefield, 2005), 91. It is important to note that Joseph Ratzinger served as a *peritus* or chief theological expert at Vatican II, alongside Justinae Janisch, to Josef Cardinal Frings of Cologne, Germany. In the beginning of his pontificate, Benedict made the following statement: "In laying the foundations for a renewed relationship between the Jewish people and the Church, *Nostra Aetate* stressed the need to overcome past prejudices, misunderstandings, indifference and the language of contempt and hostility . . . I have expressed my own firm determination to walk in the footsteps traced by my beloved predecessor Pope John Paul II. The Jewish–Christian dialogue must continue to enrich and deepen the bonds of friendship which have developed." Benedict XVI, "Message of the Holy Father to the President of the Holy See's Commission for Religious Relations with Jews on the Occasion of the 40th Anniversary of the Declaration *Nostra Aetate*," in *Commission for Religious Relations with the Jews: Fortieth Anniversary of Nostra Aetate* (Rome: Pontifical Commission on Religious Relations with the Jews, October 26, 2005).
50 John T. Pawlikowski, "Reflections on Covenant and Mission: Forty Years after *Nostra Aetate*," *Cross Currents* 56, no. 4 (Winter 2006–2007): 71.
51 "Notes," VI, 25.
52 Ibid., also quoting John Paul II, March 6, 1982, alluding to Romans 11:17–24, emphasis mine. This statement rejects years of theological anti-Judaism through the concept of the "Witness People." See E.H. Flannery, *The Anguish of the Jews: Twenty-Three Centuries of Antisemitism* (Mahwah, NJ: Paulist Press, 1985), 53.
53 Sergio I. Minerbi, "Pope John Paul II and the Jews: An Evaluation," in *Le Programme Juif De Destruction De L'Eglise Catholique Derniére Phase* (La Sfinge, Rome, Eté, 2006), http://www.vho.org/aaargh/fran/livres6/minerbi.pdf (accessed January 23, 2017).
54 John Paul II, "Address to the Jewish Community in Mainz, West Germany," November 17, 1980, in Philip A. Cunningham, *Seeking Shalom: The Journey to Right Relationship between Catholics and Jews* (Grand Rapids, MI: Eerdmans, 2015), 184, n. 8, emphasis mine.
55 John Paul II, "Address to Jewish Leaders in Miami," September 11, 1987, Mary C. Boys, "The Covenant in Contemporary Ecclesial Documents," in Eugene Korn and John Pawlikowski, eds., *Two Faiths, One Covenant? Jewish and Christian Identity in the Presence of the Other*, The Bernardin Center Series (Lanham, MD: Rowman & Littlefield, 2005), 81–110, at 82, emphasis mine.
56 John Paul II, "Address to the Jewish Community in Mainz, West Germany," November 17, 1980, in Philip A. Cunningham, *Seeking Shalom: The Journey to Right Relationship between Catholics and Jews* (Grand Rapids, MI: Eerdmans, 2015), 184. For Benedict's views, see Tracey Rowland, *Benedict XVI: A Guide for the Perplexed* (London: T&T Clark International, 2010), 132. Some scholars have noted strikingly anti-Semitic language in the writings of Benedict. See Matthew Lange, *Antisemitic Elements in the Critique of Capitalism in German Culture, 1850–1933* (Bern: Peter Lang, 2007), 134.
57 See E.P. Sanders, *Paul and Palestinian Judaism: A Comparison of Patterns of Religion* (Minneapolis, MN: Fortress Press, 1977), 241, and J. Haers and P.D. Mey, *Theology and Conversation: Towards a Relational Theology* (Leuven, Belgium: Peeters, 2003), 341.

58 The phrase "old covenant" appears only once in the New Testament as *palaias diathekes* in 2 Corinthians 3:14, and refers exclusively to the Mosaic covenant.
59 See Moltmann, *The Church in the Power of the Spirit*, 136–137.
60 Ruether, *Faith and Fratricide*, 16.
61 For an explication of John Paul II's paradoxical understanding of otherness and sameness in relation to the continental philosophy of Emmanuel Levinas, see Nigel K. Zimmermann, "Karol Wojtyla and Emmanuel Levinas on the Embodied Self: The Forming of the Other as Moral Self-Disclosure," *The Heythrop Journal* 50, no. 6 (2009): 982–995.
62 Bruce D. Marshall, "Elder Brothers: John Paul II's Teaching on the Jewish People as a Question to the Church," in D.G. Dalin and M. Levering, eds., *John Paul II and the Jewish People: A Jewish–Christian Dialogue* (Lanham, M.D: Rowman & Littlefield Publishers, 2008), 117–118, emphasis mine.
63 For the pope's various comments concerning the Jewish people as "partners," see John Paul II, et al., in *Spiritual Pilgrimage: Texts on Jews and Judaism, 1979–1995* (Chestnut Ridge, NY: Crossroad, 1995), 105–109.
64 Marshall, "Elder Brothers: John Paul II's Teaching on the Jewish People," 116.
65 See *Lumen Gentium* 7.
66 Ruth Langer, "A Jewish Response," in S.J. Pope, C.C. Helfling, and Fidei Catholic Church, Congregatio pro Doctrina, eds., *Sic Et Non: Encountering Dominus Iesus* (Maryknoll, NY: Orbis Books, 2002), 130–131.
67 The phrase "without hope" (ἐλπίδαε μὴ ἔχοντες) points to the Ephesians' alienation from the community of Israel and by default, the promises of God, but it also carries with it eschatological connotations: the Ephesians were without the hope of the resurrection which was shared by first-century Jews. P.S. Williamson, *Ephesians* (Ada, MI: Baker Publishing Group, 2009), 70.
68 The Catholic Catechism states that ". . . in her [the Catholic Church] subsists the fullness of Christ's body united with its head; this implies that she receives from him "the fullness of the means of salvation" which he has willed: correct and complete confession of faith, full sacramental life, and ordained ministry in apostolic succession. The Church was, in this fundamental sense, catholic on the day of Pentecost and will always be so until the day of the Parousia" (*Catechism of the Catholic Church*, 2nd edn (New York The Doubleday Religious Publishing Group, 2003), §830, 239.
69 Ibid., §671, 192.
70 Ibid., §672, 192–193.
71 Franz Rosenzweig spoke often of the importance of "being *in time*" for the Jewish people, almost a "homelessness in time," contrary to Hegelian idealism and in opposition to the philosophy of the "All-encompassing Protocosmos," as Rosenzweig discusses in the third part of the *Star of Redemption*. For a commentary on Rosenzweig's views on the importance of time in reference to God's mystery and the human experience of it, particularly in Jewish–Christian dialogue, see Barbara Galli, "Rosenzweig Speaking of Meetings and Monotheism in Biblical Anthropomorphisms," *Journal of Jewish Thought and Philosophy* 2, no. 2 (1993): 221.
72 *NA*, no. 4, in Flannery, *The Conciliar and Post Conciliar Documents*, 573.
73 Philip A. Cunningham, *Sharing the Scriptures* (Mahwah, NJ: Paulist Press, 2003), 7–8.
74 "*NA*, for all practical purposes, begins the Church's teaching . . . concerning a theological or, more precisely, a doctrinal understanding of the relationship between the Church as 'People of God' and 'God's People' Israel." Eugene J. Fisher, "The Evolution of a Tradition: From *Nostra Aetate* to the *Notes*," in *International Catholic–Jewish Liaison Committee, Fifteen Years of Catholic–Jewish Dialogue: 1970–1985* (Rome: Libreria Editrice Vaticana and Libreria Editrice Lateranense, 1988), 239.

75 "Notes," VI.25.
76 Secretariat for Catholic–Jewish Relations (U.S.), United States Catholic Conference. Adult Education Section, and B'nai B'rith. Anti-defamation League. Interfaith Affairs Dept. "Within Context: Guidelines for the Catechetical Presentation of Jews and Judaism in the New Testament: Prepared in Cooperation with the Secretariat for Catholic–Jewish Relations, National Conference of Catholic Bishops, Adult Education Section, the Education Department, U.S. Catholic Conference, and the Interfaith Affairs Department, Anti-Defamation League of B'nai B'rith," (Morristown, NJ: Silver Burdett & Ginn, 1987), §5, ¶ 3, found at http://www.ccjr.us/dialogika-resources/documents-and-statements/interreligious/770-usccb-adl1986, accessed on May 22, 2011.
77 Boys, "The Covenant in Contemporary Ecclesial Documents," 82, emphasis mine.
78 Benedict claims that Christians ". . . should also acknowledge God's providence, which has obviously given Israel a particular mission in this 'time of the Gentiles.'" Benedict. *Many Religions, One Covenant: Israel, the Church, and the World* (San Francisco, CA: Ignatius Press, 1999), 104. Ironically, the fact that Jews have existed since the advent of Jesus Christ had not made their ongoing mission in the world "obvious" during the period of Christendom.
79 See E.I. Cassidy, *Ecumenism and Interreligious Dialogue: Unitatis Redintegratio, Nostra Aetate* (Mahwah, NJ: Paulist Press, 2005), 254.
80 "The faith and religious life of the Jewish people as they are professed and practiced still today, can greatly help us to understand better certain aspects of the life of the Church." Pope John Paul II, "Address to Experts Gathered by the Pontifical Commission for Religious Relations with Jews" (March 6, 1982), quoted in "Reflections on Covenant and Mission: Consultation of the National Council of Synagogues and the Bishops Committee for Ecumenical and Interreligious Affairs," *The Hebrew Catholic* 77 (August 12, 2002): 39–40.
81 See Pontificium Consilium pro Dialogo inter Religiones, "Dialogue and Proclamation," *Bulletin* (1991) 26: 77, 210–250.
82 See Jacques Dupuis, S.J., "The Church's Evangelizing Mission," *Pastoral Review* 1 (2005): 23.
83 Francis Cardinal George, "The Decree on the Church's Missionary Activity, Ad Gentes," in *Vatican II: Renewal within Tradition*, 299.
84 See D.J. Harrington, *The Light of All Nations: Essays on the Church in New Testament Research* (Bates City, MO: M. Glazier, 1982), 116.
85 Ibid., 302.
86 Ramesh Khatry, *The Authenticity of the Parable of the Wheat and the Tares and Its Interpretation* (Boca Raton, FL: Universal Publishers, 2000), 110.
87 "Evangelization and the Jewish People," in Consultation of the National Council of Synagogues and the Bishops Committee for Ecumenical and Interreligious Affairs, *Reflections on Covenant and Mission*, August 12, 2002, http://www.bc.edu/bc_org/research/cjl/Documents/ncs_usccb120802,html, accessed October 7, 2011.
88 The 2002 document entitled "The Jewish People and their Sacred Scriptures in the Christian Bible," issued by the Pontifical Biblical Commission makes a strong positive statement regarding the Jewish witness to the messianic reign of God's kingdom. Refer to the view of Donald Senior, in "Rome Has Spoken: A New Catholic Approach to Judaism," *Commonweal* 130, no. 2 (January 31, 2003).
89 "Evangelization and the Jewish People," in USCCB, "Reflections on Covenant and Mission." See further USCCB, "A Note on Ambiguities contained in Reflections on Covenant and Mission," (2009) a document that came into existence 'clarifying' the 2002 "Reflections," after some believe pressure was put on the U.S. Bishops for espousing theological and ethical ideas contrary to the later *Dominus Iesus*.

Nostra Aetate *and its reception* 83

M. Saracino, *Being About Borders: A Christian Anthropology of Difference* (Collegeville, MN: Liturgical Press, 2011), 83. In reaction to the note issued by the USCCB, David Berger, Ph.D., head of the Jewish Studies Department at Yeshiva College made the following comment: "Orthodox Jews can tolerate any Christian view on the necessity of faith in Jesus Christ as savior of all, but they cannot agree to participate in an interfaith dialogue that is a cover for proselytism." See USCCB Press Release, July 1, 2009, accessible at http://www.usccb.org/comm/archives/2009/09-153.shtml.

90 S. McFague, *Models of God: Theology for an Ecological, Nuclear Age* (Minneapolis, MN: Fortress Press, 1987), 34.
91 Boys, "The Covenant in Contemporary Ecclesial Documents," 102, emphasis mine.
92 Cardinal Ratzinger, now Pope Emeritus Benedict XVI, published *Many Religions* originally in German in 1998 under the title *Die Vielfalt der Religionen und der Eine Bund*. It was written as an essay for the Jewish–Christian meeting of Jerusalem in February 1994.
93 See Edward Idris and Cardinal Cassidy, "The Future of Jewish–Christian Relations in Light of the Visit of Pope John Paul II to the Holy Land," address delivered at the Annual General Meeting of the Interreligious Coordinating Council in Israel, Jerusalem, March 13, 2001 and Cardinal Walter Kasper, "*Dominus Iesus*," §2. Joseph Cardinal Ratzinger placed Judaism outside the scope of "another religion," making "*Dominus Iesus*" inapplicable to Judaism. See Joseph Ratzinger, "L'eredità di Abramo dono di Natale," in *L'Osservatore Romano* (Dicembre 29, 2000), 1. Jewish scholar David Berger claims that "*Dominus Iesus*" does indeed apply to the Jews, yet Berger identifies two forms of supersessionism explicit in the text: one endorsed by Ratzinger, which does *not* view Judaism as espousing "... narrow, petty legalism pursued in the service of a vengeful God and eventually replaced by a vital religion of universal love." David Berger, "On Dominus Iesus and the Jews," in Pope, *Sic et Non*, 39.
94 *Dominus Iesus* emphasizes and makes mandatory for the Catholic faith belief in "... the unicity and salvific universality of the mystery of Jesus Christ, *the universal salvific mediation of the Church, the inseparability*—while recognizing the distinction —of *the kingdom of God, the kingdom of Christ, and the Church*, and the subsistence of the one Church of Christ in the Catholic Church." Congregatio pro Doctrina Fidei, *Dominus Iesus: Declaration on the Unicity and Salvific Universality of Jesus Christ and the Church* (Ithaca, NY: Traces, 2000), §4, emphasis mine.
95 *Dominus Iesus* consistently speaks of salvation in terms consistent with personal transcendence—a view foreign to the Jewish mind, which views salvation as a communal phenomenon. For the changes initiated by Vatican II concerning the Church and salvation in relation to other religions, see J.B. Barla, *Christian Theological Understanding of Other Religions According to D.S. Amalorpavadass* (Rome: Editrice Pontificia Università Gregoriana, 1999), 119.
96 Decree *Unitatis redintergatio*, 4 as quoted in Catholic Church, Declaration "*Dominus Iesus*: On the Unicity and Salvific Universality of Jesus Christ and the Church," §16, accessible at http://www.vatican.va/roman_curia/congregations/cfaith/documents/rc_con_cfaith_doc_20000806_dominus-iesus_en.html.
97 See Joseph Ratzinger, "Necessità della missione della chiesa nel mondo," in *La Fine della Chiesa come Società Perfetta* (Verona: Mondatori), 1968, 69–70.
98 For the dangers of such conceptions expressed in *Dominus Iesus*, see R.M. Bennett, *Dominus Iesus: Rome Exalts Her Throne: A Verbal Reappearance of the Inquisition* (Edmonton, AB: Still Waters Revival Books, 2000), 2.
99 The *Imprimi Potest*, or official permission to publish the Catholic Catechism, was authorized and physically signed by Joseph Cardinal Ratzinger, under the authority of Pope John Paul II.

84 *Supersessionism and* Nostra Aetate

100 See Georges Florovsky, "The Limits of the Church," accessed October 27, 2011, found at http://www.wcc-coe.org/wcc/who/crete-01-e.html. The Reformed tradition has stressed that there is indeed one Church founded by Christ, but has maintained a logical distinction between the visible and invisible Church. See Brian Schwertly, "The Visible vs. the Invisible Church," accessed October 27, 2011, found at http://www.monergism.com/thethreshold/articles/onsite/visible.html. For an understanding of the correlation of the topic of the invisible Church and interreligious dialogue, see Cassidy, *Ecumenism and Interreligious Dialogue*, 74.
101 "The Church is simultaneously *the means and the goal of God's plan*: prefigured in creation, prepared for in the Old Covenant," *Catechismus Catholicae Ecclesiae* (Rome: Libreria Editrice Vaticana, 1997), §778, emphasis in the original.
102 Boys, "The Covenant in Contemporary Ecclesial Documents," 91.
103 Pope Benedict, XVI, and P. Seewald, *God and the World: Believing and Living in Our Time* (San Francisco, CA: Ignatius Press, 2002), 208–210. Likewise, Ratzinger has made the following claim: ". . . all nations, *without the abolishment of the special mission of Israel*, become brothers and receivers of the promises of the chosen people." (Ratzinger, "Reconciling Gospel and Torah: the Catechism," an address given at the International Jewish–Christian Conference, Jerusalem, 1994, emphasis mine.
104 J. Ratzinger, "Interreligious Dialogue and Jewish–Christian Relations," *Communio: International Catholic Review* 25 (Spring 1998): 29–40.
105 Benedict, *God and the World*, 150.
106 It was not until after *Dominus Iesus* was released that Walter Kasper made the claim that the document "does not apply to the Jewish people." Nothing in the document itself articulates that the Jewish people are exempt of the Church's mediatorial role for salvation.
107 Ratzinger does mention that *NA* was intended as a declaration on Catholics and Jews only, and laments that it was prematurely broadened to include all world religions—a point with which I agree, due to the negative implications for dialogue between Jews and Christians. Joseph Ratzinger, *Theological Highlights of Vatican II* (Mahwah, NJ: Paulist Press, 2009), 157. Nevertheless, the absence of the declaration's impact in the text is theologically irresponsible considering the book treats the "highlights" of Vatican II.
108 F.J. Coppa, *The Papacy, the Jews, and the Holocaust* (Washington, DC: Catholic University of America Press, 2006), 292.
109 Pope Benedict XVI, *Many Religions—One Covenant: Israel, the Church, and the World* (San Francisco, CA: Ignatius Press, 1999), 22–23.
110 Ibid., 36.
111 Ibid., 55–56, emphasis mine.
112 D. Hartman, *A Heart of Many Rooms: Celebrating the Many Voices within Judaism* (Woodstock, VT: Jewish Lights, 1999), 262.
113 Pope Benedict XVI, *Many Religions*, 55.
114 Ibid., 53.
115 Ibid., 70–71, emphasis mine.
116 Ibid., 68.
117 J.A. Davies, *A Royal Priesthood: Literary and Intertextual Perspectives on an Image of Israel in Exodus 19.6* (London: T&T Clark International, 2004), 118.
118 Boys, "The Covenant in Contemporary Ecclesial Documents," 105, emphasis mine.
119 Ratzinger states that certain interpretations of 2 Corinthians 3 create too strong an antithesis between the two covenants and that ". . . it has largely been forgotten that other Pauline texts portray the drama of God's history with men in a much more nuanced way." Pope Benedict XVI, *Many Religions*, 54.
120 Ratzinger states that God ". . . has obviously given Israel a particular mission in this 'time of the Gentiles,'" but fails to clarify what that mission is. Ibid., 104. In one section it reads that through the Jews' ". . . witness to the one God, who cannot be

adored apart from the unity of love of God and neighbor, they should open the door into the world for this God so that his will may be done and so that it may become on earth 'as it is in heaven': so that 'his kingdom come.'" Ibid., 46.
121 Ibid., 28.
122 See Gerhard Nachtwei, *Dialogische Unsterblichkeit: Eine Untersuchung zu Joseph Ratzingers Eschatologie und Theologie* (Leipzig: St. Benno-Verlag, 1986).
123 Joseph Ratzinger, *The Ratzinger Reader: Mapping a Theological Journey*, ed. Lieven Boeve and Gerard Mannion (London: T&T Clark International, 2010), 87. According to Richard McBrien, the intention of the authors of *Lumen Gentium* 5 was to avoid the triumphalism of the past and ". . . to counteract this residual habit of equating the Church with the kingdom of God." Richard McBrien, Vatican II themes: The Church as an eschatological community," accessed October 27, 2011, found at http://ncron line.org/blogs/essays-theology/vatican-ii-themes-Church-eschatological-community.
124 Pope Benedict XVI, *Jesus of Nazareth*, 41.
125 Modern Judaism, borrowing from traditional elements, has stressed the connection between the earthly and the heavenly Jerusalem, and the complete rebuilding of the sacred city is a central part of restoration theology and Jewish religious identity. "The Heavenly Jerusalem and the Earthly Jerusalem" in H. Schwartz, *Tree of Souls: The Mythology of Judaism* (New York: Oxford University Press, 2004), 414.
126 Joseph Ratzinger, *Eschatology: Death and Eternal Life* (Washington, DC: Catholic University of America Press, 2007), 58.
127 Aidan Nichols, "Note on the Current Volume" in Ratzinger, *Eschatology: Death and Eternal Life*, xvii.
128 Ratzinger, *Eschatology: Death and Eternal Life*, 58–59. he, pinnacle, and telos of all, pinnacle, and telos of all kingdom related language. in relation to replacement theology is no.
129 W.R. Herzog, *Jesus, Justice, and the Reign of God: A Ministry of Liberation* (Louisville, KY: Westminster John Knox Press, 2000), 219ff.
130 Ratzinger, *Eschatology: Death and Eternal Life*, 55–56.
131 For example, Moltmann speaks of the ". . . ruthless persecution of the Jews, who still wait for the Messiah, and of dissidents unable to recognize in . . . [the] . . . Roman ecclesiastical rule Christ's messianic kingdom of peace." Moltmann, *The Coming of God*, 180.
132 C.H. Dodd, *The Parables of the Kingdom* (New York: Scribner, 1961), 164.
133 Ratzinger, *Eschatology: Death and Eternal Life*, 55.
134 Dale C. Allison, *Jesus of Nazareth: Millenarian Prophet*, 69.
135 S.M. Bryan, *Jesus and Israel's Traditions of Judgement and Restoration* (Cambridge: Cambridge University Press, 2002), 2.
136 See also, Pope Benedict, XVI, and P. Seewald, *God and the World: Believing and Living in Our Time*, 344. Also, Ratzinger often quoted A. Loisy, claiming that ". . . the opposition of kingdom and Church has no factual basis." Alfred Loisy, *L'évangele Et L'église* (Paris: A. Picard et fils, 1902). See also Benedict, and Hans Maier, *Demokratie in Der Kirche: Möglichkeiten Und Grenzen* (Limburg: Lahn-Verlag, 2000) for Ratzinger's views on the kingdom, contemporary politics and the existence of the Church.
137 Ratzinger claims that ". . . what Jesus' message immediately announced was not the Church but the kingdom of God . . ." Benedict XVI, *Called to Communion: Understanding the Church Today* (San Francisco, CA: Ignatius Press, 1996), 21, but Ratzinger often has clarified that the Church was intended by Christ to be viewed as the kingdom on earth. See Benedict, XVI and V. Messori, *The Ratzinger Report: An Exclusive Interview on the State of the Church* (San Francisco, CA: Ignatius Press, 1985), 48, in which Ratzinger emphasizes the definition of the Church in *Lumen Gentium*, no. 3, referring to ". . . the Church, or, in other words, the kingdom of Christ now present . . ."

Part II
Millenarianism

A valid part of Church history

3 Millenarianism explored

In the Chapter 2 of this book, I argued that the theology of supersessionism has been questioned by some contemporary Roman Catholic theologians, especially since the inception of *NA*. We gave a cursory definition of millenarianism, positing the overall thesis of this book: that a modified chiliastic (millenarian). Eschatology provides a means to overcoming supersessionism, especially considering that eschatological exploration has been encouraged in Roman Catholic circles regarding Jewish–Catholic dialogue. Some scholars may question why a 'means beyond supersessionism' is necessary, considering that so many Christian denominations have either already rejected the theory, or have adopted more pluralistic solutions. The reality is that the majority of 'confessional' Christian Churches, in our case, the Roman Catholic Church, have not formalized the rejection of supersessionism—in spite of reforms made by Protestant Churches and Vatican II in Catholicism. In addition, most if not all mainline Churches, including the Roman Catholic Church, have informally adopted amillennialism as their eschatology of choice—millenarianism has neither been taken seriously, nor fully explored by theologians in relation to supersessionism.

Ultimately, a significant problem arises if eschatological exploration utilizes millenarian categories, since such thought has been relegated to the fringes of theological research, is perceived as an eschatological system adopted solely by Fundamentalists or revolutionary thinkers, and has been portrayed in Catholic circles as having no biblical or traditional roots.[1] Many Catholic theologians go so far as to call the eschatology heretical. Therefore, in this chapter, I will focus on showing the validity of millenarian eschatology, arguing for its biblical legitimacy and place in traditional, orthodox doctrine. Further, I will seek to explain the factors that contributed to the original millenarian eschatology being replaced by amillennialism.

The purpose of this chapter is to show that millenarianism was a legitimate, uncontested theology in the early Church era, is validly part of the biblical narrative, and was exchanged late in Church history by an amillennial view that was foreign to the original eschatology of the Church. The ways I will fulfill the purpose of this chapter are as follows. First, I intend to define millenarianism and explore a limited history of its expression in the early Christian tradition,[2] utilizing a survey of modern biblical and theological literature. Second, I will show how millenarianism is considered by many respected scholars to be a valid biblical principle (in John's Revelation, in the ideas of Jesus, and in the work of Paul), while at the same time exegetically critiquing the *amillennial* view. Next I will illustrate how millennialism was both the normative and orthodox eschatology of the early Church, and was held by numerous early Church Fathers. I will briefly discuss some of millenarianism's earliest retractors (beginning in the middle of the third century) and give an account as to why they refuted the eschatology. Included in this section will be a refutation of contemporary scholarship that seeks to portray chiliasm and amillennialism as equally primitive and original Christian eschatologies. Last, I will argue that a massive shift occurred in the eschatology of the Roman Catholic Church during the era and work of Eusebius and Augustine—primarily due to political reasons. With Augustine, the "Thousand Years Reign" of Revelation 20 became associated explicitly with the Roman Catholic Church, and the amillennial view became more dominant.

For a theologian to attempt to define millenarianism in totality, it would be tantamount to a historian embarking on the delineation of an entire political phenomenon such as "Americanism" in one brief work. Though the analogy may break down due to disparate time periods between millenarian religious ideas and American political concepts, the point remains valid. Expressions of both millenarian and Americanist occurrences are so divergent and polyvalent that the task would be as unfruitful as it would be impossible. Wide brush strokes must be used in describing millenarianism, in order to do justice to its various incarnations in Christian history and consciousness. For the purpose of this project, the terms "millenarianism" and "millennialism," derived from the Latin, and "chiliasm," derived from the Greek, will be used synonymously—all coming from the root words for "thousand." John M. Court claims that distinctions between the nuanced terms referring to Christian millennialism, though advocated by historical scholars primarily for polemical reasons, ". . . cannot be maintained across the whole range of historical examples, and it is better to agree with the dictionary and regard the . . . terms as virtually interchangeable."[3] Millenarian language and the Book of Revelation which inspired its spread was utilized more in theological dialogue in the Latin West than in the East during the first several centuries of Christianity,[4] though Eastern Christianity had its later share of profoundly chiliastic views. That which was missing from the early Church in the first few centuries, across the geographical spectrum, was any structured or codified formulation of what would today be called amillennialism.

Before we define millenarianism as a theological reality, it is important that we position the term in its holistic religious and cultural context. Biblical scholar Dale Allison has outlined 19 "recurring attributes" of millenarian groups that span history, expressed in Judaism, Christianity, Islam, Buddhism, and a majority of non-Western religious and cultural phenomena. In an effort to contextualize early Christian millenarianism, it is necessary to enumerate some of the more important themes in millenarian views of history, which include the following concepts: appeal to those "martyrs" experiencing persecution or misfortune due to a period of social or political change and hardship including poverty and socio-religious oppression, a view that present history is an era of unparalleled suffering, a divinely instituted vindication of those who have been wronged, communal living in a newly transformed earth which maintains the essential goodness and subsequent renewal of material existence, specifically during a new "Golden Age," a reintroduced sense of asceticism balanced with the critique of traditional religious customs, the centrality of a charismatic religious or political leader, the death and return of the charismatic leader, a wide spectrum, either of violent overtones or pacifistic patience, a restored paradise, the reality of disappointed expectations, and the reversal of power—the weak and vulnerable "reign" with their leader, indicating their vindication.[5] We will explore how the attributes above are expressed specifically in Christian millenarian religious writings, but first we will define how millenarianism is conceived in Christian circles.

Millenarianism defined and contextualized

Millenarianism is defined as ". . . the belief that there will be a period of peace and righteousness on the earth associated with the Second Coming of Christ."[6] Central to our definition of the term is that the millennium, the "era of peace," is viewed as *future-temporal*—indicating a period of time in between the Parousia which occurs first, and the general resurrection. Most premillennial biblical scholars today have flexible views regarding whether the millennial period must be viewed as strictly earthly in nature, or alternatively as a "first installment" of the newly re-created order (the "new earth"). Likewise, contemporary millennial scholars are content with stating that the purpose of the Parousia, which to them initiates the interregnum period,[7] is one of judgment leading to a general resurrection—stressing the biblical narrative as a single, unified event. Therefore, many contemporary millennialists do not envision a stark contrast between the Parousia and the first resurrection,[8] and the final judgment and general resurrection which it precedes. Regardless of nuance, all Christian millenarian views are based on complex readings of numerous biblical texts, the most important of which is Revelation 20:1–10.[9] For our purposes, the literal period of one thousand years ascribed in early millenarianism is less important than the concept that the period is an interstitial era between messiah's Second Coming and the final judgment/ complete end of historical time.

The earliest Christian expressions of eschatology contain within them explicit links to the polyvalent religion from which it sprouted during the Second Temple period. The Jewish influence from which early Christian millenarianism is derived placed emphasis on either six 1,000-year periods, spanning back to the creation of the world, and moving toward the final, seventh 1,000-year period associated with the seventh day of creation—the cosmic Sabbath[10]—or alternating periods of 700 or 400 years,[11] associated with remembrances of the Exodus[12] or the Babylonian captivity.[13] Associated with Old Testament passages such as Isaiah 2 and 11, Jeremiah 31–33, Ezekiel 36–37, Daniel 7, and Micah 4, early Christian millennial expectation borrowed deeply from the Jewish understanding of the "age to come," a materially abundant era of peace in which the original Edenic reality, whereby Yahweh would once again dwell among his people as monarch, and justice would be reestablished in Zion, or the rebuilt Jerusalem, the new spiritual capital of the world. Though not exhaustively, the narrative of Christian millennialism finds its roots in Second Temple Jewish-inspired apocalyptic texts such as *4 Ezra* 7:26–31, *2 Bar.* 29:1–30:5; 40:1–3, *I Enoch* 37–71, *The Apocalypse of Weeks* (*I Enoch* 93:1–10; 91:11–17), *The Apocalypse of Abraham* 29:8–12, *4Q246* (*Aramaic Apocalypse*), and *1QSa 2:12–15* (in the *Rule of the Congregation*).[14]

Certainly, some elements of both "realized eschatology" and an imminent, yet future realization of the kingdom of God were expressed in earliest Christianity. Nevertheless, the stress was on an imminent, earthly return of Jesus, whereby Christ would reign temporally after a first resurrection comprised of those whom God chooses, to be followed by a final, general resurrection. The concept of two resurrections was the most consistent early eschatology, in line with chiliastic expectations. First-century texts such as the *Didache* reveal several "materialistic" expectations for the kingdom of God that have been interpreted as commensurate with chiliastic thought, rather than later amillennial expressions.[15] Primitive texts such as the *Epistle of Barnabas* are explicitly chiliastic in content.[16] As we will see later, Charles Hill claims that *two* early Christian eschatologies vied for power in the fledgling early Church—one chiliastic, expecting two resurrections and a material establishment of God's kingdom on earth for a thousand years, and one that interpreted Revelation 20 as referring to an immediate, personal judgment in line with one common resurrection and final consummation.[17] We will critique Hill's thesis later, arguing instead that millenarianism is representative of the earliest Jewish–Christian eschatology, one uniformly affirmed until the third century.[18] Overall, Millenarianism was the most primitive eschatological understanding in Jewish–Christianity, is traceable to our earliest extant sources, and was held normatively through the first half of the third century.[19] The amillennial interpretation of Revelation was utterly foreign to the consciousness of most Christians during the apostolic era, save among heretics.

Until this point in the project, it has been unnecessary to utilize or define the modern terms "premillennialism," "postmillennialism," and "amillennialism," as these stark distinctions were foreign to the collective mind of the early Church, though they were later categorized by dispensationalists and modern Protestant evangelicals in America. Nevertheless, it will be a good exercise in clarification to make such distinctions for the modern reader. Timothy Weber writes that Pre-millennialists "... advocate that the Parousia will occur *before* the start of the millennium," Post-millennialists "... place the Second Coming *after* a long period of gradual and incremental 'gospel success' " in which the vast majority of humanity is converted to Christ," and finally, Amillennialists "... believe that OT prophecies about a future golden age were fulfilled in the coming of Christ and the Christian Church ..."[20]

In the early Church, the most primitive eschatology was the belief in two resurrections, one for the martyrs and "those who had not received the mark on their foreheads," and a general resurrection of all the dead, followed by a universal judgment.[21] In primitive Christian theology, it was understood that there would be an "historical" period of time involving the earth or a renewed earth—one that took place in between the two resurrections—the Thousand Years' era of peace. Later in the Church's history, the two resurrections were conflated into one general resurrection and judgment, and the Thousand Years' era of peace was interpreted as the era of the Church itself, and thus the precursors to modern amillennialism were born.[22] According to E.C. Dewick, "the Alexandrian theology (with an allegorical understanding of Scripture) on the one hand, and on the other hand the Augustinian conception of *the Church as the kingdom of God on earth*, alike contributed to render it ... [millenarianism] ... less acceptable to the Christian mind."[23]

Millenarian principles and narrative are traced explicitly to the texts of the New Testament. In particular, John's Revelation (Apocalypse) is a millenarian text, especially when one explores the details described in its twentieth chapter. Likewise, the Gospels exhibit millenarian language, primarily in the words of Jesus. It is not simply that the Synoptic Gospel writers borrowed the language, but more so that chiliastic themes were original parts of Jesus' discourse. Pauline literature, specifically the Epistle to the Romans, 1 Thessalonians, 1 Corinthians, and Philippians, contains chiliastic principles, such as chronologies of the return of Christ that express an intermediate time of reign, language concerning saints and martyrs that is found solely in chiliastic literature, and explicit language regarding two distinct resurrections, a major theme in chiliastic thought. We will briefly explore these themes in the following section seeking to illustrate a trajectory of millenarian theology in the above three sources.

Revelation 20: An intentionally chiliastic text

The biblical passage essential to Christian millenarian interpretation is Revelation 20: 1–10, which reads:

> Then I saw an angel coming down from heaven, holding the key of the abyss and a great chain in his hand. And he laid hold of the dragon, the serpent of old, who is the devil and Satan, and bound him for a thousand years; and he threw him into the abyss, and shut it and sealed it over him, so that he would not deceive the nations any longer, until the thousand years were completed; after these things he must be released for a short time. Then I saw thrones, and they sat on them, and judgment was given to them. And I *saw* the souls[24] of those who had been beheaded because of their testimony of Jesus and because of the word of God, and those who had not worshiped the beast or his image, and had not received the mark on their forehead and on their hand; and they came to life and reigned (βασιλεία)[25] with Christ for a thousand years. The rest of the dead did not come to life until the thousand years were completed. This is the first resurrection (*protos anastasis*). Blessed and holy is the one who has a part in the first resurrection; over these the second death has no power, but they will be priests of God and of Christ and will reign with Him for a thousand (*chilia*) years. When the thousand years are

completed, Satan will be released from his prison, and will come out to deceive the nations which are in the four corners of the earth, Gog and Magog, to gather them together for the war; the number of them is like the sand of the seashore. And they came up on the broad plain of the earth and surrounded the camp of the saints and the beloved city, and fire came down from heaven and devoured them. And the devil who deceived them was thrown into the lake of fire and brimstone, where the beast and the false prophet are also; and they will be tormented day and night forever and ever.
(Revelation 20:1–10, NASB, modified)

The primary debate concerning millennialism and amillennialism may be narrowed down to the question of a literal or allegorical reading of the above passage.[26] In the millennial view, the martyrs and confessors are interpreted as they who, in light of the *first* resurrection, "... will rule with Christ (cf. Matt 19:28; I Cor 15:20–28; 6:2–3; Dan 7:22, 27) in his messianic kingdom as "priests of God and of Christ" (20:4–6). This corresponds to the realistic millennial expectation of the coming thousand-year reign."[27] We see within the context of Revelation 20, and in light of other NT[28] and OT passages associated with it,[29] that there appears no intention given by the author to suggest a metaphorical or non-literal reading of the passage.[30] The literal character of the Apocalypse and the influence for a millenarian view becomes evident when compared to the Hebrew Bible and various Second Temple texts—primarily the Book of Ezekiel,[31] 4 Ezra,[32] and I Enoch.[33] The narrative of the two resurrections in the passage,[34] the earthly beloved city "camp" of those saints (Jerusalem)[35] and those who did not receive the mark of the beast reigning with Christ for a period of time prior to the final judgment, and the initial, justified postponement of resurrection for those who are opposed to God or oppress those who belong to Christ—these give no logical reason supportive of an allegorical reading of the text in Revelation 20.[36] The importance of the millenarian interpretation of Revelation 20 has more to do with the literal reading of the chronology than that of a literal 'thousand-year' time period, though the thousand-year era of peace appears often in Jewish literature, along with variations on the theme. The point of importance in the millenarian reading of Revelation 20 is that in it the reign of Christ occurs during a period in the future that is *not* the current era of the Church, but a future era of the Kingdom of God.

In Revelation 20, John speaks of "thrones" on which those who are to judge are seated. The theological function of this pericope is to express vindication for those who have given up all earthly comfort and safety for the sake of God's cause, in spite of on-going persecution. John sees two groups of people reigning with Christ, and each of these groups is divided among people who lived before and after the tribulation. There is one group to whom judgment is given, and another group comprised of martyrs. In each case, the place of honor is reserved not for the representatives of a conflated institution of Church and State, as was established at the time of Constantine, but for those who remained faithful to the Lord through times of persecution, refusing to commit idolatry:

Millenarianism explored 95

> Then I saw thrones, and they sat on them, and judgment was given to them. And I *saw* the souls of those who had been beheaded because of their testimony of Jesus and because of the word of God, and those who had not worshiped the beast or his image, and had not received the mark on their forehead and on their hand; and they came to life and reigned with Christ for a thousand years.
>
> (Revelation 20: 4)

The text above is language borrowed from other millenarian sources, and the amillennial view of the text, which we will explain momentarily, is not justifiable in terms of relating the "reign" of the saints with the current Church era.

The language of "thrones," indicative of authority and reign, functions in a specifically millenarian manner in the Book of Revelation. Natural to the millenarian interpretation is a view of history that refrains from equating the "reign of the saints" with any moment in past or present history, or any strictly defined grouping of people, such as the predominately Gentile Church. John speaks of the throne of God, the throne of Jesus (the Lamb), and even the throne of Satan, but speaks of "thrones" in the plural only one other time in the Book of Revelation.[37] In Revelation 4:4, similar to Revelation 20, John has a vision of:

> a throne standing in heaven and One sitting on the throne. And He who was sitting was like a jasper stone and a sardius in appearance; and there was a rainbow around the throne, like an emerald in appearance. Around the throne were twenty-four thrones; and upon the thrones I saw *twenty-four elders* sitting, clothed in white garments, and golden crowns on their heads.
>
> (Revelation 4:2b–4)

The text above was influenced heavily by Jewish millenarian-apocalyptic— particularly the imagery of the *Merkabah* throne of Ezekiel 1, Isaiah 6, Psalm 110, and Daniel 7.[38] The question of the fourth chapter of Revelation has to do with its connection to its twentieth chapter, assuming that the passages refer to two different groups of enthroned individuals—one described as being in heaven in the fourth chapter, and the others reigning from the beloved city on earth, in the twentieth chapter. Both visions of the "thrones" include details that should not be overlooked, that align the text with a chiliastic intent. At minimum, the amillennial interpretation of the text, i.e., that the "reign" of Christ and his saints is the "era of the Church," is difficult to sustain, premised on the text alone. The expression of 24 thrones for 24 elders in Revelation 4 is significant because it represents the 12 apostles *and* the 12 tribes of Israel,[39] worshipping God *together*.[40] As Brian K. Blount describes it:

> A heavenly subscribed position contends that the 24 represent the combined presence of the 12 tribes and the 12 apostles. In them the wholeness of the people of faith is represented ... Just as each of the seven Churches is

represented by an angel in chapters 2–3, so too are the tribes and the apostles represented on the heavenly throne by surrogate angels.[41]

This description of Revelation 4 expresses a profound theological reality. Surrounding the great throne of heaven are representatives that cannot be equated explicitly with the Church, though amillennialist scholar J. Ford attempts to synthesize the groups into Jewish and Gentile believers composite of the "New Israel."[42] According to millenarian interpretations, the text above is read in a different manner: those around the throne of Revelation 4 convey a composite faith community representative of both the Church and the synagogue,[43] with the intention of a diversity inclusive of explicitly Jewish identity. The entire enthronement scene in Revelation 4 harkens back to the covenant ceremony at Sinai, also utilized in pre-Christian Jewish millennial texts.[44]

In Jewish Apocalyptic texts dealing with theophanic throne scenes, angels are said to mediate in presenting the prayers of saints before the throne of God,[45] but they are never termed "elders." Other scholars identify the 24 elders as the OT saints or their representatives,[46] or the 24 courses of Levite priests who represent the whole of Israel, as in 1 Chronicles 24:3–19.[47] Early Jewish tradition, the primary source available to and used by John, evolves to interpret the term "24 elders" as referring to Israel's human elders—a point based on the ancient understanding of the phrase.[48] According to Beale, Rabbinical Midrashim have consistently compared "... Isa 24:23 to Exod. 24:1 and applied [the texts] to the messianic time to come, when Israel's elders will sit as *part* of God's court."[49] Jewish traditional understanding illustrates that the 24 elders in Revelation 4 refer, at least in part, to Jewish elders as a group distinct from the Church.[50] The throne scenes of Revelation 20 and Revelation 4 both indicate that the author intentionally borrowed Second Temple chiliastic imagery from Jewish sources, while amillennial interpretations appear utterly foreign to the text's content and the author's intent.

There appears to be a connection between the groups around the throne, either those in Revelation 4 or Revelation 20, and other parts of the New Testament narrative, considering the words that Jesus addressed to the disciples in Luke 22: 29–30: "... just as My Father has granted Me a kingdom, I grant you that you may *eat and drink* at My table in My kingdom, and you will sit on thrones judging the twelve tribes of Israel."[51] Eating and drinking hardly appear allegorical in the context of Luke's Gospel, as in the amillennial interpretation, considering Jesus' promises take place during the institution of the Last Supper—from which Roman Catholics typically draw a very literal understanding. Such material imagery is not the product of an allegorical intention by the author of Luke–Acts, but a reference to the earthly kingdom to be established at the eschaton.[52] Luke 22: 29–30 holds striking similarity to I En. 108:12[53] and previous chapters of this Enochic literature describe the future kingdom in explicitly millenarian terms.[54] Luke 22, I En. 108, and the millennial scene of Revelation 20 carry significant similarities, describing the messianic 'age to come." Again, in Matthew 19:28, it is written: "And Jesus said unto them, Verily I say unto you, that you which have followed

Me, in the restoration (παλιγγενεσία)[55] when the Son of man shall sit in the throne of His glory, you also shall sit upon twelve thrones, judging the twelve tribes of Israel." These passages too are related to prior Jewish Apocalyptic writings that envisioned an earthly, millennial reign of the Lord, in which God's whole people will participate—a point in almost complete harmony with Revelation 20.[56] All the texts above contain parallels to the themes echoed in Revelation 20, thus pointing to a chiliastic thread of thought running throughout. The literal, chiliastic interpretation of the text of Revelation 20, which is most consistent with an honest exegesis of the passage, views the reign of Christ as an event that has not yet occurred—it will occur in the future, in an interstitial space of time, on earth.

The amillennial interpretation of Revelation 20 is flawed

The modern Roman Catholic interpretation of Revelation 20, by contrast to the early millenarian view held by individuals during the apostolic era, is focused on the point that the reigning of the martyrs mentioned in the above text refers to their bodiless souls alone, as they reign with Christ now, in heaven, or more specifically, to their initial regeneration and conversion to the Catholic faith.[57] The Catholic view stresses the current, heavenly, spiritual reality of the saints—in line with the typological reading of Scripture, over and against the future, earthly, bodily interpretation.[58] Such an interpretation does not take into account the fact that the first resurrection in Revelation 20 means exactly that—the unification of the body with the soul, after which, the prospect of further bodily death is no longer a threat. The text of Revelation 20 is explicit in claiming that "the rest of the dead [those who were not the martyrs, or 'those who had not worshiped the beast or his image'] did not come to life until the thousand years were completed" (20:5). The Catholic, amillennialist view that the individuals described in Revelation 20 are simply souls[59] and that ". . . the 'first resurrection' refers to the regeneration of the believer at the point of conversion . . . understood as the initiation unto the Christian life of the present age,"[60] is inconsistent with a proper exegesis of Revelation. For example, of the 42 times that it is used in the NT, "resurrection" (ἀνάστασις) *never* refers to regeneration, as in the Catholic interpretation—instead, it refers to bodily resurrection. Further, the Greek word *zao* ("to live") used in Revelation 20 is used 139 times elsewhere in the NT, with it referring to spiritual life after physical death only twice—both different in context from that of Revelation 20.[61] In refutation of the Catholic interpretation of Revelation 20, Charles Feinberg states, "When believers die, they can die in only one realm—the physical; when they come alive, they do so in one area only—the physical. Where does Scripture teach otherwise?"[62]

There also exists a logical fallacy in the modern Catholic, amillennial interpretation of Revelation 20, having to do with the chronology of the text, and the fact that the first resurrection deals specifically with *martyrs*. If the first resurrection is interpreted to be the moment a person becomes a Catholic believer, i.e., conversion, does this not mean that, ". . . the individuals described in verse 4 are not regenerated by the Holy Spirit until after they are martyred for their faith in Christ?"[63] Such an interpretation makes little sense in light of the plain meaning of the text itself. Thus, the amillennialist interpretation of Revelation 20:4 presents "... the absurdity of having souls being [spiritually] regenerated *after* they had been beheaded for their faithfulness to Christ."[64] A common amillennialist argument is that if John intended to speak of a physical resurrection, he would not have used the term "souls" to describe the martyrs. Such an argument holds no validity, as the term "soul" is used multiple times in Scripture to refer both to those who are living, prior to any death or resurrection, and those who have died and are indeed resurrected.[65] Further, in 1 Thes 4:16, Paul writes that "the dead in Christ shall rise *first*."[66] Bible expert Robert H. Mounce frames the argument regarding the plurality of resurrections in these terms:

> The strong presumption is that the verb in v.4 should be taken in the same sense as it is in v. 5. In the second case the statement, "The rest of the dead did not come to life until the thousand years were ended," certainly refers to a bodily resurrection at the close of the millennial period. If "they came to life" in v. 4 means a spiritual resurrection to new life in Christ, then we are faced with the problem of discovering within the context some persuasive reason to interpret the same verb differently within one concise unit. No such reason can be found. Alford's much-quoted remark is worth repeating: "If, in a passage where *two resurrections* are mentioned . . . the first resurrection may be understood to mean *spiritual* rising with Christ, while the second means *literal* rising from the grave;—then there is an end of all significance in language, and Scripture is wiped out as a definite testimony to anything."[67]

One argument made in this book is that there *is* a motive behind why Roman Catholic exegetes reject the concept of two resurrections in Revelation 20,[68] in spite of there being "no persuasive reason" to do so in light of the plain meaning of the text. To admit of two resurrections is to simultaneously admit of a period of historical time after the Church era, but before the judgment and general resurrection—an intermediate existence categorized as the establishment of Christ's temporal reign on earth—what millenarians call "the millennial reign."[69]

The Catholic reading of the "two resurrections" text as one that is spiritual in kind (conversion to the Church) and the other physical in kind (the general resurrection) is rooted in a desire to maintain that the Church's existence in history and the millennial reign of Christ are synonymous.[70] The amillennialist view is almost uniformly accepted in Catholic circles despite the fact that it is inconsistent with the plain and proper exegesis of Scripture, and in spite of the reality that "... with one exception [Gaius] there is no Church Father before Origen who opposed the millenarian interpretation,[71] and there is no one before Augustine whose extant writings offer a different interpretation of Revelation 20:1–15 than that of a future earthly kingdom consonant with the natural interpretation of language."[72] Adherents of modern Roman Catholic eschatology, rooted in the shift to amillennialism that took place with Augustine's legacy,[73] view the "thousand years" of Revelation 20 as referring to the period of the historical Church since the ascension of Jesus.[74] The Roman Catholic acceptance of fourth century amillennial propositions has caused a spiritualization of Revelation 20 that is found nowhere in the text itself, thus promoting the concept ". . . that the kingdom is the *regnum Christi* or domain of spiritual salvation. This kingdom is not spatial, political, or national, but spiritual, finding expression in the present earthly and heavenly Church."[75] The problem with the dominant Catholic view is the contextual evidence in Revelation 19–20 itself, which is chronologically, or *sequentially* accurate as it stands as an extended pericope, pointing to the fact that the millennial reign is not the current Church age, but a future period of time.[76]

Amillennialists, including many modern Catholics theologians, uphold the recapitulatory view of Revelation 19–20, i.e., that the events of Revelation 20:1–6 precede those of 19:11–21.[77] The implications of the sequential view (millennialism) in contrast with the recapitulatory view (amillennialism) are important, because if the events of Revelation 20: 1–6 follow Christ's Second Coming in Revelation 19, the millennium, the fullness of the kingdom of God, *cannot* be said to exist (at least fully) in present history through the Church.[78] The sequential interpretation of Revelation 19–20 is validated for several reasons. First, Revelation 20:7–10 is seen to follow the future millennial kingdom of Ezekiel 36–37 and Revelation 20:1–6, illustrating a corresponding influence in the Hebrew Bible as the pattern for the sequential events.[79] Second, the binding of Satan in Revelation 20:1–3 cannot be reconciled with the New Testament's portrayal of Satan's activities in the present age.[80] Third, the resurrection at the beginning of the Thousand Years is bodily in nature,[81] establishing that the "thousand years" do not refer to the present age, as people are not currently in a resurrected state.

In the modern Roman Catholic view there is an insistence that now is the time of the "chaining of Satan," thwarting the deception of the nations.[82] According to the amillennialist view, the "deception of the nations" by Satan is what occurred in the old dispensation—the Jewish one—prior to the proclamation of the Gospel by the Church.[83] According to amillennialism, as long as the Church has latitude to proclaim the Gospel, Satan is not "deceiving the nations."[84] Similar to the Jewish critique of the fullness of the realization of the creation's redemption and the total, historical defeat of evil with the advent of Christ, so too, one must ask, "Where is the proof of the chaining of Satan during the 'Church age'?—why do the nations *appear* to be so influenced by evil and deceived?" Were there exceptions of this deception during particularly evil periods in world history, such as the Second World War and the Holocaust? Biblical exegete Matthew Waymeyer states that, ". . . the binding of Satan in Revelation 20 indicates that the devil will be completely inactive on the earth during the thousand-year period, but the testimony of the New Testament indicates that Satan is quite active on the earth in the present age,"[85] subverting the amillennial interpretation. The concept that Satan will be bound during a period of time, coinciding with the messianic era of peace figures prominently in Second Temple Jewish literature and had a major influence on the earliest Christian writers who borrowed from it—including in the NT[86] and the Book of Revelation,[87] specifically. For example, J.W. Bailey writes that "In Jubilees 23:26–31 we have a description of the messianic time—the most vivid in the book—when men 'will draw nigh to one thousand years', 'and no Satan or evil destroyer will be in the land.' "[88] One Catholic author, seemingly unaware that he is deviating from the traditional Catholic view of the text, admits of a thousand-year period which includes the binding of Satan, but is alternative to the Church age: "In St. John's outlook, however, *the end of the world could not have been included* in the 'hour of temptation' because a thousand years must *intervene between the days of Antichrist and the end of the world.*"[89] In such an interpretation as above, in order to claim that the present Church era is the Thousand Years (which the author does not), the author would have to admit that the time of Antichrist has already occurred in history. The text above, which ascribes to chiliastic views of history, received both the *Nihil Obstat* and the *Imprimatur*—an obvious oversight on the part of Joseph Mueller, the Bishop of Sioux City, considering the text's departure from Augustinian Catholic interpretations of the Book of Revelation.

Overall, the Catholic amillennial reading of Revelation 20 is inconsistent with the biblical text itself, whereas the millenarian reading is an intrinsic part of it— the text was written with millenarian motifs in mind, and used to express an early chiliastic expectation among Christians. The motive behind an amillennial reading of Revelation 20 in the Roman Catholic tradition will be explored later in this book.

Millenarianism in the Gospels and Pauline corpus

There are varied views of the kingdom of God expressed in the Synoptic Gospels, particularly by Jesus in the narratives. At one point Jesus states that the kingdom of God is to some extent "fulfilled," indicating its nascent presence (Mark 1:15), while at other points Jesus makes the materialistic claim that he will have to wait to drink wine again, for he will do so in the future kingdom of God (Mark 14:25; Matthew 26:29; Luke 22:16). Jesus commands his disciples to pray that the kingdom *will* come (Matthew 6:9–13; Luke 11:2–4). Jesus insists that Abraham, Isaac and Jacob, as well as "many from the east and the west" will recline at table together in the kingdom (Matthew 8:11). One thing to which modern scholarship testifies is the inherently eschatological dimension of Jesus' teaching and its parallels with Jewish Apocalyptic and Second Temple millenarian ideas. Whereas Albert Schweitzer argued for a Jesus who embraced "consistent eschatology"— an expectation that God's kingdom would come within the first year of Jesus' ministry in the form of a visible "golden age," then revised to a near future, C.H. Dodd spoke in opposing terms of a "realized eschatology," arguing that Jesus believed that the kingdom was being fulfilled in earnest as he ministered, albeit not in the visible manner consistent with Jewish Apocalyptic expectations.[90] Joachim Jeremias saw in Jesus' words and the Gospel accounts an eschatology that was in the process of being realized, basically consistent with the Vatican II emphasis of a kingdom fulfillment that is simultaneously "already" and "not yet."[91] E.P. Sanders, in his groundbreaking work, *Jesus and Judaism*, argued that Jesus' primary eschatological vision was the material restoration of Israel.[92]

It was not until the work of Dale Allison in his recent *Jesus of Nazareth: Millenarian Prophet* that Schweitzer's thesis of Jesus' expectation and prophetic inauguration of an imminent, visible manifestation of the kingdom began to be taken seriously again in the scholarly community. Allison intensely argues that Jesus was a *millenarian ascetic* and that we see in the words and expectations of Jesus the ". . . standard pattern of Jewish messianism," and overall consistencies with worldwide millenarian religious sensibilities, specifically connected with the central goal of the eschatological restoration of Israel.[93] Although the "disappointments of history" took form, i.e., the kingdom was not manifest in the life of Jesus in the ways Jewish people expected, Allison argues that there was a consistency between Jesus' original message and the doctrines of the Church in early, though later centuries, carried on by the Apostles—through their chiliastic tradition. Thus, "Jesus' death and resurrection were *later* interpreted as the inauguration of a longer process of eschatological fulfillment . . .",[94] one that "nourished the belief that eschatological promises had begun to be fulfilled."[95] Nowhere in the early Gospel tradition is it implied that eschatological promises were fulfilled in their entirety, in or through the mechanism of the Church as a historic-political entity. Generally, the Gospel traditions likewise avoid the outlandish claims of triumphalism prominent in some *contemporary* millenarian movements,[96] insisting on the Jewish-influenced martyrdom aspect of the kingdom, that ". . . entry into the kingdom is associated with suffering, as in Matt. 5:10."[97] In early Christian consciousness, particularly the Gospel traditions, the ideal state of the last things was one of spiritual reality, but this certainly did not exclude ". . . visions of last things that were concrete, sensible, and imminent,"[98] often associated with the early Christian expectation for restoration of the people of Israel and the revival of a physical Temple beyond the Christian community itself.[99] Such chiliastic hopes did not exclude the concept that the final consummation would bring in spiritual blessings, but held such ideas in tension with God's vindication of the martyrs of history and the restoration of the created order in an earthly, temporal sense. Overall, the Gospels contain chiliastic language, imagery, hopes and expectations that appear to be quite different from the amillennialism that replaced its original eschatological pattern in the fourth century.[100]

In light of Jesus' words in the Gospels, certain scholarship has likewise pointed to St. Paul as one who espoused millenarian concepts in his writings.[101] These Pauline texts do not merely borrow such Jewish messianic concepts, but appear to be driven by them.[102] In addition to 1 Thessalonians 4:16,[103] discussed earlier, one such passage, 1 Corinthians 15:20–24 has been interpreted as pointing to the same millennial scenario as Revelation 20.[104] It reads:

> But now Christ has been raised from the dead, the first fruits of those who are asleep. For since by a man *came* death, by a man also *came* the resurrection of the dead. For as in Adam all die, so also in Christ all will be made alive. But each in his own order: Christ the first fruits, after that those who are Christ's at His coming, then *comes* the end, when He hands over the kingdom to the God and Father, when He has abolished all rule and all authority and power.

According to the millennial interpretation of the text above:

> Christ Himself is resurrected as the first fruits (23a). Then, Christians are resurrected at His Parousia (23b). Finally, at the end of the millennium, the rest of the dead are raised (24a). The quotation of Psalm 110:1 . . . and the picture of Christ handing over the kingdom . . . [is] . . . understood with reference to the millennial age, at the very end of which death itself is destroyed.[105]

Referring to 1 Corinthians 15, Zuck states that Paul's use of the Greek phrases *epeita* ("after that . . .") and *eita* ("then"), as they are always used in the NT, involve an interval of time, pointing to a millennial chronology: Christ's resurrection, "after that" the resurrection of the saints and martyrs at His coming, "then" the end of the mediatorial kingdom, and then the state of eternity.[106] Lietzmann takes the "end" or *telos* referenced in the passage as pointing to a period of millennial rest prior to the general resurrection.[107] 1 Corinthians 15:22 states that "in Christ, all will be made alive," with vs. 23 stating, "But each in his own turn." The Greek word for "turn" here is *tagmati*, meaning "rank" or "squad," suggesting a distinction in event, chronology and priority, and further multiplicity of resurrection: first Christ (at his first advent), then those "in Christ," and then all of humanity.[108] That Paul would utilize the concept of dual resurrections is significant, not only for his understanding of bodily resurrection, but also for his stress on a certain view of history:

> Paul's scathing sarcasm later in 4:8–11 is directed precisely at such persons who have collapsed into the present what for Paul remains future, namely already sharing the kingdom: "Already you are satiated, already you have become rich, apart from us you have reigned!" So there are some Corinthian believers who have vaunted that they have already arrived at the fullness of the life of faith that Paul expects only at the Parousia. They hold that they have advanced beyond their former peers in the faith.[109]

Thus, Paul's *critique* of the community at Corinth was directed toward those who equated the "newness of life" of regeneration in Christ with resurrection itself—a point strikingly similar to amillennial readings of the "first resurrection" of Revelation 20. Regardless of the nuance of the interpretation of 1 Corinthians 15:23, the passage suggests that ". . . until the end of time it is Christ, not believers, who reigns . . ."[110] Such a rendering of 1 Corinthians deals a significant blow, both to images of the kingdom that are closely linked to the Church of history, and forms of realized eschatology that function contrary to millenarian eschatology.

Though millennialist interpretations of Pauline texts have been ridiculed in the past,[111] modern research suggests a close relation between early Pauline interpretations of the Old Testament phrase most quoted in the New Testament,[112] Psalm 110:1 (The LORD says to my lord: "Sit at my right hand until I make your enemies a footstool for your feet"), and the expectation of a millennial reign of

Christ on earth.[113] "Progressive millenarians," exemplified by David R. Anderson's exhaustive work on the subject of Psalm 110 and the NT, claim "Jesus has inaugurated the kingdom of David but will return to the earth to consummate this kingdom with a millennial reign from Jerusalem."[114] The fact that Paul quotes Psalm 110 in 1 Corinthians 15 suggests a connection between his eschatological chronology and early millenarian expectations.[115] 1 Corinthians 15 is related to the millennial idea that there is a ". . . need for a time when Christ will be glorified within history . . ."[116] and that there must come a time within history when a ". . . period of 'refreshing' will correspond with and counterbalance the time of oppression which God's people experienced."[117] The passage likewise seeks a mediating position between the differing opinions regarding the resurrection of the body during Paul's time among Jews, stressing the physical aspect, and Gentiles, stressing the spiritual nature.[118] In this sense, millennial thought in Paul, as in his later interpreters, serves a theological function—the restoration of that which was lost, i.e., primordial creation, by others, on account of their loyalty to the divine commands.[119] It is likewise evident in 1 Corinthians 15, as in Revelation 20, that the writer envisions two resurrections and not one—consistent with a chiliastic interpretation.[120]

Biblical interpreters see clues present in other Pauline texts such as Phil 1:23,[121] Phil. 3:11,[122] and 2 Corinthians 5:1–5[123] that are indicative of an intermediary period after death, yet prior to the general resurrection of judgment—pointing to the probability of a millennial state. Such an intermediary period has been associated with a first and second resurrection, as in the Book of Revelation, but scholars had not illustrated the overall importance of a Pauline rendering of two resurrections for eschatology and ecclesiology until the work of Moltmann.[124] Moltmann pays particular attention to Phil. 3:11, which uses the term "resurrection *from* the dead" (εχἀνάστασις)—the sole time the specific compound occurs in the NT or LXX.[125] Philippians 3:11 contains a phrase that scholars take to be used by Paul in an intentional distinction from the "resurrection *of* the dead," pointing to two resurrections separated by an interstitial period of time.[126] Though "resurrection from the dead" occurs only once, "life from the dead," referring to the future resurrection of God's people, occurs in Mark 12:25; Luke 20:35; Acts 4:2; and Ephesians 5:14. In the expert opinion of Richard Bauckham, ". . . the distinction in meaning between the two phrases [resurrection *from* and *of*] is valid."[127] Some scholars consider the Pauline emphasis on two resurrections as referring specifically to a first resurrection of the martyrs, as in Revelation 20, while others see it as referring to a resurrection of martyrs who are representative of *all* those in covenantal connection with God.[128] Of particular importance for this book is that the term "life *from* the dead" is used in Romans 11:15, not in reference to the Church, but to Israel—a point emphasized by Moltmann and reiterated in his critique of Luther's translation of the Bible which reads "resurrection *of* the dead" for all phrases, ". . . probably deliberately so, in order to exclude millenarianism."[129]

Romans 11:15 reads as follows: "For if their [the Israelites'] rejection brought reconciliation to the world, what will their acceptance be but life *from* the dead?"

Thus, the phrase in Romans is consistent with the concept expressed throughout the NT, pointing to the reality of two resurrections. Romans 11:15 carries with it the unique exception that the resurrected are a direct reference to "all Israel," as reiterated in Romans 11:25–27. The important point is that the concept of two distinct resurrections, directly connected to a chiliastic view of history, appears often in the New Testament, especially within the Pauline corpus. Indeed, the distinction in resurrections mentioned in Romans is not a novel idea in the New Testament. For example, Matthew 27:52–53 reads that immediately after Jesus' death on the cross, "The tombs broke open and the bodies of many holy people who had died were raised to life. They came out of the tombs, and after Jesus' resurrection they went into the holy city and appeared to many people."[130] The writers of the *Didache* take up this passage in a way that supports our theory of the early Christian chiliastic belief in two resurrections.[131] There are multiple New Testament passages that describe resurrection in apocalyptic terms,[132] describe a resurrection in history that is a prolepsis to the general resurrection of the dead on the last day, and put the resurrection in the context that more than one would occur. Nowhere in the Matthew text, in parallel to Paul's letters, does it state that the resurrection was more of a "resuscitation" whereby those who rose died again, and perhaps more importantly, the text describes those who rose as "holy people."[133] These were most obviously Jewish people, namely, Jewish "saints," and the text gives no indication that they had believed in Jesus as the messiah at any point in their lives.[134] Moltmann points to the connections among New Testament texts and their support of millenarian eschatology. According to Moltmann, the Gospel and Pauline ". . . witnesses of Easter do not recognize the risen Lord in a *blaze of heavenly, supra-worldly eternity*, but in the foretaste and dawn of his *eschatological future for the world*."[135] Further, Moltmann insists that millenarian thought exhibited in Paul is most consistent with the early orthodox rejection of Marcionism, Gnosticism, and Docetism.[136]

In sum, Paul's writing coheres well with the Second Temple understanding of Jewish eschatology and use of chiliastic language—especially in light of Romans 11 and the early orthodox Church's use of millennial belief in refutation of certain Christological heresies. Specifically, the Epistle to the Romans utilizes categories most recognizable as Jewish restoration eschatology, of which millennialism was a significant part, while other Pauline texts utilize chiliastic imagery in support against heretical, early Christian beliefs regarding bodily resurrection.[137]

Notes

1 "Millennium and Millenarianism," in J. Kirsch, ed., *The Catholic Encyclopedia* (New York: Robert Appleton Co., 1911), emphasis mine.
2 Rosemary Radford Reuther claims that Jewish Apocalyptic, including its millenarian ideas, was influenced by Zoroastrianism. See Rosemary Radford Ruether, "Eschatology in Christian Feminist Theologies," in J.L. Walls, ed., *The Oxford Handbook of Eschatology* (Oxford: Oxford University Press, 2008), 329. Cf. G. Scholem, arguing against Martin Buber's claim that messianism in Judaism borrowed extensively from Persian sources. See G. Scholem, *The Messianic Idea in Judaism and Other Essays on Jewish Spirituality* (New York: Schocken Books, 1995), 1–36.

3 J.M. Court, *Approaching the Apocalypse: A Short History of Christian Millenarianism* (London: I.B.Tauris, 2008), 42.
4 Brian E. Daley, "Apocalypticism in Early Christian Theology," in Bernard McGinn, Stephen Stein and John J. Collins, eds., *The Continuum History of Apocalypticism* (New York: Continuum, 2003), 222. See also Dionysius of Alexandria, *Ex libro de promissione*, 3–7 in Alexander Roberts and James Donaldson, eds., *The Writings of Gregory Thaumaturgus, Dionysius of Alexandria and Archelaus: Ante Nicene Christian Library Translations of the Writings of the Fathers Down to AD 325, Part Twenty* (Whitefish, MT: Kessinger Publishing, LLC, 2004), 170. A notable exception to millenarianism being held primarily in the Latin West is that of St. Ephrem the Syrian, the fourth century Doctor of the Church, whom Jerome "classified . . . as millenarian." Leroy Froom, *The Prophetic Faith of our Fathers* (Washington, DC: Review and Herald), 1950, 337.
5 Allison, *Jesus of Nazareth: Millenarian Prophet*, 78–94. On aspects of martyrdom in millenarian movements, see *The World's Religions: Continuities and Transformations*, ed. Peter Clark and Peter Beyer (Abingdon: Taylor & Francis, 2009), 354. For examples of both violent and pacifist influence exhibited in Christian millenarianism, see Reinaldo L. Roman, "Christian Themes: Mainstream Tradition and Millenarian Violence," in M. Barkun, ed., *Millennialism and Violence* (London: Frank Cass & Co., 1996), 52–82.
6 Timothy P. Weber, "Millennialism," in *The Oxford Handbook of Eschatology*, 365.
7 R. Schnackenburg, *God's Rule and Kingdom* (New York: Herder and Herder, 1968), 346.
8 D.C. Smith, "The Millennial Reign of Jesus Christ: Some Observations on Rev. 20:1–10," *ResQ*, 16 (1973): 219–230.
9 Weber, "Millennialism," 365.
10 See Rachel Elior, *The Three Temples: On the Emergence of Jewish Mysticism* (Oxford and Portland, OR: Littman Library of Jewish Civilization, 2004), 211–212.
11 T.B. *Sanhedrin* 99a; Midr. *Tanhuma*, Ekeb 7.
12 F. Weber, *Jüdische Theologie auf Grund des Talmud und verwandter Schriften*, ed. F. Delitzsch and G. Schnedermann (Leipzig: Dörffling Franke, 1987), 371–373.
13 Oded Irshai, "Dating the Eschaton: Jewish and Christian Apocalyptic Calculations in Late Antiquity," in Albert I. Baumgarten, ed., *Apocalyptic Time* (Boston, MA: Brill Academiclishers, 2000), 147.
14 James C. VanderKam, "Messianism and Apocalypticism," in McGinn *et al.*, *The Continuum History of Apocalypticism*, 120–132.Cf. Karina Martin Hogan, *Theologies in Conflict in 4 Ezra: Wisdom, Debate, and Apocalyptic Solution* (Leiden: Brill Academic, 2008), 201 and M.C de Boer, "Paul and Apocalyptic Eschatology," in McGinn *et al.*, *The Continuum History of Apocalypticism*, 190.
15 Brian Daley, *The Hope of the Early Church: A Handbook of Patristic Eschatology* (Cambridge: Cambridge University Press, 1991), 12. See further, Allison, *Jesus of Nazareth: Millenarian Prophet*, 166–167.
16 J.A. Kleist, *The Didache, the Epistle of Barnabas: The Epistles and the Martyrdom of St. Polycarp, the Fragments of Papias, the Epistle to Diognetus* (Westminster, MD: Newman Press, 1948, 180, n. 160, and also Brian Daley, "Eschatology in the Early Church Fathers," in *The Oxford Handbook of Eschatology*, 93.
17 Hill, *Regnum Coelorum: Patterns of Future Hope in Early Christianity*, Oxford Early Christian Studies (Oxford and New York: Clarendon Press and Oxford University Press, 1992), 92.
18 Jean Danielou, *The Theology of Jewish Christianity* (Darton, Longman & Todd, 1964), 395. Cf. John G. Gager, *Kingdom and Community: The Social World of Early Christianity* (Englewood Cliffs, NJ: Prentice-Hall, 1975), 33.

19 Paul L. King, "Premillennialism and the Early Church," in K. Neill Foster and David E. Fessenden, eds., *Essays on Premillennialism: A Modern Reaffirmation of an Ancient Doctrine* (Camp Hill, PA: Christian Publications, 2002), 1–12.
20 Weber, "Millennialism," 367–368.
21 Georg Strecker, *Theology of the New Testament* (Louisville, KY: Walter De Gruyter, 2000), 543.
22 John F. Walvoord, *The Millennial Kingdom: A Basic Text in Premillennial Theology* (Grand Rapids, MI: Zondervan, 1983), 37–47.
23 E.C. Dewick, *Primitive Christian Eschatology* (Cambridge: Cambridge University Press, 2011), 373, emphasis mine. On the distinction between early Christian eschatology and Dispensationalism, see John D. Hannah, *An Uncommon Union: Dallas Theological Seminary and American Evangelicalism* (Grand Rapids, MI: Zondervan, 2009), 121. Cf. Crawford Gribben, *Writing the Rapture: Prophecy Fiction in Evangelical America* (New York: Oxford University Press, USA, 2009) and Arthur William Wainwright, *Mysterious Apocalypse: Interpreting the Book of Revelation* (Nashville, TN: Abingdon Press, 1993), 21.
24 See John H. Walton, *Ancient Near Eastern Thought and the Old Testament: Introducing the Conceptual World of the Hebrew Bible* (Grand Rapids, MI: Baker Academic, 2006), 210.
25 Alexandrinus, in an attempt to dispute the future tense of the Greek verb "reign," renders it in the present tense in his commentary. This served the purpose of envisioning an early, already inaugurated version of the saints reigning with Christ metaphorically in the Church. G.K. Beale, *The Book of Revelation: A Commentary On the Greek Text* (Carlisle, Cumbria: Eerdmans, 1999), 1016.
26 Christopher C. Rowland, "The Book of Revelation: Introduction, Commentary, and Reflections," in *The New Interpreter's Bible*, Vol. 12, 709.
27 Strecker, *Theology of the New Testament*, 543.
28 "Even if Christianity has come to be identified with a spiritual messianism, there are important strands in the history of Christianity that bear witness to a political messianism akin to that which is characteristic of Judaism. Both forms of messianism are endemic to Christianity. There are *significant strands* with the New Testament that exhibit the 'chiliastic mentality.'" Rowland, "The Book of Revelation," 709, emphasis mine.
29 E.C. Dewick, "Eschatology: The Jewish Background of Ideas," in James Hastings, John A. Selbie, and John C. Lambert, eds., *Dictionary of the Apostolic Church* (New York: C. Scribner's Sons, 1916), 354.
30 Even Augustine claimed that the millennial reign of Christ, a time after the Church era but prior to the general resurrection, was allowable, provided that the saints enjoyed spiritual privilege and not carnal privilege. Augustine, *The City of God*, XX, 7. For others who see John's words as intentionally literal based on an early Jewish–Christian understanding of the millennium, see Walvoord, *The Millennial Kingdom*, 219; Beale, *The Book of Revelation*, 1018; and George Eldon Ladd, Robert G. Clouse and Anthony A. Hoekema, *The Meaning of the Millennium: Four Views* (Downers Grove, IL: IVP Academic, 1977), 67–68. For an excellent defense of the Millenialist view of Revelation 20, see Craig A. Blaising, "A Premillennial Response to Robert B. Strimple," in S.N. Gundry and D.L. Bock, eds., *Three Views on the Millennium and Beyond* (Grand Rapids, MI: Zondervan, 2010), 150–155.
31 Daniel I. Block, *The Book of Ezekiel: Ch. 25–38*, Vol. 2 (Grand Rapids, MI: Eerdmans, 1998), 492.
32 J. Webb Mealy, *After the Thousand Years* (Journal for the Study of the New Testament Supplement) (Sheffield: Sheffield Books, 1992), 231.
33 John D. Ladd, *Commentary on the Book of Enoch* (Maitland, FL: Xulon Press, 2008), 323; 144. Ladd states that *Barnabas 13: 3–5* along with several passages in *I Enoch*,

Millenarianism explored 107

were interpreted in early Christianity, uniformly, as referencing the Thousand Year reign of Jesus. Also, in *I Enoch*, the fallen angel Azazel is described as being bound and cast into a dark abyss (Cf. I Enoch 10:4–6; 12–13; 88:1–3; 90:25, and 54:1–6).

34 The term "first resurrection" in this passage implies that there will be another, later resurrection, as the narrative unfolds. Some scholars, following the later Augustine, view the "first resurrection" as applying to living Christians as a "resurrection of the soul," while the second resurrection is the general resurrection of the bodies of the dead. See W.A. Jurgens, *The Faith of the Early Fathers*, Vol. 3 (Collegeville: Liturgical Press, 1998), 103.

35 Mealy adds that ". . . consistent both with previous and with subsequent promises in Revelation, the kingdom over which the resurrected 'saints'" (20:6) were to reign for the millennium was interpreted as the realm of creation, as at the beginning of the world (cf. Genesis. 1:26–28; Revelation 5:10). Thus, the saints/martyrs are to reign from Jerusalem, over all the created order. Mealy, *After the Thousand Years*, 238.

36 Mealy, *After the Thousand* Years, 16. Further, Thomas, writing on the four sense of Scripture, insists that a literal interpretation of any given doctrinal text, particularly Scripture, may be used to prove a doctrine, provided that the plain sense of the text is not diminished by an obviously allegorical character within the passage as a whole or its surrounding context: "In Holy Writ no confusion results, for all the senses are founded on one—the literal—*from which alone can any argument be drawn, and not from those intended in* allegory" (*ST* I:1:10 ad 1).

37 Joseph L. Trafton, *Reading Revelation: A Literary and Theological Commentary*, rev. ed. (Macon, GA: Smyth & Helwys Publishing, 2005), 187.

38 Timo Eskola, *Messiah and the Throne: Jewish Merkabah Mysticism and Early Christian Exaltation Discourse* (Tübingen: Abm Komers, 2001), 12.

39 J.D. Hays, J.S. Duvall, and C.M. Pate, eds., *Dictionary of Biblical Prophecy and End Times* (Grand Rapids, MI: Zondervan, 2009), 165. Some commentaries suggest that the 24 elders represent the 24 cycles of Aaronic priests, but many also suggest that it is indicative of the 12 tribes of Israel and the 12 apostles together, as a composite. See James L. Resseguie, *Revelation Unsealed: A Narrative Critical Approach to John's Apocalypse* (Boston, MA: Brill Academic, 1998), 68.

40 Connecting those on the throne with the 144,000 of Revelation 7, Moltmann makes the following statement: ". . . the 'Thousand Years' empire' of Revelation 7 and 20 must then be conceived of—in spite of the anti-Jewish utterances in Rev. 2.9, 3.9., and 11.8—as *the messianic kingdom of Jews and Christians*." Moltmann, *The Coming of God*, 198, emphasis mine.

41 Brian K. Blount, *Revelation: A Commentary* (Louisville, KY: Westminster John Knox, 2009), 90.

42 J. Massyngberde Ford, *Revelation* (New York: Doubleday, 1995), 73.

43 In Revelation 7:13, one of the 24 elders asks John who those described as a ". . . great multitude that no one could count, from every nation, tribe, people and language, standing before the throne and before the Lamb." This group, obviously representative of the Gentiles who came through the Tribulation, is set off as a distinct group from the 24 elders. This does not necessarily mean that the 24 elders are Jews who are not part of the Church, but it is a possibility, as the exact identity of the 24 is "unclear." Resseguie, *Revelation Unsealed*, 68.

44 Jacques B. Doukhan, *Secrets of Revelation: The Apocalypse through Hebrew Eyes* (Hagerstown, MD: Review & Herald Publishing, 2002), 56.

45 See *Tob* 12:12, 15; *Test. Levi* 3:5–7; *Test. Dan* 6:2; *I En.* 9:3; 40:6; *3 Bar* 11:4; and *Apoc. Paul* 7–10.

46 Beale, *The Book of Revelation*, 324.

47 A. Feuillet, *Johannine Studies* (New York: Alba House, 1965), 214.

108 *Millenarianism: valid Church history*

48 See *Sifre* Num. §92; *m.'Aboth* 6:8; *b. Baba Bathra* 10b; *b. Aboth* 6:8; and *Kallah Rabbati* 54a–b.
49 Beale, *The Book of Revelation*, 324. See *Midr. Rab.* Exod. 5:12; *Midr. Rab* Lev. 11:8; and *Midr. Rab* Eccles. 1.11, §1.
50 Herman A. Hoyt, *Studies in Revelation* (Quezon City, Philippines: BMH Books, 2006).
51 See James M. Scott, ed., *Restoration: Old Testament, Jewish, and Christian Perspectives* (Boston, MA: Brill Academic, 2001), 476.
52 Modern biblical scholarship points to a connection between Luke 22:29–30 and Zechariah 14:9: ". . . and the Lord shall be *king over all the earth*." See Joel Marcus, *The Way of the Lord: Christological Exegesis of the Old Testament in the Gospel of Mark* (New York: T&T Clark International, 2004), 157.
53 Walck, "The Son of Man in the Parables of Enoch and the Gospels," 322–324.
54 "Millennialism" in Geoffrey W. Bromiley, ed., *The International Standard Bible Encyclopedia*, 4 Vols. (Grand Rapids, MI: Eerdmans, 1995), 357.
55 This word is to be rendered as "restoration," on the analogy of Josephus. See Josephus, *Ant.* 11.66.
56 W.D. Davies and Dale C. Allison, *A Critical and Exegetical Commentary on the Gospel According to Saint Matthew* (London: T&T Clark International, 2004), 60–63. Allison points out the strikingly "*chiliastic* generalization" expressed in the Matthean passage above, borrowed from Jewish Apocalyptic, yet expressed in an explicit way in the Book of Revelation.
57 William Kurz, *What Does the Bible Say About the End Times?: A Catholic View* (Cincinnati, OH: St. Anthony Messenger Press, 2004), 152–173. This text carries the *Nihil Obstat* and the *Imprimi Potest*. It is significant to point out that the amillennialist view is the modern expression of Roman Catholic eschatology. Early Christianity espoused millennialism as its original eschatology, and the amillennialist position held now by most Catholics, though introduced by Eusebius and Augustine, was not more formally codified until recently. Donald W. Wuerl, *The Teaching of Christ: A Catholic Catechism for Adults*, 5th ed. (Huntington, IN: Our Sunday Visitor, 2005), 480.
58 It is interesting to note that the contrast between the spiritual and the earthly kingdom gave rise to anti-Catholic rhetoric during the time of the Reformation. For example, the Geneva Bible reads that ". . . as the kingdom of Christ is from heaven and bringeth men thither: so the Pope's kingdome is of the earth and leadeth to perdition (note on Revelation 13:11).
59 For support of the claim that Catholic theology upholds amillennialism and the view that the first resurrection of Revelation 20 is referring to an individual's conversion to Christ and the Church while they are alive on earth, see Walvoord, *The Millennial Kingdom*, 105.
60 Matt Waymeyer, *Revelation 20 and the Millennial Debate* (Woodlands, TX: Kress Christian Publications, 2004), 34. Cf. Sydney H.T. Page, "Revelation 20 and Pauline Eschatology," *Journal of the Evangelical Theological Society* 23, no. 1 (March 1980): 31–43.
61 Waymeyer, *Revelation 20*, 39.
62 Charles Lee Feinberg, *Millennialism: The Two Major Views*, 3rd ed. (Chicago, IL: BMH Books, 1985), 335.
63 Waymeyer, *Revelation 20*, 38.
64 Alva J. McClain, *Greatness of the Kingdom* (Winona Lake, IN: BMH Books, 1974), 488.
65 B. Knepper, *Satan Bound: or Resurrection, Judgment and the Happiness of the Future World Considered* (State College, PA: Pennsylvania State University Press, 1860), 22.

66 Scholarship suggests that Paul is pulling, in this text, from the earliest eschatological ideas of the Jesus movement, namely, the concept of resurrection concurrent to and following the Parousia. Colin R. Nicholl, *From Hope to Despair in Thessalonica: Situating 1 and 2 Thessalonians* (New York: Cambridge University Press, 2004), 40. On Paul and the two resurrections of 1 Thessalonians, see W.D. Davies, *Paul and Rabbinic Judaism: Some Rabbinic Elements in Pauline Theology*, 4th ed. (Philadelphia, PA: Fortress Press, 1980), 289.

67 Robert H. Mounce, *The Book of Revelation*, rev. ed. (Grand Rapids, MI: Eerdmans, 1998), 364, emphasis in original. For a rebuttal of Alford, suggesting that the first resurrection of Revelation 20 is spiritual, and a subsequent and authoritative response to that same rebuttal, see Beale, *The Book of Revelation*, 1005–1006. Beale states that even if the first resurrection of Revelation 20 refers to a spiritual resurrection, verses 4–6 speak of a historical period *immediately prior* to the consummation (Beale, *The Book of Revelation*, 1009).

68 See Anthony C. Garland, *A Testimony of Jesus Christ: A Commentary on the Book of Revelation*, vol. 2 (Hustisford, WI: SpiritandTruth, 2007), 310.

69 That which is important for contemporary millenarians like Moltmann is not the length of time associated with this reign (a literal thousand years), but that the period of time is *not* to be viewed as synonymous with the Church era.1 Moltmann states, "If [the] Christian Imperium is interpreted as the "thousand-year Reich," then the saints must reign with Christ and judge the nations. In the millennium, resistance to Christ cannot be tolerated. So in the Christian imperium sacrum there was no justice for dissidents, people of other beliefs—and Jews. Jürgen Moltmann, *The Way of Jesus Christ: Christology in Messianic Dimensions*, 1st Fortress Press ed. (Minneapolis, MN: Augsburg Fortress Publishers, 1995), 31.

70 "Millennialism," in *Eerdmans Dictionary of the Bible* (Amsterdam: Amsterdam University Press, 2000), 900.

71 Some scholars insist that Clement of Alexandria definitively rejected chiliastic thought. Though Clement was not a chiliast (in *Paedagogus I. vi. 2.8.3* he states that "the end is reserved till the resurrection of those who believe") there is no hint of a formal rebuttal of chiliasm in his work. Thus, up through the first quarter of the third century, chiliasm went unchallenged.

72 George E. Ladd, *Crucial Questions about the Kingdom of God* (Grand Rapids, MI: Eerdmans, 1952), 23.

73 "Allegorical methods, adopted by the third-century Origen, led Augustine to develop the amillennial view—that Jesus was to rule *spiritually* rather that literally. This view ultimately became the dominant view of the Roman Catholic Church." Chuck Missler, *Prophecy 20/20: Profiling the Future through the Lens of Scripture* (Nashville, TN: Thomas Nelson, 2006), 93.

74 Pasquini, *True Christianity: The Catholic Way* (Bloomington, IN: iUniverse, 2003), 134. Pasquini states that the Roman Catholic tradition rejects both premillennialism and postmillennialism.

75 Mark Saucy, *Kingdom of God and the Teaching of Jesus: In 20th Century Theology*. Dallas, TX: W Publishing Group, 1997, 98.

76 Roy B. Zuck, *Vital Prophetic Issues: Examining Promises and Problems in Eschatology* (Grand Rapids, MI: Kregel Academic & Professional, 1995), 74–75.

77 Waymeyer, *Revelation 20*, 61.

78 "Does Revelation 20:1–10 refer to the present age?" in Zuck, *Vital Prophetic Issues*, 74.

79 Ronald L. Farmer, *Revelation* (St Louis, MO: Christian Board of Publication, 2006), 124.

80 Mounce, *Revelation*, 361. See Mounce's argument based on the previous work of Walvoord.

81 M. Eugene Boring, *Revelation: Interpretation: A Bible Commentary for Teaching and Preaching* (Louisville, KY: Westminster John Knox Press, 2011), 203.
82 Ralph E. Bass Jr., *Back to the Future* (Little Rock, AR: Living Hope Press, 2004), 432.
83 "In the Old Testament era, the nations were in darkness, but the redemptive work of Christ and the binding of Satan 'paved the way for successful proclamation of the gospel throughout the world.'" Sam Hamstra, "An Idealist View of Revelation." In C. Marvin Pate and general editor, *Four Views on the Book of Revelation* (Grand Rapids, MI: Zondervan, 1998), 120.
84 Cf. http://www.catholic.com/tracts/the-rapture.
85 Waymeyer, *Revelation 20*, 18.
86 George J. Brooke, *Dead Sea Scrolls and NT Cloth* (Minneapolis, MN: Augsburg Fortress Publishers, 2005), 33.
87 Beale, *The Book of Revelation*, 504.
88 J.W. Bailey, "The Temporary Messianic Reign in the Literature of Early Judaism," *Journal of Biblical Literature* 53, no. 2 (1934): 170–187, at 174–175.
89 H.B.F.L. Kramer, *The Book of Destiny: An Open Statement of the Authentic and Inspired Prophecies of the Old and New Testament* (Rockford, IL: Tan Books and Publishers, 1975), 101, emphasis mine.
90 Cf. A. Schweitzer, and J. Bowden, *The Quest of the Historical Jesus* (Minneapolis, MN: Fortress Press, 2001); Dodd, *The Parables of the Kingdom*.
91 See further J. Jeremias, *The Parables of Jesus* (Norwich: SCM, 2004), and N. Perrin, *The Kingdom of God in the Teaching of Jesus* (Norwich: SCM Press, 1963).
92 E.P. Sanders, *Jesus and Judaism* (Minneapolis, MN: Fortress Press, 1985), 340. Marcus Borg argues that *most* scholars today do not believe that Jesus expressed an expectation of the world's end in his own day. In light of the most contemporary scholarship, this statement becomes increasingly debatable. See M.J. Borg, *Jesus, a New Vision: Spirit, Culture, and the Life of Discipleship* (San Francisco, CA: Harper, 1987), 14.
93 Allison, *Jesus of Nazareth: Millenarian Prophet*, 48.
94 D.B. Gowler, *What Are They Saying about the Historical Jesus?* (Mahwah, NJ: Paulist Press, 2007), 74–75, emphasis mine.
95 Allison, *Jesus of Nazareth: Millenarian Prophet*, 149.
96 For example, contemporary Jehovah's Witness, or more fundamentalist fringe groups such as the "Cargo Cults." See G.W. Trompf, ed., *Cargo Cults and Millenarian Movements: Transoceanic Comparisons of New Religious Movements* (New York: Mouton De Gruyter, 1990). Historical, Patristic millenarianism is distinct from these contemporary groups, both in literary content and views of history.
97 G. Vermes, *The Religion of Jesus the Jew* (Minneapolis, MN: Fortress Press, 1993), 150–151. Vermes likewise points out that Paul, in Colossians 4:11, makes reference to Jews ("men of circumcision") who are Paul's "fellow workers for the kingdom of God." This language is quite different from later supersessionist readings of the kingdom in relation to Jew and Gentile.
98 Eugen Weber, *Apocalypses: Prophecies, Cults, and Millennial Beliefs through the Ages* (Cambridge, MA: Harvard University Press, 2000), 155.
99 Timothy Wardle, *The Jerusalem Temple and Early Christian Identity* (Tübingen: Error, 2010), 223–224.
100 David Van Meter, *The Apocalyptic Year 1000: Religious Expectation and Social Change, 950–1050*, ed. Richard Landes, Andrew Gow, and David C. Van Meter (New York: Oxford University Press, 2003), 246.
101 T.G. Darling, "The *Apostle Paul and the Second Advent*," *PTR*, 2 (1904), 197–214.
102 Robert Gnuse states that "the New Testament contains a wide range of millennialist texts. These include numerous passages in the apostle Paul's letters . . ." Robert Gnuse,

"Ancient Near Eastern Millennialism," in Catherine Wessinger, ed., *The Oxford Handbook of Millennialism* (New York: Oxford University Press, 2011), 140. Likewise, Albert Schweitzer held a firm belief that Paul was influenced by Jewish Apocalyptic and espoused a unique form of millennialism. Albert Schweitzer, *The Mysticism of Paul the Apostle*, Johns Hopkins paperbacks ed. (Baltimore, MD: The Johns Hopkins University Press, 1998), 94.

103 For more on the connection between 1 Thessalonians and millennialism, see Robert Jewett, *The Thessalonian Correspondence: Pauline Rhetoric and Millenarian Piety* (Philadelphia, PA: Fortress Press, 1986).

104 Robert D. Culver, "A Neglected Millennial Passage from Saint Paul," *Bibliotheca Sacra*, 113, no. 450, April, 1956, 142.

105 Ralph Allen Smith, "The Eschatological Debate: 'A Neglected Millennial passage from St. Paul,'" found at http://www.berith.org/essays/cor/, accessed November 30, 2011. Cf. Frederic Louis Godet, *Commentary on First Corinthians* (Grand Rapids, MI: Kregal, reprint, 1977), 787.

106 Zuck, *Vital Prophetic Issues*, 73.

107 H. Lietzmann, *An die Korinther I, II* (Tübingen: Mohr-Siebeck, 1931), 80.

108 Ben Witherington, *The Indelible Image: The Theological and Ethical Thought World of the New Testament* (Downers Grove, IL: IVP Academic, 2010), 226, n. 32.

109 J. Paul Sampley, "The First Letter to the Corinthians: Introduction, Commentary, and Reflections," in *The New Interpreter's Bible*, Vol. 10, 980.

110 Ibid., 981.

111 See Robert A. Morey, *The End of the World according to Jesus* (Maitland, FL: Xulon Press, 2010), 159.

112 Larry W. Hurtado, *The Earliest Christian Artifacts: Manuscripts and Christian Origins* (Grand Rapids, MI: Eerdmans, 2006), 128.

113 See the connection between the citing of Psalm 110 in the NT, the Book of Enoch, and Jesus' millennialist understanding of a future political kingdom based on Jewish Apocalyptic in Risa Levitt Kohn and Rebecca Moore, *A Portable God: The Origin of Judaism and Christianity* (Lanham, MD: Rowman & Littlefield Publishers, 2007), 167–169.

114 David R. Anderson, *The King-Priest of Psalm 110 in Hebrews* (New York: Peter Lang Publishing, 2001), i.

115 R. Fowler White, "Agony, Irony, and Victory in Inaugurated Eschatology: Reflections on the Current Amillennial-Postmillennial Debate," *Westminster Theological Seminary* 62, no. 2 (2000): 161–176, at 163.

116 Robert L. Saucy, *The Case for Progressive Dispensationalism: The Interface between Dispensational & Non-Dispensational Theology* (Grand Rapids, MI: Zondervan Publishing House, 1993), 290.

117 Hendrikus Berkhof, *Christ the Meaning of History* (Eugene, OR: Wipf & Stock, 2004), 167.

118 Joost Holleman, *Resurrection and Parousia: A Traditio-Historical Study of Paul's Eschatology in I Corinthians 15* (Leiden: Brill Academic, 1996), 35–40.

119 "The Millennial Kingdom," in James L. Mays, *The HarperCollins Bible Commentary*, rev. ed. (San Francisco, CA: HarperOne, 2000), 1200.

120 Walter C. Kaiser, "The Two Resurrections in I Corinthians 15:22–24," in *What's So Important about Pre-Millennialism*, found at http://www.walterckaiserjr.com/Israel%20and%20pre-millennialism.html, accessed December 20, 2011.

121 Gerald F. Hawthorne, *Word Biblical Commentary*, Vol. 43: *Philippians* (Nashville, TN: Thomas Nelson, 1983), 50.

122 Veronica Koperski, *The Knowledge of Christ Jesus My Lord: The High Christology of Philippians 3:7–11* (Kampen, the Netherlands: Peeters Publishers, 1996), 276–277.

123 Oscar Cullmann, *Immortality of the Soul or Resurrection of the Dead?: The Witness of the New Testament* (Eugene, OR: Wipf & Stock, 2000), 52–55.
124 Randall E. Otto, "The Resurrection in Jürgen Moltmann" *JETS* 35/1 (March 1992), 81–90, at 82. Moltmann was primarily concerned with rooting the idea of two resurrections in Pauline Scripture and not solely in Revelation 20. See Moltmann, *The Coming of God*, 150–151, 194–195. Dewick claims that Paul's eschatology is "completely Judaic (read millenarian) in form." E.C. Dewick, "Eschatology" in Hastings, *Dictionary of the Apostolic Church*, 362. Otto writes that the "Johannine doctrine of two resurrections (John 5:29) was known also to Paul." Ottos as quoted in Fredrik Lindgård, *Paul's Line of Thought in 2 Corinthians 4:16–15:10* (Tübingen: J.C.B. Mohr (P. Siebeck), 2005), 362.
125 Moisés Silva, *Philippians*, 2nd ed. (Grand Rapids, MI: Baker Academic, 2005), 168. The only Old Testament text associated with Philippians 3:11 is Hosea 6:3, a possible connection to early (8th century B.C.E.) Jewish eschatological thought: "Let us acknowledge the LORD; let us press on to acknowledge him. As surely as the sun rises, *he will appear*; he will come to us like the winter rains, like the spring rains that water the earth." Some early manuscripts read that the Lord will appear "in the former and the latter times," suggesting the possibility of a double advent.
126 John Albert Bengel, *Gnomon of the New Testament* (Cambridge, MA: Harvard University Press, 1862), 860, n. 25; Robert C. Tannehill, *Dying and Rising with Christ: A Study in Pauline Theology* (Eugene, OR: Wipf & Stock, 2006), 120.
127 Bauckham, *God will be All in All*, 144. Cf. R.H. Lightfoot, *Saint Paul's Epistle to the Philippians* (London: Macmillan, 1868), 151.
128 Ernst Lohmeyer, *Die Briefe an die Philiper an die Kolosser und an Philemon* (Göttingen: Vandenhoeck & Ruprecht, 1964), 141. Cf. H.M. Matter, *De brief can Paulus aan de Philippenzen en de brief aan Philemon* (Kampen: Kok, 1965), 86–87.
129 Moltmann, *The Coming of God*, 195. Lutheranism, to this day, is highly suspect of millenarianism and as some argue, chiliasm has been officially declared heretical by the Augsburg Confession—though the eschatological view has never been formally declared heresy in Roman Catholicism. Martin Luther's critique of chiliasm was directly related to his problems with Thomas Münzer, his chiliastic opponent during the Peasants' War. J.M. Porter, "Luther and Political Millenarianism: The Case of the Peasants' War," *Journal of the History of Ideas* 42, no. 3 (July—September, 1981), 389–406, at 389.
130 Thomas refutes this passage as a proof of true resurrection in addition to the general resurrection of the dead. Unknown to Thomas was the modern biblical scholarship that proves that the passage was original to the text of Matthew and not a later gloss. Thomas' argument likewise envisions a "resusitation of the dead," whereas the Greek points to a true resurrection of the dead. Likewise, Thomas argues that the Matthean writer was likely referring to a future resurrection, but again, proper exegesis of the text suggests otherwise: "Jerome, in a sermon on the Assumption [*Ep. x ad Paul. et Eustoch*, now recognized as spurious], seems to be doubtful of this resurrection of the saints with Christ, namely as to whether, having been witnesses to the resurrection, they died again, so that theirs was a resusitation (as in the case of Lazarus who died again) rather than a resurrection such as will be at the end of the world—or really rose again to immortal life, to live forever in the body, and to ascend bodily into heaven with Christ, as a gloss says on Mat. 27:52. The latter seems more probable, because, as Jerome says, in order that they might bear true witness to Christ's true resurrection, it was fitting that they should truly rise again. Nor was their resurrection hastened for their sake, but for the sake of bearing witness to Christ's resurrection: and that by bearing witness thereto they might lay the foundation of the faith of the New Testament: wherefore it was more fitting that it should be borne by the fathers of the Old Testament, than by those who died after the foundation of the

Millenarianism explored 113

New. It must, however, be observed that, although the Gospel mentions their resurrection before Christ's, we must take this statement as made in anticipation, as is often the case with writers of history." Thomas Aquinas, *Summa Theologia*, III, Q.77, A. 2, found at http://www.ccel.org/ccel/aquinas/summa. XP.iii.XP_Q77.XP_ Q77_A1. html?highlight=millenarian#highlight accessed on June 16, 2012. Ambrose of Milan pictures the resurrection of Matthew 27 to be a true, physical resurrection and not resuscitation. See Ambrose, *On Belief in the Resurrection*, ii., 83–84, found at http://www. monachos.net/content/patristics/patristictexts/73?start=1.

131 "Should we . . . understand that the framers of the Didache envisioned the resurrection of the righteous—one at the death of Jesus and one prior to the coming of the Lord upon the clouds?" Milavec, *The Didache: Faith, Hope, & Life of the Earliest Christian Communities*, 733.

132 See D.A. Hagner, "Apoclayptic Motifs in the Gospel of Matthew: Continuity and Discontinuity" *HBT* 7 (1985), 56.

133 This pericope in Matthew is common to all extant copies and was not a later interpolation. For an excellent summary of the text, see Daniel M. Gurtner, *The Torn Veil: Matthew's Exposition of the Death of Jesus* (New York: Cambridge University Press, 2007), 150–152, esp. 150, n. 55 and 151, n. 60.

134 M. Eugene Boring, "The Gospel of Matthew: Introduction, Commentary, and Reflections," in *The New Interpreter's Bible*, 493, n. 599.

135 Jürgen Moltmann, *Theology of Hope: On the Ground and the Implications of a Christian Eschatology*, 1st Fortress Press ed. (Minneapolis, MN: Fortress Press, 1993), 86. Thus, Moltmann agrees with W. Kreck that millennialism helps to ward off the temptation for eschatological constructs to become saturated in Docetism. W. Kreck, *Die Zukunft Des Gekommenen: Grundprobleme Der Eschatologie* (Evang: Verlagsanstalt, 1968).

136 Moltmann, *The Coming of God*, 193.

137 Pablo T. Gadenz, *Called from the Jews and from the Gentiles: Pauline Ecclesiology in Romans 9–11* (Tübingen: Error, 2009), 322–323. For the point that millennialism was a major aspect of Jewish restoration eschatology, see H. Wayne House, ed., *Israel, the Land and the People: An Evangelical Affirmation of God's Promises* (Grand Rapids, MI: Kregel, 1998), 149–151. Bagatti suggests that both millennial expectation and the concept of multiple resurrections were common among Jews and Christians immediately after the time of Christ. B. Bagatti, *The Church from the Circumcision: History and Archaeology of the Judaeo-Christians* (Jerusalem: Franciscan Press, 1971), 11, 92.

4 Millenarianism and early Church tradition*

It is almost a foregone conclusion in Roman Catholic theological circles that millenarianism is an eschatology that for centuries has been outside the parameters of acceptable belief, at least in non-Protestant Churches. By contrast, we intend to show that millenarianism was not merely a "tolerated" viewpoint among early Christians—it was held uniformly until a very specific point in the middle of the third century. Further, millenarianism was a part of the apostolic deposit defended by its proponents—an eschatological reality passed down by Jesus, the Apostles, the Fathers, and the early bishops of the Church, over wide geographical areas. In the sections that follow, we will illustrate these points: the post-apostolic and Ante-Nicene Fathers claimed that chiliasm was apostolic tradition, chiliasm was normative and universally held until the third century, contemporary attempts to prove otherwise are problematic, Justin Martyr, Papias, and Irenaeus bear testimony representative of the whole of early Christianity on behalf of chiliasm as original eschatology, and finally, the primary opponents of chiliasm—appearing 250 years into the history of the Christian Church—were predominately, though not exclusively, heretical.

Millenarianism as orthodox eschatology

Paula Fredriksen writes that:

> Millenarianism cohered effortlessly with the points and principles in proto-orthodox doctrine. Its emphasis on bodily resurrection and historical redemption, and its focus on Jerusalem, in particular, resonated with these orthodox Churches' affirmation of Christ's incarnation, his bodily resurrection, and the physical resurrection of believers.[1]

Justin Martyr in his *Dialogue with Trypho* makes clear that millenarianism is a perfectly orthodox belief, held by a wide range of early Church persons,[2] yet Thomas Falls, in a note on the translation of Justin's text makes the following claim: "The belief in the millennium was not as general as Justin's words imply. The only other early supporters of this doctrine were Papias of Hierapolis and Irenaeus."[3] Falls' assessment is incorrect. Among the apostolic and later Fathers, both Latin and Greek through the early fourth century, in addition to Papias (d.~120), Justin (d. 165), and Irenaeus, we see pre-millenarian testimony or influence in Clement of Rome (d. ~99),[4] Pseudo-Barnabas,[5] Hegesippus (~110–180),[6] Julius Africanus (ca.160–ca. 240),[7] Pothinus (d.~177) the martyr from Lyons,[8] Melito of Sardis (d.~180),[9] the Egyptian bishop Nepos,[10] Polycrates of Ephesus,[11] Tertullian (d. 225) prior to his Montanist period,[12] Hippolytus (d. 235),[13] Cyprian (d. 258),[14] Lactantius (d.~320),[15] Victorinus,[16] Commodian,[17] Methodius of Olympus (d. 311),[18] Ambrosiaster (~366),[19] and several others.[20] Another noteworthy proponent is St. Ephrem the Syrian, the fourth-century doctor of the Church, whom Jerome "classified . . . as millenarian."[21] In addition to the evidence gleaned from well-respected early theologians, various pieces of non-textual evidence have surfaced, many of which point to chiliastic expectation in the earliest Christian communities: ". . . studying funeral monuments [of early Christians] we find ourselves face to face with very many signs which lead us to millenarian iconographic repertoire . . ."[22]

Theophorus (Ignatius), pupil of Peter and John, never in detail described chiliasm as an eschatology, but often referred to the kingdom as an imminent reality, utilizing language that mimicked patterns found in early chiliastic writings. The writer of "The Shepherd," Hermas, is said to espouse millenarian ideas.[23] Other scholars see millenarian emphases in the *Didache* (50–70 C.E.), specifically because of its use of Jewish ethical and eschatological categories, with the consummation viewed as taking place within end-time history. The *Didache*'s end-time scenario saw history's ". . . consummation to be a restored material creation . . ."[24] Likewise, the *Didache* appears to directly subscribe to a chiliastic understanding,[25] specifically of resurrection:

> And then shall appear the signs of the truth: first, the sign of an outspreading in heaven, then the sign of the sound of the trumpet. And third, the resurrection of the dead—*yet not of all*, but as it is said: "The Lord shall come and all His saints with Him." Then shall the world see the Lord coming upon the clouds of heaven.[26]

Some scholars take the above passage as a reference to a chiliastic chronology espousing two resurrections—one for the saints at the coming of Christ,[27] and one general resurrection after Christ's reign. In the *Didache*, there is no mention whatsoever of a Day of Judgment at the coming of Christ. Others see the pointedly chiliastic form of the prayers for the eschatological gathering of Israel in chapters 9–10 of the *Didache* as a sign of the millenarian scope of the entire document.[28] The Eucharistic prayers, particularly in ch. 9, point to common features in early Jewish–Christian chiliastic texts[29]—the sharp division between the kingdom of God on earth and the Church, which will be gathered into the kingdom at the eschatological, earthly reign of Christ.[30] Chiliastic leanings are most likely present in Polycarp (d. 155), bishop of Smyrna and disciple of the Apostle John,[31] insofar as Irenaeus, a chiliast, was his pupil and borrowed eschatological concepts extensively from him.[32] Polycarp's eschatology, overall, cannot be firmly affiliated with either a chiliastic or amillenarian view.[33] Nevertheless, Polycarp's influence on Irenaeus is significant in determining how eschatology was passed down from mentor to pupil,[34] and there is no documentation that illustrates bishops as early as Polycarp ever refuted chiliasm or offered an alternative to it.[35] After exhaustive research, and convinced that millenarianism was the normative view of the apostolic Fathers, the seventeenth-century theologian Joseph Mede wrote: "... the dogma of the thousand years regnum was the general opinion of all orthodox Christians in the age immediately following the apostles ... and none were known to deny it but heretics ... This was why Irenaeus ardently maintained it in his book *Contra Heresies* and Tertullian against the Marcionites."[36] To this day, the Ethiopian Orthodox Church affirms chiliastic eschatology, following the model of St. Giyorgis of Sagla as codified in his work entitled *Metshafe Mestir*,[37] and the chiliastic line of thought in *Enochic literature*, which they view as canonical.

One of the earliest extant sources for chiliasm comes from the writings of Papias,[38] "... an ancient man, who was a hearer of John, and a friend of Polycarp."[39] Papias claims that he received his chiliastic eschatology directly from the Apostle John,[40] describing the 'Thousand Years' era of peace in detail, while insisting on the apostolic origin of the view.[41] Several modern scholars claim that Papias' account is accurate, handing down a tradition that was normative in the apostolic community[42]—"... a weighty testimony to primitive Christian eschatological beliefs."[43] Philip Schaff makes the same claim in the following terms: "Papias, and *most of his contemporaries* [maintained] the pre-millenarian views which were subsequently abandoned as Jewish dreams by the Catholic Church."[44] Those contemporaries of Papias that Schaff does not mention were not amillennialists—they were simply silent on the issue of the interpretation of Revelation 20.

Irenaeus of Lyons (d. 202 C.E.), too is known for his embrace of chiliastic eschatology,[45] namely as he used it to combat the rejection of the bodily resurrection and created matter, and the dualistic tendencies in Gnosticism.[46] Modern scholars, uncomfortable with Irenaeus' eschatology, claim either that it surfaced solely in service to his polemic against the Gnostics,[47] or portray it as 'an honest mistake.'[48] A more reasonable understanding of the chiliastic ending of *Against Heresies* is achieved if we attribute, "... the chiliasm of Irenaeus to his high respect for tradition, the 'rule of faith.'"[49] Irenaeus refers to apostolic tradition when he defends chiliasm against the Gnostics, and he warns that anyone who rejects both the bodily resurrection and the literal "millennial" reign of Christ are to be considered heretics.[50] Irenaeus strongly emphasized the importance of apostolic succession, the succession of presbyters, and significantly, the role of the bishops in safely guiding the interpretation of Scripture and the guardianship of apostolic doctrine, which for him, included millenarianism.[51] The lack of a consistent, orchestrated rebuttal of Irenaeus' chiliastic eschatology until late into the third century suggests that its roots were apostolic,[52] while its replacement was a later development.

Overall, we see a stream of millenarian tradition within the first few centuries of the Church, yet what is conspicuously missing is a parallel stream of amillennial thought. There is no evidence of an early, competing alternative to chiliasm.[53] A non-chiliastic concept of the eschaton and interpretation of Revelation 20 does not appear in the writings of early Christians until late in the second century and do not enter into the consciousness of the Church until about 170 C.E., rooted in the ideas of Marcion. Though there were some heretical sects, such as the Montanists, who later held to severely distorted versions of the otherwise apostolic chiliasm, the eschatology is found firmly rooted in orthodox apostolic tradition.[54]

Responding to the refutation of chiliastic normativity

In 2001, a book by Charles Hill was published under the title *Regnum Coelorum* (the Kingdom of Heaven). In it, Hill, the first scholar of the contemporary period to dispute the normativity of chiliasm in the first three centuries of Christianity, suggests that there were two lines of apocalyptic thought that vied almost equally in the apostolic period—a chiliastic view that conceived of two resurrections and an earthly reign of Christ prior to final judgment, and an amillennialist view which conceived of souls entering heaven immediately upon death, with no millennial kingdom.[55] The text argues for the existence of a formalized, amillennial eschatology in *all* centuries prior to Origen, Tyconius, and Augustine. Hill states that ". . . a solidly entrenched and conservative, non-chiliastic eschatology was present in the Church to *rival chiliasm from beginning to end*."[56]

The problem with Hill's thesis is twofold. First, in order to have a "rivalry," one must see definitive, long-standing, competing eschatologies from the time of the apostles through the fourth century. By contrast, scholarship shows either a wide level of chiliasm, or silence in the first century into the late second century of the Christian witness.[57] There are no documents that consider chiliasm problematic prior to the mid third century, and there are no documents that espouse a specific eschatology identifiable with amillennialism, traceable to that time either.[58] There is either strong support of chiliasm as the orthodox eschatology, or silence in the formalized, historical records until the time of Origen in the East and Augustine in the West, an opposition Erickson considers "early."[59] Cohn tells us that:

> the third century saw the *first* [formalized] attempt to discredit millenarianism, when Origen, perhaps the most influential of all theologians of the early Church, began to present the kingdom as an event which would take place not in space or time but only in the souls of believers.[60]

In what sense is historical opposition to millenarianism "early" when one considers that 250 years passed with almost perfect silence on the issue? How do scholars account for the nearly unanimous support for chiliasm in the early apostolic and early Ante-Nicene period?

The second problem with Hill's thesis has to do with the internal logic of his research. Hill claims that multiple early chiliasts believed that disembodied souls (with the exception of those of the martyrs, in some writers) would remain in Hades until the establishment of the millennial kingdom, forming *possible* links based on the influence of two writings: *II Baruch* and *IV Ezra*.[61] Using this "interpretive key," Hill makes the general claim that for Christians living in the Ante-Nicene period, ". . . belief that the Christian (or his soul or spirit) at the time of death departs to heaven where Christ is . . . ought to be counted as *evidence* of a non-chiliastic eschatology."[62] If the beliefs of the Ante-Nicene Christians regarding their views of "the intermediate state" is the *sole* marker for chiliastic versus non-chiliastic assent, Hill's thesis is spurious at best. Hill explains that his hermeneutic about the intermediate state vs. the immediate journey of the soul to heaven has unlocked the "key" to the minds of early chiliasts, illustrating that what really set them apart from the "amillennialists" of the second century was their belief in the intermediate state of the soul outside of heaven.[63] If Hill is correct, what of the evidence that belief in purgatory and prayers for the dead (borrowed from Judaism) was popular among some Ante-Nicene Fathers (though not universally held)?[64] What would be the point of praying for souls if they could not attain paradise from their sub-earthly, Sheol-like vaults until the millennium?

Hill emphasizes the idea that *most* chiliasts believed that disembodied souls occupied Hades as opposed to the witness of Revelation 6:9–11, which suggests that souls, particularly those of the martyrs, occupied a space beneath the altar of heaven, awaiting their resurrection and future reign with Christ.[65] Though there is some evidence to suggest that Irenaeus and other chiliasts wrote of souls awaiting resurrection in Hades (belief in an "intermediate state")[66] their interpretation did not preclude belief in the ability of the soul to enter heaven immediately, or preclude belief in a *purgatorial intermediate* state followed by admittance to heaven.[67] It is incorrect, as does Hill, to draw a stark contrast between the chiliasts that believed souls went directly to Hades, and (later) amillennialists, who believed souls went directly to heaven.[68]

Some of those amillennialists who came to deny the Thousand Years reign likewise denied that the soul immediately apprehended God in heaven upon death, again putting Hill's thesis in question. For example, Augustine, during his amillennialist period, in his *Sermon on the 36th Psalm*, claimed that "after this brief life, thou shalt not yet be where those are who hear the Lord's invitation at the end of the world." Again, in *City of God*, xii.9: ". . . the souls of the dead rest in secret habitations." Likewise, we see that ultimately some scholars argue that the chiliast ". . . Irenaeus lends no support to those who speak of the departed as always excluded from the vision of God until the resurrection and yet he teaches that they may already be in a place called Paradise."[69]

Overall, Andrew Chester states the following about Hill's assessment: "It is not clear . . . that Hill's argument disposes of chiliasm, or removes it from its position of central importance in the early Christian tradition, in the way that he implies. Thus, it is not incongruous or logically inconsistent to hold belief in a millennium along with that of an intermediate [purgatorial] state."[70] Further, some chiliasts believed not only in an intermediate state aside from Hades (what we would now refer to as 'purgatory') but also that many of the departed souls went directly to heaven. Thus, F. Stanley Jones also puts Hill's thesis into question, insofar as he produces evidence of chiliasts who believed that "when souls are separated from their bodies and long for God, they are born into his bosom"—suggesting immediate apprehension of God in heaven.[71] Thus, Hill's argument, which rests on the assumption that those who did not believe in an intermediate state within the first few centuries C.E. were amillennialists, and those who did were chiliasts, has been shown to be untenable. Likewise, some chiliasts believed that souls went directly to heaven—a belief that Hill claims drew a stark contrast between millennial and amillennial thought in the first several centuries of the Church. Evidence from the first two centuries, by contrast, suggests that no Christians from that time period held to what would now be discerned as amillennialism.

A proper way to understand the chiliastic interpretation is not that its adherents necessarily saw the millennium as a means for disembodied souls to move from Hades to Heaven, but that they saw a need for the martyrs to be given justice in the face of their oppressors during the interregnum period, within history, and that their expectations of the return of Christ were imminent. Hill's thesis is incorrect in asserting that the early and later chiliasts were hermeneutically forced to posit an earthly millennium to operate as a means for disembodied souls to make the move from Hades to Heaven, as many chiliasts, including Hermas,[72] Irenaeus,[73] Tertullian,[74] and Ambrose of Milan,[75] believed that a purgatorial cleansing could fulfill that function. Granted, Irenaeus, Tertullian, and Justin saw an initial conflict between claiming a future, earthly millennium for the martyrs, and the direct journey of the soul to heaven at the time of death.[76] Nevertheless, a subterranean waiting place for the souls of the departed was held by some *amillennialists* as well as some early chiliasts. Ambrose, who wrote during the fourth century, was a proponent of 'two resurrection eschatology,' suggesting he was a chiliast, wrote of a purgatorial cleansing, while at other times he simply wrote on the apprehension of heaven by the soul immediately upon death.[77] There is good evidence to show that Ambrose was borrowing these ideas from earlier sources, including chiliastic ones.[78]

Chiliasts likewise had a view of history that followed earlier Jewish conceptions of the "weeks" of history, followed by a "Sabbath rest," not necessarily adopting outright the concept of an intermediary space for souls apart from Christ.[79] Oftentimes, in order to allay the fears of a Christian usurpation of Roman authority, writers of the chiliastic ideology would clarify that they believed heaven itself, along with Christ and the martyrs, would come down to earth for the future reign, meaning they conceived of souls as already with Christ upon the initiation of the millennial kingdom. Overall, in spite of Hill's detailed research and fine contribution to the debate, his interpretive framework fails to show that amillennialism was an eschatological view that rivaled chiliasm in the early Church. As Glenn R. Kreider puts it: ". . . Hill's entire thesis seems to depend on his interpretive key. Without that key, he claims that drawing any conclusions is

Millenarianism and early Church tradition 121

difficult since the second and third-century Fathers are 'practically silent or seemingly ambiguous on the matter of millennialism.' (p. 6). Of course Hill is aware that interpreters find strong support for millennialism in the Fathers."[80] As H. Corrodi wrote, "at that time [up through the middle of the third century] the number and respectability of its [chiliasm's] supporters was not small."[81]

Another problem with Hill's assessment is that he categorizes many Fathers of the Ante-Nicene period (Clement of Rome, Ignatius of Antioch, Polycarp of Smyrna[82] [A Quartodeciman[83] and mentor of the chiliast Irenaeus], Hermas, and Melito of Sardis) as amillennialists, while their actual writings point to either explicit or implicit chiliastic leanings, or are completely silent on the issue.[84] For example, in his section on Clement of Rome, Hill invalidates his own case: ". . . we are left somewhat in the shadows of the relationship of his (Clement's) eschatology to chiliasm if we must rely solely on explicit statements about the resurrection or the kingdom."[85] Hill's work is riddled with such quotations, which makes his readers wonder if there is anything but circumstantial evidence in support of his thesis. On the other side, there are ample explicit statements about the resurrection and the kingdom' in the writings of the chiliastic Fathers (virtually all the Fathers prior to Origen), to support the thesis that chiliasm was the predominant, normative view of the early Church. I will quote at length the words of Donald Fairbairn, who summarizes our point well:

> First, there is clear evidence of chiliastic expectation in the early part of the patristic period. *Second, arguments that nonchiliastic eschatologies were also common during this period are largely based on silence*, but the silence of many second-century authors about an earthly kingdom can easily be explained without assuming that these authors held to a view other than premillennialism. Third, because there are no explicit rejections of chiliasm before the third century, one should regard the later prominence of amillennialism as a shift in patristic eschatology . . .[86]

The earliest detractors of chiliasm: Marcion, Gaius, Origen

Thus far, we have illustrated that millenarianism, with its roots in the New Testament, was considered not merely a valid eschatology in the first two and a half centuries of the Christian tradition—there was no other competing eschatology, because chiliasm was believed to be handed down from the Apostles. The question must then be posed as to when chiliasm began to be challenged, and why. The seventeenth-century theologian Joseph Mede wrote: ". . . the dogma of the thousand year regnum was the general opinion of all orthodox Christians in the age immediately following the apostles . . . and none were known to deny it but heretics . . . This was why Irenaeus ardently maintained it in his book *Contra Heresies* and Tertullian against the Marcionites."[87]

Marcion (~85–160), the heretical bishop of Sinope, rejected chiliasm[88] in light of his understanding of the god of the Old Testament, whom he named the "Demiurge," and to this god, Marcion dualistically ascribed creation of the material universe in stark contrast to the spiritualized God of Jesus Christ and the Church.[89] Chiliasm stressed the material nature of creation, the importance of bodily resurrection, continuity with Jewish eschatology, and made room for a future carnal kingdom for Old Testament saints—all of which was unacceptable in terms of Marcionite principles. Marcion's universal god of compassion and love was viewed as diametrically opposed to the old order of the covenant, to the point that Marcion discounted the entire Old Testament, rejected Jewish interpretations of religion, and sought to reinvent the Gospel of Luke. Thus, Marcion's rejection of what would become significant parts of the canon, along with his hermeneutic of salvation history, earned the censure of the chiliastists Justin,[90] Irenaeus[91] and Tertullian.[92] Marcion's aversion to chiliasm was rooted in his desire to reject the value of the material world, invert otherwise orthodox notions of bodily resurrection, and deny the importance of Christian principles, eschatological or otherwise, that remotely resembled the Second Temple Judaism from which they developed.

Though the Gnostic Marcionites were implicitly opposed to chiliasm during the decades of the early Church, a sect that flourished in the 170s in Asia Minor, the *alogia*, known for their rejection of Jesus as the divine *logos*, were the first open enemies of chiliasm in Church history.[93] In an effort to deny the excesses of the sect with which it competed geographically—the Montanists—the *alogia* went to the other extreme, rejecting the movement of the Holy Spirit entirely, and ultimately, consistent with their Gnostic roots, denying the incarnation of the divine Word of God. The *alogia*, like other Gnostic sects in history, focused on the disowning in the community of the "limitations" of the material order,[94] making chiliasm the group's enemy number one. In light of chiliasm's stress on eschatological community for society's oppressed outcasts (martyrs, and those wronged through religio-political oppression), and its insistence on the inherent value of the material order and its regeneration, the *alogia* waged a strategic attack on its adherents. Though historically unfounded, the *alogia* denied Johannine authorship of both the Gospel of John and Revelation, and began an accusation that would reverberate through future centuries of anti-chiliastic rhetoric: that the Book of Revelation was written by a heretic named Cerinthus.[95] Irenaeus faithfully kept to the chiliastic tradition he had received, using its main points to refute the Gnostic tendencies of both the Marcionites and the *alogia* sect.[96]

Perpetuating some of the accusations that originated in Asia Minor, Gaius of Rome, who flourished during the first quarter of the third century, attacked chiliasm relentlessly. Viewing Montanism as an affront to Roman ecclesial authority, Gaius waged a war against it, focused on propagating the rejection of an ambiguous aspect of Montanist belief that could be easily confused with traditional chiliasm—the expectation that the New Jerusalem would descend from the sky into Phrygia, where Montanus prophesied.[97] Along with the *alogia*, Gaius rejected the canonicity of the Book of Revelation[98]—for which the Roman writer ultimately gained the reputation as a heretic in the West[99]—and perpetuated the rumor that chiliasm was connected with the heterodox Cerinthus, who had Gnostic tendencies.[100] Gaius had an influence of Dionysius' more practical rejection of chiliasm, focused on what he thought was too trivial of a hope in a predominantly material kingdom of God.[101] Overall, Gaius is an important figure in the history of Christian eschatology, because there is virtually no evidence to suggest that Patristic authors, East or West, viewed chiliasm as associated with heresy, prior to his time.[102]

Origen Adamantius (ca. 185–253/254), adopting an almost exclusively allegorical and spiritualized hermeneutic,[103] was the first of the respected Patristic authors to reinterpret apocalyptic texts and imagery in an effort to debunk chiliasm.[104] Origen rejected the chiliastic interpretation of Scripture for two reasons: first because it was a "useless holdover from Judaism,"[105] and second because he believed only a "realized eschatology"[106] could portray Christ and the souls which make up the Church as the fulfillment of messianic hope. Though there are multiple examples of spiritualized eschatology in the New Testament, the dominant eschatology of the early Patristic period shifted so much vis-à-vis Origen's re-construal, that Eastern views of the kingdom became synonymous with "individual eschatology,"[107] in which ". . . prophecies about the future kingdom were fulfilled spiritually in the human soul."[108] In sum,

> Origen's allegorical interpretations, including his views on Bible prophecy, gained wide acceptance in the Church of his day. His influence, followed by Constantine's acceptance of Christianity and Augustine's teaching in the fourth century, are usually cited as the principle causes of premillennialism's eventual replacement by amillennial eschatology.[109]

Although chiliasm was validated by the fact that it was the normative eschatology of the Church for 250 years, Origen's influence is so widespread, even to this day, that Pope Emeritus Benedict XVI considers it one of only "three dimensions" of the Church Fathers' valid interpretations of the Kingdom of God.[110] Benedict mentions two others under the rubric of Tyconius and Augustine, while the obvious chiliastic authors who exclusively dominated the Church's eschatological view for two and a half centuries after the death of Jesus are ignored.

Notes

* A portion of this book chapter was originally published as "Newman's First Two Notes on Development and Patristic Millenarianism," in Newman Studies Journal 11, no. 2 (2014), Copyright © [2014]. Reproduced by permission of the National Institute for Newman Studies®, owner and publisher of Newman Studies Journal.

1 Paula Fredriksen, "The Diaspora Synagogue and the Origins of Christianity," in David S. Potter, ed., *A Companion to the Roman Empire* (Blackwell Companions to the Ancient World) (Boston, MA: Wiley-Blackwell, 2009), 604.

2 See Justin Martyr, *Dialogue with Trypho*, found at http://en.wikisource.org/wiki/Ante-Nicene_Fathers/Volume_I/JUSTIN_MARTYR/Dialogue_with_Trypho/Chapter_LXXX.

3 Thomas Falls, St. *Justin Martyr*, 277, n.5. Falls takes "early" here to mean the overall Christian legacy of the first three centuries.

4 It is said that Clement was the first pope, ordained by Peter as bishop (Tertullian, *De Praescript.*, xxxii; Jerome, *De Viris Illustribus*, 15). See also Justin, *Fragment XV*,

with commentary by Anastasias. Cf. Horatius Bonar, "The Apostolocity of Chiliasm," *The Quarterly Journal of Prophecy* 2 (April, 1850): 141–161, at 159.

5   *Epistle of Barnabas*, XV. James Carleton Paget, *The Epistle of Barnabas: Outlook and Background* (Tübingen: J.C.B. Mohr, 1994), 170.

6   Peters, *The Theocratic Kingdom of our Lord Jesus Christ*, 495–496. Hegesippus lived in the sub-apostolic age and was a Hebrew Christian. Some scholars claim that Irenaeus was his pupil and that Irenaeus learned of the imminent understanding of eschatology and the material reign of Christ on earth under Hegesippus's tutelage. See W. Telfer, "Was Hegesippus a Jew?" *The Harvard Theological Review* 53, no. 2 (1960): 143–153, at 53. Grier claims that Hegesippus was *not* a chiliast. See W.J. Grier, *Momentous Event* (London: Banner of Truth, 1976), 23–24. Cf. Justin, *First Apology*, 11.52.

7   Greg Carey, *Ultimate Things: An Introduction to Jewish and Christian Apocalyptic Literature* (St. Louis, MO: Chalice Press, 2005), 232. Cf. Pier Franco Beatrice, *Anonymi Monophysitae Theosophia: An Attempt at Reconstruction* (Boston, MA: Brill Academic, 2001), xxxviii.

8   W.D. Killen, *The Ancient Church: Its History, Doctrine, Worship, and Constitution* (Teddington, UK: Echo Library, 2010), 267. Cf. Peters, *The Theocratic Kingdom of our Lord Jesus Christ*, 495.

9   David S. Katz and Jonathan I. Israel, eds., *Sceptics, Millenarians, and Jews* (New York: Brill Academic, 1990), 180. Melito likewise subscribed to Quartodecimanism, though the controversy over the celebration of *Pascha* did not always coincide with millenarian eschatology. Guennadius classifies Melito as one of the early Fathers who espoused chiliasm (*De Dogm. Eccles.* C.52). Jerome, too, relates Melito to millenarianism in *Comm. on Ez.* 36. It should be noted that in some of Melito's writings, he stresses a spiritualized concept of Jerusalem and an ecclesialized understanding of God's kingdom-presence. Nevertheless, many Church historians consider him to be of the camp of early chiliasts. Frend states that Melito ". . . was regarded in later tradition as a millenarian whose view of God tended toward the anthropomorphic." W.H.C. Frend, *Rise of Christianity* (Philadelphia, PA: Fortress Press, 1986), 240. Both Jerome and Gennadius refer to Melito as a "decided millenarian." See Jerome, *Comm. on Ezek.*, 36. and Gennadius, *De Dogm. Eccl.*, 52.

10 Karl R. Hagenbach, *History of Christian Doctrine*, 3 vols (Whitefish, Montana: Kessinger Publishing, LLC, 2006), Vol.1, 139.

11 Margaret M. Mitchell and Frances M. Young, eds., *Origins to Constantine* (New York: Cambridge University Press, 2006), 320.

12 Tertullian, *De anima*, 55.2–4. Cf. "Millenarianism," in Porter, *Dictionary of Biblical Criticism and Interpretation*, 227.

13 Brian Daley argues that Hippolytus was "not a millenarian." Daley, "Eschatology in the Early Church Fathers," 96. J.N.D. Kelly disagrees with this assessment based on valuable textual evidence rarely addressed by the scholarly community. See J.N.D. Kelly, *Early Christian Doctrines*, 5th ed. (London: Continuum, 2000), 468–469. Cf. Mal Couch, ed., *A Bible Handbook to Revelation* (Grand Rapids, MI: Kregel Academic & Professional, 2001), 27. Though copies of *Against Heresies* attributed to Irenaeus, but in Hippolytus's library, showed an absence of the original millenarian language, this is thought to be a redaction by a later scribe. Indeed, a copy of Irenaeus's *Against Heresies* found in 1547 seems to suggest that someone had tampered with Hippolytus's manuscript, which would have contained the original millenarian references. Overall, on the subject of eschatology, Hippolytus agreed with his teacher, Irenaeus.

14 Peters, *The Theocratic Kingdom of our Lord Jesus Christ*, 496, n. 3b. Cyprian likewise subscribed to the "millennial week" eschatology with an historical, Sabbath millennium to follow. Cyprian, *Treatise 11; Preface, 2; On the Exhortation to Martyrdom*, 11.

15 Lactantius, *Divine Institutes*, in A. Roberts and J. Donaldson, eds., trans. W. Fletcher, *Ante-Nicene Christian Library: Translation of the Writings of the Fathers down to A.D. 325*, Vol. 21, *The Works of Lactantius*, Vol. 1 (Edinburgh, 1871), 480. Cf. Jeffrey K. Jue, *Heaven upon Earth: Joseph Mede (1586–1638) and the Legacy of Millenarianism* (Dordrecht: Springer, 2006), 121.

16 "And in Matthew we read, that it is written Isaiah also and the rest of his colleagues broke the Sabbath -that that true and just Sabbath should be observed in the seventh millenary of years ... Wherefore, as I have narrated, that true Sabbath will be in the seventh millenary of years, when Christ with His elect shall reign." Victorinus, *On Creation of the World*, in Alexander Roberts, ed., *The Ante-Nicene Fathers: The Writings of the Fathers Down to A.D. 325*, Vol. 7: *Fathers of the Third and Fourth Century-Lactantius, Venantius.Teaching and Constitutions, Homily, Liturgies* (New York: Cosimo Classics, 2007), 342.

17 Commodian, *Writings*, 44.

18 Methodius of Olympus, *Banquet*, IX, 5. Cf. "Millenarianism," in Jean-Yves Lacoste, ed. *Encyclopedia of Christian Theology*, 2 vols (New York: Routledge, 2005),1031.

19 "For Ambrosiaster, however, the collapse of the Roman empire was the sign of the approaching end of the world. Antichrist would then appear, only to be destroyed by divine power, and Christ would reign over His saints for a thousand years." Ferguson, *Encyclopedia of Early Christianity*, Vol. 1, 2nd ed., 479, 239.

20 Jean Daniélou, *The Origins of Latin Christianity* (London: The Westminster Press, 1977), 123. Among some of the other early millenarians are Coracian.

21 Leroy Froom, *The Prophetic Faith of our Fathers* (Washington, DC: Review and Herald), 1950, 337.

22 Bagatti, *The Church from the Circumcision: History and Archaeology of the Judaeo-Christians*, 298.

23 This Hermas, the author of "The Shepherd," was possibly the same one mentioned in Romans 16:14, though likewise it is possible that he was the brother of the later Pope Pius I (reigned as pope from ~140–152).

24 Dunn, *Jews and Christians*, 286–288, at 286. Cf. O'Hagan, *Material Re-Creation in the Apostolic Fathers*, 29, and also Aaron Milavec, *The Didache: Faith, Hope, & Life of the Earliest Christian Communities, 50–70 C.E.* (Mahwah, NJ: Paulist Press, 2003), 110.

25 G. Ladd, "The Eschatology of the Didache," unpublished Harvard Thesis, 1949.

26 *Didache*, XVI: 6–8 in Alexander Roberts, ed., *The Ante-Nicene Fathers: The Writings of the Fathers Down to A.D. 325*, Vol. 7, 382, emphasis mine.

27 T.H.C. van Eijk, *La Résurrection des Morts chez les Pérres Apostoliues* (Paris: Beauchesne, 1974), 25.

28 O'Hagan, *Material Re-Creation in the Apostolic Fathers*, 18–30.

29 Ronald E. Diprose, *Israel and the Church* (Waynesboro: GA: Paternoster, 2004), 218, n.30.

30 John Lawson, *A Theological and Historical Introduction to the Apostolic Fathers* (New York: Macmillan, 1961), 86.

31 See Polycarp, *Epistle to the Philippians*, 5.2, J.B. Lightfoot, trans., found at http://www.earlychristianwritings.com/text/polycarp-lightfoot.html. The original Greek of Polycarp's Epistle is intact in fragments, up through the 9th section, which is currently extant only in Latin. Cf. Chafer, *Systematic Theology*, 272. Chafer suggest that another scholar, gleaning information from one of Polycarp's fragments, sees Polycarp "... locating the reign of the saints after the coming of Jesus and the resurrection of the saints, but before the general resurrection."

32 Irenaeus, *Adv. Haer.*, 3.3.4.

33 For the concept that Polycarp's eschatology was highly ambiguous, illustrating neither a firmly chiliastic or amillennial view, see Frederick Grant, "The Eschatology

of the Second Century," *The American Journal of Theology* 21, no. 1 (1917): 193–211, 198. Francis Gumerlock tells us that though there are extant fragments on eschatology from the second century, there are no extant commentaries specifically on the Book of Revelation from that period. See Francis X. Gumerlock, "Patristic Commentaries on Revelation: The Problem of Accessibility" *Kerux* 23, no. 2 (September 2008): 3–13, at 2, n.5. Cf. Hill, *Regnum Caelorum*, 252.

34 Irenaeus documents his relationship with and knowledge of Polycarp on multiple occasions, including in *Adv. Haer.*, 33.4, iii.3.4, in his letters to Florinus and Pope Victor.

35 Borrowing from Pauline literature, Polycarp spoke of the eschatological promises available to the righteous believers in Christ: "For if we be well pleasing unto Him in this present world, we shall receive *the future world* also, according as He promised us to *raise us from the dead*, and that *if* we conduct ourselves worthily of Him *we shall also reign with Him*, if indeed we have faith." J.B. Lightfoot, trans., Polycarp, *The Epistle of Polycarp*, 5.2.

36 Joseph Mede, *The Works of the Pious and Profoundly Learned Joseph Mede, B.D., sometime Fellow of Christ's College in Cambridge*, 4th ed. (London: Roger Norton, 1677), 602. Chiliasm has survived as the dominant orthodox eschatology in the Ethiopian Orthodox Church to this day. See Gianfrancesco Lusini, "Eschatology" in Siegbert Uhlig, ed., *D-Ha*, vol. 2 of *Encyclopaedia Aethiopica* (Wiesbaden: Otto Harrassowitz Verlag, 2005), 153–154.

37 Robert Beylot, "Le Millénarisme, Article de Foi Dans L'eglise D'ethiopienne Au Xvème Siècle", *dans Rassegna di Studi Etiopici* 25 (1974): 31–43.

38 "The Fragments of Papias," in Schaff, *History of the Church*, Vol. 2: *The Ante-Nicene Fathers*, accessible at http://www.ccel.org/ccel/schaff/anf01.vii.i.html. Cf. Irenaeus, *Adv. Haer.*, 5. 33; *II Baruch* XXIX.

39 Eusebius, *Hist. Eccl.* III, 39. Cf. "The 'Papias' Fragments and Conclusions as to Jesus and Joses," in Robert H. Eisenman, *James the Brother of Jesus: The Key to Unlocking the Secrets of Early Christianity and the Dead Sea Scrolls*, reprint ed. (London: Penguin (Non-Classics), 1998).

40 There has been some debate as to whether Papias is referring to his conversations with John the Apostle, or another "John." The evidence is overwhelmingly in favor of Papias' text as referring to John the Apostle, *presbyter* in Ephesus. Eusebius, an ardent critic of millenarianism (who at one point refers to Papias as a literalist and man of 'small faculty"), attempted to make a distinction between the John Papias referred to and another person, namely because of his opposition to millenarianism. Eusebius is disputed on the grounds of his statement that Papias "was not himself a hearer and eye-witness of the holy apostles" insofar as it is logically inconsistent with a passage in Eusebius' *Chronicle*, which expressly calls the Apostle John the teacher of Papias. Interestingly, Eusebius assigns John the Presbyter, in contrast to John the Apostle, with the authorship of the *Book of Revelation*, of which Eusebius disputed canonical authority. Jerome later follows Eusebius on the same topic. The *Catholic Encyclopedia* challenges Eusebius' distinction on the grounds that "the distinction, however, has no historical basis." For a thorough argument regarding Papias's claim that he knew and spoke with the Apostle John, see D.A. Carson and Douglas J. Moo, *An Introduction to the New Testament*, 2nd ed. (Grand Rapids, MI: Zondervan, 2005), 233–234.

41 *Fragments of Papias*, IV, in Philip Schaff, *The Apostolic Fathers with Justin Martyr and Irenaeus*, Vol. 1 (Oxford: Benediction Classics, 2010), 1745.

42 R.C. Foster, *Studies in the Life of Christ: Introduction, the Early Period, the Middle Period, the Final Week* (Joplin, MO: College Press, 1995), 173–174. According to Foster, some of Papias' information came from relatives or student of the apostles, or relatives of disciples, including the daughters of Philip the evangelist. For another

argument for the validity of first or second degree sourcing in Papias' information, see Michael Newman, *The Didache: The Epistle of Barnabus, the Epistles and the Martyrdom of St. Polycarp, the Fragments of Papias, the Epistle to Diogenes: Ancient Christian Writers* (Mahwah, NJ: Paulist Press, 1948), 108–110.

43 B. Bandstra and S.S. Stuart, "Millennium," in Geoffrey W. Bromiley, ed., *International Standard Bible Encyclopedia*, Vol. 3: *K-P* (International Standard Bible Encyclopedia), rev. ed. (New York: Eerdmans, 1995), 358.

44 Philip Schaff, *History of the Christian Church. Complete in Eight Volumes*, Vol. 3, 57, emphasis mine. The contemporaries of Papias to whom Schaff refers include Barnabas, Justin Martyr, Irenaeus, Tertullian, Methodius, and Lactantius, among others.

45 Irenaeus, *Adv. Haer.*, 4.38; 5.28.3, accessible at http://www.newadvent.org/cathen/08130b.htm.

46 M.C. Steenberg, *Irenaeus on Creation: The Cosmic Christ and the Saga of Redemption* (Leiden: Brill Academic, 2008), 52. The use of the imagery of a chiliastic kingdom worked well to refute the Gnostic notion that the future, isolated for a chosen few, would lay apart from world history. The Gnostics, contra Irenaeus, ". . . interpreted Christian resurrection hope in entirely spiritual terms." Daley, "Apocalypticism in Early Christian Theology," 225.

47 Eduard Schwartz, "Johannes und Kerinthos," *Zeitschrift für die Neutestamentliche Wissenschaft* 15 (1914): 210. Cf. Daniélou, *The Theology of Jewish Christianity*, 386. Daniélou struggles more with Irenaeus' texts on chiliasm, open to the idea that it was one of two acceptable echatologies at the time.

48 Christopher R. Smith, "Chiliasm and Recapitulation in the Theology of Irenaeus." *Vigiliae Christianae* 48, no. 4 (1994): 313–331, 316.

49 Ibid., 314.

50 Irenaeus, *Adv. Haer.*, 5.31; 5.35. Some scholars have claimed that Irenaeus' support of chiliasm leaves him with a weak Christology and soteriology, insofar as it may be conceived that Jesus fulfilled none of the prophecies regarding redemption. See Herman-Emiel Mertens, *Not the Cross, but the Crucified: An Essay in Soteriology* (Louvain: Peeters Press, 1992), 65–66.

51 Irenaeus, *Adv. Haer.*, 4.26.

52 Jaroslav Pelikan's *The Emergence of the Catholic Tradition (100–600)*, vol. 1 of *The Christian Tradition* (Chicago, IL: University of Chicago, 1971), 125. Eusebius, in a section on Dionysius' debate with chiliasts of Egypt, claims that it was not merely 'bishops, elders, and doctors' of the Church who held to the chiliastic eschatology early on, but also their congregations. Eusebius, *Hist. Eccl.* 7.23.

53 For example, Walter Bauer speaks of Justin's formulation for proper Christian belief. There are some, says Justin, who believe, but "only in a general way share the pure and holy outlook," whereas other are described as *"orthodogñomones kata panta,"* having right knowledge in "all particulars." It is to the latter group that chiliasts belong. Walter Bauer, *Orthodoxy and Heresy in Earliest Christianity*, 2nd ed. (Mifflintown, PA: Sigler Press, 1996), 129.

54 History tells us that opposition to Montanism had nothing to do with chiliasm, or its expression as a legitimate element of the early Church: "Montanism's earliest opponents did not accuse it of chiliastic enthusiasm. No extant oracle speaks explicitly of chiliasm." Neither Jerome nor Eusebius, both skeptical of chiliasm, condemn Montanism on the grounds of chiliastic belief, though they do condemn it.

Christine Trevett, *Montanism: Gender, Authority and the New Prophecy* (Cambridge; New York: Cambridge University Press, 2002), 96. Modern scholarship suggests that the heresy of Montanism was based almost solely on its ". . . rejection that the first-century gospels could constitute any final and complete form of revelation." Court, *Approaching the Apocalypse*, 54. There is likewise evidence that Montanism was

rejected because of a flawed view of the Trinity. Some contemporaries of Montanus suggested that the sect even baptized in the name of "the Father, the Son, and the Lord Montanus." Overall, the rejection of Montanism had nothing to do with chiliasm. Scott, ed., *Restoration: Old Testament, Jewish, and Christian Perspectives*, 535. Cf. John C. Poirier, "Montanist Pepuza-Jerusalem and the Dwelling Place of Wisdom," *Journal of Early Christian Studies* 7, no. 4 (1999): 491–507.
55 Hill, *Regnum Coelorum*, 249–253. Cf. Daley, "Apocalypticism in Early Christianity," 224.
56 Ibid., 253, emphasis mine.
57 "Chiliasm," in Hans J. Hillerbrand, ed., *The Encyclopedia of Protestantism* (New York: Routledge, 2004), 630.
58 Millard J. Erickson, *Contemporary Options in Eschatology: A Study of the Millennium* (Grand Rapids, MI: Baker Book House, 1977), 76; Sung Wook Chung and Craig L. Blomberg, eds., *A Case For Historic Premillennialism: An Alternative to "Left Behind" Eschatology* (Grand Rapids, MI: Baker Academic, 2009), xiii. Hill argues that there was an amillennialist "tradition" prior to the time of the Alexandrian school, but offers no documentation to support that claim. He likewise points to the unfair assessment of labeling the amillennialism of some third-century fathers as "Greek," "spiritualizing," or "allegorical." Though not all amillennialism from the third century was "Greek," in almost every case it adopted Platonic presumptions and was "allergic" to the more materialistic understanding of creation and resurrected order. Conversely, many early "Greek" theologians were millenarians. Hill refers to the opposition to chiliasm as "early," but no such opposition occurred prior to the time of Gaius. Hill, *Regnum Coelorum*, 251.
59 Millard J. Erickson, *A Basic Guide to Eschatology: Making Sense of the Millennium*, rev. ed. (Grand Rapids, MI: Baker Books, 1998), 96.
60 Norman Cohn, *The Pursuit of the Millennium: Revolutionary Millenarians and Mystical Anarchists of the Middle Ages* (Oxford: Oxford University Press, 1970), 29, emphasis mine.
61 Hill, *Regnum Coelorum*, 50.
62 Ibid., 6, emphasis mine.
63 Ibid.
64 Gerald O'Collins and Mario Farrugia, *Catholicism: The Story of Catholic Christianity* (New York: Oxford University Press, USA, 2004), 36.
65 Michael Barber, *Coming Soon: Unlocking the Book of Revelation and Applying Its Lessons Today* (Steubenville, OH: Emmaus Road Publishing, 2006), 98. Cf. Joseph A. Seiss, *Apocalypse: An Exposition of the Book of Revelation* (Peabody, MA: Kregel Classics, 2000), 147. Seiss points out that Irenaeus simply claims that all disembodied souls are in ". . . the place assigned them by God," whereas another prominent chiliast, Tertullian states ambiguously that the souls are ". . . in peace under the altar," making no reference to their status as martyrs.
66 Irenaeus, *Adv. Haer.* 31:1–2.
67 The later chiliast, Methodius, believed that disembodied souls went to heaven: ". . . our souls shall be with God until we shall receive the new house which is prepared for us." Methodius, *Fragments on the Resurrection*, 2.15.7.
68 Some scholars find strong evidence in Paul's Epistles (see 1 Corinthians 15:18 and 1 Thessalonians 4:13–17) for the concept of an intermediate state of the soul, connected to his terminology of "sleep." See William Barclay, *The Apostles' Creed* (William Barclay Library) (Louisville, KY: Westminster John Knox Press, 1998), 179.
69 R.E. Hutton, *The Soul in the Unseen World: An Inquiry Into the Doctrine of the Intermediate State* (Memphis, TN: General Books LLC, 2010), 181. Cf. Irenaeus, *Adv. Haer.*, 5.31.

Millenarianism and early Church tradition 129

70 Andrew Chester, "The Parting of the Ways," in Dunn, *Jews and Christians: The Parting of the Ways, A.D. 70 to 135: The Second Durham-Tübingen Research Symposium on Earliest Christianity and Judaism, Durham, September 1989*, 270.
71 F. Stanley Jones, "Jewish–Christian Chiliastic Restoration in Pseudo-Clementine Recognitions 1.27–71," in Scott, ed., *Restoration: Old Testament, Jewish, and Christian Perspectives*, 529–571 at 546, n. 33.
72 Hermas, *Pastor Vis.* I, iii, 7.
73 Irenaeus, *Contra Haer*, v. 35, 36.
74 Tertullian, *De Anima*, lviii.
75 Ambrose, *De Spir. San.*, I, 170. Ambrose subscribed to two physical resurrections during the final stages of history—one leading to the intermediate temporal reality, and the other leading into eternity. (See Ambrose of Milan, *On the Belief in the Resurrection*, ii. 108).
76 Hill, *Regnum Coelorum*, 187–188.
77 Thomas W. Petrisko, *Inside Purgatory: What History, Theology and the Mystics Tell Us about Purgatory* (Pittsburgh, PA: St. Andrew's Productions, 2000), 18.
78 For example, elements of chiliasm brought from Oriental liturgical sources to Milan tended to influence Ambrose in some of his writings. See Geir Hellemo, *Adventus Domini: Eschatological Thought in 4th-Century Apses and Catecheses* (New York: Brill Academic, 1997), 250. Henry Lea states that Ambrose "proposed an eschatological theory which assimilated him to the Chiliasts." Henry Charles Lea, *A History of Auricular Confession and Indulgences in the Latin Church, Part Three* (Whitefish, Montana: Kessinger Publishing, LLC, 2004), 302.
79 See J.A. Kleist, *The Didache, the Epistle of Barnabas: The Epistles and the Martyrdom of St. Polycarp, the Fragments of Papias, the Epistle to Diognetus*, 179.
80 Glenn R. Kreider, Review of *"Regnum coelorum: Patterns of Millennial Thought in Early Christianity," Bibliotheca Sacra* 160, no. 638 (April 1, 2003): 253.
81 Corrodi Heinrich, *Kritische Geschichte Des Chiliasmus* (Frankfurt and Leipzig: Dritten Theils, 1901), Vol. 2, Part 3.
82 Paul Hartog, in an exhaustive study of Polycarp's Epistle to the Philippians (the bishop's only extant writing), he claims that the prevalence of chiliastic eschatology in Asia Minor during the second century, combined with Polycarp's ardent defense of the celebration of Passover against the Roman Church, points toward Polycarp embracing the early eschatology. Hartog writes: "... some have suggested that Polycarp disagreed with the chiliasm of the Apocalypse; but this conjecture is not only unprovable, but also improbable." Paul Hartog, *Polycarp and the New Testament: The Occasion, Rhetoric, Theme, and Unity of the Epistle to the Philippians and Its Allusions to New Testament Literature* (Tübingen: Paul Mohr Verlag: 2002), 188.
83 Epiphanius of Salamis, *de Fide*, vi. 9.7., in Frank Williams, *The Panarion of Epiphanius of Salamis* (New York: Brill Academiclishers, 1997), 411.
84 See Hill, *Regnum Coelorum: Patterns of Future Hope in Early Christianity*, 78–102.
85 Ibid., 79.
86 Fairbairn, "Contemporary Millennial/Tribulational Debates: Whose side was the Early Church on?," in *A Case For Historic Premillennialism: An Alternative to "Left Behind" Eschatology*, 105–132, at 117, emphasis mine.
87 Mede, *The Works of the Pious and Profoundly Learned Joseph Mede*, B.D., 602.
88 William R. Farmer, ed., *The International Bible Commentary: A Catholic and Ecumenical Commentary For the Twenty-First Century* (Collegeville, MN: Liturgical Press, 1998), 113.
89 Moll, *The Arch-Heretic Marcion*, 40. Marcion's utter rejection of all "Judaic principles" made him unique among the early heretics. Hans Jonas, *The Gnostic Religion: The Message of the Alien God & the Beginnings of Christianity*, 3rd ed. (Boston, MA: Beacon Press, 2001), 137.

130 *Millenarianism: valid Church history*

90 Justin, 1 *Apol.* 26.8. Cf. Helmut Koester, *From Jesus to the Gospels: Interpreting the New Testament in Its Context* (Minneapolis, MN: Fortress Press, 2007), 69.
91 Irenaeus, *Adv. Haer.*, 4.27–32. Daley tells us that Irenaeus ". . . sensed the need both to affirm the public continuity of Christian teaching, as the belief of a worldwide community with a recognizable history, and to resist the attractions of more inward, individualistic forms of Christianity." Daley, "Apocalypticism in Early Christian Theology," 225.
92 Andrew Gregory, *The Reception of Luke and Acts in the Period Before Irenaeus: Looking for Luke in the Second Century* (Tübingen: Paul Mohr Verlag, 2003), 185–186.
93 "The *alogia* denied the Johannine authorship of both the Gospel of John and Revelation, attributing the latter to the heretic Cerinthus." James Gardner, *Faiths of the World*, Part 1 (Whitefish, Montana: Kessinger Publishing, LLC, 2003), 69. Epiphanius was the first to coin the term "alogia" in reference to the group. Epiphanius, *Haer.*, 67.
94 Eric Voegelin, *Science, Politics, and Gnosticism* (Chicago, IL: Henry Regnery, 1968), 85–88.
95 Gardner, *Faiths of the World*, Part 1, 69.
96 Bart D. Ehrman, *Lost Christianities: The Battles for Scripture and the Faiths We Never Knew* (New York: Oxford University Press, 2005), 121.
97 William Tabbernee, "Portals of the Montanist New Jerusalem: The Discovery of Pepouza and Tymion," *Journal of Early Christian Studies* xi/1 (2003), 92–93.
98 "Millennium" in W.R. Chambers, *Chambers's Encyclopædia: A Dictionary of Universal Knowledge for the People*, Vol. 6 (Charleston, SC: Nabu Press, 2010), 469.
99 MS, *Cod. Paris. Syr.* 67, fol. 270, r°, col. 2, contained in the *Bibiotheque Nationale* in Paris. See also J.D. Smith, "Gaius and the Controversy over Johannine Literature," PhD dissertation, Yale University, 1979. It appears that Gaius actually thought that Cerinthus was the author of the Book of Revelation, "passing it off as the work of an apostle," seeing as the Roman theologian could not conceive of chiliasm being rooted in what would become a canonical book of the Bible.
100 Kurt Rudolph, *Gnosis: The Nature and History of Gnosticism* (Edinburgh: T&T Clark Int'l, 2001), 165. Cf. Simone Petrement, *A Separate God: The Christian Origins of Gnosticism* (New York: Harpercollins, 1990), 308–311. New Testament scholar Raymond Brown rejects the concept that Cerinthus was a chiliast, and attributes the statement to purely polemical sources. See Raymond E. Brown, *The Epistle of John* (New York: Doubleday, 1982), 770. Irenaeus accused Cerinthus of heresy, but it had nothing to do with chiliasm, of which Irenaeus himself was an adherent. See *Adv. Haer.*, 3.3.4. It appears that Irenaeus was alluding to the idea that Cerinthus was guilty of Valentinianism. See Matti Myllykoski, "Cerinthus," in Antti Marjanen and Petri Luomanen, eds., *A Companion to Second-Century Christian "Heretics"* (Leiden: Brill Academic, 2008), 213–246 at 226. For specific material regarding Irenaeus on Cerinthus, see *adv. Haer.*, 1.26.1, in A.F.J. Klijn and G.J. Reinink, *Patristic Evidence for Jewish–Christian Sects* (Leiden: Brill, 1973), 103.
101 Dionysius, aware of chiliasm's roots in apostolic tradition, offered a rather practical reason for its critique: Chiliasm did ". . . not permit our simpler brethren to have any sublime and lofty thoughts concerning the glorious and truly divine appearing of our Lord . . . but, on the contrary, lead them to a hope for small things and mortal things in the kingdom of God." Dionysius, *On the Promises*, as quoted in Eusebius, *Hist. Eccl.* 7.24–25.
102 Johann Lorenz Mosheim, *Commentaries on the Affairs of the Christians before the Time of Constantine the Great*, Vol. 1 (Memphis, TN: General Books LLC, 2012), 139.

103 Daley, "Apocalypticism in Early Christian Thought," 230. Ironically, Eusebius states that Origen, an extreme ascetic, castrated himself based on a *literal* reading of Matthew 19:12. Eusebius, *Hist. Eccl.*, 6.2.9. Burrus regards Origen's reinterpretation of earlier biblical concepts as "hermeneutical supersessionism," based on an "embarrassment of the flesh." Virginia Burrus, *Begotten, Not Made: Conceiving Manhood in Late Antiquity* (Stanford, CA: Stanford University Press, 2000), 26.
104 Erickson, *A Basic Guide to Eschatology: Making Sense of the Millennium*, 96. For Origen's most exhaustive rebuttals of chiliasm, see *De principiis*, 2.11 (on the holy city of Jerusalem, about which Origen claims there is a universal curse, stretching over all creation), *De Princ.*, 2.11.2, 4.3.7–8, 4.2.1, and *HomNum.* 28.2.
105 Origen, *De Princ.*, 2.11.
106 Clayton Sullivan, *Rethinking Realized Eschatology* (Macon, GA: Mercer University Press, 1988), 139, n.15.
107 Jacob Taubes, *Occidental Eschatology* (Stanford, CA: Stanford University Press, 2009), 76.
108 Weber, "Millennialism," in *The Oxford Handbook of Eschatology*, 369. We notice that Weber describes Origen's non-millennial apocalyptic ideas as the *exception* through the third century. See Brian Daley, "Eschatology in the Early Church Fathers," in *The Oxford Handbook of Eschatology*, 98–99 and C.E. Hill, *Who Chose the Gospels?: Probing the Great Gospel Conspiracy* (New York: Oxford University Press, USA, 2010), 44.
109 Larry V. Crutchfield, "Origen," in Mal Couch, ed., *Dictionary of Premillennial Theology* (Grand Rapids, MI: Kregel Publications, 1997), 289.
110 Benedict XVI, *Jesus of Nazareth*, 41. For Benedict, the first two valid eschatological expressions are taken directly from Origen: first, that Jesus himself is the kingdom, and second, that man's soul or "interiority" is the location of the kingdom. Benedict's third Patristic interpretation is radically generalizing, even in light of Augustine, borrowing almost directly from Tyconius: the Church and the kingdom are "brought into almost exclusively synonymous proximity."

5 A shift in eschatology
The Church becomes the kingdom

Thus far, we have argued that millenarianism, or chiliasm, was an eschatological framework expressed vividly in the New Testament and adopted exclusively during the first two and a half centuries of Christianity. The early Patristic period saw the development of a robust chiliastic eschatology, while every orthodox writer of note held to the belief in an intermediate period of Christ's reign on earth to take place between the first resurrection, and the second resurrection and universal judgment, or was relatively silent on the issue. Though some heretical sects early in Church history also believed in chiliasm, it is noteworthy that both sects that began the denial of millennial orthodoxy were Gnostic: the Marcionites and the *alogia*. Eventually, more accepted retractors of chiliastic eschatology such as Origen and Gaius were likewise declared heretical for their eschatological beliefs—Origen for his views on *apokatastasis* and denial of orthodox conceptions of resurrection,[1] and Gaius for his rejection of the canonicity of John's Revelation. In the following section, we will explore three Latin writers whose works mark the shift from the original, apostolic millennial eschatology, to an amillennialism directly attributable to the political phenomenon of the birth of Constantine's Christendom. Eusebius, Tyconius, and Augustine, in different ways, birthed an alternative to Christian eschatology that was foreign to the minds of early Christians, and at odds with their conception of salvation history.[2]

Adherence to millenarianism began to decline in earnest in the late fourth and early fifth centuries, in response to two specific historical-theological realities. First, Jesus Christ had not yet returned and some of the eschatological promises related by the Apostles were viewed as either disappointed, deferred, misinterpreted, or already fulfilled during the time of Jesus Christ.[3] Second, Christianity was transforming from an unorganized, persecuted offshoot of Judaism to an organized, politically powerful and institutionalized religion. There was no room for expectations of an historical, earthly kingdom initiated by God[4] if it was to be seen as something extra, or outside the auspices of the Church as an historical institution. Christianity had became "official":

> As Christianity became the official religion of Rome and the Church became a powerful institution, such teaching [amillennialism] gave the Catholic Church authority to see itself as God's fulfillment of His purposes. This

authority was used to oppose all who questioned the social status and power of the Church ... In short, it was that she had become God on earth ... The development of Christendom ... promoted the acceptance of post-and amillennialism.[5]

We will now seek to explain why the earlier Christian eschatology shifted, primarily due to the influences of Eusebius, Tyconius, and Augustine, while continuing to maintain the validity of the Church's traditional chiliastic trajectory.

Eusebius (ca. 263–339 C.E.): The Church and the Roman kingdom

Eusebius, well-known Church historian and bishop of Caesarea, was a staunch opponent of millenarian eschatology, and is the father of what would become known as "Imperial ecclesiology."[6] On the one hand, Eusebius saw problems with chiliasm, insofar as he interpreted it to mean that the messianic kingdom was completely "on hold" until Jesus' return, prompting questions from Jewish and pagan critics alike as to the "visible proof" of the kingdom and its messianic fulfillment. On the other hand, Eusebius believed that an allegorical eschatological interpretation, internalizing the kingdom in the human soul, did little to help prove that Jesus and the present Church were fulfillments of God's salvation history: "Origen sought to resolve the 'problems' of the chiliasts by spiritualizing redemption, so Eusebius sought to resolve the deficiencies in Origen's spiritualization by relocating redemption in history—in the form of the newly converted Roman Empire."[7] Eusebius's solution did not merely situate redemption within the history of the Roman Empire, but the consummation of the kingdom of God, in a political sense, was also seen to take place through the institutional auspices of the new Christendom.[8] As Bader-Saye puts it, "Eusebius sought to answer the Jewish challenge by affirming that redemption was both visible and present in the empire ... baptizing the rule of Rome as the visible evidence of the messianic age ..."[9] Eusebius conflated earlier Christian expectations for a peaceable, chiliastic, messianic kingdom, with the newfound success that the Church was achieving in its partnership with the Roman Empire. If the messianic age was "presenting" itself in the empire, that age needed a messiah, thus, for Eusebius, the messiah-vicar was the Emperor Constantine.[10]

Eusebius' motivation for rejecting chiliasm was rooted in his form of Church-history apologetics, insofar as he sought to illustrate that his own contemporary Christianity, grounded in ancient sources but gaining momentum in the newly birthed Christendom, was God's tool for establishing the kingdom on earth. Therefore, Eusebius' approach to history adopted a realized eschatology that he believed would quiet both Jewish and pagan critics of the Christian Church.

Scholars have discerned a pattern that suggests Eusebius was known for flip-flopping on important theological issues, if the inconsistency would help his apologetic cause.[11] Like the later Augustine, the bishop from Caesarea had not always adhered to a realized, amillennial view of the Last Days.[12] The early

Eusebius, prior to the victory of Constantine at the Milvian Bridge in 312,[13] adopted and accepted elements of apocalyptic, millenarian eschatology:

> There is something like a consensus in contemporary Eusebian scholarship that the first Church historian was flexible on questions of eschatology. When the persecutions of Maximin called for the more "primitive" apocalyptic conceptions of traditional Christianity . . . [chiliasm] . . . Eusebius was willing to use them. But with the triumph of Christianity at the Milvian bridge, he conveniently "shelved" other-worldly aspirations and praised with "unconcealed" joy the establishment of God's rule on earth in the form of Constantine's empire.[14]

Eusebius' initial acceptance of traditional chiliastic beliefs, and subsequent rejection or misuse of them, reflect less a desire to maintain an "orthodoxy" within the Church and more so an attempt to force-fit the trends of the time into a panoramic that portrayed Roman Christian history as God's eschatological *telos*.[15] Knowing that chiliasm was the eschatology of Christian antiquity, Eusebius re-appropriated its language to describe what he claimed was God's historicized eschatological working within Romanized Christianity—as he had done with other theological premises to which he at one point adhered.[16] Eusebius borrowed the details of apocalyptic and millenarian rhetoric and applied them to the Roman Emperor's reign, the inauguration of the Pax Romana[17] in conjunction with the "Thousand Years" peace,[18] and the participation of the members of the Roman Catholic Church in relation to the reception of the chiliastic kingdom by the saints.[19]

In sum, Eusebius was the first among the Latin writers to successfully circumvent the traditional, apostolic, chiliastic eschatology, while simultaneously applying the language of chiliasm (associated with the Thousand Years' reign, kingdom authority, and the fulfillment and consummation of the kingdom), to the Roman Empire. According to both Moltmann and Ruether, Eusebius initiated a form of *political millenarianism* that was utterly foreign to the early, apostolic Church, and contrary to its eschatological trajectory.[20] Some of Eusebius's themes were taken up by Tyconius, who applied the concept of the messianic reign to the Church of his own time—a point adopted by Augustine.[21]

Augustine (354–430 C.E.): The Church and the kingdom of God

The purpose of our forthcoming section is to give a modest summary of Augustine's eschatology in order to point out the shift that occurred from the chiliasm of the apostolic Church to the amillennialism that took root in the fourth and fifth centuries. As we have established, Origen's work was the first to legitimately challenge chiliasm since its apostolic inception, but had significant detractors because of the Alexandrian school's almost exclusively allegorical hermeneutic.[22] Augustine's work figured to discredit the ancient expectation of the messianic kingdom at a new level, as the bishop and Doctor of the Church's influence on Roman Catholic ecclesiology and eschatology is essentially unrivaled to this day, perhaps only with the exception of Thomas Aquinas. As one scholar writes, "Augustine was a principal factor in the rise and acceptance of amillennialism and the consequent decline ... of the premillennial doctrine that until his time was regarded as a settled point of orthodoxy in early patristic eschatology."[23]

The primary text from which we gain access to the connection between eschatology and ecclesiology in Augustine is his *De Civitate Dei* (*City of God*), in which he points to the struggle between the Church as the representative of the eternal City of God, and the "city of the devil," which coexists with the Church, and even shares its members in certain cases.[24] By interpreting the historical plane as an admixture of divine, human, and demonic events, Augustine gave the Church a new centrality in salvation history, and more importantly, a claim to be the sole reflection and embodiment of a realized eschatological reality.[25]

The early Augustine was a staunch and ardent supporter of chiliasm and its view of history, following the apostolic tradition that was accepted at the time.[26] Like Eusebius, it appears Augustine changed his mind with the new fortunes experienced by both the empire and the Church, though this was tempered by the events that led to the writing of the *City of God*—the sack of Rome by the Goths in 410 C.E., and the claim of the Donatist party to a pure, martyr-Church which was free from earthly impurities.[27] Unlike Eusebius, Augustine was highly skeptical of drawing explicit parallels between the empire's success and ecclesiological advancements, but nevertheless developed a reading of Revelation 20 in which the earthly Church was either continuous with, or synonymous to, the kingdom of God.[28]

Augustine took the "thousand years" in Revelation 20 as corresponding specifically to the Church era, over time. According to Augustine, the first "six-thousand-year" period was the time before Christ, while the "thousand-year reign" is symbolically read as the time of the Church, established since the first advent of Christ, and lasting until his return.[29] Augustine likewise reinterpreted the "two physical resurrections" tradition of Revelation 20 as meaning one spiritual resurrection and one physical,[30] claiming that Satan was "bound" in a certain sense during this spiritual millennium, but still able to seduce the Church.[31]

In his reinterpretation of Revelation 20, Augustine drew a one-to-one correspondence between the Church and the messianic reign of Jesus. Augustine wrote, "Therefore the Church even now is the kingdom of Christ, and the kingdom of heaven. Accordingly, even now His saints reign with Him ... they reign with Him who are so in His kingdom that they themselves are His kingdom."[32] This close identification of the Church and the kingdom had lasting consequences, insofar as the kingdom was conceived as a present reality, whereby the Church was considered its sole custodian.[33] Augustine replaced the early tradition that claimed the kingdom was something to be awaited from God in a future orientation, with an almost completely realized eschatology.[34]

Despite his reinterpretation of the millennial reign of Christ, Augustine was sympathetic to a modified millenarian reading of Revelation 20—one that stressed spiritual instead of carnal blessings during the era of peace: "And this opinion would not be objectionable,[35] if it were believed that the joys of the saints in that Sabbath shall be spiritual, and consequent on the presence of God; for I myself, too, once held this opinion."[36] Augustine had apparently come in contact with forms of millenarianism, different from the early forms advocated by Justin and Irenaeus, that were so materialistic, sensual, or carnal, that he was compelled to reject them. But a careful reading of the above quote shows that Augustine did tolerate millenarianism in a spiritual form, provided that the kingdom was established as an extension of God's presence among the saints. Though Augustine reinterpreted the two resurrections of Revelation, viewing the first as referring to the current state of Christian existence after baptism, and the other as the general, physical resurrection, he did not deny the validity of viewing the end of history as a "Sabbath rest," with an intermediary period in the presence of the Lord—obvious markings of a chiliastic reading of the text.[37]

Regardless of Augustine's ability to make space for the early millennial interpretation of the Last Days, the bishop's amillennial interpretation gained so much momentum during the fourth century that the normativity of eschatology in the Roman Catholic Church shifted. What was once the Church's hope for a future kingdom of Christ changed when "Augustine's version of realized eschatology drew out the eschatological within history through identification with the Church."[38] This shift in understanding, from the early chiliastic Christian hope of the New Jerusalem and era of messianic peace, to the realized ecclesia-eschatology, since Augustine, has become the most influential philosophy of salvation history for Roman Catholicism. Despite efforts since Vatican II to portray the Roman Catholic Church as a "pilgrim Church,"[39] ". . . the contents of the statements reveal only little change in the magisterium relative to the identity of Church and kingdom."[40] Any changes regarding the Church and the kingdom that appear to be evident in the documents of Vatican II are negated by the famous phrase declaring that the Church is the ". . . kingdom of Christ now present in mystery."[41] Avery Dulles confirms the enduring influence of Augustine on Catholic eschatology when he states that "In the documents of Vatican II . . . the Church is not simply a sign or pointer to the kingdom of God, nor is it a mere servant of the kingdom. The Church is either identical with or at least central to the kingdom."[42] Thus, the "already-not yet" balance of eschatology in Roman Catholicism has been so deeply influenced by past realized eschatologies, that the "already" of the Kingdom takes form in the Church's conception of itself.

In concluding our section on Augustine, we point to the reality that there was a shift in the eschatology of the Church from the first to the fourth century C.E.—one which cannot be explained away by claims to a legitimate "development of doctrine."[43] Quite the contrary, the eschatological shift that occurred in the work of Augustine (with its roots in Eusebius and Tyconius) is foreign to that of the early Church, insofar as nothing remotely similar to his ecclesial interpretation of Revelation 20, even taking into account Origen and the Alexandrian legacy, existed prior to the *City of God*. It is likewise important to state that the shift that occurred with Augustine may be misinterpreted because it is labeled as "amillennialism."[44] Advocates of a pure "amillennialism" would insist on a completely allegorical interpretation of the "Thousand Years reign," whereas with Augustine, the reign is both literal and historical, but refers to the time of the Church. Thus, Augustine's ideas simply transformed early eschatology into a wholly different variety of millenarianism: from *eschatological millenarianism* to *historicized (presentative)* millenarianism, with an emphasis on ecclesiological concerns.[45]

In summarizing our work thus far regarding eschatology, we began by defining what we mean by "millennialism," "millenarianism," and "chiliasm," and illustrated how the major themes of chiliasm are validly extracted from Scripture by worthy biblical exegetes. While validating the millennial interpretation of Scripture, we likewise pointed to flaws and weaknesses in the amillennial position, focusing primarily on the twentieth chapter of Revelation. Next, we detailed the way in which chiliasm was considered the universal orthodox opinion of the early Church, pointing to the work of multiple early Church Fathers who held the belief, while exposing the weaknesses of the thesis of Charles Hill, the only scholar who has argued extensively and definitively for a well-developed amillennialism prior to the fourth century. We likewise positioned the earliest retractions of chiliastic eschatology to the year 250 C.E., traced to several heretical sects, and the allegorical work of Origen and the Alexandrian school. Finally, we argued that a significant shift occurred in the Latin West with the thought of Eusebius of Caesarea and Augustine of Hippo, insofar as the "Thousand Years Reign" of Christ and the eschatological kingdom of God was re-construed to refer to the present era of the Roman Catholic Church.

Notes

1 "The Anathemas against Origen," in Alexander Roberts, James Donaldson, Philip Schaff, and Henry Wace, eds., *Nicene and Post-Nicene Fathers*, Second Series, 14 vols (Buffalo, NY: Hendrickson, 1994), found at http://www.ccel.org/ccel/schaff/npnf214.xii.ix.html. I. Beckwith claims that Origen's view of the resurrected body amounted to a nuanced version of Gnosticism. See Isbon T. Beckwith, *The Apocalypse of John* (London: Macmillan, 1919; repr., Grand Rapids, MI: Baker Book House, 1979), 323. John Patrick Donnelly and Joseph C. McLelland, *Philosophical Works: On the Relation of Philosophy to Theology* (Kirksville, MO: Truman State University Press, 1996), 115.
2 Walvoord, *The Millennial Kingdom: A Basic Text in Premillennial Theology*, 19. Cf. Jonathan Frankel, ed., *Studies in Contemporary Jewry*, Vol. 8: *Jews and Messianism in the Modern Era: Metaphor and Meaning* (Oxford: Oxford University Press, 1991), 69.
3 Douglas Wilson, *Heaven Misplaced: Christ's Kingdom on Earth* (Moscow, ID: Canon Press, 2008), 93–97.
4 Cohn states that as of the Constantinian era, ". . . the Catholic Church was now a powerful and prosperous institution, functioning according to a well-established routine; and the men responsible for governing it had no wish to see Christians clinging to out-dated and inappropriate dreams of a new earthly Paradise." Cohn, *The Pursuit of the Millennium*, 29.
5 Sang Taek Lee, *Religion and Social Formation in Korea: Minjung and Millenarianism* (Berlin: Mouton De Gruyter, 1996), 11.

A shift in eschatology 139

6 *Hist. Eccl.*, 7.24–25, 3.39, 12–13. Cf. Vincent Twomey, *Apostolikos Thronos: The Primacy of Rome as Reflected in the Church History of Eusebius and the Historico-Apologetic Writings of Saint Athanasius the Great* (Münster: Aschendorff, 1982), 390.
7 Bader-Saye, *Church and Israel after Christendom*, 59.
8 Eusebius's preoccupation with Constantine is seen most vividly in his Panegyric writings, such as *Hist. Eccl.*, *De laudibus Constantini*, and *Vita Constantini*. For an excellent summary of Eusebius's attitude toward Constantine and connection of theological rhetoric with the Roman Empire, see Sabine MacCormack, "Latin Prose Panegyrics," in Thomas Alan Dorey, ed., *Empire and Aftermath: Silver Latin II* (London: Routledge & Kegan Paul Books, 1975), 168.
9 Bader-Saye, *Church and Israel after Christendom*, 59.
10 Eusebius, *Vit. Const.*, 5.19, 20. Cf. Jonathan Bardill, *Constantine, Divine Emperor of the Christian Golden Age* (Cambridge: Cambridge University Press, 2011), 342. On the emperor as portrayed as the vicar of Christ, see Glenn F. Chesnut, *The First Christian Histories: Eusebius, Socrates, Sozomen, Theodoret, and Evagrius*, 2nd ed. (Macon, GA: Mercer University Press, 1986), 154.
11 Barnes mentions significant deficiencies in the historical writings of Eusebius, and suggests a connection in the midst of shifts in the relationship between the Church and the state and the "back and forth" nature of his opinions. See Timothy D. Barnes, *Constantine and Eusebius* (Cambridge, MA: Harvard University Press, 1981), 140.
12 Barnes, *Constantine and Eusebius*, 168. Cf. D.S. Wallace-Hadrill, *Eusebius of Caesarea* (Cambridge, MA: Mowbray, 1960), 177; H.C. Frend, *Martyrdom and Persecution in the Early Church* (Oxford: Blackwell, 1964), 544, Jean Sirinelli, *Les vues historiques d'Eusebe de Cesaree durant la periode preniceenne* (Dakar: Universite de Dakar, 1961), 472. In a similar manner, Eusebius initially adopted and defended the beliefs and practices of Quartodeciminism, knowing that they had roots in apostolic and episcopal tradition. Yet when such beliefs proved incompatible with Constantinian sensibilities, he publicly and literarily opposed the Asian practice, despite supporting it previously. See William L. Petersen, "Eusebius and the Paschal Controversy," in Harold W. Attridge, ed., *Eusebius, Christianity and Judaism* (Detroit, MI: Wayne State University, 1992), 320.
13 Michael P. Speidel, *Riding for Caesar: The Roman Emperor's Horse Guard* (Cambridge, MA: Harvard University Press, 1997), 116. Eusebius's famous *Ecclesial History* was written after the Milvian victory, around 325 C.E.
14 Frank S. Thielman, "Another Look at the Eschatology of Eusebius of Caesarea," *Vigiliae Christianae* 41 (1987): 226–237, at 226.
15 D.S. Wallace-Hadrill, *Eusebius of Caesarea* (London: Mowbray, 1960), 174–175. Wallace-Hadrill explains Eusebius' historical view as ". . . the ordering of the world being a graduated hierarchy, God—Christ—Constantine . . .".
16 Kim Riddlebarger claims that Eusebius was simply reviving what was an already latent and orthodox amillennial tradition. Kim Riddlebarger, *A Case for Amillennialism: Understanding the End Times* (Leicester, UK: Baker Books, 2003), 67. For an overall rebuttal of Riddlebarger's claim, see C. Odahl, "The Use of Apocalyptic Imagery in Constantine's Christian Propaganda, *Centerpoint 4* (1981), 9–20.
17 Eusebius, *Demonstratio Evangelica*, 2.3, 3.7. In these sections, Eusebius relates the era of the *Pax Romana* in terms of the re-establishment of the messianic kingdom. Cf. Michael J. Hollerich, *Eusebius of Caesarea's Commentary on Isaiah: Christian Exegesis in the Age of Constantine* (Oxford: Oxford University Press, 1999), 189.
18 Eusebius, *Vit. Const.*, 16.7–8.
19 At one point, Eusebius relates Constantine's nepotistic practice of extending ruling privilege to family members throughout the empire with the apocalyptic prophecy of Daniel 7:18: "the saints of the Most High will receive the kingdom." Eusebius, *Oration in Honor of Constantine 1–3* in Maurice Wiles and Mark Santer, eds., *Documents in Early Christian Thought* (Cambridge: Cambridge University Press,

140 *Millenarianism: valid Church history*

1977), 233. Eusebius likewise borrowed ancient Christian imagery, such as the martyr's cross, and used them as symbols for imperial victory. See "The Cross and Religious Imagination" and "The Vision of Constantine," in Carroll, *Constantine's Sword*, 172–194.

20 Moltmann draws a distinction between two types of historical millenarianism: *politischer Millennarismus*, predominant in European history and traceable to Eusebius, and *kirchlicher Chiliasmus*, traceable to the ecclesial eschatological interpretation of Tyconius and Augustine. Timothy Harvie, *Jürgen Moltmann's Ethics of Hope: Eschatological Possibilities for Moral Action* (Aldershot: Ashgate, 2009), 155. Ruether claims that Eusebius' primary argument that ". . . the gentile Church is a messianic fulfillment [sic] takes on a new political tone . . . the ecumenical empire comes to be identified with the millennial reign of the Messiah over the earth . . ." Reuther's point is that Euesbius drew a one-to-one correspondence between the Church as situated in and protected by the Roman empire, and the chiliastic reign of Christ on earth.

21 Allison summarizes the importance of Tyconius's ideas, which he describes as "new": "Tyconius and his chief follower Augustine established amillennialism as the reigning eschatological view. Tyconius paved the way for this new understanding by means of his *Book of Rules* for correctly interpreting the prophecies of Scripture: they will be fulfilled *spiritually*, not *literally* as premillennialists imagined. When he applied this method to Revelation 20: 1–6, Tyconius focused on a spiritual millennium corresponding to the current Church period. Those pictured as reigning with Christ are believers who overcome sin and live righteously." Allison, *Historical Theology*, 688. Cf. Kenneth B. Steinhauser, *The Apocalypse Commentary of Tyconius: A History of Its Reception and Influence* (Frankfurt am Main: Peter Lang, 1987), 131, and Daley, "Eschatology in the Early Church Fathers," 99–100.

22 Cohn, *The Pursuit of the Millennium*, 29. Cf. Gerard O'Daly, *Augustine's City of God: A Reader's Guide* (New York: Oxford University Press, 2004), 160–161.

23 Ibid.

24 Augustine, *De Civitate Dei*, 20.11. Augustine relates the earthly manifestation of the City of God (the Church) to Jerusalem, while the earthly city is related to Babylon. Cf. Ernest L. Fortin, "City of God," in Allan D. Fitzgerald, ed., *Augustine through the Ages: An Encyclopedia* (Grand Rapids, MI: Eerdmans, 1999), 196–202, at 198.

25 There is, in Augustine's thought, a sense in which there is an eschatological fulfillment yet to come, but ultimately for Augustine, ". . . the Church is the historically visible form of the kingdom of God." There cannot be any historical, visible form of the kingdom of God, save for the Church. Donald G. Bloesch, *Jesus Christ: Savior & Lord* (Christian Foundations) (Downers Grove, IL: IVP Academic, 2005), 213.

26 Augustine, *De Civitate Dei*, 20.7ff. Cf. Folliet, "La typologie du sabbat chez Saint Augustin: son interprétation millénariste être 388 et 400," 371–390. The early Augustine followed the sexta/septamillennial tradition that was common up through the fourth century, in which history was viewed in terms of six 1,000-year periods, followed by a Sabbath rest conceived as the millennial kingdom of peace. See also Jeremy Cohen, *Living Letters of the Law: Ideas of the Jew in Medieval Christianity* (Berkeley, CA: University of California Press, 1999), 46.

27 Joseph C. Schnaubelt and Frederick Van Fleteren, *Augustine: Biblical Exegete* (New York: Peter Lang, 2001), 286.

28 "History" in Allan D. Fitzgerald, ed., *Augustine through the Ages: An Encyclopedia* (Grand Rapids, MI: Eerdmans, 1999), 433.

29 Augustine, *De Civitate Dei*, 20.9. Cf. Catherine Gunsalus González and Justo L. González, *Revelation* (Louisville, KY: Westminster John Knox Press, 1997), 132.

30 The same verb used in Revelation 20, referencing the "first resurrection," *zaō*, refers also to Christ's physical resurrection from the dead in Revelation 1:18 and 2:8. There

is near unanimity among modern exegetes that to take one resurrection as spiritual and the other as physical deviates from an honest reading of the text in context. See Stephen S. Smalley, *The Revelation to John: A Commentary on the Greek Text of the Apocalypse* (Downers Grove, IL: IVP Academic, 2005), 509–510; James L. Resseguie, *The Revelation of John: A Narrative Commentary* (Grand Rapids, MI: Baker Academic, 2009), 315; George Eldon Ladd, *A Commentary On the Revelation of John* (Grand Rapids, MI: Eerdmans, 1972), 265–266.

31 Augustine, *De Civitate Dei*, 20.8.
32 Ibid., 20.9.
33 Ronnie Littlejohn, *Exploring Christian Theology* (Lanham, MD: University Press of America, 1985), 427.
34 There is an aspect of "futurity" within Augustine's eschatological writing, but this has developed into an almost exclusively realized conception of the kingdom. See Mike Higton, *Christ, Providence, and History: Hans W. Frei's Public Theology* (Edinburgh: T&T Clark International, 2004), 130.
35 The Latin, *utcunque tolerabilis* should be rendered "And this opinion would be to a degree tolerable . . ." Following a misunderstanding of Augustine's nuance, Philiaster claimed that chiliastic thought was considered generally heretical, whereas Augustine differentiated between the mitigated millenarianism (a spiritual type of earthly reign of Christ with spiritual benefits, and the more carnal type falsely attributed to Cerinthus). See Philiaster, *de Haeres.*, 59.
36 Augustine, *De civitate Dei*, 20.7.
37 Modern scholars understand Augustine to have been quite congenial to multiple interpretations of one biblical text: "Augustine argued that Scripture's obscurity may lead to the possibility of multiple orthodox interpretations." William Harmless, ed., *Augustine in His Own Words* (Washington, DC: Catholic University of America Press, 2010), 190–191.
38 Francis Schussler Fiorenza and John P. Galvin, eds., *Systematic Theology: Roman Catholic Perspectives*, 2nd ed. (Minneapolis, MN: Fortress Press, 2011), 628. Lerner makes the following claim regarding the influence of Augustine's realized eschatology: ". . . Augustine reprehended any hope for miraculous collective betterment on earth. Since faith and charity required Christians to despise delight in earthly existence and to love solely for the end of enjoying God in heaven, there could be nothing superior to the Church militant as an earthly institution designed to forward that end. Therefore it followed that when Saint John told of a thousand-year earthly reign of Christ and the saints (Apoc. 20:1–6), he could not have been referring to a coming dispensation but had to be telling of the present Church." Robert E. Lerner, "The Medieval Return to the Thousand Year Sabbath," in Emmerson and Bernard McGinn, eds., *The Apocalypse in the Middle Ages*, 52. Cohn reiterates this interpretation of Augustine's work: ". . . the kingdom of God had been realized, so far as it ever could be realized on this earth, at the moment the Church came into being, and that there never would be any millennium but this." Cohn, *The Pursuit of the Millennium*, 109.
39 Since Augustine, the Church has consistently viewed itself as God's kingdom. Some examples include the writings of Pope Gregory the Great (540–604 C.E.) in his *Homilia* XXXII:6 in Jacques-Paul Migne, *Patrologiae Cursus Completus: Seu Bibliotheca Universalis, Integra, Uniformis, Commoda, Oeconomica, Omnium* Ss *Patrum, Doctorum Scriptorumque . . . Innocentii III (Anno 1216) Pr.* (Greek Edition) (Charleston, SC: Nabu Press, 2011), 76:1236–1237. The modern era saw the continuation of Augustine's scheme in the work of Pope Pius XII, in *Mystici Corporis*, §65, found at http://www.vatican.va/holy_father/pius_xii/encyclicals/documents/hf_p-xii_enc_29061943_mystici-corporis-christi_en.html, in which he claims that "the kingdom of the Son" *is* the Church.

142 *Millenarianism: valid Church history*

40 Saucy, *The Kingdom of God in the Teaching of Jesus*, 270.
41 *De ecclesia*, 5.
42 Avery Dulles, *The Reshaping of Catholicism: Current Challenges in the Theology of Church* (San Francisco, CA: Harpercollins, 1988), 138.
43 John Henry Newman, following Vincent of Lérins' thought, "... described the emergence and amplification of Christian doctrine as a process of 'development,' a quasi-organic evolution in which what develops later is the flowering of what was contained at the inception of revelation: as living things grow to fullness without surrendering their identity." John McDade, "Development of Doctrine," in Adrian Hastings, Alistair Mason, and Hugh Pyper, eds., *The Oxford Companion to Christian Thought* (Oxford: Oxford University Press, 2000), If amillennialism is to be considered a valid development of doctrine, one must contend with two hurdles: first, why is anything like it missing from the Apostolic Witness? And second, how can a doctrine develop, essentially, into its *opposite*?
44 I have termed Augustine's eschatology 'amillennialism' because it is common form, and simplifies the distinctions between chiliasm and later Christian eschatologies.
45 Moltmann, *The Coming of God*, 146.

Part III
Millenarianism, heresy, and contemporary Catholic theology

6 The hermeneutics of heresy

As the early Church longed and struggled for unity in its doctrine, we see certain essential doctrines either defined in vague terms, or not fully defined—even through the fifth century C.E.[1] Even today, some Roman Catholic doctrines are well specified, while others have gone without episcopal or papal definition. For the greater part of Christian history, the specific essentials[2] of eschatology have included (a) a belief in the return of Jesus Christ in glory from the "right hand of God the Father," (b) a belief in the universal resurrection, (c) the resurrection of the body after death, (d) a final judgment for all human beings, both those alive and dead, (e) the consummation of the world, and (f) the ushering in of an eternal existence with God for all the "righteous."[3]

As I have shown in previous chapters, during the Church's earliest doctrinal history, the interpretation and chronology of the events described above was chiliastic.[4] I have shown that "the Apostolic Church was premillennial and for over 200 years, no other view was entertained, and the writings of the Church Fathers abound in evidence of that fact."[5] After the Augustinian eschatological shift of the mid-fourth century, a level of flexibility was embraced in regards to eschatology, considering that amillennialists and millennialists could agree on the *essential* eschatological points as defined in the Apostles' and Nicene creeds:

> The doctrine of the kingdom, although prominently in the Bible, is not specifically treated in the early Confessions, as e.g. the Apostles', Niceno-Constantinopolitan, and Athanasian. General expressions, without entering into details, are employed, to which both millenarians and anti-millenarians could subscribe.[6]

The statement above coincides with the thesis of the second part of this book, in which I claimed that a shift occurred in eschatology during the fourth century at the same time some of the earliest creeds were codified, and Ecumenical Councils were held. If the Church, functioning through its episcopal authority, intended to declare chiliasm heretical and replace it with the re-interpretive scheme of amillennialism, one would expect that Ecumenical Councils of the fourth through fifth centuries would have offered the best opportunities to take such action. Yet no such action took place.

The goals of the section to come are as follows: first, I will use the 'Vincentian canon' as a standard for evaluating the validity of chiliasm as an understanding of eschatology within Roman Catholicism. I will then contend that although many scholars assume that millenarian eschatology has been declared heretical through the Church's ecumenical and conciliar processes, this is not the case. Instead, we see heresies that have nothing to do with chiliasm, condemned at Councils, and which mistakenly come to be associated with chiliastic eschatology. Chiliastic eschatology itself was never declared heretical.

My exploration will include the language of the major creeds, as these statements of faith have functioned as definitive guideposts and interpretations for proper dogma, and historically they are the fruit of conciliar agreement. Additionally, the major creeds have been used by amillennialist apologists as "proof texts" to show that millenarian eschatology has been officially rejected by the Church. The conciliar history on the topic of chiliasm is important, because by illustrating that chiliasm is apostolic, and by showing that it is not considered heretical in an ecumenical sense, a strong case may be made for its future theological exploration in Roman Catholic circles, specifically in light of Jewish–Catholic relations.

Second, I will show how the Roman Catholic Church did not make a definitive, negative statement regarding millenarianism until 1944, vis-à-vis a one-sentence declaration by Pope Pius XII. This statement had an aim other than excluding millenarianism as a theological option. Specifically, the statement was made in response to the atrocities of Second World War, is highly contextualized, and is ambiguous in its content. Insofar as millenarianism goes undefined, the statement does not state whether the eschatology may be held as a private opinion, or be explored by theologians.[7] I will argue that in light of confronting the elements that made the *Shoah* possible, Pius sought to reject any eschatological system that could be used to justify establishing a "Reich" on earth, and his aim was not millenarianism as a theological option.[8] I will further show how Hitler's conception of the establishment of an earthly reign has more in common with the Church's "traditional," historical millenarian (amillennial) view, than with Patristic chiliasm.

Last, I will explore contemporary catechesis regarding millenarianism vis-à-vis comments by the Church's recent Magisterium. Since the pope's declaration in 1944, millenarianism, or "mitigated millenarianism,"[9] as the 1994 Catechism refers to it, has been dismissed by the Magisterium. The statement of Pius XII regarding millenarianism was reiterated in the 1994 Catechism, along with a brief explanation that millenarianism has "been rejected" by the Church, and is dangerous because it welcomes the deceptions of an antichrist by claiming that the kingdom of God may take on a historical form, centered on the figure of a Messiah.[10] I will compare the text in the Catechism with recent statements made by Pope Benedict in response to a form of "spiritualized" millennialism, which stresses the Eucharist and sacerdotal role of the Church—a concept to which the pope appears openly congenial. Ultimately, I argue that the Magisterium is agreeable to elements of chiliasm, provided those elements help to promulgate the idea that the Roman Catholic Church is God's kingdom on earth, and that ecclesial authority cannot be superseded—even by the return of Jesus the Messiah within history.[11]

Again, I am bracketing the overall thesis of this book, namely that a modified millenarianism is able to overcome supersessionism, here only establishing that millenarian eschatology is a viable option for Catholic Christians, in the face of contemporary magisterial skepticism.

The point of our current argument is that modern and contemporary authors have sought to illustrate that the hierarchical Church condemned millenarian eschatology as a heresy, or at least a "grave error,"[12] often claiming that certain Councils explicitly rejected it, denying it as a an opinion permissible, among orthodox ones.[13] In what follows, I will expose a pattern that became evident when one examines the occasions in which some theologians of the Church (both past and present) have stated that conciliar gatherings or creedal statements in the Church's history were specifically formulated in order to refute chiliasm. The pattern is that what some scholars believe was a refutation of chiliasm in conciliar or creedal statements is in reality a refutation of some other condemned heresy which is linked to chiliasm.

Scholars who are experts in the details of conciliar history, who come from a wide range of Christian traditions, have formulated a consensus in reference to the claim that chiliasm was pronounced a heresy, either in creed or council, though this present study is the first to enumerate the reasons why. By the fourth century, though millenarianism was waning in popularity and had its detractors, and though some individual writers disparaged it as a heresy, it was never formally declared so:

> [In the fourth century], Orthodoxy fought against these [chiliastic] ideas; but as they were openly expressed in many passages of the Fathers, they were never strictly qualified as heresies. St. Epiphanius, who was a man of most strict research, who tried to enlarge his catalogue of heresies by making two or three sects out of one, has not devoted a special chapter to millenarians.[14]

Modern Eastern Orthodox scholars corroborate the quote above, referring to ancient sources. Though some orthodox theologians find millenarianism somewhat incompatible with their tradition, they admit that "... there is scant evidence that chiliasm has ever been condemned by an Ecumenical Council."[15] The doctrine of chiliasm was never condemned, and even Protestant scholars who reject millennialism say as much.[16] Roman Catholic theologian and Patristic expert Brian Daley claims that "... any mention of an official condemnation is conspicuously missing from what appear to be otherwise thorough works on the history of millennialism."[17]

In this section, using Vincent of Lérins' popular standard for determining heresy versus authentic doctrine, I argue that in spite of the skepticism regarding chiliasm after the time of Constantine, the Church has never formally denounced the millenarian interpretation of the kingdom of God and history, save for one relatively recent and contextually tempered papal statement.

We will ask then if the fact that millenarianism was never formalized as a heresy opens the door for its wholesale acceptance by the faithful. That chiliasm is so firmly rooted in the primitive traditions of the Fathers, was accepted at the time as the normative interpretation of Sacred Scripture, and was never declared improper eschatology by an ecumenical body, warrants its further exploration—particularly by Roman Catholic theologians.

St. Vincent of Lérins: Determining valid doctrine

There exists a certain tradition, a "hermeneutic of heresy,"[18] whereby Roman Catholics are able to discern what has been condemned in terms of theological dogma, and what has not. That tradition, often revived and cited by modern and contemporary Roman Catholic scholars, is the "Vincentian canon." In perhaps his most often quoted statement, the Gallic Christian writer Vincent of Lérins (d. 445), in his *Commonitory* of 432 which was written with the intent of creating ". . . a general rule whereby to distinguish Catholic truth from heresy," claims that in ". . . the Catholic Church itself, all possible care must be taken that we hold that faith which has been believed everywhere, always, by all."[19] Specifically, Vincent states that in order to ascertain the proper doctrine of the Church, the Council of Ephesus thought it would suffice ". . . to show the agreement of ten fathers or principal doctors of the Church."[20] As Catholic theologian J.C. Fenton explains, in order for the consent of the early Church Fathers to be "unanimous":

> we need not demand an explicit declaration on the point from every one of the Fathers of the Church. There is such consent when at least a moral unanimity of the fathers *who have actually dealt with this subject*, teach the same doctrine as having been revealed by God . . . the apposition of one, or even of an inconsiderable number, to the teaching which is common with the rest, does not prevent common teaching from enjoying certain unanimity. The united voice of the fathers constitutes a real rule of faith.[21]

Vincent's writing, which is respected in both Eastern and Western circles, specifies a sequence of study if one is to determine if a certain belief system is heretical, in serious error, or by contrast, encouraged within the pale of orthodoxy. Vincent makes the following claim:

> What if in antiquity itself two or three men, or it may be a city, or even a whole province be detected in error? Then he will take the greatest care to *prefer the decrees of the ancient General Councils, if there are such*, to the irresponsible ignorance of a few men. But what if some error arises regarding which nothing of this sort is to be found? Then he must do his best to *compare the opinions of the Fathers and inquire their meaning, provided always that, though they belonged to diverse times and places, they yet continued in the faith and communion of the one Catholic Church; and let them be teachers approved and outstanding*. And whatever he shall find to have been held,

approved and taught, not by one or two only but by all equally and with one consent, openly, frequently, and persistently, let him take this as to be held by him without the slightest hesitation.[22]

It must be reiterated that premillennialism as a system is in a unique situation, insofar as it was held widely, in multiple provinces, as the view of the early Church, and held so by Fathers of the Church, Saints recognized in both the East and West, and was held by some Doctors of the Church.[23] The circles in which chiliasm flourished prior to the late third century were so wide and influential that there is no evidence to suggest an alternative even existed: ". . . all of the earliest Church Fathers of the first and second centuries, whose eschatology can be discerned with any degree of certainty, were chiliasts. They awaited the restoration of the creation at the coming of Christ, and His reigning over the nations from Jerusalem."[24]

If, as Vincent suggests, we must first look for a consensus among the well-respected Fathers as a test case for heresy, we are left at a loss concerning the view that chiliasm was heretical. In reality, the opposite is true, insofar as there is no evidence to suggest that amillennialism was the universal eschatology of the early Church.[25] Among the Doctors of the Church, Ambrose kept to a dual-resurrection and chiliastic eschatology,[26] while the early Doctor of the Church, Augustine, was a defender of chiliasm[27] until, like Eusebius,[28] he changed his mind.[29] Like Augustine, Jerome, though opposed to the chiliastic reading, refrained from declaring the system heretical because of its early status and popularity among the earliest Fathers.[30]

In order to follow Vincent's rule regarding the viewpoint of the early Church Fathers, it is important to review a major point that I covered previously—that chiliasm was held normatively by the Church. For example, recent scholarship proves that the Pseudo-Clementine "romance" work entitled the *Recognitions* is of Jewish–Christian origin, explicitly chiliastic, and dated as early as 70 C.E.[31] We must also add the multiple chiliastic saints who remained in communion with the Catholic Church, including St. Barnabas, St. Papias of Hierapolis, St. Justin Martyr, St. Irenaeus, and St. Melito,[32] among others, along with the more ambiguous, but nevertheless noteworthy, commentary on the six-week construct of eschatology by SS. Polycarp and Ignatius—a system indicative of chiliastic ideology. Fathers such as St. Tertullian,[33] St. Hippolytus,[34] and Lactantius[35] cannot be overlooked, and early writers, such as those who penned *the Shepherd* and the *Second Epistle of Clement* held to chiliasm.[36] Two Doctors of the Church explicitly ascribed to chiliastic elements, five saints describe and expand on chiliastic ideas explicitly, a plethora of saints allude to it with their descriptors of the kingdom, proximity to, and blessing of, chiliastic proponents, their understanding of the divisions of history, and their borrowing of millenarian Jewish apocalyptic language. Perhaps most telling is the fact that not one Father of the Church explicitly or implicitly rejects millennialism until the late third century, let alone calls it an error or heresy.

Those who lived prior to the late third century, who did not appear to explicitly adhere to chiliasm, also did not condemn it. Neither did they offer an alternative

150 *Contemporary Catholic theology*

that was similar to Origen's total spiritualization of the kingdom,[37] or Augustine's amillennialism. As D. Earl Cripe states, "The oldest interpretive scheme . . . [of eschatology] . . . was known as Chiliasm. This doctrine goes back to the beginning of the Church."[38]

The significant point for our project is that the opposing eschatological interpretive scheme, now known as amillennialism, surfaces nowhere in historical documentation until the time of Gaius in the West (whom Schaff dates at "the first quarter of the third century")[39] and Origen in the East[40]—relatively late for an eschatology that would later become dominant in all of Christendom. Though it seems almost inconceivable that a theological system that carried such weight in the early centuries of Christianity would come to be considered heretical by some Fathers by the fifth century (though not formally declared so), this is precisely what happened in the case of chiliasm, due to the early influences of Gaius, the Alexandrian school, and a series of misconceptions and misrepresentations of the original eschatology.[41] Gerhard Maier makes the following salient point: ". . . nearly all researchers are united in this, that the end-time conception and doctrine designated . . . as chiliasm, dominated the whole Church until the great Alexandrians, and the West even into the third and fourth centuries."[42]

The primary cause of the eschatological shift, in addition to an increased spiritualizing Hellenism that was diametrically opposed to early Jewish–Christian doctrine,[43] is associated with the fact that the Christian Church transformed from a fledgling, organic community composed of persecuted and marginalized outcasts in need of a future hope for justice in the material world, to a triumphalist institution married to the Roman State, embarrassed of the material abundance already in its possession. Desiring to control the "keys to the Kingdom," the Church, vis-à-vis Augustine's near solidification of amillennialism, changed the conception of that kingdom into a heaven beyond the earthly realm—the entrance to which could be managed by the sacramental activities of the Church, which took on the role of the sole custodian of the kingdom. As Cohn puts it, "early in the fifth century, St. Augustine propounded the (amillennial) doctrine which the *new condition demanded*."[44] Augustine, influenced by the earlier work of Gaius and ecclesiocentric thinkers such as Tyconius and Eusebius, and encouraged by the strong Platonist, spiritualizing tendency that grew in the Christian tradition,[45] inspired future generations to associate chiliasm solely with those heretical groups. It is noteworthy that the Bishop of Hippo himself did not go so far as to condemn early millenarianism, at one point stating that it was "acceptable" in a certain form.[46]

Since the time of Blessed John Henry Cardinal Newman, who followed Vincent's canon and adapted it, Catholics may consider such apparent changes in belief processes to be the fruit of the "development of doctrine," yet Newman states explicitly that doctrine cannot develop in such a manner as to negate a past consensus or normative doctrine of the Church.[47] The Newmanesque view of doctrine is anticipated in Vincent's oft-ignored "second rule":

> But someone will perhaps say: is there no progress of religion in the Church of Christ? Certainly there is progress, even exceedingly great progress.

For who is so envious of others and so hateful toward God as to try to prohibit it? Yet, it must be an advance [*profectus*] in the proper sense of the word and not an alteration [*permutatio*] in faith. For progress means that each thing is enlarged within itself, while alteration implies that one thing is transformed into something else [*aliquid ex alio in aliud*]. It is necessary, therefore, that understanding, knowledge, and wisdom should grow [*crescat*] and advance [*proficiat*] vigorously in individuals as well as in the community, in a single person as well as in the whole Church and this gradually in the course of ages and centuries. But this progress must be made according to its own type, that is, in accord with the same doctrine, in the same meaning, and in the same judgment.[48]

In light of Vincent's canon and Newman's reevaluation of it, both of which have been used often by Roman Catholic apologists to support doctrinal developments such as purgatory, the Immaculate Conception, and papal infallibility,[49] we must ask whether chiliasm's decline in popularity was a matter of the way eschatology came to be formulated and legitimately evolved, or if the issue is *over the actual matter or content of the eschatology itself*.[50] All indicators would point to the fact that the stark move from premillennial eschatology among the early Church Fathers to a strict anti-millennialism after Origen in the East, and Augustine in the West, was more of a total *change in doctrine*, than a development of it.[51] Thus, the apostolic tradition itself morphed into an allegorical and symbolic system of eschatology that had once been taken to be literal, temporal, and historical.

It can be said with a great degree of certainty that scholars have illustrated that premillennialism was held widely, and in a basic sense, universally, within multiple geographical provinces prior to Origen. By contrast, amillennial literature is non-existent and leaves one with "silence" during the first two centuries.[52] Walvoord claims, in an exhaustive work on the concept of the kingdom in the Patristics, that "the first century is barren of any real support for the amillennial viewpoint . . . [and] . . . is a lost cause for amillennialism. The second century, like the first, is devoid of any testimony whatever for amillennialism, except at its close."[53]

In relation to Vincent's rule, we see that:

> Catholics rightly point back to Vincent's dictum that "progress requires that the subject be enlarged in itself." They argue that, in order for the Church truly to possess a "living" tradition, the tradition must be capable of being modified, even greatly modified, *without radical "alteration" of its essence*.[54]

Thus, the question arises as to how a doctrine may develop in a manner that reflects a total and undeniable shift in content.[55] The most plausible explanation is that the apostolic deposit, in reference to eschatology, carried forward the customary, second-century Jewish view of the Last Days. This early Christian teaching expected some kind of restoration of Jerusalem at the time of an interregnum period at the historical coming of the Messiah—a time when the nations would flood into the Holy City.[56] This framework was retooled in Christian circles to illustrate that Jesus would return as messianic king, a Davidic figure who would vindicate the martyrs and consummate the earthly, created order during an historical interregnum period, with Jerusalem at its center.[57]

We must ask if it is enough to say that because later prominent theologians disavowed chiliasm that the Church as a whole is justified in rejecting its earliest normative eschatological belief. If no Ecumenical Councils condemned the 2,000-year-old chiliastic doctrine, we must ask whether very recent papal rejections of chiliasm are innovative attempts at maintaining an ecclesio-centric eschatology.[58] In the following material, it will become clear that chiliasm meets Vincent's standards for orthodoxy, insofar as it was held normatively in many provinces by multiple ancient Fathers, was never declared heretical by an Ecumenical Council, and has maintained a significant place in the *sensus fidelium*.[59]

Roman Catholicism has always held to some form of millenarianism, whether the kind critiqued by Moltmann, namely the "historical millenarianism" of Tyconius, or spiritualized versions such as Pope John Paul II's Apostolic Letter entitled *Tertio Millennio Adveniente*.[60] Millenarian articles were produced consistently through the sixteenth and seventeenth centuries and legitimatized in the Roman Catholic tradition. For example, Blasius Viega's (1554–1599) *Commentarii Exegetici in Apocalypticism* unapologetically adopted elements of ancient Christian chiliasm. Despite Cornelius a Lapide's critique of the millenarianism of the seventeenth century as "untraditional and suspect because 'it makes history out of prophecy,'"[61] this is precisely what the Augustinian model did by equating the historical period of the Church with the prophetic utterances of the Old and New Testaments. In the case of Patristic chiliasm, such historical and temporal manifestations are reserved for the time of Jesus' Second Coming, and are to come about only by an act of God, relegating the Church to act as an instrument of peace rather than an instrument of triumphal conquest on the way to the eternal kingdom of God. If we are to consider amillennial belief, that eschatological system was certainly *not* "believed everywhere, always, by all."

Continuing to follow Vincent's protocol, in the following section I will explore the language of the creeds and the pronouncements of the major Ecumenical Councils (in addition to some minor ones), to determine if they support millennialism, condemn it as heretical, or remain ambiguous. Previously we argued that a great number of the Ante-Nicene Fathers held to chiliasm and wrote extensively to defend it. But this reality alone does not make chiliasm an acceptable doctrine, as it is the Church that decides which aspects of Patristic tradition are to be retained as authentic Christian teaching and which ones are in error. When we say that the Church decides on doctrine, we mean the ecumenical Church throughout the ages, with special emphasis on the role and function of the bishops, as gathered for the purpose of defining or clarifying doctrine, as well as the faithful populace. When one considers the whole of ecumenical, conciliar history, whether in the Latin West or the East, it is impossible to show that chiliasm was ever rejected outright.

Notes

1 For the treatment of the subordination of pneumatology and eschatology to Christological concerns, see John Panteleimon Manoussakis and Neal Deroo, *Phenomenology and Eschatology: Not yet in the Now*, ed. Neal DeRoo (Aldershot: Ashgate, 2009), 76–77. On apocalyptic eschatology, see John J. Collins, "Introduction: Towards the Morphology of a Genre," in John J. Collins, ed., *Apocalypse: The Morphology of a Genre* (Missoula, MT: Scholars 1979), 1–20.
2 The Moravian bishop Comenius is credited with the phrase: "In essentials unity, in non-essentials liberty, and in all things, charity." Comenius' quote serves us well in describing the nature of eschatological discourse in the early Church, even after the Augustinian turn to amillennialism. Augustus Schultze, *Christian Doctrine and Systematic Theology* (Bethlehem, PA: Moravian Church, 1914), iv.
3 Mark J. Edwards, ed., *We Believe in the Crucified and Risen Lord* (Downers Grove, IL: IVP Academic, 2009), 169.
4 For information on the "intervening space" of chiliasm, see "A Divine Milieu: A Middle Way," in Mark C. Taylor, *Erring: A Postmodern A/theology* (London: University of Chicago Press, 1987), 112–118. For the spiritual and earthly balance within Patristic chiliasm, see Alessandro Scafi, *Mapping Paradise: A History of Heaven on Earth* (Chicago, IL: University Of Chicago Press, 2006).
5 Clarence Larkin, *The Second Coming of Christ* (New York: Cosimo Classics, 2010), 44. See also Bagatti, *The Church from the Circumcision: History and Archaeology of the Judaeo-Christians*, 202, 297–298. Cf. Sylvester John Saller and Emmanuele Testa, *The Archaeological Setting of the Shrine of Bethphage* (Jerusalem: Franciscan Press, 1961), and Fulcanelli, *Fulcanelli: Master Alchemist: Le Mystere Des Cathedrales, Esoteric Intrepretation of the Hermetic Symbols of The Great Work* (New York: Cosimo, 1984), 166. Cf. Jay Weidner and Vincent Bridges, *The Mysteries of the Great Cross of Hendaye: Alchemy and the End of Time* (Rochester, VT: Destiny Books, 2003), 37. A lengthy section of this text is dedicated to illustrating the prolific nature of chiliastic archaeological evidence prior to the third century.
6 Peters, *The Theocratic Kingdom of our Lord Jesus Christ*, 128.
7 The Decree of Pope Pius XII reads, rendered in English: "In recent times on several occasions this Supreme Sacred Congregation of the Holy Office has been asked what must be thought of the system of mitigated Millenarianism, which teaches, for example, that Christ the Lord before the final judgment, whether or not preceded by the resurrection of the many just, will come visibly to rule over this world." Answer according to Pope Pius XII: "The system of mitigated Millenarianism cannot be taught safely." "Decree of the Holy Office," July 19, 1944, confirmed by Pope Pius XII, July 20, 1944 (DS3839).
8 John Cornwell, *Hitler's Pope: The Secret History of Pius XII*, repr. ed. (New York: Penguin Books, 2008). Cf. John Roth and Carol Rittner, *Pope Pius XII and the Holocaust* (Leicester History of Religions) (London: Continuum, 2004).
9 The term "mitigated millenarianism" refers to a spiritual millennium, with Jesus nevertheless reigning on earth during a period of time.
10 *Catechism of the Catholic Church*, #676.
11 The Catechism, in its treatment of millenarianism, openly states that its modern resistance to the chiliastic eschatology is based on the view that amillennialism better insulates the Catholic hierarchy against threats to its authority. No such alternate authority may exist until the final judgment given by Christ. Ibid., 668–669.
12 Manuel Lacunza, *The Coming of Messiah in Glory and Majesty* Vol. 1 (St. Paul, MN: Seeley, 1827), 128. Lacunza's book was banned by the Holy Office of the Roman Catholic Church on September 6, 1824, yet Menendez Pelayo claims that the ban did not mention millenarian eschatology at all, but instead banned the book due to "... statements against the Roman Curia or statements offensive to the Fathers of

the Church or in praise of Judaism." Ovid Need, *Death of the Church Victorious* (Mulberry, IN: Sovereign Grace Publishers, 2002), 465. A priest commissioned by a Vicar General to examine the book for error speaks rather objectively on the eschatology espoused in it, mentioning the point that millenarianism had few opponents among the Church Fathers up through the fifth century. See ibid., 41–68.

13 David F. Noble, *Beyond the Promised Land: The Movement and the Myth* (Toronto, ON: Between the Lines, 2005), 53.
14 Ernest Renan, *The History of the Origins of Christianity: The Reign of Hadrian and Antoninus Pius, A.D. 17–161* (Memphis, TN: General Books LLC, 2010), 51.
15 Wendy Paula Nicholson, "Eschatology," in John Anthony McGuckin, ed., *The Encyclopedia of Eastern Orthodox Christianity* (Maldin, MA: Wiley-Blackwell, 2011), 225. One Orthodox scholar makes the claim that millenarianism was "thoroughly examined at the Second Ecumenical Council . . . and condemned," but there is no evidence of such condemnation in the canons of the Council itself. Dennis Eugene Engleman, *Ultimate Things: An Orthodox Christian Perspective on the End Times* (Ben Lomond, CA: Conciliar Press Ministries, 2005), 115–116. A popular website dedicated to answering questions regarding the Orthodox faith lists the following answer regarding chiliasm: "it does not seem that millenarianism is—from an historic Orthodox perspective—strictly speaking a condemned heresy (on account of these venerable fathers who taught it) but rather a tolerable private opinion." See http://www.orthodoxanswers.org/answer/4/. Cf. Roger E. Olson, *The Westminster Handbook to Evangelical Theology* (Louisville, KY: Westminster John Knox Press, 2004), 232.
16 ". . . from the third to the fifth centuries Chiliasm was vigorously fought and ruthlessly put down, although it was not officially declared a heresy. It was all really rather awkward, because previously *nearly everybody of note* had been a Chiliast . . . between Chiliasm and the charge of heresy stands the canonization of Justin Martyr and Irenaeus." C. Cooper, "Chiliasm and the Chiliasts," *Reformed Theological Review* 29 (1970): 12.
17 Brian Daley, *The Hope of the Early Church*, as cited in Michael J. Svigel, "The Phantom Heresy: Did the Council of Ephesus (431) Condemn Chiliasm?" *Trinity Journal* 24 (2003): 105–112, at 108.
18 See James K. Smith, *The Fall of Interpretation: Philosophical Foundations For a Creational Hermeneutic*, 2nd ed. (Grand Rapids, MI: Baker Academic, 2012), 170, and James K. Smith, "Fire from Heaven: The Hermeneutics of Heresy," *Journal of Theta Alpha Kappa* 20 (1996): 13–31.
19 Vincent of Lérins, *Commonitory*, 2.6, found at http://www.newadvent.org/fathers/3506.htm., and see Jaroslav Pelikan's *The Emergence of the Catholic Tradition (100–600)*, vol. 1 of *The Christian Tradition*, 333–339.
20 C. Journet, *The Church of the Word Incarnate: The Apostolic Hierarchy* (Lanham, MD: Sheed and Ward, 1955), 537.
21 Joseph Clifford Fenton, *The Concept of Sacred Theology* (Milwaukee, WI: Bruce Publishing Co, 1941), 136, emphasis mine.
22 Vincent of Lérins, *Commonitory*, 3.7–8. Vincent lists numerous heretics in his writing, including the sacramental heresy of Agrippinus, and the Trinitarian and Incarnational heresies of Arius, the Donatists, Nestorius, Valentinus, Apollinaris, and Photinus. Chiliasm is not mentioned, although Vincent held up Ambrose as an exemplar of the faith. As ascertained previously in this project, Ambrose held to two resurrections at the eschaton.
23 Bethune-Baker, *An Introduction to the Early History of Christian Doctrine: To the Time of the Council of Chalcedon*, 69.
24 Timothy Warner, "The Source of the Corruption of Apostolic Eschatology," *ODJ* 5, no. 1 (2008): 1–6, http://olivetdiscourse.com/index.php?option=com_content&task=view&id=315&Itemid=43 (accessed June 29, 2012), 1.

25 If discerning the original apostolic deposit means basing such assumptions on evidence, the apostolic Church, as its normative view, believed in a "thousand year" reign of Christ in Jerusalem prior to the general resurrection of the dead.
26 See J. Derambure, "Le millénarisme de S. Ambroise," *Revue des études anciennes* 17 (1910): 545–556.
27 D. Earl Cripe, *Seven Trumpets Asounding: A Commentary on the Book of Revelation in the Historic, Orthodox Tradition of the Christian Church* (Bloomington, IN: AuthorHouse, 2006), 1.
28 "Eusebius was a writer who changed his mind about the Apocalypse; in his early days his views were close to those of the chiliasts." Wainwright, *Mysterious Apocalypse: Interpreting the Book of Revelation*, 34.
29 Notably, Augustine never condemned spiritual chiliasm, as he did with his earlier infatuation with the Manichaeism heresy. "Augustine and Manichaeism," in Samuel N.C. Lieu, *Manichaeism in the Later Roman Empire and Medieval China: A Historical Survey* (Manchester: Manchester University Press, 1985), 152–153.
30 "In the fourth century, Jerome, who did not believe in it [chiliasm], did not dare condemn it in light of the many pious and learned advocates it had found in former centuries." "Millennium," in Frederick C. Beach, *The Americana: A Universal Reference Library*, Vol. 14 (New York: Scientific American, 1912).
31 "Within the Ps. Clementine Recognitions, 1.27–71 has been isolated as a Jewish–Christian source, which can possibly be dated to ca. 100–15 C.E., somewhere in the traditional land of Israel . . . Arnold Stotzel dates the source between 70 and 135 C.E. because it expects a future return to the land." James M. Scott, *Geography in Early Judaism and Christianity: The Book of Jubilees* (Society for New Testament Studies Monograph Series) (Cambridge: Cambridge University Press, 2005), 97. Cf. F. Stanley Jones, "Jewish–Christian Chiliastic Restoration in Pseudo-Clementine Recognitions 1.27–71," 529–571.
32 See Polycrates in Eusebius, *Hist. Eccl.*, v. 24.
33 Tertullian, *adv. Marc.*, iii and *de Res. Carn.*
34 Hippolytus, *Dan.*, iv.3.
35 Lactantius, *Inst. Div.*, vii § 11ff., esp. § 24.
36 Bethune-Baker, *An Introduction to the Early History of Christian Doctrine: To the Time of the Council of Chalcedon*, 70; 68, n. 2.
37 Couch, *A Bible Handbook to Revelation*, 57.
38 Cripe, *Seven Trumpets Asounding: A Commentary on the Book of Revelation in the Historic, Orthodox Tradition of the Christian Church*, 1.
39 Schaff, *History of the Christian Church*, Vol. 2: *Ante-Nicene Christianity, A.D. 100–325*, §184, found at http://www.ccel.org/ccel/schaff/hcc2.v.xv.xxvi.html.
40 Origen wrote *On First Principles*, in which he condemns chiliasm, in Alexandria Egypt, circa 225 C.E.
41 For an excellent summary on precisely how the normative theology of chiliasm became associated with error, see Fairbairn, "Contemporary Millennial/Tribulational Debates: Whose side was the early Church on?," in *A Case For Historic Premillennialism: An Alternative to "Left Behind" Eschatology*, 105–132.
42 Gerhard Maier, *Die Johannesoffenbarung und Die Kirche* (Tübingen: Mohr, 1987), 87.
43 Bietenhard, "The Millennial Hope in the Early Church," *Scottish Journal of Theology* 6 (1953): 12–30, at 14–16.
44 Cohn, *Pursuit of the Millennium*, 29, emphasis mine.
45 Bauckham, "Millennium," 130.
46 Augustine, *De Civitate Dei*, 20.11. In sum, chiliasm began to decline for two reasons. First, in the East, the anti-Judaic, spiritualizing tendencies of the Alexandrian school could not tolerate a Christian doctrine that was so obviously influenced by Second

Temple Judaism. Second, in the West we see Augustine seizing the opportunity to formulate an eschatology more conducive to a renewed relationship between the Church and the State. Overall, as Edwards puts it, "... we see the unfortunate fate of chiliasm in getting mixed up with heresies with which it, as such, had nothing to do." Edwards, *The Transformation of Early Christianity from an Eschatological to a Socialized Movement*, 12.

47 John Henry Newman, *Roman Catholic Writings on Doctrinal Development* (Kansas City, MO: Sheed & Ward, 1997), 23. See John Henry Newman, *An Essay on the Doctrine of Development*, found at http://www.newmanreader.org/works/development/. Daniel J. Lattier confirms this notion when he states that for Newman, "... developments of doctrine are not augmentations of Tradition, but are expressions of the one, infinite mystery contained within Tradition ..." Daniel J. Lattier, "The Orthodox Rejection of Doctrinal Development," *Pro Ecclesia* 20, no. 4 (Fall, 2012): 389–410, at 394.

48 Vincent of Lérins, *Commonitorium* 23.1–12. For the translation of the original Latin, see Thomas Guarino, "Tradition and Doctrinal Development: Can St. Vincent of Lérins still Teach the Church?" *Theological Studies* 67 (2006): 34–72.

49 Dave Armstrong, *Development of Catholic Doctrine: Evolution, Revolution*.

50 See Pannenberg on Vincent in Wolfhart Pannenberg, *Systematic Theology*, 3 vols, trans. Geoffrey Bromiley (Grand Rapids, MI: Eerdmans, 1991), 1:11.

51 See Walter Kasper, *Theology and Church*, trans. Margaret Kohl (New York: Crossroad, 1989), 103. We must ask then, how does doctrine develop from one sense or direction (premillennialism) to another that is its opposite (amillennialism)?

52 "... When it [the Book of Revelation] was first delivered it was understood to be millenarian, since the early chiliasts were the only interpreters who denied neither its canonicity, nor its value for the early Church." Jue, *Heaven upon Earth: Joseph Mede (1586–1638) and the Legacy of Millenarianism*, 112.

53 Walvoord, *The Millennial Kingdom*, 43.

54 Craig Payne, *What Believers Don't Have to Believe: The Non-Essentials of the Christian Faith* (Lanham, MD: University Press Of America, 2006), 17, emphasis mine.

55 There are currently two primary scholars who argue that chiliasm and amillennialism were present from the beginnings of the Christian community in the first century. One is Charles Hill, whose work we have determined hinges upon a rather unstable hermeneutic. The second author, Clementina Mazzucco, follows Hill in his argument. Neither use actual, primary Patristic sources to support his case. See Clementina Mazzucco, "Ill millenarismo cristiano delle origini," in Renato Uglione, ed., *"Millennium": L'attesa della fine nei primi secoli cristiani. Atti delle III giornate patristiche torinesi* (Turin: CELID Editrice, 2002), 145–182. No reliable scholars argue that chiliasm was an entirely absent or unimportant part of the early Church. Quite the contrary, there is almost universal agreement that chiliasm *was* early eschatology.

56 William Horbury, *Messianism among Jews and Christians: Twelve Biblical and Historical Studies* (Edinburgh: T&T Clark, 2003), 281.

57 See for example, Jones, "Jewish–Christian Chiliastic Restoration in Pseudo-Clementine Recognitions 1.27–71," 529–571.

58 See Erik Ranstrom, "Dialogue as Communio: Recovering the Eschatological Dimension of the Eucharistic Church," paper presented at the 67th Annual Convention of the Catholic Theological Society, Miami, FL, June 7, 2012, http://www.ctsa-online.org/Convention&202012/CTSAProgramAbstract4-13-12.pdf (accessed January 30, 2013). Ranstrom confirms the trend of an ecclesio-centric eschatological posture among the Catholic hierarchy—one that exists in order to safeguard against a more open approach that affirms the Church's provisional nature.

The hermeneutics of heresy 157

59 Ormond Rush states that "... the *sensus fidelium* is a corporate organon at work in the Church, enabling the one Church throughout the world to receive revelation faithfully and meaningfully, and then to tradition it effectively." Ormond Rush, *The Eyes of Faith: The Sense of the Faithful and the Church's Reception of Revelation* (Washington, DC: Catholic University of America Press, 2009), 241. For examples of popular and ascetic millenarianism in the Roman Catholic tradition, see Kottman, *Millenarianism and Messianism in Early Modern European Culture, from Savonarola to the Abbé Grégoire* Vol. 2: *Catholic Millenarianism*, especially the essay by Bernard McGinn entitled "Forms of Catholic Millenarianism"; and "En Route to the Marian Kingdom: Catholic Apocalypticism and the Army of Mary," in Hunt, *Christian Millenarianism: From the Early Church to Waco*, 149–165.

60 Abbas Amanat and Magnus Bernhardsson, *Imagining the End: Visions of Apocalypse from the Ancient Middle East to Modern America* (London: I.B.Tauris, 2012), 167.

61 Ibid., 165. A. Lapide, among others, openly admitted "... a number of early commentaries had taught that Apocalypse 20 referred to the *refrigerium sanctorum* after Antichrist." Ibid., 164.

7 Millenarianism
Creeds, Ecumenical Councils, and heresy?

Applying Vincent of Lérins' system, the purpose of the section that follows is to explore the earliest and most influential creeds of the Latin and Greek Churches, along with the most prominent Ecumenical Councils, in light of their eschatology. In particular, I look to determine if chiliasm was ever condemned by any of the Ecumenical Councils and to examine its relationship to the earliest creedal system of Christianity. It is true that Ecumenical Councils did not exist in order to systematically list heretical doctrines, especially if such doctrines did not need to be censured due to previous condemnations by Fathers or Doctors of the Church. My contention is that while chiliasm fell out of popularity, it was never formalized as a heretical belief by any ecumenical ecclesial authority that held the power to speak on behalf of the entire Church, whether East or West. If it were a dangerous heresy, one would expect it to have been condemned outright.

Chiliasm was present in seed form at the formation of the Apostles' Creed, and though it fell out of favor after the Augustinian recapitulation of eschatology, it was never declared an eschatology that was outside the bounds of orthodoxy, let alone formally condemned as heresy. The amillennialist idea that the present era of the Church is completely equal to the reign of Christ on earth is utterly foreign to the apostolic kerygma. Ayer makes the claim that during the period of Diocletian (303–313 C.E.), "... the Church cast off chiliasm which had lingered as a part of a primitive Jewish conception of Christianity and adapted itself to the actual condition of this present world."[1] Though there is truth to the idea that chiliasm fell out of favor in the fourth-century Church, one would expect the ruling of an Ecumenical Council if the rejection of chiliasm were as definitive as Ayer suggests. Instead, we see what appears to be a concerted effort to *not* define too much about the specific nature and unfolding of the Last Days. Many of the creedal statements are rather ambiguous on the topic of eschatology in general, and say nothing on the chronological details of the Second Coming of Christ, or the chronology of the resurrection of the dead. Essentially, the creeds claim that belief in Christ's Parousia, his judgment of both the living and the dead, and the bodily resurrection of all persons, is essential Christian doctrine. The one creedal formulation that mentions the kingdom does so in response to a Trinitarian and Christological heresy, and not a faulty eschatology, as we will see.

Not a single canon of any Ecumenical Council mentions chiliasm. If chiliasts were viewed as far outside of the mainstream of early Christian tradition, or as holding to an erroneous or heretical doctrine, why would millennialism not be named explicitly as such in a canon or note of the Councils? Would not its threat to the Church warrant such censure, as was the case with Arianism, Apollinarianism, Docetism, or even the potentially schismatic practice of the Quartodecimans? Instead, we see that chiliasm was still very much alive through the fifth century and beyond, without censure, most likely because it was normative in the early Church.

The Apostles' Creed

"If there is one statement of the Christian Church, it is contained in the Apostles' Creed," writes William Barclay.[2] While the authority of the Apostles' Creed in the early Church goes without saying, it was not the sole Christian creed, and it was interpreted in more diverse ways than once thought.[3] The exact origin of the Apostles' Creed is ambiguous, but it appears that it finds its seeds in some of the earliest statements of faith and baptismal formulations of the Church.[4] Additionally, the origins of the creed suggest that it was not, as once thought, used originally as a single standard for complete orthodoxy or "Church membership." Arnold Ehrhardt claims that the creed ". . . appears as the form of witness of the 'Church of the Martyrs,' and not as a form of 'adherence' for internal use."[5] Some authors draw the original language of the Apostles' Creed from the "Old Roman Symbol" traceable to the fourth-century Sabellian writer, Marcellus of Ancyra,[6] who was condemned by the Council of Nicaea.[7] Yet it is unlikely that Marcellus's work was the first iteration of the symbol. The origins of the Apostles' Creed are far older than the fourth century, though not traceable to the Apostles themselves in any explicit sense.[8] The first explicit rendering of the Apostles' Creed (*Symbolum Apostolicum*) as we know it today appears in a letter written in a Council of Milan to Pope Siricius, circa 390 C.E.,[9] though this was a shorter version of what we have now, which was expanded in the *De singulis libris canonicis scarapsus* of St. Pirminius in the eighth century.[10] The article of the creed that is interesting, for the purposes of this project, reads as follows: "and he (Jesus Christ) will come again to judge the living and the dead."[11] The dispute in question revolves around whether Jesus's second coming, as rendered in the creed, precludes a distinction in timing or chronology as to when the living and the dead will be raised, whether Jesus could legitimately be viewed as returning and establishing a temporal interregnum period upon which the "saints," or as we have argued, the Jewish people, would be resurrected in distinction from the general resurrection, and also whether Jesus's "judgment" of both groups necessarily implies one act in time. William Shedd describes the amillennialist viewpoint regarding the creed in the following:

> The doctrine which the Church very early derived from the Scriptures, respecting Christ's second coming, is found in the statement of the Apostles' Creed . . . According to this statement, there is no corporeal advent of Christ upon earth after his resurrection, until he leaves his session with the Father

and comes directly "from thence" to the last judgment. The doctrinal statement in the Apostles' Creed, consequently, precludes a premillennial advent of Christ . . . that it [premillennialism] could not have been the catholic and received doctrine is proved by the fact that it forms no part of the Apostles' Creed, which belongs to this period, and hence by implication is rejected by it.[12]

Though Shedd's contentions appear logical on the surface, there are several errors in his thought. First, because the interregnum period of chiliasm is not explicitly mentioned in the Apostles' Creed does not mean, a priori, that chiliasm was not part of the apostolic tradition. A parallel example in Roman Catholic theology would be that the explicit doctrine of the continual existence of purgatory is found nowhere in the creed, despite its article that claims that Jesus "descended to the dead."[13] The same may be said about the sinless nature of Jesus, the sinless nature of Mary, the Immaculate Conception, the primacy of the pope, and various other important doctrines. It would be unwarranted to assume that because the doctrines mentioned above are missing from the Apostles' Creed that they held no part in apostolic tradition, or were never handed down orally as part of the apostolic deposit.

It appears instead that although chiliasm was indeed the early and thoroughly orthodox eschatology of the Church (as mentioned earlier, Justin Martyr claimed that those who denied the millennial reign were outside the bounds of orthodoxy),[14] the most important aspect of the creed is its succinct and pointed nature. The creed does not overtly define something unless a definition is necessary to proclaim a doctrinal truth or refute a serious error. Instead, the nature of the creed is seen in its very brief statements on the Holy Spirit, the Church, the communion of saints, the resurrection of the dead, and eternal life. The Apostles' Creed's statement on resurrection is so succinct and general that one could legitimately argue that Origen's conception of resurrection is consistent with it. Thus, Councils and further declarations on the nature of resurrection were necessary to further redefine or censure doctrines that were considered to be heretical.[15] Scholarship has indeed pointed to a polemical purpose that drove the development of the creed, but this polemic was not against chiliasm. Instead, ". . . the entire Apostles' Creed was pointed against Marcion,"[16] a point made obvious by the development of its strong Christological formulae[17] and its independent precursors in the Oriental form which identified belief "in one Lord Jesus Christ, the only Son of God, who was of the Father *before all aeons, through whom all things came into being* . . ."[18]

Shedd's statement that the Apostles' Creed precludes a premillennial reading of the Last Days is not as clear as he expresses. The article which claims that "from thence" (the seated place at the right hand of the Father) Jesus will come to "judge the living and the dead," does not exclude the possibility of an interregnum period, nor does it necessarily imply that all the events described in the article occur in the chronological sequence in which they are written. This is attested by the fact that the early chiliasts *embraced* the statement that Jesus would, "from thence come to judge the living and the dead."[19] Scholarship has shown that there were multiple forms of the creed that existed prior to the old "Roman Symbol,"[20] stemming from both Western and Oriental sources, while the most recent scholarship suggests that there was a single origin to the diverse articles of the creed. Everett Ferguson calls this symbol "proto-R," illustrating that scholars believe the pieces of evidence ". . . point in the direction of an original form to which all known forms harken back."[21] Moehlman states explicitly that two precursors to the Apostles' Creed, the Oriental[22] and Roman symbols, are traceable to the same origin, that which he calls the "Jerusalem creed," a statement that contains the original formulation claiming that Jesus will "come again in glory to judge the living and the dead."[23] Moehlman further makes the claim that ". . . the ultimate root of both symbols is imbedded in Eastern soil . . . in Tertullian, Irenaeus, and Justin the Martyr . . ."[24] In terms of original hermeneutics in the progression of the Apostles' Creed, *all three early contributors to its development were undisputed chiliasts.*[25] Irenaeus functioned as a central figure in the development of the Apostles' Creed,[26] and his 'Rule of Faith' contains the earliest known and most explicit formulations that parallel the exact language of the creed now used.[27] Justin's "Trinitarian Rule of Faith," which acted as a significant precursor to the Apostles' Creed, assumed a specific eschatology that took for granted a chiliastic understanding of the renewal of the created order, as well as the continued significance of Hebrew prophecy for salvation history.[28] Irenaeus and Tertullian specifically expanded upon the original creedal formulation by their early additions and interpretations of the terms "Son" and "Lord" in the second article of the Rule.[29] Irenaeus's "Rule" states belief in Christ Jesus and in ". . . his appearing from heaven in the glory of the Father to comprehend all things under one head, and to *raise up all flesh of all mankind* . . ."[30] and he speaks further of "guarding diligently the ancient tradition" of the belief in the Christ who ". . . shall come in glory, the Savior of those who are saved, and the Judge of those who are judged . . ."[31] Seeing as Irenaeus fully adopted the chiliastic eschatology of two resurrections,[32] his insistence that 'all flesh of all mankind would be raised' could not have meant that all flesh would be raised up at the same time during one and the same event. Instead, Irenaeus was restating the apostolic tradition that all persons and not merely some would eventually be resurrected, avoiding the heresy of annihilationism.[33] Schaff illustrates how Irenaeus's first, second, and third form of the "Rule" correspond on multiple points to the current Apostles' Creed,[34] with no less than 14 phrases in common in the Greek.[35] For example, Irenaeus' first version of the rule begins with "We believe in God, the Father, the Almighty,"[36] while other aspects affirm the virgin birth,[37] and that Jesus "suffered, died, and was buried," rising on the third day.[38]

Tertullian mentions the Rule of Faith and contributes to it, stating that "The Rule of Faith is altogether one, sole, immovable, and irreformable . . ."[39] and includes in this statement belief that Jesus is ". . . sitting now at the right hand of the Father, coming to judge the living and the dead, also in the resurrection of the flesh." In *Against Praxeas*, Tertullian repeats the Rule, that Jesus is ". . . sitting at the right hand of the Father, to come to judge the living and the dead . . ."[40] while in his treatise, *On Prescription of Heretics*, he uses the term "Rule of Faith" a third time, this time in an apparent chiliastic sense,[41] drawing a distinction between the saints and the wicked: "... he will come again with glory to take the saints into the enjoyment of eternal life and the celestial promises, and to judge the wicked with eternal fire *after the resurrection of both*, with the restitution of the flesh."[42] We notice immediately that in Tertullian's understanding of the Rule, there is a promise of both eternal life and celestial reward, and all, both the saints and the wicked will be resurrected, but the timing of the resurrection/s is left undefined. Though other Fathers, including Novatianus,[43] Cyprian,[44] and Origen[45] rendered various forms of the Rule of Faith, and later commentaries were issued by Cyril, Rufinus, Ambrose, and Augustine,[46] the earliest forms of the creed came through, and were augmented by Justin, Irenaeus, and Tertullian.[47] Considering that chiliasm was not merely the dominant eschatology of the Ante-Nicene period, but in fact the sole eschatology that is clearly traceable through the time of Origen,[48] Shedd's contention that the article in reference to the Parousia and judgment of humanity in the Apostles' Creed existed for the purpose of precluding a chiliastic reading of the Last Days is put into serious question. It appears that the contextual basis for the development of the creed had everything to do with formulating a statement of orthodox Trinitarian belief,[49] delimiting issues within the Doctrine of God, and forming standard statements on the person and divinity of Jesus Christ.[50] Also at the center of the creed was the implicit statement that Jesus would return "in the flesh," distancing from orthodoxy any semblance of Docetism. If the three most prevalent chiliasts of the Ante-Nicene period fully embraced the earliest forms of the Apostles' Creed, including the untouched statements on the Parousia of Christ and the final judgment, and were instrumental to the progression of the creedal formulae, in what manner could the creed be considered a treatise against millennialism? In addition to Justin, Irenaeus, and Tertullian's later work, the earliest rendition of the creed came in the form of an interrogatory baptismal formulation, confirmed in the work of Hippolytus entitled *Apostolic Tradition*, composed in 215 C.E.[51] As mentioned earlier, Hippolytus was an ardent chiliast,[52] begging the question as to how or why he would continue the promulgation of the article that states Jesus will "from thence come to judge the living and the dead," if the phrase was explicitly anti-millenarian in nature. Overall, the creed itself was adopted and significantly developed by early Christian millenarians who saw the Rule of Faith as a permanent and unchanging symbol of orthodoxy. The absence of explicit premillennial language in the Apostles' Creed must be tempered by the fact that any explicit amillennialist language is likewise missing, and the symbol is ambiguous on the topic of eschatological chronology and resurrection. As we examine further creedal formulae and the assemblage of various councils, we must heed the reminder of Joseph Ayer regarding the roots and development of eschatology in Christianity:

> So long as chiliastic expectations were the basis of the Christian's hope and his judgment of the order of this present world, the Christian felt he was but a stranger and sojourner in the world, and that his real home was the kingdom of Christ, soon to be established on earth. With such a view the Christian

would naturally define his relation to the world as being in it, yet not of it. As time passed, the opinion became more common that the kingdom of Christ was not a future world-order to be set up on His return, but the Church here on earth. This thought, which is the key to the *City of God* by St. Augustine, *was not to be found in the first century and a half of the Church*.[53]

If, as sound scholarship suggests, the orthodox principles of the early creeds and the decisions of the Councils had their roots in apostolic and early post-apostolic beliefs,[54] in what sense would chiliasm have been excluded in its influence on creedal and conciliar eschatology, let alone condemned by it?

An early Council responding to Montanism, not chiliasm

Some authors claim that with the refutation of Montanism, the Church unilaterally condemned chiliastic expectations: "Premillenarianism was the first heresy condemned by a Church Council. Montanism, which was largely premillenarianism, was condemned by a Synodical Council in Asia Minor about 178 A.D . . . the first Church creed, the Apostles' Creed, rules it out."[55] Again, *no* Church Council has ever condemned eschatological millenarianism, including the Ecumenical Councils at Ephesus and Constantinople.[56]

Though we are illustrating the contrast between chiliasm and Montanism, it must be noted that Montanism was misrepresented by a wide list of contemporary detractors—a list that includes Eusebius, Athanasius, Epiphanius, and even Tertullian prior to his conversion to the movement.[57] Contemporary scholarship points to a widespread motive among the enemies of Montanism—one that has little to do with either eschatology or Trinitarian theology. Current scholarship points to accusations leveled against the Montanists by orthodox forces—accusations including that of orgies, incest, and the consumption of the blood of infants (ironically, an accusation also made concerning the Jews of the second century).[58] Though none of the accusations are actually provable, prominent feminist authors show how the underlying motive becomes clear, that these statements were made in order to discredit a movement that grew primarily because of the leadership of women—a point highly threatening to the dominant patriarchal system of orthodox Christianity.[59]

In response to the quote above, which claims that chiliasm was condemned along with Montanism, we simply point to the fact that we have already treated the Apostles' Creed and its eschatology, which may be interpreted as a chiliastic statement. There is no evidence that suggests Montanism was a chiliastic belief system at all, though it borrowed from some millenarian expectations. Montanism's heretical elements, which were indeed condemned, had nothing to do with chiliasm.[60] The quote above, apparently referring to the second meeting of a local council in Asia Minor, is vaguely attested in a fragmentary Greek document entitled the *Libellus Synodicus*, the earliest copy of which is dated to the ninth century.[61] The document reveals only a general condemnation of Montanist activity at the time, but makes no mention of Patristic millenarianism. The

Montanists were charged with a wide range of errors, some associated with the Trinity, pneumatology, and an eschatological outlook in which dates for the end of the world were calculated[62] and Phrygia was posited as the new landing place for the coming messiah, instead of Jerusalem.[63] Nevertheless, chiliasm was not on the radar when it came to the Asian condemnation of Montanist doctrine.

Whether true or not, Montanism was referenced in the canons of the Council of Constantinople using the terminology of "Phrygians," and officially described it as a condemned belief system in 381 C.E.[64] Based on the Council's seventh canon, the pronouncement makes an explicit link between Montanism and the heresy of monarchianism—the rejection of distinctions between Father, Son, and Spirit which are permanent.[65] In some instances, "monarchianism" is used in reference to Montanism insofar as it was believed that the sect conceived of an era of the Holy Spirit that was utterly detached from the workings of the Father and Son, in different historical dispensations—a kind of modalistic interpretation.[66] At other times, the Montanist monarchical heresy was associated with the idea that God the Father possessed a "sole rule"—one which was simply shared with God the Son. In the heresy of monarchianism, there is a denial of an 'eternal Triad,' in reference to God's existence, replacing the concept with an "eternal Monad." If early Jewish–Christian elements, including any chiliastic tendencies, were not grounds for the rejection of Montanism, its later development into a monarchist renewal movement would have tipped the New Prophecy over the edge into the realm of the heretical.[67] J. Massyngberde Ford, in her study on the roots of Montanism, argues that it was not the primitive, Jewish–Christian elements that were problematic for the movement, but by contrast, what it evolved into later—a frenzied state of prophetic utterances that appeared to draw a wedge between the "dispensation" of the Holy Spirit and the activity of the three Persons of the Trinity in a more unified way.[68]

Nicaea (325 C.E.) and Rome (382 C.E.)

The synodical and ecumenical process has a basis in the New Testament, which testifies to its role and authority, even as early as the Jerusalem "Apostolic Council"—though the Council recorded in the Book of Acts was not "ecumenical" in the strict sense of the term.[69] In determining whether a certain doctrine was considered orthodox—or at minimum, *not* considered heretical—it is imperative to glean specific information from the early Councils of the Church, as St. Vincent's canon subscribes. Because we are using Vincent's rule as a guide, we follow his view that when it comes to a doctrine that was not agreed upon by Church Fathers of the fourth century (i.e., chiliasm), the next place to look for clarification or proof of the belief's acceptability is the ecumenical, conciliar history.

It has been the modus operandi of amillennialists of the modern, and especially contemporary periods, to make the claim that chiliasm and all forms of millennial belief were condemned early in the Church's conciliar history. The reality of the matter is that no Council in the history of the Church has ever claimed that chiliasm was a heretical eschatology.[70] Gumerlock claims that amillennialists:

in an attempt to strengthen their position and disparage the validity of premillennialism, have focused upon early Church councils, citing several that have allegedly opposed chiliasm. On the surface these historical citations appear to be trump cards demonstrating the doctrinal superiority of amillennialism. But upon closer scrutiny, the claims suffer from a severe lack of substantiation.[71]

In the sections that follow, we will seek to expose the patterns we briefly mentioned earlier, in the written history of those who have claimed that millenarianism was denounced as heretical by the doctrinal authorities of the early Church—namely the bishops of the Ecumenical Councils. The pattern of amillennialist polemicists is such that various authors have, whether intentionally or not, claimed that chiliasm was deemed heretical simply because persons who subscribed to a particular heresy *also were millennialists*. These people, such as Apollinaris (an anti-Arian bishop) and Montanus, among others, were certainly sanctioned by Ecumenical Councils, and their beliefs were indeed condemned— but the condemned beliefs had nothing to do with their adherence to chiliasm. Apollinaris' conception of the Divine Logos, not his supposed chiliasm, was so strongly rejected, that it was eventually banned through an Imperial Edict in 388 C.E. Apollinarianism:

> was condemned by synods at Rome in 377, at Antioch in 379, and at the Ecumenical Council of Constantinople in 381. In its essence, Apollinarianism asserts that there is only one mind, will, and soul of the Second Person of the Trinity. The human aspect of the human Jesus is limited solely to his bodily flesh.[72]

The problems with Apollinarian thought, or at least its logical consequences, become apparent when one considers the balance expressed in orthodoxy regarding the divine and human natures of Christ. Apollinarianism, by contrast, implies that:

> the body of Christ, by its unity with the Word and lack of a human soul, is so divinized as to be "unearthly," not a human body at all . . . [and there was also] . . . the problem of Christ's sufferings: Apollinarianism would have to maintain either that the divine nature suffered or that no Passion, and no Atonement took place.[73]

Conciliar condemnations of Apollinarianism illustrate an important point. Very few, if any early Councils were held in response to controversies surrounding the nature of the kingdom of God or the chronology of Jesus' second coming. Instead, the Councils tended to focus on Trinitarian, Christological, and incarnational debates. The eschatological elements of the Councils, and the creeds they produced, typically focused on the importance of the bodily resurrection and the fact that Jesus' return would be truly corporeal. As with the conciliar condemnations against Apollinaris, the rejection of Montanus and his beliefs have nothing to do with his highly modified chiliasm. Instead, the condemnations are likely focused on the Phrygian heresy that too closely identified Montanus and his prophecy with the Person and prophetic function of the Holy Spirit.[74] While scholars differ as to whether Montanism was condemned for doctrinal or purely disciplinary and practice-related reasons,[75] they agree that the primary error leveled against Montanism was Trinitarian in scope because it disregarded the role of the institutional Church as a mediator for the Holy Spirit. Further, early detractors of Montanism made claims that Montanus or one of the prophetesses of Phrygia were believed to actually embody the Holy Spirit, and that the Montanist revelation superseded even that of the Holy Spirit. According to J. Hefele:

> Apollinaris, the holy Bishop of Hierapolis in Asia, and twenty-six of his colleagues in the episcopate, held a provincial council at Hierapolis, and there tried and condemned Montanus and Maximilla the false prophets, and at the same time Theodotus the currier (the celebrated anti-Trinitarian).[76]

Hefele also goes on to report: ". . . the *Shepherd of Hermas*, which was certainly anterior to 151 . . . seems already to oppose Montanism."[77] This is of interest to us because, according to Jerome, Apollinaris of Hierapolis was a chiliast[78]—likely having the tradition handed down by Papias, another bishop of the same province. The *Shepherd of Hermas* is a traditionally chiliastic text. Why would Apollinaris and the writer of the *Shepherd* oppose Montanism, if chiliasm were the central theme of what was perceived as a heresy among the Phrygians?

Certainly, eschatological expectation was a major part of Montanist spirituality, but there is nothing to suggest that this was the focus of its censure.[79] It appears that the "error" of Montanism, according to the early synod, was associated with claims regarding its adherents' view of how the Holy Spirit works, whether they baptized in the orthodox Trinitarian formula,[80] and whether there might be a further revelation of the Spirit in Phrygia that replaced the institutionalized Church. Tertullian, both a chiliast and a Montanist, defended the sect's asceticism and rigorism while maintaining orthodoxy on all fronts.[81] The Council of Nicaea did not condemn Montanism, though the Phrygians did receive a dishonorable mention.[82] The seventh canon of the Council of Constantinople rejected Montanist and Sabellian baptisms while accepting Arian baptism.[83] Again, Trevett tells us that, "in 381, the Council of Constantinople condemned Montanism on the grounds of Monarchianism."[84] The Council of Laodicea (364 C.E.), in its eighth canon, makes the following statement:

> those who are converted from the heresy called that of the Phrygians (Montanism), even if they be among those whom they account as clergy or even among those called their great ones—after they have been very carefully instructed, they are to be baptized by the bishops and presbyters of the Church.[85]

The censures above are likely due to the fact that at least later Montanists were suspected of baptizing in the name of "the Father, the Son, and the Lord

168 *Contemporary Catholic theology*

Montanus."[86] Overall, when authors such as Columba Flegg claim that "the heresy of chiliasm was eventually condemned in 381 by the Second Ecumenical Council,"[87] they are likely referring to the condemnation of the Sabellianist or Monarchinian heresy associated with Montanism, while conveniently leaving out the specifics. Amillennialist authors may likewise be referring to other heresies of Apollinaris of Laodicea, unrelated to his chiliasm. There is no direct mention of chiliasm in any Ecumenical Council, nor may it be inferred that chiliasm, based on the original sources and histories of the Councils and creeds, was the subject of debate at an Ecumenical Council. Later in this section, we will more closely explore the Ecumenical Councils in order to discern why scholars of the past confusedly believed that millennialism was declared heretical. It will become evident that when an amillennialist claims that millennialism was condemned at an Ecumenical Council, it is really meant that "Apollinaris," or "Montanus," or "Joachim" was condemned, glossing over, or conveniently ignoring, the specific *reasons* for their condemnations.

The first Ecumenical Council held at Nicaea, Bithynia, in 325 C.E., convened by the Roman Emperor Constantine, had as its aim the unification of the multiple parts of Christendom under one basic consensus and system of doctrine, representing most, if not all, the provinces of the Christian Church.[88] Doctrinally and liturgically, the Council's function was to discern Christological theology in light of the Arian controversy,[89] settle the calculation of the date of the celebration of Easter,[90] construct the first part of the Nicene Creed (which is the Eastern form of the primitive creed),[91] and promulgate a new code of canon law.[92] It is often argued that because the Nicene Creed, the original of which was formulated at the first Ecumenical Council, includes the phrase, "I believe in the resurrection of the dead and the life of the world to come," that the "resurrection of the dead" is to be interpreted as the general resurrection and judgment, followed by the ushering in of the eternal kingdom, as in amillennialism.[93] This interpretation would preclude any concept of two resurrections, and eliminate the possibility that any of the Council's bishops took seriously the chiliasm that was so prevalent in the early Church.[94] The view above appears to claim that, "after the Council of Nice [*sic*], none gave utterance to anything in sympathy with chiliasm."[95] But according to Peters, the extensive study of the canons and acts of the first Ecumenical Council by Gelasius Cysicenus,[96] there exists an interesting note in the *acta* of the first Ecumenical Council, in reference to the article on the resurrection of the dead. The bishops state, in reference to the 'resurrection' article of the original Nicene Creed, that:

> The world was made inferior because of foreknowledge, for God foreknew that man would sin. Therefore we expect new heavens and a new earth according to the Holy Scriptures; the Epiphany and Kingdom of the Great God and our Savior Jesus Christ then appearing. And as Dan says (ch. 7:18), "the saints of the Most High shall then take the kingdom. And there shall be a pure and holy land, the land of the living and not the dead," which David, foreseeing with the eye of faith, exclaims, "I believe to see the goodness of

the Lord in the land of the living[97]—the land of the meek and humble." "Blessed," sayeth Christ (Matt. 5:5) "are the meek, for they shall inherit the earth." And the prophet sayeth (Isa. 26:6), "the feet of the meek and humble shall tread upon it."[98]

On the surface, the quote above may not appear to have any explicit millenarian elements, but read within its context, it is a presentation of chiliastic interpretation[99] because this note on the article of the Nicene Creed regarding eschatology is an explicit parallel, both linguistically and thematically, to Lactantius,[100] whose seventh chapter of the chiliastic work, the *Divine Institutes* ". . . presupposes the edict of Milan in 313."[101] According to Valentin Fabrega, the fourth century:

> Lactantius stands with his chiliasm in the ground of a firm biblical and Churchly tradition. As in other spheres so is he also in this point a collector of handed-down opinions. That the chiliastic doctrine was contested among orthodox theologians is a concept which Lactantius, with the decided chiliasts, never once intimates.[102]

The note on the resurrection article from the creedal formula ascribed to the first Ecumenical Council, borrows not only Lactantius' language, but also his interpretive framework of the Old Testament prophecies, use of the words of Christ in reference to the inheritance of the land, and understanding of the correlation of meekness, the presence of the kingdom on a renewed earthly Jerusalem, and the special resurrection promised to the saints.[103] Lactantius' entire interpretive system is chiliastic, and adopted in the episcopal notes regarding the creed's eschatology. Peters argues that, contrary to the assumption made by amillennialists that the creedal phrase "I believe in the resurrection of the dead and the life of the world to come" must refer to one general resurrection, coinciding with the final judgment and consummation of the world, the testimony of the context of the creed itself illustrates that many chiliastic bishops interpreted the phrase alternatively.[104] Chiliasm was still quite popular in Western orthodox circles during the time of the first Ecumenical Council,[105] and its absence from the original Nicene Creed in an explicit sense is akin to the absence of an explicit amillennialist interpretation of the same. Nowhere in the canons or creedal system is it implied that the Church is to be equated with the kingdom, or that the reign of Christ is to be interpreted as beginning with his first advent, precluding any further reign during his second.

By the fourth century, chiliasm began falling out of popularity, but it was never censured or even discussed at the first Ecumenical Council. By contrast, there appear to be bishops who understood the eschatology of the Council in a moderately chiliastic sense. Overall, the Council of Nicaea fervently condemned Arianism as incompatible with orthodox Christological and Trinitarian understanding,[106] and likewise condemned Quartodeciminism, primarily on political grounds, regardless of the legitimacy of the practice since before the time of Polycarp.[107] Nowhere in the canons or extensive notes of the Council of Nicaea was chiliasm mentioned, and any connection between the statements on judgment and resurrection in the Nicene Creed[108] and purported rejection of chiliasm is unfounded.[109] As we will see later, the phrase "And His Kingdom will have no end," taken from the Gospel of Luke, was added to the Nicene Creed at the Council of Constantinople in 382,[110] after extensive and disruptive arguments over multiple Trinitarian issues ensued among the Nicene Council's bishops.[111] Thus far, our thesis stands, succinctly described by Michael J. Svigel: "The oldest tradition of writers on the history of millennialism appears to be ignorant of any alleged condemnation of Chiliasm in any official and dogmatic capacity in early Christian history."[112]

Although we will be exploring the Second Ecumenical Council held in Constantinople in 381 C.E., and its extended creedal statement, it is important that we consider a lesser-known Council, not of an ecumenical nature, that occurred during the same period—the Council of Rome (382 C.E.). Certain themes inherent in the Council of Rome were being discussed *prior to* the Council of Constantinople, and thus influential upon it.[113] Pope Damasus, a staunch defender of Roman primacy,[114] called and moderated the synodical meeting and wrote a decree based on its decisions, incorporating them into a *Tome*—parts of which are still in existence.[115] The reason the Council of Rome is important is because at least one scholar has claimed that the Council condemned chiliasm: D.T. Taylor wrote that, "The Council of Rome under Pope Damasus, in A.D. 373[116] formally denounced Chiliasm."[117] Taylor gets his claim from the sixteenth-century Roman Catholic historian Baronius, and also likely from Lorinus of Avignon's *Commentary on Acts*, in which the author writes of ". . . the heresy of chiliasm, which Pope Damasus had *condemned in Apollinaris*."[118] Although the bulk of the accounts of the Roman synod held under Pope Damasus are no longer extant, there is little doubt that Apollinaris was condemned there.[119] The important point for our purposes is that Apollinaris was not condemned because he was a chiliast, but because of his view of the personhood of Jesus:

> Those who denied the perfect humanity of Christ included some also who claimed that he did not have a real human soul. The best known authors of this heresy are Arius and Apollinaris of Laodicea, "the young." They are both under the influence of the Logos-Sarx approach to Christology which owes its starting point to Origen.[120]

It is well known that Basil rejected Apollinaris on the point of Christology, and sent two presbyters to Damasus asking the Roman bishop to immediately condemn the position, along with Apollinaris personally.[121] The deposition of Apollinaris was so serious that the Council of Rome likewise condemned his two closest disciples, Vitalis and Timotheus, directing the angst of the Council against the Christological error: "By the same Council (Rome) it was defined, that Jesus was 'true Man and true God' and whoever maintained or asserted anything to be wanting either to his Humanity or Divinity, was declared an Enemy to the Church."[122] Certainly, if that which the Council of Rome wanted to condemn regarding

Apollinaris was his chiliasm, we would see a condemnation of the same beforehand, deposing the earlier Commodian, Lactantius, or Victorinus of Patau—all prolific writers before the time of Apollinaris.[123] We likewise see plentiful examples of individuals who were chiliasts after the Councils of Rome and Nicaea, all of whom went on about their business without censure. We see a very wide tolerance of the chiliastic views so that by the time of Apollinaris, conciliar focus was upon the Trinitarian and Christological heresies of the time. There is no evidence whatsoever that the Council of Rome intended to condemn chiliasm along with Apollinaris.[124] Further, there is still scholarly debate as to whether Apollinaris of Laodicea was a chiliast at all, as Eusebius accuses him of a chiliastic 'Jewish fervor,'[125] while Epiphanius argues the opposite.[126]

Constantinople (381 C.E.): "Whose kingdom shall have no end"

It is a common claim among amillennialists that the Second Ecumenical Council held at Constantinople, by adding the phrase "and His kingdom shall have no end"[127] to the Nicene Creed, formally condemned the chiliastic eschatology, as held by Apollinaris.[128] Again, it is debatable as to whether Apollinaris, who was influenced by Origenism vis-à-vis his exposure to Athanasius' Alexandrian theology,[129] held to chiliasm, though his opponents polemically claimed so in dramatic terms.[130] As with the Council of Rome, it appears that Apollinaris and chiliasm have become synonymous, though without cause: "In this case, as in others mentioned, we see the unfortunate fate of chiliasm getting mixed up with heresies with which it, as such, had nothing to do with."[131]

Roman Catholic, Protestant, and Orthodox authors alike have spread the misconception that:

> the bishops gathered at the Council of Constantinople in 381 specifically condemned the chiliast teaching of Apollinaris of Laodicea (d. 390); and in order to curb his teachings about the thousand year reign of Christ, they inserted into the creed the words "His kingdom will have no end.[132]

For example, Catholic writer Joe Kennedy states that "... the words in the Nicene Creed, 'whose kingdom shall have no end,' were specifically intended to oppose ... chiliasm."[133] Even one popular Protestant theologian who has worked in accord with Moltmann's eschatological framework, Wolfhart Pannenberg, has perpetuated the fallacy regarding chiliasm and the phrase in the Nicene Creed: "The Lordship of the Son is not, as the chiliasm of the Montanists et al. thought, a special epoch in salvation history ... for this reason it can be said of the Son that his kingdom will have no end."[134] Pannenberg is correct in his Trinitarian theology, but incorrect in stating that either the Montanists or chiliasts were conclusively modalistic. Orthodox Protopresbyter Michael Pomazansky offers a more specified accusation, pastorally forbidding even the private opinion of chiliastic eschatology:

If it was at one time possible to express chiliastic ideas as private opinions, this was only until the Ecumenical Church expressed its judgment about this. But when the Second Ecumenical Council (381), in condemning *all* the errors of the heretic Apollinarius, condemned also his teaching of the thousand-year reign of Christ and introduced into the very Symbol of Faith the words concerning Christ: *And His Kingdom will have no end*—it became no longer permissible at all for an Orthodox Christian to hold these opinions.[135]

In spite of the certainty with which Fr. Pomazansky claims the ecumenical censure of chiliasm, two questions must be posited in reference to his claim. First, did the Council of Constantinople condemn everything Apollinaris taught, or did the bishops have a specific censure in mind? Second, was the addition of the phrase "And His kingdom will have no end," though added for a specific purpose, intended as a statement against chiliasm? The first canon of the Council of Constantinople reads as follows:

> The profession of faith of the holy fathers who gathered in Nicaea in Bithynia is not to be abrogated, but it is to remain in force. Every heresy is to be anathematized and in particular that of the Eunomians or Anomoeans,[136] that of the Arians or Eudoxians,[137] that of the Semi-Arians or Pneumatomachi,[138] that of the Sabellians,[139] that of the Marcellians,[140] that of the Photinians[141] and that of the Apollinarians.[142]

We notice that in the canon above, heresies are identified by groups, associated with those who purportedly spread the errors. Further, we notice a specific commonality among each heresy listed in the first canon, corresponding to the general purpose for which the Council was called by Theodosius, that is, to solidify adherence to Nicene Trinitarianism and Christology.[143] Gumerlock astutely recognizes that:

> *all* of the heretics mentioned in Canon 1 in some way contradicted the Nicene faith with respect to the doctrine of God, more specifically to the nature and relationship of the Son and Holy Spirit within the Godhead. The Apollinarians were no exception, as they too were teaching doctrine contrary to the Nicene faith.[144]

According to Gumerlock, Apollinarianism,[145] though not Apollinaris personally, was harshly condemned at Constantinople, but the addition of the phrase "His kingdom will have no end"[146] was not directed toward the Apollinarians. Instead, the phrase "who came down and became incarnate from the Holy Spirit and the Virgin Mary" was specifically added to refute the Apollinarian teaching that Jesus was not fully human.[147] Gumerlock further explains the addition of the phrase "And His Kingdom will have no end" into the Nicene Creed: "The Council of Constantinople did insert this phrase into the creed, but according to the best patristic scholarship it had nothing to do with the millenarian teachings of Apollinaris. Rather, it was a reaction to the unorthodox Christology of Marcellus . . ."[148] According to Marcellus, God was a Monad who split into a Dyad at creation, with the Logos becoming "Son" only at the incarnation.[149] During Easter, or, according to some of Marcellus' adversaries, Pentecost, God became a Triad with the sending of the Spirit.[150] The key to Marcellus' teachings in relation to the Nicene Creed is that according to the heresy, ". . . *at the end of time Christ will hand over the Kingdom to the Father, and God will be all in all, once again a Monad.*"[151] William Brackney summarizes the point as follows:

> Increasingly associated with his student, Photinus (?-376), who rejected the preexistence of Christ, Marcellus, along with Photinus, was condemned at the Council of Constantinople in 381. In refutation of Marcellus's interpretation of I Corinthians 15:24–28, the Nicene Creed was modified to read, "whose kingdom shall have no end."[152]

All indications point to the fact that millenarianism, whether associated with Apollinaris or not, was never discussed at the Council of Constantinople. Apostolic millenarians did not teach that a formal "end" or "terminal point" would occur in reference to the messianic kingdom,[153] because a majority of them perceived the "thousand-year reign" as a kind of symbol—albeit one with an historical referent different from Augustine's ecclesiastical view. The thousand-year reign, to them, would lead directly from the historical reign of Christ and the resurrected saints, to the destruction of Satan, the general resurrection and final judgment, into eternity. The eschatological event of the ushering in of the kingdom would flow seamlessly into eternity with God.

For the Council of Constantinople and its changes to the Nicene Creed, all language associated with the eschatological kingdom of God was treated in holistic proximity to the eternal economy of the Persons of the Trinity and their interrelations, particularly associated with creation, incarnation, and the eternal reign of the Persons of the Trinity, who were understood as co-eternal, co-substantial, and co-equal. Contra Marcellus and Photinus, the kingdom of Christ would have no end because it, like the Divine Logos, was, and is, eternal. Gumerlock states that ". . . as for the early councils, *none* explicitly addressed the belief in an earthly millennial kingdom."[154] Constantinople I addressed Marcellus and Apollinaris, among others, Ephesus, as we will see, does not speak a word of chiliasm, and Constantinople II (553) ". . . anathematized anyone who maintained that Christ's kingdom would have an end, but . . . this statement was not directed against chiliastic beliefs . . ."[155]—instead it was set as a defense against Origen's concept that all will be temporally cycled and reabsorbed into the Godhead.

Gumerlock suggests that Canon 18 of the Council of Hiereia (754), which met at the height the iconoclasm controversy, states that the kingdom of heaven will not end, but, "as is the case of the councils mentioned previously, chiliast beliefs were not the subject of attack . . ."[156] Likewise, according to Pelikan, official conciliar censure was not directed against millennialism:

> Most ... eschatological speculation, however, escaped official anathema. The condemnations of Montanism were not directed principally against its apocalyptic teachings, and the attack against Gnosticism was mentioned, but did not concentrate upon, its millenarian tendencies.[157] *Eschatology that denied the creed was anathematized as heresy; eschatology that merely went beyond the creed was tolerated . . .*[158]

Millenarian eschatology went "beyond the creed" in the sense that it explained in detail that which was left undefined, especially in reference to the chronology of the events of the Second Coming and specifics regarding the resurrection of the dead. Nevertheless, millenarian eschatology was tolerated because it never transgressed or contradicted any articles of the ecumenical creeds, and carried with it the support of so many well-respected Patristic figures. Thus, it is unlikely that the Ecumenical Councils simply ignored the eschatology because some Fathers of the fourth century considered millennialism a misreading of Revelation 20. Quartodeciminism is similar to millennialism, in the sense that it was practiced by a wide range of orthodox Fathers and officially supported in their writings, particularly in citing appeals to apostolic tradition.[159] Millennialism could have suffered the same ecumenical censure as did both the dogmatic and liturgical aspects of the celebration of Easter according to the Jewish calendar, but it did not. Some believe that millennialism was ecumenically tolerated because it would have been impossible to argue that it did not come from apostolic sources: ". . . history records the fact that such a premillennial belief was the *universal* belief of the Church for two hundred and fifty years after the death of Christ."[160]

Ephesus (431 C.E.): No direct or indirect reference to millenarianism

The First Ecumenical Council at Nicaea met to settle Trinitarian issues, formalize a creed, and enforce a standard day for Easter celebration, while the Second Ecumenical Council at Constantinople gathered to reinforce the primacy of *homousian*, Nicene Christianity over and against Arianism, and reject the reactionary teachings of Apollinaris and various other forms of monophysitism and Logos–sarx Christology.[161] The crumbling of the Roman Empire historically led to the First Council of Ephesus, or the Third Ecumenical Council, which met in seven sessions, primarily to deal with the Nestorian controversy.[162] One aspect that was heavily emphasized at Ephesus, Christological at root, was the use of the term *Theotokos* in reference to the Virgin Mary, contrary to the thought of Nestorius, who wanted to emphasize that Jesus comprised two separate persons, and Mary was the mother only of his human person.[163]

Similar to what was discussed earlier concerning the Council of Constantinople, modern scholars such as Andrew Bradstock have stated that the Council of Ephesus declared millennialism as heretical, issuing a statement on the topic, as if it was an historical and dogmatic fact:

Following Augustine, the Church had long believed that the reign of the saints foretold by Revelation was already in operation through its own good offices, and shown little enthusiasm for the idea that Christ would return imminently to set up an earthly kingdom: *indeed, the Council of Ephesus declared such a belief heretical in 431.*[164]

In 2003, Svigel explored the validity of the statement above, publishing his findings in *The Trinity Journal*.[165] We take note that in Bradstock's quote above, he specifically ties together the Augustinian view of the millennium, which was compiled and distributed by Augustine himself about a decade prior to the Council of Ephesus, and the "decision" of the bishops of the Council to "condemn" chiliasm. The problem that we are attempting to emphasize is that the bishops never condemned premillennial eschatology. Despite claims to the contrary, there is not a single canon or note associated with the Council of Ephesus, or its history, that touches upon the topic of chiliasm.[166] Following a thorough study of the roots of historical, Patristic millennialism in relation to conciliar declarations, Steven Matthews states that the "interpretation of the Council of Ephesus which claims that chiliasm was clearly condemned there in 431 is *highly debatable.*"[167] A detailed examination of the original Greek text of the eight canons of the Council of Ephesus illustrate condemnations of Nestorius[168] in canons three, four, five, and seven, condemnation of Celestius[169] in canon one, and a condemnation of an exposition brought to the floor by the Presbyter Charisius[170] in canon seven—none of which have anything to do with chiliasm.[171] Contemporary, authoritative studies on the Council of Ephesus stress its preoccupation with Nestorianism and properly defining the "hypostatic union," whereby Jesus' divine and human nature are to be conceived as held together in one person.[172]

The idea that chiliasm was addressed at Ephesus, though unfounded in any primary sources, may have stemmed from the connection of Apollinaris and apocalyptic eschatology, considering the Council of Ephesus likely reiterated some of the points of Constantinople.[173] Nevertheless, systematic scholarly texts that detail the events of Ephesus did not begin to associate the Council with a condemnation of chiliasm until the appearance of a work by the French writer Leon Gry, published in 1904.[174] Gry's work contains an ambiguous footnote in which he claims that St. Cyril (the president of the Council of Ephesus) was questioned by Oriental bishops in reference to the third anathema regarding past ecumenical condemnations. In the case of Cyril at Ephesus, the interrogation apparently involved the divine and human natures of Christ, traceable to the work of Apollinaris—particularly in reference to the heretic's view of the Eucharist.[175] It is Gry who connects the line of questioning with the anti-materialistic rhetoric prominent at the time, in line with anti-chiliastic sentiments. Norman Cohn, in his popular yet scholarly work entitled *Pursuit of the Millennium*, either misquoted or mistranslated Gry's footnote, interpreting it to mean that the Council of Ephesus formalized against chiliasm.[176] Cohn's statement then became a widespread source of thought on chiliasm in general. The extent to which Cohn's statement on chiliasm and its erroneous allegation of a condemnation at Ephesus has been perpetuated would be impossible to measure, but Svigel alone lists at least six books that repeat the error, in which the authors cite Cohn either directly or secondarily.[177] The following summarizes the extent of the damage:

> As can be seen from the reconstruction of the history of the claim that the Council of Ephesus condemned Chiliasm in 431, the original source records no such condemnation, anathema, decree, or declaration . . . Having been made by able scholars with a far-reaching influence in popular volumes, this error . . . [that Ephesus condemned chiliasm] . . . has now reproduced itself at the popular level with no hope for restraint.[178]

The dissemination of Cohn's error developed quickly into statements that not only claimed that millennialism was condemned by the bishops, but that the ". . . Council of Ephesus in 431 accepted amillennialism as orthodox eschatological teaching."[179]

Despite the absence of any condemnations of millenarian eschatology traceable to the Council of Ephesus, one might ask of the probability of the subject being treated at the Council, without an official anathema or documentation being rendered. Perhaps the *intention* of the 250 bishops of the Council was to reject the eschatology, without giving formal censure for one reason or another. The problem with this hypothesis is that the Council of Ephesus would have been the perfect occasion for such a rejection of chiliasm vis-à-vis the formalized adoption of the then new, but well known, amillennial view. It is well known that "Augustine began work on *The City of God*, said to be the first philosophy of history ever written, in response to the sacking of Rome by the Visigoths in A.D. 410."[180] Dana Gould tells us that Augustine conversed with Marcellinus and Volusianus about the decline of the Roman Empire, and wrote *City of God* between 413 and 424.[181] By 431, the year the Council of Ephesus was called, the amillennialism of the *City of God*, and Augustine's view of the Church was known widely in multiple geographical areas.[182] Augustine, whose amillennial influence was both profound and wide, was invited to the Council of Ephesus, but he died before he could receive the invitation.[183] Robert Clouse, perpetuating the misnomer of heresy discussed earlier, claims that Augustine's ". . . teaching was so fully accepted that at the Council of Ephesus in 431, belief in the millennium was condemned as superstitious."[184] Thus, in light of Clouse's repetition of the charge, a question arises: *if* the bishops of the Council were considering chiliasm, there certainly were a number of contemporaries, such as St. Methodius of Olympus (d. 311), Victorinus (d. 304), and Lactantius (d. 320), whose strong millenarian legacies into the fourth century could have conceivably been tried and condemned. Such a condemnation would likewise accompany a formalization of the Origenist, allegorical reading of Revelation 20, or the adoption of an Augustinian interpretation of the eschatological phrases of the creeds. But such a condemnation is thoroughly missing, not only from the proceedings of the Council of Ephesus, but from all of our conciliar history—precisely because no such explicit intention existed among the bishops as they were gathered ecumenically. What is fascinating

Creeds, Ecumenical Councils, and heresy? 177

about the false claim that chiliasm was condemned at Ephesus is that the bishops certainly were aware of Augustine's amillennialism but chose *not* to formally pronounce it as the only acceptable and orthodox eschatology for the Church.

Notes

1 Joseph Cullen Ayer, *A Source Book for Ancient Church History* (Teddington, UK: Echo Library, 2010), 163.
2 William Barclay, *The Lord's Prayer* (Louisville, KY: Westminster John Knox Press, 1998), 115.
3 Piotr Ashwin-Siejkowski, *The Apostles' Creed: The Apostles' Creed and Its Early Christian Context* (London: T&T Clark International, 2009), 26.
4 Carl E. Braaten, *Who Is Jesus?: Disputed Questions and Answers* (Grand Rapids, MI: Wm. B. Eerdmans Publishing Company, 2011), 116.
5 Arnold Ehrhardt, "Christianity before the Apostles' Creed," *The Harvard Theological Review* 55, no. 2 (1962): 73–119, 73. By contrast, Schaff suggests that the Apostles' Creed "... still surpasses all later symbols for catechetical and liturgical purposes, especially as a profession of candidates for baptism and Church membership." Philip Schaff, *The Creeds of Christendom*, Vol. 1: *The History of Creeds*, 6th ed. (Grand Rapids, MI: Baker, 1998), 15.
6 John Baron, *The Greek Origin of the Apostles' Creed Illustrated* (Oxford: Oxford University Press, 1885), 34.
7 Archibald Robertson, *Regnum Dei* (Whitefish, MT: Kessinger Publishing, 2004), 52.
8 J.N.D. Kelly, *20. Rufinus: A Commentary on the Apostles' Creed* (Ancient Christian Writers) (Mahwah, NJ: Paulist Press, 1978), 101–102, n. 8. Cf. "Apostles' Creed," in *Oxford Dictionary of the Christian Church* (Oxford University Press, 2005), 90.
9 See http://www.tertullian.org/fathers/ambrose_letters_05_letters41_50.htm#Letter42.
10 Kelly, *Early Christian Creeds*, 398–430.
11 The Latin rendering is as follows: "inde venturus (est) judicare vivos et mortuos," while the Greek is rendered as: "εκειθεν ερχόμενον κρῖναι ζωντας και νεκρούς."
12 William Greenough Thayer Shedd, *Dogmatic Theology*, Vol. 2 (Charleston, SC: Forgotten Books, 2010), 642.
13 Shedd traces both chiliasm and purgatory to errors of "Jewish influence" and argues that neither is found in the Apostles' Creed. Shedd, *Dogmatic Theology*, Vol. 2, 596.
14 Thomas Petrisko, *The Kingdom of Our Father* (Pittsburgh, PA: Saint Andrew's Productions, 1999), 52.
15 Such clarifications are still necessary, as attested by the following statement in the Catholic Catechism that claims that the Christian idea of resurrection includes "... not only that the immortal soul will live on after death, but that even our 'immortal body' will come to life again." *Catechism of the Catholic Church*, §990, 258.
16 Conrad Moehlman, "The Origin of the Apostles' Creed," *The Journal of Religion* 13, no. 3 (July 1933): 301–319, 310.
17 Moehlman holds that "... the late second century Apostles' Creed recorded a development in which an expanded triune baptismal formula had been synthesized with an expanded Eucharistic Christological confession through the liturgy of the Church. The polemical element was secondary." Ibid., 311.
18 See Hans Lietzmann, *Die Anfänge Des Glaubensbekenntnisses: Festgabe Zu A.v. Harnacks 70* (Tübingen: Mohr Siebeck, 1921), 226ff.
19 H.B. Swete, *The Apostles' Creed: In Relation to Primitive Christianity* (Cambridge: Cambridge University Press, 1899), 92, n.3.
20 Ibid.

178 *Contemporary Catholic theology*

21 Everett Ferguson, "Creeds, Councils, and Canons," in Susan Ashbrook Harvey and David Hunter, eds., *The Oxford Handbook of Early Christian Studies* (Oxford: Oxford University Press, 2008), 431.
22 The Oriental form of what would later become the Apostles' Creed ". . . had assumed somewhat definite form before the middle of the second century and independently of the Western development." Ibid., 314.
23 Moehlman, "Origin of the Apostles' Creed," 316.
24 Ibid., 313.
25 Hill, *Regnum Coelorum*, 11–20, 27–32.
26 "Irenaeus's Use of the regula fidei as a Framework," in Brevard S. Childs, *The Struggle to Understand Isaiah as Christian Scripture* (Grand Rapids, MI: Eerdmans, 2004), 47–48.
27 "At the heart of his doctrine was the question of the 'rule of faith' and its transmission. For Irenaeus, the 'rule of faith' coincided in practice with the Apostles' Creed . . . in fact, the gospel preached by Irenaeus is the one he was taught by Polycarp, bishop of Smyrna, and Polycarp's gospel dates back to the Apostle John, whose disciple Polycarp was." Pope Benedict XVI, *Great Christian Thinkers: From the Early Church through the Middle Ages*, 1st Fortress Press ed. (Minneapolis, MN: Augsburg Fortress Publishers, 2011), 13.
28 Paul R. Hinlicky, *Divine Complexity: The Rise of Creedal Christianity* (Minneapolis, MN: Fortress Press, 2011), 129. For the articles of the creed as espoused by Justin, see *Apol.*, I.c.10, 13, 21, 42, 46, 50.
29 Moehlman, "Origins of the Apostles' Creed," 307.
30 Irenaeus, *Contra Haer.*, I.10, §1, emphasis mine. The fact that Irenaeus believes that all people will be resurrected directly refutes those who claim that the later Athanasian Creed precludes a millenarian reading because it claims that at Christ's coming "all men will rise with their bodies." Like the Apostles' and Nicene creeds, certain theologians have sought to link articles of the Athanasian Creed with an explicit refutation of chiliasm. The brief eschatological statements of the Athanasian Creed, in addition to borrowing the statement from the Apostles' and Nicene Creed, "From thence He shall come to judge the quick and the dead," adds the phrase, "Ad cujus adventum omnes resurgere habent cum corporibus suis et reddituri sunt de factis propriis rationem" ("At whose coming all men shall rise again with their bodies; and shall give account of their own works."). Peters claims that the chronology of the Athanasian Creed on the Second Coming coincides well with Irenaeus, an ardent chiliast.
31 Ibid., III.4.§§ 1,2.
32 Scott M. Lewis, *So That God May Be All in All: The Apocalyptic Message of 1 Corinthians 15, 12–34* (Rome: Pontificia universita gregoriana, 1998), 173.
33 Ibid., Cf. William C. Irvine, ed., *Heresies Exposed* (Whitefish, MT: Kessinger Publishing, 2003), 18. According to T.L. Tiessen, annihilationism was condemned at the Fifth Ecumenical Council of Constantinople in 553. See T.L. Tiessen, "Hell," in W.A., Dyrness, V.M. Karkkainen, and J.F. Martinez, eds., *Global Dictionary of Theology: A Resource for the Worldwide Church* (Downers Grove, IL: IVP, 2008), 374. Looking at Jewish apocryphal sources, the *Apocalypse of Moses*, in contrast to the Christian heresy of annihilationism, suggests that some will be raised at a different time from others, but all will ultimately be raised from the dead. Like Christian chiliasm, Second Temple Jewish Apocalyptic anticipated two resurrections—a point never formally declared heretical by the Church. See *Apoc. of Moses*, 13:3–5. Cf. Lester L. Grabbe, *Judaic Religion in the Second Temple Period: Belief and Practice from the Exile to Yavneh* (New York: Routledge, 2000), 264.
34 Schaff, *The Creeds of Christendom*, Vol. 2: *The Greek and Latin Creeds*, 12–16.
35 See Schaff's chart, ibid., 52–53.

36 The Greek is identical with later versions: εἰς ἕνα Θεὸν, Πατέρα παντοκράτορα.
37 The Greek phrase is καὶ τὴν ἐκ Παρθένου γέννησιν.
38 For the entire rule and its development, see Irenaeus, *Contra Hæreses*, Lib. I. cap. 10, § 1.
39 Tertullian, *On the Veiling of Virgins* (Whitefish, MT: Kessinger Publishing, LLC, 2010), Ch. 1, 3. *On the Veiling of Virgins* was written during his Montanist period, unlike some of his other chiliastic writings.
40 Tertullian, *Against Praxeas*, ii, in Evans, *Tertullian's Treatise against Praxeas*.
41 Johannes Quasten, *Patrology: The Ante-Nicene Literature after Irenaeus*, vol. 2, of *Patrology* (Trumbull, CT: Spectrum, 1950), 412. *On Prescription of Heretics* is filled with explicit chiliastic language.
42 Tertullian, *On Prescription of Heretics*, xiii.
43 See Novantius, *De trinitate s. de regula fidei*.
44 See Cyprian, *Ep. Ad. Mag.* and *Ep. Ad Jan.*
45 See Origen, *De principiis*, I. praef. § 4–10.
46 Schaff, *The Creeds of Christendom*, Vol. 1: *The History of the Creeds*, 18, n. 3.
47 Thomas C. Oden, *Classic Christianity: A Systematic Theology* (Ventura, CA: HarperOne, 2009), xiii. Cf. Ashwin-Siejkowski, *The Apostles' Creed: The Apostles' Creed and Its Early Christian Context*, 71.
48 Ibid., 810.
49 Columba Stewart, "Christian Spirituality during the Roman Empire," in Arthur Holder, ed., *The Blackwell Companion to Christian Spirituality* (Hoboken, NJ: Wiley-Blackwell, 2010), 73–89, 75.
50 Hans Schwarz, *Christology* (Grand Rapids, MI: Eerdmans, 1998), 144.
51 Robert A. Krieg, "The Apostles' Creed," in Richard P. McBrien, *The HarperCollins Encyclopedia of Catholicism* (San Francisco, CA: HarperSanFrancisco, 1995), 75.
52 Bietenhard, "The Millennial Hope in the Early Church," 19. Cf. Danielou, *The Theology of Jewish Christianity*, 401.
53 Ayer, *A Source Book for Ancient Church History*, §11, "The Church and the World," emphasis mine.
54 Berard L. Marthaler, *The Creed: The Apostolic Faith in Contemporary Theology*, rev. ed. (Mystic, CT: Twenty-Third, 2007), 2.
55 William Rainey Harper, *The Biblical World*, Vol. 6 (Memphis, TN: General Books LLC, 2010), 172.
56 Manuel Lacunza, *The Coming of Messiah in Glory and Majesty*, Vol. 1, 60–65.
57 Virginia Burrus, "The Heretical Woman as Symbol in Alexander, Athanasius, Epiphanius, and Jerome," *HTR* 84 (1991) 229–248.
58 "Montanists at Rome were also accused of sorcery and black magic, mixing of the blood of infants with flour to bake communion bread . . . [and] . . . holding drunken orgies at Eucharist . . ." Robert Benedetto, *The New Westminster Dictionary of Church History* (Louisville, KY: WJK, 2008), 444.
59 Gail Corrington Streete, "Women as Sources of Redemption and Knowledge in Early Church Traditions," in Ross Shepard Kraemer and Mary Rose D'Angelo, eds., *Women & Christian Origins* (New York: Oxford University Press, 1999), 344.
60 "Montanism's earliest opponents did not accuse it of chiliastic enthusiasm. No extant oracle speaks explicitly of chiliasm." Trevett, *Montanism: Gender, Authority, and the New Prophecy*, 96. Neither Jerome nor Eusebius, both skeptical of chiliasm, condemn Montanism on the grounds of chiliastic belief, though they do condemn it. Modern scholarship suggests that the heresy of Montanism was based almost solely on its ". . . rejection that the first-century gospels could constitute any final and complete form of revelation," and had nothing to do with chiliasm. Court, *Approaching the Apocalypse*, 54, and Scott, ed., *Restoration: Old Testament, Jewish, and Christian Perspectives*, 535. Cf. John C. Poirier, "Montanist Pepuza-Jerusalem

180 *Contemporary Catholic theology*

and the Dwelling Place of Wisdom," *Journal of Early Christian Studies* 7, no. 4 (1999): 491–507. Cf. Eusebius, *Hist. Eccl.*, 5:16:10, and David F. Wright, "Why Were the Montanists Condemned?" *Themelios* 2, no. 1 (September 1976): 15–22, at16.

61 Karl Joseph von Hefele, *A History of the Christian Councils, from the Original Documents, to the Close of the Council of Nicaea, A.D. 325* (Charleston, SC: Nabu Press, 2010), 222–224.

62 The chiliast Irenaeus rejected the idea that calculating the date of the end of the world could be part of a proper eschatology.

63 Trevett, *Montanism: Gender, Authority and the New Prophecy*, 77–150, 214.

64 See the reasons behind the Phrygian condemnation in Council of Constantinople, 381 C.E., Canon 7, in "Early Church Texts: The Canons of the Council of Constantinople (381)—the original Greek text with English Translation and Latin version," found at http://www.earlyChurchtexts.com/public/constantinople_canons.htm.

65 For a more detailed understanding of monarchianism and the wide uses of the term, see Justo L. González, *Essential Theological Terms* (Louisville, KY: Westminster John Knox Press, 2005), 114.

66 Jerome points toward monarchian, Sabellian, and modalistic breaches of the Rule of Faith as the source of the condemnation of Montanism. See *Les Sources de l'Histoire du Montanisme*, 167–168.

67 Some ancient sources tell us that Montanism was banned because its adherents baptized "in the name of the Father, the Son, and the *Lord Montanus*."

68 Ford argues that Montanism did ". . . not seem to have been a heresy in its beginnings." J. Massyngberde Ford, "Was Montanism a Jewish–Christian Heresy?," *Journal of Ecclesiastical History* 17 (1966):145–158, 145.

69 P. Kariatlis, *Church as Communion: The Gift and Goal of Koinonia* (Wayville, SA: ATF Press, 2011), 171–176.

70 See Daley, *The Hope of the Early Church: A Handbook of Patristic Eschatology*. The most thorough histories of the Ecumenical Councils omit any mention of premillennialism whatsoever.

71 Francis X. Gumerlock, "Millennialism and the Early Church Councils: Was Chiliasm Condemned at Constantinople?" *Fides et Historia* 36, no. 2 (Summer/Fall 2004): 83–95, 85.

72 Gary Macy, "Apollinarianism," in Orlando Espin and James B. Nickoloff, eds., *An Introductory Dictionary of Theology and Religious Studies* (Collegeville, MN: Liturgical Press, 2007), 67–68, at 67.

73 Stephen Thomas, *Newman and Heresy: The Anglican Years* (Cambridge: Cambridge University Press, 1991), 91. Newman's theory is that Apollinarianism, despite the good intentions of its founder, ultimately results in Sabellianism and Patripassionism.

74 See William Tabbernee, *Fake Prophecy and Polluted Sacraments: Ecclesiastical and Imperial Reactions to Montanism* (Leiden: Brill, 2007).

75 See Mary Rose D'Angelo, "'I Have seen the Lord': Mary Magdalen as Visionary, Prophecy, and the Context of John 20:14–18," in Deirdre J. Good, ed., *Mariam, the Magdalene, and the Mother* (Bloomington, IN: Indiana University Press, 2005), 95–101, esp. 115. Cf. Davis, *The First Seven Ecumenical Councils (325–787): Their History and Theology*, 22. See also F. Forrester Church, "Sex and Salvation in Tertullian," *HTR* 68, no. 2 (1975): 82–101.

76 von Hefele, *A History of the Christian Councils, from the Original Documents, to the Close of the Council of Nicaea, A.D. 325*, 78.

77 Ibid., 79.

78 Jerome, *De Vir., Ill.*18; *Com. In Ezech.*, c. 36.

79 Rex D. Butler, *The New Prophecy & New Visions* (Washington, DC: Catholic University of America Press, 2006), 35.

80 Ibid., 29.

81 Tertullian was never excommunicated and he never considered himself a separatist from the Catholic Church. See Schaff, *History of the Christian Church*, 420.
82 Socrates, *HE* i.13.7.
83 John Anthony McGuckin, *The Orthodox Church: An Introduction to Its History, Doctrine, and Spiritual Culture* (Malden, MA: Wiley-Blackwell, 2010), 275, n. 274.
84 Trevett, *Montanism: Gender, Authority and the New Prophecy*, 218.
85 Jurgens, *The Faith of the Early Fathers*, vol. 1, 316.
86 Trevett, *Montanism: Gender, Authority and the New Prophecy*, 219.
87 Columba Graham Flegg, *An Introduction to Reading the Apocalypse* (Crestwood, NY: St. Vladimirs Seminary Press, 1999), 47.
88 Leo Donald Davis, *The First Seven Ecumenical Councils (325–787): Their History and Theology* (Collegeville, MN: Liturgical Press, 1990), 21.
89 G.L. Prestige states that a major reason for the calling of the Council was to ascertain how "... it was possible to maintain the unity of God while insisting on the deity of one who was distinct from God the Father." G.L. Prestige as quoted in ibid., 33.
90 Ibid., 68.
91 There are two main versions of the Nicene Creed—one formulated at the first Ecumenical Council, taken from the Eastern primitive creed, as the Apostles' creed developed in the West, and one which removed an anathema and added several phrases during the second Ecumenical Council. For a fuller discussion of the Nicene Creed, see Schaff, *The Creeds of Christendom*, Vol. 1: *The History of the Creeds*, 24–28.
92 R.C. Mortimer, *Western Canon Law*, 1st ed. (London: Adam & Charles Black, 1953), 9.
93 Ratzinger, *Eschatology: Death and Eternal Life*, 213.
94 Paul L. King writes that "... the earliest Church overwhelmingly maintained a premillennial viewpoint," citing multiple early Fathers. King, "Premillennialism and the Early Church," 8.
95 Peters, *The Theocratic Kingdom of Our Lord Jesus, the Christ, as Covenanted in the Old Testament and Presented in the New Testament*, 518, note to Obs. 7.
96 See John Cox, ed., *The Writings and Disputations of Thomas Cranmer Relative to the Sacrament of the Lord's Supper* (Cambridge: Cambridge University Press, 1844), 355.
97 Calvin argues that "the land of the living" here is not in reference to the heavenly realm, as is evident from the Hebrew and also the Greek in the LXX. It is in reference, instead, to an earthly, divinely established kingdom. The context is that belief, for David, constitutes a new life in the earthly "land of the living." See John Calvin, *Commentary on the Psalms* (Edinburgh: Banner of Truth Trust, 2009), commentary on Psalm 27:13–14, n. 13.
98 Gelasius Cysicenus, *His. Act. Con. Nic.*, as quoted in Peters, *The Theocratic Kingdom of our Lord Jesus Christ*, 128.
99 Cf. Hagenbach, *History of Christian Doctrine*, Vol. 3, 356.
100 Lactantius, *Divine Institutes* vii.24. Cf. *Epit.*, 72.
101 Quasten, *Patrology: The Ante-Nicene Literature after Irenaeus*, Vol. 2, 397.
102 Valentin Fabrega "Die Chiliastische Lehre Des Laktanz," *JAC* 17 (1975): 126–146, at 142.
103 See George Günter Blum, *Offenbarung und Berlieferung* (Göttingen: Vandenhoeck & Ruprecht, 1971), 356.
104 It is worth quoting Peters at length on this point: "... it would appear that many, at least, of the three hundred bishops composing the Council were Millennarian—for this statement [of the bishops, inspired by Lactantius] is *purely chiliastic*—and that the influence and teaching of Lactantius and others was not forgotten. Let us add that the extract [recorded by Gelasius Cysicenus] is valuable in indicating *how anciently* such expressions in the creed which simply expressed a belief in the resurrection of

the dead, were understood, namely: not necessarily to imply a simultaneous resurrection of all at one and the same time. This again shows . . . that the leading creeds, as the Apostles' and Niceno-Constantinopolitan, as well as the brief formulas of Irenaeus and Tertullian were in direct sympathy with chiliasm." Peters, *The Theocratic Kingdom of Our Lord Jesus, the Christ, as Covenanted in the Old Testament and Presented in the New Testament*, 518, emphasis in original.

105 Karlfried Froehlich, "Interpretation of History," Bruce M. Metzger and Michael David Coogan, eds., *The Oxford Companion to the Bible* (New York: Oxford University Press, 1993), 314.

106 See Marthaler, *The Creed: The Apostolic Faith in Contemporary Theology*, 92.

107 Jeffrey VanderWilt, *A Church without Borders: The Eucharist and the Church in Ecumenical Perspective* (Collegeville, MN: Michael Glazier Books, 1998), 150. VanderWilt's point is interesting, insofar as both Quartodecimanism and chiliasm have traceable apostolic roots, and both are customs and doctrines heavily influenced by Judaism. The important point for our purposes is associated with why the Council's bishops would explicitly condemn Quartodecimanism, but make no mention of chiliasm whatsoever. If the intention of the bishops were to condemn millennialism, even for the sake of a forced unity in the midst of diversity, would millennialism not have received the same definitive censure as Quartodeciminism?

108 For the Roman Catholic polemical use of the Nicene Creed, see Jon Kennedy, *Jesus and Mary the Blessed Mother the Holy Son, and His Teachings of the Word* (East Bridgewater, MA: Word Publishing Group, 2010), 275.

109 Peters, *The Theocratic Kingdom of our Lord Jesus Christ*, 128.

110 Bradley G. Green, ed., *Shapers of Christian Orthodoxy: Engaging with Early and Medieval Theologians* (Downers Grove, IL: IVP Academic, 2010), 165.

111 See Lewis Ayres, *Nicaea and Its Legacy: An Approach to Fourth Century Trinitarian Theology* (Oxford: Oxford University Press, 2004).

112 Svigel, "The Phantom Heresy: Did the Council of Ephesus (431) Condemn Chiliasm?" 105.

113 Jurgens argues that the Tome of Damasus was actually attached to the acts of the Council of Constantinople. See Jurgens, *The Faith of the Early Fathers*, Vol. 1, 405.

114 David L. Eastman, *Paul the Martyr: The Cult of the Apostle in the Latin West* (Atlanta, GA: Society of Biblical Literature, 2011), 102–103.

115 Jurgens, *The Faith of the Early Fathers*, Vol. 1, 405. One of the primary heresies condemned at the Council was that of Patripassionism—that God the Father died. See Jacques Dupuis, *The Christian Faith: In the Doctrinal Documents of the Catholic Church* (New York: Alba House, 1982), 147.

116 Taylor borrowed both the date and the information regarding the Council of Rome from Baronius, who is incorrect in his dating of the Council which condemned Apollinaris—it took place in 382 C.E. See von Hefele, *A History of the Christian Councils, from the Original Documents, to the Close of the Council of Nicaea, A.D. 325*, 10.

117 D.T. Taylor, *The Voice of the Church on the Coming and Kingdom of the Redeemer; or, A History of the Doctrine of the Reign of Christ on Earth*, rev. and ed. H.L. Hastings (Peace Dale, RI: H.L. Hastings, 1855), 115.

118 Lorinus of Avignone, *Com. On Acts 1:6*; Peters, *The Theocratic Kingdom of Our Lord Jesus, the Christ, as Covenanted in the Old Testament and Presented in the New Testament*, 520, emphasis mine. Lorinus of Avignon was a Jesuit scholar (1559) and was known for his commentary work.

119 Taylor, referring to the Council called by Pope Damasus, rightly claims that, ". . . a great council was held in Rome, where Apollinaris, Bishop of Laodicea, was condemned and deposed." Taylor, *The Voice of the Church on the Coming and Kingdom of the Redeemer*, 43.

Creeds, Ecumenical Councils, and heresy? 183

120   F. Ocáriz, L.F. Mateo Seco, and J.A. Riestra, *The Mystery of Jesus Christ: A Christology and Soteriology Textbook* (Dublin: Four Courts Press, 1998), 58.
121   Archibald Bower, *The History of the Popes, from the Foundation of the See of Rome, to the Present Time*, Vol. 1 (Charleston, SC: Gale ECCO, 2010), 278. Apollinaris' condemnation as an individual likely came from his unwillingness to recant his doctrine. See P.C. Thomas, *General Councils of the Church: A Compact History* (Bandra, Mumbai: St. Pauls Publications, 2001), 22.
122   Ibid.
123   Schaff, *History of the Christian Church*, Vol. 2, 618.
124   Frederic J. Baumgartner, *Longing for the End: A History of Millennialism in Western Civilization* (New York: St. Martin's Press, 1999), 47.
125   Eusebius, *Hist. Eccl.*, iii.39, 13.
126   Epiphanius, *Pan.*, Lxxvii, 36.5. In Epiphanius's book of heresies, the *Panarion*, Apollinaris is accused of over-emphasizing the divine attributes of Jesus, ignoring that he was fully man. There is no discussion relative to Ebionite or "Jewish errors." It appears odd that a man condemned for embracing a heresy that emphasized the divine over the human attributes of Jesus, traceable to Origen, would likewise embrace Judaistic elements of Christianity such as chiliasm. Overall, Epiphanius claims that Apollinaris was *not* a chiliast.
127   The phrase has a New Testament basis in the Gospel of Luke's account (1:30–34) of the annunciation to the Virgin Mary: "But the angel said to her, 'Do not be afraid, Mary; you have found favor with God. You will conceive and give birth to a son, and you are to call him Jesus. He will be great and will be called the Son of the Most High. The Lord God will give him the throne of his father David, and he will reign over Jacob's descendants forever; his kingdom will never end.' "
128   Kennedy, *Jesus and Mary*, 275. Cf. Flegg, *An Introduction to Reading the Apocalypse*, 47.
129   Kelly, *The Ecumenical Councils of the Catholic Church*, 35.
130   Gregory Nazianzen, *Ep.* CII, 4, and Basil, *Ep.* CCLXIII, 4, claimed that Apollinaris held to an expectation of a grossly carnal and highly Jewish expectation of a messianic kingdom, which would include a reinstitution of the centrality of the Temple in Jerusalem. On the questionable validity of Gregory and Basil's claims about Apollinaris' eschatology, see Edwards, *The Transformation of Early Christianity from an Eschatological to a Socialized Movement*, 11–12. By contrast, Jerome puts Apollinaris in the millenarian camp of Irenaeus, Papias and Tertullian. See Jerome, *Com. Dan.*, 9.24 and Daley, *The Hope of the Early Church*, 102. Epiphanius of Salamis claims that Apollinaris is not a millennialist at all. Epiph. *Adv. Haer.*, 77.36.5, Daley, *The Hope of the Early Church*, 80.
131   Edwards, *The Transformation of Early Christianity from an Eschatological to a Socialized Movement*, 12.
132   Gumerlock, "Millenialism and the Early Church Councils: Was Chiliasm condemned at Constantinople?" 89.
133   Kennedy, *Jesus and Mary*, 275.
134   Pannenberg, *Systematic Theology*, Vol. 3, 608, n. 258.
135   Michael Pomazansky, *Orthodox Dogmatic Theology: A Concise Exposition*, 3rd ed. (Platina, CA: St. Herman Press, 2006), 173, emphasis mine. Cf. Engleman, *Ultimate Things*, 116, and Aversky Taushev, *The Apocalypse in the Teachings of Ancient Christianity* (Platina, CA: St. Herman of Alaska Brotherhood, 1995), 288.
136   Roger E. Olson, *The Story of Christian Theology: Twenty Centuries of Tradition & Reform* (Downers Grove, IL: IVP Academic, 1999), 181.
137   Ibid., 147.
138   The Pneumatomachi, or "enemies of the Spirit," subordinated the Holy Spirit, denying its divinity.

184 *Contemporary Catholic theology*

139 The Sabellians were Tritheists, insisting on three different natures among the Persons of the Trinity. Olson, *The Story of Christian Theology: Twenty Centuries of Tradition & Reform*, 183–184.
140 The Marcellians, named after their Sabellian bishop, Marcellus of Ancyra, were modalists, ". . . identifying the Father and the Son so closely that they are to be considered one and the same subsistence, or personal identity." Ibid., 163.
141 The Photinians were named after their founder, Photinus, bishop of Sirmium (d. 376). Photinus was ". . . a reputed disciple of Marcellus of Ancyra, [and] he is associated with a Monarchian type Trinitarianism, manifest in its view that the Son did not subsist until his incarnation *and that his kingdom was not eternal*." D.H. Williams, "Photinus," in Benedetto, *The New Westminster Dictionary of Church History*, 519.
142 The translation above is taken from the Greek. For the original Greek, see Hefele, *A History of the Christian Councils, from the Original Documents*, 2.1, 13–15. See also "First Council of Constantinople," in Jurgens, *The Faith of the Early Fathers*, Vol. 1, 399.
143 John W. Morris, *The Historic Church: An Orthodox View of Christian History* (Bloomington, IN: AuthorHouse Publishing, 2011), 64. The original Easter creed contained neither the phrase "And His kingdom will have no end," nor the *Filioque* that is present in its correct Latin form. See Jurgens, *The Faith of the Early Fathers*, Vol. 1, 398.
144 Gumerlock, "Millenialism and the Early Church Councils: Was Chiliasm condemned at Constantinople?" 91–92, emphasis mine.
145 Constantinople, following an earlier Council at Alexandria (362), refrained from using the name "Apollinaris" as a personal name, though it did identify the heresy with its founder by connecting him with the sect. Philip Smith, *The Student's Ecclesiastical History: The History of the Christian Church During the First Ten Centuries from Its Foundation to the Full Establishment of the Roman Empire and the Papal Power* (New York: Harper & Brothers, 1879), 350–351.
146 For the additions made to the Nicene Creed during the Second Ecumenical Council, see F.L. Cross & E.A. Livingstone, eds. *The Oxford Dictionary of the Christian Church*, 3rd ed. (New York: Oxford University Press, 1997), 1145–1146.
147 Gumerlock, "Millenialism and the Early Church Councils: Was Chiliasm condemned at Constantinople?" 91. That the focus of the Council's rejection of Apollinarianism was its Christology is affirmed explicitly in a letter sent to Rome after the Council closed. See Norman P. Tanner, ed., *Decrees of the Ecumenical Councils: Nicaea I to Lateran V* (London: Georgetown University Press, 1990), 28.
148 Ibid., 92–93.
149 Ibid., See also Aloys Grillmeier, *Christ in Christian Tradition: From the Apostolic Age to Chalcedon (451)* (Christ in Christian Tradition), vol. 1, rev. ed. (London: A.R. Mowbray & Co., 1975), 277.
150 Carl L. Beckwith, *Hilary of Poitiers on the Trinity: From de Fide to de Trinitate* (New York: Oxford University Press, 2009), 20.
151 Joseph T. Lienhard, *Contra Marcellum: Marcellus of Ancyra and Fourth-Century Theology* (Washington, DC: Catholic University of America Press, 1999), 49–50, emphasis mine.
152 "Marcellians," in William H. Brackney, *Historical Dictionary of Radical Christianity* (Historical Dictionaries of Religions, Philosophies, and Movements Series) (Lanham, MD: Scarecrow Press, 2012), 187.
153 According to Scott, this understanding is most readily seen in Irenaus' chiliasm, which borrowed extensively from the Book of Jubilees. For apostolic chiliasm, ". . . the transformation expected in the restoration will last from that time and until eternity, which is another evidence of the continuity between the third era (the messianic reign) and the eternal state." James M. Scott, *On Earth as in Heaven: The Restoration of*

Sacred Time and Sacred Space in the Book of Jubilees (Boston, MA: Brill Academic, 2005), 233.
154 Gumerlock, "Millenialism and the Early Church Councils: Was Chiliasm condemned at Constantinople?" 93, emphasis mine.
155 Paul M. Collins, *Partaking in Divine Nature: Deification and Communion* (London: T&T Clark, 2010), 102, n. 73.
156 Gumerlock, "Millenialism and the Early Church Councils: Was Chiliasm condemned at Constantinople?" 94. Depiction of the glory of God and the saints in man-made images seemed to detract from the fullness of glory in heaven, which was the focus of the Council. The Council of Heireia was overturned in 787 by a Council of Nicaea.
157 Contra Pelikan, many scholars challenge the idea that Gnosticism could have carried with it millenarian ideas, or vice versa. Cf. Bauer, *Orthodoxy and Heresy in Earliest Christianity*, 2nd ed., 85, 207; Klaus Wengst, *Häresie und Orthodoxie im Spiegel Des Ersten Johannesbriefes* (Gütersloh: Gutersloher Verlagshaus G. Mohn, 1976), 35–36; Brown, *The Epistle of John* (New York: Doubleday, 1982), 770. George MacRae denies a connection between early Gnosticism and Christian chiliasm, calling them "strange bedfellows." George W. MacRae, *Studies in the New Testament and Gnosticism* (Wilmington: Michael Glazier, 1987), 247.
158 Jaroslav Pelikan, *The Christian Tradition: A History of the Development of Doctrine*, Vol. 1, 129, emphasis mine.
159 Gerard Rouwhorst, "Liturgy on the Authority of the Apostles," in A. Hilhorst, ed., *The Apostolic Age in Patristic Thought* (Boston, MA: Brill Academic, 2004), 63–87, at 75–76.
160 J. Dwight Pentecost, *Things to Come: A Study in Biblical Eschatology* (Grand Rapids, MI: Zondervan, 1965), 374.
161 See Davis, *The First Seven Ecumenical Councils (325–787): Their History and Theology*, 33–77, 81–131, and also Grillmeier, *Christ in Christian Tradition*, Vol. 2, 308–328.
162 For an excellent summary of the Nestorian debate in the context of the Council of Ephesus, and its ensuing repercussions on the Christian Church of the fifth century, see Susan Wessel, *Cyril of Alexandria and the Nestorian Controversy: The Making of a Saint and of a Heretic* (New York: Oxford University Press, 2004).
163 Janice Poorman, "Council of Ephesus," in McBrien, *The HarperCollins Encyclopedia of Catholicism*, 470.
164 Andrew Bradstock, "Millenarianism in the Reformation and the English Revolution," in Hunt, *Christian Millenarianism: From the Early Church to Waco*, 77, emphasis mine.
165 Svigel, "The Phantom Heresy: Did the Council of Ephesus (431) Condemn Chiliasm?" 105–112.
166 Ibid.,106.
167 Steven Matthews, *Theology and Science in the Thought of Francis Bacon* (Aldershot: Ashgate, 2008), 109, n.9. For a thorough translation of the primary texts associated with the Council of Ephesus, see James Chrystal, *Authoritative Christianity: The Third World Council*, 3 vols. (Charleston, SC: Nabu Press, 2010).
168 McMahon gives an excellent, succinct reason for the theological condemnation of Nestorius, who ". . . fell into a position that did not adequately express the full union of the divine Son with the human being Jesus . . . Nestorius' ideas seemed like a form of adoptionism, and therefore a denial of the incarnation." Christopher McMahon, *Jesus Our Salvation: An Introduction to Christology* (Winona, MN: Anselm Academic, 2007), 137.
169 Celestius, a priest ordained in 415, was condemned by name at the Council of Ephesus, presumably because of his adoption of Pelagian theology and his inferred denial of Adam's fall from grace. See B.R. Rees, *Pelagius: Life and Letters* (Rochester, NY: Boydell Press, 2004), 4–5.

186 *Contemporary Catholic theology*

170 Nicholas Constas, *Proclus of Constantinople and the Cult of the Virgin in Late Antiquity: Homilies 1–5, Texts and Translations* (Leiden: Brill Academic, 2003), 123, n. 133.
171 "Canons of Ephesus," and "Notes on the Canons of Ephesus," in William Bright, *The Canons of the First Four General Councils of Nicaea, Constantinople, Ephesus, and Chalcedon, with Notes* (Oxford: Clarendon Press, 1892), xxv, 124–139. Cf. Henry Bettenson and Chris Maunder, *Documents of the Christian Church*, 4th ed. (Oxford: Oxford University Press, 2011), 510.
172 Christopher M. Bellitto, *The General Councils: A History of the Twenty-One General Councils from Nicaea to Vatican II* (Mahwah, NJ: Paulist Press, 2002), 22–24.
173 Charles E. Raven, *Apollinarianism: An Essay on the Christology of the Early Church* (Eugene, OR: Wipf & Stock, 2004), 233.
174 Leon Gry, *Le millénarisme dans ses origines et son développement* (Paris: A. Picard, 1904). See especially 106–107.
175 Svigel, "The Phantom Heresy: Did the Council of Ephesus (431) Condemn Chiliasm?" 109. Cf. Phiiippe Labbe and Gabriel Cossart, eds., *Sacrosancta concilia ad regiam editionem exacta*, 16 vols (Lutetiae Parisiorum: Societatis typographicae Librorum Ecclesiasticorum jussa Regis constitutae, 1671–1672), 3: col. 834–837. Gry appears to draw a parallel between questioning of the bishops, directed toward Cyril, regarding an error of Apollinaris associated with a claim that the Eucharistic mystery was solely a natural phenomenon without spiritual significance. It is possible that the Eastern bishops made a connection between this conception of the sacrament and the emphasis on the material over the spiritual in Apollinaris' "grossly carnal millenarianism." Nevertheless, Cyril apparently ignores the question, and refocuses attention on the topic at hand, which was that of Christological error. The third anathema of the Council of Ephesus ends with a threat of excommunication or deposition of those who continue to follow any bishops who were condemned as heretics by former Ecumenical Councils (including the condemnation of Apollinaris at Constantinople).
176 This book has been quoting from Cohn's corrected version of the text, published in 1970. For the source of the error, see Norman Cohn, *The Pursuit of the Millennium: Revolutionary Messianism in Medieval Reformation Europe and Its Bearing on Modern Totalitarian Movements* (New York: Harper & Row, 1957), 14. Here, Cohn alleges that in ". . . 431 the Council of Ephesus condemned belief in the Millennium as a superstitious aberration."
177 Svigel, "The Phantom Heresy: Did the Council of Ephesus (431) Condemn Chiliasm?" 106–108. Among the authors Svigel cites as perpetuating Cohn's mistake are Robert Clouse, Peter Toon, Andrew Bradstock, Richard Kyle, Paul Boyer, and Stanley Grenz. None of the scholars listed cite primary sources in their statements regarding the Council of Ephesus.
178 Ibid., 112.
179 Peter Toon, *Puritans, the Millennium and the Future of Israel: Puritan Eschatology, 1600 to 1660: A Collection of Essays* (Cambridge: James Clarke, 1970), 14.
180 B. Hadden and H.R. Luce, *Time* (New York: Time, 1987), 166. See also Rüdiger Bittner, "Augustine's Philosophy of History," in Gareth B. Matthews, ed., *The Augustinian Tradition* (Berkeley, CA: University of California Press, 1999), 346.
181 Dana Gould and Terry L. Miethe, *Augustine's City of God* (Nashville, TN: B&H Books, 1999), 8.
182 ". . . Augustine was known farthest and widest, beginning in the early 410s, when he was nearing 60." Eleonore Stump and Norman Kretzmann, eds., *The Cambridge Companion to Augustine* (New York: Cambridge University Press, 2001), 12, and Andrea Wilson Nightingale, *Spectacles of Truth in Classical Greek Philosophy: Theoria in Its Cultural Context* (Cambridge: Cambridge University Press, 2004), 16.

183 "... at the end of his ... [Augustine's] ... life, *his reputation had penetrated erratically into the Greek Church* and an invitation was sent for him to attend the council of Ephesus—but he had died before it could reach him in Africa." Ibid., emphasis mine.
184 Clouse, "Introduction," in Clouse and Hoekema, *The Meaning of the Millennium: Four Views*, 9.

8 Recent magisterial statements on millenarianism*

Having illustrated the historical silence of the Church in officially condemning millenarianism for the purpose of exploring the implications of Joachim's philosophy of history, we now return to the theme of ecclesial declarations on eschatology. In the sections that follow, I will focus on modern and contemporary statements by the Church's ordinary Magisterium that treat the topic of millenarianism. It will become clear that the brief and novel statements regarding millenarian eschatology, when put in proper context, open up the possibility for theological exploration of the pre-Nicene, chiliastic view of the end times. In general, the highly ambiguous statement of Pope Pius XII regarding millenarianism must be put in the context of the Second World War, while statements in the 1994 Catechism basically reiterate the earlier papal statement of 1944, and its rationale, but aim such accusations at Communism and Liberation Theologies. Overall, Pius' statement does not carry much weight as a formalized condemnation of millenarian doctrine, primarily because it was issued specifically against Nazi manifestations of originally Christian chiliastic principles, and existed as a public (though belated) refutation of Nazi aspirations to establish a political messianic kingdom on earth.

Pius XII and the declaration against millenarianism

After nearly two millennia in which the Roman Catholic Church was silent on the topic of millenarian eschatology through its formal ecumenical, episcopal, and papal authority, on July 19, 1944, Pope Pius XII[1] broke that silence. The context involved the pope's response to a question posed by the "Supreme Sacred Congregation of the Holy Office" (the precursor to today's CDF), which reads:

> 'In recent times on several occasions this . . . Holy Office has been asked what must be thought of the system of mitigated Millenarianism, which teaches, for example, that Christ the Lord before the final judgment, whether or not preceded by the resurrection of the many just, will come visibly to rule over this world.' Pope Pius answered, 'The system of mitigated Millenarianism cannot be taught safely.'[2]

The degree to which the statement above is an authoritative doctrine binding on all Roman Catholics for assent is debatable, since a wide majority of Catholic scholars agree that the pope's finalization of doctrine does not exist in a vacuum, but is confirmed by the ecumenical, episcopal process, and is reaffirmed through the *Sensus Fidelium*.[3] Pope Pius's answer was never published in an Encyclical and was never declared *ex cathedra*. Additionally, the statement is not to be placed within the category of the *universal* ordinary Magisterium, as no universal episcopal statements were made up until Pius XII's answer. No bishops have touched upon the subject of millenarianism in an official teaching, either individually or collectively. Certainly the pope's answer cannot be considered 'infallible,' but is to be respected by the faithful only as a matter of decision by the pope as he exercises authority in the sense of his ordinary teaching capacity.[4]

The one-sentence papal statement likewise begs the question as to whether the prohibition of a doctrine as "unsafe to teach" is equivalent to declaring that a specific doctrine is a heresy. We must ask if the doctrine of "mitigated Millenarianism" is acceptable as a private opinion, and most importantly for our purposes, if it is an eschatology that may legitimately be explored by Catholic theologians, considering it enjoyed universal acceptance for the first two and a half centuries of Christianity.[5] At least one Roman Catholic scholar claims that although the Holy Office judged that "premillennialism cannot be safely taught," "*the Church has not dogmatically defined this issue*."[6] It appears that Roman Catholic theologians are free to explore and discuss the concept of "mitigated millenarianism," provided that the system of eschatology is not taught as official Catholic doctrine. This autonomy comes not only from the Roman Catholic Church's traditional emphasis on religious freedom,[7] freedom of conscience,[8] and natural reason,[9] but on the Church's own designation describing the role of the theologian as one who mediates between the Magisterium and the People of God.[10] In regards to millenarianism, the Church likewise confirms that a critical approach may be taken by theologians, in an effort to express the fuller story of authentic Christian eschatology: "We can distinguish between the critical work theologians do with regard to defined dogmas, and the critical approach theologians may take toward the ordinary, non-fallible teaching of the magisterium."[11] The declaration on millenarianism falls squarely within the category of the ordinary, non-fallible teachings of the papal Magisterium, since neither the millennium, nor amillennial eschatology, is a defined dogma of the Church. In light of the work contained in this book regarding scriptural exegesis of the Book of Revelation and the Epistle to the Romans, and the already supported thesis that millenarianism was *the* orthodox eschatology of the early Church, Joseph Cardinal Ratzinger's statement on the role of theologians appears to be applicable: "Criticism of papal pronouncements will be possible and even necessary, to the degree that they lack support *in Scripture and the Creed*."[12] Certainly, there is no lack of "support" for amillennialism in the New Testament, but the exegesis of the Scriptures that results in an amillennial reading was heavily critiqued by the early Fathers, and as we have seen, a wide majority of those who framed the concepts in the creed were chiliasts.

The real issue posed by the Holy Office and taken up by Pius's answer has to do with *why* mitigated millenarianism[13] was considered an unsafe concept for eschatology. By examining the context in which the Holy Office was asked about millenarianism and the language of the pope's answer, we gain a valuable insight into the deceptive nature of certain kinds of millenarian and messianic movements, and the way these movements borrow apocalyptic language and pervert it. If we consider that the Allied powers had all but solidified victory in the Second World War by July of 1944, close to when the Holy Office published its decree regarding millenarianism, we may confidently deduce that the context of the pope's rejection of millenarianism was in response to Adolf Hitler's well-known desire ". . . to build a millennial city adequate [in splendor] to a thousand year old people with a thousand year old historical and cultural past, for its never-ending [glorious] future . . ."[14] Carroll confirms this when he writes that ". . . Nazi mythology exploited the idea of the dawning messianic era. The Third Reich corresponded to the Third Age of the millennium. It was expected to endure, as Hitler said repeatedly, for a thousand years."[15] In this sense, Hitler ". . . perverted biblical hope by proclaiming himself the Messiah . . ."[16]

When Pius XII rejected "mitigated millenarianism," his concern was with *historicized/presentative millenarianism*, in which certain views of the messiah and the kingdom too easily lead to imaginative desires for hope in the *present-historical* rather than the *future-historical* period.[17] Presentative millenarianism is a form of realized eschatology that focuses on desires that rapidly turn political, violent, and inspire aspirations for power. There is a significant distinction between Ante-Nicene Patristic chiliasm, which stressed martyr aspects of messianism in the future-historical realization of a peaceable kingdom and should be counted among the "millenarian movements [that] take a pacifist political stance because they expect the imminent intervention of God,"[18] and the violent, secular versions that conceive of a human reign that is "to be realized on this earth,"[19] in the present. It is the latter type of millenarianism that inspired aspects of Nazism.

It is imperative to understand the distinctions between the types of millenarian ideology. In Roman Catholic theology, the chiliastic impetus has been to assume that millenarianism leads to violence, when in reality, when one looks historically, millenarians typically hold to some version of non-aggression. Flinn tells us that Roman Catholic scholars have traditionally created ". . . an image of [all] millennialism as inevitably leading to violence. If anything, however, the truth is quite the reverse. Most millennial groups have been completely free of violence, and many have been pragmatically pacifist."[20] The consistent misunderstanding that has surfaced during the modern period regarding the Magisterium's view of millenarianism has to do with the confusion of the two forms of millenarianism—historicized/presentative versus future-historical. Every Father of note prior to 250 C.E. believed in a future-historical millennium,[21] when ". . . Christ the Lord before the final judgment . . . will come visibly to rule over this world"—precisely the belief labeled as unsafe to teach by the Holy See. The distinctions in terminology are imperative: historicized forms of presentative millenarianism are ideologically commensurate with the Tyconian–Augustinian "amillennialist" view that the Church, or some other entity such as the Roman empire, is in some way presently the historicized "Thousand Years Reign of Christ." Adherents of early Patristic millenarianism viewed the reign of Christ as an historical reality, set in a future, "eschatological age" holding in tension the concepts of hope for a divine future in history with a strong ethic of Christian charity for the present moment.[22] It is the historic millenarian model (mislabeled "amillennialism"), associated with Eusebius, Tyconius, and Augustine, and not the future-imminent chiliastic form, that inspired horrific events such as the First Crusade.[23] Like the modern, presentative millenarianism that is a ". . . peculiar blend of the political and religious,"[24] the Eusebian model adopted by the fourth-century Roman Catholic Church in place of the earlier Patristic chiliasm, implicitly promoted ". . . political or revolutionary action to 'force' the coming of paradise."[25] This point is particularly evident in Eusebius' one-to-one correspondence between the kingdom of God and the Roman empire—an ideology ultimately rejected by Augustine, but transferred for all intents and purposes to the Church of history in the Catholic tradition.[26] Presentative/historical millenarianism, advocating the view that one's own religious or political community could incarnate or establish the divine kingdom, influenced the formation of German National Socialism in the 1930s. The resistance to radical, secularized millenarianism by the Holy See was conditioned further by the adoption of "millenarian" principles in the context of a growing Socialist and Communist populace in Europe—points that contributed to solidifying the fears of the Magisterium.[27] By contrast, for the early Church's future-historical millenarian disciples, the only preparation for, or realization of the Thousand Years Reign, was prayer, peaceful dissent, and martyrdom.[28] The Vatican's rejection of a realized, historicized, presentative eschatology was correct, while its association of this realizable form with the Patristic millenarianism that envisioned that "Christ the Lord before the final judgment . . . will come visibly to rule over this world," was erroneous, reactive, and incommensurate with the earliest, normative traditions of the Church.

The 1994 Catechism and millenarianism

Pius XII's post-Second World War statement was the first papal or magisterial declaration on the issue of millenarianism. Up until that declaration, the history of millenarianism in the Church vacillated between embracing this understanding of eschatology and fearing it, but never formally rejecting it.[29] The 1994 *Catechism of the Catholic Church* picked up on and appropriated the erroneous rejection of Patristic millenarianism that came in 1944. Citing Pius XII's answer to the Congregation of the Holy Office, the Catechism reads:

> The Antichrist's deception already begins to take shape in the world every time the claim is made to realize within history that messianic hope which can only be realized beyond history through the eschatological judgment. The Church has rejected even modified forms of this falsification of the kingdom to come under the name of millenarianism, especially the "intrinsically perverse" political form of a secular messianism.[30]

Those who drafted the Catechism, like Pius XII, were rightly thinking of the misuses of some messianic and millenarian principles in justifying the false hopes associated with charismatic dictators such as Hitler,[31] along with early, violent forms of Marxism.[32] The words of the 1994 Catechism, to some extent, are aimed at rejecting the use of the language of "kingdom," "reign," and "messianic domination" by dictators and totalitarian regimes with evil intent.[33] While the Church did well in repeating Pius' concerns and reaction against a historicized, politicized, messianic eschatology, the continued mistaken application of these perverse forms to the chiliastic traditions of the early Church has perpetuated a significant misunderstanding: that millenarian traditions are foreign to the Catholic faith and in themselves, dangerous.[34] The millenarian phenomena linked to both Hitler and some Marxist revolutionary groups were almost exclusively associated with a blend of millennial hopes and already latent and violent nationalistic ideologies[35]—ideas foreign to Patristic forms of eschatology that were focused on the model of a martyr-messiah. The Ante-Nicene Church exhibited a purely pacifistic chiliasm in which its hopes were set on a future-historical era of peace in Jerusalem, under the Lordship of its martyr-king, Jesus of Nazareth.[36] The chiliastic, eschatological hope rejected in the Catechism was profoundly believed, vigorously defended, and normatively held by the Patristic community. By contrast, is not the impetus to "realize within history that messianic hope which can only be realized beyond history through the eschatological judgment" precisely what the Catholic Church has adopted in its rejection of early chiliasm and its adoption of a now normative, historicized, ecclesio-centric model?[37]

Despite the Catholic Church's progress in articulating an already, not-yet model whereby the Church is to be considered a "pilgrim in history,"[38] the concept that the Church possesses the only full expression of salvation in history[39] betrays its commitments that it is the sole, legitimate custodian of the kingdom of God.[40] Oscar Cullmann draws a significant correlation between this ". . . Catholic absolutizing of the period of the Church" and "the reference of the thousand year kingdom (Revelation 20:4) to the Church, a view that goes back to Tyconius."[41] Frank Flinn's commentary on the subject likewise confirms the connection between the Tyconian–Augustinian model and contemporary Catholic eschatology:

> Augustine of Hippo . . . abandoned his early hope in a millennial kingdom and turned his attention to the present: the Church with its sacraments. Pope Benedict XVI, as Cardinal Joseph Ratzinger, followed this Augustinian line of reasoning in claiming that orthodox belief "tears eschatology from time." What he is left with is the Church, particularly the hierarchical Church. Ratzinger incorporated this opinion into the 1994 *Catechism of the Catholic Church* (676).[42]

The Catechism, in its attempt to expose the dangers of the realization of the coming messianic kingdom "within history," implicates the Church itself for its replacement of a primitive, burning expectation for the visible return of Jesus in

194 Contemporary Catholic theology

future history with a present-historical, ecclesial presence of Christ in the Eucharist and "papal vicarage."[43]

The earliest Church Fathers had no problem holding in tension the presence of Christ in the Eucharist with a future-historical reign of Jesus on earth.[44]

It appears that attempts, consistent with the Bible and early Church tradition, to envision a future, yet imminent eschatological messianic age on earth, are forbidden by the Catechism, because they place that era within a historical framework in a way that may promote premature trust in secular or Satanic deceptions, or may too quickly turn violent. But the Church, in its attempt to maintain institutional and sacerdotal power, continues to claim that *it* is the embodiment of that messianic reign, within history, as its sole possessor—a view consistently reiterated and justified by the hierarchy.

It would be academically dishonest to claim that the Roman Catholic Church has made *no* progress ". . . to counteract a residual tendency in the direction of triumphalism, that is, the identification of the Church with the Kingdom of God."[45] Nevertheless, it is apparent that attempts to return the Church to a triumphalist posture, both subtle and explicit, permeate contemporary theological dialogue. A prime example of the return to the pre-Vatican II understanding of the Church and the kingdom, consistent with the Catechism's denial of Patristic chiliasm, is the declaration *Dominus Iesus*. In it, the CDF argues vehemently against theologians who claim ". . . that certain truths have been superseded; for example . . . the universal salvific mediation of the Church . . . these theses are contrary to Catholic faith because they deny the unicity of the relationship which Christ *and the Church* have with the kingdom of God."[46] Though the writers of *DI* strain in their language to draw a distinction between the institutional Church and the eschatological kingdom, ultimately, they claim that the Church cannot tolerate any instantiation of the Kingdom of God in history, beyond itself. When the Catholic hierarchy, whether through the Catechism or *DI* reiterates that the Church is the kingdom's ". . . sign and instrument in history," it is meant to convey that the Church is the kingdom's *sole* sign and instrument in history.[47] Thus, as expressed in the Catechism, a millenarian doctrine that claims that the kingdom of God is expressed proleptically in the Church, but is to be fulfilled in a future history beyond the Church, is highly threatening to those in ecclesial authority.

Benedict XVI and the spiritual, Eucharistic millennium

In 1990, eminent Catholic theologian Fr. Marino Penasa asked Cardinal Joseph Ratzinger about an imminent, intermediate, millenary reign of Jesus Christ, prior to the final judgment.[48] Cardinal Ratizinger's answer was succinct, but consistent with the argument of this book: "Giacché la Santa Sede non si é ancora pronunciata in modo definitivo" ("the Holy See has not yet made any definitive pronouncement in this regard").[49] There is a degree of debate as to whether Cardinal Ratzinger was stating that the past declaration on millenarianism (Pope Pius XII in 1944) was not a definitive proclamation, or if the Cardinal thought Penasa was referring to a millenary reign of the Church, but not a non-carnal, spiritualized era of peace constituting a personal, eschatological reign of Jesus Christ in his resurrected body, i.e., Patristic millenarianism. It is Fr. Penasa's version of millennialism that makes one question the exact context of his interaction with the pope, as Penasa himself adheres to and openly promotes a spiritualized version of Patristic chiliasm that includes a chronology of an "intermediate Parousia" of Christ in the body, and an "earthly joyous millennium."[50] Massimo Introvigne, in his essay on "Modern Catholic Millennialism," refers to the:

> book published by Father Martino Penasa claiming that Catholics could believe in an imminent "intermediate coming" of Jesus Christ on Earth to inaugurate a thousand-year reign of the saints prior to the final judgment ... Although the terminology was different, Penasa's ideas appeared to be more similar to classical Christian premillennialism ... .[51]

It is entirely possible that Cardinal Ratzinger knew the context of Penasa's question and the priest's theological commitments, and simply admitted that the Church had not declared on the matter in such a way as to formally denounce millenarianism as heresy. The more likely scenario is that Ratzinger believed Penasa was asking about a form of contemporary Catholic millennialism that is different from Patristic millenarianism only insofar as the former does not admit of an earthly reign of Jesus, while the latter does. In this form of acceptable Catholic millennialism, theologians allow for a new, millennial age prior to the final judgment, sometimes conceived as an era of the reign of the Virgin Mary (supported by Pope John Paul II),[52] a reign of the Holy Spirit, or a reign of Jesus Christ in his Eucharistic presence. That which is common to all three "approved" versions of Catholic millennialism is that the Roman Catholic Church is conceived as *expanding* during the future interregnum millennial age, gaining in charisma, popularity, converts (particularly Jewish), and power. In spite of the beauty of some of its linguistic descriptions and the centrality of love and peace in endorsed Catholic millennial writers, this version replaces the traditional, bodily, intermediate millennial reign of the messiah, held and defended by the early Fathers, with a purely ecclesiocentric model in line with protecting the authority of the hierarchy.

Much of the new wave of Catholic millennialism is associated with the work of Fr. Joseph Iannuzzi, who in his book entitled *The Triumph of God's Kingdom in the Millennium and End Times*, claims that though it is undisputed that the early Fathers believed in an interregnum millennial period as part of the *regula fidei*,[53] they considered it to be marked by the reign of Christ in the Eucharist, and did not associate it with the Parousia.[54] The Roman Catholic Magisterium is open and supportive of Iannuzzi's work, although his thesis is patently incorrect: *all* the early millennialists from Papias to Lactantius believed that at the center of the intermediate millennial age was Jesus' visible return and reign with the saints in a renewed Jerusalem.[55] While the early chiliastic Fathers held to a profound Eucharistic devotion, none of them connected the future millennial reign to Christ's *Eucharistic* presence, except to say that the Eucharist was a prolepsis of the coming millennial banquet.[56]

Thus, the question must be posed as to why the Roman Catholic Church would on the one hand be open to an alternative to Augustine's standard amillennialism in which a future, millennial, messianic age associated with resurrected believers, the Eucharistic presence of Christ, and an outpouring of the Holy Spirit (consistent with Joachim's system), but on the other hand, be intolerant of a millennial age in which it is conceived that Jesus Christ and the martyrs would be physically present on earth during an intermediate period of peace, prior to the final judgment. Upon further scrutiny, it becomes evident that millenarianism as expressed by the earliest Church Fathers is highly threatening to the Roman Catholic Church as an institution, precisely because the return of Christ to earth for any period of eschatological history would make the pope, the episcopal college, and the sacerdotal function of the priestly clergy obsolete, creating space for another as yet unknown, historical expression of the kingdom of God. If, as is taught in Patristic millenarianism, Christ's intermediate bodily presence is central to future eschatological history, the sacrifice of Christ as represented in the Mass ceases to exist in the conditioned form believers now experience.[57] Pope Leo the Great (d. 461) conceived of the institution of the Mass by Christ (handed down to be a function of the "real priesthood"), as an event which ". . . brought to an end the Old Testament,"[58] because "in Christ's sacrifice, the figures of the Old Law found their fulfillment and consummation,"[59] so too the return of Jesus Christ to earth would bring to an end the sacrament of the Mass and usher in the period of the eschatological messianic banquet.[60]

We recall that the pope and bishops had never universally condemned Joachim's Trinitarian version of history, the adherents of which conceived of a millennial era of the Holy Spirit and a new expression of the Christian faith (though prior to the bodily return of Jesus). The Church, in a provincial gathering, did not begin to take issue with Joachim until the local hierarchy realized there was a threat to its institutional existence—that Joachim's new messianic era of the Spirit would decentralize episcopal and clerical power and put it in the hands of a new monastic order. The new Catholic millennialism, one which is almost identical to Joachim's version, is counted as an acceptable alternative to Augustine's "traditional Catholic" view of the millennium because, although it places the millennium in the historical future, the Church is still viewed as central to it and serves a vital function: there is no Eucharistic reign of Christ without the priests, bishops, and the Bishop of Rome.

The reification of eschatological reality in Catholic, traditional (Augustinian) and contemporary ("Eucharistic reign") doctrine is central to the thesis of the fourth part of this project: re-apprehension of the early apostolic millenarian eschatology, one that rejects the concept that the Church is and will remain as the sole expression of the kingdom of God up through eternity, is the most promising way to overcome supersessionism. Millenarian eschatology, in light of its solid roots in Patristic theology, creates various opportunities—opportunities original to the Roman Catholic tradition—that allow a critique of replacement theology and emphasize a positive point of dialogue with the Jewish people.

In summarization of our recent themes, we began by looking at the "hermeneutics of heresy," i.e., the ways in which doctrines are accepted or rejected in Catholic tradition. In particular, we applied Vincent of Lérins' canon to the historical and ecclesial reality of millenarianism, and discussed how chiliasm is an expression of apostolic faith, while Origenist and Augustinian amillennialism finds no precursors in the earliest eschatological thought of the Church. We argued that amillennialism should not be considered a legitimate "development of doctrine," as doctrines do not develop in a manner that radically changes the core, primitive deposit of faith. To be considered valid doctrinal development, scholars should be able to find something resembling an amillennial reception of Scripture and tradition within the first three centuries of the Church, but they cannot.

Next, we undertook an exploration of the creedal and conciliar system of the Church up through the fifth century, in respect to millenarianism. Despite the perpetuation of misinformation on the subject, the Church never declared that millenarianism was a heretical belief. Although multiple opportunities existed for the universal Church or the pope to speak on the subject, it was never addressed— most likely because millenarian eschatology was held by the Church Fathers. The Church's ecumenical creeds were either written or inspired by chiliastic Fathers. Declarations of heresy that appear on the surface to apply to chiliasm, in reality have nothing to do with it, but refer to other heresies, particularly those of the Trinitarian or Christological variety.

In our previous section, we discussed the moment in history when it is said that millennial belief and Ecumenical Councils coincided. We looked at the work of Joachim of Fiore in relation to the Fourth Council of the Lateran, showing that the Council did not reject either Joachim's view of history, or his eschatology, but denounced his view of the Trinity in relation to Peter Lombard. Though a provincial Council formalized a rejection of Joachim's "Trinitarian history" due to its threat to Church authority and influence on French monastic groups, this was not an anathema directed against millennialism specifically, and is not to be conceived as a binding statement for the universal Church.

We finished our chapter by exploring modern and contemporary papal and catechetical statements, marking the first time a document associated with the Magisterium has cited millenarianism. Our research suggests that the ambiguous ruling by Pope Pius XII that "mitigated millenarianism cannot be taught safely," when put in context, was directed against a dangerous version of millenarian belief that seeks to establish a messianic reign through political means—at that time, it was fascism. By falsely attributing realized, presentative, and historicized millenarian principles to the beliefs of earliest Christian millenarians, the pope claimed that the Church's original eschatological heritage could not be taught as official Catholic doctrine. The 1944 teaching was borrowed by Cardinal Joseph Ratzinger, and applied to the Catechism of 1994, which connected Pius XII's rejection of historicized millenarianism to Pius XI's rejection of Marxist and Liberation theologies and their proclivity to accept millennial dogma, continuing the negative caricature of Patristic millenarian eschatology. Finally, we briefly surveyed a form of spiritualized millennialism centered on the Eucharist—one that is gaining wide acceptance in Catholicism, even at the level of the Vatican. We argued that the Eucharistic millennialism is acceptable because it safeguards the authority and function of the Church, instead of threatening it.

Our primary point is that millenarian eschatology has never been formalized as a theology that cannot be explored by theologians, or even held as a private opinion, despite the Magisterium's most recent denunciations. We must likewise consider the context of the modern and contemporary papal and catechetical statements, and admit that not all millenarian eschatologies lead to "unsafe," violent, or revolutionary acts. Quite the contrary, millenarian belief has enabled oppressed groups to maintain hope during trial and persecution, and was adopted by the Church Fathers and early martyrs as a worthwhile part of Second Temple Judaism. Though theologians cannot teach chiliasm as the official doctrine of the Catholic Church (although it was regarded as just that during first three centuries), its ancient tenets offer multiple points for dialogue in relation to Jewish–Catholic dialogue and supersessionism, as we will see.

Notes

* A portion of this book chapter was originally published as "One Step Forward, Two Steps Back: Supersessionism and Pope Benedict XVI's Eschatological Ecclesiology concerning Israel and the Jewish People," in *Journal of Ecumenical Studies* 49, no. 4 (2014), Copyright © [2014]. Used by permission.
1 Pope Pius XII held the office of the papacy from 1939 to 1958.
2 "Decree of the Holy Office," July 19, 1944, confirmed by Pope Pius XII, July 20, 1944 (DS3839).
3 Those aligning with the Gallican tradition, as opposed to the Ultramontane position, see the infallibility of the pope as exercised solely when "fortified by the consent of the Universal Church, the only depository conjointly with him, of irrefragable authority." Richard F. Costigan, *The Consensus of the Church and Papal Infallibility: A Study in the Background of Vatican I* (Washington, DC: Catholic University of America Press, 2005), 138. In reference to the Sensus Fidelium, the Catechism validates what was issued in *Lumen Gentium*, stating: "By this appreciation of the faith, aroused and sustained by the Spirit of truth, the People of God, guided by the sacred teaching authority (Magisterium) . . . receives . . . the faith, once for all delivered to the saints . . . the People unfailingly adhere to this faith, penetrate it more deeply with right judgment, and apply it more fully in daily life." *Catechism of the Catholic Church*, §93.
4 "The pope . . . is only said to be infallible when he speaks *ex cathedra* in the act of defining a doctrine of faith or morals with the intention of binding the whole Church to that doctrine." Keith A. Mathison, *The Shape of Sola Scriptura* (Moscow, ID: Canon Press, 2001), 263. See also Francis A. Sullivan, "The Meaning of Conciliar Dogmas," in Daniel Kendall, Stephen T. Davis, and George Carey, eds., *The Convergence of Theology: A Festschrift Honoring Gerald O'Collins, S.J.* (New York: Paulist Press, 2001), 84.
5 "What is meant by 'mitigated' or 'mild' millennialism and by the qualifier 'safely' renders the official answer ambiguous." Svigel, "The Phantom Heresy," 1, n.1.
6 Ibid., emphasis mine.
7 See Pope Leo XIII, *Libertas: Encyclical of Pope Leo XIII on the Nature of Human Liberty*, found at http://www.vatican.va/holy_father/leo_xiii/encyclicals/documents/hf_lxiii_enc_20061888_libertas_en.html. Cf, *Gaudium et spes*, §52.

Magisterial statements on millenarianism 199

8   Charles E. Curran, *Loyal Dissent: Memoir of a Catholic Theologian* (Washington, DC: Georgetown University Press, 2006), 227.
9   James C. Livingston and Francis Schüssler Fiorenza, *Modern Christian Thought* (Minneapolis, MN: Fortress Press, 2006), 252–255.
10 "The theologians' function can be described as one of mediating in both directions—between the magisterium and the people of God." Francis A. Sullivan, "The Magisterium and the Role of Theologians in the Church," in Gerard Mannion *et al.*, eds., *Readings in Church Authority: Gifts and Challenges for Contemporary Catholicism* (Burlington, VT: Ashgate, 2003), 402–409, at 403.
11 Ibid., 405.
12 Joseph Ratzinger, *Das neue Volk Gottes: Entwürfe zur Ekklesiologie* (Munich: Patmos, 1969), 73.
13 One author limits the definition of "mitigated millenarianism" solely to a view that denies that the Church may go through any kind of tribulation by positing a "rapture theology." Other authors believe that "mitigated millenarianism" refers to only a carnal view of the millennium, leaving room for more spiritual expressions of it. Bernhardsson, *Imagining the End*, 167.
14 Hitler on the establishment of the "Third Reich": Speech 27 November 1937. The German reads: "*einem tausendjährigen Volk mit tausendjähriger geschichtlicher und kultureller Vergangenheit für die vor ihm liegende unabsehbare Zukunft eine ebenbürtige tausendjährige Stadt zu bauen.*" Adolf Hitler, *The Speeches of Adolf Hitler, April 1922–August 1939* (New York: H. Fertig, 1969). For Hitler's ideology and how Nazism borrowed historical millenarian principles, see David Redles, *Hitler's Millennial Reich: Apocalyptic Belief and the Search for Salvation* (New York: NYU Press, 2005).
15 Carroll, *Constantine's Sword*, 256.
16 Ibid.
17 Bauckham, *God will be All in All*, 131.
18 Elisabeth Schüssler Fiorenza, *Jesus and the Politics of Interpretation* (New York: Continuum, 2001), 110. It was this kind of political pacifism that was a mark of the early Jesus movement and its chiliastic ideology.
19 Thomas Idinopulos, "Nazism, Millenarianism, and the Jews," *Journal of Ecumenical Studies* 40, no. 3 (2003): 296–302, at 296.
20 F.K. Flinn, "Eschatology," in F.K. Flinn, *Encyclopedia of Catholicism* (New York: Infobase Publishing, 2007), 454.
21 Chung, *A Case for Historic Premillennialism*, ii.
22 Moltmann, *The Coming of God*, 154. Moltmann views the future messianic kingdom as encompassing elements of both history and eternity. This viewpoint engages Christians on an ethical level: "For Christians this [transcendent element of hope] is both a promise and a demand, a present grace and a future still to be attained. Christians therefore live in a tension between faith and hope." Jürgen Moltmann, *Man: Christian Anthropology in the Conflicts of the Present* (Minneapolis, MN: Fortress Press, 1974), 58.
23 Michael Signer, "The Christian Millennium in Jewish Historical Perspective: Implications for Dialogue and Joint Social Action," *Sidic Periodical* 32, no. 1 (1999): 2–5.
24 Robert Ellwood, "Nazism as a Millennialist Movement," in Catherine Wessinger, ed., *Millennialism, Persecution, and Violence: Historical Cases* (Syracuse, NY: Syracuse University Press (Sd), 2000), 241.
25 Ibid., 245.
26 Kevin J. Vanhoozer, ed., *Theological Interpretation of the New Testament: A Book-by-Book Survey* (Grand Rapids, MI: Baker Academic, 2008), 238.

27 James M. Rhodes, *The Hitler Movement: A Modern Millenarian Revolution* (Stanford, CA: Hoover Institution Press, 1980). Pope Pius XI condemned political forms of secular messianism, paving the way for Pius XII's rejection of what he incorrectly thought to be the seeds of Nazi messianism—mitigated millenarianism. Pius XI called the particularly Marxist forms of messianism "intrinsically perverse," a formula repeated verbatim in the Catechism. See Pius XI, *Divini Redemptoris: Encyclical on Atheistic Communism* (Rome: Liberia, 1937), §8.
28 Hunt, *Christian Millenarianism*, 2–3.
29 As mentioned previously, chiliasm is tolerated as a private opinion in most Eastern Orthodox circles. See http://www.orthodoxanswers.org/answer/4/.
30 *Catechism of the Catholic Church*, §676. For the possibilities for violence instituted by liberation theologies in Catholic circles, see Gordon Zahn's ideas in Rael Jean Isaac and Erich Isaac, *The Coercive Utopians: Social Deception by America's Power Players* (Chicago, IL: Regnery Gateway, 1984), 148.
31 Some recent studies have come to attribute certain elements of Bavarian Catholic thought as foundational for the beginnings of Nazi philosophy, contrasted with any millenarian underpinnings. See Derek Hastings, *Catholicism and the Roots of Nazism: Religious Identity and National Socialism*, repr. ed. (New York: Oxford University Press, 2011). It is interesting that Hastings traces the roots of Nazi ideology to elements in "liberal, reform Catholicism"—elements that seemed associated with persons who wanted to replace the centralized authority of the pope with more nationalistic aspirations. Most scholars agree that if there was a religious phenomenon that acted as a catalyst to Nazi ideology, it was the occult and paganism.
32 Barkun, *Millennialism and Violence*, 110.
33 Pius XII's warning against the misuses of messianic and millenarian principles has been reused recently by Pope Benedict XVI in application to Liberation Theologies, specifically refuting the work of Jürgen Moltmann in this regard. For example, Benedict, one paragraph removed from his opinion of Moltmann, writes that, "the kingdom of God, not being itself a political concept, cannot serve as a political criterion, by which to construct in direct fashion a program of political action and to criticize efforts of other people." Ratzinger, *Eschatology: Death and Eternal Life*, 58. Allen sees in this quote, among others, a pattern in which Benedict seizes on opportunities to debunk Liberation Theologies as misapprehensions of eschatology vis-à-vis the application of political principles to concept of the kingdom of God. In particular, Benedict appears keen to 'overcome' the influence of Marxism on Christian theology, insisting that the kingdom of God is bracketed in almost exclusively ethical terms, with no firm grounding in a body politic. For Moltmann, by contrast, if Christian ethics fail to take on some kind of political form, it ceases to be Christian. Moltmann's conception is that in Jesus Christ, we see God's theocratic politic as a preferential option for the poor and the movement of the Holy Spirit in moving oppressors to repentance and advocacy for the "least of these." Allen, *Cardinal Ratzinger: The Vatican's Enforcer of the Faith*, 100–101.
34 Wuerl, *The Teaching of Christ: A Catholic Catechism for Adults*, 480.
35 John Christian Laursen and R.H. Popkin, eds., *Millenarianism and Messianism in Early Modern European Culture*, Vol. 4 (Boston, MA: Springer, 2001), xviii.
36 Most scholars claim that early Christian chiliasm was pacifistic, while its later realized and secular-political incarnations became totalitarian and violent. The Catechism makes the error of treating both kinds of chiliasm as interchangeable. See James H. Toner, *The Sword and the Cross: Reflections On Command and Conscience* (New York: Praeger, 1992), 150, n. 37.
37 Sullivan, *Rethinking Realized Eschatology*, 11.
38 Paul Avis, *Reshaping Ecumenical Theology: The Church Made Whole?* (London: T&T Clark, 2010), 46.

39 While the Catholic Church admits to being a "pilgrim" in history, Catholic theology has always maintained the strict concept that the Latin Church is objectively necessary for salvation. See Gavin D'Costa, ed., *The Catholic Church and the World Religions: A Theological and Phenomenological Account* (London: T&T Clark, 2011), 8.

40 "The tendency towards realized eschatology and de-eschatologizing in Catholic theology has also been found in the Roman Catholic concept of the Church as the body of Christ. Everything seems to be fulfilled in the Church. Does this leave room for expectation of the coming Kingdom?" Berkouwer, *Studies in Dogmatics: The Return of Christ*, 146.

41 Cullmann, *Christ and Time: The Primitive Christian conception of Time and History*, 146–147.

42 F.K. Flinn, "Eschatology," 259.

43 Berkouwer, *Studies in Dogmatics: The Return of Christ*, 144.

44 Though there was a deep conviction among the chiliastic Fathers that the Presence of Christ was accessible through the Eucharist, there was nevertheless an emphasis on prolepsis—the Eucharist would one day be replaced by the coming banquet in the Kingdom of the messiah. See Dennis J. Billy, *The Beauty of the Eucharist: Voices from the Church Fathers* (Hyde Park, NY: New City Press, 2010), 11–75, 86–97.

45 Richard P. McBrien, *The Church: The Evolution of Catholicism*, 1st repr. ed. (New York: HarperOne, 2009), 4.

46 Congregatio pro Doctrina Fidei, *Dominus Iesus: Declaration on the Unicity and Salvific Universality of Jesus Christ and the Church*, §4 and §19, emphasis mine.

47 *Lumen Gentium: Dogmatic Constitution on the Church*, n.1.

48 The final question asked by Fr. Panasa was ". . . what of an imminent, future era of vital Christianity?," but the context of the discussion and of Fr. Panasa's work was that of an imminent, future, and peaceful reign of Jesus Christ on earth.

49 Martino Panasa, *Il Segno del Soprannaturale* 30 (1990): 1–15, 10.

50 See Martino Penasa, *Viene Gesù! La Venuta Intermedia Del Signore* (Udine, Italy: Edizioni Segno, 1994).

51 Massimo Introvigne, "Modern Catholic Millennialism," in Wessinger, *The Oxford Handbook of Millennialism*, 549–566, 549–550.

52 John Paul II explicitly backed the work of Catholic millennialist St. Grignion de Montfort (1673–1716). Montfort wrote of a "reign of Christ" in the last days (though not in the flesh), and a millennial "age of Mary." John Paul's motto of Marian devotion, "All Yours," came directly from the work of Montfort. Jean Seguy, "Millénarisme et 'Ordres Adventistes': Grignion de Montfort et les Apôtres des derniers temps," *Archives des Sciences Sociales des Religions* 53 (1982): 23–38.

53 Iannuzzi is correct in that the early chiliast Fathers defended the millennial reign as a notion to be included in the apostolic and sub-apostolic deposit of faith. See J.A. Cerrato, *Hippolytus between East and West: The Commentaries and the Provenance of the Corpus* (Oxford: Oxford University Press, 2002), 229.

54 Referring to Lactantius' millennial doctrine, Iannuzzi claims that when the Father states that "Christ will be engaged among men a thousand years," he ". . . does not refer to Christ's carnal reign in the flesh but to his universal reign in the Eucharist." Iannuzzi, *The Triumph of God's Kingdom in the Millennium and End Times*, 40.

55 Jerome confirms that Papias taught ". . . of the millennium . . . in which our Lord is to reign in the flesh with his saints." Jerome, *De Viris Illustribus*, 18. For another example, we see Justin in the *Dialogue with Trypho* is asked whether Christians "really believe that this place Jerusalem shall be rebuilt, and do you actually expect that you Christians will one day *congregate there to live joyfully with Christ*, together with the patriarchs, the prophets, the saints of our people (the Jews) and those who became proselytes before your Christ arrived?" Justin's answer: "I have declared to you earlier that I, with many others, feel that such an event will take place." Justin,

Dialogue with Trypho, ch. 80. Jerome confirms that Justin held to millenarian elements. Further, we see that Irenaeus drew a direct correlation between the millennial reign and Christ's Second Coming, insisting that Jesus would reign with the saints after the first resurrection but prior to the general resurrection. For example, Irenaeus' exegesis of Daniel, the Apocalypse, 2 Thessalonians 2, Matthew 24, and Luke 18 point to a theology that is both millenarian and eschatological in reference to a future, earthly, historical period of Christ's reign on earth. Cerrato, *Hippolytus between East and West*, 229. Irenaeus makes three central arguments for a millennial kingdom on earth *after* Christ's return, the first of which is rooted in Matthew 26:29: "I tell you, I will not drink from this fruit of the vine from now on until that day when I drink it new with you in my Father's kingdom." Chung and Blomberg, *A Case for Historic Premilleniallism*, 11. See Lactantius in Di Berardino, *We Believe in One Holy Catholic and Apostolic Church*, 164. See *ANF*, 7:219, and "The Epitome of the Divine Institutes," LXXII in Roberts, *ANF*, Vol. 7, 254. Cf. Irenaeus, *Proof of the Apostolic Preaching*, chs. 43–48 on theophanies, in light of the argument regarding chiliasm made by Arkadi Choufrine, *Gnosis, Theophany, Theosis: Studies in Clement of Alexandria's Appropriation of His Background* (New York: Peter Lang, 2002), 162. The majority of prominent Patristic scholars believe that the early millennialists were also chiliasts proper: they believed that Christ would physically reign in his resurrected and glorified body during an intermediate period on earth after the Parousia, but prior to the final judgment. See Wilken, "Early Chiliasm, Jewish Messianism, and the Idea of the Holy Land," 298–307, Hill, *Regnum Coelorum*, 1; 21–43, and Olson, *Will Catholics be Left Behind?*, 143.

56 For an excellent summary of the apocalyptic and eschatological dimension of the early understanding of the Eucharist, see Paul Vu Chi Hy, "Towards a Constructive Retrieval of the Eschatological Dimension of the Eucharist," *AEJT* 3 (August 2004): 1–22, 1.
57 Pope Paul VI, *Constitution on the Sacred Liturgy: Sacrosanctum Concilium*, §7–8.
58 Pope Leo the Great, *Serm*. LVIII, *de Passione Dom*. VII, ch. 3, in St. Leo the Great, *Sermons* (Washington, DC: Catholic University of America Press, 1996).
59 Nicholas Gihr, *The Holy Sacrifice of the Mass V1: Dogmatically, Liturgically, and Ascetically Explained* (Whitefish, MT: Kessinger Publishing, LLC, 2006), 114.
60 The *Catechism of the Catholic Church* refers to the Eucharist as "a pledge of the life to come," (1402) an "anticipation of eternal life," (1326) and an "anticipation of the final Passover of the Church in the glory of the kingdom" (1340). It likewise claims that the Church will celebrate the Mass ". . . *until Christ returns*" (1337, 1341, 1344). Though the celebration of the Mass is in concert with the communion of saints in heaven, it, as a historically conditioned reality, will one day cease.

Part IV
Millenarianism and post-supersessionism

9 Prolegomena to a Christian millenarian theology of Judaism

In Part II, we set out to show that millenarian eschatology is deeply rooted in the Hebrew Bible and New Testament, was held as the normative eschatology in the early Church, and was never declared heretical in any official way. At worst, millenarian eschatology is a belief system frowned upon by the Roman Catholic hierarchy. At best, millenarianism is an ancient belief system with ample promise for contemporary Catholic theology, if only it was explored and experimentally applied to areas in the field of systematic theology. Millenarianism has the ability to inspire Christians to more deeply affirm Judaism as a sister religion, and get to know Jesus as the Son of God and the messiah of the world in ways that take serious the Jewish roots of the "Man of the cross." The work that follows may only be useful as a remedial exercise, but in a world in which anti-Semitism is still very real, the use of millenarian categories in this book may also be useful as a creative resource for Christian affirmations of comparative theology. This project will be most useful to "Confessing Christians" who reject the pluralistic hypothesis[1] as a valid means of interreligious dialogue, but nevertheless want to affirm the theological value of Judaism as a tradition intentionally founded by God and continuing as an aspect of the divine will. As we recall, the reason we focused on the Roman Catholic tradition is because of calls from the Church's hierarchy, after Vatican II, to explore eschatology as a way forward in Roman Catholic theologies of Judaism. Our overall purpose in this project is thoroughly a matter of Christian theology and is not meant as a foundation for Jewish–Catholic dialogue, though it may prove useful to those engaged in such work. The purpose of this chapter is to prove the initial thesis that was introduced in the first chapter of this book: that a modified form of millenarian eschatology has the potential to greatly improve Christian and specifically Catholic attitudes toward Judaism as a religion in relation to the eschatological hopes both communities share, before the one God as understood generally in both traditions. As part of this thesis, we seek to illustrate that Catholic amillennialism perpetuates supersessionist claims.

We established that supersessionism is a theology still alive in the Roman Catholic tradition, although the reception of *NA* by various Catholic theologians and high-ranking clergy has compelled them to call for ways beyond it. While various Vatican departments have advocated eschatological and ecclesiological theological exploration in order to improve views of the Jewish community, the

Church generally refuses to reevaluate its Augustinian, amillennial position that became dominant in the fourth century C.E.

To review, advocates of supersessionism claim:

> the view that the Church is the new and/or true Israel that has forever superseded the nation Israel as the people of God. The result is that the Church has become the sole inheritor of God's covenant blessings originally promised to national Israel in the Old Testament. This rules out a future restoration of the nation Israel with a unique identity, role and purpose that is distinct in any way from the Christian Church.[2]

Because so many of the promises to the people of Israel—and by default, the contemporary inheritors of the Jewish religious identity—have to do with the "kingdom of God,"[3] it becomes clear that the amillennial view which claims that the Church is currently the kingdom of God *in toto*, is supersessionist, at least in its presumptions. If the Church is the kingdom leading into eternity, there is no hope that the people of the Synagogue will ever inherit the kingdom, or that it would even have a participatory role in the kingdom, though such an expectation is affirmed by many Jewish eschatological traditions, including the Bible itself.[4] By contrast, if as millenarians insist, the kingdom is something that will, *in future history and time*, envelop the imperfect Church, and also in a sense overshadow it, certainly one could say that another provisional, historical expression of the divine covenant might also lead to that same kingdom of God, in the future.[5] This is especially true considering that the Sacred Scriptures held by the Roman Catholic Church may legitimately be interpreted as promoting a view that holds an expectation for Jews to participate in the kingdom, after the first coming of Jesus, depending on their response during his Second Coming.

The millenarian view admits that the kingdom is typologically (and topologically) nearby, a point affirmed by Jesus, but also insists that the Church cannot make the sole and final claim to it. It is Jesus Christ who is the final arbitrator of the kingdom, including its future permutations. Jesus promised that the gates of hell would not prevail against the Church (Matthew 16:18), but he likewise spoke of the prevailing of the kingdom of God in this world, even over aspects of the Church itself[6]—a welcome and anticipated concept among the early Christian community. Since Vatican II, the Church has attempted to walk the fine line between the "already" synthesis of institutionalized Christianity and the kingdom of God, and the "not yet" expectation for a full consummation of the kingdom of God. The problem, as already discussed at length in this project, is that the Church wields a very heavy bias toward the "already" of the kingdom, in part because of its sedimentation[7] of an over-spiritualized, and transcendent eschatology,[8] and in part because it conceives of itself as the kingdom in the "here and now".[9] Indeed, Paul Boyer argues that the strand has been "... designated amillennial (*non-millennial*), since it envisions a transcendent, spiritual fulfillment of the apocalyptic texts ... and became the doctrine of the Roman Catholic Church."[10] Liberation theologian, Vitor Westhelle claims that amillennialism is the view that:

the Church be identified in its essence with the kingdom as such, only lacking in plentitude, a position associated with the Roman Catholic Church where the Church and the history in which it is inserted as salvation history is essentially connected to the kingdom (*ecclesia triumphans*) and only incidentally to the world (*ecclesia militans*).[11]

How amillennialism contributes to supersessionist theologies of the Jewish people, and how millenarianism detracts from such ideas and offers an alternative, is the subject of the text that follows. We will begin part four by providing a prolegomenon to our millenarian, post-supersessionist thesis. Looking at general eschatological categories held by some sub-traditions within Judaism, we will paint a picture of what one Jewish eschatological hope might be, and what kind of Christian theology would affirm it, or simply utilize it. Though there is no such thing as one, monolithic "Jewish eschatological hope,"[12] what we are anticipating is the construction of a Christian hope for the Jewish people (which for the Christian is epitomized in the person and work of Jesus Christ)—one that takes seriously some of early and contemporary Judaism's most well established conceptions of the 'world to come,' that were also at play in Jesus' words.

We will then define a contemporized, modified version of millenarian eschatology posited, though never fully developed by Moltmann, and point out some similarities and differences between it and Patristic millenarianism. We will also link Moltmann's millenarian eschatology to his concept that the Church is in service to, and provisional to, the kingdom of God, and briefly point to Moltmann's claim that adherents of millenarian eschatology in the history of Jewish–Christian relations have, by and large, rejected supersessionism. Millenarian thinkers have developed positive theological roles for Judaism within the Christian narrative, producing a historical warrant for the suggestion of this project, that millenarian eschatology provides a fecund resource for the Christian affirmation of Judaism as a religious system closely related to itself.

Second, we will look at how amillennial and millennial eschatologies differ significantly regarding their theology of history and time. We will show that amillennialism makes it impossible to affirm a theologically positive role for Judaism in the future, apart from the Church, while by contrast, such a role is intrinsic to the millenarian view.

Third, we will determine how amillennialism perpetuates the three forms of supersessionism, while millenarian eschatology is able to move past the three types—economic, punitive, and structural. Millenarianism overcomes economic supersessionism by promoting a consummative element within the economy of salvation that affirms God's promises to the Jewish people. Millenarianism overcomes punitive descriptions of God's interactions with the Jewish people by supplying a positive theological role for Israel—the Jews are not punished for various reasons, but will be blessed in specific ways by virtue of their election and witness to the righteousness of God for the nations, in light of the person of Jesus. Moltmann's millenarianism makes structural supersessionism obsolete by returning God's actions with Israel to the forefront of Christian eschatology in a way that does not simply demand the conversion of Israel to the Church, but does so specifically through its hermeneutic of the biblical narrative regarding the irrevocable promises of the God of Israel.

Weber succinctly describes the point we will unpack in detail in the sections that follow, when he writes that:

> a theological pre-understanding that informs ... amillennialism is "supersessionism," the belief that with the Jews' rejection of Jesus as Messiah, God created a new Israel, the Church, and transferred all OT prophecies to it. In practical terms, this means that supersessionists see *no future role* for the old Israel in God's program. Most modern premillennialists, on the other hand ... think that God has unfinished business with Israel, which will finally be concluded at the Parousia and in the millennial kingdom.[13]

We must again take note that amillennialism is the dominant Roman Catholic eschatology, despite the early Church's record. The reason why defenders of amillennial eschatology are likewise supersessionists follows logically from their view of salvation history, their view of the way God works or does not work *in time*, and the aforementioned view of the current Church as equivalent or nearly equivalent to the kingdom of God. By looking to the specifics of Moltmann's millenarian ideas, we seek to point out the ways that millenarian principles are indeed opposed to a supersessionist understanding of the theological place and role of Israel.

Throughout the bulk of the part that follows, I will argue that Christian eschatological millenarianism overcomes supersessionism, in part because it leaves a theological space in time and history for Jewish eschatological expectations to take place. This millenarian "surplus in meaning," both in terms of a theology of history and exegesis of Scripture, is post-supersessionist for two main reasons. First, it does not conceive of divine eschatological or messianic promises as exhausted by fulfillment in the Church of history—instead, there is plenty of God's covenantal assurance to go around. Second, millenarianism is a consummative theology that does not seek to *turn Israel into the Church*. This does not mean that the Church refrains from holding up faith in and obedience to Jesus as the means of salvation, but instead that it views the Church itself as an entity distinct from the people of Israel—to whom belong the covenant as well. Soulen confirms this post-supersessionist theological reality when he states that:

> The Church is commissioned to make disciples of all the nations (*panta ta ethné*) (Matt 28:19). It has no comparable commission to seek the 'conversion' of the Jewish people. This is especially true of the gentile Church. Nothing in the Apostolic Witness remotely suggests the validity of a gentile-Christian mission to non-Christian Jews.[14]

The mission of the Church is simply to witness to the work of Jesus Christ through proclamation, dialogue, and service, understanding the eschatological Scriptures that affirm God's future plans with Israel. This does not mean that

Christians must refrain from conversionary efforts regarding individual Jewish people, only that the conversion of the Jewish people *as a whole* will be the direct work of God. Soulen also affirms that a truly post-supersessionist theology must take seriously God's separate but valid consummative economy for the people Israel,[15] yet he does not mention the value of millenarian eschatology, the advocates of which consistently promote his own view on God's consummative economy for the Jewish people. Soulen's writing, which is highly constructive in terms of post-supersessionism, could benefit from a renewed appreciation of what millenarian eschatological offers for a positive Christian theology of Judaism. One of the weaknesses of contemporary post-supersessionist theology in general is that its proponents seek to construct a positive role for Israel in eschatological salvation history, yet ignore the traditionally Christian millenarian eschatology that provides such a construction, and the amillennial view that prohibits it. This is likely an oversight on the part of theologians who engage in formulating a theology of Judaism insofar as the once well-regarded and traditional millennial approach has been pushed to the margins of systematic, dogmatic study in mainline Christianity.

In order for us to conceive of the ways that millenarian eschatology opens a door for the consummative future of Israel, we must be able to enumerate, to some degree, the eschatological expectations of the Jewish people. Ultimately, it is up to the Jewish community and their philosophers and scholars, to define and describe a "Jewish eschatological hope". Since this project concerns the promotion of a post-supersessionist, positive, *Christian* eschatological theology of Israel,[16] its primary aim is not for the purposes of Jewish–Christian dialogue, though such dialogue is of crucial importance. The aim of this project is to internally overcome the series of poor and dangerous presuppositions adopted through amillennialism, because theologically, supersessionism is a problematic posture *for the Church* to adopt. Further, this project may be used as a resource to help Christians become interested in comparative theology, through which *Judaisms* will be encountered on their own terms instead of being reduced by the Church to another "expression of the self," vis-à-vis the philosophical and historical tendencies of Christianity toward totalization. We will apply the categories of our study specifically to the Roman Catholic tradition.

Jewish eschatological hope in relation to supersessionism and millenarianism

There is no more a uniform, homogeneous "Jewish eschatological hope" than there is a Christian one. Such eschatological concepts are highly diverse, especially over time and strains and sub-traditions within Judaism, and it is impossible to describe a system that would fully encompass such views. Nevertheless, Christian supersessionists have managed to replace, negate, or ignore virtually *all* uniquely Jewish hopes for a future restoration of the world and usurp their messianic traditions, justifying such theology by simply saying that the promises God made to the Jewish people as attested in the Hebrew Bible now apply to the Church of history.[17] According to amillennialists, if the Jews want to make a viable contribution to the coming kingdom of God, which is allowably conceived almost solely as a transcendent heaven prior to the final judgment of Christ and an a-temporal, "new creation," the best they can do is convert to the Catholic Church directly.[18]

In an attempt to illustrate how the millenarian principle expresses a rejection of such supersessionist claims, we will first outline some general points that appear to be most common to many Jewish visions of God's coming kingdom. According to Jewish scholar and rabbi David Novak, there are three areas that surface extensively in rabbinical sources that are broadly indicative of Judaic thought: the world to come (*olam ha-ba*), the resurrection of the "dead body," both personal and corporate (*tehiyyat ha-metim*), and the messiah (*ha-meshiah*).[19] In the context of our research interest, we will focus primarily on the first area, the eschatological "world to come," treating the other two areas in light of it.

Rabbi Simcha Paull Raphael tells us that in early Pharisaic-rabbinic thought, the three categories above were held as one strand, with the messiah's coming resulting in the beginnings of the establishment of the world to come and the resurrection of the righteous, *who would inhabit it*.[20] The messianic age was not viewed as something diametrically opposed to the earth upon which humans now dwell—but as a divine transformation of it, prior to the final consummation and the fullness of the world to come. One Jewish philosopher who has published extensively on the notion of the "world to come," Steven Nadler, claims that "the dominant view among those who adopt a post historical understanding of the world to come is that it will arrive after the end of the Messianic era, and after the resurrection of the body and its reunion with the soul."[21] We notice that in much Jewish thought, it is the world to come that is ahistorical, not the messianic era. Jewish historian, Joseph Klausner, claims that though there is divergence among "modern Jews" regarding the degree of difference between this world and the world to come, both Reform and Orthodox Jews project the "Golden" messianic age into *future history*.[22] Likewise, a wide majority of rabbinic statements on the messianic golden age focus on its qualities as a time period when a great, divine banquet will be given for the righteous.[23] In some strands of Judaism, the entire messianic age and the world to come are historical realities, whereas in other strands, the distinction between the two is maintained. Nadler mentions that a point of contention and divergence within rabbinic thought and modern Jewish philosophy is the relationship between the world to come and the messianic age.[24] But there seems to be little divergence regarding the fact that the age of the messiah, for those who expect his coming or for those who expect a divine "era" without a personal human messianic agent, will be during a future historical period on earth. Included in the "Statement of Principles for Reform Judaism" associated with the 1999 Central Conference of American Rabbis, is a section on the Jewish responsibility of *tikkun olam*, or "repairing of the world": "Partners with God in (*tikkun olam*), repairing the world, *we are called to help bring nearer the messianic age*."[25] Jon Bloomberg argues that the concept of the historical, earthly, messianic age, leading to the eternal *olam ha-ba*, is so central to Reform Judaism that Reform Jews take on, personally and communally, the burden of ethical responsibility to assure it happens.[26] Of course, from the Christian perspective, no human person knows "the day or the hour," and the full spectrum of the messianic age is in the sovereign hand of God, but human participation in it is central, whether through witness to Christ, or service to humankind.

The three aspects of Jewish eschatology mentioned above are considered to be *sequential* in both early rabbinic and contemporary Jewish exegesis.[27] In other words, the messiah will bring to this earth the "world to come" in a preliminary form as a "first installment" continuous with the messianic age—a precursor to the final resurrection of the dead and the judgment of the righteous and wicked, and those events will be followed by the consummation of the universe and the divine plan of salvation.

The three Jewish categories were affirmed and developed by Jesus, and likewise adopted in early Christian millenarian eschatology—themes that were only later criticized as being too "Jewish."[28] Along with these strands were the detailed and incontrovertible ideas that hell (Gehennah, Hades, Tartaros) awaited the wicked—those who were not righteous before the judgment throne of God. Though the early Christians believed that Jesus, as messiah, had initiated the process leading to the world to come and the resurrection, through his own death and resurrection, they awaited a further event whereby the messianic kingdom would be exposed as a more "historically complete" precursor to its absolute fullness—during the millennial age at the end of history, but still within it.[29] This earliest Christian eschatology was focused on a physical, in-breaking of the kingdom, and was not, contrary to amillennialism, limited to a non-temporal, transcendent, heavenly existence for souls upon death, only to be followed by judgment, resurrection, and a renewed creation (as an afterthought).[30] Early Christian thought was heavily influenced by Jewish eschatology, which sought to answer the question of why those who do righteousness and abide by faithfulness should suffer without vindication.[31] The answer was to be found in the ". . . resurrection of the dead and the life of the world to come" which was embedded in the Christian creeds, in reference to a place both within time and upon a renewing earth that saw God's righteousness and peace overcome and vindicate the poor, the oppressed, and the martyrs. In this sense, Second Temple Jewish eschatology and its early Christian inheritance had much in common with contemporary Christian Liberation theology and its millenarian antecedents, with the exception that Liberation theologies of today reduce the atoning work of Christ to a footnote in the overall process of salvation.[32] The Talmud asks about a person's promised "length of days" in the circumstance in which one followed Torah devoutly, but their life unjustly or prematurely came to an end. The answer comes in a reference to the "first deposit," within time, of the world to come—"in a world altogether long; in a world altogether good."[33] According to Meryl A. Walker, Jewish:

> descriptions of the world to come include illustrations of a utopian *Olam Ha-Zeh*, meaning *this world*. In the world to come, for example, a single grape will yield thirty measures of wine. But more importantly, Olam Ha-Ba is the final exoneration of the people of Israel, the response of God to the past oppressions, persecutions, and injustices of history . . .[34]

The precursor period described above—one that is a participation in, but distinct from, the consummative *world to come* in Jewish eschatology, is the same world affirmed in Christian millenarian hermeneutics (we recall the abundant grape illustration in the work of the Christian chiliast, Papias). Yet the system of eschatology just described is dismissed in amillennialist texts as a "Jewish dream."[35] For Catholic amillennialism, there is a *conflation* of what Jewish scholars would call Olam Ha-Zeh, which in Catholic eschatology is conceived of as an eternalized, ahistorical, but renewed creation, and the coming *Olam Ha-Ba*, the final end. In the amillennial paradigm, there is no opportunity for this world and the world to come to overlap within history or time, no matter how briefly. There is no "parenthesis" in amillennial eschatology—there is only either existence on earth, or existence on a renewed earth, in eternity, after the judgment of souls.

The concept of the "world to come," in the majority of rabbinic literature includes a heavenly type of existence that may neither be calculated nor imagined—but one that is preceded by another kind of earthly existence referring to a "first deposit"[36] of that world—"... some sort of *future redemption* ... and *a time less than the time of the incomparable world to come.*"[37] According to much rabbinic exegesis, the time mentioned above was a literal period within a historical, yet future-imminent reality. For example, Rabbi Yohanan concedes that the fullness of the world to come will not resemble this world, but the first installment of such a world would be a time when the "... righteous sit with crowns on their heads and enjoy the splendor of the divine Presence. As it says, 'They beheld God and they ate and they drank' (Exodus 24:11)."[38] This "time less than the time" is also the language of the millennium according to the Christian Patristics.[39] Thus, millenarians believe in a future time of redemptive history not yet known, while amillennialists believe it is a time that is already apprehended, solely by the Church. There is no admission of a "time less than the time" of the world to come, according to the amillennial reading, for in it there is either redemption now, through the Church's auspices, or some non-temporal, non-historic, transcendent means of attaining redemption,[40] such as through purgatorial cleansing—an exception which too is reserved for *members of the Roman Catholic Church* who have already died.[41]

The traditionally Jewish, intermediary age of redemption and restoration prior to the "world to come" (what early Jewish–Christians viewed as the millennium) is what makes it possible for *all Israel* to have a place in the world to come, and this too opens a place for the "nations," despite a lack of conversion to Judaism, according to rabbinic tradition.[42] In traditional Judaism, even Christians were considered to be a sect of Judaism (a group that strayed from normative Judaism into "suspicious doctrines"), and many rabbis saw a place for Christians in the world to come.[43] Gentiles were often perceived as permitted to enjoy the world to come, provided they adhered to the Noachide law—a point the early Church wrestled with during the Jerusalem Council of Acts 15:19–29.[44] No such category exists for the Jews in official modern Catholicism, save for a Vatican II reading that lumps the Jewish people as a whole in with all other "Non-Christian Religions," and views them as "possibly" being saved in the future, by virtue of a "Baptism of desire."[45] According to this reading, the salvation of the Jews, if it happens, has nothing to do with them being Jewish and heirs to the promises of God. Worse, it has nothing to do with covenantal election, nullifying the possibility of a mass conversion of the Jewish people to Christ in the future.

Millenarian approaches to messianic eschatology, resurrection, restoration, and the "world to come" have been widespread within modern Jewish traditions, especially because the system has been acknowledged as a primary philosophy adopted by those who experienced and survived apocalyptic levels of violence, oppression, and genocide.[46] The post-Second World War concept of "hope" (*tikvah*) in Judaism was directly related to a prospect for the messianic age in which Torah, people, and land would miraculously converge.[47] The eschatological, yet historical "intermediary period" prior to the fullness of the world to come, a significant aspect in traditional Judaism (and early Christian millenarianism), is respected among modern Reformed Jews as well, despite their emphasis on the "immortality of the soul" and a personalized, transcendent heaven after death. Reform Judaism and its Conservative counterpart adopt an even deeper regard for the eschatological intermediary period because it replaces the expectation for a personalized messiah and redeemer (*go'el*) with a future, "messianic age," which will be the age of peace and "redemption" (*ge'ulah*).[48] Kabbalistic sources express,[49] and contemporary Jewish Zionists have adopted, the messianic principles that were common among Jews and Christians in the first three centuries.[50] For more traditionalist Jews, a restoration of the Temple in Jerusalem, an emphasis on the land inheritance, and a literal re-gathering of those in diaspora is central to any eschatological conception—all events allowable to occur in Moltmann's millenarian concept of eschatology, which of course, will be ushered in by Jesus Christ.

Jewish conceptions of the world to come are connected to the resurrection of the dead and messianic hopes. In general, the concept of the resurrection of the dead is intertwined with Jewish liturgical and prayer practices (*ha-tefillah*).[51] If the term *lex orandi est lex credenda* has any bearing on official Jewish theologies, physical resurrection of the dead body (and not merely an immortality of the soul) is thought to be essential to belief. The Mishnah's few exceptions to those who have a place in the world to come include those who deny the resurrection of the dead.[52] In traditional Jewish theology, the ". . . body is *ensouled* just as the soul is *embodied*."[53] In Reform Judaism, the immortality of the soul is stressed, and while some scholars claim that Reformed Jews completely deny bodily resurrection, there are many within this expression of Judaism that hold tightly to the doctrine.[54] The concept of bodily resurrection has been dramatically revived among Reform Jews worldwide, primarily because of the resurgence to *ad fontes* theology within their expressions of the faith.[55] The Conservative Jewish prayer book, *Sim Shalom*, maintains the original Hebrew translation of the phrase regarding the God who "resurrects the dead," as do the Orthodox Jewish liturgical guides.[56]

Perhaps the most important point, in relation to our discussion of Christian millenarianism, is that Jewish conceptions of resurrection stress the nationalistic elements of the doctrine, in line with the messianic age of eschatological history.[57]

Non-secular Jews, by and large, believe that with the coming of the resurrection of the dead by God, the resurrection and restoration of the Jewish people as a nation (as a theological phenomenon and communal event near the end of time), will also come about.[58] During the Jewish intermediary messianic period, God will resurrect the righteous and will set up *a dwelling* among the people in Jerusalem. The traditional Jewish (and early Christian) understanding of resurrection conceived of the event as deeply embedded in time and treated it as a final stage within history.[59]

Millenarian eschatology has safeguarded many of the elements of Jewish belief in the resurrection,[60] careful not to give in to solely, other-worldly, or overly materialistic conceptions of the messianic age.[61] In the amillennial view, resurrection must come after any historical or temporally conditioned era because Jesus' Parousia is seen in ahistorical terms. In amillennialism, the return of Jesus brings the rupture, and thus the end, of history, in an instant.

Like the concept of resurrection, Jewish hope for the messiah and messianic age is indicative of a nationalistic impetus, in balance with a desire for spiritual renewal, and it is oftentimes conceived in ethical terms.[62] Depending on its kind, Jewish messianic hope may alternately stress a unique individual who will take up the Davidic role as God's agent of restoration for Israel—the apocalyptic Son of man who will hand the kingdom to God and vindicate Israel—or a "non-personified" era of messianic benefit, unrelated to a specific "messiah" per se.[63] Rabbis have debated and continue to debate what kind of powers the messiah might have when he comes to initiate the world to come—and whether he would have an authority nearly equal to God, or even an authority to *abolish the need for Torah observance*.[64] Within the *Chabad* movement in America, there is a significant group who believe that the last Rebbe[65] was and is the messiah, and some believe that he lives on in a "resurrection body" that is spiritual rather than physical, although this last Rebbe reportedly died in 1994.[66] Nevertheless, the point is that there is great expectation among many contemporary Jewish people for the coming of the messiah.

What is common to Jewish conceptions of messianic hope is that the messianic ideal is to result in concrete events that benefit the Jewish people and the nations. To my knowledge, no kind of contemporary Judaism, save "messianic Christian Judaism," admits of an incarnation of the Godhead in a human being, though some kinds of Second Temple Judaism came very close. For example, A.F. Segal has identified a rather significant sect of rabbis who lived during the Second Temple period, who held to a "two powers in heaven" belief system—a system vehemently rejected as heretical by the majority rabbinic establishment.[67] Though Segal's work seeks to connect the rabbinic accusation of heresy to early Christians and Gnostics, he admits that the concept of a sharing of divinity among "powers in heaven" was not limited to these groups, but was applicable to various Jewish rabbis, and various sects of Judaism as a whole.

The continued Jewish rejection of Jesus as messiah directly correlates to Jewish reality—Jesus did not bring to the Jewish people the kind of national restoration that was expected, and unfortunately, Christianity brought to the Jews consistent and incalculable harm.[68] The primary problem with "Jesus as the messiah," according to rabbinic Judaism, is that they cannot accept a resurrected messiah.[69] Millenarian Christians argue that such issues may only be resolved eschatologically, after the first resurrection, whereas amillennialists believe the "first resurrection" refers to the resolution in terms of conversion directly to the Church through baptism.

Two kinds of messianic expectations have existed since the time of the rabbis —an "apocalyptic" variety in which the resurrection of the dead was conceived as co-relative to the coming of messiah, and a "projective" variety in which the messiah would raise the righteous from the grave, after which a period of intermediary time would take place. During the intermediary state of projective messianism, the Jewish messiah would consummate the covenantal blessing to national Israel, redeem Israel by the forgiveness of sin and the gathering of the exiles back to Jerusalem, and re-establish worship in the Temple—all prior to the general resurrection.[70] In general terms, in Judaism, ". . . the role of the messiah is essentially political (taken in the deepest sense): he is to both bring and forever maintain the kingdom of God, centered in Jerusalem but extending throughout the whole earth."[71] Thus, the question that arises for Christian theologians is whether Jesus, as messiah, inaugurated the kingdom of God, specifically within the auspices of the Church, in a way that makes a future consummation of the kingdom utterly obsolete for those Jewish people who are alive at that time. Millenarian theologians almost unanimously claim that Jesus' inauguration of the kingdom, as real as it was, does not preclude a future expression of it outside of the Gentile Church.

The thesis that arises in our study of Christian millenarianism, that it overcomes supersessionism, does not demand a one-to-one correspondence between Jewish and Christian eschatology (which would be difficult—essentially impossible, in light of Christological and Trinitarian concerns)[72]—indeed, such a construct would partially negate the distinctions between Israel and the Church that we have thus far attempted to safeguard. The real point is that Jewish messianic expectations, no matter how spiritualized in modern expressions, contain a temporal and historical dimension. The Jewish hope for the kingdom is that God will redeem and restore Israel, as Israel.

Soulen's insight on this point is exactly correct, although he once again fails to connect the point to the failures of amillennial Christian eschatology and the opportunities provided by millennialism. I will quote at length because of its importance. Soulen states that it is:

> appropriate to *distinguish* between the "historical" and the "cosmic" dimensions of God's one eschatological blessing. The historical dimension of final consummation concerns the climax of the history that unfolds between the Lord, Israel, and the nations. The cosmic dimension concerns God's establishment of a new heaven and a new earth . . . The rabbis operated with

a similar distinction in their understanding of "the world to come" ... the *inauguration* of God's own reign in creation ... *God's historical fidelity toward Israel is the 'narrow gate' that opens the new creation ... God's consummating work does not engage the human family 'immediately.'* God's consummating work engages the one human family in its covenantal identity as Jew and Gentile, as Israel and the nations, and *in this way* engages the human creature and human creation as a whole. The path from creation to new creation goes by way of the open-ended story that unfolds among God, Israel, and the nations.[73]

In the pages that follow, we will illustrate that in the Catholic amillennial model, there is a conflation of the historical element of God's consummation—which is very important to Jewish theology—and the cosmic. By conflating the historical economy of the present Church with the consummative and final economy of the new heavens and the new earth, amillennialism presents the Church as leading directly, or "immediately" into the new creation,[74] substituting the Church for the kingdom, and sidestepping the necessary "narrow gate" of God's redemptive and restorative interactions with the Jewish people, through the person of Jesus. As amillennialists insist, if God reigns in the Church now, there is no hope for a future kingdom beside it, on this side of eternity. Yet we must either ask if our definition of 'the Church' is too narrow, or if in fact God's plans for the Jewish people, outlined in biblical detail, hold the answer. Adherents of the amillennial paradigm claim that, upon Jesus's return, history and time will cease, all will be resurrected, judged according to their deeds, and ushered directly and immediately into the new creation/new earth.[75] We must ask, in reference to the amillennial paradigm, in what way, shape or form did or does Israel play an active role in salvation history, apart from *becoming* the Church? In the millenarian paradigm, there is conceived to be an *intervening period within time and history*, yet also between temporality and eternity, during which God through Jesus Christ will reign, the saints will be resurrected, and the consummation will be inaugurated. As such, millenarian eschatology leaves space for God's distinctive interactions with the Israel of the future, and the mutual blessing between Israel and the nations. Contemporary millenarian thought also has a tendency to view the Church as a provisional entity in history, rather than an incarnation of the kingdom that will last through the Last Days and usher directly into a heavenly reality. Because "the gates of hell will not prevail against it" does not mean that the Church holds the monopoly on eternity—quite the contrary, because God is a God of covenantal promise, the gates of hell will be crushed once and for all.

The two important elements of millenarianism—the ability to leave space for a valid theological role regarding the Jewish people in relation to God, and the propensity to view the Church as conditioned by history, are two functions described in detail by Jürgen Moltmann and applied to the Jewish–Christian question of supersessionism. In our next section, we will explore Moltmann's unique contribution to post-supersessionist theology in light of millenarian categories.

Moltmann's mitigated millenarianism and the provisional Church

Before we enumerate the ways in which millenarianism as a general eschatology rejects supersessionist thought and opens new possibilities for a truly positive Catholic theology of Judaism, we must now decide on which specific incarnation of millenarianism would be most helpful to our thesis. Christian millenarianism, as we have described, is rooted in Judaism, in the words of Jesus and the Apostolic Witness, and is traceable throughout the works of the early Fathers. Jürgen Moltmann's version of millenarianism maintains virtually all the elements of Patristic millenarianism, but avoids the apocalyptic thematic components that may too easily be misappropriated and applied to further violent expressions like that of its competitive counterpart, realized eschatology.[76] Moltmann wants to avoid any hint of a triumphalist, violent millennial reign in the here and now or conceivable future, established by people who hold power in the conventional political sense—precisely the problem with "historical millenarianism," conventionally called amillennialism.[77] Likewise, there is an intentional avoidance of violent uprising by the masses of oppressed in the world. Moltmann states that:

> When the imperial theologians transferred . . . [the traditionally millenarian] . . . apocalyptic promises to the *imperium christianum*, which came into being before their very eyes, they conferred upon that kingdom a messianic sense of mission which has never wholly disappeared from the political or civil religions of Christianity down to the present day.[78]

Referring to the amillennial scheme, Moltmann states that even the cross was converted into a symbol of militant and triumphalist victory—no longer a sign of victory over sin and death, but over those guilty of deicide, the Jews.[79] It is this triumphalism that Moltmann's approach successfully removes as a possibility. It must be noted that some, though not all of the early chiliasts, in light of their context and polemic against the Jewish people, did make the claim that the millennial age was only for Christians and not Jews.[80] Moltmann's millenarianism, by contrast, makes the presence and participation of the Jewish people *constitutive* of the messianic age, insofar as the Hebrew Bible's prophetic words regarding such a kingdom are addressed to Israel directly and are still in effect for the future role that Israel will play.[81]

What Moltmann posits instead of the politicized "historical millenarianism" (conventionally called amillennialism), is an eschatological expectation that takes seriously the ethical imperative to embody the kind of ministry that Jesus himself embraced—servanthood, encompassing a bold witness to the Gospel, combined with a "mission" to the hurting, oppressed, and marginalized, in which the greatest expression of power would come about through a cruciform, martyr-oriented existence.[82] Moltmann's understanding of the millennium, taken primarily from his works entitled *The Coming of God*[83] and *The Church in the Power of the Spirit*, is firmly rooted in his earlier "Theology of Hope," which contains certain features regarding the nature of the Church and the people Israel.[84] For Moltmann:

Old Testament promises were never superseded by historical events, but were constantly modified and expanded. Of course, some were realized within history. Yet, the promises were not completely resolved in any event, but there remained an overspill that pointed to the future . . . Moltmann sees the same feature in the New Testament, because the revelation in Christ is at the same time good news and promise . . . The Old Testament history of promise does not simply find its fulfillment in the gospel, but finds its future in the gospel. Because the gospel is promise, it is a guarantee of the promised future.[85]

Moltmann's eschatological millennium and its primary features are considered the "space" for the "overspill"[86] of divine promise that exists for both the Church and Israel.[87] This is precisely why Moltmann's millenarianism is set firmly in a future that may only come about by an act of God (resisting well-intentioned but oftentimes misguided human attempts at progressively establishing the kingdom),[88] resists apocalyptic excesses by removing violence as a means of participating in the kingdom now (establishing an ecclesial ethic of humble service to Israel and the world, while rejecting "escapism"),[89] and insists that the future messianic age is a period in which both Israel and the Church are involved in worshipping God together, without one converting to the other as institutional entities. Moltmann rejects contemporary dispensationalism as ". . . antimodernist, fundamentalist *apocalypticism,*"[90] namely because of its use in American political banter and the rise of the "moral majority."[91] For Moltmann, the Church and Israel are "partners in history" now because they both have a calling to serve the world and witness to God by leading the nations to the eschatological millennium, *without one becoming the other.*[92] This does not remove the impetus of conversion to Jesus, but merely makes the claim that a Jew who believes in Jesus need not become a Gentile Christian but can maintain elements of Jewish particularity. Moltmann says that God's *parousaic* and consummative economy ". . . means that all Israel will not through faith become Christian, but through sight will be redeemed"[93]— a point associated with the apocalyptic promises to the Jewish people found in Daniel 7:13, whereby they will simply recognize the *Shekinah*, Presence of God and at that point be resurrected. This corresponds to the Jews who are on earth during the return of Jesus, who will look upon him as their Deliverer. Whereas the Patristic millenarians (Justin, Irenaeus, etc.) initially adopted supersessionism as a posture in order to differentiate Christianity from Judaism, Moltmann uses the millenarian principle to offer an alternative eschatological hope for Israel that is not synonymous with the Church.[94]

Perhaps the single most important feature of Moltmann's contemporary millenarian conception, which is in many ways consistent with the ancient Patristics, is that the Thousand Year's Reign and penultimate installment of the kingdom of God is *future, terrestrial, temporal, and historical.*[95] Moltmann describes the difference between amillennialism[96] (which he calls, alternately, "historical," or "presentative," taking on sub-categories of political or ecclesiastical millenarianism), and the eschatological millenarianism he advocates, as that between the *time-eternity dialectic* (amillenailism) and the *historical dialectic* (eschatological millenarianism).[97] In the amillennial worldview, when Jesus returns, time will end abruptly and eternity will begin, whereas in the millenarian viewpoint, the millennial age will be a bridge between history and eternity,[98] a time labeled as *eschatological future history*. Eschatological future history includes an element of "surprise" connected to particularity, temporality, and the conditions of history[99]—something that cannot be said of the amillennialist, time-eternity dialectic. We will explore why this temporal distinction is important in the section entitled "Catholic amillennialism is necessarily supersessionist." For now, it is sufficient to say that if the only salvific period of history that exists is the *present age*, in which the eschaton has been "imported" solely through the auspices of the Church, there can be no simultaneously eschatological and temporal contribution of the Jewish people to a Christian view of salvation history for the future. If the present age of the Church is viewed as an incarnation of the kingdom that leads directly into the final judgment and then eternity, supersessionism is the only viable option regarding Christian eschatology and ecclesiology, and the Jewish people, as Jews, are without hope in the sense that a future encounter with the living Christ would literally be an "impossible dream."

Moltmann's most polemical discussion on the millennium takes place within the context of the dangers of traditional amillennialism (historical or presentative millenarianism). Moltmann believes that the German dialectical theologians, like traditional Catholic amillennialists, viewed redemption as a ". . . redemption from history and time into the eternity of God"[100] (thus, at the eschaton, time ends abruptly with the coming of Christ and therefore, eternity ruptures history), whereas typical modern Jewish thinkers (and Christian millenarians) embrace the fact that ". . . the messianic interpretation of the experience of the moment that ends and gathers up time is the *redemption of the future* from the power of . . . [oppressive] . . . history."[101] History is only of benefit to those who control it, for ". . . the power of history is exercised by the mighty. They have to extend their victorious present into the future in order to augment and consolidate their power. *Their* future is without an alternative, and devoid of surprises."[102]

The abuse of the eschatological future at the hands of Western power is also the story of the amillennial, supersessionist, anti-Jewish tradition in the Roman Catholic Church, and its alternative is ". . . the redemption of the future from the power of history in the *kairos*[103] of conversion."[104] What then, is the intermediary time of conversion for the Church, in light of God's future, which is coming to the world? In the amillennial paradigm, all historical entities convert to the Church, including Israel, while the Church feeds history directly into eternity—with no surplus of meaning other than what the Church *already has in its possession*. Here the Church converts to nothing, for the Church is the penultimate to eternity, and historically defines eternity. Moltmann puts it this way: "If the Church hopes for something greater than itself, it can then draw Israel into its hope. If the Church considers itself to be the fulfillment of all hopes, it then shuts Israel out."[105] The "something greater than itself" for which the provisional Church hopes is the messianic kingdom in eschatological history—the future millennium, or the Thousand Years Reign of Jesus Christ, advocated in Patristic chiliasm.[106] The Church, according to millenarian tradition, is provisional to the messianic kingdom, because it is provision to Christ, who is its head, and is called continually to *convert* to Christ and convert to a renewed service to the kingdom. Likewise, if Israel is to convert, it is not to the Church of history, but to a renewed understanding of YHWH and to the coming kingdom of their God—the nature of which is consistent with the promises of the Hebrew Bible as ascertained by the rabbis. The Christian witness always has been, and always will be, that the conversion to YHWH is likewise a conversion to the Son of God, Jesus of Nazareth.

Moltmann struggled extensively with the question of supersessionism and how to overcome it. He asks:

> does the divine history of Israel merge into Church history in such a way that Israel, as 'the ancient people of God,' has been superseded and rendered obsolete by 'the new people of God'? Or does Israel retain its own particular 'vocation for salvation,' side by side with the Church, *down to the end of history*?[107]

What Moltmann is really asking is if Christians, and Christian theologians, are able to conceive of a Church that ceases to hate its own "not yet"[108] (a future which will include particularly Jewish expressions in the Community of the Redeemed). Are Catholic theologians able to imagine a Church that is acceptable in terms other than ". . . the kingdom of God on earth in absolute form,"[109] in the form which it exists currently? Moltmann's conception of the eschaton, which includes a hope for a future kingdom that embraces *justice*, the *humanizing of men and women*, the *socializing of humanity*, and *peace for all creation*,[110] unlike the work of Ruether and van Buren,[111] does not demand that Christians do away with their doctrine that the God of Israel is Trinity, that Jesus is a member of that Trinity, or that Jesus died on a Roman cross to redeem sinners and was raised from the dead in victory over death itself.[112] To do away with these basic doctrines is to advocate for a religiosity that is so different from what Christians have always believed and practiced that it ceases, in fact, to be Christian at all.[113] Moltmann's millenarian expression simply demands that Christian theologians admit that God's future cannot exclude the people of Israel, and that the Church cannot now be conceived as the only expression of the kingdom of God within history—a kingdom yet to be consummated on earth, in time. The mutual hope of Jews and Christians is one in which all parties take responsibility—it is a realistic hope in the midst of the sufferings of this world and one which takes seriously the questions of the systemic evils of the past and present.[114] Thus, the Christian hope for both the Church and Israel is the same Jesus who engaged in a ministry of suffering on behalf of the suffering.

Supersessionism is specifically an ecclesiastical and eschatological problem because the Church has viewed itself as the sole eschatological hope for the world, ignoring the election and calling of the Jewish people as a valid expression of an alternative messianic hope, awaiting the return of Jesus Christ.[115] Moltmann calls the theological interdependence of Christians and Jews the "salvation-historical thesis," a school of thought popularized by resurgence in millenarian eschatology through Reformed Federalist Theology, Pietist theology, and the Lutheran "Erlangen" school.[116] According to Moltmann, the Christian theological schools that have conceived of a positive role for the Jewish people in salvation history are ones that have embraced millenarianism.[117] From the perspective of this "salvation-historical" model, Jesus embodied the visible aspects of the messianic kingdom in his lifetime, but because we await Jesus' return, there is still divine promise that is yet to be fulfilled within history. Because the Church is provisional to, and waiting upon, the fulfillment of promises made by God in both the Hebrew Bible and the New Testament, it cannot make an *exclusive* claim to the kingdom of God. Moltmann explains that the:

> salvation-historical thesis is closely connected with millenarianism, the hope that Christ will rule for a thousand years before the end. But we 'shrug our shoulders over the chosen people and hence over millenarianism as well.' From the time of Tyconius and Augustine onwards this thousand-year rule of Christ was continually interpreted as the era of the Church following Christ's resurrection and ascension. But if the Church understands itself as the messianic kingdom of Christ, then it cannot acknowledge Israel's separate existence alongside itself. Since in the millennium Christ and his followers are to 'rule' over his enemies, they must, according to this way of understanding themselves, view the unbelieving Jews as their enemies and suppress them ... the Jews must surrender their hope of a Messiah.[118]

Since the "... Old Testament must be seen as the book of promises of present-day Israel,"[119] Christians have yet to fully understand how the Jewish people contribute positively to the eschaton, but must affirm that they do currently, and will in the future, in light of the Judaic nature of almost all the future-oriented promises in Sacred Scripture. If the Church is not related to Israel in a one-to-one sense (i.e., if the Church has not *become* Israel, as we have already argued it has not), and the Church cannot claim to be the kingdom of God on earth without alternative, supersessionism cannot stand as a consistent and theologically honest approach. Contemporary amillennialists claim that the Church is the New Israel, and that the Old Israel no longer serves any theological function.[120] Amillennialists also claim the Church possesses the kingdom of God until the end of time, and that any apocalyptic promises given to the Jewish people, by God, now apply to the Church.[121] Amillennialists have sought to do away with the threat posed by millenarians, designating it as a "Jewish dream," specifically because millenarianism insulates and protects a Jewish hope for the future—one that cannot be reduced to the Church.[122] Millenarian eschatology threatens the position of power in the predominantly amillennial Church because that Church is among those institutions which proclaim:

> that their own political or ecclesiastical present is Christ's Thousand Years' empire [and] cannot put up with any hope for an alternative kingdom of Christ

besides . . . but post-millenarian eschatologies of this kind are based on a false definition of the location of the present in the context of salvation history.[123]

Theologically, the Church's proper indicator for the placing of the present and future of salvation history is its inseparable binding to, and attitude regarding, present-day Israel, for ". . . it is only the millenarian hope in Christian eschatology which unfolds an earthly and historical future for the Church and Israel."[124] The goal of the sections that follow is to point to the specific relationship between millenarianism and non-supersessionist theology, and explore the means by which millenarian eschatology helps to overcome supersessionist attitudes in Christian theology.

Three problematic questions

Before we are able to prove our thesis in a fuller sense, there are three problematic questions that arise for Christian theology that must be addressed regarding the millenarian view in relation to supersessionism: (1) If millenarian theology envisions an economy of salvation for the Jewish people apart from the Church, what does this say about the cross of Jesus Christ and God's economy of redemption for the world according to Christian tradition? (2) If the Thousand Years' reign of Revelation 20 is conceived as a future reign of *Jesus Christ* with the martyrs, does this not negate any Jewish contribution to, or participation in it, particularly one that is acceptable either to Jews or Christians? (3) How is it possible to envision a future, Jewish–Christian messianic kingdom in virtue of the fact that Christians believe Jesus is God the Son incarnate, and will worship him as God during the messianic reign, while Jews currently appear to deny the concept altogether?

We will explore these three questions in turn, but it is important to note that although soteriology, Christology, and Trinitarianism are deeply connected to eschatology and ecclesiology, these themes are not the precise focus of this book. Granted, each must be dealt with, as any Christian theology of Judaism must partake in the task while holding firmly to the divinity of Jesus and the unicity of salvation through his work on Golgotha and his resurrection power. We mention them here only because questions will linger in the minds of theologians regarding the interdependency of the various aspects of doctrine upon the claims we are making. The purpose of this book is essentially to prove the thesis that millenarianism as defined and nuanced by Moltmann largely overcomes the problem of supersessionism in its three forms, particularly through its philosophy of time and its view of the kingdom of God as a reality that is not bound by contemporary human conceptions of "Church." The biblical understanding of the term "Church" must take into consideration its separateness and service to the kingdom of God.

Supersessionism is defined as the notion that the Church takes over God's covenantal promises to the Jewish people, oftentimes described as "Israel," in our text. Whether Jews remain "Jewish" but convert to Jesus in the eschaton, thus gaining a form of soteriological merit that itself is foreign to Jewish theology (and if it is possible to be considered a Jew if one believes that Jesus is the messiah)[125] or Christians accept the Sinai covenant as the defining and transcendent moment of salvation history, as some more liberal theologians claim, making Christology and atonement theory secondary[126]—these things are outside the exact scope of this project. That said, any orthodox conception of Judaism must include the idea that the Jewish people will one day see in Jesus, in a subjective sense, the fulfillment of their own messianic hopes. Further, it is not the purpose of this project to create some sort of forced syncretism of Jewish and Christian belief, though we will advocate for an eschatological end that includes both the Jewish people as a distinct commmunity, and Gentile Christians, worshipping together with the Lamb at the center of the glorification process. Overall, we will work to allow the primary differences between Judaism and Christianity to remain, even in our conceptions of the millennial age, but where the New Testament makes space for common ground, we will pursue such ground theologically. Following the advice of Jewish scholar and ecumenist Terry Bookman, we will seek to avoid ". . . liberal attempts to either include those who do not profess their faith under their particular salvific formulation or to relativize all truth away."[127] Bookman's point is important, simply because Jews and Christians do not view redemption in the same way, but nevertheless, Jews and millenarian Christians share significant themes in common regarding the world to come. The overarching purpose of touching on the three problematic questions above is simply to show that we have responsibly taken them into consideration.

First, millenarians, because they present space in time for a consummative work of God that is differentiated from, complimentary to, and in some ways, interrelated with the redemptive economy in Jesus Christ that is proclaimed by Christians, they are able to confirm a theological future for Israel. The confirmation of a final, consummative work of God in history for the purpose of the redemption and restoration of the Jewish people need not be viewed as mutually exclusive to the exclusive, universal, and redemptive cross of Jesus Christ, if the cross is conceived as God's confirmation that Israel is elect forever, that human atonement is constitutively tied to the Jewish people, and that God's election of Israel vis-à-vis the Abrahamic promise is *ratified as a blessing for the nations* through the cross of Jesus. Soulen argues that ". . . the gospel proclaims Jesus' life, death, and resurrection as the proleptic enactment of God's eschatological fidelity to the work of consummation, that is, to fullness of mutual blessing (among Jews and Christians) as the outcome of God's economy with Israel, the nations, and all creation."[128] In this sense, the cross of Jesus is the divine, non-violent means whereby violence and the curse of human sin is banished, overcome, and exchanged for *shalom*[129] and the blessing of the peaceable kingdom,[130] a peace and blessing intended by God from the beginning to be given to Israel, and through Israel, the nations.[131] Because God ordained this peace from the beginning for Israel prior to the cross of Jesus, it is part of God's permanent, irrevocable consummative economy of salvation. The resurrection of Jesus is the divine means whereby those who are righteous—especially those who have been persecuted or killed for the sake of righteousness—are proleptically restored unto new life,[132] a life that the God of Israel originally promised to Israel, but has yet to fulfill in totality. Jesus' death on the cross and resurrection from death by the power of the Holy Spirit make clear the point that the God of Israel has revealed the Gospel to the world that proclaims YHWH's coming reign—a reign that will once and for all overcome the curse of sin and the violent consequence of death.[133] But this Christian theological reality by no means negates God's original purpose in bringing to fulfillment the divine covenant with the people of Israel, and this is the case regardless of the *current* Jewish position in reference to the Gospel that we just defined: "... from the standpoint of God's choice they are beloved for the sake of the fathers; for the gifts and the calling of God are irrevocable" (Romans 11:28–29). The Christian hope for the Jewish people is the hope that the Jewish people, in a corporate sense, will see Jesus for who he is: the messiah of the world, the Son of God, and the hope of nations. But that hope is tied to the realization among the Jews as a whole that Jesus fulfills these aspects as the *Jewish* messiah as well. This point is precisely why the Second Coming of Jesus is so closely tied to specifically Jewish messianic expectations, both the Epistle to the Romans, and the Book of Revelation.

In order to avoid Marcionism on the one hand, and contemporary supersessionism on the other, Christians (as the community of Christ-followers) must simultaneously affirm the exclusive Gospel that focuses on the cross and resurrection of Jesus, the importance that the God Christians worship is the same God of the Jews—the God *of Israel*, and the reality that there is a coming reign of God that will resolve the theological problems while maintaining and affirming the differences and particularities among Jews and Christians. An understanding of the cross and resurrection as *real but proleptic*[134] safeguards many of the traditional Christian beliefs while leaving room for a consummative future. Through Christian disciples, the entire world participates in the real yet proleptic blessings of Jesus' cross and resurrection, as Christians embody sacrificial love, take up their own crosses, and witness to the unique value of the entire human person in God's salvific drama through the atoning work of Jesus as Son of God. In reference to atonement and forgiveness of sin, Jesus is viewed as the sole means of forgiveness and redemption, but it must be remembered that God had supplied a means for righteousness to be "imputed" upon the Jewish people prior to the cross of Christ, that being the irrevocable, unconditional covenant made directly with the people of Israel through the patriarch Abraham in Genesis 15, and also Genesis 17:6. "Then Abraham believed in the LORD; and He reckoned (וַיַּחְשְׁבֶהָ) it to him as righteousness" (Genesis 15:6). Thus, this unconditional covenant which existed prior to Jesus' incarnation will find its *telos* in the return of Jesus.

Ultimately, Christian biblical and apostolic tradition has maintained two primary propositions that traditional Judaism has denied: Jesus is God incarnate, and Jesus is messiah. If Christian theologians deny either of these propositions, the very core of the Christian tradition is augmented in an unacceptable manner. From an ethical standpoint, Christians should not be pressured into rejecting their own traditional Christology any more than Jews should be pressured into accepting it in the contemporary moment. But this does not mean that such traditionalist Christians, particularly Catholics, cannot *affirm a shift in ecclesiology and eschatology* that envisions a further chapter in the story of God's salvation history with Israel. The millenarian shift in eschatology denies that the Church is the kingdom of God *in toto*, therefore pointing to the Jewish community (despite its plurality) as another, alternative instantiation of God's reign for the future. Likewise, millenarian eschatolology supports the belief that the messianic kingdom, as expressed in the biblical narrative in Revelation 20, will incorporate virtually all of the expectations that the Jewish people have for the messianic age and the messiah. Because supersessionists, as we have argued, claim that the Church usurps the divine promises meant for Israel, millenarian eschatology denies such a concept as incompatible with Christian theology—in particular its ecclesiological and eschatological dimensions, for it is likewise incompatible with the Jesus whom Christians worship, and also with the doctrine of election.

The second theological challenge involves the millenarian idea that the interregnum period is a reign of *Jesus*, at least according to Revelation 20: 1–15. We will explore this further when we briefly discuss the nature of the messianic kingdom through an exegesis of Revelation 20 and Romans 11, but for now, it is sufficient to say that a close reading of the text of Revelation confirms that one may interpret the passage as referring to two groups of people worshipping the same God in different ways, with one group apparently *emphasizing* a deeper understanding of the God of Israel as Father, and the other, a deeper understanding of the God of Israel as Son, Jesus—the one whom Christians believe to be the second Person of the Trinity: ". . . And I saw the souls of those who had been beheaded because of their testimony about Jesus *and* because of the word of God . . . they will be priests of God and of Christ and will reign with him for a thousand years" (Revelation 20: 4,6). Why did the writer care to distinguish between the group that had given testimony to Jesus and those who gave testimony to God's word?[135] Why did John distinguish between "priests of God," and "priests of Christ"? I argue that a millenarian, post-supersessionist reading of the text affirms Jews and Christians worshipping the God of Israel in eschatological community, albeit both groups are worshipping both the Father and Jesus, the Lamb. Most modern Jews acknowledge that followers of Jesus Christ worship the God of Israel.[136] Most modern Christians acknowledge that Jews are in covenant relationship with the God of Israel, *as Jews*, in some sense that is maintained as a mystery.[137] Does not the millenarian reading of Revelation affirm that these two seemingly opposed groups currently witness to the same consummative economy of God's blessing in the eschaton, regardless of the combined Presence of YHWH and Jesus Christ in the narrative? Is this not preferable to the amillennial position, which reads the entire Revelation 20 episode as already fulfilled in the historical Church, and limits the value of Judaism to the time prior to the advent of Jesus? Ultimately, if the Jewish people and the Church are to be conceived as sharing together any portion of the world to come, room must be made for a narrative that is inclusive of both the God of Israel and the Presence of Jesus. Moltmann's millenarianism promotes such a view, without sacrificing traditional Christian sentiments that Jesus Christ is uniquely the Lord of all creation.[138]

While the Christological, and thus Trinitarian issues of Christian dogma underlie all dialogue regarding the Last Days, a reassessment of Christian eschatology and the Church's view of its own role should take priority. If the Church cannot see anything beyond itself as the expression of the God of Israel's reign and economy of salvation in this world, debate about Christological issues, the messianic identity of Jesus, and the precise eschatological solution to the problem of how Jews and Christians will worship, will lead nowhere.

The final primary question that arises in relation to our thesis relates to our second question regarding the identity of Jesus in the eschaton. If Christians worship Jesus in the millennial reign, how can this be a true community in terms of Jewish participation in it? Does this not constitute idolatry for the Jew? The 2002 document produced by the National Jewish Scholars Project entitled *Dabru Emet—A Jewish Statement on Christians and Christianity*, though not uniformly representative of all Jewish opinions, is indicative of wide trends in Jewish ecumenical dialogue with the Church. It contains two statements that have significant bearing on our thesis. The first states this:

> Jews and Christians worship the same God. Before the rise of Christianity, Jews were the only worshippers of the God of Israel. But Christians also worship the God of Abraham, Isaac, and Jacob; creator of heaven and earth. While Christian worship is not a viable religious choice for Jews, as Jewish theologians we rejoice that, through Christianity, hundreds of millions of people have entered into relationship with the God of Israel.[139]

The focus of our project at hand is whether Christians believe that through Judaism, "hundreds of millions of people have ... [likewise] ... entered into relationship with the God of Israel," despite a temporary rejection of Christian messianic claims that appear to be the will of God directly (see Romans 9–11). Supersessionists state, and amillennialists imply, that Judaism no longer has to do with the God of Israel at all, though the Church does. Millenarian theology denies these implications by claiming that the Jewish people are a constitutive part of the future millennial kingdom based on an eternal covenant, and therefore contribute to it regardless of the Church's existence. But in envisioning the eschaton, how can Jews tolerate the worship of Jesus, and how can Christians envision a liturgical community in which Jesus is not worshipped in the same way the Gentile Church worships him? The writers of *Dabru Emet* saw this question as a theological conundrum, so therefore they concentrated on *what they could affirm* based on real history: that a relationship with Jesus has in fact (not merely in principle) allowed millions of people to enter into valid relationship with the God of Israel, despite Christian worship of that God as Trinity.[140] Christians, like Jews, do not claim to worship more than one God, but make distinctions as to the Persons within the Godhead and the means of unique incarnation. Christian theologians may learn from this by pointing to the historical reality that prior to the advent of Jesus, Judaism led millions of individuals into a relationship with the God of Israel, despite Judaism's non-Trinitarian, strictly monotheistic doctrine,

Christian millenarian theology of Judaism 227

in terms of development of the religion *at that time*. Judaism likewise made space for theophanic phenomena, and in many cases argued that God could, in a mysterious way, become visible and corporeal.

Jewish scholar Michael Wyschogrod has successfully argued that the doctrine of the incarnation is a focused and intensified augmentation of the original Jewish doctrines of *divine indwelling*.[141] The Jews, to a large degree, believe that God specifically made a divine indwelling in the community/people of Israel, among whom the incarnated Jesus was a member. For Christians, Jesus' incarnation was and is entirely unique, as he is the incarnation of the Logos, the divine Son of God, sharing in one substance with the Father. As Jacob Neusner has argued, Jewish rejection of Christianity's "particular framing" of incarnation is *a rejection in fact, but not in principle—an issue over degree and not kind*.[142] If there is space for Jewish forbearance regarding the incarnation of Jesus among some of its leading theologians, is there not space for a Christian eschatological conception that makes as the basis for relationship God's indwelling in the Jewish people during the millennial age, simultaneous with the Christian worship of Jesus, Son of God and Jewish man? In other words, the Christian hope that the Jewish people will corporately worship Jesus at the eschaton is directly related to God's past practice of indwelling among the very flesh of the Jewish people. Yet in Christ, the God of Israel *took on Jewish flesh*—an even more powerful expression of God's faithfulness and election of the Jewish nation and community.

Ultimately, in its second statement related to our project, *Dabru Emet* affirms that the eschaton will bring with it, simultaneously, the answer to the deep mystery of Jewish and Christian religious hope, while at the same time leaving a current space for disagreement and instantiating a post-supersessionist reality: "The humanly irreconcilable difference between Jews and Christians will not be settled *until* God redeems the entire world as promised in Scripture."[143] For the Christian, God has redeemed the entire world (the cosmos, though not all individually) through the Person and work of Jesus. That work is yet to be consummated.

Notes

1 The pluralistic hypothesis for interreligious reality is described by John Hick: ". . . the great post-axial faiths constitute different ways of experiencing, conceiving and living in relation to an ultimate divine Reality which transcends all our varied visions of it." John Hick, *An Interpretation of Religion: Human Responses to the Transcendent* (New Haven, CT: Yale University Press, 2005), 235–236. For more on the development of recent debates regarding pluralism and interreligious dialogue, see Aimée Upjohn Light, "Harris, Hick, and the Demise of the Pluralist Hypothesis," *Journal of Ecumenical Studies* 44, no. 3 (Summer 2009): 467–470, and John Hick, "A Brief Response to Aimée Upjohn Light," *Journal of Ecumenical Studies* 44, no. 4 (Fall 2009): 691–692. See also, Steven Aguzzi, "The Problematic of Totalization in Hick's Pluralist Thesis: Arguing for an Open Eschatological Inclusivism" (paper presented at *Symbolon* in the Theology Department of Duquesne University, Pittsburgh, PA, November 6, 2009), 1–21.

2 Michael J. Vlach, "Variations within Supersessionism," in *The Conference of the Evangelical Theological Society* (San Diego, CA, 2007). Diprose questions why the Church, in amillennialism, is conceived as an inheritor of the blessings of Israel, but

not an inheritor of the punishments associated with straying from the holiness required of God's chosen people. See Diprose, *Israel and the Church*, xi.
3   B. Klappert, "Fellow Heirs and Partakers of the Promises," in Didier Pollefeyt, ed., *Jews and Christians, Rivals or Partners for the Kingdom of God?: In Search of an Alternative for the Theology of Substitution* (Louvain: Peeters, 1998), 38–61, esp. 58. See 2 Samuel 7:11–19; 1 Chronicles 17; Psalm 89:3–4; Isaiah 9:6–7; Jeremiah 30:9–10; 33:14–17; Ezekiel 37:22–25; Hosea 3:4–5; Zechariah 14:9. For the concept of a literal restoration of the political kingdom of David, see 2 Samuel 7:18–27 and 2 Chronicles 6:14–16.
4   George Eldon Ladd, *The Gospel of the Kingdom: Scriptural Studies in the Kingdom of God* (Grand Rapids, MI: Eerdmans, 1990),113.
5   Gerard Mannion and Lewis S. Mudge, eds., *The Routledge Companion to the Christian Church* (Routledge Religion Companions) (New York: Routledge, 2008), 203–204.
6   In Matthew 26:29, Jesus claims that he ". . . will not drink of the fruit of the vine from now on until that day when I drink it new with you in my Father's kingdom." This passage, located in the middle of the Last Supper discourse, is interpreted by millenarian scholars as pointing to a new, earthly dispensation of Christ's kingdom that supersedes even the Church, and conditions the Church's sacerdotal power within history.
7   Walvoord, *The Millennial Kingdom*, 108.
8   Paul Boyer, "The Growth of Fundamentalist Apocalypticism in the United States," in McGinn, *The Continuum History of Apocalypticism*, 516–544, at 518. Cf. Vitor Westhelle, "Liberation Theology: A Latitudinal Approach," in Walls, *The Oxford Handbook of Eschatology*, 311–372, 319.
9   Westhelle, "Liberation Theology: A Latitudinal Approach," 311.
10 Boyer, "The Growth of Fundamentalist Apocalypticism in the United States," 518.
11 Westhelle, "Liberation Theology: A Latitudinal Approach," 311.
12 "Since there was no single Judaism, there was no single Messianic idea or Messianic doctrine." William Jacob Neusner, William Scott Green, and Ernest S. Frerichs, eds., *Judaisms and Their Messiahs at the Turn of the Christian Era* (Cambridge: Cambridge University Press, 1988), front panel. Cf. Scott Green, "Messiah in Judaism: Rethinking the Question," in ibid., 1–14, esp. 3–4.
13 Timothy P. Weber, "Millennialism," in Walls, *The Oxford Handbook of Eschatology*, 368–369, emphasis mine.
14 Soulen, *The God of Israel and Christian Theology*, 173.
15 Ibid.,130–132.
16 Pamela Vermes, *Buber* (London: Grove Press, 1988), vii. See also Amy-Jill Levine, *The Misunderstood Jew: The Church and the Scandal of the Jewish Jesus*, rep. ed. (New York: HarperOne, 2007), 115, 212.
17 Riddlebarger, *A Case for Amillennialism: Understanding the End Times*, 87. Cf. Hoekema, "Amillennialism," in *The Meaning of the Millennium*, 172.
18 John Phillips, *Exploring Galatians: An Expository Commentary* (Grand Rapids, MI: Kregel Academic & Professional, 2004), 223, n. 2.
19 Novak, "Jewish Eschatology," in Walls, *The Oxford Handbook of Eschatology*,124.
20 Simcha Paull Raphael, *Jewish Views of the Afterlife*, 2nd ed. (Lanham, MD: Rowman & Littlefield, 2009), 129.
21 Steven Nadler, *Spinoza's Heresy: Immortality and the Jewish Mind* (New York: Oxford University Press, 2001), 58.
22 See comment on Joseph Klausner in Louis Jacobs, *The Book of Jewish Belief* (New York: Behrman House, 1984), 228.
23 Ibid.
24 Nadler, *Spinoza's Heresy: Immortality and the Jewish Mind*, 58–59.

Christian millenarian theology of Judaism 229

25 Central Conference of American Rabbis, "A Statement of Principles for Reform Judaism" (paper adopted at the 1999 Pittsburgh Convention Central Conference of American Rabbis May 1999-Sivan 5759, Pittsburgh, PA, October 27, 2004), https://ccarnet.org/rabbis-speak/platforms/statement-principles-reform-judaism/ (accessed April 10, 2013).
26 Jon Bloomberg, *The Jewish World in the Modern Age* (Jersey City, NJ: Ktav Pub, 2004), 94.
27 Novak, "Jewish Eschatology," in Walls, *The Oxford Handbook of Eschatology*,124.
28 Extensive studies on the apocalyptic words of Jesus "... suggest that *although referring to the future ... [the eschatological promises do] ... not have in view the eternal state.*" Diprose, *Israel and the Church*, 145, emphasis mine. See also Dale Allison, "Jesus & the Victory of Apocalyptic," in Carey C. Newman, ed., *Jesus & the Restoration of Israel: A Critical Assessment of* N.T. *Wright's Jesus and the Victory of God* (Downers Grove, IL: IVP Academic, 1999), 129. Cf. Michael E. Fuller, *The Restoration of Israel: Israel's Re-Gathering and the Fate of the Nations in Early Jewish Literature and Luke-Acts* (New York: De Gruyter, 2006), 264, n. 265.
29 Madigan and Levenson, *Resurrection: The Power of God for Christians and Jews*, 29–30.
30 Oden, *Classical Christianity: A Systematic Theology*, 806–807.
31 David Novak, "Jewish Eschatology," in Walls, *The Oxford Handbook of Eschatology*, 115.
32 Ibid., 1–21, esp. 12.
33 B. Hullin, 142a. Cf. Joshua L. Moss, *Midrash and Legend: Historical Anecdotes in the Tannaitic Midrashim*, 2nd ed. (Piscataway, NJ: Gorgias Press, 2004), 329.
34 Sean M. O'Shea and Meryl A. Walker, *The Millennium Myth: The Ever-Ending Story* (Atlanta, GA: Humanics Trade Group, 1998), 61.
35 The Roman Catholic, amillennial view was and is so pervasive that the early Reformers, both Lutheran and Calvinist, viewed Christian millennial categories as holdovers of a "Jewish opinion" in eschatology, or a "Jewish hope" for a better world to come, within time and history. See the *Augsburg Confession*, §17, and the *Second Helvetic Confession*, §11.
36 Marcus Jastrow, *Dictionary of the Targumim, Talmud Bavli, Talmud Yerushalmi and Midrashic Literature* (New York: Judaica Pr, 2004), 1454.
37 Ibid., 116, emphasis mine. Cf. *B. Shabbat* 30b re Eccl. 1:9; *B. Sanhedrin* 90b-91a.
38 See *Bemidbar Raba* 2.25; *Peskita de Rav Kahana* 26.9; *Vayikra Raba* 20:10; *Midrash Tanhuma Aherei* 6.
39 The "time less than the time" of the world to come is, in a sense, part of the world to come, but also in a sense, antecedent to it, in time and history.
40 Moltmann, *The Way of Jesus Christ*, 12.
41 *Catechism of the Catholic Church*, §1031.
42 M. Sanhedrin 10.1 re Isaiah 60:21. See Rabbi Joshua's commentary on Gentiles having a place in the world to come. Cf. David Novak, *The Image of the Non-Jew in Judaism: The Idea of Noahide Law*, 2nd ed., ed. Matthew Lagrone (Oxford: Littman Library of Jewish Civilization, 2011). A contrast to Rabbi Joshua's more congenial view, which is held widely among Jews today, is the stricter view of Rabbi Eliezer, which claims that if a Gentile does not convert to Judaism, he or she is destined for *she'ol*, or other-worldly punishment. Novak claims this is a kind of 'Jewish' *extra ecclesiam nulla salus*.
43 *T. Shabbat* 13.5; *P. Berakhot* 1.8/3c.
44 McGrath tells us that Jewish–Christians abided by every aspect of Second Temple Judaism, with the important addition of belief in Jesus as the messiah. Alister McGrath, *Christianity: An Introduction* (Hoboken, NJ: Blackwell Publishing, 2006), 174.

45 David Martin, *Vatican II: A Historic Turning Point: The Dawning of a New Epoch* (Bloomington, IN: AuthorHouse, 2011), 104. Such a concept makes no sense logically if applied to Judaism, as Judaism is divinely inspired religion. Much of the leniency of Vatican II as it regards salvation outside of the Church was influenced by Karl Rahner's concept of anonymous Christianity. See Soulen's view that Rahner maintains a structural supersessionism in his theology, in Soulen, *The God of Israel and Christian Theology*, 94–103.
46 See "Jewish Millenarian-Messianic Movements: Comparisons of Aschkenazim, Sephardim, and Italian Jews," in Stephen Sharot, *Comparative Perspectives on Judaisms and Jewish Identities* (Detroit: Wayne State University Press, 2011), 91–104.
47 David Patterson, *Emil L. Fackenheim: A Jewish Philosopher's Response to the Holocaust* (Syracuse, NY: Syracuse University Press (Sd), 2008), 138.
48 Chaim Stern, *Gates of Repentance: The New Union Prayerbook for the Days of Awe* (translation *of Shaarei Teshuva*), rev. ed. (New York: Central Conference of American Rabbis, 1996), 30, 104, 260, 309.
49 Sharot, *Comparative Perspectives on Judaisms and Jewish Identities*, 115.
50 Ibid., 252. The *haredim* do not attached messianic significance to the modern State of Israel, as do the Zionists, but most branches of Judaism adopt an historical intermediary period of redemption that is to signify a messianic reality—either nationalistically or spiritually, but predominantly historically.
51 *Daily Prayer Book*, ed. and trans. P. Birnbaum (New York: Hebrew Publishing, 1949), 83, 265.
52 M. Senhedrin 10.1.
53 Novak, "Jewish Eschatology," in Walls, *The Oxford Handbook of Eschatology*, 123.
54 Eugene B. Borowitz and Naomi Patz, *Explaining Reform Judaism* (New York: Behrman House, 1985), 89.
55 Jon D. Levenson, "The Modern Jewish Preference for Immortality," in Levenson, *Resurrection and the Restoration of Israel*, 1–22.
56 Novak, "Jewish Eschatology," in Walls, *The Oxford Handbook of Eschatology*, 123.
57 Wright, *The Resurrection of the Son of God*, 204. N.T. Wright traces two Second Temple Jewish interpretations of "resurrection," one literal and one metaphorical.
58 Levenson, *Resurrection and the Restoration of Israel: The Ultimate Victory of the God of Life*, 156.
59 Madigan and Levenson, *Resurrection: The Power of God for Christians and Jews*, 257.
60 Levenson affirms that while not all Jews believe in resurrection, "many Jews and Christians have shared and do today affirm belief in the resurrection of the dead." Ibid., 3.
61 Moltmann claims "... it is only the millenarian hope in Christian eschatology which unfolds an earthly and historical future for the Church and Israel." Moltmann, *The Coming of God*, 197.
62 Hermann Cohen, *Religion of Reason out of the Sources of Judaism* (Atlanta, GA: Oxford University Press, 1995), 329.
63 Novak, "Jewish Eschatology," in Walls, *The Oxford Handbook of Eschatology*, 125.
64 See for example, *B. Niddah* 61b, regarding Psalm. 88:6. Jewish scholar Julius H. Greenstone's *The Messiah Idea in Jewish History*, though rather dated, remains an authoritative source on the subject, and affirms the debate over the powers attributable to the messiah in biblical through modern Judaism. See Julius H. Greenstone, *The Messiah Idea in Jewish History* (Berkeley, CA: University of California Libraries, 1906). Many adherents of Lubavitch Hasidism, for example, claim that the messiah "... differs from them [others who live their lives as 'arks for the Torah'] only by having been born into his role." Harris Lenowitz, *The Jewish Messiahs: From the*

Galilee to Crown Heights (New York: Oxford University Press, 2001), 217. Lubavitch Hasidism, one of the largest Hasidic movements, has experienced disunity since the death of its leader, Lubavitcher Rebbe (R' Menachem Mendal Schneerson), in 1994. The source of division is precisely among messianists and anti-messianists, that is, those who believe Schneerson was and is the Mosiach. Representative of some Jewish intellectuals, Martin Buber rejected the possibility of a divine messiah, though he upheld a version of the deity of Jesus on the basis of a universally accessible deification. Martin Buber, *Two Types of Faith: A Study of the Interpretation of Judaism and Christianity* (New York: Harper & Row, 1961), 112, 115–116.

65 Rabbi Menachem Mendel Schneerson was a very brilliant scholar, eloquent speaker, and perhaps the most globally influential rabbi of the past century. He was attributed with bringing deep Torah interpretation to a very wide international audience, sending emissaries to various countries, and amassing a very large following of faithful Jews.

66 Gil Student, *Can the Rebbe Be Moshiach?: Proofs from Gemara, Midrash, and Rambam* (Boca Raton, FL: Universal Publishers, 2002), 23–26.

67 Alan F. Segal, *Two Powers in Heaven: Early Rabbinic Reports about Christianity and Gnosticism* (Boston, MA: Brill Academic, 2002), 3–4.

68 Amy-Jill Levine has made the claim that ". . . the idea of 'Jesus as messiah' is less controversial within the Jewish community than the idea of 'Jesus as G-d.'" Amy-Jill Levine, "Five Questions for Amy-Jill Levine," *Havurah* 15, no. 2 (Fall 2012): 1–5, http://www.jewsforjesus.org/files/pdf/havurah/havurah-15–02.pdf (accessed April 8, 2013).

69 Shaye J.D. Cohen, *From the Maccabees to the Mishnah*, 2nd ed. (Louisville, KY: Westminster John Knox Press, 2006), 167–168.

70 Novak, "Jewish Eschatology," in Walls, *The Oxford Handbook of Eschatology*, 125.

71 Ibid., 124.

72 Daniel Boyarin, *Border Lines: The Partition of Judaeo-Christianity* (Philadelphia, PA: University of Pennsylvania Press, 2004), 90, 105.

73 Soulen, *The God of Israel and Christian Theology*, 133–134, emphasis mine in part.

74 Jürgen Moltmann, *Sun of Righteousness, Arise!: God's Future for Humanity and the Earth*, 1st Fortress Press ed. (Minneapolis, MN: Fortress Press, 2010), 72.

75 Riddlebarger, *A Case for Amillennialism: Understanding the End Times*, 180.

76 "In more recent decades, J. Moltmann ns W. Pannenberg promoted a 'theology of hope,' which revived notions of realistic eschatology by considering the historical Parousia and the establishment of God's kingdom on earth without resorting to apocalyptic excesses." Weber, "Millennialism," in Walls, *The Oxford Handbook of Eschatology*, 379. Cf. Hans Schwarz, *Eschatology* (Grand Rapids, MI: W.B. Eerdmans, 2000), 146.

77 Moltmann, *The Church in the Power of the Spirit*, 351.

78 Moltmann, *The Coming of God*, 162.

79 Ibid.

80 See for example, Justin Martyr, Melito of Sardis, Irenaeus, and Tertullian as quoted in David W. Bercot, ed., *A Dictionary of Early Christian Beliefs: A Reference Guide to More Than 700 Topics Discussed by the Early Church Fathers* (Peabody, MA: Hendrickson, 1998), 375–376. Vlach argues that while supersessionism was a part of early Christian chiliast thought, it represented a temporary and not permanent rejection of Israel, and that Israel would be eschatologically restored as Israel, apart from the Church. See Vlach, "Rejection then Hope: The Church's Doctrine of Israel in the Patristic Era," 56.

81 Michael Gilbertson, *God and History in the Book of Revelation: New Testament Studies in Dialogue with Pannenberg and Moltmann* (New York: Cambridge University Press, 2005), 197–199.

82 According to Moltmann's view of Revelation, it is the Beast who makes absolute claims to power. While the martyrs appear to be defeated in this world, their historical vindication is the peaceable messianic kingdom. Moltmann, *The Coming of God*, 139, 152–153, 194–195. Cf. Bauckham, *God will be All in All*, 146.
83 While the *Coming of God* contains one of Moltmann's most thorough treatments of millenarianism, he has mentioned the concept in earlier works, including: P. Lapide and J. Moltmann, *Israel und Kirke: ein gemeinsamer Weg? Ein Gespräch* (Munchen: Kaiser, 1980), 26–32, J. Moltmann, *The Trinity and the Kingdom of God: The Doctrine of God* (London: SCM Press, 1981), 235, n. 44, and J. Moltmann, *History and the Triune God: Contributions to Trinitarian Theology* (London, SCM Press, 1991), 96, 108–109.
84 Moltmann is one of a handful of contemporary theologians who have taken seriously the millenarian interpretation of Scripture, pulling it in from the margins of theology to which it has been assigned by mainstream Christianity.
85 Schwarz, *Eschatology*, 147.
86 Likewise described as "surplus" in this project.
87 God's promises to both Israel and the Church involve the phrase that God will "never leave nor forsake" the covenant people (Deuteronomy 31:6; Hebrews 13:5). God's promises also include the divine imperative to bring to completion the redemptive and consummative economies of divine interaction within human history.
88 Moltmann dismisses progressive millenarianism (oftentimes associated with Protestant postmillennialism or secular millenarianism influenced by the Enlightenment) as "epochal millenarianism." Moltmann especially points out that Enlightenment teleology is essentially the application of humanistic principles to the Christian millennium. Moltmann, *The Coming of God*, 134–135, 184–192. The only sense in which Motmann's millennium comes about progressively is by virtue of the fact that disciples share in the resurrection of Christ. Moltmann claims that Christian hope ". . . sees in the resurrection of Christ not the eternity of heaven, but the future of the very earth on which his cross stands." Moltmann, *Theology of Hope*, 21.
89 Molmann's millenarianism is deeply political and ethical, calling for a sense of action and commitment against the oppressive powers of the world, especially those aligned against the poor and marginalized, and it is focused on theologies sympathetic to liberationist, feminist, and ecological concerns. Some claim that Moltmann's "Theology of Hope" was a significant and unique precursor to liberation theology, and his millenarian eschatology that conceives of a future and transformative earthly kingdom has transformed later concepts of eco-theology. Moltmann's millenarian eschatology is distinct from "dispensationalist millenarianism," which Moltmann himself calls an "apocalyptic flight from the world." Moltmann, *The Coming of God*, 159. Moltmann states that ". . . because original Jewish and Christian millenarianism was a martyr eschatology, it is the precise opposite of every eschatological escapism, and of every know-all assumption based on a salvation-history concept." Moltmann, *The Coming of God*, 201.
90 Ibid., 158–159.
91 Ibid., 159.
92 Moltmann's view of the coming, future kingdom of God is unique in that he maintains that the Church and Israel are moving toward the same eschatological history, but Israel is one of the historical partners that ". . . are not the Church and will never become the Church." Israel holds a unique place because it is ". . . Christianity's original, enduring, and final partner in history." Such partnership stresses the unique and particular means by which both Israel and the Church serve the kingdom without converting one to the other. Moltmann, *The Coming of God*, 134–135.
93 Ibid., 198.
94 Ibid., 201.

95 Moltmann, *The Coming of God*, 146.
96 Stanley J. Grenz, *The Millennial Maze: Sorting out Evangelical Options* (Downers Grove, IL: IVP Academic, 2007), 150–151.
97 Moltmann, *The Coming of God*, 147.
98 "The Israelo-centric kingdom of Christ forms the organic transitional link between the present state of the world and the completion of the world that will one day come about." Moltmann, *The Coming of God*, 199.
99 Rosenzweig, *The Star of Redemption*, 54.
100 Moltmann, *The Coming of God*, 44.
101 Ibid., 45.
102 Ibid.
103 *Kairos*, the qualitative counterpart to the Greek term for quantitative, linear time, *kronos*, ". . . signifies a time between, a moment of indeterminate time in which something special happens." For Moltmann, this is the eschaton. Eric Charles White, *Kaironomia: On the Will-to-invent* (Ithaca, NY: Cornell University Press 1987).
104 Moltmann, *The Coming of God*, 46.
105 Ibid., 197.
106 "The rediscovery of the relevance of the Old Testament, the new discovery of Christianity's own provisional nature in the framework of the still unfulfilled hope of the messianic kingdom, and the recognition of Israel in a partner-like relationship are the elementary presuppositions for a Christian abolition of ecclesiastical triumphalism." Moltmann, *The Church is the Power of the Spirit*, 137.
107 Ibid.
108 Rosenzweig, *The Star of Redemption*, 197.
109 Moltmann, *The Church is the Power of the Spirit*, 136.
110 Moltmann, *Theology of Hope*, 329.
111 Bader-Saye, *Church and Israel after Christendom*, 78.
112 Schwarz, *Eschatology*, 148.
113 See Diprose, *Israel and the Church*, 184–185. Part of Diprose's argument is that the pluralistic approach to dialogue among various traditions ultimately fails, insofar as its claim to represent all religions, it in reality totalizes religions into a "least common denominator" and legitimately represents no religion.
114 See Bauckham, *God will be All in All*, 138. Cf. Rollan McCleary, *A Special Illumination: Authority, Inspiration and Heresy in Gay Spirituality* (Oakville, CT: Equinox Publishing, 2004), 103.
115 "Right down to the present day, there is no Christian creed which expresses an eschatological hope for Israel, and with that the recognition of Israel's divine calling, apart from the Church." Moltmann, "The Hope of Israel and the Anabaptist Alternative," in Bauckham, *God will be All in All*, 150.
116 Moltmann, *The Church in the Power of the Spirit*, 138.
117 "Up to now I have seen no positive Israel theology on the Christian side that fails to integrate Christ's chiliastic kingdom of peace into the eschatology." Moltmann, "The Hope of Israel and the Anabaptist Alternative," in Bauckham, *God will be All in All*, 151.
118 Ibid.,138–139.
119 Ibid., 138.
120 Vlach, *Has the Church Replaced Israel?*, 123.
121 Ibid., 79–83.
122 "This designation of the millennium as a Jewish dream is generally explained historically: it is supposed to have been due to movements within the Judaism of the time. But I understand it theologically. Christ's kingdom of peace is evidently associated with hope for Israel's future in the fulfillment of God's promises to Israel in the kingdom of the Son of man (Daniel 7)." Moltmann, "The Hope of Israel and the Anabaptist Alternative," in Bauckham, *God will be All in All*, 150.

123 Moltmann, *The Coming of God*, 194.
124 Ibid., 197.
125 See for example the early Christian response to Zionism that sought to safeguard future Jewish belief in Jesus, but somehow deny that the Church supersedes Israel. Carlo Antonio Zanini, *La Vedetta Cristiana*, II/14, 15 (July 1871): 109. See also Daniel F. Moore, *Jesus, an Emerging Jewish Mosaic: Jewish Perspectives, Post-Holocaust (Jewish & Christian Text)* (London: T&T Clark, 2012), 237.
126 Paul van Buren envisions a theology whereby the Mosaic Covenant on Sinai is the central and most authoritative covenant for both Jews and Christians. R. Diprose, conversely, demands that Christians "... obey the missionary mandate which he [Jesus] entrusted to his followers (Matthew 28:18–20)." It is worth noting that Matthew 28 says nothing of a gentile mission to Jews, but only a mission to "the nations." The term *ethonos* has always been understood as intentionally differentiating between Jew and non-Jew.
127 Terry W. Bookman, "The Holy Conversation: Towards a Jewish Theology of Dialogue," *JES* 32 (1995): 212–213.
128 Soulen, *The God of Israel and Christian Theology*, 112.
129 "I will make a covenant of peace with them; it shall be an everlasting covenant with them; and I will bless and multiply them, and will set my sanctuary among them forevermore" (Ezekiel 37:25–28).
130 Micah 4:1–4.
131 Genesis 22:18, *Pesichta Rabbati* 45b. See the rabbinical view that the election of Israel is intended by God as a blessing to all the nations, in *Sifre Deut* §40.
132 Ezekiel 37:1–14.
133 Soulen, *The God of Israel and Christian Theology*, 156–157.
134 Reuther, *Faith and Fratricide*, 250.
135 We will see later that a further exploration of the text equates one of these groups with the "144,000," who are from the tribes of *Israel*.
136 *Dabru Emet: A Jewish Statement on Christians and Christianity*, found at http://www.jcrelations.net/Dabru+Emet+-+A+Jewish+Statement+on+Christians+and+Christianity.2395.0.html?L=3.
137 Ibid.
138 Moltmann, *The Coming of God*, 156.
139 *Dabru Emet: A Jewish Statement on Christians and Christianity*, found at http://www.jcrelations.net/Dabru+Emet+-+A+Jewish+Statement+on+Christians+and+Christianity.2395.0.html?L=3.
140 Douglas H. Knight. *The Eschatological Economy: Time and the Hospitality of God* (Grand Rapids, MI: Eerdmans, 2006), 62–63.
141 "Incarnation of God's Indwelling in Israel," in Wyschogrod, *Abraham's Promise: Jewish and Jewish–Christian Relations*, 178.
142 Jacob Neusner, *The Incarnation of God: The Character of Divinity in Formative Judaism* (Atlanta, GA: University of South Florida, 1992), 6.
143 *Dabru Emet: A Jewish Statement on Christians and Christianity*, 3, emphasis mine.

10 Millenarianism, supersessionism, and the messianic kingdom

The purpose of this final chapter is to describe in more detail the ways that millenarianism, specifically Moltmann's non-violent, modified form, rejects and moves beyond the idea that the Church replaces Israel in salvation history. Two concepts frame Moltmann's thesis for accepting chiliasm and rejecting the amillennial paradigm. First, by rejecting the time-eternity dialectic, millenarianism returns time to its rightful place as a conditioning agent for the Church, making it impossible for the Church to claim that it exercises the sole monopoly regarding participation in the eternal kingdom of God.[1] Certainly, under the millenarian paradigm, the Church no longer is able to claim being utterly equivalent to the kingdom of God. The Church is essential, but provisional to the kingdom itself. By adopting the millenarian worldview, Christian theology makes room for a Judaism that in its contemporary expression, and despite its mutually exclusive claims to Christianity, walks side by side with the Church as a positive participant, leading to the future of salvation in light of the return of Christ.[2] Second, part of the very fabric of the millenarian narrative is the language and conceptual framework of Israel's hopes, but unlike the amillennial view, millenarianism refrains from applying those hopes solely to the Catholic Church or some far-off dimension in a heavenly eternity. Instead, the structure of the millenarian interpretation of the story of the messianic kingdom is one that allows Jewish people to remain Jewish, and maintains a biblical imagery that is intrinsically positive regarding God's future interactions with national Israel and individual Jewish people. Amillennialism simply reinterprets the positive, future elements of the messianic kingdom and applies them to the Church,[3] while at the same time it conveniently refrains from adopting the challenges and punitive warnings that accompany the responsibilities associated with being God's "chosen people."

We recall that we described three varieties of supersessionism that have permeated Christian theology: economic supersessionism, for which adherents claim that "... carnal Israel's history is providentially ordered from the outset to be taken up into the spiritual Church";[4] punitive supersessionism, for which adherents claim "... that God has rejected carnal Israel on account of its failure to join the Church"[5] while replacing blessing with punishment; and a final form labeled "structural supersessionism." Structural supersessionism is most recognizably aligned with the viewpoint of the ancient heretic Marcion, as Marcionite adherents interpreted the entire scriptural narrative regarding salvation history in a manner that rendered the Hebrew Scriptures as indecisive in relation to the way Christians are to understand God's redemptive and consummative work.[6] In the sections that follow, we will treat the three forms of supersessionism in reference to how amillennialism upholds their central claims and how millenarianism overcomes them.

Millenarianism, amillennialism, and economic supersessionism

Economic supersessionists insist that in the providential ordering of salvation history, God has seen fit to make Israel, including the Jewish people of the contemporary moment, obsolete in light of the new Christian covenant, specifically and inextricably expressed as the Church. In this scheme, the economic relationship[7] between God and Israel is transferred to the Church, as exemplified by the words of the ancient supersessionist Melito of Sardis, ". . . the people was made void when the Church arose."[8] Economic supersessionism is a position that views Israel and the synagogue as provisional, but the Church as eternal, in spite of the fact that Jews and Christians both worship the same covenanting God (YHWH), and Christianity itself was birthed out of Judaism. Economic supersessionists believe that ". . . Israel's essential role in the economy of redemption is to prepare for salvation in its spiritual and universal form."[9] Amillennialists, typically supportive of economic supersessionism, take this "spiritual and universal form," for which Israel is a preparatory entity, as applying to the Church of today—the realized kingdom of God in history. Many amillennialist authors go so far to say that ". . . believing Israel in the Old Testament was the Church in its infancy,"[10] drawing the replacement of Israel back into a deeply rooted yet flawed tradition. Any distinction between the Church and Israel today cannot be tolerated in the amillennial paradigm because according to adherents of that view, the kingdom of God, although it has not yet come in its absolute, eternal form, comes through the *new, ecclesial* "Israel" alone.

Millenarian theologians like Moltmann (to be contrasted with the premillennial dispensationalism of more fundamentalist strands of Protestantism), would agree that Israel exists to "prepare for salvation in its spiritual and universal form," but the spiritual and universal form of salvation is not limited to a purely redemptive construct, and is not to be equated with the Church.[11] Additionally, the binary nature of both amillennialism and supersessionism is rejected in the millenarian framework: the term "spiritual" is not viewed as the opposite of "material," and the term "universal" in not viewed as the opposite of "particular." The millennial age will consist of a material spirituality that universally encompasses the world without destroying divinely established particularities—including the distinction between Israel and the nations.[12] Moltmann's critique of the "condemnation" of premillennial principles by a predominantly amillennial Church has to do with the economic supersessionist concept that Israel's role leads directly into the Church as its all-encompassing horizon and *telos*. Thus, what amillennialism has ". . .

theologically condemned is the idea that the Christian hope includes a future for the Jews as Jews."[13]

The fullness of salvation, according to millenarian principles, comes with the consummation of the world and not with its preliminary expression[14] of redemption for the nations in Christ, though these two aspects of salvation history work in tandem because the cross of Christ and his resurrection are the real and eternal means whereby the eschaton "breaks in" to human history and illuminates it. Contemporary millenarian eschatology, in spite of the supersessionism held by some of early millennial Patristic advocates, supports the claim that the participation of modern Judaism plays a role in the consummation of the world, because without Judaism, there is no future messianic kingdom. In this Christian scheme, the present age is viewed as an extension and transformation of the inaugural but real instantiation of the kingdom ushered in by Jesus's death and resurrection, and sacramentally available in the Church.

This contemporary millenarian system is well represented by the words of Robert Jenson, who claims that the divine, consummative economy is in particular a work of the Holy Spirit. Douglas Knight solidifies this point in the following claim:

> It is not individuals that correspond to types, but community, this specific community ... [Israel] ... that is elect. We should then identify God by focusing, not on Jesus Christ *as individual*, but on Jesus *and the community the Holy Spirit gives to him*. To identify God by the Holy Spirit is to refuse to abstract from God's concrete self-determination to be for Israel ... Consummation, not redemption, is the proper model for understanding Israel's relationship with God. Attempts to ask about Israel's salvation submit Israel to an inappropriate logic, one in which an unredeemed community is replaced by a redeemed community. This is the logic of supersessionism.[15]

Knight's conception that consummation and not "redemption"—as understood solely in the Christian terms of liberation from sin and evil—is a correct theological category in reference to the Jewish people, based on the conceptions of the Hebrew Bible. But for many of the Jewish people, consummation *is* redemption, insofar as consummation is the anticipated visible and political aspect of liberation and redemption,[16] associated with the coming of the messiah and the establishment of Zion as the central worshipping community for the both Israel and the nations. Further, it is not as if redemption from sin is *not* important to Jews—the Day of Atonement functions as the primary means for this purification. The overarching point that we take from Knight's comment is that the consummation of the world means future, visible redemption for Israel, and a renewed Christian understanding of the role of the Holy Spirit, providing the theological function of keeping God's consummative and Christian, redemptive economies somewhat distinct.

Joachim of Fiore, within his unique millenarian paradigm, was correct in arguing that the Holy Spirit would play a significant role in bringing about the world to come, for both Jew and Christian.[17] The millenarian interpretation of the Valley of the Dry Bones prophecy is indicative of this point:

> This is what the Sovereign Lord says: My people, I am going to open your graves and bring you up from them; I will bring you back to the land of Israel. Then you, my people, will know that I am the Lord, when I open your graves and bring you up from them. I will put my Spirit in you and you will live, and I will settle you in your own land.
>
> (Ezekiel 37:12–14)

The resurrection of the Jewish people in Ezekiel 37 is directly associated with the miraculous work of the Holy Spirit, as in the resurrection of Jesus, and is proximate in time to the "peaceable kingdom."[18] Yet the kingdom is not driven solely by a salvific economy that stresses the spiritual, but also is bodily in emphasis. All Christian millennialists insist that Jesus will return in the flesh to inaugurate the visible kingdom of God, a concept held precisely to refute the amillennial idea that the Church of history *is* that visible instantiation in the present moment, in replacement of Israel. Jesus comes as the first fruit of all Israel—an Israel that will be resurrected as a nation as well as individuals.[19] As the "electing God,"[20] it is the Holy Spirit who is working in the Church and the synagogue, moving both toward the consummative reality of the world to come—a point emphasized by Moltmann in the millenarian schema he promotes in the chapter entitled "The Church of the Kingdom of God," of *The Church in the Power of the Spirit*.[21] According to this schema, the Holy Spirit does not work alone, but in alignment with the will of the Father and the Son, and the Church works not for its own existence, but in service to the millennial kingdom that the Holy Spirit is establishing on earth. Moltmann states that:

> Israel has a "call to salvation", independent of the Church, which remains to the end . . . the messianic promises of the Old Testament are only in principle fulfilled through the appearance and history of Christ; and only provisionally and partially through the eschatological gift of the Spirit . . . this salvation-historical thesis is closely connected with millenarianism, the hope that Christ will rule for a thousand years in history before the end.[22]

It is this millenarian paradigm that has left space for such a post-supersessionist conception of the eschaton and the Church, through its refusal to collapse the consummative economy of God into the redemptive economy verified through Jesus. Because Jesus is to rule on earth for a thousand years, within history *before the end*, the Church cannot claim to *be the end*. Therefore "the Church is not in a position to put itself in the forefront of the imperfect, natural orders as a perfect society . . . it cannot be the Church's commission to form the world after its own image."[23]

The millenarian "economic approach," borrowed by Moltmann, is traceable back to Irenaeus and his concept of the election of the literal seed of Abraham and the millennial kingdom. Though in some places Irenaeus equates the "seed of Abraham" with the Church, this is not normatively the case. Concerning the consummation of the world, Irenaeus claims the following regarding Christian *heretics*:

they are both ignorant of God's dispensations, and of the mystery of the resurrection of the just, and of the earthly kingdom . . . and it is necessary to tell them respecting those things, that it behooves the righteous first to receive the promise of the inheritance which God promised to the fathers, and to reign in it, when they rise again to behold God in this creation which is renovated, and that the judgment should take place afterwards . . .[24]

In this section, Irenaeus simply reiterates the orthodox, chiliastic view of the eschaton, arguing that Jesus will return bodily in order to "renew the inheritance of the earth," and initiate the messianic banquet that was proleptically expressed during the Last Supper.[25] But for whom will Christ renew this inheritance and to whom was the inheritance of the earth promised in the first place? Certainly, Irenaeus believes that the inheritance will be renewed for "the meek," who will inherit the earth, and for the disciples of Christ—particularly those who were martyred for the faith. The quote above suggests that the disciples of Christ will share in the inheritance that belonged to "the fathers." But Irenaeus does not appear to limit this inheritance to the Church alone:

Thus, then, the promise of God, which He gave to Abraham, remains steadfast. For thus He said: "Lift up your eyes, and look from this place where now you are, towards the north and south, and east and west. For all the earth which you see I will give to you and to your seed, even forever." Genesis 13:13–14 . . . Now God made promise of the earth to Abraham and his seed; yet neither Abraham nor his seed do now receive any inheritance in it; but they shall receive it at the resurrection of the just.[26]

The question that arises with Irenaeus' millenarian language is whether or not the Jews after the time of Jesus are to be considered inheritors of the promise of the messianic kingdom, its vindication, and the consummative element of resurrection.[27] If we answer this in the affirmative, a post-supersessionist reading would apply the principles of the Christian millennium to the Jewish people, as Jews, in light of the revelation of Christ to them. B.D. Marshall, in his study on Irenaeus, reiterates this point:

When the tradition affirmed that Israel worshipped the true God before the Emmaus road and Pentecost, it allowed for the genuine worship of this God by Abraham's children even when they were not in a position to identify him as Trinity. If we can make sense of this affirmation, then it should be straightforward on a post-supersessionist outlook, to extend it to Abraham's children after Christ as well as to those before.[28]

Assuming Marshall's assessment of Irenaeus' view and the early tradition is correct, the millenarian Christian view is open to seeing the inheritance of the land promised by Christ (Matthew 5:5) as applicable to modern-day Jews.

We have established that *"God's historical fidelity toward Israel is the 'narrow gate' that opens the new creation . . ."*[29] Amillennialists seek to bypass this narrow gate in one of two ways. The amillennialist paradigm either draws the eschatological, consummative economy of salvation into the current "era of redemption," which belongs to the Church as the custodian of sacramental participation in Jesus Christ's redemptive work, or views "God's historical fidelity toward Israel" as equal to God's historical fidelity to the predominantly Gentile Church, since the Church is viewed as the new and superior Israel. In the millenarian view, the narrow gate of God's historical fidelity to Israel is safeguarded because the future-historical millennium is Judeo-centric in scope. In the amillennial view, ". . . everything that characterized the economy of salvation in its Israelite form becomes obsolete and is replaced by its ecclesial equivalent."[30] The Jewish features safeguarded by millenarian eschatology include aspects of the Law of Moses, circumcision, the legitimacy of Torah obedience in relation to the Sinai covenant, and the promises made by God to Abraham for land, progeny, and *blessing to the nations* vis-à-vis modern Judaism.[31] Certain forms of millenarian theology hold that the practice of the Law and liturgy in Judaism is valid,[32] not as a replacement of the work of Jesus, but as a witness to what will one day be a Jewish–Christian messianic era (the future Thousand Years' reign). Millenarian theologians are quick to point out that the Law is never expressed as entirely superseded in the New Testament.[33] Essential to the Jewish–Christian messianic era is both the people of Israel themselves and their sacred traditions as commended to them by God. This is the case, regardless of Israel's initial, but temporary rejection of the Gospel. This point becomes clear in Christian millenarian writings:

> Nothing, not even their opposition to the gospel, could cancel the special love of God for his people. It is this election of Israel which makes her eschatological salvation certain. Likewise, her status as an elect people explains why, in present time . . . *Israel contributes to the enrichment and the reconciliation with God of the other nations of the world.*[34]

Unlike in the Augustinian, amillennial tradition, whereby Israel's role as a "witness people" points to the punitive removal of God's election and transference of that election to the Church, millenarian writers view Israel's liturgical faithfulness, observance of Torah, and even their temporary rejection of the Gospel, as a *confirmation* of their election and future participation in the reign of God on earth. As Paul states explicitly in the Epistle to the Romans, Israel's rejection of Jesus acts as an entry point to the covenant for Gentiles. But this rejection of Jesus on Israel's end is not permanent, and any rejection they face on the divine end is likewise impermanent. What is permanent is God's election of the people of Israel as a nation. Amillennialists, as economic supersessionists, must deny any future dimension of redemptive history, even in consummative history, ". . . because the ultimate obsolescence of carnal Israel is an *essential* of God's one overarching economy of redemption for the world . . ."[35] The millenarian model makes Israel's election and spiritual contribution constitutive of the Church, and thus finds ways in which to describe the future reign of God on earth in Jewish eschatological terms, consistent with a Jewish reading of John's Apocalypse.[36] Millenarianism protects Jewish expressions of faith in Christian theology by viewing the biblical tradition of God's election of the Jewish people as an abiding and irrevocable promise that will fully take place during the future messianic era. This promise holds that the Jewish people continue to be a "kingdom of priests" (Exodus 19:6), that they are unique recipients of God's revelation (Deuteronomy 4:5–8; 6:6–9) and confirms the original witness of the Jewish people as inheritors of the monotheistic religion of YHWH (Isaiah 43:10–12). The Jewish contribution to the economy of salvation is their own divinely instituted, yet future redemption from a world that has either oppressed them as a people or treated them as aliens in a foreign land (Augustine reiterated the idea of the Jews as an "alien race" in his amillennial *City of God*),[37] and their restoration as a people visibly receiving God's earthly and spiritual blessings, through the ministry of Jesus Christ. The economy of consummation in chiliastic eschatology shows how the Jewish people's redemption is likewise redemption *for* the world, insofar as it confirms that the God of Israel seeks the well-being and salvation of the nations as well. For the millenarian theologian, Israel's national redemption and restoration from diaspora, as conceived in many Jewish expectations, is a *precondition* to the future messianic kingdom (Leviticus 26:40–42; Jeremiah 3:11–18; Hosea 5:15–16:3; Zechariah 12:10–13:1; Matthew 23:37–39), while others see Israel's redemption and the initiation of the messianic kingdom of Jesus as simultaneous events.

Amillennialists tend to believe that the messianic kingdom has already come and is to be found in the Church alone, or is part of a future solely dependent upon a worldwide judgment against those who are not part of the Church.[38] Therefore, any future hope for the Jewish people, let alone any participation they might have in God's work of consummating the created order and redeeming the human race from sin, violence and death, is automatically negated in the amillennial worldview.

Jewish journalist, author, and social commentator Melanie Philips drew the same conclusion after years of studying nuanced relations between Jews and Christians today, when she wrote that the *source* of much modern-day hatred of the Jews is "... replacement theology. In essence, it says that the Jews have been replaced by the Christians in God's favor, and so all God's promises to the Jews, including the land of Israel, have been inherited by Christianity. The spirit of Augustine lives on."[39] What aspect of Augustine lives on, that Philips, a secular Jew, would connect his ancient work with a contemporary understanding of replacement theology? Is it not Augustine's amillennial view that the kingdom of God, along with all its messianic promises, has been apprehended by the Church to the point that the Jews are permanently replaced in the economy of salvation?[40] Did not the amillennial threat to the early Christian belief in the millennium take away a venue whereby the Church might continue to imagine a future hope for the Jewish people while allowing the Jewish people to retain at least some of that which makes them Jewish?

There is a dual problem, emblematic of the amillennial, economic view of salvation history. Because Roman Catholic amillennialists believe the kingdom of God is apprehended by the Church they likewise believe that the covenantal economy of God in relation to Sinai is *replaced* fully and not simply expanded, intensified or fulfilled (as opposed to *abolished*) by the new covenant mediated by the Church.[41] Conversely, because amillennialists believe the covenant on Sinai has been replaced by the new covenant initiated by Jesus, it is assumed that any claim to be part of God's kingdom made by the Jewish people is transferred to the Church, as it is the covenant community of Jesus.

The problematic principles related to the amillennial position on "covenant replacement" and the realized kingdom of God are evident in a variety of relatively recent Catholic statements, indicating that the Church has adopted or continues to strongly rely on the same supersessionist logic its modern theologians desire to overcome.[42] *Lumen Gentium* for example, citing Jeremiah 31:33, includes the following statement: "all these things [the details of the Mosaic covenantal structure] . . . were done by way of preparation and as a figure of that new and perfect covenant"[43] instituted and ratified by Christ. Pope Emeritus Benedict XVI, when acting as Prefect for the CDF confirmed the 'traditionalist strand' of economic supersessionism as he advocated a strict amillennialism and claimed that the original Christian eschatology regarding the kingdom of God should be narrowed down to the thought of Origen (who eventually was declared a heretic), and Augustine.[44] Benedict writes: "God, according to the Prophet, will replace the broken Sinai covenant with a New Covenant that cannot be broken . . . [it] . . . is replaced by the *unconditional covenant* in which God binds himself irrevocably."[45] To be fair, Benedict here seems simply to be reiterating the essence of the prophetic witness making the claim that the Mosaic covenant had conditions attached to it. Likewise, Benedict made statements in which he ascribed a unique and continual mission to the current Jewish people. Nevertheless, in light of his influence on documents such as *Dominus Iesus*, one must wonder if Benedict sees a real, abiding theological efficacy for this people, rooted in the pre-Mosaic, Abrahamic covenant, aside from that covenant functioning as the core and foundation for the superior new covenant, found *solely* in the Church. Indeed, it is curious that a theologian with such a thorough knowledge of the nuances of biblical covenant theology would not see the intrinsic connection between the unconditional Abrahamic covenant, its ratification at Sinai, and its future fulfillment with the Jewish people. It is less that the Sinai covenant was replaced and more that the Sinai covenant is simply an extension of the unconditional, Abrahamic promise. What is certain is that Benedict's overarching theological presupposition is one that relies almost exclusively on the philosophy of substance metaphysics, and in a Thomistic manner, makes the Catholic Church the supreme *telos* of reality: "Ratzinger derives . . . [his] . . . priority from the ontological which saw first creation as having an inner teleology leading to the Church . . ."[46] Within Benedict's amillennial framework, the consummative divine economy, initiated but fully apprehended by God at creation, leads directly through the redemptive divine economy, apprehended by the Church as its end. The Church then possesses the "unconditional covenant in which God binds himself irrevocably."

When we refer to "substance metaphysics," we do so because the philosophies of totalization that are rooted in the desire to somehow "know" substance, share at a foundational level the same kind of deterministic, finalistic language and concepts as amillennial, realized eschatology. Substance metaphysics carries with it weighty ". . . commitments to timelessness, immutability, pure actuality with no potentiality, and being unaffected by relations to other beings."[47] In a similar way, amillennialism seeks to dislodge itself from time by claiming that the Church enacts the eternal attributes of the kingdom in a way that makes it triumphant and dominant over other historically conditioned entities. Similarly, Soulen draws a correlation between supersessionism and the amillennial rejection of temporality in light of its stress on a transcendent kingdom, whether in the form of a completely transcendent heaven, or the earthly Church. This eschatological form of ". . . supersessionism depicts salvation as deliverance—not from creation—but nevertheless from that temporal form of God's economy characterized by God's Israel-relatedness."[48] As the realized eschatological counterpart to replacement theology, amillennialism depicts salvation as a deliverance from both God's workings with Israel, *and* the temporal, created order, insofar as amillennialists primarily conceive of a renewed and consummated earth only after time and history have ceased, after the return of Christ and the judgment. In part, this is because the sedimentary, realized eschatology stresses concern with God's identity within the category of being, more so than God's irrevocable, covenantal relationship with the Jewish people, or how this relationship affects Christian theologies of communion. In this sense, the amillennialism espoused by Benedict is ". . . *eo ipso* forced to think 'eternal identity' in one-sided reliance on YHWH's dialectical shadow, *ousia*."[49]

Millenarianism, by contrast, carries with it a hope for an eschatological future within the person of Christ, but outside of the Church, the nature of which is temporally conditioned as an earthly reality within history. In the amillennial paradigm, there is a degree to which the Church's apprehension of the kingdom is a pure actuality with no potentiality—the Church is viewed as a messianic *telos* unto itself. In the millenarian view, there is no telos but the consummation of all things, and its only precursor is the future messianic kingdom of the saints. Even the Church cannot aspire to such heights—it may only participate as a conditioned entity alongside others, though it is indeed a central vehicle for the kingdom's apprehension. The realized, amillennial view categorizes the Church as utterly unique (as in the encyclical *DI*), making it the narrow gate whereby all people, including the original chosen people, the Jews, must enter before apprehending the divine presence. In this sense, the realized eschatological view evokes an almost idolatrous position, replacing the narrow gate of Jesus Christ with the utter necessity of the Gentile Church as it exists today, within history. Such a view exasperates already strained relations with the Jewish people, confirms a commitment to tired and uncreative replacement theologies, and above all, demands that the interrelations between covenantal "religious others" be synthesized into the sameness which is the Church. Moltmann's millenarian principle, instead of totalizing otherness, challenges Christian theologians to conceive of the Jewish people as a dialogical and ethical community, i.e., *eternally distinct* "partners" who are constitutive and integral to any Christian concept of the age to come.

To a large degree, Benedict bases his view on Jesus' words of institution over the Eucharistic cup,[50] and relates this negatively to Jeremiah 31:31–34 which begins with the phrase "They [the Jewish people] broke my covenant." Benedict repeats himself, emphasizing that, ". . . the conditional covenant, which depended on man's faithful observance of the Law, is replaced by the unconditional covenant in which God binds himself *irrevocably*."[51] Along with Jeremiah, Exodus 24: 3–8 does indeed make clear that the specific benefits of the Mosaic covenant are dependent upon the obedience of its hearers, but does this necessarily mean that the Mosaic covenant, which may be considered to some extent *an extension of the former, unconditional, Abrahamic covenant*, is utterly superseded by the new, especially in light of the fact that Benedict's entire thesis is that Jews and Christians somehow abide in one, unitary, eternal covenant? Certainly, faithful Jews do not view such an interpretive mechanism as convincing, simply because the amillennialist, supersessionist paradigm draws a stark and unwarranted distinction between the Abrahamic covenant, which they call "irrevocable," and the Mosaic covenant, which many Jewish people view as a continuation, memorialization, and liturgical ratification of that original covenant.[52] Most millennial Christian authors admit that there is a degree of *discontinuity* between the irrevocable, Abrahamic covenant and the Mosaic, but likewise insist that the Mosaic ". . . is *continuous* with the Abrahamic covenant of promise in terms of its individual application of redemption and initial *fulfillment of the kingdom promise* in the promised land . . ."[53] Though the peoples' assent is "required," the Mosaic covenant, like the Abrahamic, ". . . is Jehovah's covenant exclusively."[54] Thus, the entire covenantal narrative of the Bible, from beginning to end, emphasizes *God*'s election, faithfulness, and steadfast determination to keep the promises made to the chosen people.

Indicative of the amillennial pattern of biblical exegesis, Benedict fails to mention key parts of the Jeremiah citation that point to very real aspects of God's promise for Israel's earthly, eschatological future—parts emphasized in the millenarian model, and clearly not applicable to the Church. First, God states in the passage that the divine love and care of Israel, qua Israel, is non-negotiable and eternal, regardless of apparent conditional elements in the covenantal structure: "'Only if the heavens above can be measured and the foundations of the earth below be searched out will I *reject the descendants of Israel because of all they have done*,' declares the Lord" (Jeremiah 31:37). Regardless of any inability on Israel's part to maintain the precepts of the Law, God will not reject them, and certainly will not replace them. Second, God's promise for Israel is not solely for a future "forgiveness of sins" (Jeremiah 31:34), but the writer of Jeremiah also uses apocalyptic language that functions as an eschatological vision and promise for a share in a divine, earthly kingdom, in line with the prophet Isaiah: '"They will return from the land of the enemy. So there is hope for your descendants," declares the Lord.' "Your children will return to their own land" (Jeremiah 31:17), and ' "The days are coming," declares the Lord, "when I will plant the kingdoms of Israel and Judah . . ."' (Jeremiah 31: 27). ' "The days are coming," declares the Lord, "when this city will be rebuilt for me from the Tower of Hananel to the Corner Gate ... The city will *never again* be uprooted or demolished"' (Jeremiah 31:38, 40). God makes another promise to Israel, using language associated with the establishment of a renewed, Edenic paradise on earth—interpreted as the messianic kingdom in rabbinic circles,[55] claiming that Israel will once again be able to say to one another "'The Lord bless you, you prosperous city, *you sacred mountain*'" (Jeremiah 31:23).[56] In this passage, there are allusions to the millennial grape–eating so common in Jewish apocalyptic writings. Most importantly, all these eschatological promises are associated *with the same Mosaic covenant God initiated and vowed to eschatologically 'repair'*: "'Only if these decrees vanish from my sight," declares the Lord, "will Israel ever cease being a nation before me'" (Jeremiah 31:36. Cf. Isaiah 11:12, Zecheriah 10:6, Isaiah 26:19, Ezekiel 16:55).

Benedict's amillennial interpretation appears to be overly selective in its use of certain sections of Scripture. Many modern Jews, skeptical of Christian typological readings, could interpret such selective use of the Hebrew Bible as serving the purpose of removing the possibility of any future consummation of God's economic covenant with Israel outside the Church—although the biblical text explicitly points to such a reality with no mention or implication of a Gentile Church whatsoever. Any admission that there is an economic dimension by which God would save and restore carnal Israel at the eschaton, particularly one associated with the land, progeny, and the themes of Jewish apocalyptic, would threaten the Church's claim that it alone is the fulfillment of all Jewish hopes and covenantal promises—the replacement of the salvific economy of God for the Jews.

Such supersessionist and amillennialist themes are incompatible with various elements of the Apostolic Witness as well as the Hebrew Bible. Jesus states in the Gospel of Matthew the following: "Don't misunderstand why I have come. I did not come to abolish the Law of Moses or the writings of the prophets. No, I came to accomplish their purpose" (Matthew 5:17, NLT). The word in the passage for "abolish," *kataluō*, infers an overthrowing or replacement of the former. Jesus states he did *not* come into the world to destroy or replace the Mosaic Law. The word in the passage for "accomplish," *plēroō*, means "to make full." Jesus had no intention of superseding the Law, but he did intend to augment it, point to a deeper meaning, and embody it in a perfected manner. Indeed, Jesus' other statements on the subject seem to imply that even apocalyptic events would not remove the importance of the same Law that was ratified at Sinai, in its ceremonial, judicial, and moral principles: "For truly I say to you, until heaven and earth pass away, *not the smallest letter or stroke shall pass from the Law of Moses until all is accomplished*" (Matthew 5:18, NLT). Though Jesus claims that his mission of salvation for the nations is accomplished through his work on the cross (John 19:30), God's final accomplishment will be consummative: heaven and earth will one day pass away—but until then, the Law remains, as do the synagogue and the Church.

Benedict is correct when he states that Jesus initiated a new covenant in his blood, and instituted that covenant in a special way through the Eucharist: "This is the cup of the new covenant in my blood" (Luke 22:20).[57] The word for "new" in Luke's Gospel, *kainos*, is repeated, eschatologically speaking, by Jesus in Revelation 21:5: "I am making *all things new*." It is important to note that in the 'consecration text' in the Gospels, Jesus never explicitly refers to the new covenant sealed in his blood as 'everlasting,' in spite of the fact that the Roman Catholic words of Institution quote him as referring to ". . . the new and everlasting covenant." The term "everlasting covenant" is used in the Hebrew Bible, first in reference to the post-flood reality in Genesis (Genesis 9:16; 17:7; 17:13; 17:19), and then again a number of times, all in reference to God's covenant with the people of Israel (Numbers 18:19; 2 Samuel 23:5; I Chronicles 16:7; Psalm 105:10; Isaiah 24:5; 55:3). Reference is made to the eternal covenant in Hebrews 13:20 as related to Jesus' blood sacrifice, but this is not explicitly linked to the Church's Eucharistic ritual. Rather, Jesus' blood sacrifice is rendered as a spiritually eternal reality for the faithful. The millenarian reading of the Eucharist as *proleptic* of the eschatological, messianic banquet, maintains the tension that confirms that the Church is not a replacement of Israel, but indeed is provisional to the kingdom of God in its fullness: "Blessed are those who are *invited* to the marriage supper of the Lamb" (Revelation 19:9). The Eucharistic reality is certainly a participation in the marriage feast of Christ, but it also acts as a constant reminder that it is provisional to the consummative supper of the Lamb. Moltmann's millenarian description of the 'Thousand Years' as a messianic kingdom of Jews and Christians implies that Jews, in an inexplicable and mystical sense, are chosen for the messianic banquet, along with other groups, the members of which the Church may not expect (Matthew 22: 1–14). This reality poses challenges to traditional Christian theological categories, as faith in Jesus the messiah will act as a prerequisite to participation in the messianic banquet, yet the details of such faith and the exact means by which the Jewish people, at the eschaton, come to understand Jesus' divinity and salvific Personhood, remain undefined. Recent interpretations of the Epistle to the Hebrews clarifies, as millenarians have always maintained, that the old and new covenants need not be juxtaposed for the purpose of pointing out exclusivity, but must be contextualized in light of eschatology.[58] Benedict's amillennial view seems to require an abandonment of Jesus' Jewishness in order to argue that the new covenant replaces the Mosaic in a way that makes the latter utterly void, useless and obsolete.[59] By deemphasizing Patrology,[60] the amillennial paradigm removes from the Sinai covenant and the Christian covenant that which is common to them both—the belief that God the Father is sovereign and that the messiah comes to participate in the consummation and full establishment of the kingdom of God:

> Then the end will come, when he [Jesus] hands over the kingdom to God the Father after he has destroyed all dominion, authority and power. For he must reign until he has put all his enemies under his feet. The last enemy to be destroyed is death. For he "has put everything under his feet." Now when it says that "everything" has been put under him, it is clear that this does not include God himself, who put everything under Christ. When he has done

this, then the Son himself will be made subject to him who put everything under him, so that God may be all in all.

(1 Corinthians 15:24–28; cf. Psalm 8:6).

We notice that the enemies of Jesus in this passage are not a specific people group or a nation, but the spiritual and political structures of power and domination in the world, with the final power being death. Thus, the millenarian reading sees an economy of both restoration and resurrection for the Jewish people, fulfilled by God the Father. The divine, economic activities of God vis-à-vis the Mosaic covenant with the Jewish people are not one of the authority structures to be *overcome* by Jesus, though in Jesus they are in the process of a continuing and further fulfillment, whereby the Gentiles may come into relationship with the God of Israel. "According to the New Testament, the fulfillment of some aspects of the Messianic hope awaits the second advent of Christ (Matt. 13:36–43; Mk. 14:60–62; Lk. 19:11–27; Acts. 3:19–21; 14:21–23; 17:30–31)."[61]

The replacement of the economy of God's consummative will in relation to the Jewish people with the blood covenant ratified by Jesus is a key feature of amillennialism. Though millenarians take seriously the view that Jesus died on the cross for the redemption of human sin, this is not viewed as exclusive of the future, consummative and irrevocable covenant God has made with Israel particularly. As Evangelical theologian, Robert Diprose summarizes:

> it is not surprising that the traditional claim of Christendom to embody the promised messianic kingdom is an embarrassment to Christians involved in dialogue with Jewish people . . . if the view according to which the Church incarnates the promised messianic kingdom is a corollary of replacement theology, it follows that the widespread repudiation of this view should lead Christian theologians to also re-examine the grounds for realized eschatology.[62]

I too am arguing explicitly that economic replacement theology may be overcome only by a repudiation of amillennial, realized eschatology. The means for overcoming this eschatology is already possessed by the Church in its earliest, apostolic expression of Patristic millenarianism—an eschatology that has been refined and modified for the contemporary moment in the work of Jürgen Moltmann through the fruit of his Jewish–Christian dialogue.

Millenarianism, amillennialism, and punitive supersessionism

Economic supersessionism is but one of the three major types of replacement theology that is promoted by amillennial eschatology, but rejected by millenarian principles.[63] Our purpose in the following section is to describe punitive supersessionism in further detail, show how it is an extension of Augustine's amillennialism (among other offshoot traditions), and explore the ways in which the millenarian view of salvation history offers an alternative to it.

Punitive supersessionists (also called *retributive supersessionists*) claim that Israel's right to God's covenant promises—especially eschatological promises—have been forfeited due to the nation's wicked actions against God[64] and *temporary* rejection of Yeshua as messiah.[65] As a reaction to Israel's disloyalty, hardness of heart, and blindness to the truth, punitive supersessionists claim that God has transferred Israel's promises of blessing to the Church, and is currently in the process of punishing Israel for their iniquities, both corporate and personal. When we speak of "blessings" in reference to Israel, we mean the blessings of God's loyalty and forbearance (Genesis 17:7; Deuteronomy 7:9; Leviticus 26:44), land promises (Genesis 13:15; Amos 9:15), promises for restoration after harm (Deuteronomy 30:1–5, Isaiah 49:15), promise for future resurrection (Ezekiel 37:1–14), the generational blessing of the offspring of the particular covenant people (Genesis 12), God's blessing to use the covenant people as a witness to God's care for the world (Zecheriah 8:23), and for the ultimate consummation and messianic deliverance of the kingdom of God to that people as an eternal blessing (2 Sam. 7:12–16), spilling over to the nations (Gal. 3:8).

The "punishment" that is operative in punitive supersessionism is conceived in terms which assume that God's punishment upon Israel will last *through the final judgment, into eternity*. For most amillennialists, the primary means of punishment for the Jews, whether in response to their rejection of Jesus, or the responsibility they took in "killing God,"[66] was that the kingdom and its blessing was transferred to the Church, and God's protection of the Jews was removed, permanently replaced by God's punitive posture: "God's promises to Israel are viewed as having been fulfilled with the Church; therefore, amillennialists see no specific future for national Israel."[67] Contemporary millenarian scholars deny that God has permanently rejected Israel and are critical of any posture that claims an eternal, irreversible punishment of the Jews for their initial rejection of Jesus as messiah. For eschatological millenarians such as Evangelical writer, Michael Vlach, the NT ". . . denies the possibility of Israel's being permanently rejected by God."[68]

Moltmann, during the pioneering phase of his work on the Jewish–Christian millennium, maintains the same view, that "Israel's promises remain Israel's promises. They have not been transferred to the Church. *Nor does the Church push Israel out of its place in the divine history*."[69] From the millenarian perspective, Israel's distinct mission to the nations remains until their participation in the establishment of the kingdom of God is accomplished. God's *ultimate* intention for the covenant people is blessing and not punishment.

While some early Patristic millenarians adopted punitive supersessionism in their polemical writings through competition with Jewish interlocutors,[70] it resulted in a logical inconsistency in light of the fact that the early chiliast impetus was to safeguard some sort of Jewish messianic hope, believing that the return of Jesus was imminent and that he would at that time, "restore the kingdom to Israel" (Acts 1:6).[71] In one sense, the early millenarians, if they were to maintain vigorous polemics against the Jews, had only punitive supersessionism to adopt, as a harsh economic supersessionism could not conceivably be held alongside their view that the Church was not the final instantiation of the kingdom, and that God had unfinished work with the Jewish people as a whole. Scholarship has confirmed that the Patristic millenarians, representing the earliest expression of eschatology, held a tension between God's *temporary* rejection of the Jewish people through the destruction of the Temple—an extension of the "Deuteronomic program"— and hope for the future restoration of the kingdom of God to Israel and the Church.[72] Post Augustine, amillennialists typically held to a paradigm of *permanent rejection* and transference of all eschatological hope regarding the kingdom, from Israel to the Church.[73]

The Eastern Father who was the primary precursor to Augustine's Western amillennial theory, Origen, utilized the anti-Jewish polemic of deicide, and espoused a form of punitive supersessionism that took God's retribution upon Israel to a new level—*making the punishment and not the covenantal promises permanent and irrevocable*: "And we say with confidence that they [the Jews] will *never* be restored to their former . . . [blessed] . . . condition. For they committed a crime of the most unhallowed kind."[74] The later Patristic amillennialists and punitive supersessionist influence on Christianity is so thorough that it is traceable through the Middle Ages and up through the Reformation. Martin Luther, who borrowed extensively from both Origen and Augustine, adopted amillennialism in a *semi-official* sense for his tradition[75]—a sense that is curiously missing from official Roman Catholic decrees and connects the destruction of the Temple with God's rejection of the Jewish people, unable to conceive of the possibility of a future restoration in line with the millenarian interpretation of Ezekiel 37:24–28, Jeremiah 31:31–34, etc.:

> Listen, Jew, are you aware that Jerusalem and your sovereignty, together with your temple and priesthood, have been destroyed . . .? For such ruthless wrath of God is sufficient evidence that they assuredly have erred and gone astray . . . Therefore *this work of wrath* is proof that the Jews, surely rejected by God, are no longer his people, and neither is he any longer their God.[76]

It appears that for Luther, the economic principles (meaning the 'management of the household') of God's salvific work with the Jews is reduced to a work of wrath expressed as a punitive principle. For Luther, God's wrath, as a theological reality for the Jewish nation is based upon "proof" regarding the plight of the Jews in history: diaspora, destruction, removal of the Temple, and marginalization and ultimate replacement of the priesthood by a new priesthood. Yet what interests us is that Luther's examples in this writing regarding the punitive elements of God's covenantal status with the Jews point specifically to things that the Hebrew Bible states will be restored in the future, eschatologically—things permanently connected to Jewish expectations for the messianic kingdom: "Jerusalem and your sovereignty," "temple and priesthood," have been destroyed and transferred. The primary notion that could confirm to Luther that these elements of Jewish religious life had been destroyed *permanently* is amillennialism, for in this paradigm, the kingdom itself is apprehended in the Church, with no possible future expression beside its own,[77] let alone a *Jewish* expression.

As we have already discussed, Augustine's unique theory of the Jews as the "witness people" may have saved thousands of lives in the fourth through sixth centuries, leading Church leaders and politicians alike to spare the race of people,[78] so that they might "bear witness to God." For an amillennial theologian such as Augustine to admit that the ". . . Jews had not yet fulfilled their role in God's plan," seems as remarkable as it is unlikely, until one realizes what this "Jewish role" in salvation history is—to be used in service to, and for the good of, the Church:

> it was God's will that Jews not be slain, so that they might bear witness to the triumph and truth of Christianity. If Jews had a continuing place in the drama of divine salvation, it was *solely* as a witness people, to vindicate the truth of the new religion . . . they were permitted to practice Judaism *only* as a service of witness to the Church.[79]

It is no coincidence that when Augustine described the "witness" concept explaining the continued existence and religious observances of the Jews, that the concept also unapologetically adopted and promoted a punitive supersessionism. At the same time, Augustine likewise became the Father of amillennial eschatology in the West, which in principle advocated the idea that as punishment, the kingdom was taken from the Jews and given to the Church. It becomes clear that in Augustine's worldview, as far as the Jews are concerned, the time approaching the eschaton exists solely for their conversion to the Church (what Augustine calls the Jewish "*telos* in history").[80] Jewish participation in any future expression of God's kingdom (besides the eternal expression) is the same as the Jews' historical participation: to witness by suffering through the punitive consequences of rejecting Jesus and resisting membership in God's earthly kingdom, until ultimately they become subsumed by the Church, or are condemned.

Biblical scholar Magne Sæbø, who in his 1969 doctoral dissertation advocated for a millenarian reading of Zecheriah 9–14, astutely points out the punitive legacy of the thought of a number of amillennial theologians from the third through fifth centuries:

> Christian theologians, such as Origen in the third century, Eusebius of Caesarea in the fourth, and Augustine in the fifth, argued that since Jews were obstinate in their refusal to accept the Divinity of Christ and the Gospels, they were denied the divine promises of being the elected people. Christian theologians emphasized that the Exile of the Jews was the divine punishment inflicted upon them for having denied Christ, stressing however that their repentance, by conversion to Christianity, was the sole way for their salvation.[81]

What Sæbø points out is one element of the replacement concept. The other, Augustinian concept, which is the primary focus of this book, is that admittance into the Church, and not simply belief in the Christian kerygma or Jesus himself, a requirement for Jewish salvation. The eschatology adopted by Augustine, along with the punitive elements of his view, point to the amillennial hermeneutic that is limited to the typological reading of Scripture: "The Jews failed to understand that everything in their Law pointed to Christ" (*C. Faust.*, 12.2–3). As a result, they misunderstood their Scripture, and their temple was destroyed and they were *punished with exile and subjugation.*"[82] Yet Augustine went beyond simply claiming that the Hebrew Scriptures pointed to Jesus by adopting a view of *the Church's total possession of the kingdom* in place of a Jewish possession of it.[83] Augustine, following the amillennialist Origen,[84] justifies this concept based on his supersessionist reading of Matthew 21:43, in which Jesus states that ". . . the kingdom of God will be taken away from you and given to a people, producing fruit of it."[85] Since the time of Augustine, multiple scholars have successfully rebutted the typical, supersessionist reading of the Matthew passage, but the damage has been done.[86] The amillennial view that the kingdom of God has been transferred from Israel to the Church (because of God's punishment upon Israel) has become a sedimentary, reinforced, and dangerous assumption. Our point here is that Augustine's amillennial eschatology logically and naturally produces a theology whereby the Jews are punished, and their only future hope is to *convert to the Church*, the new, true, and abiding kingdom: ". . . it was simply assumed, according to the eschatological scenario laid out by Augustine, that the Jews would convert to Christianity."[87] The question must be raised as to whether Jewish people can 'convert' to the person of Christ, without being subsumed into the Church. Certainly, messianic Jews fall into this category, yet Christian eschatology is ripe with other future examples of this phenomenon.

Chiliasm, particularly Moltmann's non-apocalyptic form, rejects the punitive assumptions of supersessionism, through the themes of (1) a provisional Church[88] and a continued witness of Judaism, (2) an emphasis on the land promise given to the Jews, and (3) a reiteration of the eschatological promise of God's presence in Zion, with the people of Israel. In this millenarian scheme, Israel is seen as poised for blessing, not punishment. In reference to the provisional nature of the Church and the continued witness of Judaism, Moltmann affirms both. According to Moltmann's millenarianism, the role of Israel, as Israel, is to witness to the messianic kingdom of God, not necessarily the Church.[89] Thus, there is a *telos* for Judaism, but it is not ecclesial in form, and Israel cannot be described in punitive terms, simply because that elect community refuses to become the Church, or temporarily rejects Jesus, which according to Romans 11, is in fact *the plan of God*.[90] Contra Augustine and his amillennial view, the continued role of Israel as a "witness people" is not to testify in a national sense to God's abandonment, cosmic retribution, and replacement, but to God's constant and steadfast election, in spite of the tragedies of human history. The millenarian view of history again comes into play, insofar as it affirms a present and future for the people of Israel that is not reduced either to a forced conversion to the ecclesial body or the prospect of judgment and annihilation in any permanent sense for those who are to see Jesus as messiah in a future disbursement of God's grace and revelation.

Millenarian theology breaks "... free from the Augustinian tendency to understand salvation as redemption *from* the people constituted by God's actual, historical, interaction, the people of Israel, and so to think of redemption in terms of deliverance *from* history."[91] The amillennial tendency views the redemption accomplished in Jesus Christ not only as a redemption from sin, death, or the hands of the devil, but also as redemption from the punitive consequences of the old, carnal, historical Israel. Eschatological millenarianism instead points to a redemption from the oppressive mechanisms of this world, to a messianic age marked by peace, blessing, and the reconciliation of Jew and Christian, without one tradition's particularities being consumed by the other. This does not remove or replace the need for individuals to repent of personal sin (both commission and omission), but it does couch the redemption of Israel into a story that precedes the New Testament and comes to fulfillment for the original people of the promise. Otherwise, the covenantal narrative of the Bible is essentially hijacked by Gentiles, and then withheld from the Jewish people by the mere fact that the Church is viewed as a telos in history beyond the person of Jesus Christ, and the kingdom Jesus came to establish.

Moltmann's millenarian principles affirm that the Jewish people, regardless of their "divinely instituted" rejection of Jesus (Romans 11:7), are beloved by God forever. This is predicated upon the certain hope that the Jewish people will, in a significant way, share in the millennial banquet of God's future as a participation in their own anticipated redemption and restoration—within their own particular relationship with Jesus in the future.[92] Moltmann, referencing the millenarian interpretation of Romans 11:15, writes that "... both its countenance as a people, and also *the bringing to faith of individuals belonging to it*, are the earnest pledge of Israel's ultimate acceptance."[93] In this way, Moltmann views the millennial age to come, and its promises of the resurrection and restoration of Israel, as the ultimate end to which Jewish religious life leads. Israel has its own mission, whereby individuals and groups come to Jewish faith, and Israel enacts its ongoing role as a witness people in this positive sense. God's ultimate promise is that at the fullness of eschatological time, Jesus' divine identity and role as messiah will be revealed to the Jewish people. Such a concept stands against the amillennial model whereby Israel is viewed as either the recipient of God's righteous wrath, or destined for conversion to the Church of history. Mal Couch points to this inconsistency in amillennialism, for which "... the future conversion of Israel is taken literally and historically, but the Davidic kingdom reign is not taken literally."[94]

We see in much millenarian writing the idea that Israel stands as a constant and abiding witness to the future kingdom of God, making any permanent chastisement of Israel by God impossible. Horner, for example, among other millenarians, advocates a "harmony of spiritual materiality" that leaves space for uniquely Jewish expectations for participation in the kingdom intact, as opposed to a thoroughly spiritualized and allegorized conception, as in the amillennial model.[95] In this sense, the carnal expectations regarding the world to come of the Jewish people may be harmonized with the Christian chiliastic conception of the ultimate afterlife, though the meaning of 'salvation' remains different but complimentary in the traditions.[96] Pointing to this unique understanding in the premillennial view, Baruch Maoz states that:

> salvation is not to be thought of as exclusively spiritual and moral, as if Israel's living in the land had no spiritual and moral implications! The gospel message is replete with appreciation for the material realm. The New Testament makes it quite clear that the material is the arena in which ultimate salvation is to take place, thus reconfirming Old Testament expectation. Even our bodies will be redeemed.[97]

In reference to the land promises affirmed in the Hebrew Bible, the millenarian view takes such claims seriously. One of the ways that Israel is affirmed as a *positive* "witness people" to the kingdom of God, stressed by millenarians as a material *and* spiritual reality (in ways that amillennialists attempt to hold in tension but ultimately fail to do so), is precisely through their existence as *a people of the land*, a people who mark their uniqueness by enacting their covenantal origins through "carnal" or "material" means oftentimes foreign to many of today's Christian theological constructs. These include practices such as circumcision and the keeping of Torah. Catholic scholar John T. Pawlikowski, without overtly advocating the eschatological millenarian view, points critically to the punitive and supersessionist assumptions that underlie past amillennial, Catholic conceptions of the holy land, and describes them as:

> efforts by Christian theologians to replace a supposedly exclusive Jewish emphasis on "earthly" Israel with a stress on a "heavenly" Jerusalem and an eschatological Zion . . . [T]his tendency has the effect of neutralizing (if not actually undercutting) *continued Jewish claims*. The bottom line of this theological approach was without question that the authentic *claims to the land* had now passed over into the hands of the Christians. Jerusalem, spiritually and territorially, now belonged to the Christians.[98]

When Pawlikowski refers to the stress on a "heavenly" Jerusalem, he is (without claims to do so) referencing the amillennial, overly allegorized readings of land-promise texts from traditionally apocalyptic Jewish sources. When he refers to "an eschatological Zion," the assumption is that the eschatological Zion envisioned by Christians is far-off and other-worldly, and not open for admittance to Jews and Jewish expectations regarding its features, whereas Moltmann's millenarianism takes this into account, essentially advocating the view that Gentile Christians will participate in the eschatological Zion that God will prepare *specifically for Israel and the Church*: "The Church of Christ can only understand its historical consciousness of its own nature in accordance with the kingdom, and messianically, if it grasps its relationship to Israel, to the Old Testament, and to the divine future."[99]

Those holding to the amillennial view, despite their attempts at safeguarding bodily resurrection and an earthly consummation, neglect the same Jewish elements of the kingdom that they seek to usurp within history, justifying such an approach through the default category of divine punishment. Jeffrey Siker describes the historical millenarian (amillennialist) impetus in these terms: "The Jews have been evicted from the holy land as a result of God's punishment, and the land is now the promised inheritance of Christians."[100] The punitive element of amillennialism is so strong that it appears to be capable of conceiving of a divine punishment upon the Jews that leads to their total and permanent destruction, related to the usurpation of their land. In regards to God's abiding presence with the elect people of Israel, millenarian eschatology affirms that such a reality exists now, though in a limited fashion, and will again in its fullest fashion in the messianic kingdom. Moltmann interprets Daniel 7:24 as descriptive of the Jewish and Christian messianic kingdom, for which God makes the promise: "I will set my sanctuary in the midst of them for evermore."[101]

In the amillennial view, God has permanently lifted the divine presence from the people of Israel as a punishment for their (God ordained) rejection of the Gospel, and God's presence instead has become embedded *in its totality* within the new temple, individual Christians and the Body of Christ, which is the Church. Because the kingdom is the Church according to this understanding, God's presence will never again grace the Jewish people. An example of this comes from a popular amillennial source that claims that the absence of the divine, protective presence was a sign of God's punitive posture toward the Jews during the destruction of the Temple and the siege of Jerusalem: "The circumstances of the Jews trapped in Jerusalem was unique in all of history. God had withdrawn his presence ... it was a tribulation suffered only by those Jews who had rejected Christ. Those who believed Jesus' prophecy were saved from the disaster of A.D. 66–70."[102] Not only is the statement above historically incorrect (early messianic Jews did not *cease* worshipping in the Temple), but it also casts a shadow upon the ethical motivations of Christian amillennial eschatology. By contrast, Soulen points to the consummative principles within millenarianism that insist that God's presence has not left the Jewish people—a point confirmed in the resurrection of Jesus as a prolepsis of the resurrection of *all* Jews.[103] Robert Jenson explains this millenarian concept further when he makes the powerful statement that, "What the Lord does to Israel he does to himself, in that the *shekinah* shares Israel's lot and the Lord's being."[104] If God is indeed present with the people of Israel, a punitive view makes sense only in terms of a *temporary* withdrawal of the divine presence, as in the Hebrew Bible, and not a permanent withdrawal, rejection, and replacement, as in punitive supersessionism.[105] Within Moltmann's millenarian view of the 'world to come,' the Christian hope for the people of Israel coincides with the Jewish hope: that God will be present with carnal Israel, within a renewed Zion. Moltmann aligns this with the primary means of Jewish religious expression: "Obedience to the Torah cannot be legalistically deprived of its legitimacy, for the Torah is the prefiguration and beginning of the divine rule on earth."[106]

Modern chiliasts, following Moltmann's logic, believe that a future, Jewish participation in the Thousand Years' messianic kingdom illustrates that the Jewish people are not due punishment, but blessing, alongside the Christians who will worship Jesus upon Zion. God's blessing upon Israel takes many forms, but

The messianic kingdom 255

ultimately results in a further blessing of the nations through Israel. Robert Whalen illustrates the millennial affirmation when he writes that there is "... a clear ideological affinity between Christian millennialism and Yahweh's expected promise of a coming era of blessedness for humanity which will center upon Israel."[107] For millenarians, the consummative will of God the Father is an economy that should not be conflated with God's redemptive process as it is inextricably linked to the Church of history. Therefore, "The difference between ... [the amillenialists and the] ... premillennialists is that this possibility ... [of the restoration of Israel] ... is *not seen as requiring an earthly millennium; it places elect, ethnic, natural Israel in the Church, which has now become true Israel.*"[108] In Moltmann's millenarian paradigm, the earthly millennium requires the presence and participation of the Jewish people who come to believe in Jesus as messiah, as constituted *apart* from the Church.

Because millenarian hermeneutics allows for an alternative reading of the prophetic promises of the Hebrew Bible, it permits a view that promotes a future blessing that involves land, progeny, resurrection, and restoration.[109] Instead of focusing solely on the Hebrew Bible's punitive prophecies regarding the Jewish people, chiliasts take the apocalyptic stories as part of a holistic framework, insisting that the narrative of God's interactions with the Jews did not end with the Church or the mission of the Jewish–Christians given at Pentecost.

Millenarianism, amillennialism, and structural supersessionism

In addition to the economic and punitive forms of supersessionism supported by amillennialist eschatology, structural supersessionism is perhaps the most stubborn form to eradicate because the rejection and replacement of the Jewish people is a necessary part of its hermeneutic of the Hebrew Bible and its view of the salvation story in general. In an article on the economic Trinity and the Christian theology of Judaism, Soulen offers this nuanced definition: "Precisely expressed, structural supersessionism refers to the fact that the classical model, taken as a whole, *portrays God's enduring and universal purpose for creation in a manner that simply outflanks God's history with carnal Israel.*"[110]

The logical outcome of structural supersessionism appeared early in the Church, in the thought of Marcion—particularly in his desire to rid the canon of the Hebrew Scriptures, making it indecisive for how Christians view salvation history. Granted, whereas Marcion eliminated the entire Hebrew canon, contemporary supersessionists tend to view the Hebrew Bible as directly inconsequential, gaining its importance only in light of that to which it points: a de-Judaized version of the Apostolic Witness or the Church. Marcion's removal of the Hebrew Scriptures ultimately led him to reject the idea that Jesus could possibly have been the incarnation of the same God the Jews worshipped. Marcion was one of the first heretics to reject chiliastic orthodoxy because chiliasm confirmed Jewish prophetic themes and left space for a future in which the promises God made in the Hebrew Bible concerning the Jewish people might be literally fulfilled in a future messianic kingdom, *within temporal history*, and according to Jewish expectations.[111] Indicative of his supersessionistic impact on Trinitarian theology, "Marcion believed that the Jewish god was a poor bumbling deity, while Christ was a good and saving God, completely independent from, and superior to, the God of the Old Testament."[112] We bring up Marcion as an example because, regardless of the fact that his views were condemned as heretical,[113] his influence left its mark, though sometimes subtle, on the more extreme forms of structural supersessionism in the Christian tradition, particularly in relation to contemporary amillennialism. It is outside the scope of this project to trace all of Marcion's influences on modern Christian theology, but it is sufficient to say that some scholars have seen ". . . a widespread revival of Marcionism in the modern Church,"[114] and have established that ". . . many well-meaning Christians are to all intents and purposes Marcionite in their attitude to the Old Testament."[115] Jeffrey C.K. Goh, a Catholic theologian, expert on ecclesiology, and judge on the Ecclesiastical Tribunal of the Archdiocese of Kuching, has this to say about Marcion's legacy on ecclesiology: "The most extreme version of supersessionism was that of Marcion. For Marcion . . . the God of the Old Testament was not the same as the God of the New Testament. Quasi-Marcionite views have . . . become persuasive in ecclesiology."[116] E.C. Blackman also traces the historical development of Marcion's influence on the Catholic Church's theology, in his work entitled *Marcion and His Influence*. Though Blackman claims that Adolf von Harnack over-emphasized the legacy left by Marcion, there was still a significant mark left, specifically regarding the discontinuity between the interrelation (though not the synonymous nature) of the Hebrew and apostolic narratives.[117] Despite the polemics against Marcion, initiated by Tertullian and Irenaeus, his influence was significant enough for the movement to last through the fifth century,[118] and for the Catholic Church to retain, largely intact, his original codifications of the New Testament canon, though necessary changes were eventually discerned and made.[119] As we will see, the logical disconnect and utter lack of influence or continuity between the Hebrew Bible and the Apostolic Witness is the hallmark of *structural* supersessionism, as it was at one point, the central theme of Marcion's theology. Knight tells us that structural supersessionism is ". . . present whenever the Old Testament does not determine Christology,"[120] but a more accurate description is that, in this form of supersessionism, the Old Testament determines *almost nothing* in relation to the New.[121]

The fact that Marcion was one of the first non-chiliasts is significant, insofar as supersessionism was upheld by the early Church Fathers but their anti-Marcionite, millenarian eschatology functioned as a buffering or tempering factor in reference to the mystery of God's ultimate posture toward the Jews. By contrast, Marcion's structural supersessionism, combined with his rejection of the earliest Christian millenarian eschatology[122] influenced his view that the Jews did indeed await their own, *lesser* messiah. As Tertullian describes it, "between these . . . [messianic realities] . . . he . . . [Marcion] . . . sets up a great and absolute opposition, such as between justice and kindness, between law and gospel, *between Judaism and Christianity*."[123] Thus, Marcion's specific form of supersessionism was not one that typologically applied and then replaced the promises of God to the Jews, but instead conceived of a Hebrew testament that held no bearing on Christianity whatsoever, because the God of the Hebrew people was in fact a different God altogether. This thought process, though tempered by the Church's official condemnation of Marcion, still has ties to structural supersessionism, insofar as structural supersessionists claim that the Hebrew Bible is decisive for Christian theology, but largely ignore it in ways that would naturally interpret a permanence or eternal validity to its prophetic utterances in any sense that is not *figurative*. Though most modern millenarians insist on the *distinctions* between Israel and the Church, especially in light of God's particular and eternal covenant with the Jewish people, they simultaneously insist that the God of Jesus, worshipped by Christians, is the same God of Abraham, Isaac, Jacob, and all of Israel.

Marcion's legacy is evident when one notes the utter absence of any positive theological role attributable to Israel in the majority of Christianity's most official, documented history: "Christianity in these authoritative forms ... [creeds, confessions, ecumenical councils, dogmatic text books, etc.] ... does not appear to regard the Old Covenant's distinctive testimony to God as *strictly indispensable* for the purpose of articulating God's economy in its normative dogmatic shape."[124] We likewise notice the patterns that connect Marcionism with modern-day amillennialism: "The ancient heresy of Marcion—with its separation of Old from New, of God from Jesus, of creation from redemption, and of material from spiritual—has persisted throughout the history of the Church."[125] The legacy is not that amillennialists, like Marcion, have literally thrown out the Old Testament and changed the canon, but that in the amillennial paradigm, God's "past" as expressed in the Old Testament is reduced to God's "future" as expressed in the New Testament—to the point whereby the God of the Hebrew people becomes unrecognizable as the God of Jesus, who is known only through a new, special, and divinely revealed *gnosis*.[126] In a strange change of sequence, amillennial theology does not see the past of the New Testament as historically expressed in a Church that is not then again reduced to God's future as expressed in the anticipated, consummated world. Instead, in amillennialism, God's future is consumed by the Church's present through the elements of a realized, historicized, and presentative millenarian reality.[127] If structural supersessionism ". . . relegates to the past that whole sphere of divine action whose central object was carnal Israel,"[128] amillennialism relegates to the Church any manifestation of the divine action for the future.

Structural supersessionists and amillennialists alike use the Hebrew Bible in an almost strictly allegorical[129] and typological sense, to support a very narrow vision of the economy of salvation—one which makes us question why it is important that Christians worship the *God of Israel* at all, or include the Hebrew Bible in the Christian canon.[130] Amillennialism is the eschatological extension of the structural view of the biblical narrative,[131] insofar as ". . . the great bulk of the Hebrew Scriptures, and above all God's history with Israel and the nations, is rendered ultimately indecisive for shaping conclusions about how God's works as Consummator and Redeemer engage creation in enduring and universal ways."[132] Amillennialism ultimately fails in addressing how God, as Consummator of the created order, works in the present and future to bless Israel directly, and thus bless all the nations and the world through Israel, as promised in the Scriptures. Amillennialists essentially claim that God's blessing "through Israel" comes solely through the Church, as it is the single entity that rightly represents Israel, thus advocating a structure of replacement. The world receives its blessing through the Body of Christ, the Church as the new Israel, vis-à-vis conversion to it. Because there is no further consummative economy involving Israel as Israel, the very *narrative structure* of the amillennial Christian tradition fails to answer the question of how the Hebrew Bible is directly decisive for theological thought and reality outside of a solely typological function. As Soulen describes it, the correlation between amillennialism and structural supersessionism becomes clear, as both systems adopt a view that:

> consists in the sequence: creation, fall, Old Covenant, New Covenant, final consummation. Alone among the economy's great divine works, the Old Covenant—*taken according to its 'letter' or manifest form*—is not only *temporal* but *temporary*, i.e. divinely destined to be left behind the inexorable logic of *signum* and *res*.[133]

What Soulen means by "letter or manifest form" is the direct application of prophetic eschatological promises to the religious community for which the Hebrew authors originally intended—the Jewish people. Soulen affirms the *manifest form* of Hebrew biblical hermeneutic by envisioning a consummative era which results in a permanent *shalom* and permanent reign of God on earth for the Jewish people. Moltmann's millenarian view is consistent with this, applying various Hebrew Bible narratives directly to the messianic era. Soulen uses the same Scripture passages cited by Moltmann to prove the same point:

> They shall live in the land that I gave to my servant Jacob ... I will make a covenant of peace with them; it shall be an everlasting covenant with them ... My dwelling place shall be with them; and I will be their God and they will be my people. Then the nations shall know that I the Lord sanctify Israel, when my sanctuary is among them forevermore.
> (Ezekiel 37:25–28)

Soulen takes the passage above as a manifestation of "... God's self-identification with the Jewish people ... [here God] ... confirms it and manifests it before the eyes of the nations."[134] This passage above from Ezekiel refers to the messianic era when the Spirit and the prophetic word are made manifest in God's consummative economy: "So in this way the people itself [Israel], in its historical and everyday life, is to become the 'temple' of God's Spirit, and the Shekinah of the most high."[135] Though the Church is the "Temple of the Holy Spirit" (1 Corinthians 6:19), the Ezekiel passage refers to the Jewish people directly, upon the beginning of the consummative order. The Hebrew Scriptures describe a future day when God will directly, through the indwelling of the Jewish nation upon Zion, redeem the people: God's *Shekinah* is "... the means through which Israel is redeemed: God himself is the 'ransom' for Israel."[136] This, in its most basic sense, is what connects the future, carnal Israel, with Jesus Christ.

Both Soulen[137] and Moltmann (in his millenarian exegesis)[138] view Micah 4:1–4 as referring to Israel's direct eschatological restoration in terms whereby both Israel and the nations will be present to worship God. Moltmann's millenarian exegesis is a primary example of the post-structural supersessionist, "letter" or "manifest" exegesis of the Hebrew Bible, particularly of passages such as Jeremiah 31:33–34,[139] and Ezekiel 37:1ff., wherein the locus of God's salvific means for the Jewish people is shifted to a future, resurrecting event.[140] The millenarian principle here takes seriously the claim that the Hebrew Bible promises redemption to Israel directly as a community, and this redemption is connected with the *land*. Therefore, "... if Israel is to possess the land forever, they must exist forever,"[141] and not be replaced by the Church through an allegorical interpretation of their own scriptural texts.

In the structural supersessionism adopted by amillennial eschatology, the old covenant, and therefore the prophetic word of the Hebrew Bible, flows directly into the new covenant, because its *sole* prophetic purpose is to typologically support and prove the claims of the new covenant, during Second Temple Judaism and the rise of early Christianity. To state that the Hebrew Bible has a positive prophetic voice for the Jewish people of today or in the future is met with extreme skepticism and defensiveness in some amillennial circles. Specifically, in the amillennial view, the new covenant, expressed predominantly in ecclesial terms, and the final consummation, are practically interchangeable—the first advent brings with it the only historical and temporal expression of the kingdom of God. As we concluded in part two, in the Augustinian/Thomistic amillennial tradition, the consummation of salvation history leads in a specific sequence: the old Law is superseded by the era of the Church, and the Church leads directly into eternity.

So we must ask, how does Moltmann's millenarian understanding stand against amillennialism's structural replacement of Israel? It is precisely through its ability to take the old covenant "... according to its 'letter' or 'manifest' form ..."[142] and apply the Hebrew Bible narrative of God's covenantal promises not only to the Church, but to a consummative reality that emphasizes the temporal dimensions of the Thousand Year reign of Christ on earth, associated with God's permanent, eternal interactions with Israel. Moltmann identifies in no uncertain terms the precise problem with structural supersessionists, for whom "... it was usual to try to separate the Jewish idea of God from the Jewish people, in order to adopt the Old Testament's monotheism while despising the Jews ..."[143] Now is the time for "... the recognition of the abiding vocation of the people of Israel."[144] Such an abiding vocation means that the people of Israel "... are not the Church and *never will become the Church*."[145] In this sense, instead of submitting to a flawed structural supersessionism for which Israel is simply a precursor step to the

Church, Israel is viewed as an historical participator, moving within history toward the messianic kingdom. Moltmann's new structural narrative is conceived in terms of an Israel that the Church neither "succeeds"[146] nor "supplants."[147]

For millenarian eschatology, the connection between the Jewish understanding of an eternal kingdom associated with a "this worldly" Son of man (Daniel 7), and the Christian conception of the Thousand Years' messianic empire (as mentioned in Ezekiel 38:8 and Isaiah 24:21f.), is held in tension, positing ". . . an Israel-centered messianism and a human universalism,"[148] in the sense that the Gospel message of Jesus Christ is open to all—Jew first, and then Gentile, and that the presence of God during the Thousand Year period is one of unrivaled *shalom*. Essentially, the future messianic kingdom will bring about the completion of a multitude of Jewish expectations for the messianic era and their worship of YHWH on Mt. Zion, Jesus will be present simultaneously as receiving the worship of Jews and Christians, yet neither group will *become* the other. Unity will be maintained in the midst of plurality and particularity. The Jew need not cease being Jewish in spite of his connection and belief in Jesus. Moltmann conceives of this messianic era in two realities: Israel will be brought out of diaspora in "foreign lands," and the nations will no longer be alienated from the God of Israel's direct presence:[149] ". . . at that time shall they call Jerusalem the throne of the Lord and all the nations shall be gathered into it" (Jeremiah 3:17).[150] Moltmann states that "If messianic hope is linked with Israel's sense of mission, then the fulfillment of that hope must also mean the fulfillment of Israel's mission for the nations, and hence the abolition of that particular historical role. The messianic kingdom includes Israel, and more than Israel in its historical form."[151] Israel, alongside the Church, is in possession of an historical 'mission' to witness to God and the kingdom, though initially without the 'conversionary impetus' typically associated with the Church.[152] The conversionary principle becomes intensified as a direct act of God the Father, by the Holy Spirit, as history leads into the messianic rule of Jesus Christ. In this conception, the future millennium is within history but on the cusp of eternity, and therefore the mission of Israel to the nations cannot be reduced solely to the historical realm, but instead is constitutively related to the transcendent, divinely instituted salvific economy of humankind. Millenarianism's Jewish and Christian messianic era, emphasizing eschatological community[153] in spite of difference, is conceived in terms deeply reminiscent of the work of Jewish philosopher, Franz Rosenzweig:[154]

> The whole economy . . . is based on the transition from personal existence, dominated by Revelation, to collective existence, which alone can bring Redemption. This is conceived in terms of a utopia as a final condition of the world, hence of history, and there are really two collective entities, that is, Christianity and the Jewish people, who are agents of this advent . . . This history outside history, *this temporality without becoming*, this sociality without wars or revolution defined Rosenzweig's ideal space, which is that of the Jewish people.[155]

In the chiliastic view, the *structure* of the divine salvific economy cannot possibly exclude either the Jewish people or the Christian witness, for the two entities point to the same end, but by different means—though ultimately, Christ will prove to be both the end and the means. The one religious end of the messianic kingdom is structurally related by two respective economies: the redemptive economy of Jesus, intended as a blessing for the nations, and the consummative economy of Israel, also to bless the nations. Yet when the two economies meet, the Jewish people will be blessed by the redemptive economy of Jesus, and the Jewish people will bless the nations through God's act of consummation. This is why Moltmann states that "when the Church talks about hope, it is talking about *the future of Israel*, for it proceeded from Israel, and only together with Israel can its hope be fulfilled."[156] Judaism and Christianity, in this way, are both historically conditioned, yet also *metahistorical* entities in relation to the kingdom of God.

Overall, Moltmann is content with the mystery of such a millennial thesis, not concerned with creating an absolute, one-to-one correspondence or synthesis between the Christian Thousand Years' empire and Jewish expectations for the messiah inspired by the rabbis.[157] This would assume that the rabbinic eschatology that most easily corresponds to the millenarian Christian view, the rabbinic, is to be treated as normative for all Jews, a point contested by modern scholars.[158] Some, though not all, rabbinic millennial conceptions are inconsistent with Christian ones, claiming that the part of the time leading to the golden age consists of a messiah who dies but never comes back to life,[159] a messianic era of extreme suffering,[160] and an eventual revitalization of the Temple sacrifice, though one excluding human priests.[161] For Moltmann, it is enough that the Christian millennial tradition is able to imagine an eschatological era stressing both a Jewish and Christian participation that overcomes structural supersessionism by taking seriously the apocalyptic prophecies of the Hebrew Bible *for modern Jews*. The structure of the Hebrew Bible's narrative may no longer be reduced merely to a promise-fulfillment typology or a truncated, supersessionist vision of the standard model's creation-fall-redemption-consummation scheme, but must instead be interpreted in light of the future ". . . messianic kingdom of Jews and Christians."[162] Moltmann ". . . maintains this version of millenarianism to include a future salvation for Israel as a nation . . ."[163] because it takes seriously the permanent, Judeo-centric features of the messianic age and conceives of the participation of modern Jews in light of their permanent election by the God of Israel,[164] who will at that time ". . . reign in Mt. Zion, and in Jerusalem and *before his ancients gloriously*" (Isaiah 24:23; 9:7).

Two aspects in particular set Moltmann apart in his conception of the millennial era, both involving what he does *not* say in reference to the eschaton. These elements challenge structural supersessionism by opening the eschaton, and thereby the Christian narrative, to a Judeo-centric reality. First, Moltmann adopts a language of "surprise"[165] and mystery involving the exact time and means by which Israel will be resurrected and restored. He states explicitly that the final redemption of Israel and their entrance into the messianic kingdom may only be described in mystery: ". . . when and how, God alone knows."[166] Moltmann sees

Israel's resurrection to the kingdom mentioned throughout Hebrew apocalyptic as referring to the same temporal kingdom mentioned in Revelation 20,[167] and consequent to the events described in Romans 11.[168] Second, while maintaining that from a Christian perspective Jesus of Nazareth is messiah, Moltmann refers to the messiah of the Jewish people as *"their* messiah": ". . . the special mark of Christian pre-millenarianism . . . is the Church's dream for the Jews—not for their conversion to the Church, but for their resurrection into the kingdom of *their messiah.*"[169] The idea here is that the dawning of the messianic age means divinely initiated, physical resurrection for the Jewish people, both individually and as a distinct community, and their communal participation with a messiah who fulfills their expectations and does not transgress their consciences in terms of authentic belief—or with another messiah besides.[170] For the majority of Jews, neither Jesus as *moshiach*, nor the divinity of any man is an acceptable prospect, so the millenarian kingdom overcomes supersessionism by a means different from a forced synthesis. Though this difference in theology cannot be overcome, Moltmann's millenarian concept that Jesus is messiah in an ". . . eschatologically anticipatory and provisional way,"[171] leaves enough space for Christians to embrace Jesus as the messiah without demanding from Jews an inauthentic assent to something they find both blasphemous (worship of a man) and incongruent with historical reality: "Judaism impresses on Christianity the experience of the world's unredeemed nature."[172] Moltmann refers to both the Christian apprehension and Jewish hope for the messiah as a "permanent incompleteness,"[173] pointing to the mysterious nature of the eschaton and the provisional nature of the Church and synagogue. For the sake of dialogue and comparative theology, the tension is not resolved, but from Moltmann's unapologetically Christian perspective, the messiah who will come and redeem Israel in the eschatological era is none other than Jesus.

Millenarianism allows for a non-ecclesiastical messianic era (equivalent to the 'world to come'), within future history, that envisions Jews and Christians worshipping the God of Israel side by side, without demanding a purely synthesized or homogeneous religious community. Since a wide majority of rabbinic commentary affirms that Gentiles will have a place in the world to come and that Jewish restoration includes the worship of YHWH by "the nations," this aspect opens the door for a realistic theology.

Constructing ideas on the nature of the millennial age

In this final, constructive section of the book, we will apply millenarian exegesis to the goal of envisioning the eschatological millennial age in a post-supersessionist manner, pointing to a "messianic kingdom of Jews and Christians."[174] We will look at some New Testament passages (a sampling from the Book of Revelation, and Romans 11) that are interpreted in Moltmann's millenarian paradigm as referring to God's consummative work with the Jewish people, in addition to the Church, and explore the ways in which supersessionist assumptions might be replaced by a positive theology.

According to Moltmann's millenarian exegesis, Revelation 20 speaks of two groups of people: (1) those Jewish and Gentile Christians who were martyred for their testimony to Jesus, and (2) those *Jews* who refused to bow to the beast and suffered for it, connected to the 144,000 of the tribes of Israel who were "sealed" with the mark of God as "servants." In Moltmann's chiliastic reading, the 144,000 are not limited in application to only those who are alive at the time of the end of world history—the term is referring to an aspect of eschatological restoration, including both national and individual resurrection.[175] Moltmann claims that Revelation 20:4, which refers to those primary participants in the messianic Thousand Years' age, includes "Israel's martyrs and the martyrs of the Christian faith," both groups acting as representative agents for the whole of Jewish and Christian communities. Some amillennial Christian commentators dismiss the distinctions between the groups by claiming that the 144,000 refers only to a small remnant of Jews who follow Jesus—and early on in Christian history, simply become part of what we call the Church.[176] Such a vision of the 144,000 is unwarranted by the text itself. The text states the exact identity of the 144,000, referring to them as "from the twelve tribes of Israel." According to millennial exegetes, it is appropriate to consider this a group separate or distinct from the Gentile Christian community, or even the early Jews who founded the Church.[177] Twice in the Book of Revelation there is mentioned a group of "144,000." One reference to the group occurs in chapter 7, which reads:

> Then I saw another angel coming up from the east, having the seal of the living God. He called out in a loud voice to the four angels who had been given power to harm the land and the sea: "Do not harm the land or the sea or the trees until we put a seal on the foreheads of the servants of our God." Then I heard the number of those who were sealed: 144,000 *from all the tribes of Israel*.
>
> (Revelation 7:2–4)

This group is explicitly singled out as separate from the "great multitude" that is the "nations" (ἔθνος),[178] i.e. the Gentiles, and as Rowland mentions, "The 144,000 is composed of people from every tribe *of Israel*. The Jewish identity of this group is indicated by the fact that there is another multitude in v. 9 that comes 'from every nation,' suggesting that those mentioned in v. 5 are Jews, proper."[179] Moltmann too believes that the group mentioned in chapter 7 refers exclusively to Jews: "... they ... [both groups] ... will be called together for the end-time, 144,000 from the twelve tribes of Israel, and afterwards 'the great multitude' from every nation."[180] The group of 144,000 is mentioned again in chapter 14, which reads: "Then I looked, and there before me was the Lamb, *standing on Mount Zion*, and with him 144,000 *who had his name and his Father's name* written on their foreheads ... And they sang a new song before the throne and before the four living creatures and the elders" (Revelation 14: 1;3). The fact that the 144,000 (later associated in the text with the charism of celibacy) are standing with the Lamb on Mt. Zion is an explicit description of a "millennial scene."[181] We notice immediately that the members of this group had "*his [the Lamb's] name and his Father's name*" on their foreheads. This negates the possibility that those in this group were given the mark of the beast, or were even capable of being deceived into following the antichrist, as is the case with other persons in the narrative. Because this group had the Lamb's name written on their foreheads does not necessarily imply that they somehow became like the Gentile Christians, but simply that they were set aside as belonging to God, vis-à-vis the Lamb's intervention, and not the beast, as those who come to believe in Jesus as messiah—a sort of consequence of the *Sonderweg* accomplished by God on their behalf, i.e., through election.[182]

One millenarian commentator, Thomas Nixon, links the distinction in salvific means with the term "sealed" that is used in reference to the Jewish 144,000: "This 'sealing' is evidently different from the 'sealing' of new [gentile-Christian] believers . . . This 'sealing' evidently is to identify the 144,000 as a special group among the redeemed."[183] In this sense, the Jewish people represent "a special group among the redeemed" because they are redeemed in a special way—directly by the hand of YHWH, and eschatologically through the intervention of Jesus, who will "redeem Jacob," as is testified repetitively in the Hebrew Bible.

The beatitude thematic of Revelation 20:6 picks up what is likewise a potential distinction between groups of holy individuals: "Blessed and holy are those who share in the first resurrection. The second death has no power over them, but they will be *priests of God and of Christ* and will reign with him for a thousand years." As the 24 elders seated on thrones in Revelation 4 relate a composite of both "Christian and Jewish" representation, it is my contention that the millennial vision of Revelation 20 describes the Lamb, Christian martyrs, and the Jewish nation as occupying a place of authority and judgment/vindication over the world in which they were victimized.[184] Thus, the 144,000 represent the consummation and completion of the nation of Israel—both those who are alive during the tribulation, and those who are resurrected at the Parousia of Christ, upon their visualization of Jesus the Jewish messiah, testifying to their past intention to await the messiah as Old Testament saints.[185] According to Elisabeth Schüssler Fiorenza, ". . . it is likely that in Rev 7:1–7, the twelve tribes (the 144,000) signify the *eschatologically restored Israel* . . ."[186] but this restoration does not by default imply Israel's conversion *to the Church* as we know it today, though it does imply a conversion to Jesus the Christ. For many of the contemporary Jewish faithful, national, eschatological restoration and resurrection are synonymous,[187] and deeply rooted in the apocalyptic texts of the Hebrew Bible, again insinuating a direct intervention by the God of Israel to eschatologically and Christologically redeem all of Israel. The millenarian exegesis of the Book of Revelation treats the "144,000" mentioned in chapter 7 as symbolic, but nevertheless representative of the whole of Israel, and not merely the martyrs of Israel.[188] Certainly, the 144,000 is not in reference to the Gentile Church.

The Roman Catholic Church has already claimed that those who are "outside of the Church" may attain salvation, but by this statement specifically, Israel is lumped in with the remaining "non-Christian" nations, eliminating the theological priority of their particular election.[189] By contrast, one may interpret the *Catechism of the Catholic Church* eschatologically, as referring to a composite of those inside and outside the traditional Church as occupying a place of authority in the New Jerusalem, insofar as it makes the claim that "... those who are *united with Christ* will form the community of the redeemed, 'the holy city' of God, 'the Bride, the wife of the Lamb' ... she will not be wounded any longer by sin, stains, self-love, that destroy or wound the earthly community."[190] The millenarian reading of the Book of Revelation suggests that there will be, in the messianic age, those who are mystically "united with Christ" who are neither "Christianized" in terms of adopting particularly Gentile Christian traditions, nor are they part of the Church,[191] namely those among the elect who refused to bow to the beast or worship his statue—the group that earlier texts refer to as the 144,000 "from the tribes of Israel." Referring to the 144,000 of the tribes of Israel, Moltmann in his millenarian exegesis states that "... the 'Thousand Years' empire' of Revelation 7 and 20[192] must then be conceived of—in spite of the anti-Jewish utterances in Revelation 2.9, 3.9., and 11.8—as *the messianic kingdom of Jews and Christians*."[193] The special election of these two groups does not deny entrance to others in Christ, regarding past history, of those outside the two specific groups, as the entire purpose for the blessing of Israel and the function of Christianity is the unique witnessing to the blessings of YHWH *to the nations*. It is part of what Moltmann calls "... the abiding vocation of Israel."[194]

According to the majority of millenarian biblical interpretation, the messianic reign that occurs in the eschatological scenes expressed in the Book of Revelation refer to an existential reality that comprises both Jews and Christians, each maintaining their own theological particularity and significance.[195] Because the events in the Book of Revelation suggest an eschatological *telos*, the millenarian reading puts modern-day Judaism in a kind of partnering relationship with the Church, ushering in the millenary kingdom of God, all under the messianic authority of Jesus.

Beyond the millenarian exegesis of the Book of Revelation are treatments of various other passages that millenarian exegetes view as having special significance for the Jews, such as Mark 30:30; Luke 24:21; 1 Corinthians 6:2; and 2 Timothy 2: 12.[196] Perhaps the most important of these texts is Paul's Epistle to the Romans, chapters 9–11, which explore the eschatological redemption of Israel specifically. Moltmann's millenarian interpretation of Romans 9–11 overcomes the supersessionist reading of history by envisioning an eschatological millennial age with the people of Israel and Zion at its center, engaged with the reigning Christ. Moltmann essentially makes the claim that Revelation 20: 1–4 (the millennial kingdom) and Romans 11:25–32 (the eschatological redemption of Israel) *refer to the same event*.[197]

Though the Romans 9–11 text is often read as evidence *for* supersessionism in amillennial circles,[198] it was used by some early Christian writers to point to the future salvation of Israel *qua* Israel.[199] In more recent scholarship, it has been shown that certain interpretations of the Romans text definitively overcome elements of ecclesiological supersessionism, the form which states, as we have discussed at length, that Israel must become part of the Church of history specifically, in order to be in relationship with God, or to have theological value.[200] As shown previously, the text of *NA* and its later reception puts ecclesiological supersessionism into serious question, but it is our challenge now to determine if Romans 11 is compatible with a millenarian view that upholds the eschatological consummation of the Jewish people as part of God's coming future, within history—particularly through the process of national and corporate resurrection. Paul's primary goal in Romans 9–11 is to wrestle with the paradox at hand: Jesus (*Yeshua*) is believed to be the Son of God and messiah by the Christian community, composed of few messianic Jews and very many Gentiles, but his messianic identity is rejected by the majority of the Jewish people (though primarily on the premise of function).[201] Millenarian exegete Mark Kinzer makes the claim that "Paul [in Romans] sees the community of Israel, *even in its state of unbelief* in Yeshua, as a holy people, a nation in covenant with God. He identifies with Israel as his people and maintains solidarity with them."[202] This is not to say that Paul does not conceive of the Christian Gospel as the further, fuller and perfect revelation of God's Word, but it does suggest that Paul believed there was a continued spiritual value to Judaism that would ultimately result in a national and "carnal" salvation—i.e., resurrection and participation in the world to come, upon Jesus' return to earth and the Jewish acceptance of Jesus as messiah. Further, Kinzer points out that nowhere in Romans, or in the Pauline corpus, does Paul refer to the Jewish people as *unbelievers*, despite their initial unbelief or rejection of Jesus as the messiah.[203] The unbelief and rejection are considered temporary elements of God's elective purposes and economy of salvation. This does not mean that Paul claims that no transformation of the Jewish people needs to take place in order for the "Jewish nation" to be or remain in right relation with Yahweh, yet Paul says the same thing of Christian believers.[204] Paul's overarching argument is that God has implemented a temporary "hardening" of the Jewish people that serves a soteriological purpose: the entry of the Gentiles into the covenant, through Jesus Christ (Romans 11:11–12, 30–31). Paul gives little indication as to exactly how the salvific plan of God will unfold for the Jewish people since Paul presents the entire eschatological scenario as a "mystery." What Paul does maintain firmly is that the "Deliverer" will appear from Zion, and that their ['Israel's'] sins will be taken away (9:26–27).[205] In a strange sense, the Jewish rejection of Jesus, mentioned in Romans 11, is part of God's missionary call for them, as a *gift* to the Gentiles.[206] Siker explains the phenomenon this way:

> Why has God made this provision for unbelieving Jews? Paul provides the rationale for 11:28b in 11:29: "For the gifts and the call of God are irrevocable." To what is Paul referring by "gifts" and "call"? When we examine Paul's use of "gifts of God" (*charismata tou theou*) elsewhere in Romans, we see that they function as instruments of salvation.[207]

Thus, those Jewish people who do not initially believe that Jesus of Nazareth is the messiah play a vital role in future salvation history. According to Romans this group of Jewish people have a "call" (*klesis*, one of the root words that form the word *ekklesia*, the name for the early Christian Church) to live into the plan of God, considering the term "call" is inseparable from *election* and *salvation* in Romans. Paul's argument hinges on drawing a correlation between Christian faith in Jesus and God's election of the Jewish people, tracing back to the covenantal reality of the patriarch Abraham—a covenant based on faith and later ratified through the Law, the call to obedience.[208]

When Paul claims that "all Israel" will be saved, it is to be taken ". . . as a term that strongly implies the restoration of the whole nation, including all twelve tribes,"[209] i.e., the 144,000 mentioned in Revelation 7 and 14. "All Israel," as N.T. Wright claims, does not refer to a combination of Jewish *and* Christian believers in the Gospel of Christ, but to Christ's Israel.[210] The problem with Wright's amillennial interpretation is that he also claims "all Israel" refers only to individual Jewish people who *convert to the Church* in the here and now, claiming that the verse does not apply to Gentile Christians. Wagner refutes this amillennial view when he writes that "Allison (1999) makes a convincing case that in his resurrecting of Second Temple Jewish eschatological expectations, Wright dramatically misreads the evidence in attempting to downplay the importance of future eschatology . . ."[211] by interpreting the "all Israel" of Romans as any Jew who becomes part of the Church now, i.e., the amillennial formula. Essentially, this does not match well with Paul's primary concern in Romans 9–11, which struggles at a deep theological level with how the people of Israel historically, and at least temporarily, reject belief in Jesus, while at the same time are elect in some permanent and irrevocable manner.

As we recall from our treatment of Allison's work, Second Temple Jewish eschatological expectations, adopted by Jesus, had in view a millenarian understanding of history—the consummation and ultimate redemption of the Jewish nation with the coming of a Deliverer to, and then out of, Zion.[212] The verb "to be saved," σώζω, is a direct correlation to the Jewish understanding of salvation, i.e., ". . . that Yahweh would restore his people and establish his rule ἐκ Σιὼν."[213] Of utmost significance is that Paul, in Romans 11:26 quotes Isaiah 59:20 of the LXX, which reads "the redeemer will come for the sake of [heneken] Zion," as the following: "the redeemer will come out of Zion." Douglas J. Moo rightly states that Paul's translation of Isaiah 59 ". . . differs also from the Hebrew text and from every pre-Pauline text and version."[214] Some authors attribute the phrase to pre-Pauline, Jewish, apocalyptic sources, many of which contain explicitly millennial motifs.[215]

The question that surfaces relates to why Paul would deliberately change the existing texts, in order for the phrase to read "out of Zion." As H.L. Ellison observes, "the Deliverer cannot come out of Zion unless He has first come to it,"[216] thus posing the probability that the reference is to God or God's vice-agent (Jesus) coming from heaven, establishing a place in Zion, and then "coming out of Zion" in order to establish the era of peace—the theme central to millennialism.[217] In all cases in the Hebrew Scriptures and New Testament, with the possible exceptions of Hebrews 12:22 and Revelation 14:1, the Bible uniformly renders "Zion" literally as a material, earthly reality, not exclusively as a purely spiritual, heavenly city.[218]

Both the concept that either a messianic agent, or Yahweh, would arrive, and that a consummative act of resurrection would accompany the beginning of the "age to come," are deeply imbedded in Jewish tradition, though the latter idea has been replaced by a more individualistic and general "immortality of the soul" in some modern Jewish expressions.[219] For first-century Judaism specifically, the restorative eschatology most commonly accepted was that of the chiliastic view—that Yahweh, the messianic agent, or both, would establish an era of peace on earth, a "millennium," immediately prior to, but leading into the "age to come."[220] The eleventh chapter of Paul's Letter to the Romans draws a significant correlation between the "mystery" of the salvation of all Israel and the eschatological expectations evident within Second Temple Judaism, and the Book of Revelation, namely millennialism.[221]

Romans 11:11–15 reads as follows: "for if their [Israel's] rejection brought reconciliation to the world, what will their acceptance be but life from the dead?" Fitzmyer, among others, argues that Israel's temporary rejection of the Gospel (interpreting "their" in the subjective genitive) is what brings reconciliation to the world, whereas God's eschatological acceptance of Israel will be nothing less than their resurrection from the dead.[222] In this sense, the eschatological consummation of the Jewish people will take place simultaneously with their physical resurrection as a nation—their "acceptance," i.e., the consummation of their election, will result in new bodily life and the restoration of the entire nation of Israel, upon their recognition and acceptance of Jesus as the Jewish messiah.[223] Moltmann argues that these events will take place upon the return of Jesus, at the inception of his millennial reign on earth—but this "acceptance," though dependent upon Israel's recognition and recognition and acceptance of Jesus as messiah, will not require the conversion of the Jewish people to the Church.[224] The Church at that time will cease being the primary gospel-proclaiming vehicle because it will, essentially, be obsolete. Jesus Christ will physically be present, within an eschatological history. The messianic kingdom of peace becomes a tertiary reality, which is the hope of both the Church and the synagogue, removing the possibility that one could supersede the other.[225]

Yet the question remains as to whether Paul envisioned a national conversion of Israel prior to the consummation of history, during the millennial reign of Christ. According to Fitzmyer, the exegesis of Romans 11:26 may legitimately be interpreted in one of two ways: the theological, in which sōthēsetai, "shall be saved" is understood in the passive: Israel will be saved "by God," or, in the Christological sense: Israel will "be converted" by the Deliverer, who is interpreted as Jesus.[226] Joseph Sievers points out that ". . . the citation of Rom. 11:28b-29 forms a link between past, present, and eschatological future, expressed in theological and not Christological terms through the quote from Zephaniah."[227] Whereas Ruether believes that ecumenists, though well-intentioned, are inaccurate in their exegesis of Romans if they read in it that God has not rejected those who follow the Mosaic covenant,[228] Daniel Harrington states that "What is clear . . . is Paul's endorsement of the continuing nature of God's election of Israel, even of those Israelites who have refused to accept the Gospel."[229] Such an understanding is consistent with Krister Stendahl's interpretation of Romans 11:26 in which he points out that Jesus Christ is not mentioned in the surrounding chapters, Jesus is not specified by Paul as the "deliverer who will come out of Zion," and most importantly, Paul ". . . doesn't say Israel will accept Jesus Christ."[230] Stendahl insists that we must finally rid ourselves of the concept ". . . so totally absent from Romans . . ." that

"... salvation means we win and others become like ourselves ..." i.e., the foundational idea of supersessionism.[231] Stendahl is correct in limited aspects of his interpretation of Romans, but the question remains as to whether Christians must rid themselves of all Christological creeds, and the notion that the Church's witness to the Jewish people is that Jesus Christ is identical with the eschatologically revealed messiah, in order to overcome supersessionism. For some theologians and biblical scholars, the answer is indeed found in a Christological reading of Romans 11:26 that identifies "the deliverer" with the parousaic Christ, who is none other than the returning Jesus, but does not read into Romans a conversion of the Jewish people to a predominantly Gentile Church[232]—and this is the view of the author of the current project. It is less so that God provides a Sonderweg for the salvation of all Israel, envisioning that God "... saves all Israel without a preceding 'conversion' of the Jews to the gospel,"[233] but that God provides a Sonderweg beyond the current Church of history, namely, the Jewish people, as Jews, similar to the entity that existed immediately after Jesus' first coming, prior to the mission to the Gentiles initiated by Paul the Apostle. This modification to the traditional ecclesiological and eschatological views of the Church is one that is neither radically pluralistic nor radically exclusivist[234] in the sense that it pluralizes the method (the Church of today or an eschatological, particularly Jewish community) but not the means (Jesus of Nazareth as messiah, ruler, and Lord). Contemporary scholars emphasize the reality that "... for Paul, the initial and ultimate goal of Torah is the inclusion of the Gentiles. And through Christ this goal is realized—he is 'the fulfillment of God's promises concerning the Gentiles.'"[235] This is one aspect that will be revealed to Jewish people near the end of history—that God legitimately has worked through Jesus Christ to the benefit of the Gentiles—a benefit to the nations that will be consummated through the mediation of Israel during the "Last Days."[236] Beyond this, the revelation will take place that Jesus of Nazareth is indeed the fulfillment of what was once viewed as the pinnacle of Jewish religion: the Temple cult. Perhaps a more important revelation is that Jesus the Christ is also mashiach ben David, and specifically, the cosmic Akedah for the atonement of the sins of humankind.

Moltmann's millenarian interpretation of Romans 11:25–27 views the event of "the deliverer coming from Zion" explained in Romans 11: 26 specifically, as referring to the same historical time-period as the historio-eschatological establishment of the interregnum period, foreshadowed in Revelation 14 and explicitly described in Revelation 20.[237] Precisely how the Jewish people are saved, and whether this will involve a special kind of interaction between them and the returning Jesus, will remain a matter of speculation in light of Romans 11:25, which reiterates the entire eschatological scene as a mystery. The importance emphasized by considering the reality of the Thousand Years' reign of Christ in light of Romans 11 is that the salvation of the Jewish people will take place within history, but outside the bounds of "the Church," and some faith/sight relationship will occur between Jesus and his people. The Jewish conversion to the Church, distinct from the Jewish acceptance of Jesus, is not required in the millenarian scheme, as it is in amillennial supersessionism. As David F. Ford states:

> Supersessionism sees the Church as superseding the Jews as the people of God . . . the key point is that the theology of supersessionism opens the way for writing the Jews out of any positive role in the 'divine economy' of history. A contemporary way of putting it might be that Judaism has generally been an anachronism in the Christian metanarrative: Jews have no good future unless they become Christians.[238]

In contrast to Ford's description, Moltmann's understanding of the millennial reign of Jesus Christ acts as a counter to such views of history because a conversion to the Church on the part of the Jews is not a necessary aspect of the metanarrative—though openness to the surprise of God's future in history in Christ is, for both the Church and Israel.[239] Moltmann envisions the millennial reign, which he claims is a connected thread in the messages of Jesus, Paul, and John in the Book of Revelation,[240] as a moment within future history, precisely as an alternative to the supersessionist idea that the Church of history is the messianic kingdom:

> The fact that this messianic hope of those who believe in Christ opens up an *analogous future for Israel*, seems to be the special mark of Christian pre-millenarianism. It is the Christian dream for the Jews–not for their conversion to the Church, but for their resurrection into the kingdom of their Messiah.[241]

"Their Messiah" is none other than Jesus, but he becomes the direct vehicle of their [Israel's] deliverance, not the Church, with its historical limitations and sometimes, unbridled arrogance. "Israel's martyrs and the martyrs of the Christian faith . . ."[242] will share in worship during the millennial era,[243] representing what will eventually take place for all the people of God. When Romans speaks of a "reversal of blindness" for the Jewish people, Moltmann believes it is referring to the acceptance of an understanding that Jesus came to the world as a Jewish man, for the sake of the world—living out and modeling an aspect of the Jewish mission to the nations.[244] Referring to Romans 11:15, Moltmann claims that, ". . . all Israel will not through faith become Christian but through sight it will be redeemed."[245] This should not be interpreted to mean that the Jewish people will continue to reject belief in Jesus, but simply that their redemption will take place upon the visual connection of their expectations of messiah, and the physical, bodily return of the resurrected Christ. It will also include an understanding that Jesus Christ is the final and perfect atonement for sin. Moltmann is convinced that the modern Jewish critique of Christianity is less so a rejection of Jesus and more so a rejection of the "claims of traditional Christianity"[246]—i.e., the amillennial foundation of supersessionism that makes the interpretation that the Church is the messianic, Davidic kingdom foretold in the Hebrew Bible, to the exclusion of any other expression of it.

Moltmann insists that the churches that appear to reject eschatological millenarianism and espouse historical millenarianism, the Orthodox, Roman Catholics, and mainline Protestants, are intolerant of any eschatological hope other than their own—particularly an alternate messianic hope for Israel.[247] This view, most commensurate with historical millenarianism, is one that conceives of the "Thousand Years" reign of Jesus Christ as happening within history *now*, in the institution and office of the Church:

> those who proclaim that their own political or ecclesiastical present is Christ's Thousand Years' empire cannot put up with any hope for an alternative kingdom of Christ besides, but are bound to feel profoundly disquieted and called into question by such hope. We have seen that eschatologies developed in the context of a presentative reign of Christ, or at its end, can visualize only the apocalyptic catastrophe of 'Gog and Magog' and the great Judgment on the Last Day. But post-millenarian eschatologies of this kind are based on a false definition of the location of the present in the context of salvation history.[248]

Moltmann's alternate conception is that the present is simply a bridge to God's future, which is coming toward the Church and the world, along with the eschatological presence of God, as a tertiary reality—a bridge that is currently occupied by the Church and synagogue in a complimentary, parallel, and expectant fashion.[249] Eschatological millenarianism is "... the un-crossable barrier which Moltmann attempts to erect in the way of any notion that the Church could ever become the universal kingdom."[250] Thus:

> the Church has "partners in history who are not the Church and will never become the Church" (CPS 134). These are Israel, which the Church cannot "succeed" (CPS 148) or "supplant" (CPS 351)[251]

Millenarianism acts as a guarantee against this kind of triumphalism[252] and "... those enthusiastic dreams of realizing the universality of God's kingdom through a universal Christian state or by supplanting Israel."[253]

Moltmann's use of premillenarian categories[254] has to do with the emphasis on the "... this-worldly character of Christian hope," a point important in contemporary ecological theology. Though Moltmann's discussion of forms of Christian pantheism were certainly intended to show the importance of millenarianism for a proper view of creation,[255] one which avoids Docetism,[256] those who critique his use of premillennialism miss his entire point—to show that both the Church and Israel have a theological role in history which leads to the divine kingdom, a kingdom which will supplant both of them: "Israel and the Church have distinct divine callings *in history*, by which they complement each other and which they can only fulfill by *not being each other* (CPS 147–9; cf. HD 208–13). Each witnesses to the kingdom of God in its distinctive way ... (CPS 148)."[257] This kingdom is one that is "future and surprising" in the sense that the Church experiences it in an anticipatory manner.

Whereas the hallmark of amillennial eschatology is to make sedimentary a certain and definable understanding of the kingdom of God and situate that kingdom within the auspices of the Church's power, millenarianism rejects such notions and maintains a kingdom that is yet to be realized and must be awaited with great anticipation, in light of the Church's earthly and metaphysical limitations. The millenarian apprehension of the kingdom of God takes on an ethical imperative[258] that, for the Christian, is reflected in the face of Jesus, the martyr. Ford puts it best when he describes the ethical dimensions and the ability to overcome supersessionism through a specific eschatological understanding—which for Moltmann is embodied in premillennial eschatology alone:

> To face Jesus Christ means . . . to follow his gaze of love towards his own people. It is also to be open to radical surprise. Christians have no overview of how Jesus Christ relates to other Christians or even themselves, let alone to Jews . . . Christians trust that he relates in ways that are good beyond anything they or anyone can imagine. But what about Jews who reject him as messiah and await the true messiah? Neither can claim a total overview. Both Jews and Christians agree in radical ways that the category of surprise is inseparable from eschatology.[259]

Ford asks the question that is vital to any positive Christian theology of Judaism: "what about Jews who reject him [Jesus] as messiah and await the true messiah?" Are we as Christians capable of permitting and supporting a surprising future for God's original covenant people, or must we retreat back to the patterns that have relegated the Jews, and therefore the God who is for Israel, to the fringes of history, making them irrelevant? Or are we able to imaginatively conceive of a space for both Jew and Christian, in God's future of *shalom*, in and through a revelation of Jesus Christ as deliverer of the Jewish people at the eschaton?

In review of our final section, we began with a prolegomena to the concept of Moltmann's Jewish and Christian messianic kingdom, specifically by defining concepts within Jewish eschatology that relate to, but are distinct from, Christian millenarianism. We looked at Moltmann's modified form of millenarianism in contrast to that of the early Fathers, and explained his view of the Church as a provisional entity within history. Throughout the chapter, we critiqued the ways in which amillennial eschatology formulates a view in which the Church is seen as its own end, both one which totalizes and universalizes history, and one which transcends history, at the expense of the Jewish people. We explored the question of whether amillennialism is necessarily supersessionist, and using the work of Richard Bauckham, we showed why Moltmann's millenarian is necessary and illustrated how the approach is poised to overcome various aspects of supersessionism.

Pointing to distinctions in the philosophy of history and time between millennialists and amillennialsts, we illustrated how amillennialist schemes perpetuate the idea that the Church is the kingdom, while the millenarian theology of temporality and salvation history leave space for and encourage an alternate Jewish hope for the messianic age. We then explored the three forms of supersessionism and discussed how millenarian eschatology puts each into question and offers a non-supersessionist alternative.

Last, using the millenarian exegesis of Moltmann and others regarding both Revelation 20, and Romans 11, we began to envision and construct a Christian, post-supersessionist view of the eschatological world to come. Overall, in this final chapter we illustrated that a millenarian reading of history, allowable in the Roman Catholic tradition, may envision an alternative Jewish messianic hope that is not equated with the Church as institution.

My hope is that this final chapter, though specifically an exercise in Christian theology, has exposed the need for a further reassessment of the state of Jewish–Christian dialogue, beginning with a more critical self-reflection on the part of Christian, specifically Roman Catholic theologians. As Canisius Mwandayi puts it, "inter-religious dialogue, as is evidently clear, does not originate from tactical concerns or self-interest, but is rather an activity with its own guiding principles, requirements, and dignity."[260] We must ask in what ways a thorough reassessment of both eschatology and ecclesiology might assist representatives from both the Church and the Jewish community, and be used in service to some of the principles outlined in Leonard Swindler's publication entitled *The Dialogue Decalogue*.[261] In Swindler's concise yet influential work, he outlines some "laws for dialogue" that have a direct relation to the thesis of this project. For example, Swindler's fifth commandment states that each participant must *define himself or herself*. This project has been an attempt to maintain a theology that is recognizably Christian, while simultaneously seeking to critique the Church's self-identification with certain harmful eschatological and ecclesiological positions, precisely because supersessionist and amillennialist positions make the identity of the Jewish religious *other* both unnecessary and theologically indecisive. Swindler's seventh commandment is that dialogue must take place *between equals*. Yet both supersessionism, and the inner logic of amillennialism, insists that the Jewish people are *not* equals, and that the Jewish community essentially has no reason for existence, save for conversion to the Church, or some function of service to the Gentile Church in history. The eighth commandment calls for *mutual trust*, but how would such trust exist between Jews and Christians in light of the Church's triumphalist posture and history of forced conversion—realities directly related to supersessionism and realized eschatology? Swindler's ninth commandment requires participants in dialogue to be *at least minimally self-critical*. Since Vatican Council II, the Roman Catholic Church has begun a long and difficult process toward self-critical theological exploration, but has failed to see the true ramifications of its own replacement theology and totalizing eschatology. Until the Church disengages from theologies of replacement and views of the Last Days that import the consummation of the world into the present Church as a totality, Christian theology has little hope for authentic and transformative dialogue with the Jewish people.

It may seem absurd that in this day and age we would require a theological project that re-evaluates the Church's view of God's covenant with the Jewish people and the relation of eschatological presumptions connected with that covenant, but this book clearly shows that negative, supersessionist, and triumphalist views are either implicitly or directly held in both contemporary theology and among the hierarchy of the Church. Overall, this book is a remedial project meant for intra-Christian theological conversation, so that theologians may more fully and self-critically engage the crucial, ethically mandated formulation of a positive Christian theology of Judaism. My hope is that this work will be used by experts in the field of interreligious dialogue, so their work may be advanced, by offering a comparative and critical theological foundation for their contributions.

Notes

1. Reuther, *Faith and Fratricide*, 246.
2. Jonathan Karp and Adam Sutcliffe, eds., *Philosemitism in History* (New York: Cambridge University Press, 2011), 108, n. 81.
3. Ruether, *Faith and Fratricide*, 246.
4. Soulen, *The God of Israel and Christian Theology*, 181, n. 6.
5. Ibid.
6. Vlach, *Has the Church replaced Israel?*, 16.
7. In early Christian theology and in the New Testament, the term "economy" (οἰκονομία) refers to the management, handling or disposition of God in reference to the divine interactions in the history of creation, redemption, and consummation, for all of Creation.
8. Melito and Alistair Stewart-Sykes, *On Pascha*, 48.
9. Soulen, *The God of Israel and Christian Theology*, 29.
10. Riddlebarger, *A Case for Amillennialism*, 118.
11. Scott Bader-Saye, *Church and Israel after Christendom*, 58.
12. "In the perspective of the gospel, Israel has by no means become 'like all the nations.'" Moltmann, *The Way of Jesus Christ*, 35.
13. Moltmann, *The Coming of God*, 156.
14. Robert Jenson states "until the Last Judgment and our resurrection, Christ has not yet come in the way that fully consummates Israel's history." Robert W. Jenson, *Systematic Theology*, vol. 2 (New York: Oxford University Press, 2001), 336.
15. Knight, *The Eschatological Economy: Time and the Hospitality of God*, 65.
16. S. Leyla Gürkan, *The Jews as a Chosen People: Tradition and Transformation* (New York: Routledge, 2009), 71.
17. See Iannuzzi, *The Triumph of God's Kingdom in the Millennium and End Times*, 40.
18. Weber, "Millennialism," 365.
19. "The name Jesus Christ may thus not unreasonably be said to contain internal reference to the name YHWH and to the triune shape of the evangelical history as this history is packed into the title Christ. The resurrection is the resurrection not of an individual, but of Israel, and by it Israel is vindicated and established." Knight, *The Eschatological Economy: Time and the Hospitality of God*, 66.
20. Robert W. Jenson, "You Wonder Where the Spirit Went," *Pro Ecclesia* 2, no. 3 (1993): 300–302.
21. Moltmann, *The Church in the Power of the Spirit*, 133–196. Moltmann states ". . . we shall then no longer be able to see co-operation between Christians and non-Christians in their endeavors to free the world from misery, violence and despair as purely fortuitous and without theological significance. They too are made possible and brought about by the Holy Spirit, who purposes life and not death." (192).
22. Ibid., 138.
23. Ibid., 167.
24. Ireaneus, *Adv. Haer.*, 4.32.1, in Roberts, *et al.*, *Irenaeus and Hippolytus: Ante Nicene Christian Library*.

25 Irenaeus, following Papias, claims that "... for this reason, when about to undergo His sufferings, that He *might declare to Abraham* and those with him the glad tidings of the inheritance being thrown open, after He had given thanks while holding the cup, and had drunk of it, and given it to the disciples, said to them: '*Drink all of it: this is My blood of the new covenant, which shall be shed for many for the remission of sins. But I say unto you, I will not drink henceforth of the fruit of this vine, until that day when I will drink it new with you in my Father's kingdom.*' Matt. 26:27. Thus, then, He will Himself renew the inheritance of the earth ... He promised to drink of the fruit of the vine with His disciples, thus indicating both these points: the inheritance of the earth in which the new fruit of the vine is drunk, and the resurrection in the flesh ... He cannot by any means be understood as drinking of the fruit of the vine when settled down with his above in a super-celestial place; nor, again, are they who drink it devoid of flesh, for to drink of that which flows from the vine pertains to flesh, and not spirit." Irenaeus, *Adv. Haer.*, 5.33.1.
26 Irenaeus, *Adv. Haer.*, 5.32.1, 2.
27 J.D.G. Dunn claims that Irenaeus refers to Israel as the primary subject of blessing and promise, but that the Church is also included: Irenaeus "... cites (33.4) a number of Old Testament prophecies that he interprets as referring to bodily resurrection and the restoration of the people to the land; these and other promises are made *not just to Israel* but also to the Church and the Gentiles." J.D.G. Dunn, *Jews and Christians: The Parting of the Ways*, 266, emphasis mine.
28 B.D. Marshall, "The Trinity," Colin E. Gunton, ed., *The Cambridge Companion to Christian Doctrine* (Cambridge Companions to Religion) (Cambridge and New York: Cambridge University Press, 1997), 93.
29 Soulen, *The God of Israel and Christian Theology*, 133–134, emphasis mine.
30 Ibid., 29.
31 According to amillennial scholars, the way that modern Israel blesses the nations is through their witness of converting to the Church. Riddlebarger, *A Case for Amillennialism*, 222.
32 Van Buren, *A Theology of the Jewish–Christian Religion*, vol. 2, 231.
33 Novak, *Talking with Christians: Musings of a Jewish Theologian*, 82. Biblically speaking, the Council of Jerusalem, as well as the narrative of Acts 21, act as examples of the fact that elements of the Mosaic Law were held in high regard among early Jewish Christians. By contrast, Gentile Christians were not bound by the Mosaic Law.
34 Diprose, *Israel and the Church*, 20–21, emphasis mine. For other scholars who affirm the millenarian view of the election and the continual contribution of Israel to the eschatological consummation, see C.K. Barrett, *The Epistle to the Romans* (New York: Harper & Row, 1957), 225 as quoted in Horner, *Future Israel*, 295, n. 9. Holwerda, in reference to Romans 11:28, confirms God's continued salvific election of modern Israel: "Nowhere in Romans 11 does the apostle withdraw from unbelieving Jewish Israel the reality of being the people of God or the fact of their election." D.E. Holwerda, *Jesus and Israel: One Covenant or Two?* (Grand Rapids, MI: Eerdmans, 1995), 164.
35 Soulen, *The God of Israel and Christian Theology*, 29, emphasis mine.
36 See John W. Marshall, *Parables of War: Reading John's Jewish Apocalypse* (Waterloo, ON: Wilfrid Laurier University Press, 2001). Marshall successfully argues that John's Apocalypse cannot be separated from its antecedents as a Jewish Apocalypse, written in part for a Jewish, non-Christian audience.
37 For a thorough study on the connection between Augustine's amillennialism and the idea of the Jews as an alien race, burdened by the mark of Cain until their future conversion, see Russell Jacoby, *Bloodlust: On the Roots of Violence from Cain and Abel to the Present* (New York: Free Press, 2011), 82–83.

38 Weber, "Millennialism," in Walls, *The Oxford Handbook of Eschatology*, 368.
39 Melanie Phillips, "Christians who hate Jews," *The Spectator* (February 16, 2002), 1. Cf. Horner, *Future Israel*, 358.
40 Rikk Watts, "Israel and Salvation," in McDermott, *Oxford Handbook of Evangelical Theology*, 178–179. Cf. Diprose, who states that Augustine believed that "Israel's eschatological hopes were figurative . . . now the exclusive inheritance of the Church . . ." Diprose, *Israel and the Church*, 162.
41 Harrison, "The Liturgy and 'Supersessionism,'" 1.
42 See Philip A. Cunningham, *A Story of Shalom: The Calling of Christians and Jews by a Covenanting God* (Studies in Judaism and Christianity) (Mahwah, NJ: Paulist Press, 2001), 4.
43 *Lumen Gentium*, §9.
44 Benedict XVI, *Jesus of Nazareth*, 41.
45 Ratzinger, *Many Religions, One Covenant*, 63, emphasis mine.
46 Maximilian Heinrich Heim, *Joseph Ratzinger: Life in the Church and Living Theology: Fundamentals of Ecclesiology with Reference to Lumen Gentium* (San Francisco, CA: Ignatius Press, 2007), 507.
47 Stephen T. Davis, Daniel Kendall, and Gerald O'Collins, eds., *The Trinity: An Interdisciplinary Symposium on the Trinity* (New York: Oxford University Press, 2002), 195. See in this text William P. Alston's critique of this view of substance metaphysics, pointing to nuances in Aristotle's philosophy.
48 R. Kendall Soulen, "YHWH the Triune God." *Modern Theology* 15, no. 1(January 1999): 25–54, at 30.
49 Ibid., 50.
50 Ibid., 64.
51 Ibid., emphasis mine.
52 Christopher M. Leighton, "Holocaust Theology," in Kessler and Wenborn, *A Dictionary of Jewish–Christian Relations*, 194.
53 Jeong Koo Jeon, *Covenant Theology: John Murray's and Meredith G. Kline's Response to the Historical Development of Federal Theology in Reformed Thought* (Lanham, MD: University Press of America, 2004), 232, emphasis mine.
54 Geerhardus Vos, *Biblical Theology: Old and New Testaments* (Eugene, OR: Wipf & Stock, 2003), 121–122.
55 Jacob Neusner, *Rabbinic Judaism: The Theological System* (Boston, MA: Brill, 2003), 122.
56 The term "sacred mountain" has a threefold reference in the Hebrew Bible: Eden, Sinai, and Zion (Jerusalem).
57 See Joseph Cardinal Ratzinger, *God is near Us: The Eucharist, the Heart of Life*, ed. Stephan Otto Horn (San Francisco, CA: Ignatius Press, 2003), 59.
58 Zenger, "The Covenant that was Never Revoked: The Foundations of a Christian Theology of Judaism," in *The Catholic Church and the Jewish People*, 95.
59 ". . . the risen, glorified Christ never declared that His Jewishness would ever be abandoned, though a supersessionist hermeneutic would tend to require this." Horner, *Future Israel*, 192.
60 Ibid.
61 Diprose, *Israel and the Church*, 182.
62 Ibid., 168.
63 David Novak, "The Covenant in Rabbinic Thought," in Korn, *Two Faiths, One Covenant?: Jewish and Christian Identity in the Presence of the Other*, 65–80.
64 Vlach, *Has the Church Replaced Israel?*, 13.
65 Soulen, *The God of Israel and Christian Theology*, 30.
66 See Origen, *Con. Cel.*, 4.22.
67 Couch, *Dictionary of Premillennial Theology*, 107.

68 Vlach, *Has the Church Replaced Israel?*, 200.
69 Moltmann, *The Way of Jesus Christ*, 35, emphasis mine.
70 See Hippolytus, *Treatise against the Jews* 6, *ANF* 5:220, Lactantius, *The Divine Institutes* 4.11, *ANF* 7:109, Justin Martyr, *Dialogue With Trypho* 11, *ANF* 1:200, Tertullian, *An Answer to the Jews*, chapter 3.
71 Bader-Say, *Church and Israel after Christendom*, 110.
72 Vlach, "Rejection then Hope: The Church's Doctrine of Israel in the Patristic Era," 56.
73 Mcconnell, *The Bones that Lived Again*, 41.
74 Origen, *Con. Cel.*, 4.22, *ANF* 4:506.
75 Olson, *The Westminster Handbook to Evangelical Theology*, 146.
76 Martin Luther, "On the Jews and Their Lies," in *The Works: Martin Luther* (Coconut Creek, FL: Packard Technologies, 2004), 47:138–139, emphasis mine. Luther was so convinced that the only good that could come from a Jewish person was conversion to the Church that he devalued the Jewish life completely: "If a Jew, not converted a heart, were to ask baptism at my hands, I would take him to the bridge, tie a stone around his neck, and hurl him into the river . . ." Ibid., cccliv.
77 "Like the medieval Church before him, Luther rejected a future millennial reign and interpreted Revelation 20 as a description of the historical Church rather than the end of history." John R. Frank, "Reformation Amillennialism: Salvation Now, Salvation Always," *Christian History and Biography* no. 61 (1999): 6–12, 8.
78 Haynes, *Reluctant Witnesses*, 33.
79 Kevin Madigan, "Augustine of Hippo," in Levy, *Anti-Semitism*, 44, emphasis mine.
80 Haynes, *Reluctant Witnesses*, 32.
81 Magne Sæbø, ed., *Hebrew Bible/Old Testament I: From the Beginning to the Middle Ages (until 1300), Part 2: The Middle Ages* (Göttingen: Vandenhoeck & Ruprecht, 2000), 50–51.
82 Allan D. Fitzgerald, "Jews and Judaism," in Allan D. Fitzgerald, ed., *Augustine through the Ages: An Encyclopedia* (Grand Rapids, MI: Eerdmans, 1999), 471.
83 Saint Augustine, *On Christian Teaching* (New York: Oxford University Press, 1999), 3:114–115.
84 "Our Lord, seeing the conduct of the Jews not to be at all in keeping with the teaching of the prophets, inculcated by a parable that the kingdom of God would be taken from them, and given to the converts from heathenism." Origen, *Con. Cel.*, 2.5, *ANF* 4:431.
85 See notes in Thomas Aquinas, *Catena Aurea: Commentary on the Four Gospels, Collected out of the Works of the Fathers,* Volume 1: *Gospel of St. Matthew* (New York: Cosimo Classics, 2013), Matthew 21.
86 For a rebuttal of the supersessionist reading of Matthew 21:43, see Davies and Allison, *A Critical and Exegetical Commentary On the Gospel According to Saint Matthew*, 189 and Boring, "The Gospel of Matthew: Introduction, Commentary, and Reflections," in *The New Interpreter's Bible*, 415. Cf. David L. Turner, "Matthew 21:43 and the Future of Israel," *Bibliotheca Sacra* 159, no. 633 (2002): 56.
87 Madigan, "Augustine of Hippo," in Levy, *Anti-Semitism*, 44.
88 Soulen, *The God of Israel and Christian Theology*, 171.
89 Moltmann, *The Church in the Power of the Spirit*, 144–145.
90 Ibid., 147.
91 Douglas H. Knight, *The Eschatological Economy: Time and the Hospitality of God*, 66.
92 Madigan and Levenson, *Resurrection: The Power of God for Christians and Jews*, 14.
93 Moltmann, *The Church in the Power of the Spirit*, 145, emphasis mine.

94 Mal Couch, ed., *An Introduction to Classical Hermeneutics: A Guide to the History and Practice of Biblical Interpretation* (Grand Rapids, MI: Kregel Academic & Professional, 2000), 227.
95 Barry Horner, *Future Israel: Why Christian Anti-Judaism Must Be Challenged* (Nashville, TN: B&H Academic, 2007), 206.
96 S. Mark Heim traces three general themes that make up the Christian conception of salvation: "... justification (righting relation with God), sanctification (righting human relations), and eternal life (restoring the relation with nature)." S. Mark Heim, *The Depth of the Riches: A Trinitarian Theology of Religious Ends* (Grand Rapids, MI: Eerdmans, 2001), 67.
97 B. Moaz, "People, land and Torah," in *The Land of Promise*, ed. P. Johnston and P. Walker (Downers Grove, IL: IVP, 2000), 196.
98 Pawlikowski, "Land as an Issue in Christian–Jewish Dialogue," 199.
99 Moltmann, *The Coming of God*, 135.
100 Jeffrey S. Siker, *Disinheriting the Jews: Abraham in Early Christian Controversy* (Louisville, KY: Westminster John Knox Press, 1991), 178.
101 Moltmann, *The Coming of God*, 149.
102 Paul T. Butler, *Approaching the New Millennium: An Amillennial Look at A.D. 2000* (Joplin, MO: College Press, 1998), 133.
103 Soulen, *The God of Israel and Christian Theology*, 165. Soulen states that Jesus' resurrection was a confirmation of God's victory and the function of ultimate blessing over curse.
104 Robert W. Jenson, *Systematic Theology*, Vol. 1: *The Triune God* (New York: Oxford University Press, 2001), 76. See also Michael Oppenheim, *Speaking/writing of God: Jewish Philosophical Reflections on the Life with Others* (Albany, NY: State Univ of New York Press, 1997), 156.
105 Feinberg tells us that "In the NT ... even after Israel rejects Christ, a future for Israel is still promised." S. Lewis Johnson and John S. Feinberg, *Continuity and Discontinuity: Perspectives on the Relationship between the Old and New Testaments: Essays in Honor of S. Lewis Johnson, Jr.* (Westchester, IL: Crossway Books, 1988), 83.
106 Moltmann, *The Church in the Power of the Spirit*, 147.
107 Whalen, "Israel," in Landes, *Encyclopedia of Millennialism and Millennial Movements*, 340.
108 "The Role of Israel," in Gundry and Bock, *Three Views on the Millennium and Beyond*, 150–155.
109 Paul Enns, "Millennial Interpretation of Ezekiel 36–37," in Couch, *Dictionary of Premillennial Theology*, 112–113. Cf. Ervin R. Starwalt, "Eschatology of Ezekiel," in ibid., 113–114.
110 Soulen, "YHWH the Triune God," 30, emphasis in the original.
111 Jonas, *The Gnostic Religion: The Message of the Alien God & the Beginnings of Christianity*, 137.
112 Woodrow Whidden, Jerry Moon, and John W. Reeve, *The Trinity: Understanding God's Love, His Plan of Salvation, and Christian Relationships* (Hagerstown, MD: Review & Herald Pub Assn, 2002), 130.
113 Moll, *The Arch-Heretic Marcion*, 44.
114 G.E. Wright, *God Who Acts, Biblical Theology as Recital* (London: SCM, 1952), 16.
115 C.R. North, *The Old Testament Interpretation of History* (London: The Epworth Press, 1946), 149.
116 Jeffrey C.K. Goh, *Christian Tradition Today: A Postliberal Vision of Church and World* (Louvain: Peeters, 2001), 544, n. 214. When Goh tells us that Marcionite views became "persuasive in ecclesiology," he means that the persuasion continued up

The messianic kingdom 279

through the Vatican II document, *Nostra Aetate*, which he subsequently quotes as a departure from Marcion's logic.
117 E.C. Blackman, *Marcion and His Influence* (London: Wipf & Stock, 2004), 44, 51, 138.
118 Moll, *The Arch-heretic Marcion*, 23.
119 E. Glenn Hinson, "Canon," in Watson E. Mills, *Mercer Dictionary of the Bible* (Macon, GA: Mercer University Press, 2001), 131–133.
120 Knight, *The Eschatological Economy: Time and the Hospitality of God*, 65.
121 As Soulen more emphatically states it in reference to the "standard model of structural supersessionism": "The mode renders the center of the Hebrew Scriptures . . . ultimately indecisive." Soulen, *The God of Israel and Christian Theology*, 16.
122 Tertullian directed his defense of millenarianism toward Marcion specifically: "We do confess that a kingdom is promised to us upon the earth . . . it will be after the resurrection for a thousand years in the divinely built city of Jerusalem." Tertullian, *Adv. Marc.*, 3.25.
123 Ibid., 4.6., emphasis mine.
124 Soulen, "YHWH the Triune God," 31, emphasis in original.
125 Willem A. VanGemeren, *Interpreting the Prophetic Word: An Introduction to the Prophetic Literature of the Old Testament* (Grand Rapids, MI: Zondervan, 1996), 85.
126 See Knight, *The Eschatological Economy: Time and the Hospitality of God*, 67.
127 Against this idea, Moltmann insists that those who wish to be followers of Jesus are to interpret the world in light of God's future for it.
128 Soulen, "YHWH the Triune God," 30.
129 It is interesting to note that Origen, attempting to distance himself from the teachings of Marcion, claimed that Marcion "prohibited allegorical interpretations of the Scripture." Origen, *Commentary on the Gospel of Matthew* 15.3. In contradictory statements to Origen's, multiple early writers including Epiphanius of Salamas and Tertullian claim that Marcion's biblical hermeneutic was in fact *almost exclusively allegorical* (like Origen's). See Tertullian, *Adversus Marcionem*, 1.2.
130 Soulen, *The God of Israel and Christian Theology*, 110.
131 McConnell, writing about certain typical means of Scriptural exegesis, claims that ". . . amillennialism is the *direct and inescapable conclusion* of supersessionism." McConnell, *The Bones that Lived Again*, 41, emphasis mine.
132 Soulen, *The God of Israel*, 19.
133 Soulen, "YHWH the Triune God," 30.
134 Soulen, *The God of Israel and Christian Theology*, 131.
135 Jürgen Moltmann, *The Spirit of Life* (Minneapolis, MN: Fortress Press, 1992), 55–56.
136 Moltmann, *The Coming of God*, 305.
137 Soulen, *The God of Israel and Christian Theology*, 132.
138 Moltmann, *The Way of Jesus Christ*, 11–13.
139 Moltmann, *Theology of Hope*, 18.
140 Moltmann, *God in Creation* (London: SCM Press, 1985), 92; 121.
141 Steven L. McAvoy, "Eschatological Implications of the Covenant," in Couch, *Dictionary of Premillennial Theology*, 32.
142 Soulen, "YHWH the Triune God," 30.
143 Moltmann, *The Church in the Power of the Spirit*, 148.
144 Ibid., 146.
145 Ibid., 134, emphasis mine.
146 Ibid., 148.
147 Ibid., 351.
148 Moltmann, *The Coming of God*, 148.

149 Moltmann's view is consistent with rabbinic interpretations of Deutero-Isaiah insofar as the messianic kingdom is conceived as "... an era of universal peace and recognition of Israel's God by all the nations." Benjamin D. Sommer, "Isaiah," in Judith R. Baskin, ed., *The Cambridge Dictionary of Judaism and Jewish Culture* (New York: Cambridge University Press, 2011), 282.
150 Moltmann, *The Coming of God*, 148.
151 Ibid.
152 Moltmann, *The Church in the Power of the Spirit*, 135.
153 "Eschatology is always only specific as relational eschatology." Ibid.,134.
154 For Moltmann's commentary on Rosenzweig, particularly in the two works associated with millenarianism, see *The Church in the Power of the Spirit*, 161, 149, 370, 379, 380, and 381, and *The Coming of God*, xiii, 30, 32, 33ff., 36, 38ff., 139, 141, 333, 345 nn.78, 81, 358 n.22, 380 n 101, 383 n. 30.
155 Stéphane Mosès, *The Angel of History: Rosenzweig, Benjamin, Scholem* (Stanford, CA: Stanford University Press, 2009), 40–41, emphasis mine.
156 Moltmann, *The Church in the Power of the Spirit*, 134, emphasis in the original.
157 The rabbinic interpretations of eschatology are still highly influential for Jewish belief today, but certainly not universally held. Dvora E. Weisberg, "Rabbinic Hermeneutics," in Baskin, ed., *The Cambridge Dictionary of Judaism and Jewish Culture*, 508. Moltmann sees the eschaton not as "Christ's future coming," but as "the future of Christ." Such a future brings surprise, thus we are conditioned by contingency, Se Stephen Chan, "Hermeneutics of Hope: A Dialogical Study of Paul Ricoeur and Jürgen Moltmann," 5, found at http://fac-staff.seattleu.edu/schan/web/PaperPDF/Moltmann&Ricoeur_Hope.pdf.
158 Steven T. Katz, ed., *The Late Roman-Rabbinic Period*, Vol. 4 of *The Cambridge History of Judaism* (New York: Cambridge University Press, 2006), 200.
159 There is ambiguity as to whether this is one messiah, or the coming of a first Mashiach ben Jospeph, followed by the eternal Mashiach ben David. See conversely, some rabbinical commentary focused on *4 Ezra* and the *Apocalypse of Baruch* envisions a "messiah to rule forever and peace and joy will rule over the whole earth." Katz, ed., *The Late Roman-Rabbinic Period*, vol. 4 of *The Cambridge History of Judaism*, 1061.
160 Ulla, *BTSanh.* 98a. Some Christian scholars have conceived of a portion of the millennial kingdom as involving suffering. For example, Karl Barth claimed the millennium of Revelation 20 is "... by no means an island of the blessed, but the kingdom of saints and martyrs built over the bottomless pit in which the old dragon is chained." "The Problem of Ethics Today" in Karl Barth, *The Word of God and the Word of Man* (Rockport, MA: Peter Smith, 1978), 158–160.
161 "The Holy Temple will in the future be re-established before the establishment of the kingdom of David." *Ma'aser Sheni 29*. There are likewise many aspects of the rabbinic view of the messianic age based on *Exod. R.* 15:21 that are agreeable to both Christians and Jews: that the messiah was present at the creation of the world (*Pes. Rab.* 152b., *Pes.* 54a. For the rabbis, this statement does not mean that the messiah is divine), the messiah's advent will "illumine the world", running water and fruit from trees in Jerusalem will be used for the "healing of the nations," (Cf. Revelation 22:2), Jerusalem will be rebuilt with sapphire, (Revelation 9:17, 21:19–20), peace will reign throughout the land, and weeping, wailing, and death will cease. (Cf. Revelation 21:4). The imagery of grapes growing large and abundantly is also present (*Ket.* 111b, *Shab.* 30b, Papias, *Frag.* 4), among images of the restoration Paradise in reference to nature and humans.
162 Moltmann, *The Coming of God*, 198.
163 Harvie, *Jürgen Moltmann's Ethics of Hope*, 155, n. 36.

164 "Israel has an enduring 'salvific calling,' parallel to the Church of the Gentiles, for God remains true to his promise." Moltmann, *The Coming of God*, 197.
165 Ibid., 221.
166 Moltmann, *The Church in the Power of the Spirit*, 145.
167 Moltmann, *The Coming of God*, 151.
168 Ibid., 197–198.
169 Ibid., emphasis mine.
170 See Peter Novak, *Original Christianity: A New Key to Understanding the Gospel of Thomas and other Lost Scriptures* (Charlottesville, VA: Hampton Roads Publishing, 2005), 219–220.
171 Moltmann, *The Way of Jesus Christ*, 32–33.
172 Moltmann, *The Church in the Power of the Spirit*, 148.
173 Moltmann, as quoted in Otto, "The Resurrection in Jürgen Moltmann," 87.
174 Moltmann, *The Coming of God*, 198.
175 See Moltmann's treatment of J.T. Beck, *Die Vollendung des Reiches Gottes: Separatabdruck aus der Christlichen Glaubenslehre* (Gutersloh: Gütersloher Verlagshaus, 1887), 63f. in *The Coming of God*, 199. Cf. Moltmann, *The Way of Jesus Christ*, 35–36.
176 David Aune expresses the typical amillennial, supersessionist interpretation of the passage: "David Aune lists the popular conclusions as to the identity of the 144,000:(1) a remnant of Jewish Christians, (2) all Christians including both Jewish and Gentile Christians, (3) Christian martyrs." Aune as quoted in Resseguie, *Revelation of John*, 137.
177 Christopher R. Smith, "The Portrayal of the Church as the New Israel in the Names and Order of the Tribes in Revelation 7:5–8," *JSNT 39* (1990): 111–118.
178 The term *ethnos* typically refers to non-Jews—the Gentiles, in distinction from the tribes of Israel.
179 Rowland, "The Book of Revelation," 620. Cf. Isa 10:20; Rom 9:27 and Rom 11:25–26.
180 Moltmann, *The Coming of God*, 151.
181 Adela Yarbro Collins, *Crisis and Catharsis: The Power of the Apocalypse* (Philadelphia, PA: The Westminster Press, 1984), 128.
182 Rowland, "The Book of Revelation: Introduction, Commentary, and Reflections," in *The New Interpreter's Bible*, Vol. 12, 709.
183 Thomas C. Nixon, *The Time in the End in the Book of Revelation* (Miami, FL: 1st Book Library, 2002), 38.
184 See Christopher Rowland, "The Theology of Liberation," in Christopher Rowland, ed., *The Cambridge Companion to Liberation Theology*, 2nd ed. (New York: Cambridge University Press, 2007), 12.
185 For a further explanation of this eschatological scheme, which is commensurate with both Revelation and Paul in 1 Corinthians 15, see Scott M. Lewis, *So That God May Be All in All: The Apocalyptic Message of 1 Corinthians 15, 12–34*, 55, esp. n. 100.
186 Elisabeth Schüssler Fiorenza, *Revelation: Vision of a Just World* (Minneapolis, MN: Fortress Press, 1998), 67, emphasis mine. Fiorenza concludes that Revelation 7 is referring to all of national Israel.
187 Levenson, *Resurrection and the Restoration of Israel*, xiii, 214.
188 Paul Helm and Carl R. Trueman, eds., *The Trustworthiness of God: Perspectives on the Nature of Scripture* (Grand Rapids, MI: Eerdmans, 2002), 105.
189 *Lumen Gentium* 16; *Gaudium et Spes* 22; *Ad Gentes* 7.
190 *Catechism of the Catholic Church*, VI, § 1045 at http://www.catholicculture.org/culture/library/catechism/index.cfm?recnum=327. It is significant that the Catechism claims that those who are "united with Christ" will form the eschatological community of the redeemed. May an individual or group be "united with Christ" without being

282   *Millenarianism and post-supersessionism*

a member of the Church? Further, the Catechism, quoting Irenaeus, claims that the earth will be returned to its "original state," pointing back to the Garden of Eden. Cf. St. Irenaeus, *Adv. haeres.*, 5, 32,1 PG 7/2, 210. Though there is no single, unified "Jewish eschatology," the eschatological concept that the age to come is to be a return to Eden is deeply imbedded in Jewish rabbinical commentary. Simcha Paull Raphael, *Jewish Views of the Afterlife*, 248.
191 Bauckham, *The Theology of Jürgen Moltmann*, 149.
192 Note that Moltmann views both Revelation chapters 7 and 20 as depicting a millenarian reality.
193 Moltmann, *The Coming of God*, 198, emphasis mine.
194 Moltmann, *The Church in the Power of the Spirit*, 146.
195 Katz and Israel, eds., *Sceptics, Millenarians, and Jews*, 179–180.
196 Moltmann, *The Coming of God*, 150.
197 Ibid., 151.
198 N.T. Wright, "Romans," in *The New Interpreter's Bible*, 689.
199 Vlach, *Has the Church Replaced Israel?*, 75. Cf. the writings of the Eastern Church philosopher Aristides in *Apologia 2*, and also *Ep. Diogn.*, 1.
200 Mark S. Kinzer, *Postmissionary Messianic Judaism: Redefining Christian Engagement with the Jewish People*, 12.
201 Gabriel Moran, *Uniqueness: Problem or Paradox in Jewish and Christian Traditions* (Maryknoll, NJ: Orbis Books, 1992), 64–70.
202 Kinzer, *Postmissionary Messianic Judaism*, 140.
203 Ibid., 141. Kinzer points to 1 Corinthians 10:27; 1 Corinthians 6:6; 2 Corinthians 6:14–15; and 1 Corinthians 7:12–15 as evidence that Paul's use of the term "unbeliever" is restricted to non-Jewish, non-Christian Gentiles. Kinzer likewise points out that though Paul speaks of a "veiling of the Gospel" among the Jewish people, causing a kind of spiritual "hardening," Paul still has respect for Jewish religion and sees a value in it—there is no "veiling of the Torah" for the Jewish people. The "hardening" that Paul refers to, more often than not, is a "hardening" toward Gentiles becoming engrafted into the elective covenant with the God of Abraham, Isaac, and Jacob.
204 N.T. Wright, "On Becoming the Righteousness of God" in *Pauline Theology*, ed. Jouette M. Bassler, David M. Hay, E. Elizabeth Johnson, 4 vols. (Minneapolis, MN: Fortress, 1991–1997), 2:205.
205 J. Beker, *Paul the Apostle* (Philadelphia, PA: Augsburg Fortress Publishers, 1984), 334. The scenario of the salvation and consummation of the Jewish people, for Paul, is entirely an eschatological prospect. The concept of delivery from Zion and the removal of the corporate sins of the people Israel, as expressed in Isaiah. 59:20, is a thoroughly Jewish concept. Cf. *b. Sanh.* 98b; *Pesiq. Rab Kah*, Supplement 6:5, and William Horbury, *Jewish Messianism and the Cult of Christ* (Norwich: SCM Press, 1998), 81.
206 This theological reading of Romans would assume an application of Rosenzweig's concept, yet from a Christian perspective toward Judaism. D.A. Carson writes: "On the Jewish side, the 'two-covenants' terminology is largely identified with Franz Rosenzweig. He argues that Christianity may providentially be doing things that Judaism cannot do; that the daughter is not necessarily the enemy of the mother; that the uniqueness of Israel's contribution does not automatically negate the uniqueness of Christianity's contribution." D.A. Carson, *The Gagging of God* (Grand Rapids, MI: Zondervan, 2002), 340. Moltmann claims it is part of God's salvific will for the Jews to reject the Gospel. See Moltmann, *The Way of Jesus Christ*, 35.
207 Siker, *Disinheriting the Jews*, 69.
208 Siker claims that "... for Paul, there are really two groups of 'descendants of Abraham,' both according to the flesh and according to faith in Christ." Ibid., 70.

209 Scott, *Restoration: Old Testament, Jewish and Christian Perspectives*, 525.
210 N.T. Wright, *Climax of the Covenant* (Minneapolis, MN: Fortress Press, 1993), 250.
211 Wagner, *Heralds of the Good News*, 279.
212 Joseph P. Schultz, *Judaism and the Gentile Faiths: Comparative Studies in Religion* (Rutherford, NJ: Fairleigh Dickinson University Press 1981), 210.
213 Scott, *Restoration: Old Testament, Jewish and Christian Perspectives*, 522.
214 Douglas J. Moo, *The Epistle to the Romans* (Grand Rapids, MI: Eerdmans, 1996), 111, emphasis mine.
215 Claude Cox and Albert Pietersma, eds., *De Septuaginta: Studies in Honour of John William Wevers on His Sixty-Fifth Birthday* (Mississauga, ON: BenBen Publications, 1984), 238.
216 H.L. Ellison, *The Mystery of Israel* (Grand Rapids, MI: Eerdmans, 1966), 157.
217 Hebrew Scripture represents the Redeemer both coming "to" and "from" Zion. Cf. Psalms 14:7; 20:2; 53:6; 110:2; 128:5; 134:3; 135:21; Isaiah 2:3; Joel 3:16; Amos 1:2. For a thorough study of the motif of God or the messiah coming "out of Zion" in relation to Judaism, millennial thought, and its influence on early Christian scriptural sources, see VanderKam, *The Jewish Apocalyptic Heritage in Early Christianity*: Compendia Rerum Iudaicarum Ad Novum Testamentum. Section 3: Jewish Traditions in Early Christian Literature. Assen, Netherlands, Minneapolis, MI: Van Gorcum and Fortress Press, 1996, 110; 112; 120. Cf. Shiu-Lun Shum, *Paul's Use of Isaiah in Romans: A Comparative Study of Paul's Letter to the Romans and the Sibylline and Qumran Sectarian Texts* (Tübingen: Abm Komers, 2002), 238. It is worthy to note that Isaiah 24:23 likewise presents the theme of "the Lord" reigning from Zion: "Then the moon that be confounded, and the sun ashamed, when the Lord of hosts shall reign in Mount Zion." As Karl Barth posits, the advent of the deliverer suggests a central place for Israel in history: "Those who are exalted by Him are Israel!" and also the centrality of the concept that the deliverer's coming will be "from the earth," or "out of Zion": "The fact that He goes out *from Zion* means that He has come into ... the world." Karl Barth, *Church Dogmatics* (London: T&T Clark International, 2004), 301.
218 Oswald T. Allis, *Prophecy and the Church* (Eugene, OR: Wipf & Stock, 2001), 305.
219 For the prevalence of these concepts in pre and post Second Temple Judaism, see Albert L.A. Hogeterp, *Expectations of the End: A Comparative Tradition-Historical Study of Eschatological, Apocalyptic, and Messianic Ideas in the Dead Sea Scrolls and the New Testament* (Leiden: Brill, 2009), 106–113. For Paul's borrowing of these Jewish eschatological themes and his understanding of the concept of "salvation" as the direct intervention of the divine in the history of the "age to come," see "The Eschatological Elements in the Messianism of Paul," in William Raney Harper, Ernest Dewitt Burton, Shailer Matthews, *The Biblical World*, Vol. 19 (Chicago, IL: University of Chicago Press, 1902), 282–287. For the concept of resurrection of the dead deeply imbedded in pre-modern Judaism and still alive in modern orthodox Judaism, see the work of Jewish biblical scholar Jon Levenson in *Resurrection and the Restoration of Israel*, 1, 3, 7, 11, 15, and 18–21.
220 Saucy, *The Kingdom of God in the Teaching of Jesus*, 225 and Lyford Paterson Edwards, *The Transformation of Early Christianity from an Eschatological to a Socialized Movement* (Menasha, WI: George Banta Publishing, 1919), 5. Cf. R.L. Wilken, "Early Chiliasm, Jewish Messianism, and the Idea of the Holy Land," *HTR* (1986), 218–307.
221 Ruth H. Bloch, *Visionary Republic: Millennial Themes in American Thought, 1756–1800* (Cambridge: Cambridge University Press, 1988), 145.
222 See Fitzmyer as quoted in Robert Jewett, *Romans: A Commentary*, ed. Eldon Jay Epp (Minneapolis, MN: Fortress Press, 2007), 62.

284 *Millenarianism and post-supersessionism*

223 J.R. Daniel Kirk, *Unlocking Romans: Resurrection and the Justification of God* (Grand Rapids, MI: Eerdmans, 2008), 192.
224 Moltmann, *The Coming of God*, 198. Moltmann argues that prior to the establishment of this messianic kingdom, a Gospel will be preached ". . . which calls people, no longer to the Church but to the kingdom—converts no longer to the Christian faith but to hope for the kingdom." Moltmann, *The Coming of God*, 199.
225 Moltmann, *Theology of Hope*, 10. Cf. Bauckham, *The Theology of Jürgen Moltmann*, 16.
226 Joseph A. Fitzmyer, *The Anchor Bible*, vol. 33: *Romans: A New Translation with Introduction and Commentary* (New Haven, CT: Yale University Press, 2008, 1993), 619. Hereafter cited as Fitzmyer, *Romans*.
227 Joseph Sievers, "God's Gifts and Call are Irrevocable: The Reception of Romans 11:29 through the centuries and Christian–Jewish Relations," in Cristina Grenholm, *Reading Israel in Romans: Legitimacy and Plausibility of Divergent Interpretations* (Harrisburg, PA: Trinity Press International, 2000), 153, emphasis mine.
228 Ruether, *Faith and Fratricide*, 106.
229 Daniel J. Harrington, *Paul on the Mystery of Israel* (Collegeville, MN: Liturgical Press, 1992), 64.
230 Krister Stendahl, *Final Account: Paul's Letter to the Romans*, 1st Fortress Press ed. (Minneapolis, MN: Fortress Press, 1995), 38.
231 Ibid., 44.
232 See F. Mussner, *Tractate on the Jews: The Significance of Judaism for Christian Faith* (London: SPCK; Philadelphia, PA: Fortress, 1984), 34; J.G. Gager, *The Origins of Anti-Semitism: Attitudes toward Judaism in Pagan and Christian Antiquity* (Oxford and New York: Oxford University Press, 1983), 261–264; B. Mayer, *Unter Gottes Heilsratschluss: Prädestinationsaussagen bei Paulus*, FB 15 (Würzburg: Echter-Verlag, 1974), 280–300.
233 Fitzmyer, *Romans*, 619.
234 Moltmann attempted to maintain a Christological basis that was faithful to the Christian tradition without negating the reality of conditioned existence on the part of the Church: ". . . ecclesiology can and must recognize the relativity of its subject and its own standpoint, without subsiding into mere relativity . . . Its worldly relationship is '. . . only in relation to other particulars.'" Bauckham, *The Theology of Jürgen Moltmann*, 126. Cf. Moltmann, *The Coming of God*, 11 and *The Church in the Power of the Spirit*, 155–157.
235 L. Gaston, "For All the Believers: The Inclusion of Gentiles as the Ultimate Goal of Torah in Romans," in *Paul and Torah* (Vancouver, BC: University of British Columbia Press, 1987), 130. Cf. Benjamin Schliesser, *Abraham's Faith in Romans 4: Paul's Concept of Faith in Light of the History of Reception of Genesis 15:6* (Tübingen: Mohr Siebeck, 2007), 234.
236 "While Christian worship is not a viable religious choice for Jews, as Jewish theologians we rejoice that, through Christianity, hundreds of millions of people have entered into relationship with the God of Israel." "*Dabru Emet*: A Jewish Statement on Christians and Christianity," §1.
237 Moltmann, *Coming of God*, 304; *The Way of Jesus Christ*, 35. Cf. Ronald B. Mayers, *Evangelical Perspectives: Toward a Biblical Balance* (Lanham, MD: University Press of America, 1987), 174.
238 David F. Ford, "Mending the Metanarrative: A Non-Supersessionist Messiah?" in L. Gregory Jones and James Buckley, eds., *Theology and Eschatology at the Turn of the Millennium* (Malden, MA: Wiley-Blackwell, 2002), 75, emphasis mine.
239 Moltmann distinguishes ". . . between Christ's *messianic rule* over the dead and the living (Rom. 14:9) and his *chiliastic kingdom*, in which the dead (the martyrs) will be raised (I Cor. 15:23; Revelation 20:1–4). Both are provisional compared with the kingdom of glory." Moltmann, *The Trinity and the Kingdom*, 235, n. 44.

240 Moltmann, *The Coming of God*, 150.
241 Ibid., 151, emphasis mine. Moltmann relates this interpretation regarding the resurrection of the Jewish people specifically to Romans 11:15.
242 Ibid.
243 Following Rosenzweig, Moltmann points to the importance of the general eschatological expectation for the future that is consistent with the experience of both Christians and Jews. For the Jews, it is the weekly Sabbath, in the Sabbath year, and in the Year of Jubilee. For Christians, it is experienced in the liturgical year, in the Sunday of the Lord's Day, and in the high feast days. Ibid., 138. Cf. Rosenzweig, *The Star of Redemption*, xiv, 329–334, 374–376.
244 Moltmann writes that "The promises given to Israel are as yet fulfilled in principle in the coming of the Messiah Jesus, and in him without conditions, and hence universally *endorsed* (II Cor. 1:20); and in the outpouring of the Spirit 'on all flesh' are as yet realized only partially, *pars pro toto*, and in trend. Through the gospel and the Holy Spirit, the divine promises given to Israel are extended to all the nations, for whom there has therefore dawned what Paul calls the time of the gospel—in the language of Maimonides, the *praeparatio messianica*." Ibid., 197.
245 Ibid., 198. In note 138 of the same citation, Moltmann, again referring to Romans 11:15, states that "faith" could hardly be expected of the dead who will rise at the beginning of the millennial reign.
246 Hayes, *Prospects for Post-Holocaust Theology*, 251.
247 Moltmann, *The Coming of God*, 192.
248 Ibid., 194.
249 Moltmann, *The Trinity and the Kingdom*, xv.
250 Bauckham, *The Theology of Jürgen Moltmann*, 149.
251 Ibid.
252 Jürgen Moltmann, *On Human Dignity: Political Theology and Ethics* (Minneapolis, MN: Fortress Press, 2007), 198.
253 Moltmann, *The Church in the Power of the Spirit*, 351. Cf. Bauckham, *The Theology of Jürgen Moltmann*, 149.
254 See Bauckham, *God Will be All in All*, 144; David Wilkinson, *Christian Eschatology and the Physical Universe* (New York: T&T Clark International, 2010), 34.
255 Moltmann, *The Trinity and the Kingdom*, 106; Bauckham, *The Theology of Jürgen Moltmann*, 186.
256 Jürgen Moltmann, *The Crucified God: The Cross of Christ as the Foundation and Criticism of Christian Theology*, 1st Fortress Press ed. (Minneapolis, MN: Fortress Press, 1993), 227.
257 Bauckham, *The Theology of Jürgen Moltmann*, 149.
258 Moltmann, *The Coming of God*, 193. Cf. Karl Barth, *Word of God and the Word of Man*, 138.
259 Ford, "Mending the Metanarrative: A Non-Supersessionist Messiah?," 86. Ford follows the work of Peter Ochs in exploring the possibilities of a view of Jesus Christ that is non-supersessionist. Cf. Peter Ochs, "Abrahamic Theo-politics: A Jewish View," in Peter Scott and William T. Cavanaugh, eds., *The Blackwell Companion to Political Theology* (Malden, MA: Wiley-Blackwell, 2004), 519–534.
260 Canisius Mwandayi, *Death and After-life Rituals in the Eyes of the Shona: Dialogue with Shona Customs in the Quest for Authentic Inculturation* (Bamberg, Germany: University of Bamberg Press, 2011), 64.
261 Leonard Swindler "The Dialogue Decalogue: Ground Rules for Interreligious Dialogue," *Journal of Ecumenical Studies* 20, no. 1 (Winter, 1983): 1–4.

Conclusion

In this book, we began by defining supersessionism as the idea that the Church has replaced Israel in God's economy for salvation and has taken Israel's covenant promises, thus drawing a very close correlation between the Church and the promised kingdom of God, leaving out Judaism's alternative relation to the kingdom. We discerned the three major forms of supersessionism, evaluated it as a hermeneutical and theological problem within the Roman Catholic tradition, and enumerated the ways that it has been challenged in both popular and official Roman Catholic documents since Vatican II. We paid special attention to *Nostra Aetate* (*NA*), its reception, the thought of Pope John Paul II, and the Roman Catholic challenge to critique and overcome supersessionist theology through eschatological and ecclesiological exploration. We introduced the concept that amillennialism oftentimes promotes and enables the view that the Church is currently the kingdom of God on earth, thus undermining and essentially eliminating any consummative and eschatological value associated with the Jewish people of today, in light of God's kingdom. In our thesis, we therefore stated that a return to the Church's original roots in the eschatological, 'Thousand Years' Reign,' millenarian tradition opens up space for the value of the Jewish people and their direct covenantal promises. This is because millenarianism, or chiliasm as it has been labeled, emphasizes that the kingdom has not yet come in the way amillennialists claim it has, and that God has yet to consummate the divine economy regarding Israel. Israel still serves a salvific purpose and witness in the world, regardless of its relation to the Church.

Next, we revisited and defined millenarianism in relation to the New Testament, and especially within the context of the early Church. We argued that millenarianism was widely held as the normative, orthodox position of the Church, exemplified in the writings of many Saints and early Church Fathers. This was the case until certain detractors such as Marcion, Gaius and Origen critiqued millenarianism for various polemical reasons. We proceeded to critique the weaknesses associated with the work of Charles Hill, who has challenged the idea that chiliasm was the normative eschatology of the early Church. We argued that Hill's argument is based primarily on silence, and that ultimately, with the connection of the Roman Catholic Church to the Roman empire, a shift occurred in the Church's normative eschatological and ecclesiological understanding. The "court theologians" such as Eusebius and Tyconius rewrote the Church's eschatology, claiming that the kingdom of God was not a future historical event, but a present historical event—a kind of "hypostatic union"[1] of the Church and State. Though St. Augustine critiqued various elements of the Church–State model, he nonetheless followed the amillennial, historical/presentative/ecclesiastical millenarian schematic established by his predecessors, and insisted both that heaven was a transcendent reality reserved for the holy, and that the Church of earth is indeed the primary, valid manifestation of the messianic kingdom of God, with the baptized taking on the part of those who "reign with Christ" in the present moment. For Augustine, there is still a "not yet," future to the kingdom, but this anticipation of a new kingdom era insists that the era is a-temporal, that the Church is its penultimate, and certainly that it has nothing to do with the Jews, save for their purpose as a "witness people," bearing testimony to the consequences of rejecting Jesus, the messiah.

In Part III, we took on the critical question of whether the original eschatological millenarianism of the Church was ever formally denounced by the Catholic Church since its shift, or ever declared a heresy. Ultimately, we sought to open a crack in what amillennial theologians have declared to be an airtight seal, regarding whether millenarian eschastology may be studied and explored in a positive manner. Though millenarianism has been looked upon with suspicion by the Church since the time of Augustine, no solid evidence suggests that it was ever declared a heresy in the strict sense, or even forbidden as a privately held doctrinal opinion. Using the Vincentian Canon, we applied its principles to the case of millenarianism, and found that no binding pronouncement (or even canon) of an Ecumenical Council, or definitive declaration by a pope has ever mentioned chiliasm directly. The Apostles' Creed itself, the symbol of the faith, was written in its most original form, by ardent chiliasts. The Councils at Nicaea, Rome, Constantinople, and Ephesus, show a pattern whereby amillennial theologians have connected chiliasm to what was the anathematizing of heresies that in fact had nothing to do with the primitive eschatology. At the end of the section, we explored the first papal statement on millenarianism issued by Pope Pius XII in 1944. Prompted by a question issued by the bishops, the pope stated that "mitigated millenarianism cannot be safely taught." We argued that the pope's statement was deeply conditioned by the fact that the Second World War had just ended, and that Hitler had borrowed some of the language and aspects of realized, presentative millenarianism and applied them to his desire to create the "Third Reich." We argued that this single episcopal statement within Catholic history does not justify relegating the original eschatological millenarian paradigm of the Church to the fringes of acceptable doctrine. The *Congregation for the Doctrine of the Faith* latched on to Pius XII's statement regarding millenarianism and influenced the 1997 Catechism (CCC) regarding the mention of the eschatological subject. The CCC paragraph on millennialism appears to target the historical millenarian aspects of liberation theology and some forms of secular or political millennialism, and not the eschatological millenarianism of the early Church, but it conflates the two concepts, adding to the ambiguity inherent in Pope Pius' statement. We ended the chapter by illustrating Pope Benedict XVI's support of a spiritualized, "Eucharistic Millennialism," regardless of the Church's amillennial stance. We argued that Benedict adopted this new eschatological millenarian concept precisely because it assures the sacerdotal power and function of the Catholic hierarchy and clergy. Essentially, we argued that the Church's recent intolerance of the original Christian eschatology is rooted in a desire to maintain that the Roman Catholic Church and its institutional existence are the only valid expressions of God's messianic reign in history. The overall point of both Chapters 2 and 3 was to show, by contrast, that millenarianism is a valid theology for Roman Catholic scholars to explore.

In our final part, we returned to the task of addressing our primary thesis, that while amillennialism either explicitly or implicitly promotes supersessionism, millenarian eschatology is able to envision a post-supersessionist Christian theology of Judaism. We began with a prolegomena to the discussion by seeking to understand some of the Jewish views of the world to come, the resurrection, and the expected messiah, addressing some of the similarities and differences between these Jewish ideas and the Christian millenarian view. We likewise showed how Moltmann's millenarianism is explicitly again a post-supersessionist view through its critique of the amillennialist desire to either incarnate the messianic reign within the historical Church, or push it to the completely transcendent realm. In either case, the Church is as necessary as God's presence itself in reference to Jewish redemption—the Jews are expected either to convert or be condemned. Moltmann rejects the more anti-Jewish elements of the early Church Fathers and ancient and contemporary Christian apocalypticism, and envisions instead a millenarian paradigm whereby the Church is viewed as a provisional entity, witnessing to the coming kingdom alongside Israel. Last, we experimented with a post-supersessionist millenarian exegesis of Revelation 20 and Romans 11, suggesting that each point toward a unified Christian–Jewish messianic kingdom while maintaining the religious particularities of both.

I believe that the threefold goal of this book was accomplished: (1) to show the shift in Roman Catholic theology, after Vatican II, regarding the Church's desire for a post-supersessionist trajectory, specifically using the fields of ecclesiology and eschatology; (2) to detail the ways that eschatological millenarianism was the Church's original eschatology and to safeguard and promote its study among Roman Catholic theologians; and (3) to outline the ways that amillennialism promotes, but millenarianism rejects, the traditions and theological foundations of economic, punitive, and structural supersessionism. We have explored some of the ways in which millenarian eschatology, and the hermeneutical assumptions upon which it is based, opens a space for the Synagogue to be conceived as a valid partner with the Church, awaiting the full manifestation of God's coming kingdom reign.

Roman Catholic theologians should continue on the path encouraged by *NA* in reference to exploring the ways that the covenant that God has established with the Jewish people is irrevocable. In light of the reception of *NA*, from modern Roman Catholic scholars to the significant statements of Pope John Paul II and various Vatican offices, younger Catholic theologians should pick up the mantle and construct eschatological and ecclesiological models that formulate and express the post-supersessionist theology that has been long overdue in the Church. Roman Catholic theologians should also reconsider the traditional, Augustinian amillennial view of the Last Days and open up venues for conversation with the millenarian theological camp, taking that expression seriously as a continuation of the Church's earliest, normative belief system. Understanding that millenarian theologians—ones as well established as Jürgen Moltmann—are not heretics will go a long way in healing the unwarranted reputation of those who hold such convictions regarding Christian eschatology. Theologians are called to discover in new ways the traditional millenarian hermeneutical principles as an exercise in *ad fontes* theology, especially in light of its promise regarding post-supersessionist, Christian theologies of Judaism.

It seems most appropriate to end this book on the subject of God's irrevocable covenant with Israel by using the words of Martin Buber, as he addressed the topic in a dialogue with the Protestant NT scholar, Karl Ludwig Schmidt:

> I do not live far from the city of Worms, to which I also feel bound through the tradition of my forebears; and from time to time I go over there. And when I'm there, I first walk to the cathedral. There you have the harmony of structural members become visible, there is a wholeness in which no part misses the perfection of the whole. I am walking around, envisioning the cathedral in perfect joy. And then I walk over to the Jewish cemetery. It consists of crooked, chopped, formless gravestones, without any direction. I put myself there and then I look up from this confusion to the beautiful harmony, and I feel as if I looked up from Israel to the church. Down here is not a bit of form; here one has only the stones and the ashes under the stones. One has the ashes, even though they may have diminished very much . . . I stood there, was united with the ashes and right across them with the ancestors. This is remembrance of the events with God, which is given to all Jews. The perfection of the Christian *space of God* cannot take me away from this, nothing can take me away from Israel's *time with God*. I stood there and I experienced everything myself, death has befallen me: all the ashes, all the chopping, all the soundless misery is mine; but the covenant has not been revoked. I'm lying on the ground, tumbled like these stones. But I have not been rejected. The cathedral is as it is. The cemetery is as it is. But we have not been rejected.[2]

Notes

1 Though the technical term ὑπόστασις is oftentimes used interchangeably with the concept of "substance," in relation to the divine and human natures of Christ, the term also carries connotations of "subsistence."
2 G. Sauer, "Eine gemeinsame Sprache der Hoffnung?" *Evangelische Theologie* 42 (1982): 152–171.

Bibliography

Aguzzi, Steven D. "Florovsky's 'The Boundaries of the Church' in Dialogue with the Reformed Tradition: Toward a Catholic and Charismatic Ecumenical Ecclesiology." *Ecumenical Trends* 39, no. 3 (2010): 8–14.

———. "John Henry Newman's Anglican Views on Judaism." *Newman Studies Journal* 7, no. 1 (2010): 56–72.

———. "The Problematic of Totalization in Hick's Pluralist Thesis: Arguing for an Open Eschatological Inclusivism." Paper presented at *Symbolon* in the Theology Department of Duquesne University, Pittsburgh, PA, November 6, 2009.

Alberigo, G., and J.A. Komonchak. *History of Vatican II: The Council and the Transition, the Fourth Period and the End of the Council, September 1965-December 1965.* Maryknoll, NY: Orbis, 2005.

Alberigo, G., and J.A. Komonchak, J.P. Jossua, J.A. Komonchak, and M.J. O'Connell. *The Reception of Vatican II*. Washington, DC: Catholic University of America Press, 1987.

Allen, John L., Jr. *Cardinal Ratzinger: The Vatican's Enforcer of the Faith*. New York: Continuum, 2001.

Allison, Dale C. *Jesus of Nazareth: Millenarian Prophet*. Minneapolis, MN: Fortress Press, 1998.

Amanat, Abbas, and Magnus Bernhardsson. *Imagining the End: Visions of Apocalypse from the Ancient Middle East to Modern America*. London: I.B.Tauris, 2012.

Anderson, David R. *The King-Priest of Psalm 110 in Hebrews*. New York: Peter Lang Publishing, 2001.

Andrews, Samuel James. *God's Revelations of Himself to Men as Successively Made in the Patriarchal*. 2d ed. New York and London: G.P. Putnam's Sons, 1901.

Armstrong, Dave. *Development of Catholic Doctrine: Evolution, Revolution, or an Organic Process?* Raleigh, NC: Lulu, 2007.

Ashwin-Siejkowski, Piotr. *The Apostles' Creed: The Apostles' Creed and Its Early Christian Context*. London: T&T Clark International, 2009.

Attridge, Harold W. *Eusebius, Christianity, and Judaism*. Detroit, MI: Wayne State University, 1992.

Augustine, R.S. Pine-Coffin, Marcus Dods, and J.J. Shaw. *The Confessions; The City of God; On Christian Doctrine*. 2nd ed. Chicago, IL: Encyclopædia Britannica, 1990.

Augustine, Saint. *On Christian Teaching*. New York: Oxford University Press, 1999.

———. *Homilies on the Gospel of John 1–40*. Works of Saint Augustine. A Translation for the 21st Century. New York: New City Press, 2009.

Aumann, Moshe. *Conflict & Connection: The Jewish–Christian–Israel Triangle*. Hewlett, NY: Gefen Books, 2003.

Aune, D.E. *The Gospel of Matthew in Current Study: Studies in Memory of William G. Thompson, S.J.* Grand Rapids, MI: Eerdmans, 2001.
Avis, Paul. *Reshaping Ecumenical Theology: The Church Made Whole?* London: T&T Clark, 2010.
Ayer, Joseph Cullen. *A Source Book for Ancient Church History.* Teddington, UK: Echo Library, 2010.
Babcock, William S. *Tyconius: The Book of Rules.* Atlanta, GA: Society of Biblical Literature, 1989.
Bagatti, B. *The Church from the Circumcision: History and Archaeology of the Judaeo-Christians.* Jerusalem: Franciscan Press, 1971.
Barber, Michael. *Coming Soon: Unlocking the Book of Revelation and Applying Its Lessons Today.* Steubenville, OH: Emmaus, 2006.
Barclay, William. *The Apostles' Creed.* Louisville, KY: Westminster John Knox Press, 1998.
———. *The Letters to the Galatians and Ephesians.* 3rd ed. Louisville, KY: Westminster John Knox Press, 2002.
———. *The Lord's Prayer.* Louisville, KY: Westminster John Knox Press, 1998.
Bardill, Jonathan. *Constantine, Divine Emperor of the Christian Golden Age.* Cambridge: Cambridge University Press, 2011.
Barkun, Michael, ed. *Millennialism and Violence*: London: Frank Cass, 1996.
Barla, J.B. *Christian Theological Understanding of Other Religions According to D.S. Amalorpavadass.* Rome: Editrice Pontificia Università Gregoriana, 1999.
Barnes, Timothy D. *Constantine and Eusebius.* Cambridge, MA: Harvard University Press, 1981.
Baron, John. *The Greek Origin of the Apostles' Creed Illustrated.* Oxford: Oxford University Press, 1885.
Barth, Karl, Geoffrey William Bromiley, and Thomas F. Torrance. *Church Dogmatics.* London: Continuum, 2004.
———. *The Word of God and the Word of Man.* Rockport, MA: Peter Smith, 1978.
Bartrop, Paul R., and Steven L. Jacobs, *Fifty Key Thinkers on the Holocaust and Genocide.* 1st ed. New York: Routledge, 2010.
Baskin, Judith R., ed. *The Cambridge Dictionary of Judaism and Jewish Culture.* New York: Cambridge University Press, 2011.
Bass, Ralph E. *Back to the Future.* Little Rock, AK: Living Hope Press, 2004.
Bauckham, Richard, ed. *God Will Be All in All: The Eschatology of Jürgen Moltmann.* 1st Fortress Press ed. Minneapolis, MN: Fortress Press, 2001.
———. *The Theology of Jürgen Moltmann.* Edinburgh: T&T Clark, 1995.
Bauer, Walter. *Orthodoxy and Heresy in Earliest Christianity.* 2nd ed. Mifflintown, PA: Sigler, 1996.
Baum, Gregory. "Dialogue between Believers and Secular Thinkers." Doctoral Colloquium, Theology Dept., Duquesne University, October 7, 2009.
Baumgarten, Albert I., ed. *Apocalyptic Time.* Boston, MA: Brill Academic, 2000.
Baumgartner, Friendrick J. *Longing for the End: A History of Millennialism in Western Civilization.* New York: St. Martin's Press, 1999.
Bayme, Steven. *Understanding Jewish History: Texts and Commentaries.* Hoboken, NJ: KTAV, 1997.
Bea, Augustin. *The Church and the Jewish People: A Commentary on the Second Vatican Council's Declaration on the Relation of the Church to Non-Christian Religions.* New York: Harper & Row, 1966.

Beale, G.K. *The Book of Revelation: A Commentary on the Greek Text*. Grand Rapids, MI: Eerdmans, 1999.

Beatrice, Pier Franco. *Anonymi Monophysitae Theosophia: An Attempt at Reconstruction*. Boston, MA: Brill Academic, 2001.

Beckwith, Carl L. *Hilary of Poitiers on the Trinity: From de Fide to de Trinitate*. New York: Oxford University Press, 2009.

Beckwith, Isbon T. *The Apocalypse of John*. London: The Macmillan Company, 1919; reprint, Grand Rapids, MI: Baker Book House, 1979.

Beker, J. *Paul The Apostle*. Philadelphia, PA: Augsburg Fortress, 1984.

Bellitto, Christopher M. *The General Councils: A History of the Twenty-One General Councils from Nicaea to Vatican II*. Mahwah, NJ: Paulist Press, 2002.

Benedetto, Robert. *The New Westminster Dictionary of Church History*. Louisville, KY: WJK, 2008.

Benedict XVI. *Called to Communion: Understanding the Church Today*. San Francisco, CA: Ignatius Press, 1996.

———. *Eschatology, Death, and Eternal Life*. 2nd ed. Washington, DC: Catholic University of America Press, 2007.

———. *Great Christian Thinkers: From the Early Church through the Middle Ages*. 1st Fortress Press ed. Minneapolis, MN: Augsburg Fortress, 2011.

———. *Jesus of Nazareth: From His Transfiguration through His Death and Resurrection*, Vol. 2. San Francisco, CA: Ignatius Press, 2011.

———. *Many Religions—One Covenant: Israel, the Church, and the World*. San Francisco, CA: Ignatius Press, 1999.

Benedict XVI, and T.P. Rausch. *Theological Highlights of Vatican II*. Mahwah, NJ: Paulist Press, 2009.

Benedict XVI, and P. Seewald. *God and the World: Believing and Living in Our Time*. San Francisco, CA: Ignatius Press, 2002.

Bennett, R.M. *Dominus Iesus: Rome Exalts Her Throne: A Verbal Reappearance of the Inquisition*. Edmonton, AB: Still Waters Revival Books, 2000.

Berkhof, Hendrikus. *Christ the Meaning of History*. Eugene, OR: Wipf & Stock, 2004.

Bethune-Baker, James Franklin. *An Introduction to the Early History of Christian Doctrine: To the Time of the Council of Chalcedon*. Boston, MA: Adamant Media Corporation, 2005.

Bettenson, Henry, and Chris Maunder. *Documents of the Christian Church*. 4 ed. Oxford,: Oxford University Press, 2011.

Bialer, Uri N. Lamdan, and A. Melloni. *Nostra Aetate: Origins, Promulgation, Impact on Jewish–Catholic Relations: Proceedings of the International Conference, Jerusalem, 30 October–1 November 2005: Essays*. Berlin: LIT Verlag, 2007.

Bietenhard, Hans. "The Millennial Hope in the Early Church." *Scottish Journal of Theology* 6, no. 1 (1953): 12–30.

Billy, Dennis J. *The Beauty of the Eucharist: Voices from the Church Fathers*. Hyde Park, NY: New City Press, 2010.

Blaising, Craig A. "The Future of Israel as a Theological Question." In the National Meeting of the Evangelical Theological Society, Nashville, TN, November 19, 2000.

Bloch, Ruth H. *Visionary Republic: Millennial Themes in American Thought, 1756–1800*. Cambridge: Cambridge University Press, 1988.

Block, Daniel I. *The Book of Ezekiel*. Grand Rapids, MI: Eerdmans, 1998.

Bloesch, Donald G. *Jesus Christ: Savior & Lord*. Downers Grove, IL: IVP Academic, 2005.

294 Bibliography

Blomberg, Craig L. *From Pentecost to Patmos: An Introduction to Acts through Revelation.* Nashville, TN: B&H Academic, 2006.

Blount, Brian K. *Revelation: A Commentary.* Louisville, KY: Westminster John Knox, 2009.

Blum, George Günter. *Offenbarung und Berlieferung.* Göttingen: Vandenhoeck & Ruprecht, 1971.

Bock, Darrell L., Walter C. Kaiser, and Craig A. Blaising. *Dispensationalism, Israel and the Church: The Search for Definition.* Grand Rapids, MI: Zondervan, 1992.

Bokser, Ben Zion. "Vatican II and the Jews." *The Jewish Quarterly Review* 59, no. 2 (1968): 136–151.

Bonar, Boratius. "The Apostolocity of Chiliasm." *The Quarterly Journal of Prophecy* 2 (April, 1850): 141–161.

Bookman, Terry W. *The Holy Conversation: Towards a Jewish Theology of Dialogue. JES* 32 (1995): 212–213.

Boring, M. Eugene. *Revelation: Interpretation: A Bible Commentary For Teaching and Preaching.* Louisville, KY: Westminster John Knox Press, 2011.

Borowitz, Eugene B., and Naomi Patz. *Explaining Reform Judaism.* New York: Behrman House, 1985.

Bower, Archibald. *The History of the Popes, from the Foundation of the See of Rome, to the Present Time.* Charleston, SC: Gale ECCO, 2010.

Boyarin, Daniel. *Border Lines: The Partition of Judaeo-Christianity.* Philadelphia, PA: University of Pennsylvania Press, 2004.

Boys, M.C., ed. *Seeing Judaism Anew: Christianity's Sacred Obligation.* Lanham, MD: Rowman and Littlefield, 2005.

———. "The Covenant in Contemporary Ecclesial Documents." In E.B. Korn and J. Pawlikowski, eds., *Two Faiths, One Covenant?: Jewish and Christian Identity in the Presence of the Other,* (Lanham, MD: Rowman & Littlefield, 2005)

Braaten, Carl E. *Who Is Jesus?: Disputed Questions and Answers.* Grand Rapids, MI: Eerdmans, 2011.

Braaten, Carl E., and R.W. Jenson, *Jews and Christians: People of God* (Grand Rapids, MI: Eerdmans, 2003).

Brandmüller, Walter. *Light and Shadows: Church History amid Faith, Fact, and Legend.* San Francisco, CA: Ignatius Press, 2009.

———. "Vatican II in the History of Church Councils." *L'Avvenire,* November 29, 2005.

Bromiley, Geoffrey W., ed. *The International Standard Bible Encyclopedia,* 4 vols. Grand Rapids, MI: Eerdmans, 1995.

Brooke, George J. *Dead Sea Scrolls and NT Cloth.* Minneapolis, MN: Augsburg Fortress, 2005.

Brown, Michael Joseph. "Jewish Salvation in Romans According to Clement of Alexandria in Stromateis 2." In Kathy L. Gaca, and L.L. Welborn eds., *Early Patristic Readings of Romans.* New York: T&T Clark, 2005.

Brown, Raymond E. *The Epistle of John.* New York: Doubleday, 1982.

Bryan, S.M. *Jesus and Israel's Traditions of Judgment and Restoration.* New York: Cambridge University Press, 2002.

Buber, Martin. *Fragmente über Offenbarung.* Darmstandt, Germany: F.S.M. Susman, 1964.

———. *Two Types of Faith: A Study of the Interpretation of Judaism and Christianity.* New York: Harper & Row, 1961.

Burkett, Delbert Royce. *An Introduction to the New Testament and the Origins of Christianity.* New York: Cambridge University Press, 2002.

Burrus, Virginia. *Begotten, Not Made: Conceiving Manhood in Late Antiquity.* Stanford, CA: Stanford University Press, 2000.

——. *The Heretical Woman as Symbol in Alexander, Athanasius, Epiphanius, and Jerome.* HTR 84 (1991) 229–248.

Butler, Paul T. *Approaching the New Millennium: An Amillennial Look at A.D. 2000.* Joplin, MO: College Press, 1998.

Butler, Rex D. *The New Prophecy & New Visions.* Washington, DC: Catholic University of America Press, 2006.

Calvin, John. *Commentary on the Psalms.* Edinburgh: Banner of Truth Trust, 2009.

Carey, Greg. *Ultimate Things: An Introduction to Jewish and Christian Apocalyptic Literature.* St. Louis, MO: Chalice Press, 2005.

Carroll, James. *Constantine's Sword: The Church and the Jews: A History.* Boston, MA: Houghton Mifflin, 2001.

Carson, D.A. *The Gagging of God.* Grand Rapids, MI: Zondervan, 2002.

Carson, D.A., and Douglas J. Moo. *An Introduction to the New Testament.* 2nd ed. Grand Rapids, MI: Zondervan, 2005.

Cassidy, E.I. *Ecumenism and Interreligious Dialogue: Unitatis Redintegratio, Nostra Aetate.* Mahwah, NJ: Paulist Press, 2005.

Catholic Church. *Acta Synodalia Sacrosancti Concilii Oecumenici Vaticani Secundi IV, part IV, Congregatio Generalis CLXIV.* Vatican City: Typis Polyglottis Vaticanis, 1978.

——. *Catechism of the Catholic Church: Revised in Accordance with the Official Latin Text Promulgated by Pope John Paul II.* 2nd ed. Vatican City: Libreria Editrice Vaticana, 1997.

——. *The Companion to the Catechism of the Catholic Church: A Compendium of Texts Referred to in the Catechism of the Catholic Church.* San Francisco, CA: Ignatius Press, 1994.

——. Pontificia Commissio Biblica. *The Jewish People and Their Sacred Scriptures in the Christian Bible.* Boston, MA: Pauline Books & Media, 2002.

——. United States Conference of Catholic Bishops. *United States Catholic Catechism for Adults.* Washington, DC: United States Conference of Catholic Bishops, 2006.

Cernera, A.J. *Examining* Nostra Aetate *after 40 Years: Catholic–Jewish Relations in Our Time.* Fairfield, CT: Sacred Heart University Press, 2007.

Cerrato, J.A. *Hippolytus between East and West: The Commentaries and the Provenance of the Corpus.* Oxford: Oxford University Press, 2002.

Chesnut, Glenn F. *The First Christian Histories: Eusebius, Socrates, Sozomen, Theodoret, and Evagrius.* 2nd ed. Macon, GA: Mercer University Press, 1986.

Childs, Brevard S. *The Struggle to Understand Isaiah as Christian Scripture.* Grand Rapids, MI: Eerdmans, 2004.

Choufrine, Arkadi. *Gnosis, Theophany, Theosis: Studies in Clement of Alexandria's Appropriation of His Background.* New York: Peter Lang, 2002.

Christiansen, Ellen Juhl. *The Covenant in Judaism and Paul: A Study of Ritual Boundaries as Identity Markers.* Leiden; New York: E.J. Brill, 1995.

Chrysostom, John. *Discourses against Judaizing Christians.* Washington, DC: Catholic University of America Press, 1979.

Chrystal, James. *Authoritative Christianity: The Third World Council*, 3 vols. Charleston, SC: Nabu Press, 2010.

Chung, Sung Wook, and Craig L. Blomberg, eds. *A Case for Historic Premillennialism: An Alternative to 'Left Behind' Eschatology.* Grand Rapids, MI: Baker Academic, 2009.

Church, F. Forrester. "Sex and Salvation in Tertullian." *HTR* 68, no. 2 (1975): 82–101.
Cleenewerck, Laurent. *His Broken Body: Understanding and Healing the Schism between the Roman Catholic and Eastern Orthodox Churches*. Washington, DC: Euclid University, 2007.
Cohen, Hermann. *Religion of Reason out of the Sources of Judaism*. Atlanta, GA: Oxford University Press, 1995.
Cohen, Jeremy. *Living Letters of the Law: Ideas of the Jew in Medieval Christianity*. Berkeley, CA: University of California Press, 1999.
Cohen, Shaye J.D. *From the Maccabees to the Mishnah*. 2nd ed. Louisville, KY: Westminster John Knox Press, 2006.
Cohn, Norman. *The Pursuit of the Millennium: Revolutionary Messianism in Medieval Reformation Europe and Its Bearing on Modern Totalitarian Movements*. New York: Harper & Row, 1957.
———. *The Pursuit of the Millennium: Revolutionary Millenarians and Mystical Anarchists of the Middle Ages*. Oxford: Oxford University Press, 1970.
Collins, Adela Yarbro. *Crisis and Catharsis: The Power of the Apocalypse*. Philadelphia, PA: The Westminster Press, 1984.
Collins, John, ed. *Apocalypse: The Morphology of a Genre*. Missoula, MT: Scholars, 1979.
Collins, Paul M. *Partaking in Divine Nature: Deification and Communion*. London: T&T Clark, 2010.
Constas, Nicholas. *Proclus of Constantinople and the Cult of the Virgin in Late Antiquity: Homilies 1–5, Texts and Translations*. Leiden: Brill Academic, 2003.
Coppa, F.J. *The Papacy, the Jews, and the Holocaust*: Catholic University of America Press, 2006.
Coppens, Joseph. *Le Messianisme Royal, Ses Origines, Son Développement, Son Accomplissement Lectio Divina*, Paris: Éditions du Cerf, 1968.
Cornille, Catherine, ed. *Many Mansions?: Multiple Religious Belonging and Christian Identity*. Maryknoll, NY: Orbis Books, 2002.
Cornwell, John. *Hitler's Pope: The Secret History of Pius XII*. Reprint ed. New York: Penguin Books, 2008.
Costigan, Richard F. *The Consensus of the Church and Papal Infallibility: A Study in the Background of Vatican I*. Washington, DC: Catholic University of America Press, 2005.
Couch, Mal, ed. *A Bible Handbook to Revelation*. Grand Rapids, MI: Kregel Academic & Professional, 2001.
———, ed. *Dictionary of Premillennial Theology*. Grand Rapids, MI: Kregel, 1997.
———, ed. *An Introduction to Classical Hermeneutics: A Guide to the History and Practice of Biblical Interpretation*. Grand Rapids, MI: Kregel Academic & Professional, 2000.
Court, J.M. *Approaching the Apocalypse: A Short History of Christian Millenarianism*: London: I.B.Tauris, 2008.
Cox, Claude, and Albert Pietersma, eds. *De Septuaginta: Studies in Honour of John William Wevers on His Sixty-Fifth Birthday*. Mississauga, ON: BenBen, 1984.
Creeds of the Hungarian Reformed Christians: The Second Helvetic Confession and the Heidelberg Catechism. 1st ed. Ligonier, PA: Bethlen Freedom Press, 1968.
Cripe, D. Earl. *Seven Trumpets Asounding: A Commentary on the Book of Revelation in the Historic, Orthodox Tradition of the Christian Church*. Bloomington, IN: AuthorHouse, 2006.
Cross, F.L. & Livingstone, E.A., eds. *The Oxford Dictionary of the Christian Church*. 3rd ed. Oxford: Oxford University Press, 2005.

Cullmann, Oscar. *Immortality of the Soul or Resurrection of the Dead?: The Witness of the New Testament*. Eugene, OR: Wipf & Stock, 2000.

Cunningham, Philip A. "Official Ecclesial Documents to Implement the Second Vatican Council on Relations with Jews: Study Them, Become Immersed in Them, and Put Them into Practice." *Studies in Christian–Jewish Relations* 4, no. 1 (2009): 1–36.

———. *A Story of Shalom: The Calling of Christians and Jews by a Covenanting God*. Studies in Judaism and Christianity. Mahwah, NJ: Paulist Press, 2001.

———. *Sharing the Scriptures*. Mahwah, NJ: Paulist Press, 2003.

Cunningham, Philip A., Johannes Hofmann, and Joseph Sievers. *The Catholic Church and the Jewish People: Recent Reflections from Rome*. 1st ed. New York: Fordham University Press, 2007.

Curran, Charles E. *Loyal Dissent: Memoir of a Catholic Theologian*. Washington, DC: Georgetown University Press, 2006.

D'Costa, Gavin, ed. *The Catholic Church and the World Religions: A Theological and Phenomenological Account*. London: T&T Clark, 2011.

Dalin, D.G. and M. Levering. *John Paul II and the Jewish People: A Jewish–Christian Dialogue*. Lanham, MD: Rowman & Littlefield, 2008.

Damascene. *Father Seraphim Rose: His Life and Works*. 1st ed. Platina, CA: St. Herman of Alaska Brotherhood, 2003.

Daniélou, Jean. *The Origins of Latin Christianity*, Vol. 3. London: Westminster Press, 1977.

———. *The Theology of Jewish Christianity*: Darton: Longman & Todd, 1964.

Davies, Alan T., ed. *Antisemitism and the Foundations of Christianity*. Mahwah, NJ: Paulist Press, 1979.

Davies, J.A. *A Royal Priesthood: Literary and Intertextual Perspectives on an Image of Israel in Exodus 19.6*. London: T&T Clark International, 2004.

Davies, W.D. *Paul and Rabbinic Judaism: Some Rabbinic Elements in Pauline Theology*. 4th ed. Philadelphia, PA: Fortress Press, 1980.

Davies, W.D., and Dale C. Allison. *A Critical and Exegetical Commentary on the Gospel According to Saint Matthew*. London: T&T Clark International, 2004.

Davis, Leo Donald. *The First Seven Ecumenical Councils (325–787): Their History and Theology*. Collegeville, MN: Liturgical Press, 1990.

Davis, Stephen T., Daniel Kendall, and Gerald O'Collins, eds. *The Trinity: An Interdisciplinary Symposium on the Trinity*. New York: Oxford University Press, 2002.

Denzinger, Henricus, ed. *Enchiridion Symbolorum: Definitionum et Declarationum de Rebus Fidei et Morum*. 36th emended ed. Edited by Adolfus Schönmetzer. Freiburg: Herder, 1976.

Dewick, E.C. *Primitive Christian Eschatology*. Cambridge: Cambridge University Press, 2011.

Diprose, Ronald E. *Israel in the Development of Christian Thought*. Rome: Instituto Biblico Evangelico Italiano, 2000.

———. *Israel and the Church*. Waynesboro: GA: Paternoster, 2004.

Dodd, C.H. *The Parables of the Kingdom*: New York: Scribner, 1961.

Dorey, Thomas Alan, ed. *Empire and Aftermath: Silver Latin II*. London: Routledge & Kegan Paul Books, 1975.

Doukhan, Jacques B. *Secrets of Revelation: The Apocalypse through Hebrew Eyes*. Hagerstown, MD: Review & Herald, 2002.

Drury, John L. "Testing the Tests: Post-Supersessionist Theology and Newman's Notes of a Genuine Development of Doctrine." The Drury Writing Blog, entry posted April 23, 2004, http://www.drurywriting.com/john/ (accessed February 21, 2011).

Dulles, Avery. "'Covenant and Mission.'" *America* 187, no. 12 (2002): 9.

———. *Models of the Church*. Garden City, NY: Doubleday, 1974.

———. *The Reshaping of Catholicism: Current Challenges in the Theology of Church*. San Francisco, CA: HarperCollins, 1988.

Dunn, James D.G. *Jews and Christians: The Parting of the Ways, A.D. 70 to 135*. The Second Durham-Tübingen Research Symposium on Earliest Christianity and Judaism, Durham, September, 1989. Grand Rapids, MI: Eerdmans, 1999.

———. *Paul and the Mosaic Law*. Grand Rapids, MI: Eerdmans, 2001.

———. *The Theology of Paul's Letter to the Galatians*. Grand Rapids, MI: Eerdmans, 1994.

Dupuis, Jacques. *The Christian Faith in the Doctrinal Documents of the Catholic Church*. 7th rev ed. New York: Alba House, 2001.

———. "The Church's Evangelizing Mission." *Pastoral Review* 1 (2005): 23.

———. *Toward a Christian Theology of Religious Pluralism*. Maryknoll, NY: Orbis Books, 1997.

Dupuis, Jacques, and J. Neuner. *The Christian Faith in the Doctrinal Documents of the Catholic Church*. New York: Alba House, 2001.

Dyrness, W.A., V.M. Karkkainen, and J.F. Martinez. *Global Dictionary of Theology: A Resource for the Worldwide Church*. Downers Grove, IL: IVP, 2008.

Eastman, David L. *Paul the Martyr: The Cult of the Apostle in the Latin West*. Atlanta, GA: Society of Biblical Literature, 2011.

Edwards, Mark J., ed. *We Believe in the Crucified and Risen Lord*. Downers Grove, IL: IVP Academic, 2009.

Ehrhardt, Arnold. "Christianity before the Apostles' Creed." *The Harvard Theological Review* 55, no. 2 (1962): 73–119.

Ehrman, Bart D. *Jesus, Apocalyptic Prophet of the New Millennium*. Oxford: Oxford University Press, 1999.

———. *Lost Christianities: The Battles For Scripture and the Faiths We Never Knew*. New York: Oxford University Press, 2005.

Eichrodt, Walther. *Theology of the Old Testament*. Philadelphia, PA: Westminster Press, 1961.

Eisenman, Robert H. *James the Brother of Jesus: The Key to Unlocking the Secrets of Early Christianity and the Dead Sea Scrolls*. Reprint ed. London: Penguin (Non-Classics), 1998.

Elior, Rachel. *The Three Temples: On the Emergence of Jewish Mysticism*. Oxford and Portland, OR: Littman Library of Jewish Civilization, 2004.

Ellison, H.L. *The Mystery of Israel*. Grand Rapids, MI: Eerdmans, 1966.

Elwell, Walter A., ed. *Evangelical Dictionary of Theology*. 2nd ed. Grand Rapids, MI: Baker Academic, 2001.

Emmerson, Richard K., and Bernard McGinn, eds. *The Apocalypse in the Middle Ages*. Ithaca, NY: Cornell University Press, 1993.

Engleman, Dennis Eugene. *Ultimate Things: An Orthodox Christian Perspective on the End Times*. Ben Lomond, CA: Conciliar Press Ministries, 2005.

Epperson, Steven. "Some Problems with Supersessionism in Mormon Thought." (Review of Robert L. Millet, and Joseph Fielding McConkie, *Our Destiny: The Call and Election of the House of Israel* (Salt Lake City, UT: Bookcraft, 1993)). *BYU Studies Quarterly* 34, no. 4 (1994): 125–136.

Erickson, Millard J. *A Basic Guide to Eschatology: Making Sense of the Millennium*. Rev. ed. Grand Rapids, MI: Baker Books, 1998.

———. *Contemporary Options in Eschatology: A Study of the Millennium*. Grand Rapids, MI: Baker Books, 1977.

Eskola, Timo. *Messiah and the Throne: Jewish Merkabah Mysticism and Early Christian Exaltation Discourse.* Tübingen: Abm. Komers, 2001.
Espin, Orlando, and James B. Nickoloff, eds. *An Introductory Dictionary of Theology and Religious Studies.* Collegeville, MN: Liturgical Press, 2007.
Ewherido, Anthony O. *Matthew's Gospel and Judaism in the Late First Century C.E.: The Evidence from Matthew's Chapter on Parables (Matthew 13:1–52).* Studies in Biblical Literature. New York: Peter Lang, 2006.
Fabrega, Valentin. "Die Chiliastische Lehre Des Laktanz." *JAC* 17 (1975): 126–146.
Fackenheim, Emil L. *To Mend the World: Foundations of Future Jewish Thought.* New York: Schocken Books, 1982.
Fackre, Gabriel. *The Christian Story.* 3rd ed. Grand Rapids, MI: Eerdmans, 1996.
Falls, Thomas. *St. Justin Martyr.* New York: Christian Heritage, 1948.
Farmer, Ronald L. *Revelation.* St. Louis, MO: Christian Board of Publication, 2006.
Farmer, William R., ed. *The International Bible Commentary: A Catholic and Ecumenical Commentary for the Twenty-First Century.* Collegeville, MN: Liturgical Press, 1998.
Feinberg, Charles Lee. *Millennialism: The Two Major Views.* 3rd ed. Chicago, IL: BMH Books, 1985.
Fenton, Joseph Clifford. *The Concept of Sacred Theology.* Milwaukee, WI: Bruce, 1941.
Ferguson, Everett, ed. *Encyclopedia of Early Christianity.* 2nd ed. New York: Routledge, 1998.
Feuillet, A. *Johannine Studies.* New York: Alba House, 1965.
Fiorenza, Elisabeth Schüssler. *In Memory of Her: A Feminist Theological Reconstruction of Christian Origins.* New York: Crossroad, 1983.
———. *Jesus and the Politics of Interpretation.* New York: Continuum, 2001.
———. *Revelation: Vision of a Just World.* Minneapolis, MN: Fortress Press, 1998.
Fiorenza, Francis Schüssler, and John P. Galvin, eds. *Systematic Theology: Roman Catholic Perspectives.* 2nd ed. Minneapolis, MN: Fortress Press, 2011.
Fisher, Eugene J. "*Nostra Aetate:* Transforming the Catholic–Jewish Relationship." *ADL* 16, no. 1–3 (April 2006): 161–163.
———, "Official Roman Catholic Teaching on Jews and Judaism: Commentary and Context." In L. Klenicki and E.J. Fisher, eds., *In Our Time: The Flowering of Jewish–Catholic Dialogue* (Mahwah, NJ: Paulist Press, 1991).
———. *Visions of the Other: Jewish and Christian Theologians Assess the Dialogue.* Studies in Judaism and Christianity. Mahwah, NJ: Paulist Press, 1994.
Fitzgerald, Allan D., ed. *Augustine through the Ages: An Encyclopedia.* Grand Rapids, MI: Eerdmans, 1999.
Fitzmyer, Joseph A. *The Anchor Bible*, Vol. 33: *Romans: A New Translation with Introduction and Commentary.* New Haven, CT: Yale University Press, 2008, 1993.
Flannery, Austin. *The Conciliar and Post Conciliar Documents, Vatican Council II.* Dublin: Dominican Publications, 1975.
Flannery, E.H. *The Anguish of the Jews: Twenty-Three Centuries of Antisemitism.* Mahwah, NJ: Paulist Press, 1985.
Flegg, Columba Graham. *An Introduction to Reading the Apocalypse.* Crestwood, NY: St. Vladimir's Seminary Press, 1999.
Fleischner, E. *Auschwitz: Beginning of a New Era?: Reflections on the Holocaust.* Jersey City, NJ: KTAV, 1977.
Flinn, F.K. *Encyclopedia of Catholicism.* New York: Infobase 2007.
Folliet, G. "La Typologie Du Sabbat chez Saint Augustin: Son Interprétation Millénariste Entre 388 Et 400." *Revue des études augustiniennes* 2 (1956): 371–391.

Bibliography

Ford, J. Massyngberde. *Revelation*. New York: Doubleday, 1995.

———. "Was Montanism a Jewish–Christian Heresy?." *Journal of Ecclesiastical History* 17 (1966):145–158, 145.

Foster, K. Neill, and David E. Fessenden, eds. *Essays on Premillenialism*. Camp Hill, PA: Christian, 2002.

Foster, R.C. *Studies in the Life of Christ: Introduction, the Early Period, the Middle Period, the Final Week*. Joplin, MO: College Press, 1995.

Foulkes, Francis. *The Letter of Paul to the Ephesians: An Introduction and Commentary*. 2nd ed. The Tyndale New Testament Commentaries. Leicester, UK, and Grand Rapids, MI: IVP and Eerdmans, 1989.

Frank, John R. "Reformation Amillennialism: Salvation Now, Salvation Always." *Christian History and Biography* 61 (1999): 6–12.

Frankel, Jonathan, ed. *Studies in Contemporary Jewry: Jews and Messianism in the Modern Era: Metaphor and Meaning*, Vol. 7. Oxford: Oxford University Press, 1991.

Fredriksen, Paula. *Augustine and the Jews: A Christian Defense of Jews and Judaism*. New Haven, CT: Doubleday Religion, 2010.

———"The Diaspora Synagogue and the Origins of Christianity," in David S. Potter, ed., *A Companion to the Roman Empire*. Blackwell Companions to the Ancient World. Boston, MA: Wiley-Blackwell, 2009.

———. "Excaecati Occulta Justitia Dei: Augustine on Jews and Judaism," *Journal of Early Christian Studies* 3 (1995): 299–324.

Frei, Hans W. *The Eclipse of Biblical Narrative: A Study in Eighteenth and Nineteenth Century Hermeneutics*. New Haven, CT: Yale University Press, 1974.

Frend, W.H.C. *Rise of Christianity*. Philadelphia, PA: Fortress Press, 1986.

Frost, Samuel M. *Misplaced Hope: The Origins of First and Second Century Eschatology*. Colorado Springs, CO: Bimillennial Press, 2002.

Fulcanelli. *Fulcanelli: Master Alchemist: Le Mystere Des Cathedrales, Esoteric Intrepretation of the Hermetic Symbols of the Great Work*. New York: Cosimo, 1984.

Fuller, Michael E. *The Restoration of Israel: Israel's Re-Gathering and the Fate of the Nations in Early Jewish Literature and Luke-Acts*. New York: De Gruyter, 2006.

Gadenz, Pablo T. *Called from the Jews and from the Gentiles: Pauline Ecclesiology in Romans 9–11*. Tübingen: Error, 2009.

Gager, John G. *Kingdom and Community: The Social World of Early Christianity*. Englewood Cliffs, NJ: Prentice-Hall, 1975.

———. *The Origins of Anti-Semitism: Attitudes toward Judaism in Pagan and Christian Antiquity*. Oxford and New York: Oxford University Press, 1983.

Gaillardetz, R.R. *Teaching with Authority: A Theology of the Magisterium in the Church*. Collegeville, MN: Liturgical Press, 1997.

Galli, Barbara. "Rosenzweig Speaking of Meetings and Monotheism in Biblical Anthropomorphisms." *Journal of Jewish Thought and Philosophy* 2, no. 2 (1993): 219–243.

Gardner, James. *Faiths of the World*. Whitefish, MT: Kessinger, 2003.

Garland, Anthony C. *A Testimony of Jesus Christ: A Commentary on the Book of Revelation*, Vol. 2. Hustisford, WI: Spirit-and-Truth, 2007.

Gihr, Nicholas. *The Holy Sacrifice of the Mass VI: Dogmatically, Liturgically, and Ascetically Explained*. Whitefish, MT: Kessinger, 2006.

Gilbertson, Michael. *God and History in the Book of Revelation: New Testament Studies in Dialogue with Pannenberg and Moltmann*. New York: Cambridge University Press, 2005.

González, Catherine Gunsalus, and Justo L. González. *Revelation*. Louisville, KY: Westminster John Knox Press, 1997.
González, Justo L. *Essential Theological Terms*. Louisville, KY: Westminster John Knox Press, 2005.
Good, Deirdre J., ed. *Mariam, the Magdalen, and the Mother*. Bloomington, IN: Indiana University Press, 2005.
Gould, Dana, and Terry L. Miethe. *Augustine's City of God*. Nashville, TN: B&H Books, 1999.
Grabbe, Lester L. *Judaic Religion in the Second Temple Period: Belief and Practice from the Exile to Yavneh*. New York: Routledge, 2000.
Grant, Frederick. "The Eschatology of the Second Century." T*he American Journal of Theology* 21, no. 1 (1917): 193–211.
Green, Bradley G., ed. *Shapers of Christian Orthodoxy: Engaging with Early and Medieval Theologians*. Downers Grove, IL: IVP Academic, 2010.
Gregg, Steve, ed. *Revelation, Four Views: A Parallel Commentary*. Nashville, TN: Thomas Nelson, 1997.
Grégoire, Henri. *Histoire Des Sectes Religieuses*. Paris: Potey, 1814.
Gregory, Andrew. *The Reception of Luke and Acts in the Period before Irenaeus: Looking for Luke in the Second Century*. Tubingen: Paul Mohr Verlag, 2003.
Grenz, Stanley J. *The Millennial Maze: Sorting Out Evangelical Options*. Downers Grove, IL: IVP Academic, 2007.
Grenz, Stanley J., and Roger E. Olson. *20th Century Theology: God & the World in a Transitional Age*. Downers Grove, IL: IVP, 1992.
Gribben, Crawford. *Writing the Rapture: Prophecy Fiction in Evangelical America*. New York: Oxford University Press, 2009.
Grier, W.J. *Momentous Event*. London: Banner of Truth, 1976.
Grillmeier, Aloys. *Christ in Christian Tradition: From the Apostolic Age to Chalcedon (451)*. Christ in Christian Tradition. Rev. ed. London: A.R. Mowbray, 1975.
Grudem, Wayne A. *Systematic Theology: An Introduction to Biblical Doctrine*. Leicester, UK, and Grand Rapids, MI: InterVarsity Press and Zondervan Publishing House, 1994.
Guarino, Thomas. "Tradition and Doctrinal Development: Can St. Vincent of Lérins still Teach the Church?" *Theological Studies* 67 (2006): 34–72.
Guder, Darrell L. *The Continuing Conversion of the Church*. Gospel and Our Culture Series. Grand Rapids, MI: Eerdmans, 2000.
Gumerlock, Francis X. "Millennialism and the Early Church Councils: Was Chiliasm Condemned at Constantinople?" *Fides et Historia* 36, no. 2 (2004): 83–95.
———. "Patristic Commentaries on Revelation: The Problem of Accessibility." *Kerux* 23, no. 2 (2008): 3–13.
Gundry, S.N., and D.L. Bock. *Three Views on the Millennium and Beyond*. Grand Rapids, MI: Zondervan, 2010.
Gunton, Colin E., ed. *The Cambridge Companion to Christian Doctrine*. Cambridge Companions to Religion. Cambridge and New York: Cambridge University Press, 1997.
Gürkan, S. Leyla. *The Jews as a Chosen People: Tradition and Transformation*. New York: Routledge, 2009.
Gurtner, Daniel M. *The Torn Veil: Matthew's Exposition of the Death of Jesus*. New York: Cambridge University Press, 2007.
Guy, Laurie. *Introducing Early Christianity: A Topical Survey of Its Life, Beliefs, and Practices*. Downers Grove, IL: IVP, 2004.
Hadden, B., and Luce, H.R. *Time*. New York: Time, 1987.

Haers, J., and P.D. Mey. *Theology and Conversation: Towards a Relational Theology*. Leuven, Belgium: Peeters, 2003.

Hagenbach, Karl R. *History of Christian Doctrine*, 3 vols. Whitefish, MT: Kessinger, 2006.

Hannah, John D. *An Uncommon Union: Dallas Theological Seminary and American Evangelicalism*. Grand Rapids, MI: Zondervan, 2009.

Hanson, R.P.C. *Selections from Justin Martyr's Dialogue with Trypho, a Jew*. New York: Association Press, 1964.

Harmless, William, ed. *Augustine in His Own Words*. Washington, DC: Catholic University of America Press, 2010.

Harper, William Rainey. *The Biblical World*. Memphis, TN: General Books LLC, 2010.

Harrington, Daniel J. *The Light of All Nations: Essays on the Church in New Testament Research*. Wilmington, DE: M. Glazier, 1982.

———. *Paul on the Mystery of Israel*. Collegeville, MN: Liturgical Press, 1992.

Harrison, Brian W. "The Catholic Liturgy and 'Supersessionism'." *Homiletic and Pastoral Review* (June 2009): 20–27.

Hartman, D. *A Heart of Many Rooms: Celebrating the Many Voices within Judaism*. Woodstock, VT: Jewish Lights, 1999.

Hartog, Paul. *Polycarp and the New Testament: The Occasion, Rhetoric, Theme, and Unity of the Epistle to the Philippians and Its Allusions to New Testament Literature*. Tübingen: Paul Mohr Verlag, 2002.

Harvey, Susan Ashbrook, and David Hunter, eds. *The Oxford Handbook of Early Christian Studies*. Oxford: Oxford University Press, 2008.

Harvie, Timothy. *Jürgen Moltmann's Ethics of Hope: Eschatological Possibilities for Moral Action*. Aldershot: Ashgate, 2009.

Hastings, Adrian, Alistair Mason, and Hugh Pyper, eds. *The Oxford Companion to Christian Thought*. Oxford: Oxford University Press, 2000.

Hastings, Derek. *Catholicism and the Roots of Nazism: Religious Identity and National Socialism*. Reprint ed. New York: Oxford University Press, 2011.

Hastings, James, John A. Selbie, and John C. Lambert. *Dictionary of the Apostolic Church*. New York: C. Scribner's Sons, 1916.

Hawthorne, Gerald F. *Word Biblical Commentary: Philippians*. Nashville, TN: Thomas Nelson, 1983.

Haynes, Stephen R. *Prospects for Post-Holocaust Theology*. American Academy of Religion Academy Series. Atlanta, GA: Scholars Press, 1991.

———. *Reluctant Witnesses: Jews and the Christian Imagination*. 1st American ed. Louisville, KY: Westminster John Knox Press, 1995.

Hays, J.D., J.S. Duvall, and C.M. Pate, eds., *Dictionary of Biblical Prophecy and End Times*. Grand Rapids, MI: Zondervan, 2009.

Hefele, Karl Joseph von. *A History of the Christian Councils, from the Original Documents to the Close of the Council of Nicaea, A.D. 325*. Charleston, SC: Nabu Press, 2010.

Heim, Maximilian Heinrich. *Joseph Ratzinger: Life in the Church and Living Theology: Fundamentals of Ecclesiology with Reference to Lumen Gentium*. San Francisco, CA: Ignatius Press, 2007.

Heim, S. Mark. *The Depth of the Riches: A Trinitarian Theology of Religious Ends*. Grand Rapids, MI: Eerdmans, 2001.

Heinrich, Corrodi. *Kritische Geschichte Des Chiliasmus*. Frankfurt and Leipzig: Error, 1901.

Hellemo, Geir. *Adventus Domini: Eschatological Thought in 4th-Century Apses and Catecheses*. New York: Brill Academic, 1997.

Helm, Paul, and Carl R. Trueman, eds. *The Trustworthiness of God: Perspectives on the Nature of Scripture*. Grand Rapids, MI: Eerdmans, 2002.

Herzog, W.R. *Jesus, Justice, and the Reign of God: A Ministry of Liberation*. Philadelphia, PA: Westminster John Knox Press, 2000.

Hick, John. *An Interpretation of Religion: Human Responses to the Transcendent*. 2nd ed. New Haven, CT: Yale University Press, 2005.

Hick, John, and Paul F. Knitter. *The Myth of Christian Uniqueness: Toward a Pluralistic Theology of Religions*. Maryknoll, NY: Orbis Books, 1987.

Hilhorst, A., ed. *The Apostolic Age in Patristic Thought*. Boston, MA: Brill Academic, 2004.

Hill, Charles E. *Regnum Coelorum: Patterns of Future Hope in Early Christianity*. Oxford Early Christian Studies. Oxford and New York: Clarendon Press and Oxford University Press, 1992.

———. "Why the Early Church Finally Rejected Premillennialism." *Modern Reformation* 8, no. 1 (1999): 16–19.

Hillerbrand, Hans J., ed. *The Encyclopedia of Protestantism*. New York: Routledge, 2004.

Hinlicky, Paul R. *Divine Complexity: The Rise of Creedal Christianity*. Minneapolis, MN: Fortress Press, 2011.

Hoekema, Anthony A. *The Bible and the Future*. Grand Rapids, MN: Eerdmans, 1979.

Hogeterp, Albert L.A. *Expectations of the End: A Comparative Traditio-Historical Study of Eschatological, Apocalyptic and Messianic Ideas in the Dead Sea Scrolls and the New Testament*. Leiden: Brill, 2009.

Holder, Arthur, ed. *The Blackwell Companion to Christian*. Hoboken, NJ: Wiley-Blackwell, 2010.

Holleman, Joost. *Resurrection and Parousia: A Traditio-Historical Study of Paul's Eschatology in I Corinthians 15*. Leiden: Brill Academic, 1996.

Hollerich, Michael J. *Eusebius of Caesarea's Commentary on Isaiah: Christian Exegesis in the Age of Constantine*. Oxford: Oxford University Press, 1999.

Horbury, William. *Jewish Messianism and the Cult of Christ*. Norwich: SCM Press, 1998.

———. *Messianism Among Jews and Christians: Twelve Biblical and Historical Studies*. Edinburgh: T&T Clark, 2003.

Horner, Barry E. *Future Israel: Why Christian Anti-Judaism Must Be Challenged*. Nashville, TN: B&H Academic, 2007.

House, H. Wayne, ed. *Israel, the Land and the People: An Evangelical Affirmation of God's Promises*. Grand Rapids, MI: Kregel, 1998.

Hunt, Stephen. *Christian Millenarianism: From the Early Church to Waco*. Bloomington, IN: Indiana University Press, 2001.

Hurtado, Larry W. *The Earliest Christian Artifacts: Manuscripts and Christian Origins*. Grand Rapids, MI: Eerdmans, 2006.

Hutton, R.E. *The Soul in the Unseen World: An Inquiry into the Doctrine of the Intermediate State*. Memphis, TN: General Books LLC, 2010.

Idinopulos, Thomas A. "Nazism, Millenarianism, and the Jews." *Journal of Ecumenical Studies* 40, no. 3 (2003): 296–302.

International Catholic–Jewish Liaison Committee, Fifteen Years of Catholic–Jewish Dialogue: 1970–1985. Rome: Libreria Editrice Vaticana and Libreria Editrice Lateranense, 1988.

Isaac, Rael Jean, and Erich Isaac. *The Coercive Utopians: Social Deception by America's Power Players*. Chicago, IL: Regnery Gateway, 1984.

304   Bibliography

Jacoby, Russell. *Bloodlust: On the Roots of Violence from Cain and Abel to the Present.* New York: Free Press, 2011.
Jaffé, D. *Studies in Rabbinic Judaism and Early Christianity: Text and Context.* New York: Brill Academic, 2010.
Jastrow, Marcus. *Dictionary of the Targumim, Talmud Bavli, Talmud Yerushalmi and Midrashic Literature.* New York: Judaica Press, 2004.
Jenson, Robert W. *Systematic Theology.* New York: Oxford University Press, 2001.
———. "You Wonder Where the Spirit Went." *Pro Ecclesia* 2, no. 3 (1993): 300–302.
Jeon, Jeong Koo. *Covenant Theology: John Murray's and Meredith G. Kline's Response to the Historical Development of Federal Theology in Reformed Thought.* Lanham, MD: University Press of America, 2004.
Jeremias, Joachim. *The Parables of Jesus.* Norwich: SCM, 2004.
Jewett, Robert. *Romans: A Commentary.* Edited by Eldon Jay Epp. Minneapolis, MN: Fortress Press, 2007.
Jewett, Robert, Larry W. Hurtado, and Patrick R. Keifert. *Christology and Exegesis: New Approaches.* Decatur, GA: Scholars Press, 1985.
———. *The Thessalonian Correspondence: Pauline Rhetoric and Millenarian Piety.* Philadelphia, PA: Fortress Press, 1986.
Johnson, S. Lewis, and John S. Feinberg. *Continuity and Discontinuity: Perspectives on the Relationship between the Old and New Testaments: Essays in Honor of S. Lewis Johnson, Jr.* Westchester, IL: Crossway Books, 1988.
Jonas, Hans. *The Gnostic Religion: The Message of the Alien God & the Beginnings of Christianity.* 3rd ed. Boston, MA: Beacon Press, 2001.
Jones, L. Gregory, and James Buckley, eds. *Theology and Eschatology at the Turn of the Millennium.* Malden, MA: Wiley-Blackwell, 2002.
Journet, C. *The Church of the Word Incarnate: The Apostolic Hierarchy.* Lanham, MD: Sheed & Ward, 1955.
Jue, Jeffrey K. *Heaven Upon Earth: Joseph Mede (1586–1638) and the Legacy of Millenarianism.* Dordrecht: Springer, 2006.
Jurgens, W.A. *The Faith of the Early Fathers*, 3 vols. Collegeville, MN: Liturgical Press, 1998.
Kaplan, Gregory. "In the End Shall Christians Become Jews and Jews, Christians?: On Franz Rosenzweig's Apocalyptic Eschatology." *Cross Currents* 53, no. 4 (2004): 511–529.
Kariatlis, P. *Church as Communion: The Gift and Goal of Koinonia.* Wayville, South Australia: ATF Press, 2011.
Karp, Jonathan, and Adam Sutcliffe, eds. *Philosemitism in History.* New York: Cambridge University Press, 2011.
Kasper, Walter. "The Church and the Jews." *America* 185, no. 7 (September 17, 2001).
———. "*Dominus Iesus.*" Paper delivered at the 17th meeting of the International Catholic–Jewish Liaison Committee, New York, May 1, 2001.
———. *Jesus the Christ.* London and New York: Burns & Oates and Paulist Press, 1976.
———. *Theology and Church*, trans. Margaret Kohl. New York: Crossroad, 1989.
Kattenbusch, F. "Kritische Studien zur Symbolik." *ThStKr* 51 (1878): 179–253.
Katz, David S., and Jonathan I. Israel, eds. *Sceptics, Millenarians, and Jews.* New York: Brill Academic, 1990.
Katz, Jacob. *From Prejudice to Destruction: Anti-Semitism, 1700–1933.* Cambridge, MA: Harvard University Press, 1980.

Katz, Steven T., ed. *The Late Roman-Rabbinic Period*. New York: Cambridge University Press, 2006.
Kelly, J.N.D. *Early Christian Doctrines*. 5th ed. London: Continuum, 2000.
———. *Rufinus: A Commentary on the Apostles' Creed*. Ancient Christian Writers. Mahwah, NJ: Paulist Press, 1978.
Kendall, Daniel, Stephen T. Davis, and George Carey. *The Convergence of Theology: A Festschrift Honoring Gerald O'Collins, S.J*. Mahwah, NJ: Paulist Press, 2001.
Kennedy, Jon. *Jesus and Mary the Blessed Mother the Holy Son, and His Teachings of the Word*. East Bridgewater, MA: Word, 2010.
Kessler, Edward, and Neil Wenborn. *A Dictionary of Jewish–Christian Relations*. Cambridge and New York: Cambridge University Press and Cambridge Centre for the Study of Jewish–Christian Relations, 2005.
Khatry, Ramesh. 1991. *The Authenticity of the Parable of the Wheat and the Tares and its Interpretation*. Biblical Stories. Council for National Academic Awards (United Kingdom). In PROQUESTMS ProQuest Dissertations & Theses A&I, http://search.proquest.com/docview/303973398?accountid=10610/ (accessed January 30, 2013).
Killen, W.D. *The Ancient Church: Its History, Doctrine, Worship, and Constitution*. Teddington, UK: Echo Library, 2010.
Kim, L. *Polemic in the Book of Hebrews: Anti-Semitism, Anti-Judaism, Super-sessionism?* Woodland Hills, CA: Pickwick, 2006.
Kinzer, Mark S. *Postmissionary Messianic Judaism: Redefining Christian Engagement with the Jewish People*. Grand Rapids, MI: Brazos Press, 2005.
Kirk, J.R. Daniel. *Unlocking Romans: Resurrection and the Justification of God*. Grand Rapids, MI: Eerdmans, 2008.
Kirsch, J. *The Catholic Encyclopedia*. New York: Robert Appleton, 1911.
Klenicki, L., and E.J. Fisher. *In Our Time: The Flowering of Jewish–Catholic Dialogue*. Mahwah, NJ: Paulist Press, 1991.
Klijn, By A.F.J., and G.J. Reinink. *Patristic Evidence for Jewish–Christian Sects*. Leiden: Brill, 1973.
Kloppenborg, John S. *The Tenants in the Vineyard: Ideology, Economics, and Agrarian Conflict in Jewish Palestine* Wissenschaftliche Untersuchungen Zum Neuen Testament. Tübingen: Mohr Siebeck, 2006.
Knight, Douglas H. *The Eschatological Economy: Time and the Hospitality of God*. Grand Rapids, MI: Eerdmans, 2006.
Knitter, Paul F. *No Other Name?: A Critical Survey of Christian Attitudes Toward the World Religions*. Maryknoll, NY: Orbis Books, 1985.
Koester, Helmut. *From Jesus to the Gospels: Interpreting the New Testament in Its Context*. Minneapolis, MN: Fortress Press, 2007.
Kohn, Risa Levitt, and Rebecca Moore. *A Portable God: The Origin of Judaism and Christianity*. Lanham, MD: Rowman & Littlefield, 2007.
Koperski, Veronica. *The Knowledge of Christ Jesus My Lord: The High Christology of Philippians 3:7–11*. Kampen, the Netherlands: Peeters, 1996.
Korn, E.B. and J. Pawlikowski. *Two Faiths, One Covenant?: Jewish and Christian Identity in the Presence of the Other*. Lanham, MD: Rowman & Littlefield, 2005.
Kottman, Karl A. *Millenarianism and Messianism in Early Modern European Culture*, Vol. 2: *Catholic Millenarianism: From Savonarola to the Abbé Grégoire*. Archives Internationales D'histoire Des Idees. Dordrecht and London: Kluwer Academic, 2001.
Kraemer, Ross Shepard, and Mary Rose D'Angelo, eds. *Women & Christian Origins*. New York: Oxford University Press, 1999.

Kreider, Glenn R. "*Regnum coelorum*: Patterns of Millennial Thought in Early Christianity." *Bibliotheca Sacra* 160, no. 638 (2003): 253.

Kurz, William. *What Does the Bible Say About the End Times?: A Catholic View*. Cincinnati, OH: St. Anthony Messenger Press, 2004.

Lacoste, Jean-Yves, ed. *Encyclopedia of Christian Theology*, 2 vols. New York: Routledge, 2005.

Lacunza, Manuel. *The Coming of Messiah in Glory and Majesty*. St. Paul, MN: Seeley, 1827.

Ladd, George E. *A Commentary on the Revelation of John*. Grand Rapids, MI: Eerdmans 1972.

———. *Crucial Questions about the Kingdom of God*. Grand Rapids, MI: Eerdmans, 1952.

———. *The Gospel of the Kingdom: Scriptural Studies in the Kingdom of God*. Grand Rapids, MI: Eerdmans, 1990.

Ladd, George E., Robert G. Clouse, and Anthony A. Hoekema. *The Meaning of the Millennium: Four Views*. Downers Grove, IL: IVP Academic, 1977.

Ladd, John D. *Commentary on the Book of Enoch*. Maitland, FL: Xulon Press, 2008.

Lamb, M.L., and M. Levering. *Vatican II: Renewal within Tradition*. New York: Oxford University Press, 2008.

Landau, Y., M.B. McGarry, L. Boadt, and K.T.P.D. Camillo. *John Paul II in the Holy Land–in His Own Words: With Christian and Jewish Perspectives*. Mahwah, NJ: Paulist Press, 2005.

Lange, Matthew. *Antisemitic Elements in the Critique of Capitalism in German Culture, 1850–1933*. Bern: Peter Lang, 2007.

Lange,r Ruth, "A Jewish Response." In S.J. Pope, C.C. Helfling, and Fidei Catholic Church, Congregatio pro Doctrina, eds., *Sic Et Non: Encountering Dominus Iesus*. Maryknoll, NY: Orbis Books, 2002.

Larkin, Clarence. *The Second Coming of Christ*. New York: Cosimo Classics, 2010.

Lattier, Daniel J. "The Orthodox Rejection of Doctrinal Development." *Pro Ecclesia* 20, no. 4 (2012): 389–410.

Laursen, John Christian, and R.H. Popkin, eds. *Millenarianism and Messianism in Early Modern European Culture*. Boston, MA: Springer, 2001.

Lea, Henry Charles. *A History of Auricular Confession and Indulgences in the Latin Church, Part Three*. Whitefish, MT: Kessinger, 2004.

Lee, Sang Taek. *Religion and Social Formation in Korea: Minjung and Millenarianism*. Berlin: Mouton De Gruyter, 1996.

Leo the Great, Pope. *Sermons*. Washington, DC: Catholic University of America Press, 1996.

Levenson, Jon Douglas. *Resurrection and the Restoration of Israel: The Ultimate Victory of the God of Life*. New Haven, CT: Yale University Press, 2006.

Levy, Richard S. *Antisemitism: A Historical Encyclopedia of Prejudice and Persecution*, 2 vols. Santa Barbara, CA: ABC-CLIO, 2005.

Lewis, Scott M. *So That God May Be All in All: The Apocalyptic Message of 1 Corinthians 15, 12–34*. Roma: Pontificia Universita Gregoriana, 1998.

Lienhard, Joseph T. *Contra Marcellum: Marcellus of Ancyra and Fourth-Century Theology*. Washington, DC: Catholic University of America Press, 1999.

Lietzmann, Hans. *An die Korinther*. Tubingen: Mohr-Siebeck, 1931.

———. *Die Anfänge Des Glaubensbekenntnisses: Festgabe Zu A.V. Harnacks*. Tubingen: Mohr Siebeck, 1921.

Lieu, Samuel N.C. *Manichaeism in the Later Roman Empire and Medieval China: A Historical Survey*. Manchester: Manchester University Press, 1985.

Lindgård, Fredrik. *Paul's Line of Thought in 2 Corinthians 4:16–15:10*. Tubingen: J.C.B. Mohr (P. Siebeck), 2005.

Littlejohn, Ronnie. *Exploring Christian Theology*. Lanham, MD: University Press of America, 1985.

Livingston, James C., and Francis Schüssler Fiorenza. *Modern Christian Thought*. Minneapolis, MN: Fortress Press, 2006.

Lo-Bue, Francesco. *The Turin Fragments of Tyconius' Commentary on Revelation*. Cambridge, MA: Cambridge University Press, 1963.

Ludlow, Morwenna. *Universal Salvation: Eschatology in the Thought of Gregory of Nyssa and Karl Rahner*. New York: Oxford University Press, 2001.

Luther, Martin. *The Works: Martin Luther*. Coconut Creek, FL: Packard Technologies, 2004.

Luz, Ulrich, and Helmut Koester. *Matthew 1–7: A Commentary*. Rev. ed. Minneapolis, MN: Fortress Press, 2007.

McBrien, Richard P. *The Church: The Evolution of Catholicism*. 1st Reprint ed. New York: HarperOne, 2009.

——. *The HarperCollins Encyclopedia of Catholicism*. San Francisco, CA: HarperSanFrancisco, 1995.

McClain, Alva J. The *Greatness of the Kingdom*. Winona Lake, IN: BMH Books, 1974.

McCleary, Rollan. *A Special Illumination: Authority, Inspiration and Heresy in Gay Spirituality*. Oakville, CT: Equinox, 2004.

MacDonald, Margaret Y., and Daniel J. Harrington. *Colossians and Ephesians*. Collegeville, MN: Liturgical Press, 2000.

McFague, S. *Models of God: Theology for an Ecological, Nuclear Age*. Minneapolis, MN: Fortress Press, 1987.

McGinn, Bernard, Stephen Stein, and John J. Collins, eds., *The Continuum History of Apocalypticism*. New York: Continuum, 2003.

McGrath, Alister E. *Christianity: An Introduction*. Hoboken, NJ: Blackwell Publishing, 2006.

McGukin, John Anthony, ed. *The Encyclopedia of Eastern Orthodox Christianity*. Malden, MA: Wiley-Blackwell, 2011.

——. *The Orthodox Church: An Introduction to Its History, Doctrine, and Spiritual Culture*. Malden, MA: Wiley-Blackwell, 2010.

McKim, Donald K. *Westminster Dictionary of Theological Terms*. 1st ed. Louisville, KY: Westminster John Knox Press, 1996.

McMahon, Christopher. *Jesus Our Salvation: An Introduction to Christology*. Winona, MN: Anselm Academic, 2007.

MacRae, George W. *Studies in the New Testament and Gnosticism*. Collegeville, MN: Michael Glazier, 1987.

Mack, Michael. *German Idealism and the Jew: The Inner Anti-Semitism of Philosophy and German Jewish Responses*. Chicago, IL: University Of Chicago Press, 2003.

Madigan, Kevin, and Jon Douglas Levenson. *Resurrection: The Power of God for Christians and Jews*. New Haven, CT: Yale University Press, 2008.

Maier, Gerhard. *Die Johannesoffenbarung und Die Kirche*. Tübingen: Mohr, 1987.

Mamet, David. *The Wicked Son: Anti-Semitism, Self-Hatred, and the Jews*. 1st ed. Jewish Encounters. New York: Schocken, 2006.

Mannion, Gerard, and Lewis S. Mudge, eds. *The Routledge Companion to the Christian Church*. Routledge Religion Companions. New York: Routledge, 2008.

Bibliography

Mannion, Gerard, Lewis S. Mudge, Richard Gaillardetz, Jan Kerkhofs, and Kenneth Wilson, eds. *Readings in Church Authority: Gifts and Challenges for Contemporary Catholicism*. Burlington, VT: Ashgate, 2003.

Manoussakis, John Panteleimon, and Neal Deroo. *Phenomenology and Eschatology: Not yet in the Now*. Edited by Neal DeRoo. Aldershot: Ashgate, 2009.

Marberry, Thomas, Robert E. Picirilli, and Daryl Ellis. *Galatians through Colossians*. 1st ed. The Randall House Bible Commentary. Nashville, TN: Randall House Publications, 1988.

Marcion, and James Hamlyn Hill. *The Gospel of the Lord: An Early Version which Was Circulated by Marcion of Sinope as the Original Gospel*. New York: AMS Press, 1980.

Marcus, Joel. *The Way of the Lord: Christological Exegesis of the Old Testament in the Gospel of Mark*. New York: T&T Clark International, 2004.

Marjanen, Antti, and Petri Luomanen, eds. *A Companion to Second-Century Christian 'Heretics'*. Leiden: Brill Academic, 2008.

Marshall, John W. *Parables of War: Reading John's Jewish Apocalypse*. Waterloo, ON: Wilfrid Laurier University Press, 2001.

Marthaler, Berard L. *The Creed: The Apostolic Faith in Contemporary Theology*. Rev. ed. Mystic, CT: Twenty-Third, 2007.

Martin, David. *Vatican II: A Historic Turning Point: The Dawning of a New Epoch*. Bloomington, IN: AuthorHouse, 2011.

Mathison, Keith A. *The Shape of Sola Scriptura*. Moscow, ID: Canon Press, 2001.

Matthews, Gareth B., ed. *The Augustinian Tradition*. Berkeley, CA: University of California Press, 1999.

Matthews, Steven. *Theology and Science in the Thought of Francis Bacon*. Aldershot: Ashgate, 2008.

Mayers, Ronald B. *Evangelical Perspectives: Toward a Biblical Balance*. Lanham, MD: University Press of America, 1987.

Mays, James L. *The HarperCollins Bible Commentary*. Rev. ed. San Francisco, CA: HarperOne, 2000.

Mealy, J. Webb. *After the Thousand Years*. Journal for the Study of the New Testament Supplement. Sheffield: Sheffield Books, 1992.

Mede, Joseph. *The Works of the Pious and Profoundly-Learned Joseph Mede, B.D., sometime Fellow of Christ's College in Cambridge*. 4th ed. London: Roger Norton, 1677.

Melanchthon, Philip. *The Augsburg Confession*. Whitefish, MT: Kessinger, 2004.

Melito, and Alistair Stewart-Sykes. *On Pascha: With the Fragments of Melito and Other Material Related to the Quartodecimans*. St. Vladimir's Seminary Press "Popular Patristics" Series. Crestwood, NY: St. Vladimir's Seminary Press, 2001.

Mertens, Herman-Emiel. *Not the Cross, but the Crucified: An Essay in Soteriology*. Louvain: Peeters Press, 1992.

Meter, David Van. *The Apocalyptic Year 1000: Religious Expectation and Social Change, 950–1050*. Edited by Richard Landes, Andrew Gow, and David C. Van Meter. New York: Oxford University Press, 2003.

Metzger, Bruce M., and Michael David Coogan, eds. *The Oxford Companion to the Bible*. New York: Oxford University Press, 1993.

Meyer, Marvin W., and Berliner Wolf-Peter Funk. *Arbeitskreis für Koptisch-Gnostische Schriften*. Coptic Gnostic Library Project. *The Nag Hammadi Scriptures*. International ed. New York: HarperOne, 2007.

Michael, Robert. *A History of Catholic Antisemitism: The Dark Side of the Church*. 1st ed. New York: Palgrave Macmillan, 2008.

Migne, Jacques-Paul. *Patrologiæ Cursus Completus [Series Græca]: Omnium Ss. Patrum, Doctorum, Scriptorumque Ecclasiasticorum Sive Latinorum Sive Græcorum*. Charleston, SC: Nabu Press, 2010.
Milavec, Aaron. *The Didache: Faith, Hope, & Life of the Earliest Christian Communities, 50–70 C.E.* Mahwah, NJ: Paulist Press, 2003.
Missler, Chuck. *Prophecy 20/20: Profiling the Future through the Lens of Scripture*. Nashville, TN: Thomas Nelson, 2006.
Mitchell, Margaret M., and Frances M. Young, eds. *Origins to Constantine*. New York: Cambridge University Press, 2006.
Moehlman, Conrad. "The Origin of the Apostles' Creed." *The Journal of Religion* 13, no. 3 (1933): 301–319.
Moll, Sebastian. *The Arch-Heretic Marcion*. Tübingen: Mohr Siebeck, 2010.
Moltmann, Jürgen. *The Church in the Power of the Spirit: A Contribution to Messianic Ecclesiology*. 1st Fortress Press ed. Minneapolis, MN: Fortress Press, 1993.
———. *The Coming of God: Christian Eschatology*. London: SCM, 1996.
———. *The Crucified God: The Cross of Christ as the Foundation and Criticism of Christian Theology*. 1st Fortress Press ed. Minneapolis, MN: Fortress Press, 1993.
———. "Das Reich Gottes und die Treue zur Erde." *Das Gespräch* 49 (1963): 3–23.
———. *God in Creation*. London: SCM Press, 1985.
———. *History and the Triune God*. New York: Crossroad, 1992.
———. *Man: Christian Anthropology in the Conflicts of the Present*. Minneapolis, MN: Fortress Press, 1974.
———. *On Human Dignity: Political Theology and Ethics*. Minneapolis, MN: Fortress Press, 2007.
———. *The Spirit of Life*. Minneapolis, MN: Fortress Press, 1992.
———. *Sun of Righteousness, Arise!: God's Future for Humanity and the Earth*. 1st Fortress Press ed. Minneapolis, MN: Fortress Press, 2010.
———. *Theology of Hope: On the Ground and the Implications of a Christian Eschatology*. 1st Fortress Press ed. Minneapolis, MN: Fortress Press, 1993.
———. *The Way of Jesus Christ: Christology in Messianic Dimensions*. 1st Fortress Press ed. Minneapolis, MN: Augsburg Fortress, 1995.
Moo, Douglas J. *The Epistle to the Romans*. Grand Rapids, MI: Eerdmans, 1996.
Moore, Daniel F. *Jesus, an Emerging Jewish Mosaic: Jewish Perspectives, Post-Holocaust*. Jewish & Christian Texts in Contexts and Related Studies 2. London: T&T Clark, 2012.
Moran, Gabriel. *Uniqueness: Problem or Paradox in Jewish and Christian Traditions*. Maryknoll, NJ: Orbis Books, 1992.
Morey, Robert A. *The End of the World According to Jesus*. Maitland, FL: Xulon Press, 2010.
Morris, John W. *The Historic Church: An Orthodox View of Christian History*. Bloomington, IN: AuthorHouse 2011.
Mortimer, R.C. *Western Canon Law*. 1st ed. ed. London: Adam & Charles Black, 1953.
Mosès, Stéphane. *The Angel of History: Rosenzweig, Benjamin, Scholem*. Stanford, CA: Stanford University Press, 2009.
Mosheim, Johann Lorenz. *Commentaries on the Affairs of the Christians Before the Time of Constantine the Great*. Memphis, TN: General Books, 2012.
Moss, Joshua L. *Midrash and Legend: Historical Anecdotes in the Tannaitic Midrashim*. 2nd Gorgias Press ed. Piscataway, NJ: Gorgias, 2004.
Mounce, Robert H. *The Book of Revelation*. Rev. ed. Grand Rapids, MI: Eerdmans, 1998.

Mussner, F. *Tractate on the Jews: The Significance of Judaism for Christian Faith.* Minneapolis, MN: Fortress Press, 1984.

Mwandayi, Canisius, *Death and After-life Rituals in the Eyes of the Shona: Dialogue with Shona Customs in the Quest for Authentic Inculturation.* Bamberg, Germany: University of Bamberg Press, 2011.

Nachtwei, Gerhard. *Dialogische Unsterblichkeit: Eine Ratzingers Untersuchung zu Eschatologie und Theologie.* Leipzig: St. Benno-Verlag, 1986.

Neusner, Jacob, William Scott Green, and Ernest S. Frerichs, eds. *The Incarnation of God: The Character of Divinity in Formative Judaism.* Atlanta, GA: University of South Florida, 1992.

———. *Judaisms and Their Messiahs at the Turn of the Christian Era.* Cambridge: Cambridge University Press, 1988.

———. *Judaism When Christianity Began: A Survey of Belief and Practice.* Louisville, KY: Westminster John Knox Press, 2002.

———. *Rabbinic Judaism: The Theological System.* Boston, MA: Brill, 2003.

Newman, Carey C., ed. *Jesus & the Restoration of Israel: A Critical Assessment of N.T. Wright's Jesus and the Victory of God.* Downers Grove, IL: IVP Academic, 1999.

Newman, John Henry. *Roman Catholic Writings on Doctrinal Development.* Kansas City, MO: Sheed & Ward, 1997.

Newman, Michael. *The Didache: The Epistle of Barnabas, the Epistles and the Martyrdom of St. Polycarp, the Fragments of Papias, the Epistle to Diogenes: Ancient Christian Writers.* Mahwah, NJ: Paulist Press, 1948.

Nicholl, Colin R. *From Hope to Despair in Thessalonica: Situating 1 and 2 Thessalonians.* New York: Cambridge University Press, 2004.

Nightingale, Andrea Wilson. *Spectacles of Truth in Classical Greek Philosophy: Theoria in Its Cultural Context.* Cambridge: Cambridge University Press, 2004.

Nixon, Thomas C. *The Time in the End in the Book of Revelation.* Miami, FL: 1st Book Library, 2002.

Novak, David. *The Image of the Non-Jew in Judaism: The Idea of Noahide Law.* 2nd ed. Edited by Matthew Lagrone. Oxford: Littman Library of Jewish Civilization, 2011.

———. *Talking with Christians: Musings of a Jewish Theologian.* Radical Traditions. Grand Rapids, MI: Eerdmans, 2005.

Novak, Peter. *Original Christianity: A New Key to Understanding the Gospel of Thomas and Other Lost Scriptures.* Charlottesville, VA: Hampton Roads, 2005.

O'Collins, Gerald, and Mario Farrugia. *Catholicism: The Story of Catholic Christianity.* New York: Oxford University Press, 2004.

O'Daly, Gerard. *Augustine's City of God: A Reader's Guide.* New York: Oxford University Press, 2004.

O'Hagan, Angelo P. *Material Re-Creation in the Apostolic Fathers: Texte und Untersuchungen Zur Geschichte der Altchristlichen Literatur.* Berlin: Akademie-Verlag, 1968.

O'Shea, Sean M., and Meryl A. Walker. *The Millennium Myth: The Ever-Ending Story.* Atlanta, GA: Humanics Trade Group, 1998.

Ocáriz, F., L.F. Mateo Seco, and J.A. Riestra. *The Mystery of Jesus Christ: A Christology and Soteriology Textbook.* Dublin: Four Courts Press, 1998.

Oden, Thomas C. *Classic Christianity: A Systematic Theology.* Ventura, CA: HarperOne, 2009.

Ogden, Schubert M. "Adversus Judaeos? A Christian Understanding of Judaism." *Process Studies* 12, no. 2 (1982): 94–97.

Olson, Roger E. *The Story of Christian Theology: Twenty Centuries of Tradition & Reform*. Downers Grove, IL: IVP Academic, 1999.

———. *The Westminster Handbook to Evangelical Theology*. Louisville, KY: Westminster John Knox Press, 2004.

Page, Sydney H.T. "Revelation 20 and Pauline Eschatology." *Journal of the Evangelical Theological Society* 23, no. 1 (1980): 31–43.

Paget, James Carleton. *The Epistle of Barnabas: Outlook and Background*. Tübingen: J.C.B. Mohr, 1994.

Paldiel, Mordecai. *Churches and the Holocaust: Unholy Teaching, Good Samaritans, and Reconciliation*. Jersey City, NJ: KTAV, 2006.

Panasa, Martino. *Il Segno del Soprannaturale* 30 (1990): 1–15.

Pasquini, John. *True Christianity: The Catholic Way*. Bloomington, IN: iUniverse, 2003.

Pate, C. Marvin. *Four Views on the Book of Revelation*. Grand Rapids, MI: Zondervan, 1998.

Patterson, David. *Emil L. Fackenheim: A Jewish Philosopher's Response to the Holocaust*. Syracuse, NY: Syracuse University Press, 2008.

Paul II, John, E.J. Fisher, and L. Klenicki. B'Nai B'rith and the Anti-defamation League. *Spiritual Pilgrimage: Texts on Jews and Judaism, 1979–1995*. New York: Crossroad, 1995.

John T. Pawlikowski, "The Christ Event and the Jewish People." In Tatha Wiley, ed., *Thinking of Christ: Proclamation, Explanation, Meaning*. New York: Continuum, 2003.

Pawlikowski, John T. "Land as an Issue in Christian–Jewish Dialogue." *CrossCurrents* 59, no. 2 (2009): 197–209.

———. "Reflections on Covenant and Mission: Forty Years after *Nostra Aetate*." *Cross Currents* 56, no. 4 (2007): 70–95.

Payne, Craig. *What Believers Don't Have to Believe: The Non-Essentials of the Christian Faith*. Lanham, MD: University Press of America, 2006.

Pelikan, Jaroslav. *The Christian Tradition, a History of the Development of Doctrine: The Emergence of the Catholic Tradition (100–600)*. New York: University of Chicago Press, 1971.

Penasa, Martino. *Viene Gesù! La Venuta Intermedia Del Signore*. Udine, Italy: Edizioni Segno, 1994.

Pentecost, J. Dwight. *Things to Come: A Study in Biblical Eschatology*. Grand Rapids, MI: Zondervan, 1965.

Peters, G.N.H. *The Theocratic Kingdom of Our Lord Jesus, the Christ, as Covenanted in the Old Testament and Presented in the New Testament*. New York; London: Funk & Wagnalls, 1884.

Petrement, Simone. *A Separate God: The Christian Origins of Gnosticism*. New York: Harpercollins, 1990.

Petrisko, Thomas, W. *Inside Purgatory: What History Theology and the Mystics Tell Us about Purgatory*. Pittsburgh, PA: St. Andrew's Productions, 2000.

———. *The Kingdom of Our Father*. Pittsburgh, PA: Saint Andrew's Productions, 1999.

Phillips, John. *Exploring Galatians: An Expository Commentary*. Grand Rapids, MI: Kregel Academic & Professional, 2004.

Pollefeyt, Didier, ed. *Jews and Christians, Rivals or Partners for the Kingdom of God?: In Search of an Alternative for the Theology of Substitution*. Louvain: Peeters, 1998.

Pontificium Consilium pro Dialogo inter Religiones. "Dialogue and Proclamation," Bulletin, no. 77; 26 (1991/2) 210–250.

Pope, S.J., C.C. Hefling, and Fidei Catholic Church. Congregatio pro Doctrina. *Sic Et Non: Encountering Dominus Iesus*. Maryknoll, NY: Orbis Books, 2002.

Porter, Stanley E., David Tombs, and Michael A. Hayes. *Faith in the Millennium*. Sheffield: Sheffield Academic Press, 2001.

Quasten, Johannes. *The Ante-Nicene Literature after Irenaeus*, Vol. 2 of Patrology. Trumbull, CT: Spectrum, 1953.

Ranstrom, Erik. "Dialogue as Communio: Recovering the Eschatological Dimension of the Eucharistic Church." Paper presented at the 67th Annual Convention of the Catholic Theological Society, Miami, FL, June 7, 2012, http://www.ctsa-online.org/Convention%202012/CTSAProgramAbstract4-13-12.pdf/ (accessed January 30, 2013).

Raphael, Simcha Paull. *Jewish Views of the Afterlife*. 2nd ed. Lanham, MD: Rowman & Littlefield, 2009.

Ratzinger, Joseph. *Das neue Volk Gottes: Entwürfe zur Ekklesiologie*. Munich: Patmos, 1969.

———. *Eschatology: Death and Eternal Life*. Washington, DC: Catholic University of America Press, 2007.

———. *God is Near Us: The Eucharist, the Heart of Life*. Edited by Stephan Otto Horn. San Francisco, CA: Ignatius Press, 2003.

———. "Interreligious Dialogue and Jewish–Christian Relations." *Communio: International Catholic Review* 25 (1998): 29–40.

———. *The Ratzinger Reader: Mapping a Theological Journey*. Edited by Lieven Boeve and Gerard Mannion. London: T&T Clark International, 2010.

———. "Remarks to the Bishops of Chile Regarding the Lefebvre Schism." Lecture, Santiago, Chile, July 13, 1988.

Rausch, Thomas P. *Towards a Truly Catholic Church: An Ecclesiology for the Third Millennium*. Collegeville, MN: Liturgical Press, 2005.

Raven, Charles E. *Apollinarianism: An Essay on the Christology of the Early Church*. Eugene, OR: Wipf & Stock, 2004.

Redles, David. *Hitler's Millennial Reich: Apocalyptic Belief and the Search for Salvation*. New York: NYU Press, 2005.

Rees, B.R. *Pelagius: Life and Letters*. Rochester, NY: Boydell Press, 2004.

Resseguie, James L. *Revelation Unsealed: A Narrative Critical Approach to John's Apocalypse*. Boston, MA: Brill Academic, 1998.

———. *The Revelation of John: A Narrative Commentary*. Grand Rapids, MI: Baker Academic, 2009.

Rhodes, James M. *The Hitler Movement: A Modern Millenarian Revolution*. Stanford, CA: Hoover Institution Press, 1980.

Richardson, Peter. *Israel in the Apostolic Church*. London: Cambridge University Press, 1969.

Ricœur, Paul. *Interpretation Theory: Discourse and the Surplus of Meaning*. Fort Worth, TX: Christian University Press, 1976.

Riddlebarger, Kim. *A Case for Amillennialism: Understanding the End Times*. Leicester: Baker Books, 2003.

Roberts, Alexander, and James Donaldson, eds. *Ante-Nicene Christian Library Translations of the Writings of the Fathers Down to AD 325*. Whitefish, MT: Kessinger, 2004.

Roberts, Alexander, James Donaldson, Philip Schaff, and Henry Wace, eds. *Nicene and Post-Nicene Fathers*. Second Series, 14 vols. Buffalo, NY: Hendrickson Publishers, 1994.

Robertson, Archibald. *Regnum Dei*. Whitefish, MT: Kessinger, 2004.

Rosenstock-Huessy, Eugen, and Franz Rosenzweig. *Judaism despite Christianity: The Letters on Christianity and Judaism between Eugen Rosenstock-Huessy and Franz Rosenzweig.* Tuscaloosa, AL: University of Alabama Press, 1969.

Rosenzweig, Franz, and Barbara E. Galli. *The Star of Redemption.* Modern Jewish Philosophy and Religion. Madison, WI: University of Wisconsin Press, 2005.

Rosenzweig, Franz, Barbara E. Galli, and Nahum N. Glatzer. *Franz Rosenzweig: His Life and Thought.* 2d rev. ed. New York: Schocken Books, 1961.

Roth, John, and Carol Rittner. *Pope Pius XII and the Holocaust.* Leicester History of Religions. London: Continuum, 2004.

Rowland, Christopher, ed. *The Cambridge Companion to Liberation Theology.* 2nd ed. New York: Cambridge University Press, 2007.

Rowland, Tracey. *Benedict XVI: A Guide for the Perplexed.* London: T&T Clark International, 2010.

Rudin, James A. *Christians & Jews–Faith to Faith: Tragic History, Promising Present, Fragile Future.* Woodstock, VT: Jewish Lights, 2010.

Rudolph, David J. "Messianic Jews and Christian Theology: Restoring an Historical Voice to the Contemporary Discussion." *Pro Ecclesia* XIV, no. 1 (2005): 58–84.

Rudolph, Kurt. *Gnosis: The Nature and History of Gnosticism.* Edinburgh: T&T Clark International, 2001.

Ruether, Rosemary Radford. *Faith and Fratricide: The Theological Roots of Anti-Semitism.* New York: Seabury Press, 1974.

Rush, Ormond. *The Eyes of Faith: The Sense of the Faithful and the Church's Reception of Revelation.* Washington, DC: Catholic University of America Press, 2009.

Sæbø, Magne, ed. *Hebrew Bible/Old Testament I: From the Beginning to the Middle Ages (until 1300).* 2 vols. Göttingen: Vandenhoeck & Ruprecht, 2000.

Sakenfeld, Katharine Doob. *The Meaning of Hesed in the Hebrew Bible: A New Inquiry.* Missoula, MT: Scholars Press for the Harvard Semitic Museum, 1978.

Saller, Sylvester John, and Emmanuele Testa. *The Archaeological Setting of the Shrine of Bethphage.* Jerusalem: Franciscan Press, 1961.

Sanders, E.P. *Paul and Palestinian Judaism: A Comparison of Patterns of Religion.* Minneapolis, MN: Fortress Press, 1977.

Saracino, M. *Being about Borders: A Christian Anthropology of Difference.* Collegeville, MN: Liturgical Press, 2011.

Saucy, Mark. *Kingdom of God and the Teaching of Jesus: In 20th Century Theology.* Dallas, TX: W Publishing Group, 1997.

Saucy, Robert L. *The Case for Progressive Dispensationalism: The Interface between Dispensational & Non-Dispensational Theology.* Grand Rapids, MI: Zondervan Publishing House, 1993.

Scafi, Alessandro. *Mapping Paradise: A History of Heaven on Earth.* Chicago, IL: University Of Chicago Press, 2006.

Schaeffer, Edith. *Christianity is Jewish.* Wheaton, IL: Tyndale House, 1975.

Schaff, Philip. *The Apostolic Fathers with Justin Martyr and Irenaeus.* Oxford: Benediction Classics, 2010.

———. *The Creeds of Christendom.* 6th ed. Grand Rapids, MI: Baker, 1998.

———. *History of the Christian Church.* 8 vols. Grand Rapids, MI: Eerdmans, 1994.

Schliesser, Benjamin. *Abraham's Faith in Romans 4: Paul's Concept of Faith in Light of the History of Reception of Genesis 15:6.* Tubingen: Mohr Siebeck, 2007.

Schmahl, Nadine. *Das Tetragramm als Sprachfigur: Ein Kommentar zu Franz Rosenzweigs letztem Aufsatz.* Tübingen: Mohr Siebeck, 2009.

Schnackenburg, R. *God's Rule and Kingdom*. New York: Herder & Herder, 1968.

Schnaubelt, Joseph C., and Frederick Van Fleteren. *Augustine: Biblical Exegete*. New York: Peter Lang, 2001.

Scholem, G. *The Messianic Idea in Judaism and Other Essays on Jewish Spirituality*. New York: Schocken Books, 1995.

Schultz, Joseph P. *Judaism and the Gentile Faiths: Comparative Studies in Religion*. Rutherford, NJ: Fairleigh Dickinson University Press, 1981.

Schultze, Augustus. *Christian Doctrine and Systematic Theology*. Bethlehem, PA: Moravian Church, 1914.

Schwarz, Hans. *Christology*. Grand Rapids, MI: Eerdmans, 1998.

——. *Eschatology*. Grand Rapids, Mich.: W.B. Eerdmans, 2000.

——. *Tree of Souls: The Mythology of Judaism*. New York: Oxford University Press, 2004.

Schweitzer, Albert. *The Mysticism of Paul the Apostle*. Johns Hopkins paperbacks ed. Baltimore, MD: The Johns Hopkins University Press, 1998.

Schweitzer, Albert, and J. Bowden. *The Quest of the Historical Jesus*. Minneapolis, MI: Fortress Press, 2001.

Scott, James M. *On Earth as in Heaven: The Restoration of Sacred Time and Sacred Space in the Book of Jubilees*. Boston, MA: Brill Academic, 2005.

——, ed. *Restoration: Old Testament, Jewish, and Christian Perspectives*. Boston, MA: Brill Academic, 2001.

Scott, Peter, and William T. Cavanaugh, eds. *The Blackwell Companion to Political Theology*. Malden, MA: Wiley-Blackwell, 2004.

Secretariat for Catholic–Jewish Relations, United States Catholic Conference. Adult Education Section, and B'nai B'rith—Anti-defamation League, Interfaith Affairs Dept. *Within Context: Guidelines for the Catechetical Presentation of Jews and Judaism in the New Testament*. Morristown, NJ: Silver Burdett & Ginn, 1987.

Segal, Alan F. *Two Powers in Heaven: Early Rabbinic Reports about Christianity and Gnosticism*. Boston, MA: Brill Academic, 2002.

Seguy, Jean. "Millénarisme et'Ordres Adventistes': Grignion de Montfort et les Apôtres des derniers temps." *Archives des Sciences Sociales des Religions* 53 (1982): 23–38.

Seiss, Joseph A. *Apocalypse: An Exposition of the Book of Revelation*. Peabody, MA: Kregel Classics, 2000.

Selby, Donald Joseph. "Changing Ideas in New Testament Eschatology." *Harvard Theological Review* 50 (January 1957): 23.

Shedd, William Greenough Thayer. *Dogmatic Theology*. Charleston, SC: Forgotten Books, 2010.

Shum, Shiu-Lun. *Paul's Use of Isaiah in Romans: A Comparative Study of Paul's Letter to the Romans and the Sibylline and Qumran Sectarian Texts*. Tubingen: ABM Komers, 2002.

Signer, Michael. "The Christian Millennium in Jewish Historical Perspective: Implications for Dialogue and Joint Social Action." *Sidic Periodical* 32, no. 1 (1999): 2–5.

Siker, Jeffrey S. *Disinheriting the Jews: Abraham in Early Christian Controversy*. Louisville, KY: Westminster John Knox Press, 1991.

Singer, David G. "Has God Truly Abrogated the Mosaic Covenant?: American Catholic Attitudes toward Judaism as Reflected in Catholic Thought, 1945–1977." *Jewish Social Studies* 47, no. 3/4 (1985): 243–254.

Smith, D.C. "The Millennial Reign of Jesus Christ: Some Observations on Rev. 20:1–10." *ResQ*, 16 (1973): 219–230.

Smith, James K.A. *The Fall of Interpretation: Philosophical Foundations for a Creational Hermeneutic*. 2nd ed. Grand Rapids, MI: Baker Academic, 2012.

Smith, Philip. *The Student's Ecclesiastical History: The History of the Christian Church during the First Ten Centuries from Its Foundation to the Full Establishment of the Roman Empire and the Papal Power*. New York: Harper & Brothers, 1879.

Smith, Wilfred Cantwell. *The Meaning and End of Religion*. Minneapolis, MI: Fortress Press, 1991.

Snodgrass, Klyne. *The Parable of the Wicked Tenants: An Inquiry into Parable Interpretation* Wissenschaftliche Untersuchungen Zum Neuen Testament. Tübingen: J.C.B. Mohr, 1983.

——. *Stories with Intent: A Comprehensive Guide to the Parables of Jesus*. Grand Rapids, MI: Eerdmans, 2008.

Soulen, R. Kendall. *The God of Israel and Christian Theology*. Minneapolis, MI: Fortress Press, 1996.

——. "YHWH the Triune God." *Modern Theology* 15:1(January 1999): 25–54.

Sparks, Jack N. *The Apostolic Fathers*. Nashville, TN: T. Nelson, 1982.

Speidel, Michael P. *Riding for Caesar: The Roman Emperor's Horse Guard*. Cambridge, MA: Harvard University Press, 1997.

Steenberg, M.C. *Irenaeus on Creation: The Cosmic Christ and the Saga of Redemption*. Leiden: Brill Academic, 2008.

Steinhauser, Kenneth B. *The Apocalypse Commentary of Tyconius: A History of Its Reception and Influence*. Frankfurt am Main: Peter Lang, 1987.

Stendahl, Krister. *Final Account: Paul's Letter to the Romans*. 1st Fortress Press ed. Minneapolis, MI: Fortress Press, 1995.

Stern, Chaim. *Gates of Repentance: The New Union Prayerbook for the Days of Awe* (translation of *Shaarei Teshuva*). New York: Central Conference of American Rabbis, 1996.

Strecker, Georg. *Theology of the New Testament*. Louisville, KY: Walter De Gruyter, 2000.

Stump, Eleonore, and Norman Kretzmann, eds. *The Cambridge Companion to Augustine*. New York: Cambridge University Press, 2001.

Sullivan, Clayton. *Rethinking Realized Eschatology*. Macon, GA: Mercer University Press, 1988.

Sungenis, Robert A. "The Old Covenant: Revoked or Not Revoked?: A Review of the PBS Documentary 'Jews and Christians: A Journey.'" *Culture Wars* (January 2008): 1–41.

Svigel, Michael J. "The Phantom Heresy: Did the Council of Ephesus (431) Condemn Chiliasm?" *Trinity Journal* 24 (2003). 105–112.

Swete, H.B. *The Apostle's Creed: In Relation to Primitive Christianity*. Cambridge: Cambridge University Press, 1899.

Tabbernee, William. *Fake Prophecy and Polluted Sacraments: Ecclesiastical and Imperial Reactions to Montanism*. Leiden: Brill, 2007.

——. "Portals of the Montanist New Jerusalem: The discovery of Pepouza and Tymion." *Journal of Early Christian Studies* 11, no. 1 (2003): 92–93.

Taubes, Jacob. *Occidental Eschatology*. Stanford, CA: Stanford University Press, 2009.

Taylor, D.T. *The Voice of the Church on the Coming and Kingdom of the Redeemer; or, A History of the Doctrine of the Reign of Christ on Earth*, revised and edited by H.L. Hastings. Peace Dale, RI: H.L. Hastings, 1855.

Taylor, Mark C. *Erring: A Postmodern A/theology*. London: University of Chicago Press, 1987.

Telfer, W. "Was Hegesippus a Jew?" *The Harvard Theological Review* 53, no. 2 (1960): 143–153.

Tertullian. *On the Veiling of Virgins*. Whitefish, MT: Kessinger, 2010.

Thayer, Joseph Henry, Carl Ludwig Wilibald Grimm, and Christian Gottlob Wilke. *Thayer's Greek-English Lexicon of the New Testament: Coded with the Numbering System from Strong's Exhaustive Concordance of the Bible*. Peabody, MA: Hendrickson, 1996.

Thielman, Frank S. "Another Look at the Eschatology of Eusebius of Caesarea." *Vigiliae Christianae* 41 (1987): 226–237.

Thomas, P.C. *General Councils of the Church: A Compact History*. Bandra, Mumbai: St. Paul's Publications, 2001.

Toner, James H. *The Sword and the Cross: Reflections on Command and Conscience*. New York: Praeger, 1992.

Toon, Peter. *Puritans, the Millennium and the Future of Israel: Puritan Eschatology, 1600 to 1660: A Collection of Essays*. Cambridge: James Clarke, 1970.

Trafton, Joseph L. *Reading Revelation: A Literary and Theological Commentary*. Rev. ed. Macon, GA: Smyth & Helwys, 2005.

Trevett, Christine. *Montanism: Gender, Authority and the New Prophecy*. Cambridge; New York: Cambridge University Press, 2002.

Trompf, G.W., ed. *Cargo Cults and Millenarian Movements: Transoceanic Comparisons of New Religious Movements*. New York: Mouton De Gruyter, 1990.

Twomey, Vincent. *Apostolikos Thronos: The Primacy of Rome as Reflected in the Church History of Eusebius and the Historico-Apologetic Writings of Saint Athanasius the Great*. Münster: Aschendorff, 1982.

Uhlig, Siegbert, ed. *D-Ha*, Vol. 2 of *Encyclopaedia Aethiopica*. Wiesbaden: Otto Harrassowitz Verlag, 2005.

Valois, Helen M. "Anti-Judaism vs. Anti-Semitism: Was Christianity Itself Responsible for the Nazi Holocaust?" *Lay Witness*, October, 1998, 1–4.

van Buren, Paul Matthews. *A Theology of the Jewish Christian Reality*. 2 vols. San Francisco, CA: Harper & Row, 1987.

———. *A Theology of the Jewish–Christian Reality*, 2 vols. Lanham, MD: University Press of America, 1995.

VanderKam, James C., and William Adler. *The Jewish Apocalyptic Heritage in Early Christianity*. Compendia Rerum Iudaicarum ad Novum Testamentum. Section 3: Jewish Traditions in Early Christian Literature. Assen, Netherlands, and Minneapolis, MI: Van Gorcum and Fortress Press, 1996.

VanderWilt, Jeffrey. *A Church without Borders: The Eucharist and the Church in Ecumenical Perspective*. Collegeville, MI: Michael Glazier Books, 1998.

VanGemeren, Willem A. *Interpreting the Prophetic Word: An Introduction to the Prophetic Literature of the Old Testament*. Grand Rapids, MI: Zondervan, 1996.

Vanhoozer, Kevin J., ed. *Theological Interpretation of the New Testament: A Book-by-book Survey*. Grand Rapids, MI: Baker Academic, 2008.

Vlach, Michael J. *The Church as a Replacement of Israel: An Analysis of Supersessionism*. Edition Israelogie (Edis). Frankfurt; NY: Peter Lang, 2009.

———. *Has the Church Replaced Israel?: A Theological Evaluation*. Nashville, TN: B&H, 2010.

———. "Rejection then Hope: The Church's Doctrine of Israel in the Patristic Era." *TMSJ* 19, no. 1 (2008): 51–70.

———. "Variations within Supersessionism." In the Conference of the Evangelical Theological Society, San Diego, CA, 2007.

Voegelin, Eric. *Science, Politics, and Gnosticism*. Chicago, IL: Henry Regnery, 1968.
Voisin, G. *L'apollinarisme: étude historique, littéraire et dogmatique sur le début des controverses christologiques*. Louvain: Typ. J. Van Linthout, 1901.
Vos, Geerhardus. *Biblical Theology: Old and New Testaments*. Eugene, OR: Wipf & Stock, 2003.
Vu Chi Hy, Paul. "Towards a Constructive Retrieval of the Eschatological Dimension of the Eucharist." *AEJT* 3 (August 2004): 1–22.
Wagner, J. Ross. *Heralds of the Good News: Isaiah and Paul in Concert in the Letter to the Romans*. Boston, MA: Brill, 2003.
Wagner, L.A. *Hitler: Man of Strife*. New York: W.W. Norton, 1942.
Wainwright, Arthur William. *Mysterious Apocalypse: Interpreting the Book of Revelation*. Nashville, TN: Abingdon Press, 1993.
Wallace-Hadrill, D.S. *Eusebius of Caesarea*. Cambridge, MA: Mowbray, 1960.
Wallis, James H. *Post-Holocaust Christianity: Paul Van Buren's Theology of the Jewish–Christian Reality*. Lanham, MD: University Press of America, 1997.
Walls, J.L. *The Oxford Handbook of Eschatology*. New York: Oxford University Press, 2008.
Walton, John H. *Ancient Near Eastern Thought and the Old Testament: Introducing the Conceptual World of the Hebrew Bible*. Grand Rapids, MI: Baker Academic, 2006.
Walvoord, John F. *The Millennial Kingdom: A Basic Text in Premillennial Theology*. Grand Rapids, MI: Zondervan, 1983.
Wardle, Timothy. *The Jerusalem Temple and Early Christian Identity*. Tübingen: Mohr Siebeck, 2010.
Warner, Timothy. "The Source of the Corruption of Apostolic Eschatology." *ODJ* 5, no. 1 (2008): 1–6.
Waymeyer, Matt. *Revelation 20 and the Millennial Debate*. Woodlands, TX: Kress Christian Publications, 2004.
Weaver, Joel A. *Theodoret of Cyrus on Romans 11:26: Recovering an Early Christian Elijah Redivivus Tradition*. New York: Peter Lang, 2007.
Webber, R.E., and D. Neff. *Common Roots: The Original Call to an Ancient-Future Faith*. Grand Rapids, MI: Zondervan, 2009.
Weber, Eugen. *Apocalypses: Prophecies, Cults, and Millennial Beliefs through the Ages*. Cambridge, MA: Harvard University Press, 2000.
Wengst, Klaus. *Häresie und Orthodoxie im Spiegel Des Ersten Johannesbriefes*. Gütersloh: Gutersloher Verlagshaus G. Mohn, 1976.
Wessel, Susan. *Cyril of Alexandria and the Nestorian Controversy: The Making of a Saint and of a Heretic*. New York: Oxford University Press, 2004.
Wessinger, Catherine, ed. *Millennialism, Persecution, and Violence: Historical Cases*. Syracuse, NY: Syracuse University Press, 2000.
———, ed. *The Oxford Handbook of Millennialism*. New York: Oxford University Press, 2011.
Whidden, Woodrow, Jerry Moon, and John W. Reeve. *The Trinity: Understanding God's Love, His Plan of Salvation, and Christian Relationships*. Hagerstown, MD: Review & Herald Publishing Association, 2002.
White, Eric Charles. *Kaironomia: On the Will-to-invent*. Ithaca, NY: Cornell University Press, 1987.
White, R. Fowler. "Agony, Irony, and Victory in Inaugurated Eschatology: Reflections on the Current Amillennial-Postmillennial Debate." *Westminster Theological Seminary* 62.2 (2000): 161–176.

Wilde, M.J. *Vatican II: A Sociological Analysis of Religious Change.* Princeton, NJ: Princeton University Press, 2007.
Wiles, Maurice, and Mark Santer, eds. *Documents in Early Christian Thought.* Cambridge: Cambridge University Press, 1977.
Wiley, Tatha. *Original Sin: Origins, Developments, Contemporary Meanings.* Mahwah, NJ: Paulist Press, 2002.
Wiley, Tatha. *Thinking of Christ: Proclamation, Explanation, Meaning.* New York: Continuum, 2003.
Wilken, Robert Louis. *John Chrysostom and the Jews: Rhetoric and Reality in the Late 4th Century.* The Transformation of the Classical Heritage. Berkeley, CA: University of California Press, 1983.
———. *The Land Called Holy: Palestine in Christian History and Thought.* New Haven, CT: Yale University Press, 1992.
Wilkinson, David. *Christian Eschatology and the Physical Universe.* New York: T&T Clark International, 2010.
Williams, Frank. *The Panarion of Epiphanius of Salamis.* New York: Brill Academic, 1997.
Williamson, P.S. *Ephesians.* Grand Rapids, MI: Baker, 2009.
Wilson, Douglas. *Heaven Misplaced: Christ's Kingdom on Earth.* Moscow, ID: Canon Press, 2008.
Wishon, Larry M. *Redigging the Wells of Our Fathers*, vol. 2. Chattanooga, TN: CreateSpace, 2010.
Witherington, Ben. *The Indelible Image: The Theological and Ethical Thought World of the New Testament.* Downers Grove, IL: IVP Academic, 2010.
Wright, David, F. "Why Were the Montanists Condemned?" *Themelios* 2, no. 1 (September 1976): 15–22.
Wright, N.T. *Climax of the Covenant.* Minneapolis, MI: Fortress Press, 1993.
———. *The Resurrection of the Son of God.* London: SPCK, 2003.
Wuerl, Donald W. *The Teaching of Christ: A Catholic Catechism for Adults.* 5th ed. Huntington, IN: Our Sunday Visitor, 2005.
Wyschogrod, Michael. *Abraham's Promise: Judaism and Jewish–Christian Relations.* Grand Rapids, MI: Eerdmans Publishing, 2004.
Wyschogrod, Michael, and R. Kendall Soulen. *Radical Traditions.* Grand Rapids, MI: Eerdmans, 2004.
Yule, Rob. "A Review of Literature on Eschatology with Special Reference to Jürgen Moltmann's Theology of Hope." *Journal of the New Zealand Theological Students Fellowship* (April 1968): 5–9.
Zakai, Avihu. "The Poetics of History and the Destiny of Israel: The Role of the Jews in English Apocalyptic Thought during the Sixteenth and Seventeenth Centuries," *Journal of Jewish Thought and Philosophy* 5 (1966): 313–350.
Zenger, Erich, "The Covenant that was Never Revoked: The Foundations of a Christian Theology of Judaism." In Philip A. Cunningham, Johannes Hofmann, and Joseph Sievers, eds., *The Catholic Church and the Jewish People: Recent Reflections from Rome.* New York: Fordham University Press, 2007.
Zeitlin, Solomon. "The Ecumenical Council Vatican II and the Jews." *The Jewish Quarterly Review* 56, no. 2 (1965): 93–111.
Zimmermann, Nigel K. "Karol Wojtyla and Emmanuel Levinas on the Embodied Self: The Forming of the Other as Moral Self-Disclosure." *The Heythrop Journal* 50, no. 6 (2009): 982–995.

Index

Abraham 43, 46, 49, 61, 64, 73, 224, 226, 238–40, 282; children of 35, 41, 239; and God's covenant with the Jewish people through 40; legacy of 41; promises of 27, 54, 223, 234, 242
Abrahamic covenant 38, 41, 44, 49, 73–4, 242, 244
Acts 1 47
Acts 1:3–8 47
Acts 1:6 248
Acts 2 47
Acts 3:19–21, 14:21–23, 17:30–31 247
Acts 4:2 103
Acts 15:19–29 212
adversus Judaeos tradition 26
Africanus, Julius 116
Against Praxeas (Tertullian) 162
Aguzzi, Steven 50, 227
Alexandrian legacy 93, 137
Alexandrian school 135, 138, 150
"all Israel" (*Romans 11: 25–27*) 9, 20, 104, 267
Allison, Dale 76, 90, 101, 105n5, 108, 140n21, 267, 277n86
Ambrose of Milan 113, 120, 129, 149, 154, 160, 163, 169
amillennial 89–90, 206–7, 209, 212, 214, 240–3, 251, 253–4, 259, 265; beliefs 152; Christian eschatology 215; Church 221, 236; concept of 4; foundation of supersessionism 269–70; influence of Augustine 176; interpretation 92, 95–7, 99, 137; interpretation of Revelation 92; reception of Scripture and tradition 197
amillennialism 98–9, 120–1, 133–6, 138–40, 149–51, 206–9, 216–18, 235–6, 257–9, 272–5; adopted by Roman Catholic and all mainline Churches 89,
249; contemporary 138, 256; modern 93; political 12; traditional 219
amillennialists 97–9, 117–21, 165, 169, 215–16, 221, 240–4, 248–9, 253–4, 257–8; apologists 146; authors 168, 236; claim that the Church is the New Israel 221; claim that the kingdom has come 287; interpretation of *Revelation* 20:4 98, 169; and millennialists 145; paradigm 212, 216, 219, 235–6, 243, 246, 257; polemicists 166; and punitive supersessionists 249; schemes perpetuating the idea that the Church is the kingdom 272; and structural supersessionists 257; themes incompatible with the Apostolic Witness and the Hebrew Bible 245; traditional Catholic 219
Amos 9:15 248
Anderson, David R. 103, 111
angels 93, 96, 183, 263, 280
Anomoeans 172
ante-Nicene 115, 118–19, 121, 123, 125–6, 163, 179, 181, 191, 193; Christians 119; Church 12, 193; Fathers 18, 115, 119, 125–6, 152; Patristic chiliasm 191; period 119, 121, 163
anti-Jewish 17–18, 41–2, 107, 219, 249, 265; Christian ideologies 41; Christian theologies 15; elements of the early Church Fathers 289; utterances 107, 265
anti-Marcionite eschatology 256
anti-millennialism 145, 151, 163
anti-Semitism 1, 14, 17, 52–4, 59, 61, 205, 277, 284
Antichrist 10, 100, 125, 146, 192, 264
Antioch 33, 121, 166
Apocalypse 93–4, 241
The Apocalypse of Abraham 92

The Apocalypse of Weeks 92
apocalyptic Jewish sources 253
apocalypticism, fulfilled and the connection with Post-Nicene Catholic ecclesiology 76
Apollinarianism 5, 160, 166, 172, 180, 184, 186
Apollinaris 154, 166–8, 170–5, 182–4, 186; and apocalyptic eschatology 175; and chiliasm 171; concept of the Divine Logos 166; deposition of 170; heresies of 168; millenarian teachings of 173; reactionary teachings of 174; rejected by Basil on the point of Christology 170
Apollinaris of Hierapolis 167
Apollinaris of Laodicea 168, 170–1
apostles 44–7, 56, 95–6, 115, 117–18, 121, 126, 145, 178, 181–2
Apostles' Creed 128, 159–64, 177–9, 288
apostolic Church 51, 106, 112, 135, 145, 155, 202
apostolic era 92, 97
apostolic Fathers 56, 117 *see also* Fathers
apostolic tradition 115, 117–18, 130, 136, 151, 161–3, 174, 224
Apostolic Tradition (Hippolytus) 163
Apostolic Witness 27, 29, 32–4, 38, 44, 72, 74, 208, 217, 255–6
Aquinas, Thomas 113, 136
Arianism 160, 169, 172, 174; baptisms 167; controversies 168
Asia Minor 122, 129, 164–5
Athanasius 164, 171, 179
Augsburg Confession 8, 16, 112, 229
Augustine 4–5, 53–5, 106–9, 133–8, 140–1, 149–51, 175–6, 191–3, 240–2, 249–52; amillennial eschatology 135, 142, 150, 177, 247, 251, 275; amillennial view of the Last Days 290; amillennial view that the Jews are permanently replaced in the economy of salvation 197, 241; conception of the Church as the kingdom of God on earth 93; discredits the ancient expectation of the messianic kingdom 135; and the early millennial interpretation of the Last Days 137; equates the historical period of the Church with the prophetic utterances of the Old and New Testaments 152; eschatological shift of the mid-fourth century 145; interprets the eschatological phrases of the creeds 176; and the Jewish *telos* 250; legacy of 98; and the recapitulation of eschatology 137, 159; teaching of 123; Western amillennial theory 249
Augustine of Hippo *see* Augustine
Augustinian interpretation of the *Book of Revelation* 100
Aune, David 52, 281
Ayer, Joseph 159, 163

Bader-Saye, Scott 134
Bailey, J.W. 99, 110
baptisms 35–6, 53, 68, 137, 177, 215, 277
Barclay, William 160
Baronius, Cesare 170
Barth, Karl 27–8, 49n16, 49, 280n160, 283n217
Basil 170
Bauckham, Richard 8, 17n15, 19n30, 20, 103, 272
Bauer, Walter 127, 185
Baum, Gregory 60, 78
Bea, Card. Augustine 60
Beale, G.K. 96, 106, 106n30, 107–10
beliefs 40, 115, 119–20, 129–30, 138–9, 161–2, 166, 173–4, 181, 229–30; authentic 262; of earliest Christian millenarians 197; heretical 175; in purgatory 119; rejection of 267, 270
"beliefs system" 148, 165, 205, 214, 290
Bercot, David W. 231
Berger, David 83
Bernhardsson, Magnus 199
Bible 21, 27, 29, 31, 33, 42, 50–2, 103, 108–9, 244; and "Churchly tradition" 169; contemporary reading of the 33; interpreters of 25, 31, 103, 278; legitimacy of 89; presuppositions of 25; prophecies of 123; scholars of 38, 269; and supersessionist formulations of ecclesiology 47; texts and traditions 91, 100, 141, 241, 245
bishops 116–17, 127, 129, 134–5, 166–7, 171–2, 175–8, 181–2, 186, 196; anti-Arian 166; of Caesarea 134; chiliastic 169; early 115; Oriental 175; of Sioux City 100; traditionalist 58
Blackman, E.C. 256, 279
Blaising, Craig A. 40
Bloomberg, Jon 128n58, 202, 210
Blount, Brian K. 95, 107
bodily resurrection 97–8, 102, 104, 115, 117, 122, 159, 166, 213, 253; *see also* resurrection
Boeve, Lieven 85

Book of Ezekiel see *Ezekiel*
Book of Jubilees see *Jubilees*
Bookman, Terry 223
Borg, Marcus 110
Boring, Eugene 39
Boyer, Paul 206
Boys, Mary C. 66, 68, 70, 74, 80n49
Braaten, Carl E. 54
Brackney, William 173
Bradstock, Andrew 175
Brandmüller, Walter 77
Bromiley, Geoffrey 34–5
Brown, Raymond 130
Bryan, Steven M. 76
Buber, Martin 104, 231, 290
Buddhism 59, 90

Calvary 49, 73
Calvin, John 181
canons 160, 165, 168–9, 172, 175, 178, 180, 186, 255, 257; of the Council of Constantinople 46, 165, 167; of the Council of Ephesus 175; of the Council of Hiereia 173; of the Council of Laodicea 167; of the Fourth Lateran Council 9
Carroll, James 49, 54, 140, 191, 199
catechism 18, 55, 70, 78–9, 146, 153, 192–4, 197–8, 200, 281–2; denial of Patristic chiliasm 194; and millennialism 192
Catholic 2–3, 5–7, 9–10, 12, 14–16, 60, 78–82, 84–5, 97–8, 198–202; catechesis 63; eschatology 10–13, 103–6, 115–18, 124–6, 135–7, 145–6, 149–51, 162–4, 189–93, 228–33; evangelization 68; hierarchy 13, 153, 156, 194, 289; history 3–4, 8, 14, 16, 19, 60, 288; and the Jewish–Catholic question of covenant 69; Magisterium 39, 195; millennialism 90, 104–6, 108–9, 111, 113, 168, 173–4, 182–3, 195, 197–201; organizations 68; relations 7, 11, 58, 60, 78, 146; scholars 99, 148, 289; theologians 4, 39, 48, 58, 67, 89, 148, 190, 198, 205; tradition 3, 11, 14–15, 48, 55, 57, 72, 127, 192, 197
Catholic Catechism 69, 71, 81, 177
Catholic Church 18–19, 59–61, 75–9, 137–8, 145–9, 189–90, 192–6, 200–2, 205–7, 287–90; acceptance of fourth century amillennial propositions 99; amillennialism 100, 205, 212, 216, 219; attitudes towards Judaism as a religion 205; conception of fulfilled messianism 11; conception of supersessionism 39; and the Eusebian model (fourth-century) 192; history with the Jewish people 2; and the Magisterium of the 3; portrays the Jews as rejected by God and cursed to live a "wandering existence" 1; and Protestant theology 58; and the rejection of millenarianism 5, 12; shifts in attitude toward the Jews (*Nostra Aetate*) 57; as the sole, legitimate custodian of the kingdom of God 193
Catholic theology 5, 14, 16, 43, 68, 108, 200–1; contemporary Roman 77; of Judaism (new) 15; modern 11; moved away from supersessionism 60; positive 217
Cerinthus 122
Chabad movement (America) 214
Charisius (Presbyter) 175
Chester, Andrew 119
chiliasm 3–8, 10–16, 89–94, 115–31, 133–8, 145–56, 163–73, 175–80, 182–6, 189–203; apostolic 118, 184; condemned 122, 154, 170, 175–6, 186; disavowed 123, 152; and early Christian beliefs 104; and the Fathers 43, 45, 121, 123, 145, 149, 154, 194, 196–8, 201; and Montanism 164; papal rejections of 152; and the teaching of Apollinaris of Laodicea 171; *see also* millenarianism
chiliastic eschatology 117, 127, 129, 133, 135, 138, 146, 149, 153, 171; economy of consummation in 241; interpretation 97, 103, 120, 123, 169; of Irenaeus 117; robust 133; traditions 101, 122, 193
chiliasts 116, 119–20, 124, 127–30, 134, 149, 154–5, 159, 167, 169–71; ardent 163, 178, 288; early 119–20, 124, 156, 161, 217; evidence of 120; modern 254; prevalent 163; teachers 171; undisputed 162
Christ *see* Jesus Christ
Christendom 16, 82, 134, 139, 150, 168, 177–9, 181, 274, 277
Christian 3, 6, 14, 63, 91, 152, 243; abuse 26; affirmation of Judaism 42, 205, 207; amillennial eschatology 254; anti-Jewish fervor 14, 42, 278; antiquity 135, 284; apocalypticism 289; apologetic 63; apprehension and Jewish hope 262; believers 127, 223, 266–7; biblical and apostolic tradition 224;

canon 32, 257; charity 192; chiliasts 116, 189, 212, 252; Church 11, 46, 50, 54, 89, 92, 155, 177, 181, 183–6; community 30, 35–6, 101, 156, 263, 266; conceptions 9, 260; concession to Jewish religious reality 6; covenant 246; creeds 211; denominations 14, 43, 89; development 76; dialogue 74, 80–1, 209, 247, 273; disciples 39, 47, 56, 96, 100, 116, 126, 170, 239, 275; doctrine 55, 124, 142, 153–5, 159, 181, 275; dogma 226; ecclesiology 40; existence 43, 64, 137; expectations 134; faith 11, 52, 72, 77, 79, 98, 263, 266, 270, 284; history 6, 18, 74, 90, 145, 184, 263, 277; and Jewish representation 26, 264; messianic era 226, 240, 260; post-supersessionism 40; premillenarianism 270; scholars and scholarship 1, 26, 29, 72, 280; tradition 3, 7, 89, 119, 159
Christian Bible *see* Bible
Christian eschatology 3, 6, 15–16, 133–4, 142, 207, 215, 222, 226–7, 230; authentic 190; earliest 211; original 90, 242, 289; regarding 219, 290
Christian–Jewish dialogue 8, 17, 278, 284
Christian martyrs 264, 281
Christian millenarian 15, 19, 90–3, 105, 213, 215, 217, 219, 232, 238; earliest 197; eschatology 209; hermeneutics 212; readings and writings 14, 240; theology of Judaism 205–27
Christian supersessionists 13, 15, 25–6, 29–39, 42–3, 45, 208–9, 219, 251, 272–3
Christian theologians 6–9, 25, 215, 220, 224, 226, 243, 247, 250, 253
Christian theology 7–8, 14, 48–50, 53–6, 183–4, 205, 222, 230–1, 234–5, 273–9; Jewish expressions of faith in 241; of Judaism 16, 26, 48, 53, 209, 222, 255, 272, 274, 276; overcoming anti-Jewish 15; overcoming supersessionist attitudes in 222; permeated by economic supersessionism 235; of post-supersessionist Judaism 289; primitive 92
Christian tradition 6, 9, 12, 25–6, 147, 184–5, 222, 224, 282, 284; amillennial 258; Gentile 265; Protestant 14
Christian understanding 14, 106; of the character of God 25; of Judaism 58; of the role of the Holy Spirit 237

Christianity 16–17, 42–4, 51–6, 106, 133, 226–7, 231–6, 249–51, 256–7, 260–2; and Augustine's teaching 123; contemporary 134; historic 6, 76; institutionalized 206; and Judaism 1, 53, 60, 139; modern 43; orthodox 164; philosophical assumptions of 1; traditional 135, 270
Christians 9–11, 40, 44, 53–4, 199–201, 217–30, 232–4, 252–5, 260–2, 269–77; baptizing Jews 68; early chiliastic 115–16, 118, 133, 137, 211, 214; millenarian 10, 215, 239, 261; thwarting Antiochian 33; traditional 224, 246; unified 289
Christological 2, 76, 153, 166, 174, 197, 215, 226, 268–9; creeds 269; orthodox 169; propositions 72; terms 268
Christology 2, 42, 72, 77, 109, 170, 172–4, 179, 183–6, 222–4
1 Chronicles 16:7 246
1 Chronicles 24:3–19 96
Chrysostom, John 26, 33, 48, 50
Church 136, 216, 243, 269; authority of the 197; ecumenical and conciliar processes 146; ecumenical creeds 197; and the Eucharist 76, 146, 175, 194–7, 245–6; hierarchical 147, 193; history and tradition 3, 5, 28, 93, 147; history of 77, 87, 89, 122, 133–4, 179, 184, 220; indebtedness to Judaism 61; institutionalized 167; mediatorial role 71; and opposition to the synagogue 26; in relation to other non-Christian religions 59, 61; and salvation outside of the 264; and state 288
The Church in the Power of the Spirit 5
Clement of Alexandria 45–6, 55, 109, 123, 149, 202
Clement of Rome 116, 121
clergy 167, 289; high-ranking 205; obsolete 196
Clouse, Robert 176
Cohn, Norman 118, 138n4, 141, 150, 175–6, 186n176
Colossians 3:11 6
The Coming of God 5
Commentarii Exegetici in Apocalypticism 152
Commentary on Acts 51–2, 79, 81, 106–7, 141, 155, 170, 181, 277, 283–4
Commission of the Holy See for Religious Relations 59

Commodian 116, 125, 171
Commonitory 148
communism 189, 192
Congregation for the Doctrine of the Faith 69
Constantine 48, 76, 124, 130, 135, 139–40, 147, 168; acceptance of Christianity and Augustine's teaching 123; and Christianity 8; and a "conflated institution of Church and State" 94; empire of 135
Contra Heresies 117, 121
conversions 3, 67–8, 97–8, 207–9, 212–13, 218–20, 250–2, 260, 268–70, 273; to Catholicism 3; to Christianity 250; of Jews 68
1 Corinthians 6:2 265
1 Corinthians 6:19 258
1 Corinthians 6:19 258
1 Corinthians 15 10–13
1 Corinthians 15:20–24 101
1 Corinthians 15:22 102
1 Corinthians 15:23 102
1 Corinthians 15:24–28 173, 247
2 Corinthians 5:1–5 103
Costigan, Richard F. 198
Couch, Mal 124, 131, 252, 278
Council Fathers 59; *see also* Fathers
Council of Constantinople 19, 45–6, 164–7, 170–5, 178, 180, 182–6, 288
Council of Ephesus 116, 126, 148, 154, 164, 173–7, 182, 185–7, 288
Council of Hiereia 173
Council of Jerusalem 275n33
Council of Laodicea 167–8, 170–1, 182
Council of Nicaea 19, 160, 165, 167–9, 171–2, 174, 180, 182, 185–6, 288
Council of Nicene 170
Council of Rome 170–1, 182
Court, John M. 90
covenant 27–8, 30, 40–4, 51–5, 62–6, 69, 71–4, 77–8, 244–6, 275–6; blessings 206; blood 247; ceremonies 96; conditional 244; divine 71, 206, 224; economic 245; eternal 65, 73, 226, 244, 246, 257; everlasting 234, 246, 258; the first born of the 64; irrevocable 290; Jehovah's 244; and mission 53, 68, 80, 82; promises 58, 248; relationships 40, 225; unrevoked 64
crucifixion 44
Crusades 76
Cullmann, Oscar 193
Cunningham, Philip 11, 66

Cyril 163, 175, 185–6
Cysicenus, Gelasius 168

Dabru Emet 226–7, 234, 284
Daley, Brian 124n13, 131, 147
Daniel 7 9, 91, 260
Daniel 7:13 218
Daniel 7:24 254
David 76, 103, 106, 123, 168, 181, 214, 228, 269, 280
Davidic kingdom 74, 76, 252, 270
D'Costa, Gavin 200
De Civitate Dei 136
death 20, 46–7, 85, 101–3, 113, 118–20, 211, 213, 223–4, 246–7; bodily 97; of Christ 174; and resurrection 11, 20, 211
Declaration on Millenarianism 190, 194
"Declaration on the Relation of the Church to non-Christian Religions" 58
declarations of heresy 197; *see also* heresy
Dei Filius 57
Dei Verbum 57
Deutero-Isaiah 42, 280
Deuteronomic theology 26, 249
Deuteronomy 4:5–8, 6:6–9 241
Deuteronomy 5:22 34
Deuteronomy 7:9 248
Deuteronomy 30:1–5 248
Dewick, E.C. 93, 106, 112
The Dialogue Decalogue 273
"Dialogue and Proclamation" 67
Dialogue with Trypho 115
diaspora 26, 213, 241, 249, 260
Didache 92, 104–5, 113, 116, 125, 127, 129
Diocletian period 159
Dionysius 105, 122, 127, 130
Diprose, Robert 17, 234, 247, 275
divine punishment 250, 254
Docetism 44, 104, 113, 160, 163, 271
doctors of the Church 18, 127, 135, 148–9, 159
doctrine 145, 147–8, 150–2, 156, 159–61, 165, 181–3, 190, 196–8, 227–8; acceptable 152, 288; apostolic 117; of chiliasm 147; monotheistic 226; orthodox 89; premillennial 136; proto-orthodox 115
documents 11–12, 57, 59–62, 66, 68–71, 77–8, 82, 84, 116, 118; confessional 8–9; Council 16; ecclesial 11, 17, 43, 58, 63, 69–70, 78; episcopal 67; Roman

324   Index

Catholic 3, 287; supersessionistic 70; Vatican 57, 63–4, 67, 69, 137, 279
Dodd, C.H. 76, 85, 100, 110
dogma 57, 77, 117, 121, 146, 190
Dominus Iesus 69–71, 78, 82–4, 194, 201, 242
Donatist party 136
Dulles, Avery 53, 55, 137, 142
Dupuis, Jacques 67

early Church 90, 92, 120–2, 137–9, 153–6, 178–81, 183, 185–6, 192–3, 287–8; Councils 165–6, 173, 180, 183–5; Councils, *see also* Ecumenical Councils; creeds 12; Fathers 75, 105, 107, 124, 148–9, 151, 181–2, 184, 195, 287; heresies 27; traditions 11, 115, 117, 119, 121, 123, 125, 127, 129, 131
early Jesus movement 34, 199
early Jewish tradition 96
early messianic Jews 254
early Patristic millenarians 248
early Pauline interpretations 102
Easter 104, 168, 174
ecclesial documents 11, 17, 43, 58, 63, 69–70, 78
ecclesiological 14, 45, 65, 69, 138, 205, 225; barriers 15; exploration 287; implications 16; interpretations 47; traditional 269; understanding 6, 287
ecclesiology 11, 15, 19, 40, 57–8, 68, 75–7, 136; elements of 77; and the Roman Catholic Church 11, 13, 108, 136; traditional Post-Nicene Catholic 76
Eckardt, Roy 42
economic supersessionism 27–9, 236, 247
economy 27, 46, 223, 241, 243, 247, 255, 257–8, 260–1, 274; of consummation 241; of redemption 27, 29, 46, 222, 236; of salvation 27, 207, 222, 226, 240–1, 257, 287
Ecumenical Councils 2–3, 145, 147, 152, 159, 161, 163–9, 173–5, 179–81, 183–7; Council of Constantinople 45, 164–5, 167, 170–4, 180, 182; Council of Ephesus 116, 126, 148, 154, 164, 173–7, 182, 185–7, 288; Council of Hiereia 173; Council of Laodicea 167; Fourth Lateran Council 9, 197
ēḏā (Hebrew word meaning assembly) 34–5

Ehrenberg, Rudolf 40, 53, 53n77
Ehrhardt, Arnold 160
Eight Homilies against the Jews 26, 33
ekklēsía 34–5, 51, 266
el-Bitar, Selah 58
elders 65, 95–6, 107, 127, 263–4; human 96; of Israel 96; Jewish 96; in *Revelation* 95–6
Ellison, H.L. 267, 283
Emmerson, Richard K. 18, 141
Emperors 135, 168
encyclicals 1, 141, 190, 198, 200, 243
Enlightenment thinkers (Immanuel Kant and Friedrich Schleiermacher) 28
1 Enoch 92, 94, 106–8, 111
1 Enoch 33 94
1 Enoch 37–71 92
1 Enoch 93:1–10 92
Enochic literature 96, 117
Ephesians 2 37
Ephesians 2: 11–12 65
Ephesians 2:13, 17 38
Ephesians 2–3 38
Ephesians 5:14 103
Epiphanius 129–30, 164, 171, 179, 183
episcopal 57–8, 67, 139, 145, 169, 189–90, 196, 288; college 196; decentralizing of 196; process 57, 190; statements 288; voting 58
Epistle of Barnabas 92
Epistle to the Hebrews 246
Epistle to the Romans 37, 61, 93, 104, 190, 224, 240; see also *Romans*
Erickson, Millard J. 128, 131
eschatological 5–6, 14–16, 47, 55–6, 60–1, 219–20, 243–4, 268–71, 283, 287; awareness 15; beliefs 133; blessings 215; chronology 103, 163; community 85, 122, 225, 260, 281; concepts 70, 116, 209, 282; era 192, 261–2, 265; expectations 33, 167, 209, 217, 268, 285; history 196, 213, 219, 232, 268; judgment 192–3; kingdom 138, 173, 194; millenarians 248, 253; millennium 5, 218; promises 43, 101, 126, 133, 229, 245, 248, 251, 258; redemption 265; restoration and resurrection 101, 263–4
eschatological millenarianism 4–5, 8, 19, 138, 218–19, 252, 271, 288–9; Christian 208; critics of 4, 8; Moltmann's 4; original 288; rejection of 270
eschatology 10–13, 103–6, 115–18, 124–6, 135–7, 145–6, 149–51, 162–4, 189–93,

228–33; amillennial 118, 123, 190, 208, 212, 247, 250, 255, 259, 271–2; apocalyptic 105, 153, 175; earliest Christian expressions of 91; ecclesiological 8, 152; heretical 89, 165; non-chiliastic 118–19, 121; original 89, 108, 115, 150, 289; orthodox 90, 115, 118, 161, 177, 190; post-millenarian 222, 271; primitive 92, 288; rabbinic 261; spiritualized 123; transcendent 206
Eschatology: Death and Eternal Life 69, 75
eternal life 161, 163
eternity 10, 102, 104, 173, 196, 199, 216, 219, 232, 259–60
Ethiopian Orthodox Church 117, 126
Eucharist 76, 146, 175, 194–7, 245–6; millenarianism 12; millennialism 198, 289; millennium 194; prayers 116
Eucharistic prayers 116
Eudoxians 172
Eunomians 172
Eusebian model 192
Eusebius (Bishop of Caesarea) 126–7, 130–1, 133–40, 149–50, 155, 164, 171, 179–80, 183, 192
Ewherido, Anthony O. 38, 52
Exodus 12 91
Exodus 19:6 241
Exodus 24:1 96
Exodus 24:3–8 244
Exodus 24:11 212
Ezekiel 1 95
Ezekiel 16:55 245
Ezekiel 36 94
Ezekiel 36:12–14 238
Ezekiel 36–37 91, 99
Ezekiel 37 238
Ezekiel 37:1 259
Ezekiel 37:1–14 248
Ezekiel 37:24–28 249
Ezekiel 37:25–28 258
Ezekiel 38:8 260
Ezra 7:26–31 92
Ezra 32 94

Fabrega, Valentin 169, 181
Fairbairn, Donald 121
faith 46, 69–70, 77–8, 80–3, 130, 148, 162–3, 180–2, 184, 197–201; apostolic 197; Catholic 46, 70, 97, 193–4; Christian 11, 52, 72, 77, 79, 98, 263, 266, 270, 284; and communion 148; doctrine of 198; of individuals 252; post-axial 227n1; rule of 117, 162–3, 178, 180
Faith and Fratricide 72
Falls, Thomas 115, 123
Fathers 12, 19, 43, 45, 145, 149, 154, 194, 196–8, 201; Ambrosiaster 116, 125; Augustine 4–5, 17–19, 53–5, 106–9, 133–8, 140–1, 149–51, 175–6, 241–2, 249–51; Clement of Rome 116, 121; Commodian 116, 125, 171; Cyprian 116, 124, 163, 179; Hegesippus 116, 124; Hippolytus 116, 124, 155, 163, 201–2, 274, 277; Irenaeus of Lyons 115, 117, 119, 121; 180; Julius Africanus 116; Justin Martyr 48, 115, 122, 149; Lactantius 125, 127, 149, 155, 169, 171, 176, 181, 195, 202; Melito of Sardis 32, 116, 121, 231, 236; Methodius of Olympus 116, 125, 127–8; Nepos 116; Novatianus 163; Papias of Hierapolis 115, 117, 149, 167; Polycrates of Ephesus 116; Pothinus 116; Pseudo-Barnabas 116; St. Ephrem the Syrian 116; Tertullian 116–17, 120–4, 127, 129, 162–4, 167, 179–83, 256, 277, 279; Theophorus (Ignatius) 116; Victorinus 116
Federici, Tommaso 68
Feinberg, Charles 97
Fenton, J.C. 148
Ferguson, Everett 125, 162, 178
Fiorenza, Elisabeth Schüssler 35, 51, 199, 264, 281
Fisher, Eugene J. 58–9, 61
Fitzmyer, Joseph A. 268
Flinn, Frank 191, 193
Florovsky, Georges 84
Ford, David F. 96, 269, 272
Ford, J. Massyngberde 107, 165, 180
Fourth Lateran Council 9, 197
fratricide 1, 17, 20, 48, 72, 79, 81, 234, 274, 284
Fredriksen, Paula 115
Frei, Hans W. 31, 50

Gaius of Rome 98, 121–3, 128, 130, 133, 150, 287
Galatians 3 36
Galatians 3:26–29 35
Galatians 3:29 41
Galatians 3–8 248
Galli, Barbara 52, 81
general resurrection *see* resurrection

Genesis 9:16, 17:7; 17:13; 17:19 246
Genesis 12 248
Genesis 13:13–14 239
Genesis 13:15 248
Genesis 15 224
Genesis 15:6 224
Genesis 15:18–21 41
Genesis 17:6 224
Genesis 17:7 41
Gentile Christians 1, 4, 35, 44, 218, 223, 263–4, 267, 275, 281
Gentile Church 33, 37–9, 43, 45, 240, 243, 245, 264, 269, 273
Gentiles 9–10, 29–30, 35–8, 40–1, 62–5, 229, 262–3, 266, 269, 281–2
George, Cardinal Francis 67
German idealism 28, 49, 52
German National Socialism 192
Giacché la Santa Sede non si é ancora pronunciata in modo definitivo 194
Giyorgis of Sagla 117
Glazier, Michael 82, 185
Gnostic Marcionites 45, 122
Gnosticism 27, 29, 44–5, 104, 117, 122, 130, 138, 174, 185
Gnostics 33, 117, 122, 127, 133, 214
God 1–12, 19–21, 25–50, 52–6, 58–77, 81–5, 92–7, 133–42, 205–85, 287–90; covenantal economy of 242; covenantal people of 38; gifts of 266; and messiah 266; *see also* kingdom of God
God will be All in All 8
Goh, Jeffrey C.K 256, 278
Golgotha 222
gospels 11, 99–101, 113, 130–1, 217–18, 223–4, 240, 267–9, 277, 284–5; accounts 100; claims 38; exclusive 224
Goths 136
Gould, Dana 176
Greek Churches 159, 187; *see also* Orthodox Church
Greenstone, Julius H. 230
Grégoire, Henri 18–19
Gregory, Andrew 183
Grudem, Wayne 37
Gry, Leon 175, 186
"Guidelines and Suggestions for Implementing the Conciliar Declaration *Nostra Aetate*" 60–1, 66, 80, 82
Gumerlock, Francis 126, 165, 172–3, 180, 183–5

Hades 119–20, 211
Harrington, Daniel 268

Hartog, Paul 129
Harvie, Timothy 140
heaven 19, 21, 93–7, 116, 118–20, 153–4, 156, 184–5, 231–2, 244–5; new 56, 168, 215–16; powers in 214; transcendent 210, 213, 243
Hebrew Bible 7–8, 27–9, 31–5, 38, 49–50, 220–1, 245–6, 253–9, 261, 264
Hebrew prophets 63
Hebrew Scriptures 1, 28, 32, 251, 255, 257, 259, 267, 279, 283
Hebrews 33–4, 44–5, 48, 53, 74, 111, 246, 256–7, 262, 267
Hefele, J. 167, 180, 182, 184
Hegesippus 116, 124
heresy 123–4, 145–9, 153–7, 159, 161–3, 165–77, 179–81, 183–5, 197, 288; anathematizing of 288; of annihilationism 162; of Apollinaris of Laodicea 168; of chiliasm 168, 170; Christological 104, 159, 171; hermeneutics of 145, 147–9, 151, 153–5, 157, 197; histological 104, 159, 171; of monarchianism 165; Sabellianist or Monarchinian 168
heretical sects 118, 133, 138
heretics 117, 121–2, 130, 154, 172, 175, 179, 185–6, 238, 242; beliefs of 159, 197; doctrines of 160; first to reject chiliastic orthodoxy 255
Hermas 116, 120–1, 125, 129, 167
Hill, Charles 92, 118–21, 126, 138, 202, 287
Hinduism 59
Hippolytus 116, 124, 155, 163, 201–2, 274, 277
Hitler, Adolf 78, 146, 191, 193, 199, 288
Hoekema, Anthony A. 37
Holocaust 40–1, 49, 53, 78, 84, 99, 153, 230
Holy Land 168, 253–4
Holy Scriptures 33, 56–7, 66, 97–8, 107, 109, 138, 190, 251, 258; *see also* Scriptures
Holy *see* 191–2, 194
Holy Spirit 46–7, 60, 97, 161, 165, 167, 172, 195–6, 200, 237–8
Horner, Barry 252
Hosea 5:15–16:3 241
Hunt, Stephen 19
Hunter, David 178

Iannuzzi, Joseph 195, 201
Idris, Edward 83

Ignatius of Antioch 116, 121, 149
II Baruch 119
Immaculate Conception 151, 161
"Imperial ecclesiology" 134
inter-religious dialogue 6, 14, 67, 69, 82, 84, 205, 227, 273–4, 285
International Catholic–Jewish Liaison Committee in Venice 68
interpretation 29, 31–2, 39–40, 51, 57–8, 76, 97–8, 117–19, 141, 145–6; bodily 97; of Jesus's words 29; millennialist 102; modalistic 165; natural 98; normative 148; of *Romans* 11:29 64, 269; sequential 99
Introvigne, Massimo 19, 195
Irenaeus of Lyons 115, 117, 119, 121, 180; and chiliastic eschatology 117; and Christian *heretics* 238; and Hierapolis 115; and millenarian language 239; and Polycarp's influence on 117; and Tertullian 162, 182
Isaac, Erich 200
Isaiah 2 91
Isaiah 6 95
Isaiah 11 91
Isaiah 11:12 245
Isaiah 24:5; 55:3 246
Isaiah 24:21 260
Isaiah 24:23; 9:7 261
Isaiah 26:19 245
Isaiah 43:10–12 241
Isaiah 49:14–16 42
Isaiah 49:15 248
Isaiah 59 267
Isaiah 59:20 267
Isaiah 59:20–21; 27:9 63
Isaiah 65:17–25 43
Isaiah 66:23 62–3
Israel 2, 14, 16, 45, 47, 55, 206, 215, 281, 287; centered messianism 260; covenant promises 287; covenantal blessings 64; disloyalty hardness of heart, and blindness to the truth 248; liturgical faithfulness 240; martyrs of 263, 270; recognition and acceptance of Jesus as messiah 268; redemption 10, 241; rejection of Christ 27, 240; role in salvation history 32, 236–7, 240
Israelites 27–8, 62, 103, 240, 268

Jacob 41–2, 64, 100, 226, 257, 282
Jehovah's covenant 244
Jenson, Robert 17, 41, 53, 274, 278
Jeremiah 3:11–18 241
Jeremiah 3:17 260
Jeremiah 31:17 244
Jeremiah 31:23 245
Jeremiah 31:27 244
Jeremiah 31:31–34 244, 249
Jeremiah 31:33 242
Jeremiah 31:33–34 259
Jeremiah 31:34 244
Jeremiah 31:35–36 41
Jeremiah 31:35–36 41
Jeremiah 31:36 245
Jeremiah 31:37 244
Jeremiah 31:38, 40 245
Jeremiah 31–33 91
Jerome 105, 112, 116, 123–4, 126–7, 149, 155, 179–80, 183, 201
Jerusalem 3, 46–7, 83–5, 151–3, 165, 213–15, 253–4, 260–1, 275–6, 279–80; "creed" (Moehlman) 162; rebuilding of 92, 195; restoration of 151; "spiritual" 32; witnesses in 47
Jerusalem Council of Acts 212
Jesus *see* Jesus Christ
Jesus Christ 1–11, 26–48, 62–72, 90–113, 159–64, 191–6, 213–27, 237–43, 250–72, 274–85; claims the Father has set a time for the restoration of the kingdom to Israel 47; commands his disciples to pray that the kingdom will come 100; death on the cross 104; divine and human nature 175; divinity and salvific personhood 246; incarnation 224, 227; messiahship 72; preaching of 76; priests of God 94; reign of 4, 9, 18, 94, 97, 117, 155, 192, 195, 201; rejected by the Jews 254; resurrection of 104, 270; return of 19, 134, 166, 216, 221, 266; Second Coming 91–2, 152–3, 159, 174, 178, 206, 224; words of 29, 100–1, 207, 244
Jesus of Nazareth 6–7, 19–20, 28–9, 40, 42–5, 85, 105, 110, 266, 269; *see also* Jesus Christ
Jesus of Nazareth: Millenarian Prophet 101
Jewish and Catholic coexistence and future 13
Jewish and Catholic traditions 15
Jewish and Christian 41, 44, 96, 216, 227, 263, 281; beliefs 223; communities 30, 263; conceptions 9; doctrine 150; eschatology 215; existence 64; messianic kingdom 254; millennium 199, 232, 239, 248; participation in a

God-ordained reality 65; reality 25; relations 5, 48, 52, 54–5, 83–4, 207, 234, 276; scholars 26; traditions 61, 282
Jewish–Catholic dialogue 89, 198, 205
Jewish conceptions of the resurrection 6, 120, 213–14
Jewish conversions 269
Jewish counter-supersessionists 26
"Jewish dream" 8–9, 11, 16, 117, 212, 221, 233
Jewish ecumenical dialogue 226
Jewish eschatological 12, 104, 122, 211–12, 228–31, 272, 282; expectations 15, 112, 207–8; hope in relation to supersessionism and millenarianism 207, 209; terms 241; traditions 206
Jewish messianic 4–5, 9, 214–15, 230, 248, 264, 268; alternative 13, 273; community 34; concepts 101; expectations 215, 224; kingdom 289
Jewish Messianism 5, 67, 101, 202, 282–3
Jewish people 37–42, 58–68, 70–4, 79–82, 207–9, 212–27, 235–9, 241–4, 257–62, 266–70; and Judaism 69; and the possibility of mass conversions to Christ 213; redemption of 241
Jewish philosophical and theological traditions 14
Jewish rabbis 64, 214
Jewish redemption 289
Jewish rejection of Jesus 56, 71, 214, 227, 266
Jewish roots 7, 43, 54, 205
Jewish scholars 25, 44, 210, 212, 223
Jewish theology 40, 48, 213, 216, 222, 226, 234, 275, 284
Jewish traditions 61, 267, 283
Jews 7–11, 25–8, 30–3, 35–45, 48–72, 78–80, 215–31, 248–57, 259–63, 272–8; and the covenant 40; and Judaism (preaching and catechesis) 54, 60–1, 66, 79, 81–2, 277; and millenarian Christians 223; non-secular 13, 36, 214, 229, 234, 281; in official Catholicism 212; wandering aimlessly in Diaspora as a "witness people" 26
"The Jews and their Sacred Scriptures in the Christian Bible" 31
Joachim of Fiore 5, 11, 18, 110, 168, 189, 196–7, 237
John (Apostle) 54, 94–6, 98, 116–17, 126, 130, 138, 141, 178, 180
John Paul II 58, 60–1, 63–6, 68, 71, 79–83, 195, 201, 287, 289

Jones, Stanley 120
Joshua 35
Jubilees 23: 26–31 99
Judah 244
Judaism 5–7, 13–17, 42–6, 48–54, 58–61, 64–7, 69–70, 81–5, 212–15, 225–30; adherents of 6; and Catholicism 15; and Christianity 6, 9, 40, 42–4, 55, 65, 223, 231, 256, 261; contemporary 60, 68, 207, 214; first-century 268; messianic Christian 214; modern 59, 61, 72–3, 75, 85, 230, 237, 240; Mosaic heritage 69; positive approach to 59; self-image of 65; spiritual value to 266; of Torah-obedience 43; traditional 212–13, 224; viewing of 45, 65
"Judaizers" 33
Judea 47
Judeo-centric features of the messianic age 240, 261
Julius Africanus 116

kainos 246
kairos 219, 233
kaleo 34
Kant, Immanuel 28–9, 45, 49
Kasper, Walter 11, 58
Kennedy, Joe 171
kingdom of Christ 19, 21, 83, 85, 108, 136–7, 163–4, 173; alternative 5, 221, 271; messianic 221
kingdom of God 5–6, 45–7, 70–1, 75–7, 134–7, 140–2, 192–4, 206–8, 220–2, 251–3; on earth 6–8, 12, 93, 116, 220–1, 240–1, 287; in history 146–7, 194, 236
Kinzer, Mark 266, 282
Klausner, Joseph 210
klesis 266
Knight, Douglas 237, 256, 274
Kottman, Karl A. 18–19
Kreider, Glenn R. 120
Kurz, William 108n57

Labbe, Philippe 106, 125, 186
Lactantius 125, 127, 149, 155, 169, 171, 176, 181, 195, 202
Landes, Richard 110, 278
Lang, Peter 202
language 36–8, 58–9, 63, 65, 72–3, 93, 95, 98, 135, 193–4; apocalyptic 149, 191, 244; of chiliasm 135; explicit amillennialist 93, 163; explicit premillennial 163

Last Supper 96, 228, 239
Latin 57–8, 70, 78, 90, 116, 125, 133, 135, 141, 159
law 29, 32, 36, 69, 73–4, 240, 244–5, 251, 256, 259; "for dialogue" 273; of faith and love 2; God given 44; and liturgy in Judaism 240; moral 28; rational 28
Lerner, Robert E. 141n38
Levenson, Jon D. 229–30, 277, 281
Libellus Synodicus 164
liberation theologians 74, 206
liberation theologies 75, 189, 197, 200, 211, 228, 232, 281, 288
Lietzmann, H. 102, 111, 177
Lindbeck, George 36
Loisy, Alfred 74, 85n136
Lombard, Peter 197
Lorinus of Avignon 170
Luke 11: 2–4 100
Luke 20:35 103
Luke 22 96
Luke 22:16 100
Luke 22:20 245
Luke 22:29–30 96
Luke 24:21 265
Lumen Gentium 19, 21, 55, 57–8, 79, 81, 85, 198, 201, 276
Luther, Martin 103, 112, 249, 277

Madigan, Kevin 49, 229–30, 277
Magisterium 16, 77, 137, 146, 190–2, 197–9; ordinary 3, 60, 77, 189–90; papal 190; Roman Catholic 39, 195; supreme 57
Many Religions—One Covenant: Israel, the Church and the World 63, 71
Maoz, Baruch 253
Marcellianism 5
Marcellians 172
Marcellus of Ancyra 19, 160, 173, 184
Marcion 28–9, 44–5, 49, 51, 104, 118, 121–2, 255–7, 279, 287; aversion to chiliasm 122; heresy of 235, 257; influence on the Catholic Church's theology 256; legacy of 256–7; official condemnation of 257; principles of 122; rejection of parts of the canon 122; removal of the Hebrew Scriptures 255; theology of 256
Marcionites 117, 121–2, 133, 235, 278; *see also* Gnostic Marcionites
Marshall, Bruce D. 64, 81, 239, 275n36
Martin, David 230n45

Martyr, Justin 25, 27–8, 32, 48, 51, 115–16, 123–4, 126–7, 161–3, 201
Martyr, St. Justin 48, 115, 122, 149
martyrs 90, 92–4, 97–8, 101–3, 116, 119–20, 122, 263–4, 270, 272; Christian 264, 281; and confessors 94; of history 101; and messianism 191
Marxism 193, 197, 200
Mary 19, 80, 161, 174, 182–3
masses 63, 196, 202, 217
Matthew 5:5 239
Matthew 5:17 29, 245
Matthew 5:18 245
Matthew 6:9–13 100
Matthew 8:11 100
Matthew 16:18 206
Matthew 19:28 96
Matthew 21:43 38, 47, 251
Matthew 22:1–14 246
Matthew 23:37–39 241
Matthew 26:29 100
Matthew 27:52–53 104
Matthews, Steven 175, 185
Maximilla 167
Maximin 135
Mays, James L. 111, 281
McBrien, Richard 85n123
McDade, John 142
McGinn, Bernard 18, 105, 141n38
Melito of Sardis 32, 116, 121, 231, 236
messiah 6, 8–11, 34–8, 210–11, 214–15, 224–5, 228–30, 261–2, 268–70, 280; expected 289; and the messianic age 214; personal 8, 213; resurrected 215; true 272
messianic 4, 7, 42, 46, 49, 63, 65–6, 192–3, 213–14, 270; agent 210, 267–8; alternative 5, 13, 220; authority 265; era 99, 191, 196, 210, 241, 258, 260–2; eschatology 193, 213; expectations 2, 6, 15, 44–5, 215; fulfillment 35, 134, 140; identity 1, 226, 266; ideology 15; kingdom 134–5, 219–22, 235, 241, 245–7, 253–5, 259–63, 267–73, 279–81, 283–5; promises 8, 60, 208, 238, 241; reign 82, 135–6, 184, 194, 197, 222, 265, 289; traditions 209
Methodius of Olympus 116, 125, 127–8
Micah 4 91
Micah 4:1–4 259
Milavec, Aaron 113, 125
millenarian eschatology 11, 134–5, 146–7, 174, 196–8, 205, 207, 209, 221–2, 288–9; condemned 147; contemporary

237; earliest Christian 256; early apostolic 196; original 89
millenarian exegesis 259, 262, 264–5; to the goal of envisioning the eschatological millennial age 262; of Moltmann regarding both *Revelation* 20, and *Romans* 11 13, 273
millenarianism 3–8, 10–16, 18–20, 89–94, 115–18, 124–6, 136–8, 146–8, 152–4, 189–97; adherence to 133; condemning of 189; defining of 11, 287; discrediting of 118; and early Church tradition 115–23, 125, 127, 129, 131; ecclesiastical 218; and non-supersessionist theology 222; and post-supersessionism 206–34, 236, 238, 240, 242, 244, 246, 248, 250, 252; secularized 192; *see also* chiliasm
millenarians 13, 89–90, 94, 112–13, 206–8, 221–3, 225, 246–8, 250–3, 265–6; apostolic 173; historical/presentative/ecclesiastical 288; and messianic movements 191; schemes 238, 251, 269; teachings 173; theology 4, 7, 13, 93, 215, 222, 226, 236, 240–1, 252; understanding of history 267
millennial age 102, 195–6, 211, 217, 219, 223, 227, 236, 252, 262
millennial beliefs 104, 110, 165, 197
millennial chronology 102
millennialism 90, 104–6, 108–9, 111, 113, 168, 173–4, 182–3, 197–201, 267–8; and amillennialism 94; political 288; rejection of 147; spiritualized 146, 197
millennialists 10, 13, 91, 110, 145, 166, 183, 272
mitigated millenarianism 12, 141, 146, 153, 189–91, 197, 199, 217, 288
"Modern Catholic Millennialism" 195
Moehlman, Conrad 162
Moltmann, Jürgen 2–5, 7–13, 15–21, 112–13, 216–22, 229–36, 258–63, 270–4, 277–82, 284–5; argument for the necessity of a "futurist" millenarian approach 10; and the concept of the Jewish and Christian messianic kingdom 12; conception of millenarianism 3, 200, 220; eschatological framework 171; eschatological millennium 218; Jewish and Christian messianic kingdom 12; language of Israel and the Church operating as "two parallel detours" in history toward an eschatological future 9; logic of 254; and the millenarian concept 213, 262; millenarian exegesis 259, 263; millenarian ideas 208, 254, 258, 272; millenarian interpretation of *Romans* 9–11 265, 269; millenarian paradigm 255, 262; millenarian principles 243, 252; and millenarianism 13, 207, 217–18, 225, 251, 253, 289; understanding of the millennium 217
Monarchinian heresy 168
Montanism 127–8, 164–5, 167–8, 174, 179–81; condemned 167; enemies of 164; heretical elements 164
Montanist baptisms 167
Montanists 116, 118, 122, 164–5, 167, 171, 179
Montanus 122, 128, 166–8
Moo, Douglas J. 267
Moore, Rebecca 111, 234
"moral majority" 218
Mosaic covenant 72–3, 78, 81, 234, 242, 244–7, 268
Mosaic Law 54, 64, 245, 275
Moses 55, 61, 64, 178, 240, 245
Mounce, Robert H. 98, 109n67
Mueller, Joseph 100
Münzer, Thomas 112n129
Mwandayi, Canisius 273, 285
Myllykoski, Matti 130n100

Nadler, Steven 210
National Jewish Scholars Project 226
National Socialism 41, 200
Nazis 18, 75, 189
Nazism 191, 199–200
Nehemiah 35
Nelson, Thomas 48, 109, 111
Nepos 116
Nestorian controversy 174, 185
Nestorianism 175
Nestorius 154, 174–5, 185
Neusner, Jacob 227
"new Israel" 35, 44–5, 50, 96, 208, 221, 258, 281
"New Jerusalem" 122, 137, 265
New Prophecy 127, 165, 179–81
New Testament 17–18, 20–1, 29–34, 36–7, 49–51, 106, 110–12, 129–30, 181–2, 256–7; multiple passages describing the resurrection in apocalyptic terms 104; and nonsupersessionist theology 15; texts and their support of millenarian eschatology 104

Newman, John Henry 30, 150–1
Nicene Council *see* Council of Nicea
Nicene Creed 19, 145, 168–74, 178, 181–2, 184
Nicene Trinitarianism 172
Nichols, Aidan 75, 85
Nihil Obstat 100, 108
Nixon, Thomas 264
non-Christian religions 58–9, 79, 212
non-Protestant Churches 115
non-secular Jews 13, 36, 214, 229, 234, 281
non-supersessionists 15, 29–30, 34, 272, 285
Norton, Roger 78, 126
Nostra Aetate 26, 28, 30, 32, 34, 36, 38, 40, 42, 56–85
Novak, David 26, 48, 210, 228–31, 275–6
Novatianus 163

Oden, Thomas C. 179, 229
Olam Ha-Zeh 211–12
Old Testament 17, 30–1, 69–72, 108, 121–2, 128–9, 181–2, 218, 256–7, 283; and the "dual significance" prophecy of the 31; in light of the New Testament 33; persons events, and prophecies fulfilled in the New Testament 32
olive trees 62–4
On Prescription of Heretics (Tertullian) 162
Oriental bishops 175
Origen 118, 121, 123, 131, 133–5, 137–8, 150–1, 249–51, 276–7, 279; and Augustinian amillennialism 197; and the conception of resurrection 161, 173; and Gaius 12, 133, 287; spiritualization of 134
Origenism 171
origins 2, 7, 44, 51, 55, 78–9, 123–5, 154, 160, 162; apostolic 117; covenantal 253
orthodox, conception of Judaism 223
Orthodox Jews 53, 83, 210, 213
orthodoxy 2, 12, 127, 135–6, 147–8, 152, 159, 161, 163, 166; complete 160; conceptions of resurrection 133; in early patristic eschatology 136; eschatology 90, 115, 118, 161, 177, 190; maintaining 167; rejecting chiliastic 255; and Trinitarian belief 163
Otto, Randall E. 112n124

pacifists 191
pagans 33, 134, 284

Pannenberg, Wolfhart 156, 171, 183, 231
papal 197–8; authority 12, 189; bulls 1; infallibility 151, 198; pronouncements 190; rejections of chiliasm 152; statements 3, 64, 69, 146–7, 189–90, 288
Papias of Hierapolis 115, 117, 126n40, 149, 167
paradise 91, 119, 192
patriarchs 40–1, 43, 46, 61–2, 64, 73, 224, 226, 238–40, 282
Patristic authors 123
Patristic chiliasm 195
Patristic history 45
Patristic millenarianism 110, 123, 164, 192, 195–6, 207, 217–18, 247, 249; and conciliar declarations 175; eschatology 197
Patristics 33, 46, 151, 219; early millennial 237; normative 25; supersessionist readings 33; theology 196; tradition 152
Paul 9–11, 35–8, 41, 50–1, 54–5, 61–3, 102–5, 109–12, 266–70, 281–5; claims that no transformation of the Jewish people needs to take place for the "Jewish nation" to remain with Yahweh 266; critical of some Corinthian believers 102; endorsement of the continuing nature of God's election of Israel 268; Epistles to the Galatians and Ephesians 35, 128, 265; and Israel's rejection of Jesus *Epistle to the Romans* 240; language of the covenant in *Romans* 64; *Letters* 50, 104, 268, 283–4; overarching argument that God has implemented a temporary "hardening" of the Jewish people 266; text in *Galatians* refers to a double-legitimacy to Abraham's legacy 41; translation *Isaiah* 59 differs also from the Hebrew text 267; words not taken as allegory but as literal eschatological reality 10
Pauline 51, 63, 103–4, 266; corpus 100, 104, 266; doctrine 62; epistles 74; literature 11, 93, 126; mission 1; reference to two resurrections 103; scripture 112; texts 63, 101–4
Pawlikowski, John T. 253
Pax Romana 37, 135, 139
Pelikan, Jaroslav 173
Penasa, Fr Martino 194–5
Pentecost 47, 56, 81, 173, 239, 255

Index

"people Israel" 7, 27, 34, 41–2, 44, 48, 54, 209, 217, 282
"people of God" 34, 66, 81
Peters, G.N.H. 111, 116, 123–4, 153, 168–9, 181–2
Pharisees 38, 74
Phil 1:23, 121 103
Phil 3:11,122 103
Photinians 172
Photinus 154, 173, 184
Phrygia 122, 165, 167
Phrygian heresy 167
Phrygians 165, 167
Pietist theology 221
"Pilgrim Church" 19, 65, 137
Pius XI 197
Pius XII 146, 189–93, 288
Platonic philosophy 43–4
Platonists 150
Pneumatomachi 172, 183
Polycarp of Smyrna 18, 116–17, 121, 125–6, 129, 149, 169, 178
Pomazansky, Michael 171
Pontifical Biblical Commission Document 31
Pontifical Council for Promoting Christian Unity 59
Pope Benedict XVI 19–20, 57, 63, 66, 80, 82–5, 131, 193–4, 200, 242–6
Pope Damasus 170, 182
Pope John Paul II 58, 60–1, 63–6, 68, 71, 79–83, 195, 201, 287, 289
Pope Leo 196, 202
Pope Paul VI 57–8, 77, 202
Pope Pius XI 197
Pope Pius XII 3, 12, 18–19, 125, 141, 146, 153, 189–94, 197–9, 288
Pope St Siricius 160
post-Holocaust theology 1, 7, 15, 20, 285
post-millennialists 92
post-supersessionism 46, 206–34, 236, 238, 240, 242, 244, 246, 248, 250
post-supersessionists 13, 39–43, 53, 64, 208–9, 225, 239, 273, 290; concept of 238; theology 25, 40–1, 55, 58, 65, 72, 77, 209, 216, 290; thesis 207; in tone and content 64, 262; understanding of 16, 69
Pothinus 116
pre-Christian, Jewish millennial texts 96
pre-Vatican II understanding of the Church and the kingdom 194
priests 93, 154, 185, 195–6, 225, 264; chief 38; human 261; kingdom of 241

primitive 90, 92, 159, 165, 168, 177, 181, 193, 197, 201; Christian eschatological beliefs 117; Christian theology 92; deposit of faith 197; eschatological understanding in Jewish–Christianity 92; Jewish conception of Christianity 159; texts 92
prophecies 19, 30, 32, 110, 123, 127, 140, 152, 167; apocalyptic 139, 261; punitive 255
prophets 29, 36, 38, 61–3, 201, 242, 245, 277; false 94, 167; Hebrew 63
Protestant Churches 89
Protestant Reformation 31
Protestant theologians 11, 13, 15
Protestant theology 58
Protestantism 14, 128, 236
Protestants 39, 171; evangelicals 92; scholars 147
Psalm 8:6 247
Psalm 30:5 29
Psalm 65:4 62–3
Psalm 105:10 246
Psalm 110 95, 103
Psalm 110:1 102
Pseudo-Barnabas 116
pseudo-Clementine "romance" work 149
punishment 26, 34, 228–9, 235, 248–51, 254; divine 250, 254; of God 34; irreversible 248; of Israel 26, 248
punitive supersessionism 26–7, 29, 235, 247–50, 254
punitive supersessionists (also called, retributive supersessionists) 248
Pursuit of the Millennium 175

qāhāl (Hebrew word meaning assembly) 34
Quartodecimans 50, 121, 160
Quartodeciminism 139, 169, 174, 182
quasi-Marcionite views 256

rabbinic Judaism 215
rabbis 8, 34, 44, 64, 212, 214–15, 220, 231, 261, 280
Rahner, Karl 27, 230n45
Raphael, Rabbi Simcha Paull 210
Ratzinger, Card. Joseph 18, 63, 69–78, 83, 190, 193–5, 197, 200, 276; advocates that the Jewish people's covenantal status has been replaced 71; assessment of the eschatology and ecclesiology of the early Fathers 75; critique of Jürgen

Moltmann's "Theology of Hope" 75; glowing review of C.H. Dodd 76; reflections on the "inner development of historic Christianity" 76; stresses Jewish *uniqueness* in order to claim its abolition 73; theology of covenant 72; understanding of the typological function of the old covenant for the new 77
Recognitions 149
redemption 27–9, 46, 52, 212–13, 219, 222–4, 236–7, 240–1, 252, 259–60; application of 244; economy of 27, 29, 46, 222, 236; eschatological 265; and forgiveness 224; historical 115; of human sin 247; intermediary age of 212; of Israel 10, 241; Jewish 289; and liberation 237; of lost humanity in Christ 32; and restoration 223; spiritualizing of 134
Reformation 8, 108, 185, 249
Reformation Churches 11, 59
Reformed Federalist Theology 221
reformed Jews, and Judaism 210, 213, 229
Regnum Coelorum 118
reign 9, 91–3, 95, 106–7, 109, 119–20, 125–6, 195, 201–2, 224–5; in creation 216; eternal 173; expected 11; historical 173, 194; implied political 75; permanent 258; temporal 98; thousand-year 136, 172–3, 195; universal 6, 201
religion 15–16, 28, 60, 69, 71, 74, 82–4, 227, 233, 275–6; civil 217; connected 1; institutionalized 133; monotheistic 241; new 250; official 133; polyvalent 91; sister 205
religious freedom 190
Renan, Ernest 154n14
replacement theology 3, 5, 11, 13–14, 17, 26, 72–3, 241, 243, 247; *economic supersessionism* 27–9, 236, 247; *punitive supersessionism* 26–7, 29, 235, 247–50, 254; refuting of 13; *structural supersessionism* 28–9, 230, 235, 255–9, 261, 289
restoration 46–7, 101, 108, 212–14, 229–30, 247–9, 252, 255, 267–8, 283; earthly 47; final 32; national 214; parallel 45; theology 8, 26, 67, 85
resurrection 10–11, 91–4, 97–9, 101–4, 106–9, 111–13, 159–63, 210–11, 213–15, 229–30; bodily 97–8, 102, 104, 115, 117, 122, 159, 166, 213, 253; of the dead by God 214; dual (Paul) 102; first 91–3, 97–8, 102–3, 107, 133, 140, 201, 215, 264; general 91–3, 98, 102–4, 106–7, 112, 116, 155, 160, 168–9, 173; in Hades 119; Jesus's death and 101, 237; and the Nicene Creed 168–9; physical 98, 113, 115, 129, 137, 140, 213, 262, 268; and restoration 214, 247, 252; spiritual 98, 109, 136
Revelation 3–5, 90–103, 106–10, 126–8, 136–8, 140–2, 224–5, 262–5, 267–70, 280–1
Revelation 4 95–6
Revelation 4:2b 95
Revelation 20 4, 13, 90, 93–9
Revelation 20:1–3 99
Revelation 20:1–10 91, 93–4
Revelation 20:1–15 98
Revelation 20:4 5, 98
Revelation 20:4–6 16
Roberts, Alexander 18n23
Roman Catholic 10, 31, 98, 136; eschatology 98; Magisterium 39, 195; official teaching of 45; scholars 191, 289; and supersessionism 48; theology 4, 13–14, 16, 69, 161, 191, 289; tradition 31, 100, 109, 152, 196, 205, 209, 273, 287
Roman Catholic Church *see* Catholic church
Roman Emperors 135, 168
Roman Empire 44, 123, 125, 134–5, 139–40, 174, 176, 179, 184, 191–2
Romans 9:4–5 62
Romans 9–11 35, 226, 265–7
Romans 11 13, 58, 64–5, 104, 225, 251, 262, 266, 269, 273
Romans 11:7 252
Romans 11:11–12, 30–31 266
Romans 11:11–15 268
Romans 11:11–32 62–3
Romans 11:15 10, 103–4, 252, 270
Romans 11:16 262
Romans 11:25 38, 63, 269
Romans 11:25–27 104, 269
Romans 11:25–32 9, 265
Romans 11:26 267–9
Romans 11:28–29 224
Romans 11:29 64
Rosenzweig, Franz 40–1, 52n74, 52, 53n77, 53, 81n71, 81, 233, 260, 280
Rowland, Christopher 106, 263
Rowland, Tracey 80n56

334 Index

rubrics 65, 123
Ruether, Rosemary 2, 11, 17, 25, 72, 104n2, 135, 140, 220
Rufinus 163, 177

Sabbath 63, 91, 120, 125, 137, 140, 285
Sabellianist, heresies 168
Sabellians 167, 172, 180, 184
Sæbø, Magne 250
sacerdotal power 194, 289
Sacra Congregatio de Propaganda Fide 59
sacraments 76, 181, 186, 193, 196
sacred scriptures 31, 50, 82, 148, 206, 221
saints 93–7, 106–7, 116, 125, 137, 160–1, 163, 168–9, 195, 201–2; and early Church Fathers 287; and martyrs 93, 102, 107, 280; multiple chiliastic 149; oppressed 9; reign of the 95; resurrected 173
Saldarini, Anthony J. 39
salvation 27, 55–6, 60–1, 65, 69–70, 83–4, 235–7, 240–1, 264–9, 277–8; amillennialism depicts 243; call to 238; carnal 266; divine 250; of God 42; spiritual 99; super-sessionism depicts 243; timetable of 10; vocation for 220
salvation history 13, 15, 27–8, 31–3, 133–4, 136–7, 207–8, 221–3, 235–7, 271–2; eschatological 209; narrative regarding 236; redemptive economies in 28
salvific 3, 37, 223, 259, 264, 282; drama 224; economy 29, 238, 245, 260; future for the Jews 2; mediation 70; personhood 246; purpose and witness 287; unification 37
2 Sam 7:12–16 248
2 Sam 23:5 246
Samaria 47
Sanders, E.P. 80, 100, 110
Sarah 43, 46
Satan 93–5, 99–100, 136, 173; activities of 99; binding of 99–100, 110; chaining of 99; deceptions of 194
Saucy, Robert L. 111, 142, 283
Schaff, Philip 16n2, 117, 126–7, 138,177n5,
Schleiermacher, Friedrich 28–9, 45, 50
Schmidt, Karl Ludwig 290
scholars 103, 107, 109–10, 116, 125, 127–8, 134, 146–7, 167–8, 185–6; amillennialist 96; contemporary millennial 91, 269; historical 90; modern 117, 141, 174, 261; respected 90
scholarship 14–15, 34, 40, 69–70, 101, 109, 118, 149, 161–2, 173; contemporary biblical 12, 47, 90, 110, 164; contemporary Eusebian 135; expert 15; sound 164
Schwartz, Eduard 85, 127
Schweitzer, Albert 100
Scott, James M. 184n153
Scriptures 33, 56–7, 66, 97–8, 107, 109, 138, 190, 251, 258
Second Coming 91–2, 152–3, 159, 174, 178, 206, 224
Second Ecumenical Council 18, 154, 168, 170–2, 174, 181, 184
Second Epistle of Clement 149
Second Temple 100, 229, 267; Jewish eschatology 211; Jewish-inspired 92; and Jewish literature 99; Judaism 15, 34–5, 122, 198, 214, 259, 268; texts 94; understanding of Jewish eschatology 104
Second Temple Period 31, 63, 65, 91, 178, 214
Second Vatican Council 5, 14, 16–17, 58–9, 66, 78
Second Vatican declaration *Nostra Aetate* 2
Second World War 2, 99, 146, 189, 191, 288
Segal, Alan F. 214
Semi-Arians 172
Sharot, Stephen 230
Shedd, William 160
Shepherd of Hermas 149, 167
Shoah (documentary film about the Holocaust) 14, 25, 146
Sievers, Joseph 268
Siker, Jeffrey 278, 282
Sim Shalom 213
sin 27–9, 49, 215, 217, 224, 237, 241, 265–6, 269, 275; forgiveness of 244; human 46, 223, 247; personal 252
Sinai 38, 44, 49, 64, 72–3, 96, 234, 242, 245, 276
Sinai Covenant 34, 73–4, 223, 240, 242, 246
Snodgrass, Klyne 38, 52
Sonderweg 264, 269
Soph 3:9 62–3
Soulen, Kendal 26–9, 32–3, 46, 48–50, 54, 56, 208–9, 230–1, 258–9, 274–9

souls 85, 93, 95, 97–8, 112, 118–20, 123, 128, 131, 210–13; believed 119; of believers 118; bodiless 97; departed 120; disembodied 119–20, 128; to heaven 119–20; human 123, 134, 166; immortality of the 213, 267
St. Augustine *see* Augustine
St. Barnabas 25, 48, 92, 105–6, 124, 127, 129, 149
St. Cyril 175
St. Ephrem the Syrian 116
St. Epiphanius 147
St. Giyorgis 117
St. Hippolytus 18, 149
St. John 100
St. Justin Martyr 48, 115, 122, 149
St. Methodius 176
St. Papias of Hierapolis 149
St. Paul 10, 101, 111, 153
St. Pirminius 160
St. Tertullian 149
Stendahl, Krister 268–9
structural supersessionism 28–9, 230, 235, 255–9, 261, 289
Sullivan, Clayton 131, 200
Sungenis, Robert 45–6, 53, 55, 55n110
supersessionism 1–4, 11–12, 14–17, 25–62, 66, 68–72, 207–9, 219–22, 235–7, 255–6; adopted 218; advocates for 45, 69; alternatives to 25; in amillennial circles 265; and the amillennial foundation of 269–70; and amillennialism 236; and anti-Judaism 1–2, 17, 43, 53; assumptions 34, 43, 253, 262; biblical roots of 29; Cardinal Ratzinger's evaluation of 71; defining 25, 287; ecclesial 7, 60; ecclesio-centric 69; ecclesiological 265; economic 27–9, 207, 235–6, 242, 247, 249; and forms of replacement theology 11; Jewish–Catholic dialogue and 198; overcoming of 13, 15, 89, 269, 272; problems associated with 27, 47; punitive 26–7, 29, 235, 247–50, 254; readings 32–4, 45, 110; rejection of 42, 58–9, 64, 207; in relation to eschatology 1, 8, 273; roots of 11, 27; structural 29, 207, 259; theological paradigm of 39; theological problem of 11, 14, 58, 68, 89, 270
supersessionists 13, 15, 25–6, 29–39, 42–3, 45, 208, 219, 251, 272–3; arguments that the Church is the complete replacement or fulfillment of Israel 34; contemporary 255; economic 236, 240; hermeneutical approach of 30; post-structural 259; punitive 248; retributive 248; traditional 13; and the use of biblical texts 36
Svigel, Michael J. 170, 175–6
Swindler, Leonard 273
Symbolum Apostolicum 160
Synodical Council in Asia Minor 164
Synoptic Gospels 52, 74, 93, 100

Talmud 105, 211
Taylor, D.T. 170
teaching 77, 81, 109–10, 142, 171–2, 176, 181–2, 277, 279, 283; apocalyptic 174; authority 57; capacity 190; common 148; doctrine 172; non-fallible 190; official 190; orthodox eschatological 176; reactionary 174
Temple in Jerusalem 1, 156, 183, 213, 230, 283
Tertio Millennio Adveniente (Pope John Paul II) 152
Tertullian 116–17, 120–4, 127, 129, 162–4, 167, 179–83, 256, 277, 279
Theodosius 172
theologians 8, 11, 14, 16, 89–90, 146–7, 152, 190, 194–5, 198–9; critical approach of 7, 190, 232; critical work of 190; dual covenant 40; evangelical 29, 247; liberation 74, 206; modern 242; modern Catholics 99; non-supersessionist 29; orthodox 147, 169; Protestant 171; in relation to supersessionism 89; responsible 25; skilled 25
Theological Highlights of Vatican II 71
theology 15, 48–51, 54, 105–6, 178–82, 184–5, 207–9, 232–4, 273–6, 284–5; biblical covenant 242; comparative 205, 209, 262; contemporary ecological 271; Deuteronomic 26, 249; non-supersessionist 15, 222; official Jewish 213; Protestant 58; restoration 8, 26, 67, 85; traditional Lutheran 10; two-covenant 40
"theology of abrogation" 69
"Theology of Hope" 75, 217, 232
Theophorus (Ignatius) 116
Theotokos (reference to the Virgin Mary) 174
1 Thes 4:16 98, 101
Third Ecumenical Council 174

Third Reich 75, 191, 199, 288
Thomas, Stephen 112n130
Thomism 72, 242
Thousand Years' age 263
2 Tim 2:12 265
Timotheus 170
tombs 104
Torah 39–40, 44, 54, 71–3, 77, 211, 213, 253–4, 278, 284; based community 34; obedience 43, 240; observance of Judaism 43–4, 214, 240
totalitarianism 75–6, 193
tradition 12, 64, 67–70, 76–7, 81–2, 117, 147–8, 156, 205, 289–90; ancient 162; anti-Jewish 219; apocalyptic 10, 51; apostolic 115, 117–18, 130, 136, 151, 161–3, 174, 224; Catholic 3, 11, 14–15, 48, 55, 57, 72, 127, 192, 197; early Gospel 101; flawed 236; modern Jewish 213; normative 192; rabbinic 212; religious 59; sacred 240; scholarly 2
Trevett, Christine 167, 179n60
Trinitarian history 19, 154, 159, 166–7, 171, 174, 197, 215, 226
Trinitarian theology 164, 169, 171, 232, 256, 278
Trinitarianism 7, 222
Trinity 165–6, 173, 184, 220, 225–6, 232, 239, 276, 278, 284–5
Tyconian–Augustinian model 193
Tyconius 18, 118, 123, 131, 133–5, 137, 140, 150, 152, 192

USCCB 61, 68, 82–3

Valentinus 45, 54, 154
value 2, 6, 31–2, 40, 42, 71, 73, 122, 282, 287; of Judaism 2, 225; religious 2; spiritual 266; unique 224
Van Buren, Paul M. 43–4, 48–9, 54, 220, 234, 275
VanderKam, James C. 283
Vatican 57, 59–61, 68, 198
Vatican Council II 57, 60, 65–7, 70–1, 77–80, 82–4, 137, 205–6, 230, 287
Vatican documents 57, 63–4, 67, 69, 137, 279

Vatican's Commission for Religious Relations with the Jews 61
Victorinus of Patau 116, 171
Vincent of Lérins 12, 142, 146–52, 154, 156, 159, 165, 197, 288
Virgin Mary 172, 174, 183, 195; *see also* Mary
Visigoths 176
Vitalis 170
Vlach, Michael 29–30, 32, 34–5, 37–8, 248
Volusianus 176
von Harnack, Adolf 256

Wagner, Ross 267
Walker, Meryl A. 211, 229, 278
Wall, Robert W. 56n117
Waymeyer, Matthew 99
Weaver, Joel A. 51n61
Weber, Timothy 92, 208
Westhelle, Vitor 206
Whalen, Robert 255
Within Context: Guidelines for the Catechetical Presentation of Jews and Judaism in the New Testament 66
Wright, David F. 267
writers 43, 68, 103–4, 113, 116, 119–20, 147, 155, 167, 170; early Christian 32, 99, 265; endorsed Catholic millennial 195; fourth-century Sabellian 160; orthodox 133; prolific 171
Wyschogrod, Michael 44–5, 54n97

Yahweh 92, 255, 266–8
Yeshua 248, 266
YHWH 41, 49, 220, 224–5, 236, 241, 243, 260, 262, 264–5
Yohanan, Rabbi 212

Zecheriah 8:23 248
Zecheriah 9–14 250
Zecheriah 10:6 245
Zecheriah 12:10–13 241
Zenger, Erich 58
Zephaniah 268
Zion 10, 42, 63, 251, 254, 259–61, 263, 265–8, 276, 282–3
Zuck, Roy B. 102